Career Assessment

Career Assessment

Integrating Interests, Abilities, and Personality

Rodney L. Lowman

 AMERICAN PSYCHOLOGICAL ASSOCIATION

Copyright © 2022 by the American Psychological Association. All rights reserved. Except as permitted under the United States Copyright Act of 1976, no part of this publication may be reproduced or distributed in any form or by any means, including, but not limited to, the process of scanning and digitization, or stored in a database or retrieval system, without the prior written permission of the publisher.

The opinions and statements published are the responsibility of the author, and such opinions and statements do not necessarily represent the policies of the American Psychological Association.

Published by
American Psychological Association
750 First Street, NE
Washington, DC 20002
https://www.apa.org

Order Department
https://www.apa.org/pubs/books
order@apa.org

In the U.K., Europe, Africa, and the Middle East, copies may be ordered from Eurospan
https://www.eurospanbookstore.com/apa
info@eurospangroup.com

Typeset in Meridien and Ortodoxa by TIPS Technical Publishing, Inc., Carrboro, NC

Printer: Sheridan Books, Chelsea, MI
Cover Designer: Anthony Paular Design, Newbury Park, CA

Library of Congress Cataloging-in-Publication Data

Names: Lowman, Rodney L., author.
Title: Career assessment : integrating interests, abilities, and personality / Rodney L. Lowman.
Description: Washington : American Psychological Association, 2021. | Includes bibliographical references and index.
Identifiers: LCCN 2021006221 (print) | LCCN 2021006222 (ebook) | ISBN 9781433836930 (paperback) | ISBN 9781433837470 (ebook)
Subjects: LCSH: Vocational interests--Testing. | Psychology, Industrial. | Counseling.
Classification: LCC HF5381.5 .L6793 2021 (print) | LCC HF5381.5 (ebook) | DDC 153.9/4--dc23
LC record available at https://lccn.loc.gov/2021006221
LC ebook record available at https://lccn.loc.gov/2021006222

https://doi.org/10.1037/0000254-000

Printed in the United States of America

10 9 8 7 6 5 4 3 2 1

To Linda and Marissa with thanks and appreciation.

CONTENTS

Preface		ix
Acknowledgments		xi
	Introduction: The Interdomain Model of Career Assessment	3
	1. Scope of Career Assessment Work	7
I.	**ASSESSING VOCATIONAL INTERESTS**	**25**
	2. Defining and Contextualizing Vocational Interests	27
	3. The "Big Six" RIASEC Interest Types	63
	4. Applications: Choosing Interest Measures, Interpreting Individual-Level Interest Results, and Case Illustrations	83
II.	**ASSESSING CAREER-RELATED ABILITIES**	**125**
	5. Career-Related Abilities: Conceptual Issues and General Intelligence	127
	6. Mechanical and Physical Abilities	147
	7. Spatial Abilities	155
	8. Artistic and Creative Abilities	169
	9. Social Abilities: Social and Emotional Intelligence	197
	10. Managerial and Leadership Abilities	207
	11. Perceptual, Computational, and Other Abilities	223
	12. Case Illustrations of Ability Profiles	235

III. ASSESSING CAREER-RELATED PERSONALITY CHARACTERISTICS — 261

13. Conceptual and Measurement Issues of Career-Related Personality — 263
14. The Five-Factor Model of Personality — 279
15. Other Career-Relevant Personality Characteristics — 311
16. Applications: Case Illustrations of Personality Profiles — 339

IV. APPLYING THE INTERDIMENSIONAL MODEL — 365

17. Relationships Across Interest, Ability, and Personality Domains — 367
18. Applying the Interdomain Model: A Step-by-Step Process for Integrating Career Assessment Data — 407
19. Client Feedback and Report Preparation — 429
20. Ethical/Legal and Technological Issues — 463

References — 485
Index — 559
About the Author — 581

PREFACE

To say that this book was a long time in the making would be droll understatement. When I contracted to write this book, it was intended to be a second edition of *The Clinical Practice of Career Assessment: Interests, Abilities, and Personality*, which was published in 1991. That book introduced my three-domain model of career assessment, and it was well-received. In fact, in his foreword to the volume, the late John Holland, father of modern occupational interest theory, stated,

> Lowman has taken the guts of three separate (perhaps "isolated" is a more fitting word) types of literature and created an integrated model or strategy for the conduct of career counseling. His integration is not a simple eclecticism. He has used the theoretical work in these divergent domains and his clinical experience as a career assessor to develop an assessment strategy that is comprehensive, explicit, and psychologically sound. . . . This book is a major contribution to a quiescent area of practice. (as cited in Lowman, 1991, p. viii)

Why did it take me so long to complete this new expanded career assessment book? For one thing, Holland's foreword set a high bar for me. For another, I had overambitiously imagined that I could prepare a second edition of the original book a couple of years after the first one was in print and while also working on other books and research articles. Mostly, however, my own career had a mind of its own, and jobs in academia, creating and running my own consulting firm, academic administrative positions on a steep upward rise, and a number of geographic moves asserted priority. The situation was a little more complicated than that because I had actually published extensively through all of those positions and relocations (I am probably one of the few people who edited a professional journal while serving as a university president, both during the Great Recession).

It was not until I retired from my professorial and academic administrative duties that I finally had some uninterrupted time to work on this project and the book latched on to me, becoming both a passion and a sentence. It's one thing if you are writing a book about a psychological model that covers one domain, but when your model aims to cover three of them (interests, abilities, and personality), plus a number of other relevant variables, not to mention integration across those areas, there is a lot to be done. Since the original volume, the literature on interests, abilities, and personality, not to mention careers, had burgeoned and with increasingly rigorous studies.

Although the structure of the current book has some similarities to the first one, the editors at APA Books and I realized that this volume is not really a second edition of my previous book; it is a new book in its own right. For one thing, this book it is longer and covers a lot more territory. It also builds on my own research in this area and over 30 years of applied career assessment work with clients experiencing a variety of career- and work-related concerns.

Throughout the zigs and zags of my own career, my interest in helping to advance this career assessment field and enhance the services clients receive has never waned. I hope that readers will find the result to be useful. At stake is nothing less than our being able to help career assessment clients have satisfying and successful careers.

ACKNOWLEDGMENTS

For a large portion of my career in academia and private consulting, I have been involved with the study and practice of career and work assessment and counseling. I have taught courses and overseen training, conducted research, and supervised internships and practicums. All of these activities have helped me anchor research and theory in practical applications. These experiences have also shaped my perspectives on career assessment, including helping me better understand what is likely to be practically useful. I gratefully acknowledge the clients, students, and fellow researchers with whom I've had the opportunity to work.

Further along in a career, perspective sets in, and one can better understand those who have had a long-term influence. My dual training in both I–O and clinical psychology at Michigan State University has advised my career persistently. From Frank Schmidt, Neal Schmitt, and the late Jack Hunter, I learned a lasting respect for the nomothetic approach to psychological research. I equally benefited from the idiographic perspectives of the late Carl Frost, who helped me learn a great deal about assessment and coaching and about consulting to organizations with a value-driven approach. John Holland's prolific work on interests and occupational environments introduced me to the field and later influenced my own work. I also enjoyed his career-long support, his forthrightness, and his slightly sardonic humor. I also learned a lot about personality from a long-standing correspondence I had with the late, always supportive, Harrison Gough. There were also a number of clinical psychology professors and mentors in graduate school, internship, and postgraduate work, who, along with consulting psychology mentors and colleagues, have influenced my understanding of the individualized method of translating theory to practice.

The book also was improved and enriched by input from professional colleagues. Anonymous reviewers and market researchers provided a number of useful ideas and suggested additions. Jim Rounds also provided suggestions and new articles from his research team relevant to the interest sections of the book. I could not begin to list all of those contributors to the research and professional practice literature on interests, abilities, and personality from whose work I have benefited. I've tried to cite a lot of their work in the book, but no doubt in a literature this expansive and with researchers this prolific, there have been omissions.

I have published a number of books, articles, and book chapters and have also edited a book series with the American Psychological Association. This time, I worked closely with Emily Ekle on contracting and market information and with APA Development Editor Beth Hatch, whose useful suggestions and enthusiasm for the project I sincerely appreciate. Thanks to Beth, the book is much more accessible than it would otherwise have been. Before that, Linda McCarter and Elise Frasier provided useful suggestions. Even earlier, Mary Lynn Skutley, the first acquisitions editor who worked with me on this project, provided support, guidance, and, particularly, patience.

People who have not themselves written books may not appreciate the many tasks associated with the production side of publishing. Just when authors think (and fervently hope) that they are done with a book, the production work begins. This includes cover designers, copyeditors, typesetters, and production editors. Here I can thank APA Production Editor Ann Butler, cover designer Anthony Paular, along with Robert Kern and his staff at TIPS Publishing Services. I also appreciate the work of the marketing team at APA Books, who are so important in connecting books with the right audiences.

Finally, my psychologist-spouse, Dr. Linda Richardson, painstakingly reviewed several versions of the manuscript, providing detailed comments and suggestions that helped to improve the book. I also appreciate her many inputs and support during times when it seemed this book would never be done. Always, she energized the work and, in the last stages, helped me get the project over the finish line. Once again, this book is dedicated to Linda and to our daughter, Marissa.

Career Assessment

INTRODUCTION

The Interdomain Model of Career Assessment

Few choices are as important in life as one's career. Career and work contribute significantly to personal and life satisfaction—and, when they are problematic, to personal unhappiness and stress. Work helps to determine people's socioeconomic status, income, personal identity, and educational level. It will also influence who one's friends and partners will likely be.

When people are unhappy in their careers and work, there are often psychological consequences. Occupational stress arises and the potential for depression and health concerns increases. Work dissatisfaction can also spill over into home and family life. For those still charting their career courses, they may lack a sense of identity about who they are and where they fit in to the world. Not inappropriately, they may move from one college major, job, or career to another, testing out hypotheses about what they are best suited to do. Partly this is associated with the normal developmental process of trying out a number of things to see where the fit feels best and the rewards—both psychological and economic—the highest. However, when this process persists year after year, one false start after another, professional help may be needed. Others, possibly more methodical, seek confirmation before pursuing training or finalizing a choice.

Contemporary searches for well-fitting and satisfying careers are made more complex by the absence of a stable work environment. Times change, as does the nature of work itself. Whereas people once saw career choice as a once and forever one, with the full career likely spent with one employer, contemporary

https://doi.org/10.1037/0000254-001
Career Assessment: Integrating Interests, Abilities, and Personality, by R. L. Lowman
Copyright © 2022 by the American Psychological Association. All rights reserved.

work may call for a number of changes of job duties and employers, including self-employment, even by those not particularly entrepreneurially inclined.

Radical change in the nature of work creates different kinds of occupations and work contexts—more rapidly changing, less structured, and often more complex and intellectually demanding. Yet, the nature of people themselves has not changed. They still face the same need to understand the types of available work and careers for which they are best suited. They need to know how their personal characteristics—their interests, abilities, and personality—relate to a changing world work and career opportunities.

You might think people would readily know what they like, what they are good at doing, and what their personality preferences are. After all, a number of these factors are at least partly built into our genetic makeup and influence behavior from an early age. For many, particularly those likely to seek out career help from a professional, however, that is often not the case. People can sometimes be pretty unaware of their personal characteristics, resulting in decisions that do not really suit them very well.

When people are motivated for it, career assessment—the systematic evaluation of characteristics of people that influence their occupational preferences and fitness for various types of work—can help. It does so by identifying aspects of people that have a demonstrated relationship with work and career outcomes. For example, general cognitive ability, or intelligence, is a powerful predictor of success in a number of careers. Spatial abilities are important in science and art. Occupational interests, preferences for particular types of work, also are very important in identifying types of careers likely to be satisfying and motivating versus those that are not. Personality variables, in turn, help determine the right niche within a particular occupation.

Those whose job it is to advise clients on career choice and change therefore have the opportunity to help people better understand themselves and to advise them on their career concerns and choices. They can help the high school student whose parents see their child struggling with lack of direction or motivation. They can help those who have not yet decided upon their best-fit careers and want better to understand why. They can also help people well established in their careers who are restive in their current career paths. And they can assist those making major life transitions such as in retirement or after experiencing financial or physical changes that necessitate new career directions. They owe to their clients knowledge of people that will affect their choice of careers, skill in translating complex assessment data to be useful to clients in making concrete decisions about their lives, and understanding and appreciation of how people change.

This book is intended to help professionals-in-training and already-trained professionals who are themselves changing career directions to learn about the content and process of career assessment. It focuses on three major types of variables (or domains)—occupational interests, abilities, and personality—each of which has proven its value in career assessment across a broad range of career concerns and with an array of presenting concerns. Each of these domains has a large literature and, in many cases, appropriate psychometric measures.

There is a lot of material in this book to master. This relates both to the volume of the literature and the areas covered in the book. Further, the process of learning career assessment requires not just understanding individual differences in the context of work environments, but also learning how clients actually experience them. Additionally, the career assessor must become skilled at providing feedback in a way that maximizes impact and at understanding the process of change.

The career assessment model used in this book is called the Interdomain Model of Career Assessment. It focuses on interests (what people like to do), abilities (what people are able to do), and personality (the persistent and preferred ways of relating to others). The three domains are not three variables but rather three collections of variables, each of which has a demonstrated track record in predicting work and career issues. Further complicating things, these domains overlap with each other and combine to form patterns, or profiles, each containing an assortment of variables within it.

There is more. Assessment is always done in service of a goal; it is not the goal itself. Applied assessment therefore involves understanding the client's purposes for undertaking the assessment, the relevant measures to be used to address the referral questions, interpreting the findings in a way that is maximally useful to the client, and providing feedback from the science-based assessments to the real-world problems of the client. "Should I change career paths?"; "I'm not happy in my college major"; "Should I move to another, better paying job, even though I'm very happy in my current one?"; "I keep changing jobs and never seem to be happy in the new ones; why, and what should I do about it?" are examples of questions to which clients seek answers and for which the assessment instrumentation needs to be relevant.

To address such questions, and to be helpful to clients, assessors will need considerable expertise. Gone are the days when knowledge of a single personality or interest measure would be sufficient to conduct competent career assessments. This book is intended to help career assessors learn in depth about major psychological factors affecting career choice and change and how clients can use them to advise real-world decisions.

1

Scope of Career Assessment Work

The choice of a career, which decreasingly is a once-and-forever decision, equals or surpasses many other major life events in its potential impact on people's lives. Career choice can dramatically influence an individual's social status, income, friends, and even core identity. Work *un*happiness can also spill over into personal unhappiness, generating stress in personal and family life.

The process of determining one's particular constellation of career characteristics (strengths and weaknesses) and deciding how they best fit into chosen work is, in many respects, comparable in importance and complexity to the process of choosing a mate. Much trial-and-error learning can be associated with both endeavors. Those who are successful in making and sustaining a match with an occupation that is personally satisfying and consistent with one's identity and life goals are fortunate. For others, however, the process of successful matching may take years. Indeed, every career choice and dilemma represent a potential plot twist in a life story filled with incipient longings and hopes, some well-placed, others not. "I want to be a physician [or a novelist]" may confront the reality of hypercompetitive fields and far fewer people actually getting into, or succeeding, in those careers compared with those who might wish to do so.

Why is it that some people can find a career early on and pursue it happily and successfully through their entire working lives while others struggle for years before they find a well-fitting career at which they can also do well? People who realized at an early age that they wanted to be, say, a scientist or a financial analyst, and for whom that dream and that identity sustained themselves over time

---

https://doi.org/10.1037/0000254-002
Career Assessment: Integrating Interests, Abilities, and Personality, by R. L. Lowman
Copyright © 2022 by the American Psychological Association. All rights reserved.

are perhaps not the norm. For many others, the process is less linear, having had few opportunities to see role models in careers they may have thought about or finding themselves lacking in self-efficacy that propels them to do the things needed to succeed in particular career pursuits.

Additionally, there can be many false starts on the way to finding a copacetic and sustained career and career identity. Early career aspirations may evaporate as reality sets in, and life circumstances may intrude on being able to pursue imagined careers. People also can be markedly ill-informed about their own strengths and weaknesses and even their interests and personality.

Career assessment professionals have much to offer those seeking career assessment and counseling. This includes knowledge of work, careers, and the assessment process. There is also the need for expertise in helping people identify and contemplate their anticipated life stories, to help them understand their passions, the role of career in their lives, and what they are likely best suited to doing. They also need help in identifying and prioritizing what needs to be done next.

This, then, is a book about helping professionals help clients make informed choices about their work and career. It is intended to help career assessors at both the beginning and more advanced stages of expertise to become more knowledgeable and competent by providing an in-depth coverage of three important and influential individual difference domains—occupational interests, abilities, and personality—and the interactions among them.

But the book is not just about evidence- and theory-based approaches to career assessment and measurement. It is also focused on how to use this knowledge to help real clients facing real career issues in real time. Such concerns do not always fit neatly into a single theory or instrument and often cannot not be addressed by research findings alone. Presenting problems are often complicated, overdetermined, and embedded in a particular context and culture. The book aims to show how assessments can be anchored in the purposes for which career assessment was sought, in characteristics of the careers and occupations being considered, and in the complex process of matching person and occupation.

TYPICAL CONCERNS

The range of problems for which career assessment and counseling is sought is wide and diverse. Many are focused on unhappiness in, or uncertainty about, career or work choices. Here is a detailed case illustration, followed by other, briefer examples.

Case 1. Kevin's Career Dilemma

To his work associates and family, Kevin was a model professional. He was exemplary in his work behavior, respected by his colleagues, and pulled more than his share of the workload as a urologist. He had done well in medical school and also obtained a PhD working on research related to an area regarded as having considerable potential to advance knowledge about the particular disease he studied.

When the client sought career assessment and counseling, he was 39 and had been working for several years in a hospital-based position which would seem to make excellent use of his training, skills, and aptitudes. Both his father and his grandfather had been physicians, and it was expected that he would pursue the same career. However, the pressure to join the "family business" was never very explicit.

Although he never shared this information with anyone, not even his family, Kevin was quite unhappy in his work and was quietly drinking to excess and had been attending an AA meeting focused on professionals. He confessed to the assessor that, despite outward appearances, he was miserable in his work and, for once, unsure of how to extricate himself from his situation. He was referred for career assessment by his mental health provider.

Kevin was supportive of the idea of career assessment. In an initial interview, he reported that he had always liked science and research but was put off by the grind of patient care. He found it repetitive and boring, and felt that his work life, and then his home life, had also become a living hell. Yet, when asked about alternative career paths in medicine, including medical administration and teaching, he was not enthusiastic, and he did not identify many alternative careers that might interest him more.

A question arose at the time of the initial interview as to whether the client was depressed and, if so, if that might affect the results. Was the timing right for a career assessment? When a client presents with possible depression it is important to consider the potential impact on the career assessment process, but also whether the work issues are likely causing the depression or vice versa. In this case, the client understood that his unhappiness was centered on his career problems and he felt ready to start, rather than to delay, the process of assessment. He also indicated that he was in his third month of sobriety and that he felt better when sober than when not.

Careful and tactful questioning about his family of origin history revealed that Kevin had been raised in a family of high achievers with very high expectations for him and in a particular career direction. Most of his siblings and cousins had become medical professionals, and the implicit pressure to achieve was high, and the unstated but clearly communicated message was that medicine was the preferred career path. Most of his time in high school had been spent in academic-related activities, and he had earned very high grades at a prestigious, very competitive high school.

Though his father and other members of the family were somewhat well known locally in their respective fields as expert practitioners, Kevin did not aspire to that. Looking back, he now saw that he liked neither clinical medicine nor working with sick people. On the other hand, he had enjoyed medical research not so much for the subject matter but for the research itself. As a scientist, he could, he stated, have been studying biochemistry or physics. He had received good reviews of his research work in his PhD program where he could spend many hours on the research itself—designing and executing the studies. He also liked to write up the results of studies, which even for many scientists, an acquired taste.

Why, then, would such a well-trained and successful professional be so unhappy in his work? A detailed initial interview revealed that his nonwork life was satisfactory, although his current career concerns were problematic for his partner. He had experienced no particularly traumatic events in his growing up, and he had always been a star performer academically. In college, he started out in a humanities area of study, but by his sophomore year, had gravitated to science. He completed the pre-med requirements, applied to, and was accepted by, several medical schools, and followed this well-structured path, but without much enthusiasm. He had pursued a joint MD-PhD program in part because he found the medical practice work too formulaic ("see one, do one, teach one") and thought he would be more stimulated and satisfied by the research activities than with medical practice. However, the medical practice training and applied work was quite demanding of his time. His parents and relatives were very pleased with his apparent career ambitions, but he never shared with them his serious unhappiness.

This hard-driving, successful young man did not know it, but he was in more career trouble than he had imagined. His early successes masked an insidious discontent that he could either confront now or, with greater difficulty, later. Compulsive in everything that he undertook, Kevin sought professional assistance with the same attention to detail that had characterized all of his work. He narrowed his list of potential career counselors to three, interviewed each over the telephone, and chose one: a specialist in career and work issues. He began the career evaluation with great energy, taking the extensive test battery that lasted for several days with few complaints.

After the extensive career assessment, Kevin reviewed the results with his assessor. What did these findings have to say relevant to his current career unhappiness? His performance on the cognitive and intellectual measures was impressive, as was his purposefulness and intensity. The psychological assessment process revealed that Kevin had all of the intellectual and cognitive abilities to be a medical doctor except one. Although he had many of the occupational interests commonly found among scientists, he was not interested in helping people or particularly in interacting with them. He was also highly introverted such that he strongly preferred working alone or in small groups. He found dealing with patients extremely draining, and he spent many hours after work alone, trying to recover from that strain, which, in turn, put stress on his personal relationships, and, until recently, led to increased drinking. Asked why he had not pursued a research career in medicine, he indicated that the demands of medical school were such that he never felt that he had time to think about career directions other than medical practice. He had actually thought that research might be a better fit for him. He also had some creative interests and enjoyed writing poetry in his spare time, but he knew that would at best be an avocation for him since it was nearly impossible to make a living that way.

Working with his career and personal counselor, Kevin developed a plan to greatly reduce the time he was spending in clinical practice and to seek out opportunities for research. It would come at a price—research jobs often pay less well than practice ones—but he realized the payment in psychological well-being would compensate for that. His partner fully supported the transition, recognizing that the current tensions associated with his career unhappiness could not persist without taking a serious toll—both on his work and on their relationship.

Typical Presenting Career and Work Concerns

This case illustrates how career and personal concerns can interact and how career concerns can be associated with psychological dysfunction. Here are two short additional examples.

Amy was referred by her parents for career assessment when she was a junior in college and still contemplating her choice of majors. She had been passionate about singing while growing up until she had suffered a career-changing injury at age 17. After that, her opportunities to further pursue singing at a professional level ceased. However, she had been a lackluster performer in academic pursuits, putting most of her energy into her avocational pursuits. Now, at age 19, she was forced to come to terms with the loss of her first career goal and to settle on a college major and specific career direction. The question was, what options would best suit her and was it time, finally, to grieve the loss of her first career interest and move on or to integrate her first love into her career in different ways?

Cassie, age 29 at the time she sought assessment help, was working as a manager in high-tech company on the West Coast. She had risen from difficult family-of-origin circumstances to obtain a degree in business from a well-regarded and very competitive institution. Subsequently she started a job in finance at a large corporation. She was considering now going back to school full time or enrolling in an executive MBA program. The trouble was, whether in school or at work, she was chronically questioning herself, feeling that she did not belong and had not earned her many, and noteworthy, achievements. Her continuous battle, too often resulting in self-sabotage and behaving in a way that snatched defeat from the jaws of victory, was mostly fought alone. Although she had read about impostor syndrome and fear of success, she did not know how it chose her or how to resolve it.

To these examples could be added many others. These include the midlevel executive, dead-ended in a current career path, who is thinking of starting a new business; the autistic son whose parents seek consultation about what careers might be appropriate for him; and the former homemaker who, in midlife, is ready to reenter a workforce that bears little resemblance to what it had been 20 years previously.

The scope of career concerns in clients is broad. In the case of career assessment of the type presented in this book, there is usually a feeling that something is wrong or missing in the current career choices or anticipated career choices and uncertainty about how to proceed. Or, for younger clients, it may be the absence of a career path that is the concern. Career guidance can help clients with these, and many other, concerns.

MAPPING THE TERRITORY

These examples are typical of the broad range of issues presented by people seeking help with their careers. It is to career assessors and counselors, who can come from a variety of professional backgrounds, that persons dissatisfied or mismatched with their careers often turn. To be helpful to clients such as these, assessors need to know how to identify and classify presenting concerns, which constructs to measure with what instrumentation, and how to translate assessment findings into practically useful career guidance. The work thus calls both for knowledge of variables and factors that influence career choice, satisfaction, and productivity as well as an understanding of how people make use of information and the process by which they change. Even when based on strong evidence, the approach needs to be individualized. This requires both knowledge of an expansive and still expanding literature and sensitivity to the affective and the cognitive components inherent in any change process.

These examples also make clear that career concerns can differ substantially even when they share common underlying issues and that they are often embedded in complex intrapersonal and interpersonal contexts. It follows that the process of career assessment is not just about coming up with a "diagnosis" or understanding of the client's career concerns. Career assessors must also be skilled at both the content and the affect associated with career assessment, feedback, and counseling.

Before elaborating some of the content of the organizing model used in this book, it is important at the outset for assessors and counselors to know that they must combine the role of providing expert information—both factual and interpretative—with helping clients identify and manage their emotional reactions to the issues and the obtained results and recommendations. Also important is the need to recognize that, no matter how good the data and the scientific basis of the predictions about career fit, it is ultimately the client's choice what to do about the data, findings, and recommendations. It is the client who must be the decision maker, the assessor/counselor, the guide.

Individual Differences, Group Tendencies, and the Idiographic Approach

"Individual differences" is the term used to refer to the psychological characteristics of people that are measured on the individual (vs. group or systemic) level and which predict various life and work outcomes. People's scores on individual difference measures reflect a range of responses, typically normally distributed, that have been demonstrated to predict relevant outcomes. Examples of individual difference variables/factors include intelligence; specific, more circumscribed abilities such as spatial and interpersonal ones; personality dimensions; and occupational interests.

Much of the individual difference literature is based on examining mean or modal differences and characteristics of groups of individuals scoring in the same range versus others scoring higher or lower. For example, there are typically differences in work performance among those scoring high, average, or low on measures of intelligence. Similarly, those scoring high versus low on measures of extraversion or introversion will likely approach work roles calling for social interaction differently. Individual difference variables tend to be relatively stable across much of the life span (though some, like intelligence, do, for most people, decline over time). This stability has been shown to be influenced by genetic components in many cases. On the other hand, individual differences also interact with one another, so it is not possible to generalize to behavior from single variables. Patterns and profiles are often important in interpreting results.

Indeed, there are a number of research studies of individual difference variables that have demonstrated work relevance (see, e.g., Farr & Tippins, 2017; Ones et al., 2018). However, much of this literature exists in silos that are not often well connected. That literature is foundational for career assessment, but it also belies the fact that group level (nomothetic) characteristics are not the same as individual, idiographic ones (to use the philosopher Wilhelm Windelband's terms). Gough (1996) captured this point well in differentiating nomothetic and idiographic approaches in stating,

> Nomothetic work—such as forecasting academic and job performance criteria . . . and identifying attributes related to creativity . . . leadership, and designative career preferences is important. However, no amount of information about groups and general trends will substitute for the interpretive skills that can only be developed by the study of case material. (p. 159)

To elaborate, in career assessment the concern is not just about scores on a variety of individual assessment measures but also about understanding people in their individual complexity, with the need to integrate knowledge-based understanding of the likely behavioral tendencies from test data with behavioral and historical evidence. This point was well described by E. D. Beck and Jackson (2020), who used the term "idiographic traits" to describe the within-person organization of (in their case) personality. They demonstrated that quantitative models can be used to capture the individual organization of personality which, their data suggest, can for some, but not all people, be consistent over time.

Career assessment and counseling of individuals, I argue, requires both group and individualized models. For example, although two assessees with managerial interest profiles may (and typically do) have similar patterns of intellectual abilities, their interests, personalities, and nonintellectual abilities may combine to make for decidedly different career paths. Career assessment and development therefore represents a complex, inevitably idiographic interaction of three major domains: abilities, vocational interests, and occupationally relevant personality characteristics. Depending on the presenting career concerns, other factors may also need to be measured.

Interest-Ability-Personality (Interdomain) Career Assessment Model

What model and, by implications, what aspects of people and what assessment measures should be used for career assessment? The answer to that question depends on the reasons for the referral and the degree to which the presenting concerns are relevant for career assessment of the type discussed in this book. The typical, but by no means the only, presenting problem for vocational counselors often boils down to a question of goodness-of-fit of person with current or potential careers. "I'm not happy in my career (or college major)," "I don't know what I should be studying," and "I think I want to be a [doctor, psychologist, entrepreneur] but am not sure about it" are typical presenting concerns. These are variations of the question of goodness-of-fit of person with career.

When fit to particular careers is the question, individual differences can be compared with those called for, or most commonly, found, among persons in occupations and the degree of fit to various careers being considered can be evaluated. For example, scientists tend to have a particular interest and ability pattern that includes abstract reasoning ability and high intelligence, and great self-discipline in pursuing the creation or applications of knowledge. If a person's interests include scientific occupations, it makes for a better fit if the abilities are also consistent with the high cognitive abilities typically found among scientists or technicians. By and large, scientists, at least of the bench scientist variety, are also more likely to be introverted than extraverted.

In other situations, even though career assessment was sought, career "fit" is not the client's primary need. These concerns, such as burnout, difficulty working with a problematic supervisor, and addressing sequelae of physical or emotional dysfunctions, are not the primary focus of this book. Sometimes these issues are symptomatic of broader concerns about work fit, and sometimes career assessment may be what is needed to understand the problem in its context. In other cases, an approach more focused on a narrow work-related issue, not a career, will be what is most appropriate. There are also situations in which the basic approach is relevant to a client's career concerns but a shorter assessment is sufficient to address the presenting problems.

Three major questions affecting people as they consider career choices are the following:

1. What do I want to do?

2. What am I good at doing?

3. What are my preferred ways of working with, and relating to, others?

Each of these questions is particularly relevant, respectively, to three career-relevant characteristics of people:

1. What do I *want* to do? – interests

2. What am I *good* at doing? – abilities

3. What are my preferred ways of working with others? – personality

This book addresses each of these important domains in considerable detail.

Interests, abilities, and personality are called *domains* because each area encompasses a variety of variables and has a particular structure among the variables. Each domain also has a demonstrated track record for work and careers and considerable evidence of its predictive power for particular work-related outcomes such as productivity or satisfaction. The book will build the case that all three of these domains typically need to be measured when career choices and goodness-of-fit is the major referral question. Each domain of variables needs to be understood in its own right, but ultimately the results have to be combined in a way consistent with evidence-based literature and with idiographic understanding.

Group differences in ability, interest, and personality unquestionably exist. The typical engineer presents a different profile in many important ways from psychologists or teachers, even though the average intelligence test scores among members of these occupations may be similar. Yet, within any occupational group (especially large ones), there will also be significant differences from one subspecialty to another and from one individual to another. A surgeon and a pediatrician or a trial lawyer and a corporate attorney share the commonalities of their respective professions but also have distinctive differences from groups of individuals from other professions. The sometimes-subtle variations within a single occupational group can nevertheless prove useful in helping a person who is dissatisfied with their career make relatively minor changes that may have a significant impact on work satisfaction.

Here each of the three major domains focused upon in this book are briefly introduced. In later chapters, each domain will be described in much greater detail and illustrated with examples from career assessment.

Vocational (Occupational) Interests

Vocational or occupational interests speak to the kinds of activities people find enjoyable and on which they want to spend time. They are predictors of the kinds of activities (both work and nonwork) and occupations that are likely to arouse motivation and to create feelings of satisfaction.

The study of vocational interests is not new. From Strong (1931, 1943) to Darley (1941) to Kuder (1948) to J. L. Holland (1985b), interests have been measured and theorized on. Many sophisticated measuring devices—both modern versions of venerable ones and those of more recent origin—currently exist and remain widely used. Most show that interests are organized into a small number of career-relevant factors and associated occupational groups.

John Holland (1997a) contributed significantly to the study of vocational interests by creating a unified theory to account for persistent findings of a recurring factor structure of occupational preferences. His theory continues to dominate the measurement of vocational interests today. Not without needs for further research, the theory of vocational interests in the context of careers is probably the most developed of the three major domains. Part I of the book (Chapters 2–4) focuses on occupational interests. In Chapter 2, I briefly review the history of vocational interest study, discuss Holland's model of interests, and note recent literature on important aspects of vocational interest theory. Chapter 3 provides detail about the Holland RIASEC (Rational, Investigative, Artistic, Social, Enterprising, Conventional) interest types, how they overlap and differ, and a variety of issues important in their interpretation, including matching interests with occupations. Special attention is given to the relation between vocational interests and occupational choice factors. Chapter 4 provides detailed examples of six illustrative cases chosen as being representative of the RIASEC types.

Abilities
Abilities refer to what one is able, or potentially able, to do rather than to what one has interest in doing. A considerable literature has been directed by psychologists and other researchers to this domain in the last 50 years. The task of mapping cognitive abilities, especially intellectual abilities, has seen considerable development in the last decades (see J. B. Carroll, 1993; E. Hunt, 2010, for reviews). Much of the literature has focused on overall general intelligence, but some promising work has focused on other more specific types of ability such as spatial and emotional intelligence.

When it comes to career choice, it is important to consider abilities beyond general intelligence. This is not to deny the special role of general intelligence; it remains the single best ability predictor for many kinds of work performance. However, the range of abilities is as wide as the types of abilities called for in different kinds of work. Abilities are covered in Part II of this volume (Chapters 5–12). Chapter 5 presents conceptual issues and a detailed discussion of general cognitive abilities, including intelligence. Chapters 7 to 11 cover a variety of career-relevant abilities from mechanical–spatial to perceptual–spatial. For each identified variable, definitions and conceptual issues are presented with information on the dimensionality of the construct, career and work implications, and measurement issues. Also discussed are relevant guidelines and suggestions for evaluating tests to determine their appropriateness for career assessment practice. Chapter 12 provides a complete summary of the measured abilities associated with the six cases introduced in Chapter 4, demonstrating what abilities add to interests in discussing careers.

Occupationally Relevant Personality Characteristics
Personality variables influence the characteristic interactions people have with others and their preferred ways of relating to the world. The conceptualization

and measurement of personality variables in the past occurred almost independently of the study of occupational applications because they did not have their origin in trying to predict career or work issues.

Additionally, there was considerable disinterest on the part of industrial–organizational (I–O) psychologists for some time (see Guion, 1987) before they determined that personality was, after all, related to work and career concerns. In the last decades, however, considerable research has examined the role of personality in career and work applications. This was particularly enhanced by the popularization of the so-called five factor model (FFM) of personality, reducing a large number of variables to five overarching factors.

It turns out, however, that broad conclusions about personality and particular occupations can be limiting, particularly when working at the individual level with people on their career concerns. Extraversion (vs. introversion), for example, is assumed to be needed to be successful in sales and introversion for scientific careers. Although such findings may represent average group tendencies, the reality can be more nuanced than that. Other factors (e.g., interests and abilities) may be of greater importance than personality in understanding career fit. However, personality may still be an important factor in determining how work roles will be implemented in particular jobs within a career.

Additional issues arise about potential differences in overall personality and work-related personality. Many personality factors have trait-like aspects, reflecting in part genetic components. But situations also matter. Introverts, who generally prefer less contact with others than do extraverts, may be at ease in many aspects of work that require interpersonal activities. But they may in their non-work lives enjoy considerable time spent alone. And again, if the fit is otherwise good in careers dominated by persons with personality types different from the assessee's, there still may be work roles in which the "against norm" personality can be effective. For example, an extraverted scientist might better enjoy a role leading a lab rather than as a bench scientist.

Much more needs to be known about personality as it relates to work before some conclusions can be reliably drawn. For example, do the relatively stable characteristics of people (e.g., extraversion-introversion, masculinity-femininity, need for dominance) generalize to work settings? Or do the requirements and expectations of work cause people to behave in prescribed ways even if they conflict with their dispositional tendencies? Psychologists know, for example, that psychopathology does not necessarily dispose people toward poor job performance (see Lowman, 1989, 1993a), contrary to what some of those who conduct preemployment screening for psychopathology may assume.

There is also a tendency to privilege some personality characteristics and look less favorably on others. Extraversion is seen by many as the desired polarity and introversion less so (though this may vary by cultures). Similarly, scoring high on neuroticism is rarely a cause for celebration, yet in some creative occupations scoring in that direction may be the norm (Lowman, 1989). Personality findings do have a role in making career choices but they are not determinative and, I argue, not the place to begin.

Part III of this volume (Chapters 13–16) covers career-related personality characteristics. Chapters 13 through 15 present conceptual and measurement issues in the personality domain. Definitions of each construct are presented that sometimes vary substantially from one approach to another. Dimensions of each factor are identified and again there is variability across approaches. This suggests that which test is used has implications for what interpretations are and are not appropriate to be made. Finally, the career and work implications of each personality factor and facet are discussed and measurement issues identified. In Chapter 16, the personality results of each of the six focal cases are presented.

Integration Across Domains

Part IV (Chapters 17–20) addresses the goal in career assessment, which is to integrate across assessment data to be able to use the data to help people address the issues for which career assessment was sought. Here there is only a still-emerging literature on which to rely and exemplary studies are reviewed in Chapter 17. These chapters suggest that there is a growing literature of interdomain relationships and that some emerging interest-ability-personality profiles are supported with even though more research studies are needed.

Career assessors are left with the practical problem of how best to combine interests-abilities-personality data with the goal of providing guidance on the issues for which career assessment was sought. A step-by-step process for combining data across domains is outlined in Chapter 18.

Client Feedback

Chapter 19 addresses issues associated with providing written and oral feedback. A lot of complicated data are typically generated in the career assessment process. This information needs to be communicated to the client in a way that is maximally useful. At the same time, it must be accurate.

The specific challenge for career assessors is how to provide detailed feedback that is consistent with the assessment data but that is also useful for the client. In seeking medical help most patients are likely to be less interested in learning all the details about what is causing their symptoms than in knowing what needs to be done to fix it. That may also be true in the case of people seeking career assessment. Career assessments do, however, need to understand the variables being measured and how they relate to real-life choices of careers. Again, it is not the job of the assessor to come up with a single career choice but rather to empower clients better to understand themselves and to translate that knowledge into the context of the careers being considered. The feedback process may also help the person consider other, uncontemplated, career paths not previously considered.

The career assessor needs to make the feedback experience be as useful as possible to the assessee. Although career assessment is said typically to involve work with "normal" populations, personal reactions to career dilemmas and concerns, as well as to career assessment results, can be wide ranging. For example, assessees may have self-perceptions that are inconsistent with their actual abilities (in either direction), or they may be experiencing a conflict between ambition and ability such that the drive to succeed blinds them to personal limitations. Alternatively, clients may need help puncturing and reshaping erroneous fantasies, often unconsciously held, of their inability or perceived lack of abilities. In addition, many clients may be experiencing clinical depression or other psychological distress, and that might have affected some of the obtained results.

Clearly, the assessor must have more than detailed knowledge of each of the three major domains discussed in this book. Comfort with the affective aspects of career assessment and feedback, sensitivity to the emotional reactions that typically accompany receiving "objective" feedback, and the intelligence to entertain and explain personal psychological dynamics as they relate to career issues are all important in successful career assessment and counseling. Precisely because occupational choice can define one's station in life and one's capacity to reach wished-for goals, feedback can be emotionally charged.

Chapter 19 also provides a sample assessment report illustrating the goal of providing a permanent record of the assessment report that can be consulted by the client over time.

Ethics and Technology

The book's final chapter, Chapter 20, expands the discussion of ethical issues in career assessment, considering ethics codes from across a number of different professional associations whose members work in the career assessment space. The ever-increasing use of technology, including in virtual assessments, finishes out the book.

CONTEXTUALIZING THE MODEL

Having introduced the three major domains that are the primary focus of this book, it may be helpful to contextualize the career assessment process. It is not just about tests and testing. In this section, several contextual factors in the career assessment process are identified, from initial contact, to assessment, to feedback. Each of the steps outlined here is further developed in subsequent chapters. This brief summary presents a series of core questions that encapsulate the overall process. The integrated assessment process, blending data with behavioral evidence, will be further discussed in Chapters 17 and 18.

The following nine questions address issues important in career assessment.

1. Why Is the Client Seeking Career Assessment at This Particular Time?

A career assessment client comes for help for one or more reasons. Those goals, though they may change or be elaborated over the course of the assessment process, drive the specific assessment. The purposes and concerns for which clients have sought out career assessment help guide the overall assessment and career counseling process. The assessor needs at the outset to explore in some depth the client's presenting problems and motives in order to determine whether the identified issues are relevant for career assessment. This includes a review of the client's career and work history to identify what has the client done so far in their work/school career and with what results? The purposes for which career assessment is most relevant have to do with career choice and change and addressing problems of unhappiness or lack of direction in one's work. This topic comes up throughout the book but is considered especially in this chapter and Chapter 18.

When career assessment is not relevant for the presenting concerns, or when the client is simply not ready for it, other types of assessment, intervention, or referral can be recommended. For example, career assessment is not the same as job-finding. When people have lost jobs that they enjoyed and were good at doing they may need job-finding counseling, although some assessment can certainly be part of that process. Career assessment and counseling, in contrast, would be relevant when the kind of work the person has done is no longer available and it is necessary to find an alternative career path.

Another issue to be considered is how motivated the client is to pursue assessment. For example, is it the client, or someone else, who thinks career assessment is a good idea? When working with teens or young adults, it is not uncommon for the parents or grandparents to fund the assessment. If the identified client is not particularly motivated to undertake the assessment, those issues will need to be explored and resolved before proceeding.

2. Is the Client Ready for Career Assessment?

Not everyone is ready for career assessment (though they may be ready for a different kind of career intervention), and it is always important to consider that issue at the outset of the process. A lot of time, energy, and expense are required for career assessment, so it is important to be sure that the time is right and that the results of assessment can be put to good use.

It is usually a good idea to evaluate how motivated the client is to pursue career assessment. For example, is it the client, or someone else, who thinks career assessment is a good idea? When working with teens or young adults, it is not uncommon for the parents or grandparents to fund the assessment. If the identified client is not particularly motivated to undertake the assessment, those issues will need to be explored and resolved before the assessment is undertaken.

Concerning readiness for career assessment, a literature has developed about readiness for career decision making, also called career decision status, or decidedness, measures (see Stoltz & Barclay, 2019). These concepts and related measures can be useful in deciding whether career assessment of the type described in this book is something the client can benefit from. Assessment measures are available to assist in this process. Some of these issues are further discussed in Chapter 18.

Even if a client is not yet ready for career assessment, or when doing an assessment is someone else's idea (such as their parents') or when other issues (such as indecision, anxiety, or depression) take priority, this doesn't mean that assessment may not be appropriate at a different time or that a different type of intervention or assessment might be needed. But it does mean that career assessment readiness is to determine whether such assessment or intervention is needed or some other approach. Enough information must be gathered from a prospective client before making a judgement about what type of assessment and intervention is needed. No type of assessment or intervention is universally relevant for all concerns. Nor are all potential clients ready to make career decisions. Therefore, a preassessment process is needed to help determine how best to proceed and whether career assessment, or some other kind of assessment of intervention, is appropriate.

3. Are There Other Aspects of the Client's Life That Are Affecting the Current Career and Work Concerns?

Another issue to be considered as part of the process is whether there are nonwork and career issues that may be affecting the career ones. Real-life cases can be complicated, and the client may be experiencing, as one example, psychological problems such as depression or anxiety. These can be the result of, or incidental to, the career concerns. Some presenting issues may need different kinds of assessment than what is covered in this book (see, e.g., Lowman, 1993a, 1997). This topic is discussed in several parts of the book including Chapters 1, 18, and 19. Because psychological issues can both cause and be caused by work issues it is important to understand whether psychological dysfunctions that may be influencing work are present. This may require expertise in mental health issues that exceeds that of a career assessor, so working with a qualified mental health professional may be needed.

The career assessor also needs to know enough about the nonwork aspects of the client's life to be sure those are not affecting work issues. If there are problems in the realm of family issues, particularly family of origin issues, or relationships, these may be affecting work and career issues. With a young adult it is important to know the family's ambitions for their child and how those have affected the assessee's perceptions; with adults, the same issues may be relevant, so the assessor should also ask about the parent's or family's goals for the client.

Current financial goals and pressures should also be considered. Is the career change or unhappiness mainly associated with external rewards such as money or with internal ones such as job satisfaction and work motivation?

The broader point here is that a number of factors need to be considered in career assessment and counseling beyond what might be revealed in testing. This type of data helps to provide a framework of the client as a person and how the testing results are congruent, or incongruent, with the rest of the client's life.

4. What Kinds of Work-Related and Other Activities Does the Client Most and Least Enjoy?

Being clear on the kind of work and nonwork activities clients like and dislike is an important part of the career assessment process. Another aspect of motivation is addressed by exploring these questions: "What problems or issues does the client want to address in their work and why?" or "In what way does the client want to make a difference in their world and in the world?" These questions speak to what a person is likely to invest time and resources into pursuing. These concerns speak to occupational interests and motivation, covered in Chapters 2 through 4 and in Chapters 13 through 15.

5. What Is the Person Best and Least Good at Doing?

What does the client see as being strengths and relative weaknesses, and is there objective evidence to support this? Are the areas of perceived weakness ones that can be learned or improved through training or practice? Abilities are the focus of Chapters 5 through 12.

6. How Are the Client's Personality Characteristics Relevant to Career Choices?

How do clients view their preferred way of relating to others? How do they view their personality as fitting in, or getting in the way of, work and career choices? These issues are discussed in Chapters 13 through 16.

7. In What Ways Are the Client's Interests-Abilities-Personality Characteristics Synergistic or at Odds?

Because interests, abilities, and personality represent different domains, the results in each area may be consistent or incongruent. Helping clients put the various aspects of their results together is an important part of the career assessor's role. Ultimately, of course, it is clients who must make career choices fitting together many aspects of themselves. How do their interests, abilities, and personality combine? Are they moving them in a consistent direction? In what ways are they not consistent? The integration of interest-ability-personality data is taken up in detail in Chapters 17 through 19.

8. With Which Occupations, or Lines of Work, Does the Client's Interest-Ability-Personality Profile Best Match?

Clients' characteristics must be matched with real-world career choices. If what they are best at doing does not match work in the real-world—or in their real world—what compromises are possible? Can nonwork and work be combined in a way that makes for an overall good fit? This topic is integrated across the book.

9. How Can the Assessed Information Best Be Communicated to the Client?

The career assessor needs to be an expert in the subject matter; the client does not. The client typically cares about what the results of assessment have to say about the problems for which help was sought but is likely to be less interested in the theory of assessment, specific measures used, and the technical details of the process. It is up to the assessor to present the findings in a way that is technically accurate but also practically focused on the issues at hand. Understanding the process of change and changing will help the assessor provide impactful feedback but at the same time help the client make effective use of the assessment findings. This topic is covered in a number of chapters but particularly in Chapters 18 and 19.

USING THE BOOK

Although considerable effort has been directed to making this book useful for people learning career assessment, there is a lot of technical as well as applied material to cover. I recommend that the chapters be read consecutively rather than taking them out of order and also that adequate time be spent on reading and reviewing the material in each chapter. Once the major points are understood, the more complicated material about interdomain findings and applications will be more easily understood and applied.

For each of the major domains, the book brings in current and sometimes classic literature findings. Evidence in each major domain is expansive. The intent is to cover major findings and to identify unresolved or still-emerging issues. Concerning applications, space does not permit detailed coverage of specific tests or their interpretation except in general terms but, as appropriate, brief comments are made about particular tests or approaches to measurement of a construct. The book does, however, present material on specific tests in its case examples. Each measure has its pluses and minuses. The case material provides examples and is not intended to advocate for use of a particular measure but rather to illustrate how complex constructs look when applied in real-life contexts.

Finally, I note that the focus of this book is on career assessment using testing. Other approaches, particularly in intervention, use more of a narrative approach (e.g., Savickas, 2019). Even when using testing, there is always the need to individualize the interactions with the client, and that is part of the art of this work, components of which are covered in the book.

ASSESSING VOCATIONAL INTERESTS

2

Defining and Contextualizing Vocational Interests

"If you didn't like it, why didn't you quit?"

"To do what? Wasn't anything I knew better than farming. I was cursed, that was the problem. Just because I didn't like it didn't mean I wasn't good at it."

"That doesn't sound like a curse to me."

"It's a curse all right . . . To be good at something you don't care about? It isn't even unusual. . ."

—THE STORY OF EDGAR SAWTELLE (WROBLEWSKI, 2008, P. 416)

Occupational interests speak to motivation. They help to identify the kinds of work and other activities about which people are likely to be passionate and to feel engaged. When it comes to career assessment, interests are an important starting point. They are also one of the oldest and most widely empirically studied psychological variables.

Research has demonstrated that neither people in jobs or college majors, nor the activities associated with jobs or college majors are randomly distributed (Cunningham et al., 1987; Gasser et al., 2007; J. L. Holland, 1997a; Logue et al., 2007; Nauta, 2011; B. Schneider, 1987). Rather, people with certain types of interest profiles are overrepresented, and those with other types of interest profiles, underrepresented, in both occupations and college majors. Because occupations and college majors can be classified on similar interest dimensions, a matching process of persons and occupations can be used to identify, at the individual level, occupations or majors in which interests are likely to be expressed.

Elsewhere (Lowman, 1993a, 1993b) I borrowed from economics the concept of the "invisible hand principle" to refer to the phenomenon by which individuals by and large do end up in occupations reasonably consistent with their interests (see J. L. Holland, 1968; J. L. Holland & Nichols, 1964a; Strong,

1931, 1938a, 1938b, 1951a). Over time, and with successive approximations, there is a general trend for many, if not most, people to match themselves well, or at least well enough, with personally relevant occupations (see, e.g., J. L. Holland, 1997a; Low et al., 2005; Lowman, 1993b; Lubinski & Dawis, 1995; Lubinski et al., 1995; Lykken et al., 1993; M. L. Morris, 2016; Tracey & Robbins, 2005). But those seeking career assessment may not actually know what their interests are or why they matter for their choice of careers or majors.

The normalcy of the matching process (individuals finding careers that fit their measured interests well) can be masked or forgotten when working with a clientele of persons unhappy or undecided in their career choices. In career assessment and counseling, it is often the exceptions—persons for whom the natural career-finding process has not worked effectively—who seek out help. Interest theories and measures, however, ideally have utility for persons whose interests are, and those whose interests are not, well suited for their current college majors or occupations.

DEFINING AND CONTEXTUALIZING VOCATIONAL INTERESTS

Before getting too far along in the discussion of vocational interests, it is useful to define the term and to understand why, important as they are, interests cannot be considered in isolation. Their relationships to other variables matter such that, ultimately, it is a profile, rather than an isolated variable, that will be most useful in understanding best-fitting career options.

Definitions

At root, interests are what provide the fuel that drives people to direct energy, knowledge, abilities, and the force of personality to a particular set of activities. More technically, a variety of definitions of the term "occupational interests" have been offered over the century-plus period in which they have been studied. One of the earliest stemmed from Strong's (1955) long line of research on interests, which he defined as

> a liking/disliking state of mind accompanying the doing of an activity, or the thought of performing the activity. (p. 138)

Rounds, one of the premiere researchers on interests, defined interests as

> traitlike preferences for activities, contexts in which activities occur, or outcomes associated with preferred activities that motivate goal-oriented behaviors and orient individuals toward certain environments. (Rounds & Su, 2014)

Elsewhere I defined interests as being

> relatively stable psychological characteristics of people which identify the personal evaluation (subjective attributions of "goodness" or "badness," judged by degree of personal fit or misfit) attached to particular groups of occupational or leisure activity clusters. (Lowman, 2003, p. 477)

Interests in Context

In this chapter, interests are explored in depth, but to some degree in isolation, so it is important to state here that they must ultimately be considered in the context of other variables, including abilities and personality. In other words, interests are not always independent (orthogonal) from other variables that matter for career choice (see Chapter 5) and therefore must be considered in relationship to them. For example, interests help to identify whether people are likely to enjoy or be engaged with particular kinds of work but not whether they have the abilities (capacity) to do that work (see Dawis, 1992, 2005) or whether their personality will be well suited to it.

Also, at least as currently measured, interests may indicate more about the appeal of broad groups of occupations than they do about narrow subcategories of occupations. For example, interests may be more useful in identifying the appeal of law and occupations emphasizing verbal persuasive job duties than, at least as stand-alone variables, for determining whether corporate or trial law would be a better fit for an individual who finds law appealing. There are certainly studies differentiating roles within occupations (see, e.g., Dunnette, 1957), but they are not comprehensive, can rapidly become dated, and usually are based on small samples even when they are tied to interests.

HISTORICAL NOTES AND CONCEPTUAL ISSUES

The long rich literature on interests, both research and application, cannot fully be summarized in a single chapter. Good early reviews of the history of the construct of interests can be found in Crites (1981; see also Super & Crites, 1962, a dated but still relevant text on vocational appraisals). More recent reviews are found in Armstrong et al., 2008; Dawis, 1991; and Lowman and Carson, 2012. Here only some of the highlights can be identified.

The pioneering nature of the early vocational researchers is well exemplified by Parsons's (1909) classic work, *Choosing a Vocation*, and by Strong's (1931, 1943) important works related to the development of a still widely used, regularly updated vocational interest measure, now called the Strong Interest Inventory (SII; Dik & Rottinghaus, 2013; Harmon et al., 1994; Herk & Thompson, 2012; Lowman & Carson, 2012). By any account, the assessment of vocational interests has provided one of psychology's earliest and most long-lasting success stories. Vocational interests have been measured with exemplary psychometric sophistication yet also have widespread practical applications. Because of early measurement and classification success, the assessment of vocational interests is appropriately regarded as an important example in the application of psychological methods to real-world issues.

Indeed, the early vocational interest assessment devices, most notably that of Strong (1931, 1943; see also Hagenah & Darley, 1955), ranked on par with early measures of intelligence for their impact on society and on the applications of psychology and for their contributions to the scientific-professional model of psychological practice. Interest measures have typically required respondents to rate occupational, school, and recreational activities, which have been empirically validated by comparison with known groups in occupations such that individual respondents' results can be compared with the criterion groups. This type of measurement set early standards for the practice of instrument development, and a number of interest measures, for example, Strong's and the Kuder Occupational Interest Inventory (Kuder, 1991; Zytowski, 1973) gained widespread use.

Although assessment instruments of this era were well grounded empirically, they were generally atheoretical and were more concerned with description and work preferences than with the development of interest theory development. As Rounds (1995) put it, "Because vocational interest theory has been underdeveloped . . . factor analysis has primarily been used to develop theoretical constructs to advance vocational interest theory" (p. 178).

The early factor studies did, indeed, provide important information. Guilford's work (J. P. Guilford et al., 1954) identified six major factors that turned out to have been remarkably similar to Holland's later RIASEC factors, namely, Mechanical Interest (similar to John Holland's Realistic factor), Scientific Interest (Investigative), Aesthetic Expression (Artistic), Social Welfare (Social), Business Interest (Enterprising), and Clerical Interest (Conventional; see Rounds, 1995, p. 179). Rounds (1995) also noted other factors, including J. P. Guilford et al.'s (1954) possible seventh factor, an Outdoor-Work interest, something that sounds like a subtype of Realistic interests. He also noted five other factors from Guilford et al.'s work: Adventure versus Security, Thinking (mathematical), Precision, Cultural interest, and Physical Fitness interests, which he felt were now established as being occupational interests.

Relatively little early effort was, however, directed toward understanding *why* obtained differences came out as they did or toward determining how the expressed preferences could be integrated into an explanatory and predictive theory (see Lowman & Carson, 2012). In contrast, the theories of interests that arose (e.g., those of Roe, Super, Bordin, and others; see D. Brown, 2002; Osipow & Fitzgerald, 1995, for summaries) were often not developed with meaningful integration of empirical data specific to the real-world context of work and careers. Not atypically, factor analysts and vocational interest theorists worked independently of each other, resulting in theory that was difficult to measure (e.g., Roe, 1956) and empirical data that were sometimes hard to interpret or contextualize. And then there is Holland's model, the theory- and empirical-based applied model that still dominates occupational interest measurement around the world.

It was the late psychologist John Holland who translated his own and others' research findings on vocational interests into an elegant and practically useful theory that meaningfully integrated the then-known empirical data. The result has been one of the most widely used theories in the world, and it is not possible to study interests without becoming familiar with Holland's widely used model. The model found widespread interest because it was (a) evidence based; (b) easy to understand and use in both practice and research; and (c) applicable both to individuals and environments, making it easy to apply in comparing people to potential occupations (or college majors, work groups, organizations, etc.).

Origin of Holland's Model and RIASEC Types

Although many career assessors use Holland's RIASEC model without thinking too much about its origin, it is important to know its derivation. John Holland was a counseling psychologist by training with particular interests in people's career choices. Holland himself was a prolific researcher but also a pianist. Among other positions, before moving to the Sociology Department at Johns Hopkins University, he worked with the American College Testing (ACT) program, which included an interest measure in its widely used college admissions test. Working with the very large data sets that such testing firms could generate, he observed from his analyses that the same six factors seemed to emerge on interests (see J. L. Holland et al., 1969). These six factors were subsequently labeled as specific interest types (Realistic, Investigative, Artistic, Social, Enterprising, and Conventional, or RIASEC for short). He integrated these factors into systematic model that he argued applied both to people and to environments. He further theorized that the interest types had a particular (hexagonal) relationship with each other and that when interests went from single types to three (or more) interest profiles, they helped to identify the types of occupations which people were likely to most enjoy and in which they were likely to be most productive.

Before getting into the practical aspects of measuring and interpreting interests, there are a number of topics to be discussed that summarize some of what is currently known about interests. These do matter for being able to apply interests in a scientifically appropriate way. For example, if interests are stable over time, that is a different situation than if they vary by age. If interests work differently by gender, ethnicity, or culture, that would also have important implications. If the types do not relate to each other in a predictable way, it will be more difficult to interpret interest profiles. Therefore, we first take up such issues at a macro level and subsequently move on to interpretation and application at the individual level.

On What Basis Do People Respond to Interest Inventories?

What is it that people are actually responding to when they complete interest inventories? What is it about them that is being tapped into?

Consider the typical interest measure. Respondents are presented with a series of items (say, the jobs of plumber, architect, or teacher, or activities such as singing, hiking, or doing volunteer work) to which they are to indicate whether they "like," "don't like," or are "indifferent." At first, it would seem implausible that many respondents would have enough information about a wide variety of occupations and other activities to respond with clear understanding and personal awareness as to liking or not liking particular occupations. How, for example, can a wide swath of high school students or young adults really know enough about the jobs of aeronautical engineers or employment counselors to have an informed opinion about liking, disliking, or feeling indifference to them? (Ask young adults about their parents' occupations, for example, and you might be surprised at how few know either what work their parents do or what that work entails.) Yet, detailed occupational information, across most ability levels, appears not to be necessary for people to reach conclusions about whether the occupation or activity is determined personally a good fit (e.g., Ferrara et al., 1985). Moreover, these responses have real predictive value in suggesting occupations in which they will spend their careers and tend to be stable over time.

So, what is it that people are responding to when completing an occupational interest measure such as those requiring responses to liking or disliking occupations or job duties for which they lack detailed information? Schoon (1978) conceptualized interest responses as being affective ones rather than responses to occupational stimuli per se. This may suggest that people can project immediately from their personal reactions to quickly respond (positively or negatively) to occupational titles or to lists of job or nonwork activities. And it may be that people are to some degree preprogrammed by genes or environment to like or dislike particular occupations.

Because the assessor does not know how and why people responded as they did to their perceptions about occupations, it is sometimes useful to ask them directly about why they have (or do not have) interest in occupations they may be contemplating. If the task is to help the client differentiate among several college majors or possible occupations being confused, it can be useful to review them one by one to understand the nature of the attraction. For example, was a particular occupation one contemplated in earlier years no longer of interest? The goal also is to help clients consider possibly well-fitting careers that they might not be aware of or have seriously considered. This is particularly important when people are rejecting from consideration occupational choices that they consider "inappropriate" or unrealistic for someone of their race/ethnicity or socioeconomic status.

Stability of Occupational Interests

Rounds and Su's (2014) definition of interests included the idea that interests are trait-like. If that is an accurate characterization, interests would be expected to be highly consistent over time. Research findings generally support that finding with some caveats.

Research has generally and persistently demonstrated that interests do not on average crystallize or become stable until around 18 to 21 years of age (Low et al., 2005; see also Super & Crites, 1962; Tracey & Sodano, 2018). This suggests that vocational interests measured in early youth must be cautiously interpreted in a manner consistent with the person's overall life interests, particularly when career immaturity and limited career knowledge is also considered (see Grotevant & Durrett, 1980). However, there is a point, usually in late adolescence or early adulthood, at which occupational interests, across many different measures, have been shown, again persistently, to be quite predictable (Rottinghaus et al., 2007; Strong, 1951b; J. L. Swanson & Hansen, 1988), although some fluctuation may be noted in response to outside influences (see Posthuma & Navran, 1970) that may broaden respondents' perspectives, or in specific types of interest patterns (Vinitsky, 1973). Reasons for this stability are intriguing, particularly since other psychological aspects of persons such as abilities and personality, do tend to change with time.

Tracey and Sodano (2008), who have extensively studied stability and change of interests in children and adolescents (Tracey & Sodano, 2015), identified a number of complexities involved in assessing the stability of interests and their changes over time. These included a variety of ways that the question of stability can be approached. Interindividual stability considers whether, over time, RIASEC scores tend on average to stay stable (as measured, e.g., by test-retest correlations). Intra-individual stability considers whether the profiles of individuals' interests (order of highest-to-lowest endorsed interests) remain stable over time. Structural stability considers whether the overall relationships of the distance and location of interests are stable over time. Also relevant is whether there are similar or different patterns of stability across the scales over time. These authors, in a number of studies and literature reviews, found systemic changes—both increases and decreases—in children's expressed interests as they grew older. As these authors noted,

> Beyond profile order stability, there are important mean differences in interests over time. There seemed to be a pattern of increasing interest scores on all scales during the elementary school years; then a drop in middle school, especially upon entry to it; and then an increase through high school, with a possible drop again toward senior year. There were clear gender differences, especially in the drop in scores with entry into middle school and in senior year in high school. These two key transitions resulted in greater drops for girls than for boys. (Tracey & Sodano, 2008, p. 59)

Some of the research paradigms can be illustrated with representative studies. Starting with early research, Strong (1931), in a cross-sectional study of the differences of vocational interests by age and occupational groups, found that the interest profiles of younger and older members of an occupation were very similar. Specifically, in this cross-sectional study, 2,340 members of eight diverse occupational groups (including engineers, lawyers, insurance salespeople, physicians, writers, and YMCA administrators) showed substantial between-group, and few within-group, differences at all age levels in endorsed preferences for various occupationally related activities. Most of the small differences within occupational groups were observed between ages 25 and 35, but, for the most part, what was liked by young members of an occupational group was also liked by older members of the same occupation. The exceptions were interests in cultural activities, in reading, and in desire for autonomy, each of which tended to increase with the age of the respondents. Of course, this was not a longitudinal study, so differences in the same respondents over time could not be measured. Nevertheless, the portrait of interests as being stable across age groups in the same occupation is noteworthy.

A number of more recent studies have examined stability of interests longitudinally. J. L. Swanson and Hansen (1988) retested a group of college freshmen 12 years after initial assessment with the Strong (specifically the Strong-Campbell interest measure). They found high stability across 12 years (and for a subset of the respondents, also across 4 and 8 years). They noted that many of those whose interests were less consistent over time were more likely to have rated themselves as being less stable over time on their interests. Lubinski et al. (1995) reported on 15-year test-retest results of Strong-Campbell interest measure among a sample that at the time of the initial assessment, when the participants were 13 years old, and were participants in a program for mathematically gifted (having scored in the top 1% of the population). The median test-retest correlation across the RIASEC themes and the Strong Basic Interest Scales was 0.57; for the six interest themes alone, 0.46. These researchers also noted that some interests (specifically, Investigative and Enterprising) were less predictable over time than the others. Considering that interests are often not stabilized until early adulthood, these interest correlations were fairly high. Low et al. (2005) examined a number of longitudinal studies that had tracked interests over time and found that after adolescence, interests became, on average, quite predictable from young adulthood through at least middle age. Like Lubinski et al.'s (1995) longitudinal study, Low et al. found that there were differences in stability across some of the interests. They found Realistic and Artistic interests to be somewhat more stable than were Investigative, Social, Enterprising, and Conventional ones. From these and other studies the conclusion seems to be that after adolescence, interests, on average, are likely to be stable through at least middle age. Other studies (e.g., Rottinghaus et al., 2007) reported similar findings. To the extent that interests are fairly predictable after young adulthood for many, if not most, individuals, it is useful to consider what might be driving that stability.

One inevitable factor to be considered in understanding the apparent stability of vocational interests concerns genetic influences. To the extent that interests emerge early (see, e.g., J. A. Johnson, 1987) and, after a certain age at least, are quite predictable over time, a genetic component could account for the trait-like nature of interests. Empirical research has explored this aspect of interests with some intriguing results.

This is not a new focus of interests research. H. D. Carter (1932) reported an average concordance rate using the then-current version of the Strong of 0.50 for identical (monozygotic) twins and 0.28 for fraternal (dizygotic) twins. A subsequent study by Lykken et al. (1993), like many such studies, also included as respondents identical and fraternal twins as well as nontwin siblings. Often the studies focus also on identical twins raised together and apart, a control of sorts of the environmental in comparison with genetic influences. (Even this characterization has become more complex as the prenatal environment may also influence genetics and child development; see Armstrong-Carter et al., 2020.) Lykken et al. found a substantial component (around 50%) of interest variance to have been heritable. Other researchers have also reported a genetic component to interest patterns (e.g., Grotevant, 1979; Grotevant et al., 1977; J. A. Harris et al., 2006). Moloney et al. (1991), using the Strong Vocational Interest Blank to measure interests, found that genetic factors strongly influenced interests (again explaining about half the variance).

Other biological bases of interests have also been reported, including from studies focusing on the effect of the exposure of the fetus to particular intrauterine hormones on. Sandberg et al. (1987) reported that adolescent girls whose mothers had been exposed to exogenous hormones during pregnancy were more likely to pursue "pioneering" careers (those that were dominated by men) and were more likely to have been tomboys who had little interest in traditional female activities. Beltz et al. (2011) reported evidence showing that women with congenital adrenal hyperplasia (CAH), which involves elevated prenatal in utero exposure to androgens, had more interest in things versus people than did unaffected female siblings. These results provided evidence for hormonal influences on interests in occupations characterized by working primarily with things versus people. There was also a dose-effect relationship such that the higher the prenatal androgen exposure, the greater the interest in things versus people. (Evidence similarly exists for hormonal effects on other abilities; see Chapter 3.)

Still other studies have also provided evidence in support of hormonal influences on interests. Hell and Pässler (2011) examined the relationship between the length of the second and fourth digits, which is hormonally influenced by prenatal testosterone exposure, and found that, for men, there were significant positive correlations with finger lengths and negative correlations with the 2D:4D ratios and Realistic interests (again suggesting hormonal influences on the preference for working with things rather than people). They also reported significant negative correlations between finger lengths and Social interests (which implied a preference for working with people versus things).

Neither genetics nor prenatal exposure to particular hormones is always destiny, of course. The various twin studies generally found that about 50% of the variance in occupational choice was explained by genetics, which means the other half was not. That still leaves a lot of opportunity for other factors, including the environment and personal preferences and choices, to be influential. Additionally, many such studies have only examined single interests rather than interest profiles.

The Structure of Interests

The structure of interests addresses how many factors best represent interest variables, how interest factors relate to one another, and the nature of their underlying positioning in space (e.g., when interest factors are visually positioned in space, what is the shape of the figure they make and are some interests positioned closer to others and others further and what accounts for that?). Some of the studies in this area are complex, and the literature is still emerging, but here some of the highlights are presented. The RIASEC factors developed by Holland and his associates derived from empirical findings (see Cole et al., 1971; G. D. Gottfredson, 1999; G. D. Gottfredson & Johnstun, 2009; J. L. Holland, 1976b). Any summary of the massive amount of research done related to the development and extension of Holland's RIASEC model will necessarily be selective and incomplete. Holland's theory, summarized and elaborated in Holland's early work (J. L. Holland, 1958, 1959, 1962, 1963a, 1963b, 1963c, 1963d, 1966, 1968, 1976a, 1976b; J. L. Holland & Nichols, 1964a, 1964b) and later in his third (and last; he died in 2008) version of *Making Vocational Choices: A Theory of Vocational Personalities and Work Environments* (J. L. Holland, 1997a), is a good place to start. Holland's last book was his most detailed elaboration of his model and supporting evidence. He also created two widely used empirical measures of vocational interests, the Vocational Preference Inventory (J. L. Holland, 1985c) and the Self-Directed Search (J. L. Holland, 1979; J. L. Holland et al., 1994; Reardon & Lenz, 2015). The most recent edition of this venerable instrument, the fifth, is called the Standard Self-Directed Search (J. L. Holland & Messer, 2017); other versions are also available. Holland's theory has inspired an enormous number of studies, including several meta-analyses of studies related to various aspects of the model (e.g., Barrick et al., 2003; Jones et al., 2020; Rachman et al., 1981; Tracey & Rounds, 1993). Here a few of the highlights of these studies are summarized.

Just as in personality research, which has spent decades reducing a larger number of personality variables into a small number of overarching, cross-situational dimensions (including the so-called Big Five models of personality; see Chapter 4), so too have interests also been reduced to a smaller number of overarching dimensions. In the case of interests, six interest factors, sometimes collectively referred to as the "Big Six," have received particular interest and widespread usage.

Each of the RIASEC dimensions is discussed in detail in Chapter 5. Here a few major and differentiating characteristics are introduced: Realistic ("real world" oriented; likes working with things more than ideas and people), Investigative (scientific, abstract, concerned with ideas), Artistic (creative, self-expressive, prefers less structured environments), Social (helpers; enjoys working with other people, especially in teaching, healing, and nurturing roles), Enterprising (enjoys managerial and leadership roles; works with and through others to help individuals and organizations achieve goals), and Conventional (likes data, precision, and numbers; more comfortable with structure, order, and predictability than with ambiguity). The model and evidence did not view the types as being orthogonal (uncorrelated) but rather saw them overlapping in a manner in which certain types were more related to each other than were others. People were viewed as being a combination of the six types, and some were more likely to be compatible with each other than others.

To start with the most popular approach to interests, Holland's model was essentially a one-dimensional, six-factor model with a specified relationship among the six interest types. Holland also maintained that the six RIASEC types were structured such that they formed a hexagonal shape (a variant of a circular model) in which variables closer to each other (e.g., Realistic and Investigative) were most similar, and those most distant from each other (e.g., Realistic and Social) were most dissimilar. The structural questions address whether the six types are related to each other in the manner Holland had hypothesized, whether some other structure best fits the data, and whether the six factors can be summarized or further reduced to a smaller number of overarching factors. However, structural models have also examined the underlying structure that occurs when multiple dimensions, rather than just one, are applied to Holland's model (see Figure 2.1).

There is considerable evidence of the existence, viability, and applied relevance of Holland's six RIASEC factors. Holland (1997a) summarized much of the literature to that point in time. Although there have been several challenges to this representation (e.g., Gati, 1991), none has yet successfully challenged the six types as being a parsimonious set of interest factors or their general circular relationship with each other. However, most of the research on which the original six-factor research was based used occupations that were representative of the broader U.S. occupations at the time but have not been updated to reflect new and emerging occupations.

FIGURE 2.1. Holland's Hexagonal RIASEC Interests Model and Underlying Structure Vectors

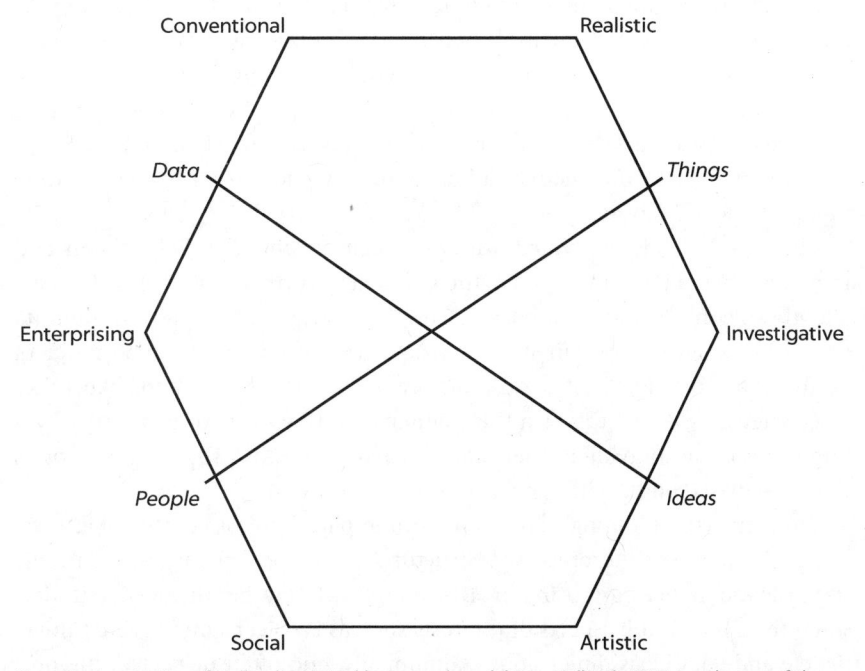

Note. Representation of Holland's original hexagonal model (see Holland, 1997a) and some of the structural vectors found in the literature (Prediger, 1982; Su et al., 2009).

More recent research has included a broader range of occupations that have developed since the earlier six-factor research. Deng et al. (2007) considered whether the research on which Holland's six-factor model had been based was sufficiently representative of the contemporary U.S. occupations. They identified a number of representative newer occupations that had not been included in the original validation of the Holland measures. When these researchers analyzed their data using only occupations included in the Holland-theory-oriented measures, they obtained the same six RIASEC factors. When they analyzed their broader collection of occupations to which their (college student) samples responded, they found the original six RIASEC factors but also some additional, structural, dimensions.

Structural analyses examine the metadimensions that underlie the six RIASEC factors. Two such dimensions were early on identified by Prediger (1982) and consisted of a "things vs. people" vector and a "data vs. ideas" vector. Deng et al. (2007), using updated occupations, found Prediger's "things vs. people" and "data vs. ideas" dimensions and an additional set of nonorthogonal factors related to prestige (desire for a high-status occupation vs. this not being important). These authors also noted the persistent sex differences between men and women, on average, on Realistic interests (men higher) and on Social interests (women higher). Other studies have found sex differences in preferences for Investigative and Enterprising interests.

A good summary of the issues associated with circular structural models is provided in a chapter called "Circular Structure of Vocational Interests" and written by two of the major researchers in this area, Tracey and Rounds (1997). The authors identified three different approaches to a RIASEC-like model, including circular (equal distances between each of the six types), circumplex (identical correlations between adjacent types, alternate types, and opposite types), and exact circumplex (in which all points on the circle have the same relationship with each equidistant points on the circle). Their research suggested that the RIASEC model had a reasonably good fit with each of these models (Tracey & Rounds, 1993).

These authors also provided a useful visual metaphor to help understand their approach. Imagining a globe, the two poles (north and south) would parallel the "People/Things" dimension. The "equator" would represent the Data versus Ideas dimension. Finally, they recognized the role and importance of occupational prestige (not a new factor; see Davies, 1952) and, like other researchers, presented this as a third dimension. However, when prestige was important to an individual, their data argued, it in effect superseded choices that were based on fit with specific interest areas.

These structural findings have important implications for vocational interest test choice and test interpretation. Structural studies do not suggest the necessity to abandon measures using the RIASEC types but rather the need to understand the overarching aspects of interests such as Prediger's underlying things-people and data-ideas dimensions. Additionally, and often neglected, the preferred prestige level people seek in their work interacts with the perceived prestige level of occupations. Thus, some people will find particular occupations of interest (think medical doctor, lawyer, airplane pilot) because of their being prestigious somewhat independently of the job or career content. Note that prestige tends to correlate well with salaries and work autonomy. Such findings also suggest that clients may need to understand how prestige needs may keep them from exploring lower prestige occupations despite having scored high on particular interests relevant for such careers. Exploring the meaning of prestige and of family or peer pressures for higher status occupations can be useful. Clients may also want to consider the higher status occupations in a field that, on average, is lower in prestige. For example, Realistic occupations include many "hands-on" lower status occupations, but the category also includes engineers and airplane pilots.

Relationship of Interests and Occupational Environments

Of particular importance, Holland's model holds that both people and environments can be measured on the same six basic occupationally relevant variables (technically, factors or dimensions). Holland's (1997a) major book on his models pointedly included "work environments" in its title. His assumption that the same variables could be used to describe people at the individual level and careers or organizations was one of the theory's most innovative and important features, for it lent itself to considerations of "fit" of persons with alternative types of work and with particular work settings.

Extrapolating from an individual difference variable like interests to an entire occupation or to a work group or organization is a risky and complicated business, and it is worth noting how such research has proceeded. Assuming Holland's RIASEC model for purposes of this discussion, the manner in which research and practice typically measure occupational interests at the group, career, or organizational level is to aggregate the interest scores. Individual scores are then compared with group scores using a variety of indices assessing fit. This is the same issue associated with examining whether there is stability in interests within the same person when measured over time.

Because Holland's model is a six-factor one, the question arises as to how many interest scores should be compared to determine degree of fit. Some studies have used only the single highest endorsed interest score while others have used the top three endorsed interests. Additionally, when examining the interests of people in a particular occupation there can be considerable variance not directly associated with interests. People can gravitate to careers for many reasons including financial rewards, occupational prestige, and the like, and people can do well in a job but not particularly like it. When measuring interests of those in particular occupations, it may therefore be important to use samples of people who are satisfied in their careers. An alternative, more complicated, and less used approach is to examine the specific job duties and make judgements about how those duties relate to particular interest characteristics.

Part of the validity of the RIASEC model of environments is whether particular occupations (e.g., those requiring primarily "hands-on" work; those focusing on science, on business, and the like), are populated by people who, on average, match the expected interest pattern. There is a fairly extensive literature in this area (see, e.g., Aranya et al., 1981; J. L. Holland, 1997b; Lowman & Ng, 2010) that generally supports the hypothesis that people in occupations tend on average to work in occupations matching their interests and that the nature of the work duties tends to be consistent with the interest types. There is variability in such research, however, and many studies only compared the highest endorsed interest type, not the three-digit pattern.

Individual Differences in Interests

The research literature on interests has considered group differences in a number of individual difference variables.[1] Here some of the major findings associated with individual difference variables are identified.

Sex

A large and often contentious body of literature (J. L. Holland et al., 1975; Horton & Walsh, 1976) has addressed the question of whether existing measures of vocational interest are sex biased in the sense that there are group differences between men and women on interest scales. "Bias" is not exactly the right word to use since it implies that the tests measure differences that either do not really exist or that result in differential validity on the basis of sex.

This matter and controversy have deep roots (e.g., Harvey & Whinfield, 1973). Some researchers (e.g., Lamb & Prediger, 1980; Prediger & Cole, 1975; Prediger & Hanson, 1974, 1976a, 1976b; see also Prediger, 1980) have argued that interest measures should be scored in such a manner that they are sex neutral, that is, with no mean differences between men and women on the items (for an illustration of the extremes of this argument, see Freeman, 1979, and Closs, 1976). Holland and his associates, in contrast, have maintained (J. L. Holland et al., 1975; see also Ghetta et al., 2018; Hansen, 1976) that there are persistent sex differences between men and women in occupational preferences and that a vocational interest inventory that does not recognize these differences is itself problematic. Other researchers have found sex differences in vocational interest factor structures (see Tuck & Keeling, 1980).

All that said, the persistent findings of sex differences in vocational interests (which appear to emerge early, see Gregg & Dobson, 1980) should not be dismissed or seen as being solely the product of societal attitudes. M. L. Morris (2016) reported on the results of a very large sample of 1,283,110 respondents who took the Strong interest measure between 2005 and 2015 (511,814 men [40%] and 771,296 women [60%], ages 14 to 63 with at least 1,500 respon-

---

[1] By "group," I mean to suggest an average or expected pattern more likely to be found in the ability or personality domain, such as high levels of intelligence on average being associated with Investigative interest patterns. On an individual level, however, interests may or may not be associated with ability or personality patterns.

dents in each of the age years). He found substantial sex differences across ages and ethnicities. Overall, women endorsed, on average, higher scores on the Social and Artistic interest variables and men had, on average, higher scores on Realistic, Investigative, Enterprising, and Conventional scales. Sex differences were found across all the age groups but tended to decrease in the older age groups.

A study by Brooks (1983) found differences in expressed interests of eighth graders no matter whether occupations were discussed in sex neutral or sex "biased" terms. Crowley (1981) reported that a career intervention program designed to increase occupational knowledge was successful in doing so, but it did not change sex-specific differences in expressed preferences. Although many women have increasingly chosen to enter traditionally male-dominated occupations (e.g., Yogev, 1983), women continue to express vocational interests that are somewhat different from those of men and vice versa (Apostal, 1991; J. Campbell, 1976; Hansen, 1988; Hansen et al., 1993; Kirkcaldy, 1988; Lunneborg & Gerry, 1977; O'Shea & Harrington, 1974; Schulenberg et al., 1991; Tétreau & Trahan, 1988; Weller et al., 1976). The relative proportion of women and men in an occupation may also affect expressed vocational interests in the occupation (Adelmann, 1989; M. E. Heilman, 1979; Krefting et al., 1978). Although the effects of occupational perceptions of male-dominated occupations for women have been widely studied, the effects of increasing feminization of occupations on men have been less examined (see M. E. Heilman, 1979). J. Collins et al. (1980), for example, found that male interest in an occupation was influenced by the perceived percentage of women in it. Levanon et al. (2009), in a longitudinal study spanning from 1950 to 2000, considered why occupations with higher percentages of women pay less than those with proportionately fewer women. This phenomenon occurs even after controlling for education and required skills. They found support for the devaluation hypothesis, which holds that occupations dominated by women tend to be devalued by employers and therefore lower paid. This in turn may affect the appeal of female-dominated occupations to men.

Men and women may also differ in how they process and approach occupational information and in their vocational maturity (to approach career choice carefully and systematically; Gade & Peterson, 1977). Women may also be more likely than men to emphasize goodness of fit of interests and personality patterns in choosing whether to further explore a particular career choice (Subich et al., 1986).

It is clearly possible to create an interest measure with no sex differences by choosing only scale items for which there are no sex differences. However, such an instrument may come at the expense of validity. If there are persistent sex differences in interests by sex, as decades of research has persisted in showing, then a measure that does not show those differences would need to demonstrate that it is still valid for its intended inferences. Although some interest scales systematically and persistently differ by gender, there is little evidence to suggest that current, widely used measures of interests are differentially valid for their intended inferences or that the structure of interests for men and women systematically differs (see Day & Rounds, 1998). As M. L. Morris (2016) noted,

> Assessments designed to minimize sex differences have their uses, but accurate measurement of sex differences is better done using measures that were developed without regard to minimizing or maximizing sex differences. During the development of the most recent Strong assessment, sex differences on the RIASEC measures were examined and deemed to be generally consistent with previous research. No intentional modifications were made to RIASEC measures based on sex differences. (p. 613)

Some recent approaches have focused on reducing sex differences at the item level without sacrificing validity. In a promising study, Pässler et al. (2014) considered some of these questions and examined whether a German interest measure that reduced sex differences at the item level would predict as well or better career choice and satisfaction. The research was suggestive in that all participants were college students and the focus was on satisfaction with college major or with work in an internship, which may not generalize to post-college career choices. The authors reported that their methodology reduced sex differences while maintaining structural consistency of the interest types, and validity coefficients were promising.

From a practice perspective, the goal of career assessment and counseling is to help clients consider all occupations relevant to their interests and not to avoid any occupations that they may consider to be "appropriate" for only one sex or another. Although the removal of barriers to entrance or advancement on the basis of sex have made substantial progress in recent decades, at least in many countries, and the perceptions of gender-linked characteristics also have changed in the United States (see, e.g., Eagly et al., 2019), perceived barriers or sex-inappropriateness can and do matter in some career choices. At the same time, if there are real differences in some of the types of work that men on average and women on average prefer then they need to be taken into account in interest assessment and feedback.

To elaborate, if a woman wants to be a nurse or a man wants to be a plumber or mechanic, those are not choices to be discouraged when their interests and other variables are a good fit. But when a man is considering health care occupations and rejects nursing because of stereotypes and preconceived notions or when a woman with Realistic interests is experiencing family pressure to reject truck driving or plumbing as not being sex-appropriate, career assessors or counselors can potentially help clients give full consideration to all relevant options. This may entail exploration of the assumptions the client is making that may be limiting career options, including helping them think through how to navigate the external pressures and influences.

Race/Ethnicity

A number of issues arise from the career assessment literature when it comes to the individual difference variables associated with race/ethnicity. Much of growing literature in this area has been focused on racial/ethnic groups associated with U.S. protected classes. These include Asian Americans (Kantamneni,

2014; Leong & Leung, 1994); Black Americans (R. P. Bingham & Walsh, 1978; R. T. Carter & Swanson, 1990; Greenlee et al., 1988; Jones et al., 2020; Strong, 1952; J. L. Swanson, 1992; C. M. Ward & Walsh, 1981), Hispanic Americans (Lattimore & Borgen, 1999), and Native Americans (Hansen et al., 2000; Kantamneni, 2014). However, there are many other categories of ethnic/racial groups than these that have rarely been studied, including Arab Americans (see Kanamneni, 2014, and Kantamneni & Fouad, 2011) and a variety of groups of people who immigrated to the United States but who retain strong ethnic/country-of-origin identities, including Israeli Americans, Chaldean Iraqi Americans, and so forth (see Lowman, 2013). Other rapidly growing groups for whom, thanks to the increasing ability to deliver services virtually (see Chapter 20), assessment services may be provided are those who reside in countries different from the assessor's. This type of service delivery raises issues not just of country-specific factors that may influence assessment results, but also within-country group differences associated with racial/ethnic groups that may differ from those in the United States. For example, a U.S.-based assessor delivering services to clients in Canada must consider large French Canadian and First Nations groups.

Concerning racial/ethnic differences, even limiting the focus to traditional U.S. categories, there are several issues to be considered. First there is the seemingly straightforward question of whether there are consistent group differences (averages) by race/ethnicity in endorsement of different interests compared with majority or other groups. However, if such differences are found, the question arises as to what factors influence why such differences occur. A second question concerns whether there are differences in the structural models that underlie interests and the implications for interest interpretation. To what extent are endorsed interests, possibly depending on the particular measure(s) used, reflective of cultural values associated with particular occupational choices, with expectations (minimized or, in some cases, excessively high), or with occupational status issues? Third, is there evidence of differential validity for the measures based on race/ethnicity? Finally, when working at the individual level, it is important to carefully consider whether factors other than the individual difference variable itself may be influencing the expressed preference. If, for example, career choices are being influenced by a lack of understanding of available options or by low self-efficacy, those may need to be addressed.

Group Differences in Endorsement of Particular Interests. In examining group differences in interests, consideration needs to be given to the size and representativeness of samples used for such comparisons. If racial/ethnic samples used in research and in norming assessment measures are small and more opportunistic than representative, this can affect the ability to draw reliable conclusions or to provide useful feedback. Nor are such groups likely to be homogeneous. Yet, many samples are based on college students or high school students taking interest measures as part of standardized admissions tests. If those are not the groups with whom the career assessor will be working, consideration must be given to the appropriateness of the reported findings or norms. Finally, there are a number of different interest measures commonly used. There may be differences from one interest measure to another in how interests are measured, which in turn may affect obtained results.

Here some of the studies done in this area will be briefly reviewed. Most made use of U.S.-based samples, U.S.-based racial/ethnic groupings, and often have used the Strong interest measures.

Fouad et al. (1997) reported racial and gender differences among racial groups using the SII. Examining the within-group averages, none of the eight groups (male and female African Americans, Asian Americans, Latinos, and Caucasians) had the same interest pattern when considering their top three endorsed interests. Only the African American groups had Social interests as the highest endorsed interest for both men and women. For each of the other three racial/ethnic groups, Artistic interests were most highly endorsed by the female groups. Male Latinos and Caucasians, on average, most highly endorsed Realistic interests, and the male Asian American group, Investigative. The male and female three-letter most highly endorsed interest codes differed significantly for Caucasian, Latino/a, and Asian American groups. However, for the African American groups, the top three codes were quite similar, with women's top three codes being Social–Enterprising–Conventional and men's being Social–Conventional–Enterprising. For all groups, women, on average, endorsed Realistic interests last and, with the exception of Asian American women, Social interests either first or second. Conversely, Realistic and Investigative interests were most highly endorsed for each of the male groups except for African Americans. Overall, these findings suggest that there are differences in the average endorsed interests across student groups and that gender and race interact to influence observed differences (see, e.g., K. A. S. Howard et al., 2011). Jones et al. (2020) conducted a meta-analysis with over 900,000 people in the combined samples comparing group differences of African Americans' and Caucasian Americans' highest measured interests. They found mean differences in Realistic and Investigative (Caucasians higher), and, like the Fouad et al. (1997) study, Social interests were more highly endorsed by African Americans, but Enterprising and Conventional interests were also higher compared with Caucasians. Moderator effects were found for education (the differences increased as education level increased, particularly after entering college), age (for Social, Enterprising, and Conventional interests), and sex (for men with Realistic and Social interests). However, they also found some evidence that these differences may be decreasing within more recent age cohorts.

Saw et al. (2018) examined interests in STEM careers in a nationally representative longitudinal study of high school students in the ninth and 11th grades. Those students who were Black, Hispanic, female, and from low socioeconomic status (SES) families were less likely to express interests in STEM careers than were White and Asian American students at both data points. Among those groups that had expressed interests in STEM careers in ninth grade, the same ethnic/gender groups were also lower in persisting in their interests from ninth to 11th grades during high school or in expressing interests in STEM occupations in 11th grade when they had not done so in ninth grade. Overall, it was a distinct minority of all respondents who envisioned themselves in a STEM career at either grade level, with overall averages being 11.4% at Time 1 (T1) and 10% at Time 2 (T2), and only 34.3% of those expressing interest in STEM occupations at T1 persisted in their STEM interests in T2, with a small group (6.9% of the overall sample) reporting STEM interests at T2 versus T1. These findings suggest an interaction of SES and race/gender in the occupations in which students express interest, at least for STEM occupations.

M. L. Morris's (2016) already-introduced study included a large, mostly U.S.-based sample, of respondents who had indicated their race/ethnicity starting in 2008, when race/ethnicity was added to the demographic options, to December 2014. The data for the race/ethnicity analyses were from 1,283,110 people who either indicated that they were located in the United States ($n = 775,070$) or who did not respond to that question but, based on other evidence, were assumed to have been U.S.-based ($n = 508,040$). Respondents were able to select more than one racial category (which 81,392 [6.8%] did). The analyzed samples included 830,530 Whites (69.1%), 150,816 Latinos (12.6%), 94,700 Native Americans and Alaskan Natives (7.9%), 81,519 Asians (6.8%), 77,856 Blacks (6.5%), 14,917 Middle Easterners (1.2%), 11,406 Indians (0.9%), 7,796 Other Pacific Islanders (0.9% of the samples since the category was added to the original choices), and 25,346 Other (2.1%). In contrast to many studies, they also included samples of Native Americans and those of Middle Eastern identity, as well as those of Indian subcontinent ethnicity/race. However, they noted that the obtained differences across groups were relatively small and far less significant than differences by sex and were also lower than age group differences. In particular, they found larger response differences by age for Blacks with lower Realistic and more data-oriented findings in the more recent samples. They also reported Blacks and Native Americans being lower on Realistic than other groups. Native American/Alaskan Native, Middle Easterners, and Asians scored higher on Investigative and Enterprising than respondents who did not specify their race. Pacific Islander groups were higher than other groups on Realistic, Artistic, and Social interests and Whites were lower on Conventional interests.

Although, to the extent they may reflect modal group/environment influences, it is worth being aware of group differences, it is also important to keep in mind that apparent racial/ethnic group differences in interests sometimes mask differences on other important variables. Sex, education, age, and SES differences are often embedded in racial differences, and these can account for some of the obtained differences (see K. A. S. Howard et al., 2011). Such interactions need to be considered when interpreting career assessment interpretation of results, and in providing clients feedback and counseling.

Structural Differences. Comparison across mean differences may be of limited value when the underlying structure of interests varies. To date there has been mixed evidence about structural differences by race/ethnicity.

Early studies of cross-cultural adaptations of various interest structures (Fouad et al., 1984) found similar factor structures for Spanish and English versions of the Strong Vocational Interest Blank. Such conclusions are mirrored in an article titled "Universality of Vocational Interest Structure Among Racial and Ethnic Minorities" by Day and Rounds (1998; see also Day et al., 1998), which used a sample of mostly college-bound test takers who had taken the ACT's unisex version of an interest measure called UNIACT. The large sample ($n = 49,450$) included 18,159 African Americans (37% of the overall sample), of whom 11,400 (63%) were women; 6,523 Asian Americans (13% of the overall sample), of whom 3,553 (54%) were women; 6,019 Mexican Americans (Latinos/as; 12% of the overall sample); of whom 3,464 (58%) were women; and 2,643 Native Americans (5% of the overall sample), of whom 1,530 (58%) were women. The sample also included 16,106 (33% of the overall sample) Caucasian test takers, of whom 9,469 (59%) were women. The authors noted that these were complete samples of those ethnic/racial groups who had completed the Strong measure in October 1989, except for the Caucasian group, which was a sample consisting of 1/12 of the much larger Caucasian group who had taken the test during that time period. Clearly, these samples were not representative of the general population (since noncollege aspirants were not included) and constituted, in effect, a convenience sample. Additionally, only one measure of interests was used.

The authors argued that inputting individual items (rather than scale scores) was more appropriate for finding structural differences. Were scale scores to have been inputted, there would only have been six variables per person rather than 90 items. The particular methodology made use of three-way individual differences scaling. The authors concluded that (a) the circular structure and predicted RIASEC order was supported for all racial/ethnic groups, (b) two dimensions (data vs. ideas and people vs. things) were also found for all groups, and (c) there were no structural differences among the groups by either race/ethnicity or sex. The authors stated, somewhat exuberantly, "In the case of vocational interest structure, the idea that racial-ethnic subgroups in the United States vary from the majority is parallel to the idea that these subgroups do not use east-west, north-south, and high-low in their thinking about geography" (Day & Rounds, 1998, p. 733).

Other studies have also provided support for the structural models of the Holland constructs with racial/ethnic minorities. For example, Kantamneni and Fouad (2011), in a small sample study also using the Strong instrumentation, found support for the circular and exact fit structure for all of the racial/ethnic groups considered except for African American women and Latino working adults.

There is not unanimity in these conclusions, however. Some studies, also using convenience samples and generally conducted with smaller samples than those of the Day and Rounds (1998) study, have found structural differences by racial group. Tracey and Rounds (1997) did not find that the various circular order models fit as well for international samples or for U.S. African American,

Latino/a, Asian American, or Native American groups as they did for the overall U.S. samples, male/female groups, and age groups, or when analyzed by specific interest measure. Leong and Hartung (2000) reviewed other structural studies and also found differences in some of Holland's structural hypotheses for U.S. ethnic/racial groups.

Given the mixed nature of the results to date for racial/ethnic groups, more research is needed before broad conclusions can reliably be drawn. Studies with larger and more representative ethnic/racial samples, making use of multiple interest measures, and with international samples will help to clarify some of the mixed findings. There have also been calls (e.g., Tracey, 2002; Pässler et al., 2014) for the use of newly constructed or still-to-be-constructed interest measures designed to address issues of varying groups, including those interested in higher versus lower levels of occupational prestige occupations and sex or ethnic/racial groups. Although some of these measures are promising, none appears yet to have a sufficiently large research base to recommend them for current usage that would substitute for some of the better-validated widely used measures currently in use.

Differential Validity. Leong and Hartung (2000) called attention to the need to understand the "cultural validity" and whether various factors associated with culture may affect career assessment results. They also addressed the need to create and validate "culture specific" assessment instrumentation. Implicitly, at least, this raises the issue of whether there is differential validity among existing, widely used career assessment measures.

The concept of differential validity is often confused as occurring when there are group differences. Clearly, as discussed, there are interest factors (Realistic and Social, to name two) on which men, on average, and women, on average, differ. However, for there to be differential validity based on that group difference, the tests would have to differentially predict relevant criterion measures. That is, when using interests measures to predict career choice or other outcome variables, the measures might predict well for the majority group but not for the minority group.

In the case of interests, the question arises about the relevant outcome criteria that would be used to assess the potential presence of differential validity. Structural studies (factor analyses and the like) provide evidence for construct validity of interests and should be similar for the groups. As for criterion-related evidence of validity, however, complicated questions arise. Whereas most differential validity studies concerning abilities use criteria such as job performance ratings or turnover, the outcomes for interests are more complicated. The purpose of measuring interests is to describe interest patterns such that people can better understand themselves and can more clearly examine their career and life choice. Interests are also used to predict careers for which people are best suited. These uses imply the need for outcome criteria that would include personal job satisfaction and perceived goodness of fit when people's interests are congruent and/or consistent. Nevertheless, interests have now been found to have relevance for use in selection, generally in combination with other predictors, particularly abilities (see Nye et al., 2012, 2017; Van Iddekinge, Putka, & Campbell, 2011).

R. T. Carter and Swanson (1990) reviewed eight studies that had used the Strong and had included Black U.S. respondents. They found group differences in scale elevation with Black Americans scoring higher than White Americans on business and social interests. Validity evidence was limited with some mixed results. Others (e.g., J. L. Swanson, 1992) found more promising results supporting the use of the measure with Black Americans.

Other empirical studies have also been promising, though different approaches to validation evidence are often used from one study to the next. Lattimore and Borgen (1999) used the "match" approach to validity, in which results of individuals used for the instrument's norming, who had completed the Strong interest measure as part of the 1994 revision to the instrument, were compared with the actual careers in which they were working. The degree of match was between the high point interest score and the respondents' current occupation. The results found comparable results across all groups, which included (relatively small) samples of African Americans, Asian Americans, Hispanic Americans/Latinos/Latinas, and Native Americans/American Indians and a much larger sample of Caucasians. These samples were all college-educated adults with mean ages in their late 30s to early 40s. Fouad and Mohler (2004) also used a data set from the Strong to examine racial differences among a group of students, working adults, homemakers, and retirees. The median age of this group was 20. Importantly, the study included 750 respondents each from the same five racial/ethnic groups used by Lattimore and Borgen (1999). The authors used a variety of methods to examine structural differences across the various groups and also included sex as a factor. Only minor differences were found by race/ethnicity (in contrast to sex differences). They concluded that their evidence supported the use of the Strong with these racial groups, at least in the U.S. context.

Career Assessment and Counseling With Members of Racially and Ethnically Diverse Groups. There is an expansive literature on the role of race in both assessment and intervention in counseling and psychotherapy (see, e.g., American Psychological Association [APA], 2017b), but the literature on race/ethnicity and career assessment and intervention is more modest and, for the most part, more recent. Still, there are studies examining the interaction of work/career factors that identify issues needing to be unpacked. Complex interactions between sex, race, and SES have been demonstrated in several studies.

Members of a racial/ethnic group are certainly not a homogeneous or monolithic group. This means the career choices of individuals may not be particularly influenced by race/ethnicity alone. Sensitivity by the assessor to the issues that are associated with career choices of minorities should lead to raising the topic of race and minority status, if the client does not raise it, and providing a safe space in which to explore how the client has experienced influences from family, the schools, peers, or the larger environment and how they may be affecting career choices. For example, if clients were raised in an underprivileged home in which aspirations may have been set artificially low (or high) and the client has experienced pressure to go into (or to avoid) a particular occupation, those assumptions may need to be examined.

Summary. Overall, a reasonable conclusion at this time is that more evidence is needed before drawing definitive conclusions about race/ethnicity and interests but to date differences by race/ethnicity appear to be small, nonstructural, and generally less strong than sex and age differences. Future research will benefit by applying the same kind of rigorous research reflected in many of the studies cited here, using adequately sized and representative samples, multiple interest measures, and disaggregating across interacting variables such as sex and age. Overall, to date, there is sufficient evidence of validity for the intended inferences to justify use of appropriate interest measures across racial/ethnic groups, at least in the United States, particularly when mean differences in particular racial groups are taken into account.

Age

Age is an important individual differences variable to be taken into account in measuring interests, especially with younger and older test takers. Considering that the major purposes of assessment are typically helping to identify college major or occupational choices, the needs of young test takers and older ones may vary. When people have retired (or are contemplating retirement) their focus for assessment is likely to be on preferences for increased leisure time or better understanding, rather than on career choice or change. If considering new career directions, their perspectives on what is possible may suppress consideration of particular occupations that realistically are not likely. Conversely, young adults or teens may imagine a broader range of choices than may be feasible or may be more swayed by popular career options.

When considering age as an individual difference variable, there are at least two factors to consider. One, already discussed, is the question of whether interests at the individual level are stable over time. The other is whether there are systematic differences of groups by age cohort such that assessing individuals' interests at certain ages may have differences as a function of age or age cohort.

As noted, interests do not become stable (or "crystallized") until the late teens or early 20s. After that, as discussed in the stability section of this chapter, they become fairly predictable at least for the working years. Rottinghaus et al. (2007) examined 30-year retest interest data whose initial sample had consisted of all juniors and seniors in a small consolidated rural high school who had taken the Kuder Occupational Interest Survey (KOIS). An impressive 89% ($n = 107$) of the initial test takers were located and their current occupations determined. Of those, 76 completed the KOIS a second time in 2005. Although KOIS was not designed around the RIASEC types, its occupational interest scales are quite similar to them. They included Outdoor and Mechanical scales (similar to Realistic interests in the RIASEC model), Scientific (Investigative), Artistic, Musical, and Literary (Artistic), Social Service (Social), Persuasive (Enterprising), and Computational and Clerical (Conventional). Each of these interest areas had moderate test-retest correlations across 30 years (mean Spearman rho = 54). Sex differences, however, were found both at the original time and in the test-retest results. The authors identified a subset of individuals whose interests changed significantly and those whose were quite stable and considered whether these phenomena may have reflected a difference in interest stability versus openness. Overall, the 1975 KOIS had fairly high predictive validity suggesting that for most, but not all, people, interests tend to be stable over time.

Why are interests not very stable before late adolescence to early adulthood? Evidence was provided in Hoff et al. (2018), an important meta-analysis of 49 longitudinal studies that examined changes in interests from early adolescence to adulthood. They found that interests generally decreased by early adolescence but then increased by late adolescence. Overall, interests in people (reflected in Social, Enterprising, and Artistic interests) increased over time and interest in things decreased (in the case of Conventional interests) or did not change (for Realistic and Investigative interests). Sex differences in interests peaked in early adolescence and decreased thereafter. This study suggests a possible basis for why interests may not be reliably predictable until young adulthood, implying that the road to trait-like predictability may be preceded by changes, possibly predictable, as children move developmentally from childhood to middle years to adolescence to adulthood. It further suggests that, in addition to demonstrating the value of longitudinal research, studies of children's interests may reflect patterns that may be different over time than at the point of data collection.

Concerning cohort differences, Strong (1931, 1951a), examined interests of men in eight occupations (including engineers and lawyers) aged 20 to 59. The breadth of interests did not decrease over the age span, but there was a small (15%) overall difference in what younger versus older men preferred. Strong noted that about half of the total differences occurred between 25 and 35, and 30% occurred between 45 and 55. Lower interests were reported by older respondents in activities involving risk, and more focus was reported on stability versus change as well as a greater liking for activities done alone. Importantly, Strong noted that the cohort differences overall were far less than the differences across those in different occupations.

Bubany and Hansen (2011) conducted a meta-analysis of aggregated vocational interest profiles by birth cohort of college students from the time period of 1976 to 2004 to see if interest patterns had changed over time. They found that Enterprising interests of women increased and Realistic and Investigative interests of men had decreased over this time period. There was also a decline in the differences between female and male Investigative, Enterprising, and Conventional interests.

Low et al. (2005) conducted a meta-analysis of stability studies including respondents from early adolescence (age 12) to middle age (age 40). They found that interests became stable and remained that way from the early 20s to around age 40, the extent of this study's focus. There were some differences in birth cohort in that those born in the 1940s (who would have reached their 20s in the turbulent 1960s) had less stability in their interests than did the other groups. The authors also found that there was greater stability in Realistic and Artistic interest than in Investigative, Social, Enterprising, and Conventional interests. Overall, the researchers noted that the stability of interests was higher than for personality variables (see Chapters 13–15).

M. L. Morris's (2016) study concerning race and sex, already discussed, also considered age differences in interests across age cohorts. Morris's research found a general pattern of older versus younger respondents endorsing more interest items, possibly reflecting a willingness to consider a broader range of occupations as they aged. Additionally, sex differences in their samples were larger in the younger groups. Leuty and Hansen (2014) examined the relationship of age and birth year cohort on interests in a sample of 1,792 adults spanning the period from 1974 to 1995 who had sought out counseling services from a university-based clinic. Neither age nor birth year predicted interests except for Realistic interests, which, contrary to Low et al.'s (2005) findings of an increase in Realistic interests, showed a small decline with age and birth cohort though there were low effect sizes. More powerful than age in predicting interests over time was sex, with men being higher on Realistic and Investigative interests and women on Artistic and Social.

Overall, there have been findings of some effects of age and birth cohort on interests, but they generally have been shown to have less impact than do other individual difference variables, particularly sex. Some of the inconsistencies in apparent interest cohort differences will require further research to sort out as will the effects of other variables that tend to be associated with stage-of-development changes. However, assessors should consider age of respondents, combined with the purpose of the testing, in interpreting interest results.

HOW VOCATIONAL INTERESTS RELATE TO OCCUPATIONAL AND OTHER OUTCOMES

A thesis of this book is that people well matched (congruent) with their occupations and with the organizations in which they work are more apt to be satisfied in their careers (and often in their jobs, assuming they are well fit to their interests), to remain in their jobs, and to be productive employees. And although there is some evidence to support this concept, at least for occupational choice satisfaction (e.g., Meir, 1988), the relationship between job satisfaction and interests appears to be complex (see Amerikaner et al., 1988; D. P. Campbell & Klein, 1975; Dipboye et al., 1978; Elton & Smart, 1988; Heesacker et al., 1988; Hoff et al., 2020; Hunter & Hunter, 1984; Klein & Wiener, 1977;

Kunce et al., 1976; Peiser & Meir, 1978; Wiener & Klein, 1978). For example, certain interest types, most notably those with high Social interests, may be the most likely to report satisfaction with their jobs, somewhat independent of the degree of congruence (Amerikaner et al., 1988; Heesacker et al., 1988), suggesting that satisfaction with careers and jobs may be multidetermined.

Additionally, how fit is measured can influence the conclusions drawn (see Wiegand et al., 2021). The most recent, and most comprehensive, meta-analysis on the relationships of interests and job satisfaction was conducted by Hoff et al. (2020). These authors corrected the correlations for unreliability and considered not just the relationship of interests with job satisfaction but also with facets of job satisfaction (job and organizational choice, and satisfaction with pay, coworkers, and the like). The results showed a significant correlation between interests and overall job satisfaction ($\rho = .19$) but much higher correlation with job choice ($\rho = .34$) and organizational ($\rho = .33$) satisfaction. The correlations with extrinsic aspects of satisfaction were much lower. It also mattered how interests were measured; a simple index of whether there was a match of the career choice and the highest interest RIASEC category resulted in the strongest correlations, higher, curiously, than with the more complex congruence indices.

Another complex question concerns whether interests also predict to job performance in work. Although past research has suggested that interests were not very predictive of job performance, especially when compared with cognitive abilities (see Nye et al., 2012; Schmidt & Hunter, 1998), abilities in general, and intelligence in particular, still take first place in predicting job outcome criteria (see Chapter 5). Sackett et al.'s (2017) review on interest research in the *Journal of Applied Psychology* noted that there had been a roller-coaster pattern of studies about interests and work outcomes. Dry spells when interests were thought to be unimportant for work outcome studies were followed by upticks in research as new approaches were employed. A recent longitudinal study by Hoff et al. (in press) found that adolescent vocational interests predicted to early career success.

Again, methodology matters. Because the amount of variance explained by interests was low when interest variables were simply correlated with work outcomes, few asked why the correlations of interests were as low as they appeared to be. Correlating Holland's six major interest types (RIASEC) one interest type at a time with job outcomes ignored the issue that interests are more based on goodness of fit with particular types of work. Thus, if interests are examined as a group without considering the nature of the job in which the work is performed, shared variance would likely be low. In an alternative approach, the theoretical or empirical coding of the interest patterns best suited to the job duties is compared with individual interest profiles. Van Iddekinge, Putka, and Campbell (2011) examined the relationships of interests and job outcomes. They found, consistent with past research, that the relationships of single interest scales and job performance were typically relatively low (0.14) in a meta-analysis of 74 studies but that they were higher (0.26) for training criteria, turnover intentions (−0.19), and actual turnover (−0.15). They also identified moderators in such relationships, including whether interests were related to actual job duties (a congruence-type concept), which measure of interests was used, and whether multiple interest scales or just one was used to assess outcomes. They (Van Iddekinge, Putka, & Campbell, 2011) went on to design and provide initial validation evidence for a selection-relevant measure of interests, which showed promising validity in predicting to several work-related criteria. Also contributing to a more complex view of interests' use in personnel selection, Jones et al. (2020) suggested that interests held potential for understanding adverse impact (differential selection ratios by protected classes) by examining whether interests predisposed members of certain protected classes from applying for jobs.

Other studies have examined the role of interests versus personality and intelligence in predicting occupational and other outcomes (see Chapter 17). In a 10-year longitudinal study of German high school students who had completed interests, personality, and general cognitive ability measures at the end of high school, Stoll et al. (2017) found that interests were useful over and above intelligence and personality variables in predicting seven outcome variables: employment, gross income, unemployment, being married, having children, never having had a relationship, and perceived health status.

Congruence

Congruence refers to the idea that a match between a person's measured interests and their work is likely to have positive work-related outcomes whereas a lack of congruence is not. The overall relationship between interest congruency and occupational or school outcomes, a measure of predictive validity, is pretty straightforward conceptually. It identifies job or school subject/major characteristics and the interests that theoretically should be related to those. The concept is that, since occupations were chosen on one's own, the closer the match between individual characteristics and the job/occupation (or for that matter, leisure and avocational activities; see Leuty & Hansen, 2013; Leuty et al., 2016) the more supported was congruence theory and also the more likely there would be positive outcomes. However, there is not a single operational definition of congruence, which is, essentially, the match of a person's interests with those found among persons in the same occupation who, preferably, are satisfied and productive in their work. A more recent approach to measuring congruence is considering the match of interests to the major job duties in particular careers. There are a variety of ways that congruence can be measured.

For purposes of research, there must be a quantitative methodology for comparing persons and jobs. Several indices have been developed for computing the match between a person's interests and the classification of the job on the same interest variables. These include the Zener-Schnuelle index (J. L. Holland, 1985a), the M Index (Iachan, 1984, 1990), and the C-Index (Eggerth & Andrew, 2006). For reviews of congruence indices and comparisons among the various measures, see S. D. Brown and Gore (1994), Camp and Chartrand (1992), Lowman et al. (2003), Subich (1992), and Xu and Li (2020).

There have been many studies on congruence and its relationship to school and work satisfaction and outcome measures published in the last few decades. An important meta-analysis of 60 years of research on the relationships of interests and work/school outcomes is found in Nye et al. (2012, 2017). The authors considered evidence as to whether congruence of interests and occupations predicted work outcomes. They noted that the likely mechanisms for any such relationships were the role of interests in focusing energy in specific areas, in increasing energy for activities related to job (or school), and in sustaining those activities over time. Their findings included a total sample size of over 15,000 individual respondents and demonstrated that, compared with studies examining only the correlations between interest scale scores and work and school outcomes, those examining congruence scores and outcomes were consistently in the moderate (rather than low) range. Overall, congruence scores were moderately correlated with Task Performance, Organizational Citizenship Behavior, and Persistence. They did not, however, predict well to Counterproductive Workplace Behavior (CWB). In the case of academic performance, congruence of interests and area of study also predicted at the moderate level both persistence and grades. These authors published a further analysis in 2017 with 92 studies (1,858 correlations) and found that interests scores alone correlated on average 0.16 but interest congruence measures, 0.32, with work-related outcomes.

Summarizing the results of his review of similar literature, Dawis (1991) concluded, "Self-report measures of interests, values, and preferences are useful predictors of occupational or job tenure and occupational or job satisfaction and can contribute significantly, if modestly, to the prediction of worker satisfactoriness"(p. 863). This summary is consistent with subsequent research findings. Much of the research on interests and work or school outcomes has used methodologies such as those just discussed. However, other studies have examined congruence/incongruence outcomes differently. Two studies are illustrative. Andrews (1975) examined whether adult students who were presently employed in full-time positions and who were attending community college for "self-improvement" or "to find a better job" were preparing to move to positions more compatible with their Holland personality types. Using a two-point Holland interest coding and a complex methodology, Andrews demonstrated that students were most likely to desire either a move to an occupation that involved no change in its congruence with their Holland type (46% of the sample) or a move to a profession that would be more consistent (37%). Only 17% of the sample were planning to enter a new occupation less congruent with their Holland personality type. Donohue (2006) found that career changers were more likely to be incongruent with their first occupations and generally moved to those more congruent. An earlier study by Robbins et al. (1978) investigated the congruence between old and new occupations for 62 primarily middle-aged male career changers, however, and found that fewer than half of the respondents moved to new careers more congruent with their Holland codes. Of note, those moving to more congruent occupations may, on average, be no more satisfied with their new career choices than were those who moved to less congruent choices (Thomas & Robbins, 1979).

Yet another methodology for studying Holland's concepts concerns who remains in, and who leaves, an occupation. Wiener and Vaitenas (1977) reported that in one sample of career changers, compared with those stable in their jobs, incongruence was only one factor that characterized the career changers. Other factors were ascendancy, dominance, responsibility, endurance, and order, on which the changers were lower. Thus, as with predicting to job performance, congruence/incongruence may need to be combined with other variables to maximize prediction and understanding.

Finally, there is evidence that interests may also be congruent with, and be predictive of, leisure activities. Melamed and Meir (1981) studied the relation between vocations and avocations for Australian and Israeli samples representing all six of Holland's occupational groupings. They concluded that people tend to select leisure activities consistent with their personality patterns. For persons working in jobs incongruent with their measured interests it is possible that leisure activities may provide compensatory opportunities. The authors suggested that nonwork, as well as work, activities should be considered in the study of occupational fit. Similarly, Mumford and Owens (1982) reported a close parallel between inventoried interests and preferred activities as measured on a biographical data blank for, in their study, three types of activities (business management, adventure, and science). Examining the life space of clients, not just their work, may therefore be important.

Consistency and Differentiation

Consistency refers to the degree of internal agreement between a person's scores on the major interest types. Holland's interests model held not only that there are six types but that they are related to each other in the order reflected in the RIASEC name (J. L. Holland, 1997a; Hughes, 1972). Realistic interests were expected to be most similar to Investigative and Conventional interests, Enterprising to Social and Conventional, and so forth around the hexagon (or circle). At the individual level, when three-interest codes are employed (e.g., Enterprising–Social–Conventional), the theory also predicted that codes with adjacent types would be more consistent and compatible than codes with types further away from each other.

Differentiation refers to how much the individuals' interest scores varied. Well-differentiated profiles, typically operationalized as the difference between the highest and lowest endorsed occupational scales, were expected to indicate greater commitment to the highest endorsed interests since they were more likely to invest their time in a smaller number of activities rather than to be distracted by competing interests.

Neither the consistency nor differentiation constructs have been uniformly supported in the empirical research literature. Compared with predictions based on congruency, consistency of interest patterns has not fared well either as a predictor of career choice or satisfaction (Nafziger et al., 1975) or in predicting to persistence in a career (Latona, 1989) or career choice readiness (Hirschi & Läge, 2007). Nauta (2010), in a review of 50 years of research on Holland's models, concluded that these constructs had received at best mixed support. Concerning consistency, the more recent research about the structural models of the RIASEC interests has suggested that the RIASEC variables may not, as the theory maintained, be equidistant from one another. Chislett (1978) reported factorial evidence for the independence of consistency, differentiation, and congruence but noted that neither consistency nor differentiation predicted to GPA, college satisfaction, or personality adjustment. Tracey et al. (2014), however, found much greater support for the consistency and differentiation constructs when using a cosine fit method of measurement. Thus, it may be that these constructs do have utility in interest assessment but that they need to be measured in a different way than Holland had espoused. Monahan (1987) also proposed a modification of Holland's differentiation calculation method.

VOCATIONAL INTERESTS MEASUREMENT IN SPECIAL POPULATIONS

Space does not permit a comprehensive review of the literature on occupational interests of persons with disabilities or special needs. Ekstrom and Smith (2002) provided valuable guidance on disability assessment across a range of disabilities. Additionally, the World Health Organization has published a diagnostic manual, *International Classification of Functioning, Disability and Health* (ICF; World Health Organization, 2001; see also Escorpizo et al., 2015) that demonstrates the wide range of disabilities that there are.

The number of people affected by disabilities is quite large. D. Taylor (2018) examined U.S. Census Bureau data showing that in 2014, among a population of 313,584,000 people, there were 72,732,000 disabled adults (age 18 and over). Of those, 47,928,000 reported a severe disability and 24,804,000 a non-severe disability. A total of 24,229,000 were reported to need assistance for their condition(s).

Substantial evidence documents that persons with disabilities are likely to be underemployed or unemployed. Shah (2016) cited evidence that disabled young people in the United Kingdom were much more likely to be unemployed, underemployed, and, for older disabled people, to be moved into early retirement. More broadly, Shahnasarian (2011) identified four areas that disabled clients, and by implication, their career counselors, need to understand: (a) less access to work opportunities, (b) the need for workplace accommodations, (c) employers' and others' bias in hiring and advancement, and (d) lower "work-life" expectancy. These factors persist despite evidence of interests and qualifications of many people who have one or more disabilities. An illustrative U.S. study by S. Turner et al. (2011) examined the career interests and self-rated abilities of 48 young adults aged 18 to 22 (median age 19) who had a range of disabilities. They found that the interests in this sample went across the RIASEC spectrum. The participants also self-rated their abilities as being relevant to a variety of work activities, yet two thirds of them were not working in a job that matched at least one of their top three interest codes or that matched their self-estimated work abilities. R. W. Cummings and Maddux (1987) similarly found few differences in the pattern and range of RIASEC interests among learning disabled and a matched group of nonlearning disabled high school students.

There is evidence that interests can be validly and reliably measured across special populations and among those who have special needs, though certain adjustments may need to be made, including choice of assessment instruments (L. S. Gottfredson, 1986d). Concerning interests, Kapes and Martinez (1999) recommended using the Career Occupational Preference System (COPS) or the Self-Directed Search (SDS) for working with many persons with disabilities. Others have suggested focusing on specific work activities rather than a career or occupation when working with individuals with intellectual disabilities (Cobigo et al., 2007; Reiter et al., 1985). In other words, consider the interests of clients in specific work activities, not just a career. Additionally, the modality of administration of interest measures may need modification such as when working with people with visual or hearing disabilities. Becker (1987) developed and validated the Reading-Free Vocational Interest Inventory for use with persons with intellectual disabilities.

Interests do appear to be persistent in the case of many with special needs. Laufer (1981), working with a group of unemployed men without homes, found occupational interest structures to be similar to those of the general population, though personality variables were found to change after a disabling condition. There is also evidence that interests are generally not affected by psychotropic medication (see Helmes & Fekken, 1986), which did, however, have a strong, negative effect on ability assessment.

Severity of impairment may affect career options and outcomes even when interests suggest a good fit with a particular line of work. Estrada-Hernández et al. (2008) found that even when interest fit was good, for high school students with disabilities the severity of disability affected employment outcomes, including earnings. Farrugia (1982) in comparing interests of 16- to 19-year-old deaf versus non-hearing-impaired students found that the deaf students were more likely to identify relatively low-level physical jobs and to see higher level ones as being out of their reach.

Concerning assessment of interests with persons who abuse substances, Levy et al. (1979) found nonalcoholic controls to show greater congruity between their occupations and interest patterns than did men who abused alcohol. H. A. Collins (1979) reported that VA heroin patients expressed occupational interests rather discrepant with their presumed skill and experience levels, identifying with socially prestigious occupations rather than with blue-collar work. Similarly, G. A. Taylor et al. (1977) reported on the Strong-measured vocational interests of a group of patients in a voluntary VA drug dependence program. This group endorsed relatively few occupations and the authors concluded that on average the group showed a "people orientation with manipulative aspirations" and that these interests were interpreted as likely to be stable over time.

Overall, the general trends are for the interests of groups of people with and without disabilities to be similar. However, the severity of their impairments may make it difficult for the disabled to find real-world career opportunities. Persons experiencing substance misuse and some other disorders may lack awareness or insight into their actual interests and realistic understanding of what occupational choices may at that time be possible. For others, career assessment feedback and counseling may help clients consider higher level and a broader range of careers than those to which they might otherwise aspire.

HOW VOCATIONAL INTERESTS RELATE TO THE VALUES, PERSONALITY, AND ABILITIES

How do vocational interests relate to other domains, in particular to personality, abilities, and values? Although interdomain relationships are discussed in considerably more detail in Chapter 17, some general trends are introduced here.

Depending on the particular definition used, there appears to be considerable overlap between the constructs of interests and values (Darley & Hagenah, 1955; Fletcher, 1966; Sagiv, 2002; Super, 1973). Values, which might be defined as those intangible or tangible qualities that a person characteristically seeks to obtain or embody, are often operationalized in a way that overlaps considerably with interests (see T. J. Smith & Campbell, 2009). Extrinsic rewards, rated higher on a values inventory than theoretical ones, for example, would be expected to have predictable correlates with certain occupational interest types, namely, Enterprising and Investigative, respectively.

Whether measurement of values adds significantly to the assessment of interests is unclear. However, there is at least some applicable research. Pryor and Taylor (1986) found a combination of interests (measured by Holland's [1985c] Vocational Preference Inventory [VPI]) and values (measured by the Work Aspect Preference Scale) was more effective than either instrument alone in predicting vocational technical students' career choices. On the other hand, between the two instruments, the Vocational Preference Inventory was more effective in the predictive task. Similarly, Hurt and Holen (1976) and Rounds (1990) have reported that a work values measure added explanatory power when interest congruence was controlled for.

Concerning personality, again, there is some overlap with interests. Indeed, in Holland's conceptualization of interests, they were conceived to be personality variables of sorts (J. L. Holland, 1973, 1997b; J. L. Holland et al., 1994). If "personality" means dispositional traits which affect a person's overt behavior, one's preferences for particular styles of relating to (or avoiding) others, then there is considerable overlap between the interest domain and the personality domain, as many recent studies (reviewed in Chapter 17) have shown.

What about occupational interests and ability variables? Because interests differ conceptually from abilities, addressing aspects of capability rather than of preferences and style, there is less overlap conceptually between abilities and interests (e.g., Barak, 1981; Barak et al., 1989). However, there appear to be patterns of abilities which, on average, are more likely to be found in particular occupational interest groupings than in others (e.g., Lowman, 1991; Randahl, 1991; Zak et al., 1979). Thus, while there is no a priori reason to think that interests and abilities are causatively associated (see Dawis, 1991), or even that the degree of overlap or correlation between the two domains is particularly high, these domains may be analogous to physical attributes of height and weight, separable even if somewhat overlapping. Again, simple correlations between these variables do not tell the whole story; patterns matter (see Chapter 17).

TRANSLATING INTEREST THEORY TO PRACTICE

At this point, with the understanding about interests in general terms, and of their relationship to important career, work, and leisure activities, the focus will be on specific interest types. Holland's six-factor model of occupational avocational interests that continues to dominate the field will be used for the interest types. This is not to suggest that Holland's types will necessarily be the final word in content-specific interests, but they remain the single most widely used interest model and are incorporated into the majority of occupational interest measures.

To elaborate Holland's theory, people who scored highest (relative to their scores on the other interest areas) were predicted, on average, to be more likely to be associated with a particular set of work and career preferences, personality characteristics, and abilities (see J. L. Holland, 1985a, 1987, 1996, and Lowman, 1987, for a complete description of the various types). In Chapter 3 I discuss each of the RIASEC types in more detail and also note the limitations of this (or any other) interest typology. When describing the average or modal properties of groups of individuals on interest measures, the task is different from what is entailed in assessing and classifying individuals. Groups define the general tendencies of people and of a social environment but do not indicate the particular issues which a career assessment client needs to understand. From a practice perspective, vocational interests are more complex than they may initially seem. On the surface, they appear to be variables that are easy to understand and apply. In fact, vocational interests are both complex and powerful, and they can identify much more than the type of work or career path that a person will likely find attractive or appealing.[2] For example, people are

---

[2] Even researchers' choice of topics they study may be influenced by interest patterns. See, for example, J. A. Johnson et al. (1988) for a description of how interests, among other personal characteristics, may influence behavioral scientists' research assumptions.

not simply a single interest type. Typically, the top three interests are interpreted in a pattern (e.g., Realistic–Investigative–Enterprising or Social–Enterprising–Artistic). If all six interest factors are considered for each person, that would create 720 different combinations of interests ($6 \times 5 \times 4 \times 3 \times 2 \times 1$), or if limited to the top three, there would still be 120 unique patterns. Pattern analysis is an important consideration when examining interest profiles.

Next, there is the issue of person-environment fit. Just because someone has an interest pattern does not mean it will always match a well-suited occupational environment (i.e., career or job). Indeed, considerable time and experience may be required for an assessor or counselor to become skilled at helping clients to understand, and to make effective use of their interests. Assessors and counselors can make a real difference in facilitating that process.

Still another complication is that interests do not stand in isolation when it comes to career choice. Many aspects of ability and personality may be important for interpreting interest profiles. Also, there are relationships across the domains such that those with particular interests are more likely, on average, to also have certain personality traits or abilities. Contrariwise, some ability and personality variables are fairly independent of interests, so the person being assessed needs to look beyond interests for a full understanding (see Table 2.1).

SUMMARY AND CONCLUSIONS

Occupational interests are one of the most venerable cornerstones of career assessment, with an impressively long history of research and application. The research literature in this area has addressed many issues, including the stability of interests, their structure, their origin, their correlates, and the many individual difference variables that affect them. Some of the many implications of this body of evidence for applied work were identified, which is explored in more detail in the next two chapters.

TABLE 2.1. Modal Characteristics of the Six Holland Vocational Interest Types

Type	Cognitive abilities	Predominant affect	People orientation	Typical jobs	Cognitive style
Realistic	Average to low	Constrained	Often avoidant	Engineer, plumber, mechanic	Concrete, practical, applied
Investigative	High	Suppressed	Reserved, cautious	Scientist, researcher, technical	Abstract, rational, logical
Artistic	Variable depending on specific occupation	Expressive; tendency to affective dysfunction	Tendency to be narcissistic, self-centered	Artist, musician, writer, actor	Divergent thinking; symbolic expression
Social	Moderately high	Warm, nurturing	Supportive, dependent	Teacher, therapist	Inductive reasoning; high emotional intelligence
Enterprising	Moderately high	Aggressive	Controlling, counterdependent	Manager, leader, business analyst	Logical, rational
Conventional	Average	Constrained	Withdrawn, avoidant	Clerk, accountant	Attentive to detail; tendency to inflexibility

3

The "Big Six" RIASEC Interest Types

This chapter considers the RIASEC (Rational, Investigative, Artistic, Social, Enterprising, Conventional) interest types one by one, as if the other types did not exist. After that, the issues associated with interest profile interpretation are discussed.

REALISTIC INTERESTS

One way for career assessors to develop an intuitive understanding of occupational interest types is to start by considering the occupations whose incumbents tend to score highest on that interest type. Examining Realistic jobs using the O*NET (see https://www.onetonline.org/explore/interests/Realistic/) demonstrates that many of these occupations are clustered in blue-collar positions and in organizations like the military.

Representative Realistic careers include the following:

- cooks
- taxi drivers
- security guards
- firefighters
- roofers
- mechanics
- assemblers

---

https://doi.org/10.1037/0000254-004
Career Assessment: Integrating Interests, Abilities, and Personality, by R. L. Lowman
Copyright © 2022 by the American Psychological Association. All rights reserved.

And, at higher required educational levels:

- engineers
- general dentists
- pilots
- surgeons

The Realistic-interest group of occupations is typically the largest grouping of occupations but one whose career opportunities have been shrinking, at least in the United States (see, e.g., Ghetta et al., 2018). Persons with strongest occupational interests in the Realistic interest area tend to like the "real" or physical world and often enjoy working with things (see Malafouris, 2020), often using their hands, or with practical, pragmatic, applied projects. Frequently, they enjoy out-of-doors work or leisure activities and are, on average, likely to have more aptitudes in this area than in cognitive or intellectual pursuits (Cegelka et al., 1974; Lowman & Ng, 2010). Women, on average, are less likely to endorse Realistic interests than are men (Su et al., 2009), but Bubany and Hansen's (2011) analysis of group averages from 1976 to 2004 on the Strong Vocational Interest measure found that men's average endorsement of Realistic interests had declined (but was still higher on average than that of women). Women in Realistic-dominated occupations tend to express similar interest vocational and preferred-activity patterns as do the men in those professions. Su et al.'s (2009) important meta-analysis confirmed the persistent finding that, on average, men prefer (endorse) Realistic and Investigative interests at a higher level than do women; M. L. Morris (2016) obtained similar results working using the Strong interest measure and with a sample of over 1,000,000 respondents. However, women in male-interest-dominated occupations are likely to endorse the same, or similar, average interests as do the men in those occupations. W. S. Cooper (1997), for example, found a group of female aviators, still a highly male-dominated occupational group, to have average interests of Realistic–Artistic–Investigative, to be very high on risk taking, and to be oriented to objects or things rather than to people or ideas. Swan (2005) similarly found the occupational interests of both female and male carpenters to emphasize Realistic interests.

Blue-collar work, predominant in the occupations associated with the Realistic type, is generally thought not to be very cognitively demanding. However, the cognitive demands on most types of work, including in Realistic occupations, have increased over the last few decades (Ansberry, 2003; Rose, 2014; Strauss, 2014). Similarly, an earlier listing of the jobs associated with the Realistic type (see G. D. Gottfredson & Holland, 1996; J. L. Holland, 1985b) showed them to be mostly blue-collar positions along with technical jobs, including engineering (Lent et al., 1989; Lowman & Ng, 2010; Nolting & Taylor, 1976).

Supporting this description, the average educational level, as computed from Holland's (1985b) *Occupations Finder*, was reported to be 4.03 on a 6-point scale (1 = *elementary school*, 6 = *college*; see Lowman, 1987), a finding consistent with Linda Gottfredson's (1980) summary of a broader sample of occupations (see also G. D. Gottfredson & Daiger, 1977). L. Gottfredson found the Realistic occupations to have the lowest prestige level and the lowest average educational level among the six occupational interest types. The O*NET used a different classification system called the Job Zone, a 1-to-5 classification system, with 5 being the highest. The ratings are based on the occupation's status, experience, and education requirements. However, the selection of occupations with Realistic as the first interest preference included 20 occupations from each of the five levels, which is not representative of the actual distribution of Realistic-interest jobs, most of which require less formal education and are lower in prestige and experience required to enter the occupation, so we will not compute averages of occupations in O*NET Job Zones in this chapter.

Realistic types are more likely than other interest types to be found in vocational/technical educational programs (R. A. Thompson, 1985), and would also appear to have a difficult time making a transition out of Realistic occupations (Dwight, 1978), should that be desired. Men are more likely than women to be in Realistic occupations (Apostal, 1991; Su et al., 2009; see also Wiernik, 2016), and are more likely to exhibit traditional male sex-specific behavioral patterns (e.g., Weis et al., 2007).

Because the Realistic world tends to revolve around things more than people and interpersonal relationships, social activities (and presumably skills) are probably not as important or plentiful among Realistic groups than they are for some of the other RIASEC types. The asocial nature (perhaps more accurately labeled social discomfiture) of the Realistic type is well illustrated by Melville's (1851/1977) description of a presumably Realistic population of whalers:

> After we were all seated at the table, and I was preparing to hear some good stories about whaling; to my no small surprise nearly every man maintained a profound silence. And not only that, but they looked embarrassed. Yes, here were a set of sea-dogs, many of whom without the slightest bashfulness had boarded great whales on the high seas . . . and duelled them dead without winking; and yet, here they sat at a social breakfast-table—all of the same calling, all of kindred tastes—looking round as sheepishly at each other as though they had never been out of sight of some sheepfold among the Green Mountains. A curious sight; these bashful bears, these timid warrior whalemen! (p. 33)

Although Tay et al. (2011) found that some people can have interests both in things and in people, Realistic jobs calling for persistent sociability and interpersonally intensive work would likely not be preferred by many with Realistic interests. Difficulties in interpersonally demanding situations that arise at work might also be encountered.

On average, Realistic types are described as being fairly stable and predictable (Hyland & Muchinsky, 1991). Male Realistic types are likely to enjoy traditional male activities such as sports and physical activities. College football athletes, for example, were reported in one study likely to express Realistic and Conventional vocational interests (M. J. Miller et al., 1985). Other occupational groups with large numbers of people with Realistic interests are found in the military (see, e.g., Lowman & Schurman, 1982). Such work settings typify many aspects of commonly encountered Realistic environments (see, e.g., Sterne, 1974). Essentially oriented to things rather than persons or ideas, work in the military focuses on equipment intensive, "real world" activities—flying airplanes, fighting with weapons in the physical world, and helping to make machines run. Prized in such settings are mechanical skills and technical expertise related to the person–machine interface. In everything from wearing uniforms to following behavioral etiquette (e.g., saluting), rules as well as positions are defined by rank. For both tactical and strategic reasons, predictability is highly prized, and military bases are known for their similarity, even in layout and physical appearance, from one to the next, and almost all tend to include large amounts of machinery, equipment, tanks, airplanes, weapons, and the like. Police work would appear to incorporate similar characteristics (Benninger & Walsh, 1980; J. A. Johnson & Hogan, 1981; Lester, 1983). The O*NET (https://www.onetonline.org/) classifies police work as Realistic–Enterprising–Conventional for police patrol officers. Police detectives were classified as Realistic–Investigative, and police supervisors had different profiles.

Persons with Realistic interests and work history may find physical impairments particularly impactful. Absent compensating abilities such as verbal/persuasive, social/interpersonal, or helping interests, they may have limited capacity to switch to other occupational roles. Rohe and Athelstan (1982), for example, reported spinal cord injury patients, who were often young males injured in accidents, to be most likely to express more interest in working with things than with data or people, creating special problems when that option becomes unavailable.

Summarizing, persons with Realistic interests tend to prefer working with things rather than with people or ideas. Their work world is typically practical and oriented to the real world. Along with such interests tend to come hands-on skills and enjoyment of outdoor and physical activities. Education is often seen as a means to an end rather than an end in and of itself. A persistent sex difference in favor of men has been found on most interest measures and in Realistic occupations, though there are certainly women with Realistic interests and occupations. Career issues arise when the jobs of people with Realistic interests are lost, as with automation and exporting of manufacturing jobs. Additionally, many Realistic jobs increasingly involve working not just with machines or one's own hands but with complex human–computer interactions.

Each of the six major interest types is illustrated in Chapter 4 with a case. Real-life vocational cases, whether examined using a qualitative approach (e.g., Cochran, 1990[1]) or, as in the cases present here, combining both quantitative and qualitative methodologies, help the career assessor learn more about the

---

[1]Cochran's (1990) story-telling, or clinically biographical, approach to studying careers of selected, mostly eminent, figures raises an interesting alternative approach to vocational study. The approach is flawed, however, by the author's wholesale rejection, if not caricature, of traditional ways of considering career issues. The methodology presented as being a superior approach for understanding career issues is less a psychological than it is a sort of literary approach. While interesting, the methods as outlined are unfortunately rather speculative, consisting primarily of a set of unvalidated premises around which are inserted a review of life events to which motives are assertively imputed.

nature of the interest type, while also seeing the form real-life career assessment data may take. These six cases were all based on actual career assessment cases. They were chosen to illustrate the interest pattern being discussed and because their assessment results were consistent across multiple measures. Other, more complicated cases are illustrated later in the chapter, when more complex interpretative challenges are considered. The data presented with each case include test results; only the names and potentially identifying background details have been modified to protect the identity of clients.

INVESTIGATIVE INTERESTS

Most of the scientific professions, almost all of which are in significant ways intellectually oriented, fall into the Investigative interest category (e.g., Dharanendriah, 1989), as do a number of medical and technical professions. A sample of representative jobs from the O*NET (https://www.onetonline.org/explore/interests/Investigative/) includes the following:

- aerospace engineers
- chemists
- research psychologists
- computer hardware engineers
- engineers (many types)
- veterinarians
- physicians

The Investigative type emphasizes ideas (classified by some researchers as "data") and things (usually combined with ideas, or abstractions) rather than people (e.g., Ormerod & Asiedu, 1991; Wai et al., 2009, 2010; Zachar & Leong, 1992). Investigative occupations tend to attract goal-directed people with high and generally abstract intelligence, who are likely to be attracted to tasks requiring logic and reasoning of a technical nature and to be somewhat indifferent to social relationships (Bachtold & Warner, 1972; Houston et al., 2015; Simonton, 1988; Wilson & Jackson, 1994). Investigative types, however, may not have the same self-perceptions. For example, Matheson and Strickland (1986) found that self-perceptions did not match others' perceptions of computer science students being introverted and socially isolated. Investigative people tend, on average, to be uncomfortable with highly emotional situations, and are likely to be perceived by others as being somewhat on the cool and distant side interpersonally, perhaps reflecting their characteristic tough-mindedness (Kline & Lapham, 1992; Lounsbury et al., 2012; Toker, 2011). They also report a high work orientation and high conscientiousness (Feist, 1998; Roe, 1952), masculinity (especially for those interested in the physical rather than biological sciences; see Kelly, 1988), tough-mindedness, and being more likely to be introverted than extraverted (Lounsbury et al., 2012; Wilson & Jackson, 1994) and to prefer independence and autonomy (Sagiv, 2002). There may also be an excess of persons with autistic spectrum disorder among scientists and those in computer science and technical occupations, especially for men (Baron-Cohen et al., 2001; Grandin & Panek, 2013). As with any such profile, these are general trends, sometimes masking subtypes (see, e.g., Gough & Woodworth, 1960). As Lounsbury et al. (2012) summarized some of these trends,

> Compared to other occupations, scientists are prone to be: pessimistic, gloomy, and cynical; less stable, anxious, and more emotionally reactive; less assertive, accommodating, and more easily swayed by dominant individuals; quieter, immersed with their own thoughts, and unaffiliative, with fewer connections to other people; nonconforming, independent minded, less rule-following, and more comfortable with lack of structure; more open to new (and sometimes radical) ideas, willing to experiment, and inclined to seek out variety and novel experience. (p. 55)

However, they also noted that scientists in their research whose personality ran counter to some of these trends tended to be more satisfied with their careers than those whose personalities were more consistent with it. Other research (e.g., Wiernik et al., 2016) found that those with Investigative interests were emotionally stable on self-report measures of personality. They were also found to be low on Agreeableness.

Although some Investigative occupations do not require extensive educational preparation, they are not plentiful. Most of the typical science, technology, engineering, and math (STEM) occupation listings on the O*NET require advanced education, often including PhD and postdoctoral work. High general intellectual ability tends to characterize the group as a whole. Investigative occupations also have the highest prestige levels of all of the six types (L. S. Gottfredson, 1980).

The preferred reward pattern for those with Investigative interest patterns is more likely to be intrinsic rather than extrinsic. Ryan (2014), for example, found in a study of research scientists found that internal self-concept motivation had a significant positive relationship on research performance across age and gender. Instrumental motivation had a significant negative effect on performance.

Just as the military and manufacturing organizations are home to many Realistic types, the modern hospital and research-oriented universities and institutes are heavily populated by Investigative types (e.g., physicians, researchers, various technicians). To the extent that medical facilities are dominated by Investigative types, the values they emphasize would indeed tend to be focused on objectivity and the dispassionate analysis of data. In the Investigative environment, empathy and the warm, nurturing acceptance of the feelings and needs of patients are seldom rewarded. (Of course, individual Investigative types may be exceptions.)

Some of the most lasting and still interesting psychological research on scientists remains the work of Ann Roe, who in several pioneering studies (Roe, 1951, 1952), examined personal characteristics of scientists, particularly eminent ones. The scientists in Roe's studies—biologists, physicists, research psychologists—tended to embody many of the features thought to be characteristic of the Investigative interest pattern: intelligent, work oriented, intense, rather independent, and asocial.

As for gender, scientists still tend to be more likely male than female in many STEM occupations, but that appears to be changing, particularly in psychology and the biological sciences (National Academies of Sciences, Engineering, and Medicine, 2020; National Science Foundation, National Center for Science and Engineering Statistics, 2019). Bubany and Hansen (2011) also reported an increase in women's average Investigative interests over time (using the Strong interest measure) and a decrease in Investigative interests among men so that the gender difference, while still favoring men, lessened in the 1976 to 2004 time period. Although women have made marked strides in recent decades in being better represented among those in Investigative occupations, they are still underrepresented in higher level STEM occupations and overrepresented in some of the lower level STEM positions. Racial minorities, on the other hand, are less likely to be found in STEM college majors and in STEM occupations (Funk & Parker, 2018). Socioeconomic issues as much as interest strongly influence minority underrepresentation, in that persons with limited means cannot afford the extensive education that is required for many Investigative occupations. Nonetheless, natural differences in ability distributions may conspire with cultural artifacts to keep the sex distribution in certain scientific occupations from being equal between the sexes (see, e.g., Beltz et al., 2011).

Though scientists as a group are generally well adjusted according to some research (see, e.g., Ludwig, 1998), Lounsbury et al. (2012) reported neuroticism scores for scientists to be higher than comparison group scores of "normal" (Big Five) personality variables. In more detailed studies, Nettle (2006b) compared relatively small samples of poets, visual artists, and mathematicians and found more evidence of signs of psychopathology (including atypical perceptions) and divergent thinking among the poets and visual artists than among the mathematicians. The latter group were more convergent in their thinking but had more evidence of autistic-spectrum symptomatology. In Post's (1996) studies of "world-famous men" (subsequently further analyzed by Simonton, 2014), scientists had the lowest average scores on rated psychopathology (in contrast to some of the other groups, especially writers). Of course scientists may also experience stress just like members of any other occupational group (e.g., Saksvik & Hetland, 2011). Because of historical and ongoing patterns of sex discrimination and more limited job opportunities, female scientists may be at greater risk for environmentally influenced psychological difficulties than others.

Overall, Investigative types enjoy working with ideas and data—knowledge, facts, theories, numbers, and the precision of information. They are attracted to learning and to education, where they tend to perform well, particularly in their areas of expertise. They are less likely to enjoy careers that involve extensive interpersonal work or helping roles. Investigative types accept the premise of a common set of rules needed to produce and verify knowledge and tend to be field independent, so they are influenced more by their knowledge than by political factors. They are persuaded by evidence, not beliefs or unfounded opinions. Many may find Investigative types to be cold and distant, but those perceptions may be influenced by the finding that they are more likely to be introverted than extraverted.

ARTISTIC INTERESTS

It is not just a stereotype to note that many are called to artistic work (i.e., have interests) but few are chosen. The number of people who make a living in full-time creative work is comparatively few. In the case of music, the College Music Society (2015) reported that, in 2011, there were 1,795 degree-granting college music programs in the United States and that 332,297 students, or 1.7% of the entire college enrollment in 2009–2010, were enrolled in those programs. The study estimated that for the same year, 45% of courses included non-music majors. Recognizing that not all musicians attend college and that the distribution of talent among those who pursue music training will vary, these data still provide evidence of musical talent and interest. Yet the Bureau of Labor Statistics (BLS) reported that there were just 187,600 people in the United States employed in music and singing jobs in 2018 (BLS, 2019g).

Similarly, there are comparatively few occupations in the visual artistic occupations. The BLS lists the following occupations in the Arts and Design Occupations (BLS, 2019e) with numbers in those occupations as of 2018: art directors (101,000), craft and fine artists (50,300), fashion designers (25,800), graphic designers (290,100), industrial designers (43,900), and interior designers (75,400). These collectively add up to 586,500. For comparison purposes, at the same time (2018 figures), there were 2,257,200 K–12 teachers, 3,059,800 registered nurses (far from the total of those in nursing), and 1,034,600 engineers (mechanical, electrical, civil, and computer hardware engineers combined).

When it comes to paid employment, dance is another rather rarefied occupation. The BLS reported as of May 2017, only 9,930 people were employed in Dance and Choreography positions (BLS, 2017a).

And in acting, BLS statistics reported that 47,430 people were employed as actors in May 2018 (BLS, 2019a), and most of those were employed in larger metropolitan areas. (This figure excludes self-employed individuals, the reality of many who work in this occupation.)

Although writers—both fiction and nonfiction—are highly revered in many societies, there are relatively few people who make their living primarily by writing. The BLS includes a category called Writers and Authors (27-3043) that, as of May 2018, included 45,210 people whose major duties were described as being to "originate and prepare written material, such as scripts, stories, advertisements, and other material" (BLS, 2019d, para. 1). However, this category excluded 50,350 technical writers (BLS, 2019c), 239,030 public relations (PR) specialists (BLS, 2019b), 38,790 reporters and correspondents

(BLS, 2017b), and 96,890 editors (BLS, 2017c). These categories may also underestimate writers to some degree (e.g., they excluded self-employed workers), but some may be overestimates in that the two largest categories, PR Specialists and Editors, may include those who do not primarily do writing as their major duty. In any event, the cited numbers of people in the United States who work as writers collectively add up to less than half a million, suggesting that jobs for writers may be in short supply compared with those wanting such careers.

It is difficult to generalize across such a broad range of occupations in the Artistic area, but a number of themes are commonly found. First, as the data illustrate, it may be hard to make a living in the arts. This reality no doubt creates situations in which those with Artistic interests will need to work at something other than their preferred jobs. Second, creative work is often not stable, so there are likely to be ups-and-downs in pursuing such work. Third, although there are those who will strike it rich in the arts, the vast majority will not.

With that as a context, there are certain common characteristics often found among those with Artistic interests. Creative and flexible rather than orderly and relatively inflexible in orientation, Artistic-interest individuals typically prefer to work with ideas and materials (e.g., words, paint, sculpture material), and their own and to express themselves in new, typically termed symbolic, ways. They value independence (Sagiv, 2002) and are typically complex (Tetlock et al., 1993), open to new experience (Barrick et al., 2003), and tend to welcome rather than to shut out new ideas (J. L. Holland et al., 1991). J. L. Holland et al. (1975) reported that relatively few Artistic occupations exist compared with the distribution of Artistic interests, something that has not changed. The prestige level of the Artistic occupations was noted by L. Gottfredson (1980) to be moderate to high and the educational level to be the second highest among the six types, but that varies by type of creative activity and work sought.

Stereotypically, Artistic types tend to flout custom and convention and to live lives that exceed the limits of normally accepted behavior. They are generally regarded as being sensitive and emotional and may experience affective disturbances at a higher rate than the general population (see Costa et al., 1984; F. K. Goodwin & Jamison, 2007; Helson, 1996; Jamison, 1989, 1996). There is some suggestion that the nature of Artistic work may be associated with the experience of neurotic conditions (see D. E. Schneider, 1979; Wittkower & Wittkower, 1963) for many of the professions in this group (or perhaps it is the other way around). For example,

> Had [Tennessee] Williams been perfectly well-adjusted, he might have grown up to spend his life as the manager of a St. Louis shoe company, playing golf on weekends and writing bad novels published by vanity presses. Possibly he would have written even better plays. One doesn't have to be neurotic to create, though it seems to help in our world. Psychological dysfunctions, if that's what they are, as well as repressive political systems, don't produce art, and truly can hobble an artist; but they also sharpen the interests and channel enormous energies. (Canby, 1990, p. 19)

Or again, Leonard Bernstein, who himself was not known for emotional quiescence, wrote in a letter to the widow of Vladimir Horowitz, saying,

> I just heard that [Horowitz] is dead. I send you loving sympathy, but let me add my admiration for you and your long years of devotion to this amazing man. He was not only a superpianist but a supermusician with all the mental fallibilities such geniuses have. You cared for him and guarded him through a series of neurotic crises the world may never know nor understand; and you returned him to us time and again, refreshed, renewed and even greater. (B. Holland, 1989, p. 13)

More interpretatively, D. E. Schneider (1979) expressed the psychoanalytical perspective on the creative artist:

> The tendency [for artists is] to wrap [themselves] in a cloak of narcissistic self-love—because [the artist's work]... *in its content* is in greater or lesser degree a transformation of [the artist's self]... This is one of the sources of that excessive selflove which destroys art and artists. (p. 140)

Artists are generally sensitive to their feelings and reactions and often use that in their creative work. Sometimes, more frequently seemingly than the general population, this is associated with psychological dysfunction. There has been significant research done over a number of years on mental disorders among creatively talented individuals, both those of eminence and in the general population.

Creative artists (broadly defined) do tend to endorse on assessment measures, and presumably to experience, psychological dysfunction—in particular, affective disorder—at a greater frequency than the general population (see F. K. Goodwin & Jamison, 2007; Jamison, 1996; Kyaga et al., 2013; Wiernik et al., 2016; and Zaman et al., 2011; see also Chapter 14, this volume). Many potential reasons for these findings have been offered, including common brain locations between creativity and psychopathology, the "ups and downs" of the creative process (Lowman, 1993a), more general tolerance for experience of strong emotions (Pufal-Struzik, 1992), and the low incomes often associated with much creative work. Although psychological dysfunction in general and affective disorder in particular appear to be more common among those with artistic/creative interest patterns and occupations than the general population, they are neither necessary or sufficient for creative productivity. Abuhamdeh and Csikszentmihalyi (2014) argued that these characteristics are not essential to successful artistic creativity, may only describe phases that artists go through, and, as the nature of the art to be created changes, so too may the desired or typical personal characteristics. Simonton (2014) also noted that there were differences across types of creators (e.g., scientists, composers, writers) and that the relationship between degree of creativity and degree of pathology varied by group. For example, the relationship between creativity and psychopathology was monotonic and linear among the writers and artists, but curvilinear among the other groups. There is also evidence of enhanced creativity among people with attention-deficit/hyperactivity disorder (Hoogman et al., 2020).

Research has examined biological bases for such connections and also for the underlying cognitive brain processes. Genetic evidence of the link between predispositions for mental illness and creativity was found by Power et al. (2015). They examined a possible genetic connection between creativity and mental disorder and reported evidence that polygenic risk scores for both schizophrenia and bipolar disorder predicted creativity in diverse samples in Iceland, Norway, and Sweden. In particular, polygenic risk scores were associated (or predicted to) research participants being in Artistic-related careers, but they did not find being in artistic/creative occupations to have been predicted by certain disease genetic risks.

Finally, there has been an emerging literature using cognitive science to study creativity. Rather than simply finding overlaps or correlations between creativity and mental disorders, some researchers have explored whether there is a common or interrelated brain mechanism between the creative process and certain mental disorders. Papworth et al. (2008), for example, found a common approach to problem solving by creative individuals and persons with serious mental illness. In particular, both groups tended to use probabilistic reasoning approaches in which conclusions were reached on the basis of limited information. Jung et al. (2010) found an inverse association between the Composite Creativity Index (a measure of creativity) and brain white matter structure in which there was overlap between particular parts of the brain that are associated with creativity and those associated with psychological dysfunction. Other mechanisms have also been suggested (e.g., K. M. Heilman et al., 2003). Since this is a book focused on career assessment, the important point is that psychological dysfunction among career assessees is not unusual and may indeed be adaptive for certain types of creative work. Still, the nature of creative work applications may be changing as it becomes more important to be innovative in a variety of different types of work, something particularly important as new knowledge and applications become more urgently needed in advanced economies.

The stereotype of the eccentric, starving artist living in a hovel and dedicated to art for its own sake despite personal hardships may be fading but still captures important aspects of many of those with strong Artistic interests: single-mindedness in devotion to Artistic endeavor and willingness to abandon traditional economic values in the pursuit of artistry. Getzels and Csikszentmihalyi's (1976) important longitudinal study of creative visual artists found that economic values did not characterize the most serious and successful of their sample. Of course this does not suggest that Artistic types have no interest in extrinsic rewards. Note the enormous wealth of the tiny fraction of highly successful artists. However, most members of the Artistic-interest professions as a group have low incomes from their professional Artistic activities. Thus, something other than (or additional to) monetary reward is presumably needed to sustain productive effort over time.

In purest form, the artist interprets or reinterprets external reality and creates things that did not exist before. Certainly there are differences between practitioners of different types of artistry (see the discussion of Artistic abilities earlier in this chapter). Yet, as a group, artists are not known for conforming to societal norms and expectations, either in their professional or their personal lives. The task of Artistic creation demands concentrated energy (Csikszentmihalyi, 1996; Getzels & Csikszentmihalyi, 1976; Roe, 1946) and, for many of the arts, selfabsorption and an element of narcissism. Moreover, because Artistic talent appears to be narrowly distributed in any population (L. S. Gottfredson, 1980), artists may hold an honored position that enhances the perception of separateness from others.

Artistic work settings are less easily described because Artistic endeavors are typically practiced alone or in small groups. Although some creative work is done in teams, in other cases it involves highly independent, "self-starting" work. Aloneness in the performance of one's work is the characteristic occupational condition of many writers, painters, and, to some extent, musicians especially given the demanding practice requirements. Even among those artists who work with others as part of their job (e.g., actors and actresses), there may be less interdependence than individualized performance in a group context. The intensity of internal concentration needed to focus deeply may have as its cost personal narcissism and estrangement from others in the realm of conventional social relationships.

SOCIAL INTERESTS

Persons high on Social interests tend to enjoy nurturing and developing others and serving in teaching, counseling, and other helping roles (Batson et al., 2007; Crandall, 1981; Kaub et al., 2016). They are the helpers of the world, those whose work gravitates around benevolence toward others, supporting, and assisting others in need (Sagiv, 2002). Persons in Social occupations are often called on by society to perform important but often underrewarded tasks. As children's television host Mr. Rogers once famously said,

> When I was a boy and I would see scary things in the news, my mother would say to me, "Look for the helpers. You will always find people who are helping." (Fred Rogers, as cited in Emery, 2019)

Social interests are also commonly found among homemakers, including those not oriented to a career outside of the home (Tinsley & Faunce, 1978). This illustrates that not all work is paid work, and a career identity can be closely tied to helping roles both that are paid and that are unpaid or volunteer.

A sample of representative jobs from the O*NET (https://www.onetonline.org/explore/interests/Social/) includes the following:

- clergy
- counselor
- crossing guard

- nurse

- teacher (K–12)

- occupational therapist

Using Van Lange et al.'s (1977) classification system of prosocial, individualistic, and competitive orientations, persons with Social interests are more likely to be prosocial in their orientation. They typically enjoy the intrinsic rewards of helping others (Conrads et al., 2016; H. W. Lee et al., 2019).

Occupations associated with Social interests involve work that entails assisting others in need, particularly the less advantaged. They are generally applied in their orientation rather than theoretical (for evidence on the separability of Social intellectual abilities, see Lowman & Leeman, 1988; Lowman et al., 1985) and prefer roles that involve working with people to help them, especially people in distress or otherwise in need of help (and may be better skilled at such work; see Gottheil et al., 1979). Because of their preference for work involving other people and their need to apply people skills in direct work with others, Social interest types tend to themselves have good interpersonal skills (see J. D. Mayer et al., 2008) and to be well-liked. Nurturance and support, not control, are prototypical characteristics. An average difference on Social interests is typically found in meta-analyses with women rating higher than men (Su et al., 2009). Social interests are also significantly correlated with extraversion (e.g., Costa et al., 1984), though it is certainly possible to be introverted, prosocial, and effective in helping roles (see, e.g., Kaub et al., 2016).

Although there are certainly exceptions, persons in helping occupations (e.g., teachers, counselors, nurses) are often highly praised for their importance to society (the social occupations nearly tied for second place in the prestige ratings of the RIASEC groups; L. S. Gottfredson, 1980), but they are not typically well rewarded financially compared to the demands and societal importance of the work roles and the amount of education that is required for career entry. Of course, many factors influence this paradox, including power issues associated with societal control over the purse strings in publicly supported institutions and the characteristic female composition of many Social occupations (see J. L. Holland, 1985a; Lowman & Leeman, 1988). However, another important factor is that those with Social interests types are often not motivated primarily by extrinsic rewards. The ability to nurture and support others, to help shape future generations, to attend to those in need, and to transmit cultural norms and expectations are of inherent value, interest, and importance to Social types. These skills have obvious societal importance in the survival of the culture, and the demand for Social-interest-related occupations appears to be increasing (see, e.g., Ghetta et al., 2018). There are also Social-interest careers at all educational levels in this interest area.

Another way to conceptualize the work of Social-interest occupations is that people typically are the end product of the work. The teacher's job is to help transform the knowledge and character of those students in their charge. The mental health worker aims to help improve psychological well-being and to help others manage mental illness. Home health care aides help assure the safety and health of their charges. Such roles often require the subordination of personal goals to those of others.

Schools, mental health centers, and hospitals embody underlying, if not always immediately apparent, values of alleviating pain and suffering, promoting health and well-being, and providing nurturance and support. Even if the modern helping institution can be overly bureaucratic, stultifying, cynical in the face of perceived helplessness, rigid, and overly concerned with legal issues (e.g., Sarason, 1972), the underlying values and basic mission are still those of assisting others in need. Additionally, because much helping is done in one-on-one relationships or in small groups such as classrooms, the Social-interest settings are often ones of closed doors and behind-the-scenes activities.

Summarizing, those who take on, and flourish, in Social-related work roles are people with strong preferences to direct their talents to the needs of others, to tackle life's difficult problems, and to help make people's lives better. They enjoy translating knowledge into action and having people contact as an important part of their job. Their social and helping natures tend to work well in teams. However, as a group, their willingness to take on life's difficult jobs may contribute to the finding that they are highly susceptible to burnout and tend to be characterized by psychological dependence (Lowman, 1993a). Taking care of their own needs is not what they typically do best.

ENTERPRISING (MANAGERIAL) INTERESTS

Like Social types, Enterprising ones are, on average, outgoing and oriented toward people (Barrick et al., 2003) rather than toward things or ideas. Those strongest in Holland's Enterprising interest type seek to exert power and control and influence others (generally in the achievement of specific goals) rather than assist or nurture them (Sagiv, 2002). As one of their most central characteristics, however, they seek to get things done, working with and through other people. In contrast to the Social interest type, the focus is on using people, along with other resources, to get a job done and to make things happen.

According to the O*NET (https://www.onetonline.org/explore/interests/Enterprising/) representative Enterprising occupations include the following:

- lawyers

- managers

- purchasing managers

- real estate brokers

- salespeople

- supervisors

Although there are assuredly Enterprising individuals who score highest on this interest scale and are great fits with the world of business and management, the term "enterprising" was perhaps not the best label with which to characterize this group. To the extent that the term "enterprising" connotes entrepreneurial interests, the name may be misleading. Or, if the enterprising term is taken to mean that people with this interest pattern are found only in business and the commercial world, that too would be misleading because such types can work in government, the not-for-profit world, and even on their own. A better term might be "managerial" or "leadership-oriented," since that better reflects the modal work done by those in these occupations. Because of its widespread use, the term "Enterprising" is retained, but "managerial" is also used as a substitute word for this interest type.

Enterprising types are generally skilled at coordinating the work of others to accomplish goals. With others, they tend to be competitive (J. M. Houston et al., 2015) and to define themselves in terms of the position they hold as compared to others. They are usually comfortable with accepting responsibility for others and with working in a hierarchical work structure where differential amounts of authority are associated with different levels of positions.

The skill at overseeing others and being a leader is exemplified in the character of Nagasawa in Haruki Murakami's (2000) novel *Norwegian Wood*. He stated,

> Nagasawa had a certain inborn quality that drew people to him and made them follow him. He knew how to stand at the head of the pack, to assess the situation, to give precise and tactful instructions that others would obey. Above his head hung an aura that revealed his powers like an angel's halo, the mere sight of which would inspire awe in people for this superior being. (pp. 39–40)

Persons in this interest type tend on average to be extraverted (Broday & Sedgwick, 1991), they can be somewhat interpersonally distant in the sense that power and control are emphasized rather than support and befriending others as an end unto itself. Interactions are more often task-oriented rather than relationship-oriented. Relationships are usually defined among Enterprising types by determining who has the right or obligation to control or influence the other. With higher level positions in organizations (where much of the Enterprising work gets done) comes more power and authority.

When control issues are clearly defined and accepted, there may be less friction than when a relationship is being created and control and dominance issues still need to be resolved. Emotional intimacy and introspection are more likely to be expressed among persons of equal power levels rather than across levels. Although Enterprising-related behavior can create a less than ideal basis for interpersonal relationships outside of work, the ability to accomplish work and organizational goals with and through other people in the workplace is inherently an instrumental, task-oriented ability (Boyatzis, 1982, 2011) that is both functional and adaptive. The Enterprising type would be expected to fit in well in large, somewhat insensitive and impersonal organizations in which the emphasis is on goal-directed behavior and coordination of the work of others.

Extrinsic rewards are especially important (e.g., Catalanello et al., 1978), particularly to the extent that they connote power relationships.

Women's expression of Enterprising vocational interests appears to be increasing (Bubany & Hansen, 2011) and certainly the numbers of women taking bachelor's and master's degrees in business have been increasing. According to the Integrated Postsecondary Education Data System (IPEDS) data from the (U.S.) National Center for Educational Statistics, from 2011 to 2012 there were almost equal numbers (189,486, men; 176,004, women) of bachelor's degrees granted to men and women. At the master's level, there were somewhat more degrees granted to men (103,245 vs. 88,286), but still they are not as lopsided as they once were. Only 2,531 doctoral degrees were granted in business in that period and again, men were slightly higher in number than women, but the overall numbers were so small that it is difficult to generalize (National Center for Education Statistics, 2013).

The Enterprising group ranked fourth (of six) in average educational level and in attributed prestige (see L. S. Gottfredson, 1980). The more recent O*NET (https://www.onetonline.org/explore/interests/Enterprising/) shows a wide range of educational levels associated with what are labeled as Enterprising occupations. Of 89 occupations, nine were Job Zone 1, and there were 20 each in categories 2 to 4. These data were intended to show representative Enterprising jobs at all levels of the spectrum and so illustrate that there are lower entry jobs with few experience and educational requirements in Enterprising jobs as well as higher ones.

Clearly managers in large companies usually require a college degree to begin their careers there. But there are many jobs in business that do not require a college degree, and it is also possible to become a manager or supervisor without a lot of higher education. However, within the managerial ranks, particularly in corporations of any size and complexity, general intelligence predicts how far one will go in management (e.g., A. Howard & Bray, 1988), and that is strongly correlated with education (see Chapter 10).

Concern with tasks to be accomplished is an essential characteristic of Enterprising types, who tend to prefer well-defined, unambiguous goals (A. Howard & Bray, 1988; Zaleznik, 1977) rather than grand but impossible-to-achieve ideals. Neither very simple ambitions nor hopeless ambitions are motivating to the prototypical Enterprising type. On the other hand, Enterprising types typically prefer ambiguity in the *accomplishment* of goals so that they are free from external influence and control in deciding how a particular goal (say, increasing the profitability of a division by 5%) will be reached.

Finally, the issue of control in Enterprising settings is an important dynamic. It is illustrated by Caro's (1989) multivolume biography of former U.S. President Lyndon Johnson. Quoting a cousin of Johnson's, Caro wrote, "Winning had always been so terribly important to him; as a boy, recalls his favorite cousin, Ava Johnson Cox, 'He had to be the leader in everything he did, just *had* to, just could not *stand* not to be'" (Caro, 1989, p. 62). Obviously, not all Enterprising types are this extreme, but the extremes can sometimes clarify the type.

Enterprising types are generally comfortable working within well-structured hierarchies of power and authority in which people's status and position are clear. Although A. Howard and Bray's (1988) still-important longitudinal studies of managers at American Telephone and Telegraph Co. (AT&T) needs for control were fairly high, particularly early to midcareer. From a psychological perspective, however, control issues may mask a counter-dependency dynamic in which the surface orientation toward power and authority mask underlying dependency needs. Such needs could help to explain the seemingly contradictory orientation toward control and authority, both in seeking out authority over subordinates and in accepting the authority of superiors. Interestingly, in one study of college students (Tryon, 1983), Enterprising types tended to avoid seeking out personal counseling, while those in Artistic or Investigative interest patterns were more likely to use such services, again suggesting the possible need to maintain personal control as well as the finding in other studies that Enterprising types, as a group, are generally well adjusted, with the possible exception of character pathology (see, e.g., Harrell & Harrell, 1973).

Enterprising types' second and third expressed codes matter for purposes of career assessment and counseling. Although Enterprising interests are commonly identified first in managerial interest patterns, there are many different 3-interest profiles. Indeed, exploring the O*NET's occupations by the key words of "managers" does identify Human Resource (11-3121.00) and Training and Development Managers (11-9151.00) with that code. Those in other areas of management have different secondary and tertiary interest codes. For example, Farm and Ranch Managers (11-9013.02) are coded as Enterprising–Realistic–Conventional, Purchasing Managers (11-3061.00) and Administrative Service Managers (11-3011.00) as Enterprising–Conventional, Medical and Health Services Managers (11-911.00) and General and Operations Managers (11-2021.00) as Enterprising–Conventional–Social, and both Chief Executives (11-001.00) and Sales Managers (11-2022.00) as Enterprising–Conventional. What all this list, and many others involving management, have in common is that all have Enterprising as their strongest endorsed interests, and Conventional is likely to be in the second or third position.

Managers differ from entrepreneurs in important ways. These are further explored in Chapter 10, but a short summary is provided here to illustrate the issues. Entrepreneurs tend to be higher on openness to new experience and conscientiousness and lower on neuroticism and agreeableness (Zhao & Seibert, 2006). Entrepreneurial self-efficacy (ESE) may mediate the relationships between perceived learning from entrepreneurial courses, risk-taking propensity, and prior entrepreneurial activities at least among MBA students (Zhao et al., 2005). When the "Big Five" personality variables plus risk-taking were examined in the context of predicting entrepreneurial intentions and entrepreneurial performance (Zhao et al., 2010), Openness and Conscientiousness predicted both intentions (openness more highly) and performance (equally). Emotional stability predicted performance comparatively highly, and risk taking predicted intentions but not performance.

Concerning sex differences, although there may be some minor differences in interest and personality patterns between them (e.g., Carland & Carland, 1991; Kepler & Shane, 2007; Sexton & Bowman-Upton, 1990), male and female managers and entrepreneurs generally appear to share much in common (Jackson et al., 1987). Managers may also combine other backgrounds, such as technical, with management. Interestingly, those who aspire to, or end up as, managers who also have technical backgrounds have been differentiated in some research. Sedge (1985) found that occupational interests within a particular occupation differentiated engineers and engineer-managers, the latter scoring higher on Enterprising interests, the former on Investigative. H. A. Hanson and Chater (1983) reported that a group of aspiring nurse managers, who did not differ in their demographics or other background variables, differed significantly from a group of nonmanagerial nurses in elevations on managerial versus pro-Social interest patterns.[2] Hill and Hansen (1986) similarly reported that male or female research managers combined scientific and Enterprising interest patterns.

Summarizing, Enterprising types are likely to be the managers and leaders of the world. They enjoy leadership roles where they can influence others and help to achieve goals, usually working with and through other people. They also manage data and other resources needed to get the job done. They usually work in organizations that are hierarchical in nature, and many aspire to move upward in the system. Although they are comfortable in systems where they wield power over others and where others have power over them, they are likely to be counter-dependent. They are also somewhat conservative, preferring incremental to radical change in most organizational contexts. Men and women are very similar in numbers in their expression of interests and increasingly in their representation in leadership roles (except, as of this writing, at the highest levels of organizations). Although entrepreneurs share some things in common with managers, they also tend to have different profiles, to be more likely to resist authority, to question existing practices, and to be less fearful about initiating radical change.

CONVENTIONAL INTERESTS

This interest type generally functions best in a well-established structure and enjoys working with detail (see J. L. Holland, 1997a). The preference is generally for working with data rather than with people or things. This attention to, and enjoyment of, working with data is an asset in careers in which accuracy is important and in which the requirement is to dig deep into data, to manage and work with it, and to recall specifics.

Conventional types tend to prefer working with data, such as numbers and symbols, and performing clerical tasks to working with ideas or people. As Stoll

---

[2]Unfortunately, these groups were based only on expressed intention to become managers, not on demonstrated success in the field.

et al. (2017) put it, "Conventional types prefer the explicit, ordered, systematic manipulation of data" (p. 170).

A sample of representative jobs from the O*NET (https://www.onetonline.org/explore/interests/Conventional/) includes the following:

- accountants
- bookkeepers
- cashiers
- clerks
- loan officers
- statisticians
- tellers

The Conventional group ranked next to last (slightly ahead of the Realistic group) in average educational level and in attributed prestige (L. S. Gottfredson, 1980). Although most statements about sex differences in the Holland typology have raised controversy (see L. S. Gottfredson, 1978; G. R. Hanson & Rayman, 1976; J. L. Holland et al., 1975; Prediger & Hanson, 1974, 1976a, 1976b), a sex difference does appear to exist in the Conventional area, with higher averages on Conventional interests found for women than men (J. L. Holland, 1985a, 1987; Su et al., 2009). For both Conventional men and women, Conventional interest patterns are associated with traditional, conservative attitudes and behavior (Sagiv, 2002; Tipton, 1976) and with a closed rather than open personality.

Conventional types tend to enjoy and do well when precision and attentiveness to detail are required. Lowman and Schurman (1982) administered an abbreviated form of the VPI to employees in six diverse federal government settings: a hospital, a defense establishment, two units of a social service agency, the national headquarters of a large regulatory agency, and a forms-processing unit of the same agency. They found that the modal employee in the forms-processing unit strongly endorsed Conventional interests.

Conventional interest types are generally found in administrative and clerical positions or in work with numbers or data such as in accounting (Aranya et al., 1981) and computer programming (https://www.onetonline.org/link/summary/15-1131.00). Aranya et al. (1981) found in a large sample of Canadian and French Canadian accountants that having Conventional–Enterprising–Social interests in the top three endorsed interests was the modal interest type, and that these scales were associated with professional and organizational commitments and career satisfaction. Extending these findings, Aranya and Wheeler (1986) found in a large sample of accountants from both Canada and California that small private practice accountants or partners were more likely to have Conventional as their highest endorsed interest but those going into large firms were more likely to have Enterprising interests first. Both interest patterns were associated with business applications.

Although some people—including career counselors—might regard adherence to authority and a need to function according to clearly defined rules and structures as not being particularly desirable characteristics, much of the world's work needs this attention to detail and disciplined compliance. A creative accountant or bookkeeper ("creative" in the sense of being imaginative, with high needs for change and variety) might concoct novel work methods that could very well lead to a tax audit or imprisonment. A rather large number of jobs are structured, with well-defined data-oriented job duties. Conventional types tend to work well in such contexts.

Concerning career assessment, one of the challenges in working with people with Conventional interests is to help them consider options that may be outside their awareness. When people have lost their jobs in a poor economy, flexibility may be needed in understanding one's strengths and applying them in new directions. Such a process may provoke anxiety in working with Conventional individuals.

Summarizing, Conventional interests tend to be associated with attention to detail and liking of data and numbers. With those interests tend to come a preference for consistency, order, and stability. Although there may be less interest in creativity or innovation, there are many more jobs that require attention to detail and working within well-defined frameworks than the opposite. Higher-end careers in this area include accounting and computer programming. There is a sex difference in many Conventional-interest jobs in favor of women. Educational levels for Conventional-level careers are generally at the high school or undergraduate college graduate level.

SUMMARY AND CONCLUSIONS

The Holland RIASEC interests are well-established trait variables. Each of the six major types speaks to real-life characteristics of groups of people and of work environments that have both theoretical and practical relevance. Valuable though these traits are, no one is a pure example solely of one interest type, and greater complexity ensues when considering patterns of interests in real-life assessment contexts. Nonetheless, these types have demonstrated their theoretical and practical value over many decades.

Assessors need to understand both theoretical and applied aspects of interests. In Chapter 4, issues associated with individual-level interest measurement are introduced, and examples are provided that illustrate variations in consistency and inconsistency across measures. Then, six cases are introduced that provide examples of interest profiles of individuals who scored highest in each of the six RIASEC areas. In later chapters, the personality and ability profiles of these same six cases are presented.

4

Applications
Choosing Interest Measures, Interpreting Individual-Level Interest Results, and Case Illustrations

Most research about interests deals with group differences. The earlier chapters on interests have reviewed a number of persistent findings from such studies, demonstrating considerable consistency across decades of study. However, career assessment is practiced primarily at the individual, not group level. General trends across even millions of people do not necessarily fit in individual cases.

This chapter begins by discussing individual-level variations in interests. Illustrating the complexity of assessing and interpreting individual level results, six detailed case examples are presented. Then, the issue of inconsistencies across various interest measures when taken by the same person is addressed, noting that different interest codes can be found across interest measures and that care should be taken when interpreting interest results on the basis of a single measure. Then, principles are identified for deciding which interest measures to use in applied work, noting the advantages and limitations of varying approaches to interest measurement. Finally, each of the RIASEC (Rational, Investigative, Artistic, Social, Enterprising, Conventional) types is illustrated with an anonymized, real-life example of individuals who scored highest on each of the six focal interest areas.

UNPACKING GROUP AVERAGES: THE INDIVIDUAL'S PROFILE VERSUS THE GROUP'S

A common analytical and interpretative technique in working with vocational profile data involves the comparison of individual interest profiles with those

https://doi.org/10.1037/0000254-005
Career Assessment: Integrating Interests, Abilities, and Personality, by R. L. Lowman
Copyright © 2022 by the American Psychological Association. All rights reserved.

obtained by people in defined occupational groups, such as engineers, managers, or nurses. Called comparing with criterion groups, the premise is that the closer the match between an individual's interests and those of an occupational group, the better the fit in terms of career happiness and productivity. This is particularly true if the group was established on the basis of comparison of responses to those of groups of productive and satisfied members of that occupation. This is the approach used, for example, by the Occupational Scales of the widely employed Strong Interest Inventory's (SII; the generic name used here for a measure that has also been called, among other former names, the Strong Vocational Interest Blank; see Harmon et al., 1994) and by the Career Assessment Inventory—Vocational Version (Johansson, 2003). A version of this approach was also used by J. L. Holland's (1985b) now dated *Occupations Finder*, in which a large number of occupations were assigned group interest profiles. However, the methodology used by many of the interest profiles in that widely used source involved translating Department of Labor data (e.g., the involvement of the occupation with data, people, and things) into the Holland interest codes without direct validation of the derived codes with empirical occupational samples.

The U.S. Department of Labor has since created and maintains a large online empirically derived data base of occupations called the O*NET (https://www.onetonline.org). It has also created, and makes available for free, a self-administered and self-interpreted interest measure called the Interest Profiler. The results of this test can be accessed anywhere in the world. The RIASEC codes from the test can then be used to find matching occupations on the O*NET.

Such individual–group occupational comparisons, when done in the context of robust empirical studies, are likely to be useful for career assessors, providing an important resource. Such data can help assessees identify occupations and occupational groups that are of interest and in confirming, or raising questions about, contemplated occupational choices. On the other hand, averages can be problematic, and care must be taken when comparing differences between an individual's scores on interest or occupation-specific scales and those of a criterion group. This is because occupations include among their satisfied members people with different interest profiles. In other words, mean interest profile scores are measures of central tendency, not an absolute indication of likely fit of individuals and occupations.

Additionally, group averages mask the fact that not everyone in an occupational group has the same interest patterns. This is illustrated by Table 4.1, which displays the average vocational preference scores of a group of successful public sector senior managers who were being assessed as candidates for a high-level, publicly visible, public sector position. The average group profile was Enterprising–Social–Conventional (ESC), consistent with the O*NET's profile coding for similar positions. However, only one individual actually had the Enterprising–Social–Conventional profile. The remainder had codes that were not exact matches and, in some cases, were rather discrepant. When it is considered that all of these individuals were functioning effectively in similar

TABLE 4.1. Average and Individual Self-Directed Search Interest Profiles for a Managerial Assessment Group

Group profile	Candidate A	Candidate B	Candidate C	Candidate D	Candidate E	Candidate F	Candidate G	Candidate H
Enterprising (37.5)	Artistic (43)	Enterprising (35)	Social (43)	Realistic (43)	Enterprising (38)	Enterprising (41)	Social (35)	Social (47)
Social (34.5)	Enterprising (38)	Social (31)	Enterprising (35)	Enterprising (35)	Conventional (36)	Social (37)	Enterprising (35)	Enterprising (43)
Conventional (28.4)	Social (37)	Artistic (21)	Investigative (34)	Investigative (35)	Artistic (30)	Conventional (30)	Artistic (32)	Conventional (40)
Investigative (28.1)	Realistic (32)	Conventional (14)	Conventional (33)	Artistic (29)	Social (27)	Realistic (29)	Investigative (30)	Artistic (39)
Artistic (27.8)	Investigative (35)	Investigative (12)	Realistic (18)	Conventional (24)	Realistic (24)	Investigative (22)	Realistic (23)	Investigative (34)
Realistic (26.5)	Conventional (26)	Realistic (8)	Artistic (11)	Social (23)	Investigative (24)	Artistic (17)	Conventional (24)	Realistic (33)
Code: ESC	Code: AES	Code: ESA	Code: SEI	Code: RE/I	Code: ECA	Code: ESC	Code: E/SA	Code: SEC

Note. Scores are raw RIASEC scores from the Self-Directed Search.

managerial positions, it must be concluded that being "misfit" on vocational preferences does not necessarily mean that one cannot be successful despite not matching the average interest group profile. It is likely, however, that when interests do not match the profile incumbents may adapt parts of the job duties to match their own interests.

For example, Candidate A was a successful manager of a city on the West Coast. He prided himself on being creative, innovative, and unusual in his approach to administration. Candidate C, in contrast, had an engineer's typical vocational preference code. As the chief administrator of a technologically sophisticated city in the Midwest, his interests were well suited to current role. However, he was regarded by many as being cold and impersonal, with little feel for, or appreciation of, the politics of the job. Candidate D was an extremely bright man with a reputation for innovation and creative solutions to problems. His other test responses suggested high creativity and imagination. To the untrained ear, his stated goals sounded somewhat grandiose, for he was concerned with such issues as world peace and creating elegant solutions to complex social problems. At the time of his assessment, he was seriously considering leaving his current position to start his own firm.

Before introducing the concept of occupational types and describing in detail common characteristics among those in the six RIASEC types, some caveats should be explicitly stated. First, few, if any, individuals are "pure" instances of a single type. As with any measures of central tendency, which is what interest groupings essentially are, the description of characteristics of high or "typical" (vs. low or "atypical") scorers can mask considerable individual variation. When assessing at the individual level, the complexity matters. Additionally, findings must be considered in the context of all interest scores and of other measured variables such as abilities and personality (see Chapters 5 and 13). This suggests the importance of profile analysis rather than looking at particular variables in isolation. Indeed, a major theme of this book is not to classify people just on the basis of a single domain (e.g., interests, abilities, personality), much less on the basis of a single variable within one domain. Still, it is necessary to examine each domain and each variable within a domain one at a time before moving to the complexities of combining across domains.

To elaborate, throughout his career J. L. Holland (1996) was an advocate of the idea that his model of what he called "occupational personalities" was an individual-level one that was also useful for assessing groups and social entities. Indeed, his view was that occupations and careers attracted like-minded individuals, that those whose interests were inconsistent with the modal ones would be less likely to stay or to be positively reinforced, and that the same variables could be used to measure both individuals and groups. However, describing groups of individuals differs from what is entailed in career assessment and counseling of individuals. Groups can define the general tendencies, but they do not indicate the particular issues that a career assessment client needs to address. External factors and abilities may make it possible or even necessary for a person to enter and remain in an occupation even when the fit is not ideal. Fortunately, interests can be expressed in ways other than in work.

All of this is to say that it is necessary to understand both group characteristics (remember that averages are measures of central tendency) *and* individual ones and not to assume that all commonly found characteristics will necessarily apply to a specific individual—or to a specific group, for that matter. Additionally, it is necessary also to be clear on the interest patterns that best characterize an individual. When multiple measures of interests are used, they may, or may not, be consistent. When they are not, clarification may be needed.

INCONSISTENCIES IN EXPRESSED VOCATIONAL INTERESTS

It is not uncommon for people to seek out career counseling, particularly after young adulthood, in an effort to better understand their interests and how to apply them. The problem can be that peoples' interests are not matched by their current work (incongruencies) or that their highest endorsed interests are not consistent with each other (inconsistency) across multiple measures of interests. Here I present four examples of ways that interests can be inconsistent in the top three endorsed interests.

Discrepancies in apparent vocational interests are not necessarily the counselor's responsibility to resolve. The apparent conflict may need to be explained to the client, along with the best evidence for the discrepancies. Once clients understand Holland's interest typology, they may be able to continue the self-exploration process on their own to better integrate the apparently conflicting aspects of the self.

Later in this chapter six cases are presented to illustrate each of the six RIASEC interest types. Those cases were chosen as being exemplars of a particular interest type. Often, however, people do not have consistent interest profiles across multiple measures of interests.

In this section, I present several cases that illustrate varieties of occupational interest inconsistencies. Each case came from an actual client (masking only the individual's identity) who was seeking help with career concerns. The aim is not to present all scales and other information associated with the various interest measures or, for that matter, full details about the cases. Rather, the goal is to illustrate how, in real-life contexts, measured interests can present a variety of challenges both in interpretation and in being helpful to clients trying to understand their obtained results. Additionally, these cases further illustrate the kinds of concerns for which career assessment is sought.

These cases identify types of inconsistencies often found in professional practice. Wherein the assessor cannot simply conclude what the interest profile is based on the results of assessment measures, even less so when only a single measure of interests was employed. It is not necessarily the assessor's job to resolve these inconsistencies but rather to help the client understand the findings and to provide suggestions about a process for understanding and working through such discrepancies.

Case 2. Marissa's Mildly Inconsistent Codes Across Interest Measures

Marissa was in her 20s at the time of her career assessment. As an undergraduate at a prestigious university, she had been a promising student in mathematics. However, as she neared the end of her junior year, she became preoccupied with the possibility that there would be few jobs available after graduation and so decided to attend law school to have a safe, "practical" career option. She was accepted by a highly prestigious law school but, as the first year of law school went by, she became very unhappy with her choice of profession and especially with her negative perceptions of lawyers, including her fellow students. Her own mild and withdrawn manner masked a genuine sociability, but she was certainly not aggressive or forceful, as she found her fellow students to be. She left a summer internship at a prominent law firm after only a few weeks and, following completion of law school, made the decision not to practice law. She was assessed in the context of her trying to decide what to do next in her career.

Marissa's measured vocational interests are shown in Table 4.2. The client's codes in this case on three different measures were varied by measure, but each included Artistic, Social, and Investigative interests. The codes themselves were reasonably consistent with one another, with the Investigative–Artistic combination suggesting preference for an intellectually demanding occupation but one in which there is considerable room for flexibility and creativity. However, the also-endorsed Social interests may suggest some application to teaching or possibly a helping-oriented profession. Clinical psychology, sociology, or a more abstract field such as philosophy might be suggested.

The virtual absence of any Enterprising interests might help to explain the client's distaste for the law. Of course, there are many roles to which law could be put, including using it to address social concerns. However, the client's own conclusion was that this was not her desired career direction, and so the question was what should she pursue instead. In this case, the inconsistencies across

TABLE 4.2. Marissa's Mildly Consistent Inconsistent Codes Across Interest Measures (Case 2)

	Self-Directed Search	Vocational Preference Inventory	Strong Interest Inventory
Realistic	14	0	35
Investigative	41	3	54
Artistic	33	11	48
Social	42	3	38
Enterprising	5	2	32
Conventional	11	1	35
Interest Code	SIA	AI/S	IAS

Note. A = Artistic; I = Investigative; S = Social.

the three measures were mild, and the two most highly endorsed codes on the Self-Directed Search (SDS) and the Strong measure were sufficiently close in magnitude of endorsement that the order could be easily reversed.

Case 3. Strom's Inconsistent Interest Codes Across Measures

Strom had come for career assessment in his early 40s because he was uncertain about how long his current job—working in sales for a large corporation—would last in a struggling economy. He was considering some options, such as starting up his own consulting business. His search for what to do next, or whether to make a change, was proceeding somewhat haphazardly.

Strom's vocational interest scores are shown in Table 4.3. In this case, none of the three measures had the same most highly endorsed interest profile three-letter interest code. However, two of the three measures had the same highest code, Enterprising, and that was also represented as the third most highly endorsed code on the Vocational Preference Inventory (VPI), consistent with his career to date in business and management. Similarly, Conventional interests were the second most highly endorsed codes on two of the measures and third most highly endorsed on the third measure. Only the SDS measure included Realistic in the top three endorsed codes, but the fourth most highly endorsed code on that measure was Social. On the basis of these results alone it is not possible to conclude that any one of the three summary codes is the definitive one, but it is likely that Enterprising and Conventional codes, and possibly Social, would be important in the occupations being considered. The Enterprising and Conventional codes point to a managerial or business-oriented career pursuit; the Social points to more of a helping one. Enterprising and Conventional interests generally identify comfort in working with well-defined, goal-directed tasks and in well-structured work; it was not clear that the client's current position would be the best fit.

TABLE 4.3. Strom's Inconsistent Interest Codes Across Measures (Case 3)

	Self-Directed Search	Vocational Preference Inventory	Strong Interest Inventory
Realistic	23	0	40
Investigative	14	1	47
Artistic	13	0	32
Social	21	9	52
Enterprising	29	6	55
Conventional	22	7	54
Interest Code	ERC(S)	SCE	ECS

Note. C = Conventional; E = Enterprising; R = Realistic; S = Social. Self-Directed Search and Vocational Preference scores are raw scores; Strong Interest Inventory scores are standardized scores (mean = 50, general population norms).

In attempting to resolve the interest measure discrepancies, a client like this would be encouraged to consider all the permutations of the codes across the three measures and to consider which identified occupations are of most interest. He would also be encouraged to understand the characteristics associated with each of the types, which may also help to sort out the interests that seem most descriptive. When, as in this case, a particular interest is represented on only one of the measures (in this case, Realistic on the SDS) it is useful to try to understand the anomaly. In the case of the SDS, although the Social–Conventional–Enterprising (SCE) or Enterprising–Conventional–Social (ECS) combinations were reasonably consistent, the Enterprising–Realistic–Conventional interest code would imply different directions, possibly to managerial roles in a manufacturing or other "hands-on" type of industry. Further clarification of the client's vocational interest scores would be needed. It can also be useful to look at each of the sections of the SDS to determine whether the results were more influenced by the vocational titles or by the self-rated abilities. In a case like this, the vocational titles may give a better understanding of the consistency of that measure with the other two.

Finally, note that someone whose current job is at risk, who is well into a career, and who has a family to support may not have the luxury of prioritizing interests. The assessor should help the client understand what the interests are suggesting as to career paths of most relevance, but finding another job will likely take precedence even if the interest fit is not ideal.

Case 4. Brenda's Widely Inconsistent Interest Results

A particularly complicated case occurs when multiple measures yield highly inconsistent vocational interest codes. In such a case, the career assessor is left with the difficult task of helping the client sort out which of the various alternatives is most descriptive of the client and, even if successful in doing so, still has the problem of understanding why the codes were so inconsistent with one another. The following case is illustrative.

The vocational interests of Brenda, the client, are shown in Table 4.4. She had been referred by her physician who was treating her for a number of medical problems that possibly had a stress-related component. She sought help to better understand her experiences of burnout after a number of years spent working in a helping profession. She had been raised in a traditional family in which her mother had been a homemaker and her father felt that women should not work outside the home. Her college major had been in the humanities, and at midlife she still needed to work to support herself and her children, but the current levels of stress needed to be lowered.

In this case, except for the consistently quite low Conventional scale scores, there was wide variability across the three measures. One profile (the SDS) made the client seem compatible with her occupation at the time of the evaluation (high school counselor), the second (the VPI) suggested engineering or science, and the third was a highly atypical combination whose codes were fairly inconsistent with each other. With such a profile, it is very difficult to counsel a

TABLE 4.4. Brenda's Widely Inconsistent Interest Codes Across Measures (Case 4)

	Self-Directed Search	Vocational Preference Inventory	Strong Interest Inventory
Realistic	19	4	39
Investigative	14	5	50
Artistic	26	3	50
Social	32	1	32
Enterprising	21	4	43
Conventional	6	1	28
Interest Code	SAE	IR/E	A/IE

Note. A = Artistic; E = Enterprising; I = Investigative; R = Realistic; S = Social. Self-Directed Search and Vocational Preference scores are raw scores; Strong Interest Inventory scores are standardized scores (mean = 50, general population norms).

client based on the interest results because there is no assurance of which, if any, of the three interest measures is the single "best" description of interests. Assessment of ability and personality characteristics can be examined in such cases to help clarify the discrepancies in the measured interests. However, it can also be useful for the client to do O*NET (https://www.onetonline.org/) searches for each of the career groups associated with the various interest permutations. This may help clarify which of the varying interest combinations fit best.

Reasons for the inconsistencies might also be explored. For example, the assessor can examine the separate sections of the SDS with the client to determine whether there was consistency across the subparts. Possibly the client was rating self-estimates of ability, which constitute 40% of the overall score (see Lowman & Williams, 1987) on the SDS, differently from how she evaluated the occupational titles. Because the SDS was intended to simulate a career assessment experience, it may hold some clues to where her primary interests lie. In examining this client's subparts of the SDS (Activities, Competencies, Occupations, and Self-Estimates), the Occupations section would have been coded as Artistic, the self-estimates as Social/Artistic. This could be discussed with the client to understand better whether she might be able to find fulfillment of some of her interests outside of work. Consideration of the other domains may also help to clarify the interest findings.

These case studies demonstrate the complexity of interpreting results across multiple measures of interests. Finally, for some young adults, it will take longer to sort out their interests, so retesting at a later date, or in the context of specific possible choices of majors or occupations, might prove helpful.

PROCEDURAL APPLICATIONS: PRINCIPLES FOR CHOOSING AND INTERPRETING INTEREST RESULTS

This section briefly outlines some of the factors to consider when choosing vocational interest measures to be used for career assessment.

Choosing Appropriate Interest Measures and Procedures for Interpretation

A variety of measures of occupational interests are available on the commercial market (see Lowman & Carson, 2012). In choosing which measure or measures to use in a particular application, careful review of the specific measure is needed. This includes consideration of the instrument's psychometric properties (see, e.g., Closs, 1976), its reliability and validation evidence for the intended inferences to be made, the population with whom the measure is to be used, and the ease with which the results of the measure can be understood by clients.

Measures of interests sometimes specialize in one population or another. Johansson's Career Assessment Inventory Vocational (Johansson, 2003; Vacc & Hinkle, 1994) was developed primarily for blue-collar and non-college-bound populations, while the Jackson Vocational Interest Survey (Jackson et al., 1984; Jackson & Williams, 1975) was validated against college majors and the Strong. Yet another measure, the American College Testing Program's Interest Inventory (G. R. Hanson, 1974; G. R. Hanson et al., 1974; Laing et al., 1984) has also been used mostly with high school and some college students. Prediger's (1981) World-of-Work Map was also promising. The Jackson measure has been criticized for some of its psychometric characteristics (Juni & Koenig, 1982). Good predictive validity has been suggested for other vocational interest inventories such as the California Occupational Preference System Interest Inventory (COPS II; Knapp et al., 1985). Conceptually, many of these instruments adopt Holland's six factor labeling structure or include dimensions that can readily be interpreted as similar constructs (e.g., Jackson & Williams, 1975; F. D. Westbrook, 1975).

Although a variety of choices exist for the measurement of interests, questions remain about the interchangeability of these measures (see Atanasoff & Slaney, 1980; Lowman et al., 2003; Savickas et al., 2002; and Slaney, 1978). Lowman et al. (2003), for example, compared interest results from participants who had completed at least two, and often three, measures of vocational interests. While correlations between same-named RIASEC scales across measures averaged 0.73, suggesting moderately high degree of convergent validity but also unique variance. When the RIASEC codes assigned to each individual were examined using the Zener-Schnuelle index, the Strong and VPI had the most overlap on the single most highly endorsed interest. The degree of overlap on the second highest code varied depending on which index was used. Additionally, the measures differed in the extent to which they produced ties in high point scores. The SDS resulted in the lowest number of ties (3.5%), the Strong the second highest (4.7%) and the VPI the highest (14.35%). More research is needed in this important area, but test users need to understand that interest measures are not interchangeable.

Other studies have also found discrepancies in the interests assigned based on the various measures of interests used. Savickas et al. (2002) concluded in their study of five commonly used vocational interest measures that "the results do raise concerns about the comparability of similarly and same-named scales" (p. 177) and "the possibility exists that using one interest inventory might only partially assess a client's interests and may even ignore measuring particular interests (e.g., musical interests, organizing interests) that could be critical in the client's decision making" (p. 179). However, they also noted that costs of administering multiple measures can, in some settings, be prohibitive. That said, given the apparent discrepancies of alternative measures of the same constructs, some caution in drawing conclusions on the basis of any single measure would seem warranted. As Dawis (1991) stated, "Multiple measurement, if not multimethod measurement, is not just desirable—at our current level of measurement technology, we cannot afford *not* to require it" (p. 862).

Currently, then, there is no single "best" instrument for assessing vocational interests. The choice of instruments may be driven by the particular population to be tested included the ages and educational levels of those being assessed, and the purposes of the assessment. However, some very good measures are available, and more measures are regularly introduced. A thorough review of the psychometric evidence for even the widely the most widely used measures of interests is beyond the scope of this book. One major development deserving further mention is the creation of a widely-accessible, free measure of interests, the O*NET Interest Profiler (Rounds et al., 1999). This solid, if basic, measure of the RIASEC constructs, available online, coupled with its potential for translating interest scores into the O*NET's extraordinary database on jobs and careers has been something of a "game changer." This source provides practitioners with tools that can easily be incorporated into practice. The Interest Profiler may not include all the features of other interest measures, but it does provide considerable utility, and some evidence has pointed (with some limitations) to convergent validity with other widely used RIASEC measures (see Eggerth et al., 2005). The Interest Profiler also includes both online and paper administration, instant scoring with the online version, the ability to be self-administered and interpreted, and availability in languages other than English.

A number of venerable measures of interests are also available. Three of the most commonly used vocational preference measures in contemporary use are the SDS (Holland, 1979, 1985c, 1987; Holland & Raymon, 1986), the VPI (Holland, 1985c, 1987), and the SII (Donnay et al., 2004). The Kuder measure (Kuder, 1991; Zytowski & Kuder, 1986), at one time widely used (Borgen, 1986), appears to have declined in usage compared with other measures. These measures also have the largest research bases, although there is always more work to be done. The Campbell Interest and Skills (CISS) measure (D. P. Campbell, 1994; Hansen, & Neuman, 1999) also has some attractive features. Still another Holland-construct based measure is Harrington and O'Shea's Career Decision-Making System Revised (Harrington & O'Shea, 2000).

Measures based on models other than Holland's are also available (e.g., for a measure based on Roe's theory, see Barak & Meir, 1974; Gati & Nathan, 1986; Lunneborg, 1979). Still other interest measures can be found in the literature (e.g., Droege & Hawk, 1977; Markham & Sugarman, 1978). Because the measurement of vocational interests has become an active and presumably lucrative industry, new measures emerge with regularity. The career assessor is advised to proceed with caution with new measures until sufficient validity and reliability literature exists to show that the measures are compatible with existing ones.

Assuming that interest measures have been carefully chosen and that they are appropriate for the particular assessment task, some general procedures can be identified for instrument administration and interpretation. Of course, each interest measure may have different scales and subscales, and each have their own identified procedures for review and interpretation. Here the focus is on a generic approach, particularly as related to the six well-researched RIASEC scale scores, preferably across multiple measures having been administered to the same client as a check on consistency.

A Procedural Approach for Interpreting Interest Results
1. Consider the Purpose of the Career Assessment
In any application, the important first step is to determine the purpose of the assessment before deciding on which vocational interest instrument is the most appropriate. Is the purpose for career assessment general ("I'm not sure what I want to do") or specific ("Should I stay as a bench scientist or become a scientific administrator?")? Is there ambiguity about the client's career motivations, for which interest assessment may be an important factor? Is the person unhappy in a college major or current occupation? What are the perceived contributors to the current unhappiness? What is the career and school history? When was the client most and least satisfied? Are there avocational interests that are important to the client?

2. Contextualize and Carefully Explain the Purpose of the Chosen Interest Measures
Test-taking orientation is important in contributing to valid results. Clients should be provided with information on the purpose of the testing and why the results are dependent on their being honest and accurate in completing the measures. Having established a helping relationship with the client will go far in assuring that the results can be appropriately interpreted and useful to the client.

3. Determine the Validity of the Obtained Profile Results
Unfortunately, many of the existing vocational interest measures do not incorporate scales for test-taking orientation. Darley and Hagenah (1955) noted long ago that perceptual distortion can be found in interest test results. The assessor should therefore review any instrument-specific internal validity indicators such as the Infrequent Responses Index (IR) and the Like, Indifferent, and Dislike indexes on the Strong, and the Infrequency scale on the VPI. Although

there are obvious incentives for a particular manner of presentation when a person is a job candidate, the possibility for biased presentation of interests when a client (or a client's family) aspires to a particular occupation should be considered.

Consideration should also be given to the pattern of test taking when there are low responders (those who find very few items to be of interest) and high responders (who find a great deal of items to be of interest). Low scorers may simply have strong interest preferences for what they like and a tendency to reject anything else as being irrelevant. Others with flat low profiles may be depressed which affects their perceptions of interests or possibilities. Still another possibility is that low scorers are resisting the assessment process by revealing as little as possible about themselves to the assessor. High scorers may genuinely find interest in a wide variety of things, reflecting a general approach of openness. Others may have manic tendencies in which they have exaggerated liking for many things and see all kinds of possibilities, perhaps unrealistically. Others have trouble deciding on some things rather than others or may be responding defensively by choosing everything as a way of masking actual interests and preferences.

When measures do include validity indicators, the assessor should determine whether a particular test-taking orientation might have affected the results. It can also be helpful to consider the validity indicators of other self-report measures, such as on personality measures to assess whether there may have been a consistent trend in self-presentation on the testing. In principle, of course, there is no reason for people not to be honest when the work is solely being done to help them. Nevertheless, some respondents may, consciously or unconsciously, distort responses or try to second-guess the instrument to present themselves in a way consistent with a career direction they (or someone in their lives) think they "should" want. If there are reasons to question the validity of some of the interest measure results, the assessor should present the basis for the concern and the interest findings to the client during the feedback, but note that further evidence may be needed to clarify the interests. Clients can be advised to interpret the results cautiously, to retake instruments then or at a later time, or to do further work to interpret their results in light of occupations being considered and actual activities at work, school, or in leisure time that may speak to interests.

Additional evidence about the validity of an interest profile can be found by comparing multiple measures of the same constructs (interest scales) and examining their consistency. When interest high point scores are inconsistent across measures, this may say more about the interest measures used than the client's unreliability. For example, some measures are based solely on job titles, some on interests–abilities–personality, and some on both work and leisure activities. The assessor can enlist the client's help in sorting out factors or reasons that may help to explain the results. If particular interest patterns have been shown to be compatible with particular career choices and the client dislikes those associated with one measured interest profile and likes those associated with another measured profile, that may provide practical evidence to help clarify the inconsistencies. Conversely, when the multiple measures all come up with the same most highly endorsed interest scores (and similar least endorsed interest scores) and those findings are reasonably consistent with the client's school, work, and avocational data, this lends strong support to the validity of the interest patterns and the value of their use in addressing the referral questions.

4. Review the Most Highly Endorsed Vocational Interests, the Pattern of the Scale Elevations, Consistencies, and Inconsistencies

What interests were most highly endorsed on the six RIASEC scales? If, as recommended, multiple measures were used, were the same high point codes obtained across the measures? In cases in which the codes are not consistent across the measures, is one (or more) code more plausible from the client's history and expressed activities? If there were ties on most highly endorsed interest patterns, were various permutations of the code considered (Strahan & Severinghaus, 1992)?

Also relevant are normative data and scores on non-RIASEC scales provided by particular interest measures. These include occupation-specific comparisons of the client's scores with those of various occupational groups and results on special interest scales (such as status or leisure activity preferences). How do the findings relate to the occupations or careers the client is considering? Are possibilities suggested that the client might not have considered? How can the client be helped to obtain additional information about career possibilities that are suggested by the interests?

When there are significant discrepancies among alternative measures of vocational interests, it is important for the client to consider why this may have occurred. The assessor should attempt to determine whether the assessee had a particular test-taking "set" (e.g., wanting to obtain a job for which psychological assessment is being done) or was motivated by other factors that needed to be taken into account in the interpretation. Of course, the results of the ability assessment will also provide an important aid in interpreting vocational interests. Thus, someone who adamantly maintains a desire to be a physician or lawyer but whose cognitive abilities are grossly inconsistent with the goal may need to explore the origins of the interest in the occupation and be assisted in reevaluating true alternative vocational interests and ability patterns.

What characteristics are known or hypothesized to be associated with the most highly endorsed interest scales? Are the most highly endorsed interest types generally consistent with each other? Are they consistent with the client's past history and with contemplated career directions? If not, are the areas of divergence consistent with known characteristics of the type? For example, Artistic types are more likely to have nonlinear career courses and, consistent with their creativity and divergent thinking, may tend to attempt a variety of occupational pursuits before settling on one that is a good match.

The slope of the profile should also be considered. The level of endorsed interests may reflect a variety of factors, including socioeconomic status. Interestingly, Omvig and Thomas (1974a, 1974b) found that disadvantaged students, compared with more affluent ones, endorsed more interests overall, possibly reflecting less belief that real choices were possible for them. More generally, "flat" profiles (high or low) are those with little differentiation among the interest patterns; either most things or few things are appealing. Flat low profiles (low endorsed interest profiles) may be differentiated in some cases by alternative measurement procedures (Meir et al., 1975; Pinkney, 1985). In one study, women with high levels of endorsed interests compared with another group of women with low levels of endorsed items were found to be more likely to have interests in expressive activities (writing and speaking, for example). Other possible explanations were previously discussed. "Peaked" profiles, in which, say, one to three interests are highly elevated compared with the other scales may indicate a pattern of well-differentiated interests. Interestingly, in a group of scientists and engineers, Arvey and Dewhirst (1979) found diversity of interests (having a wide vs. narrow breadth of interests) to be associated with greater career satisfaction and, among younger and older employees, with higher salary levels.

5. Compare Inventoried and Expressed Vocational Interests

It is generally worthwhile to compare a listing of occupations that the client has considered doing in the past (so-called expressed vocational interests, or what Darley & Hagenah, 1955, somewhat less charitably called "claimed" interests) to the inventoried interests (see Slaney & Slaney, 1986). Expressed interests appear to predict as well as measured interests (the predictions deriving from instruments) to subsequent occupational choices (Cairo, 1982). Self-ratings of interests appear to be correlated with measured interests (Athanasou, 1989) though there may be a tendency toward overestimation, particularly among young respondents (Bond et al., 1989). In some studies (e.g., Bartling & Hood, 1981; Borgen & Seling, 1978; Holcomb & Anderson, 1978; Neubert et al., 1990; Slaney, 1978) expressed interests actually predicted better than inventoried interests, and there is at least some evidence of higher overlap between the two areas than might be expected (Fabry & Poggio, 1977). When there is a discrepancy between expressed and measured interests, it may indicate a problem with career indecision (see Slaney & Russell, 1981), though academic problems of underachievement appear to be more influential, at least among late-to-decide-a-major college students (Lunneborg, 1975).

In career assessment practice, it is a simple matter to have the client prepare a list of five or more occupations said to be of interest, potentially of interest, or of interest in the past, and then to code these occupations using one of the Holland coding systems. The assessor may then systematically (e.g., Gati & Winer 1987), or in an ad hoc fashion, discuss these careers with the client to consider the degree of fit and attempt to understand the sources of discrepancy between the two groupings. Such explorations may also benefit from examining the client's self-concept (see Etzel et al., 2021) and relevant experiences, since interest-relevant experiences apparently enhance the likelihood of finding interest-congruent occupations (Prediger & Swaney, 1985).

6. Learn From the Feedback; Modify the Findings or Recommendations as Needed

Clients need to understand what interests are and how they were measured in the career assessment. After explaining the interest types, but before sharing the clients' results, the client can be asked to predict which ones were of strongest and least interest. This can help prepare the client to understand the obtained results. Understanding the client's reactions to the findings, including any inconsistencies, can be useful in better interpreting the results.

SIX ILLUSTRATIVE INTEREST CASE EXAMPLES

In this section, I present six case profiles, each representing one of the six RIASEC interest types (see Chapter 3). These cases were chosen because they scored highest on one of the six interest types across several interest measures. Background information is provided for each person, and then their interest results are shown. In later chapters, the ability (see Chapter 12) and personality (see Chapter 16) of these same individuals will also be presented.

Each of these six individuals, whose identifying information in each case has been disguised, was assessed in the context of career assessment for personal development or selection purposes. Each case illustrates real-life career assessment results. Note that in the case of assessments done for selection, complete results are reported even though some of the collected data would only have been used for career development purposes.

Case 5. Sam's Realistic Interest Profile

Sam, a rural-residing Caucasian man, was in his mid-40s at the time of his assessment as part of a selection project to choose first-line supervisors for a new highly technical facility at an industrial plant. He had been raised on a farm and had graduated from high school, at which point he went to work in a factory, which was one of the best paying companies in the area. He had come to work for his current employer about 25 years prior to the assessment and had served from time to time as a set-up supervisor, the name used for a rank-and-file employee chosen to be a part-time or acting supervisor who afterward returns to their usual duties. He was generally viewed by those with whom he had worked closely as being an excellent worker. He was described as having a good sense of humor, liking to tease the many coworkers in his circle of friends, almost all other Realistic men, and also as being self-deprecating.

On the job, he also had a reputation for creative solving of mechanical problems. He was described by supervisors with whom he had worked as being an "amazing fellow" who could make just about any mechanical device work the way he wanted it to. His creativity was manifest only in the practical domain of machine and equipment, not more generally. Overall, he was well-liked by his peers and considered to be an energetic and reliable worker, and although he did not see himself as being very good in expressing himself either in written or oral form, he brought excellent common-sense skills to the job.

His occupational daydreams from the assessment are shown in Table 4.5, and measured interests are shown in Table 4.6. The slightly elevated Infrequency score on the VPI suggests that Sam had a somewhat atypical test-taking orientation. The profile did not otherwise present apparent validity indicator problems (J. L. Holland & Messer, 2017).

The interest theme scores were fairly consistent across the three measures. His highest scores were Realistic interests on all three measures used. The next most endorsed interests after Realistic tended to be endorsed at a much lower level across the measures. There were also ties on each of the measures for either the second or third most highly endorsed interests. Nonetheless, his relative elevations on Enterprising and Investigative may orient him more to understanding the "why" of things and to asserting influence over others than may be typical of other Realistic types. Note that the Realistic–Enterprising–Investigative or the Realistic–Investigative–Enterprising interest profiles are often found among engineers and technicians. Also of note, and important to consider in evaluating interest results, are the low scores, where a person's interests are *not*. In this case, his interests appear not to be in either the Conventional or the Artistic areas.

TABLE 4.5. Sam's Self-Directed Search Occupational Daydreams (Case 5)

Occupational daydream	O*NET interest coding
Technician	Realistic–Investigative–Conventional
Carpenter	Realistic–Conventional–Investigative
Police Officer	Realistic–Enterprising–Conventional
Electrician	Realistic–Investigative–Conventional

Note. Occupational daydreams were coded from the O*NET (https://www.onetonline.org/find/).

TABLE 4.6. Sam's Realistic Interests Profile (Case 5)

	Self-Directed Search	Vocational Preference Inventory	Strong Interest Inventory
Realistic	41	8	54
Investigative	26	3	41
Artistic	8	1	30
Social	26	2	44
Enterprising	28	3	41
Conventional	17	1	17
Interest Code	REI/S	RE/I	RSE/I

Note. E = Enterprising; I = Investigative; R = Realistic; S = Social. Self-Directed Search and Vocational Preference scores are raw scores; Strong Interest Inventory scores are standardized scores (mean = 50, general population norms).

The Strong Interest Inventory (SII; the current name of a venerable measure of interests) includes scores not just on the RIASEC scales, but also reports on the match between the test taker's responses with those of members in a number of specific, representative occupations. The assessee had "moderately similar" to "very similar" scores for all but five of the Realistic occupations included on the test. Only in the Enterprising occupations did he have any other occupations in the "similar" or "very similar" areas and these (agribusiness manager, restaurant manager, and optician) were not typical managerial occupations. The Strong also provides what are called Basic Interest scales identifying interests (or lack thereof) in a number of areas related to each of the RIASEC interests. Using a midrange standard score of 50 as the cut, he had scores above this middle value for males on two Realistic-related themes (mechanical activities: 58, and adventure: 59) and on one theme included in the Social area on the Strong (athletics: 58). His profile was well differentiated, with only 19% of the overall items answered in the "like" or "yes" direction. His highest endorsed occupations on the SII, none of which were relevant to him either before or after the assessment, are shown in Table 4.7.

This table also shows the "matches" of Sam's measured codes from the O*NET for the Realistic–Enterprising–Investigative (and the more populated Realistic–Investigative–Enterprising permutation) as well as the Realistic–Enterprising–Social combinations associated with one or more of the measure's summary codes. Note that there were not many occupations associated with many of these interest codes.

In this case, the individual was not seeking a career change except for a berth in a new start-up operation in an existing manufacturing plant. He was in a blue-collar job, and the jobs that were identified were for the most part also blue-collar jobs. It is not clear, had he been seeking a change of career directions, that any of these would have been of interest to him but there are common themes.

Aspects of the values, mindset, and cognitive style of this individual are illustrated by his topic for an unstructured writing sample. He wrote on "overhauling a motor (car)." Here is his essay:

OVERHAULING A MOTOR (CAR)

First you should make sure the car is properly secure on jack, Take off the hood for easier axcess [sic]. Take off all wires, cable, brackets, and clamp. Take off all hosus [sic] and raiderations [sic]. Remove motor supports [sic], transmission supports, exast [sic] pipes. motor should then be read to take out.

Bolt chain to motor, place hoist directly above center of motor and lift out. You should then be read [sic] to disamble [sic] the motor.

With the proper tools begain [sic] taking off the caburator [sic], starter, fuelpum [sic], value [sic] pan covers, and anyother [sic]

[Time was called at this point in his writing sample.]

TABLE 4.7. Sam's Vocational Interest Measure and O*NET Interest Matches (Case 5)

STRONG INTEREST INVENTORY MEASURE HIGHEST OCCUPATIONAL MATCHES

Occupation	Strong standard score/code	O*NET code
Bus driver	63/R	RS
Optician	56/ER	ECR
Electrician	53/R	RIC
Navy enlisted personnel	52/RC	RC

Note. C = Conventional; E = Enterprising; I = Investigative; R = Realistic; S = Social. Strong scores are standard scores for same sex norms. Occupational codes are from the O*NET (https://www.onetonline.org/find/).

O*NET INTEREST MATCHES

Interest code	Job zone	BLS number	Occupation
Realistic–Enterprising–Investigative			
REI	1	45-3011.00	Fishers and related fishing workers
Realistic–Investigative–Enterprising			
RIE	3	53-2012.00	Commercial pilots
RIE	3	19-4093.00	Forest and conservation technicians
RIE	3	53-6041.00	Traffic technicians
RIE	4	19-1032.00	Foresters
RIE	4	19-1031.02	Range managers
RIE	4	17-2199.10	Wind energy engineers
Realistic–Enterprising–Social			
RES	2	27-2021.00	Athletes and sports competitors
RES	2	39-5092.00	Manicurists and pedicurists
RES	2	53-3041.00	Taxi drivers and chauffeurs
Realistic–Social–Enterprising			
RSE	1	35-3022.00	Counter attendants, cafeteria, food concession, and coffee shop
RSE	2	53-6061.00	Transportation attendants, except flight attendants
RSE	3	33-2011.01	Municipal firefighter

Note. E = Enterprising; I = Investigative; R = Realistic; S = Social.
Data from https://www.onetonline.org/explore/interests/Realistic/Enterprising/Social/ and https://www.onetonline.org/explore/interests/Realistic/Enterprising/Social/

The client's choice of topic and difficulty with written expression may mask his logical manner of thinking, thoroughness (note the care with which he identifies what should be done before removing the engine), and his no-nonsense but clear prose. It is easy to imagine that if he had had sufficient time and the services of an editor (online or otherwise), this rather uneducated but practical man might have produced a very clear guide to engine repair.

Overall, Sam's interest results suggest him to be well placed in the world of things mechanical and to have good reason to feel, as he did, that he was happily employed in a well-paying manufacturing organization, in which he had worked for a number of years. The results also illustrate how the abstract concept of Realistic interests look when they are measured using commonly used interest measures and career matching systems.

Case 6. Trevor's Investigative Interest Profile

Trevor, in his late 30s at the time of the assessment, sought help in pinpointing his career goals. He had earned an undergraduate degree in chemistry, a masters in biochemistry, and a doctorate in genetics. At the time of the assessment, Trevor was completing postdoctoral training in a specialized field of genetics. He came for assessment because he was uncertain whether to try to pursue a career in academic science or consider an applied position which would emphasize scientific administration. He found his work challenging and meaningful but disliked the long hours and what he perceived to be low rewards with little support from his supervisors or coworkers. He did not see himself becoming a first-rate researcher and sought a life where his work and personal life would be more balanced, thinking that a career in industry might be a better fit for him than one in a university.

For Trevor's School and Work Autobiography (an essay on a client's career history and current concerns), he wrote a five-page typed document (an assignment that for most clients is usually handwritten) discussing his career and school paths to date and his current career dilemma as he completed his training. He stated,

> I acknowledge that I am as much of a product of my experience as is anyone. I have discovered (by observation of myself, my likes and dislikes, etc.) that I have tendencies . . . which I would like to take account in my next job search. I enjoy exploration and problem-solving as compared to routine and repetitive work. . . . I have sought and enjoyed my organizational responsibilities in laboratory settings. . . . I take pride in my technical abilities and the concepts of accurateness and preciseness. I enjoy the nuts-and-bolts and looking for a better way to do a job. I enjoy helping people in technical matters. I tend to be a perfectionist. . . . I do not believe I have the vision which is necessary to become a top-rate researcher, and also would like to have a little more balance in my life (most top-rate scientists I know are either wed to their work or had to go through that stage at some point).

This writing excerpt well illustrates an Investigative mind at work. Oriented to detail, attentive to facts and the truth, he was analytical and balanced in his self-review. Trevor identified what he viewed as being his strengths and weaknesses and attempted (both here and later in the essay) to draw conclusions about his personal situation. An active intelligence, trying hard to understand what is best for him, is suggested.

The dilemma for this client reflected one of the problematic realities of science at the time of his assessment. He accurately observed his strengths and weaknesses as related to his career and clearly pinpointed the career challenge he presently faced. The client did not see himself as being a creative scientist (see Simonton, 1988; C. W. Taylor & Barron, 1963), though that did not mean he was not a competent one, and wondered whether he would be able to lead a lab in directions that would earn him distinction. He also was contemplating employment in an area of applied science in which he might be able to lead a less work-oriented life, though he acknowledged that he had strong needs for work that was not routine. Somehow he had set the perfectionistic standard for himself of producing at the very highest level of science, and anything less was seen as not being adequate for his own view of himself. Because he was working in an area that, at the time of his assessment, was in high demand and he had a specialized skill in short supply, it was likely that he would receive an offer at a major research institution. Trevor was at a crossroads for himself and needed assistance in deciding how to proceed.

At the time of his assessment, he listed three occupational paths he was considering (see Table 4.8). These were very specialized occupational choices that reflected his basic assessment interest: staying with an advanced lab role or moving into management.

The client's measured interest patterns are shown in Table 4.9. Two measures of vocational interests were administered, the SDS and the SII. On the Strong measure, the client had "like" and "yes" responses to an average of 26% of the test items, endorsed dislike/no to 39% of the items, and was indifferent or could not say to 34% of the items, suggesting a fairly well-differentiated profile but a fairly high number of "could not say/indifferent" items. The latter would be an issue for the assessor to explore with the client in feedback.

His occupational interest factor scores on the RIASEC measures were quite consistent, with Investigative–Realistic–Conventional being his top three scores on each measure. On the Strong general occupational theme scores (Utz &

TABLE 4.8. Trevor's Self-Directed Search Occupational Daydreams (Case 6)

Occupational daydream	O*NET interest coding
Genetics laboratory technician	Investigative–Realistic–Conventional
Biotech product line manager	Enterprising–Investigative
Pharmaceutical production manager	Enterprising–Realistic–Conventional; Enterprising–Conventional–Investigative

Note. Occupational daydreams were coded from the O*NET (https://www.onetonline.org/find/).

TABLE 4.9. Trevor's Investigative Occupational Interest Profile (Case 6)

	Self-Directed Search	Strong Interest Inventory
Realistic	30	53
Investigative	40	56
Artistic	6	30
Social	21	42
Enterprising	21	46
Conventional	23	52
Interest code	IRC	IRC

Note. C = Conventional; I = Investigative; R = Realistic. Self-Directed Search scores are raw scores; Strong Interest Inventory scores are standardized scores (mean = 50, general population norms).

Korben, 1976), Trevor's measured interests were clearly Investigative, with strong secondary and tertiary interests, respectively, in Realistic and Conventional interest patterns. His codes were highly internally consistent and also intertest consistent. His was a prototypically scientific interest profile, also consistent with some types of engineering. The strongly Realistic interest patterns presumably make science related to real-world and tangible phenomena attractive.

The client's lowest endorsed interests on both measures were on Social, Enterprising, and, especially, Artistic. Given that he was considering whether he should pursue a managerial career, his challenge in those roles would likely be on the interpersonal and interconnectedness aspects of the leadership role. This is a common problem for scientists, engineers, and technicians who may be tapped to fill, or who seek out, managerial roles as a way—sometimes the only way—to advance their careers. Such individuals may accept managerial roles and over time be at least minimally successful in such roles, but they may find them stressful or unsatisfying, particularly in the absence of managerial interests.

His most highly endorsed occupations on the Strong are shown in Table 4.10. Only one was above a T score of 50 (the standard score representing the midrange score among the normative groups used), and none of them were particularly relevant or of interest. None of the identified occupations were particularly relevant or of interest to the client, and none were particularly highly endorsed compared with the normative population. The identified choices were at too low of a level for him, and he had no interest in military service. This situation was partly an artifact of the rather small number of occupations included in the Strong, particularly problematic in new and emerging areas such as scientific occupations. In this case, it is possibly noteworthy that the endorsements for the higher level occupations in science (e.g., chemist, physicist, college professor, mathematician) were endorsed less highly than the more applied areas such as the ones listed above.

TABLE 4.10. Trevor's Strong Interest Measure and O*NET Interest Matches (Case 6)

STRONG INTEREST INVENTORY HIGHEST OCCUPATIONAL MATCHES

Occupation	Strong standard score/code	O*NET code
Radiologic technologist	51/RI	RSC
Medical technologist	45/IR	IRC
Air Force officer	47/R	Varies with specific job
Research/developmental manager	40/IR	EI (Estimated code[a])

Note. C = Conventional; I = Investigative; R = Realistic. Strong scores are standard scores for same sex norms. Strong scores are standard scores for same sex norms. Occupational codes are from the O*NET (https://www.onetonline.org/find/).
[a]E-I for Biofuel/Biodiesel Technology Production and Development Mgr.

O*NET INTEREST MATCHES

Interest code	Job zone	BLS number[a]	Occupation
Investigative–Realistic–Conventional			
IRC	5	19-1011.00	Animal scientists
IRC	5	19-1020.01	Biologists
IRC	5	15-1111.00	Computer and information research scientists
IRC	5	29-2011.02	Cytotechnologists
IRC	5	17-2081.00	Environmental engineers
IRC	5	19-1022.00	Microbiologists
IRC	5	17-2199.06	Microsystems engineers
IRC	5	29-1069.07	Pathologists
IRC	5	19-1023.00	Zoologists and wildlife biologists
Investigative–Conventional–Realistic			
ICR	5	19-1029.01	Bioinformatics Scientists

Note. C = Conventional; I = Investigative; R = Realistic.
[a]Standard Occupational Classification number from the Bureau of Labor Statistics (see https://www.Bls.gov/soc/2018/soc_2018_user_guide.pdf).
Data from https://www.onetonline.org/explore/interests/Investigative/Realistic/Conventional/?i=&z=5

The O*NET listings of occupations for this interest pattern (see Table 4.8) did a better job of identifying occupations of potential interest. Shown here are only the Investigative–Realistic–Conventional (IRC) and the ICR interest matches at Educational Level 5 (the highest educational level). In reviewing this list, note that on the O*NET, unlike on the Strong, the occupational matches are not tied to the client's specific pattern of responses. That is, all respondents with the same interest high point scores would find the same list once the highest interest groups were inserted into the O*NET search engine. Due to space limitations, only the Job Zone Level 5 occupations are shown here, but the client could also have explored Level 4 occupations associated with his interest scores.

Trevor's most highly endorsed Basic Interest Scales on the Strong interest measure included the following:

- science (60)
- mechanical activities (59)
- business management (54)
- athletics (55)
- domestic arts (51)
- mathematics (50)

Again, these are standardized scores with a mean of 50 and are of note in that science, mechanical activities, and business were all high scores for him.

These measures alone could not answer the client's rather specific career concerns. There was no indication that he was in the wrong profession, but his issues about changing to a leadership role were important ones to him and would potentially involve a change of specific career direction. Abilities and personality patterns, among others, also had to be considered in addressing the career concerns that brought him to the assessment. However, the interest patterns did not suggest that the career path he had pursued was an inappropriate one but that some fine tuning might be needed. In particular, the choice of managing a laboratory might well be appealing to him from a financial perspective more than working solely as a bench scientist, but there were some areas of misfit that would need to be managed.

Case 7. Elizabeth's Artistic Interest Profile

Elizabeth sought career assessment for assistance in resolving a difficult dilemma. Although she had, in her youth, been a skilled equestrian specializing in dressage, she had suffered a debilitating injury after years of training and work. This effectively ended her chances for a career in that area. Instead, she pursued a business major in college and somewhat accidentally fell into a marketing position after college that, although uninspiring to her, paid well enough for her to enjoy a comfortable middle-class life.

Later, as the economy suffered a major decline and work in her area dried up, she obtained paralegal training and a position in a real estate law firm. It was her job to review and fact-check particular kinds of reports, which required considerable attention to detail. Although she did not particularly like the work, it paid well, and during a recession, she felt lucky to have any job. She came to career assessment because she was not sure whether she should stay in her current occupation, switch career fields entirely, or seek another job in the same field. She noted that she would like to be "more interested and receive more enjoyment and satisfaction out of my work than I do now." She saw her strengths as including imagination, color coordination, and ability to work with animals and children. Her self-perceived weaknesses were listed as shyness, wasting time on unimportant things, and procrastination.

In her spare time, the client enjoyed painting. One of her friends, an interior decorator, asked for Elizabeth's assistance with a project when one of her employees was out sick. She had no training in this field, but her friend was surprised at how quickly she picked up the skills that were important in that line of work. She started assisting the established decorator on a part-time basis and took a few short courses. When she realized she liked the interior decorating better than her primary employment, she sought help with career assessment.

Her occupational daydreams from the SDS are shown in Table 4.11. All of these occupations had strong artistic/creative components except for physical therapist and veterinarian. Elementary education is more of a Social interest occupation, but it does have some creative aspects, since drawing and art are often part of the activities in the lower elementary school grades. Her daydreams were not very consistent with her college major or work experience to date.

Elizabeth's vocational interest scores on three different measures are shown in Table 4.12. On the Strong, she client endorsed "like" and "yes" responses to an average of 28% of the test items, responded dislike/no to 38% of the items, and was indifferent or could not say to 34% of them, suggesting a fairly well-differentiated profile. She had strongest secondary interests in Social on the Strong and SDS and on all three of the measures her tertiary high point scores were Investigative. The variations on her patterns give her a broader list of

TABLE 4.11. Elizabeth's Self-Directed Search Occupational Daydreams (Case 7)

Occupational daydream	O*NET interest coding
Photographer	Artistic–Realistic
Actress	Artistic–Enterprising
Elementary education	Social–Artistic–Conventional
Physical therapy	Social–Enterprising–Realistic
Advertising (advertising and promotional managers)	Enterprising–Artistic–Conventional
Veterinarian	Investigative–Realistic
Clothes buyer (generic buyer)	Enterprising–Conventional
Fashion designer	Artistic–Enterprising–Realistic
Interior decorator	Artistic–Enterprising

Note. Occupational daydreams were coded from the O*NET (https://www.onetonline.org/find/).

TABLE 4.12. Elizabeth's Artistic Interest Profile (Case 7)

	Self-Directed Search	Vocational Preference Inventory	Strong Interest Inventory
Realistic	8	2	39
Investigative	20	3	44
Artistic	36	7	61
Social	21	2	53
Enterprising	19	7	43
Conventional	12	0	33
Interest code	ASI	A/E	ASI

Note. A = Artistic; E = Enterprising; I = Investigative; S = Social. Self-Directed Search and Vocational Preference scores are raw scores; Strong Interest Inventory scores are standardized scores (mean = 50, general population norms).

occupations to explore but may make it difficult to identify occupations that matched all of the most highly endorsed interest permutations.

On the Strong, the client's highest interest-job matches were on flight attendant and three Artistic-related occupations (Table 4.13). Concerning her O*NET interest-matched occupations (Table 4.13), the client's "top three" most highly endorsed interest codes on two of the measures, Artistic–Social–Investigative, had no SI matches. The Artistic–Enterprising–Investigative interest combination had two matches. The various permutations of her most highly endorsed interests provided additional possibilities.

Ordinarily the focus would be on occupations in the same job zone as the client's educational level (in this case, college graduate) but there were only three occupational matches to measured interests. It was therefore necessary to go outside her educational level and to consider occupations that matched two of the three highest endorsed interests. This process identified occupations that were at least partially matched with her interests. Note that three of her nine occupational daydreams: actor, fashion designer, and interior designer, were all listed in the Artistic–Enterprising category. However, on all three measures, her Investigative interests were her third most highly endorsed pattern, and it is important to better understand how those might be fitted into her career choices.

Summarizing, in the arts and creative occupations, career dilemmas are common as talent and ambition confront the reality of limited career options, particularly when considering long-term career choices. On the other hand, clearly some will succeed in these highly competitive spaces, and some will not, at least as far as full-time careers are concerned.

Some will pursue non-Artistic full-time careers and part-time Artistic ones or find avocational outlets for their creative interests. Additionally, when a client's interests, though strong in Artistic areas, include other interests, those can also be considered in their own rights. Even in such cases, however, there needs to be a clear plan about how to handle the Artistic interests.

TABLE 4.13. Elizabeth's Strong Interest Measure and O*NET Interest Matches (Case 7)

STRONG INTEREST INVENTORY MEASURE HIGHEST OCCUPATIONAL MATCHES

Occupation	Strong code	O*NET code
Flight attendant	AE	ESC
Commercial artist	A	ARE
Photographer	A	AR
Musician	A	AES

Note. A = Artistic; C = Conventional; E = Enterprising; R = Realistic; S = Social. Strong t scores not available; codes are based on same sex norms. Occupational codes are from the O*NET (https://www.onetonline.org/find/). Strong numerical scores not available.

O*NET INTEREST MATCHES

Interest code	Job zone	BLS number	Occupation
Artistic–Social–Investigative: none			
Artistic–Enterprising–Investigative			
AEI	3	27-4032.00	Film and video editors
AEI	4	27-3022.00	Reporters and correspondents
Artistic–Investigative–Social: none			
Enterprising–Artistic–Investigative: none			
Artistic–Enterprising			
AE	2	27-2011.00	Actors
AE	2	27-1023.00	Floral designers
AE	2	39-9011.01	Nannies
AE	3	27-1012.00	Craft artists
AE	3	27-1022.00	Fashion designers
AE	3	27-4032.00	Film and video editors
AE	3	39-5012.00	Hairdressers, hairstylists
AE	3	27-1026.00	Merchandise displayers and window trimmers
AE	3	27-2041.04	Music composers and arrangers
AE	3	25-3021.00	Self-enrichment education teachers
AE	3	27-2042.01	Singers
AE	3	51-6052.00	Tailors, dressmakers, and custom sewers
AE	4[a]	25-3011.00	Adult basic and secondary education and literacy teachers
AE	4	27-1011.00	Art directors
AE	4	27-3021.00	Broadcast news analysts

(*continues*)

TABLE 4.13. Elizabeth's Strong Interest Measure and O*NET Interest Matches (Case 7)   (Continued)

Interest code	Job zone	BLS number	Occupation
AE	4	27-2032.00	Choreographers
AE	4	27-1021.00	Commercial and industrial designers
AE	3	35-1011.00	Chefs and head cooks
AE	4	27-3041.00	Editors
AE	4	27-1024.00	Graphic designers
AE	4	27-1025.00	Interior designers
AE	4	27-2041.01	Music directors
AE	4	27-2042.02	Musicians, instrumental
AE	4	27-3011.00	Radio and television announcers
AE	4	27-3022.00	Reporters and correspondents
AE	4	25-2031.00	Secondary school teachers, except special and career/technical education
AE	4	15-1199.11	Video game designers
Enterprising–Artistic			
EA	4	11-2011.00	Advertising and promotions managers
EA	4	41-3011.00	Advertising sales agents
EA	4	27-3043.04	Copy writers
EA	4	27-2012.02	Directors, stage, motion pictures, television, radio
EA	4	13-1131.00	Fundraisers
EA	4	27-2012.01	Producers
EA	4	27-2012.03	Program directors
EA	4	11-2031.00	Public relations and fundraising managers
EA	4	27-3031.00	Public relations specialists
EA	4	39-9032.00	Recreation workers
EA	4	13-1199.05	Sustainability specialists
EA	4	27-2012.04	Talent directors
EA	5	21-2011.00	Clergy
EA	5	19-3032.00	Industrial-organizational psychologists
EA	5	25-1065.00	Political science teachers, postsecondary

Interest code	Job zone	BLS number	Occupation
AE	4	27-2032.00	Choreographers
AE	4	27-1021.00	Commercial and industrial designers
AE	3	35-1011.00	Chefs and head cooks
AE	4	27-3041.00	Editors
AE	4	27-1024.00	Graphic designers
AE	4	27-1025.00	Interior designers
AE	4	27-2041.01	Music directors
AE	4	27-2042.02	Musicians, instrumental
AE	4	27-3011.00	Radio and television announcers
AE	4	27-3022.00	Reporters and correspondents
AE	4	25-2031.00	Secondary school teachers, except special and career/technical education
AE	4	15-1199.11	Video game designers
Enterprising–Artistic			
EA	4	11-2011.00	Advertising and promotions managers
EA	4	41-3011.00	Advertising sales agents
EA	4	27-3043.04	Copy writers
EA	4	27-2012.02	Directors, stage, motion pictures, television, radio
EA	4	13-1131.00	Fundraisers
EA	4	27-2012.01	Producers
EA	4	27-2012.03	Program directors
EA	4	11-2031.00	Public relations and fundraising managers
EA	4	27-3031.00	Public relations specialists
EA	4	39-9032.00	Recreation workers
EA	4	13-1199.05	Sustainability specialists
EA	4	27-2012.04	Talent directors
EA	5	21-2011.00	Clergy
EA	5	19-3032.00	Industrial-organizational psychologists
EA	5	25-1065.00	Political science teachers, postsecondary
EA	5	19-3051.00	Urban and regional planners

(*continues*)

TABLE 4.13. Elizabeth's Strong Interest Measure and O*NET Interest Matches (Case 7)   (Continued)

Interest code	Job zone	BLS number	Occupation
Social–Artistic–Investigative			
SAI	5	29-1125.01	Art therapists
SAI	5	25-1121.00	Art, drama, and music teachers, postsecondary
SAI	5	25-1122.00	Communications teachers, postsecondary
SAI	5	25-1081.00	Education teachers, postsecondary
SAI	5	25-1123.00	English language and literature teachers, postsecondary
SAI	5	25-1124.00	Foreign language and literature teachers, postsecondary
SAI	5	21-1013.00	Marriage and family therapists
SAI	5	25-1126.00	Philosophy and religion teachers, postsecondary
SAI	5	21-1011.00	Substance abuse and behavioral disorder counselors
Artistic–Social–Enterprising			
ASE	4	27-3021.00	Broadcast news analysts
ASE	4	27-2032.00	Choreographers
ASE	4	27-2041.01	Music directors
ASE	4	27-3011.00	Radio and television announcers
Artistic–Enterprising–Social			
AES	3	39-5012.00	Hairdressers, hairstylists, and cosmetologists
AES	4	27-2041.01	Music directors
AES	4	27-3011.00	Radio and television announcers
Social–Artistic–Enterprising			
SAE	3	25-3021.00	Self-enrichment education teachers
SAE	4	25-3011.00	Adult basic and secondary education and literacy teachers and instructors
SAE	4	25-2031.00	Secondary school teachers, except special and career/technical education

Note. A = Artistic; E = Enterprising; I = Investigative; S = Social.
[a]Standard Occupational Classification number from the Bureau of Labor Statistics (see https://www.Bls.gov/soc/2018/soc_2018_user_guide.pdf).
Data from https://www.onetonline.org/explore/interests/Artistic/Social/Enterprising/

With a standard score of 50 being average compared with the Strong's normative base, the client's most highly endorsed Basic Interest Scales included the following:

- music/dramatics (64)
- art (62)
- nature (60)
- social service (58)
- medical science (57)
- medical service (57)
- domestic arts (57)

To the extent that interests can drive the client's career choices, the artistic opportunities need to be considered from the perspective of real-world possibilities and earnings potential. If the creative client is highly motivated and talented enough, and willing to take on the considerable risks associated with many careers in the arts, it would still be important to have alternative career paths in mind if a preferred approach does not prove possible. At the same time, it would be important to know what the client has done with her creative interests and abilities. Has she continued to perform in her serendipitously discovered talent in the visual arts? Has this been sufficiently satisfying to her? If not, why not? Can she try increasing work in this area to see if it might become her full-time occupation? Additionally, how has she fared with her "day job" as a paralegal? Has she been performing adequately to do the job successfully? Does she enjoy the work? If so, what does she enjoy about it? If she doesn't, why not? Other career trajectories could also be considered even if a day job is necessary. Conversely, what about her Social and Investigative interests? Might she find satisfaction in a career involved, say, in one of the medical service professions and pursue her creative interests in avocational work? Could she possibly combine her interests in an occupation like art therapy? These are the types of questions, from an interests perspective, that may need to be considered with the client.

Case 8. Sarah's Social Interest Profile

Sarah's case illustrates characteristic features of the Social interest profile. The client was in her early 20s and in college at the time of her assessment. She was assessed at the request of her parents, who felt she could use some help in deciding from among alternative college majors and career paths. Her father was an engineer and her mother a homemaker.

Sarah indicated that her goal for career assessment was "to find out what occupation I would be best suited for." Her ideal job was "one with kind of flexible hours where I'm around people (preferably men)." She had held two part-time jobs while in school. She had been in the top 20 students in her large high school graduating class of nearly 400. At the time of her assessment, she had completed 1.5 years in college with a grade point average of 3.3. She was undecided about her college major but had enjoyed her education classes and was considering that as a major. Her avocational activities were "tennis, shopping, boys, being with people, my sorority." She indicated that she loves to be around children, which is one reason she was thinking of training in elementary education.

Sarah's occupational daydreams (from the SDS; J. L. Holland, 1979; J. L. Holland & Messer, 2017) at the time of the assessment are shown in Table 4.14. The interest codes came from the O*NET. All of these occupations except for flight attendant, photographer, and police officer had Social as their highest interest pattern. The secondary and tertiary interest codes for the Social occupations varied somewhat, but so did the specific codes and order of codes for the client's interests beyond the primary endorsed code.

The client's measured interest profiles are shown in Table 4.15. On all parts of the Strong measure she had 26% "like" responses, 31% "indifferent," and 42% "dislike," reflecting balance in her response to taking this measure. On the three different measures of occupational interests, Sarah endorsed Social as the strongest interest code. There was some inconsistency, however, on the measures, for the secondary and tertiary interests. Enterprising, and Artistic interests were the secondary and tertiary codes on two of the three measures. On the third measure, the secondary and tertiary endorsed scales were Conventional and Investigative. Because the interests less highly endorsed than Social were much lower than the Social interests, there is less confidence in the secondary interests. Least endorsed on all three measures were Realistic interests and (on two measures) Investigative. With such inconsistencies, the client would be encouraged to explore occupations thought to be consistent with the

TABLE 4.14. Sarah's Self-Directed Search Occupational Daydreams (Case 8)

Occupational daydream	O*NET interest coding
Elementary school teacher	Social–Artistic–Conventional
Counseling psychologist	Social–Investigative–Artistic
Flight attendant	Enterprising–Social–Conventional
Police officer	Realistic–Enterprising–Conventional
Deaf educator (special education)	Social–Artistic
Photographer, still	Artistic–Realistic
Preschool teacher	Social–Artistic

Note. Occupational codes for the daydreams are from the O*NET (https://www.onetonline.org/find/).

TABLE 4.15. Sarah's Social Interest Profile (Case 8)

	Self-Directed Search	Vocational Preference Inventory	Strong Interest Inventory
Realistic	4	0	34
Investigative	20	0	32
Artistic	5	1	43
Social	37	13	59
Enterprising	19	4	53
Conventional	21	1	37
Interest code	SCI	SEA/C	SEA

Note. A = Artistic; C = Conventional; E = Enterprising; I = Investigative; S = Social. Self-Directed Search and Vocational Preference scores are raw scores; Strong Interest Inventory scores are standardized scores (mean = 50, general population norms).

various permutations, both to consider a broader array of potentially fitting occupations and to help to clarify the code.

Table 4.16 shows interest matches with specific occupations from the Strong and from the O*NET.

The following Basic Interest Scales were most highly endorsed on the Strong interest measure. (The standard scores for the Basic Interest Scales have a mean of 50.) These scores are not only relatively high but also high compared with the normative groups for the Strong:

- social service (64)
- office practices (61)
- teaching (61)
- athletics (60)
- merchandising (59)
- domestic arts (55)
- sales (55)

On the basis of her interests (and without considering the other personality and ability data), training in a teaching or counseling role would appear to be particularly attractive. Further differentiation of her interests might be needed since the two particular interest combinations of Social–Artistic–Enterprising (and its permutations) and Social–Investigative–Conventional (and related codes) would potentially take her in quite different occupational directions.

TABLE 4.16. Sarah's Strong Interest Measure and Occupational O*NET Interest Matches (Case 8)

STRONG INTEREST INVENTORY MEASURE HIGHEST OCCUPATIONAL MATCHES

Occupation	Strong standard score/code	O*NET code
Physical education teacher	50/SR	SAC (generic teacher)
Beautician	48/E or AE	AES
Banker	47/C	ECS (financial manager)
Radiologic technologist	46/RI	RSC

Note. A = Artistic; C = Conventional; E = Enterprising; I = Investigative; R = Realistic; S = Social. Strong scores are standard scores for same sex norms. Strong scores are standard scores for same sex norms. Occupational codes are from the O*NET (https://www.onetonline.org/find/).

O*NET INTEREST MATCHES

Interest code	Job zone	BLS Number	Occupation
Social-Enterprising-Artistic			
SEA	2	27-3012.00	Public address system and other announcers
SEA	3	39-7011.00	Tour guides and escorts
SEA	4	21-1021.00	Child, family, and school social workers
SEA	4	39-9032.00	Recreation workers
SEA	5	21-2011.00	Clergy
SEA	5	25-1065.00	Political science teachers, postsecondary
Social-Artistic-Enterprising			
SAE	2	39-9011.01	Nannies
SAE	3	25-3021.00	Self-enrichment education teachers
SAE	4	25-3011.00	Adult basic and secondary education and literacy teachers and instructors
SAE	4	25-2031.00	Secondary school teachers, except special and career/technical education
Social-Investigative-Conventional			
SIC	3	29-1141.00	Registered nurses
SIC	5	25-1021.00	Computer science teachers, postsecondary
SIC	5	25-1082.00	Library science teachers, postsecondary
Social-Conventional-Investigative			
SCI	4	43-4051.03	Patient representatives

Note. A = Artistic; C = Conventional; E = Enterprising; I = Investigative; S = Social.
Data from https://onetonline.org/find

Case 9. Stan's Enterprising Interest Profile

The following case illustrates some of the common themes found with managerial interest profiles.

Stan sought career assessment after he had experienced a job loss in his 50s during an economic recession. He had attended college at a prestigious private university in the Midwest United States majoring in management and accounting. He was born into an immigrant family where there had been strong expectations of achievement and success. In college, he had been very competitive in both sports and academics. He had been in a fraternity in college and active in its leadership. His family life was stable and happy.

In his school, there had been strong pressure to get a job in large, prestigious corporations. He was successful in that goal and moved on from there to work in a series of manufacturing organizations, always responsible for overseeing a team. Over time he held senior leadership roles at the vice president level. His longest tenure in a company was for 15 years. He ultimately opened his own business, part of a larger corporation's franchise system. This was not successful, partly due to the economic recession and partly due to difficulties in leading a start-up.

At the time of his assessment, Stan saw his strength as being as a generalist who was very good at helping achieve company objectives once the objectives had been set. He felt that he was particularly good at business problem solving. He did not view himself as being particularly creative. He saw as weaknesses his impatience and his work–life balance. He also thought that his honest and direct approach was sometimes problematic in highly political work environments. Although he had felt that he was well suited to accomplish something with his life, since his job loss he felt he had lost his sense of purpose.

In this case, two themes characterized this individual's career path: the natural attraction to business and enjoyment of the financial aspects of business, and the possible misfit he had experienced with an entrepreneurial start-up.

His occupational daydreams (coded from the O*NET) at the time of his assessment are listed in Table 4.17. Note that not all of the codes provided by the O*NET were exact matches to the client's listed jobs. While the daydreams reflected variations on a theme, there were some commonalities. All of the listed occupations in some way reflected interests in business-related occupations. Beyond that, there is some diversity of the types of areas within business which the client finds appealing. However, Enterprising and Conventional interests predominate the occupations he identified as being of interest.

Stan's measured interests are shown in Table 4.18. His Holland interest themes were reasonably consistent across the three measures, with Enterprising and Conventional most highly endorsed across all three measures. The tertiary code was mixed, with Social, Realistic, and Investigative being endorsed across the three measures. The tertiary codes were much lower than the two highest endorsed interests. Perhaps the diversity of tertiary interests reflects his consideration of multiple career paths that were not always compatible. The Enterprising–Conventional code well fits financial management, which is part of several of the occupations in which he expressed interest.

TABLE 4.17. Stan's Self-Directed Search Occupational Daydreams (Case 9)

Occupational daydream	O*NET interest coding
Business manager	Enterprising–Conventional–Social (varies with specific duties)
Employee relations representatives	Enterprising–Conventional–Social (labor relations specialists)
Regulatory agency director	Enterprising–Conventional (regulatory affairs manager)
Import export agent	Enterprising–Conventional–Social (customs broker)
Announcer	Artistic–Enterprising–Social (announcement/broadcaster)
Appraiser	Enterprising–Conventional–Realistic (real estate appraiser)

Note. Occupational codes are from the O*NET (https://www.onetonline.org/find/).

TABLE 4.18. Stan's Enterprising Interest Profile (Case 9)

	Self-Directed Search	Vocational Preference Inventory	Strong Interest Inventory
Realistic	23	4	45
Investigative	22	1	54
Artistic	11	2	40
Social	32	5	46
Enterprising	44	10	67
Conventional	43	10	64
Interest code	ECS	E/CS	ECI

Note. C = Conventional; E = Enterprising; I = Investigative; S = Social. Self-Directed Search and Vocational Preference scores were raw scores; Strong Interest Inventory scores are standardized scores (mean = 50, general population norms).

The client's occupational matches on the Strong are shown in Table 4.19. All were in the business or business finance area. His occupational matches on the O*NET are also shown in Table 4.19. These matches derive from taking the summary codes from the interest measures (Table 4.18) and then finding occupations determined by the O*NET to be consistent with the interest type. Note that these are group averages but are useful in working with a client to identify occupations likely to match the measured interests. In considering the occupations on such a list, it is important also to consider the job zones of the identified occupations. Although interests may match with a particular occupation, the level of education required to pursue the career may be too high or too low for a particular client. In the current case, the assessee is a college graduate and was

TABLE 4.19. Stan's Strong Interest Inventory Measure and O*NET Interest Matches (Case 9)

STRONG INTEREST INVENTORY MEASURE HIGHEST OCCUPATIONAL MATCHES

Occupation	Strong standard score/code	O*NET code
Marketing executive	66/E-I	E-C (marketing manager)
Investments manager	64/ECI	EC (investment fund manager)
Human resources specialist	56/ESR	ECS
Financial analyst	56/CRE	IC (financial quantitative analyst)

Note. C = Conventional; E = Enterprising; I=Investigative; R = Realistic; S = Social. Strong scores are standard scores for same sex norms. Strong scores are standard scores for same sex norms. Occupational codes are from the O*NET (https://www.onetonline.org/find/).

O*NET INTEREST MATCHES

Interest code	Job zone	BLS number	Occupation
Enterprising–Conventional–Social			
ECS	4	13-1011.00	Agents and business managers of artists, performers, and athletes
ECS	4	11-3111.00	Compensation and benefits managers
ECS	4	41-3099.01	Energy brokers
ECS	4	11-3031.02	Financial managers, branch or department
ECS	4	41-1012.00	First-line supervisors of nonretail sales workers
ECS	4	11-1021.00	General and operations managers
ECS	4	13-1071.00	Human resources specialists
ECS	4	11-3051.00	Industrial production managers
ECS	4	41-3021.00	Insurance sales agents
ECS	4	13-1075.00	Labor relations specialists
ECS	4	11-9081.00	Lodging managers
ECS	4	13-1081.00	Logisticians
ECS	4	13-1121.00	Meeting, convention, and event planners
ECS	4	13-2052.00	Personal financial advisors
ECS	4	11-9141.00	Property, real estate, and community association managers
ECS	4	11-9199.01	Regulatory affairs managers
ECS	4	41-3031.01	Sales agents, securities and commodities
ECS	4	11-2022.00	Sales managers
ECS	4	41-3031.03	Securities and commodities traders
ECS	5	11-1011.00	Chief executives
ECS	5	11-9033.00	Education administrators, postsecondary

(continues)

TABLE 4.19. Stan's Strong Interest Inventory Measure and O*NET Interest Matches (Case 9) (*Continued*)

Interest code	Job zone	BLS number	Occupation
ECS	5	11-9199.03	Investment fund managers
ECS	5	11-9111.00	Medical and health services managers
Enterprising–Social–Conventional			
ESC	4	13-2071.00	Credit counselors
ESC	4	21-2021.00	Directors, religious activities and education
ESC	4	11-3121.00	Human resources managers
ESC	4	13-2071.01	Loan counselors
ESC	5	29-1141.04	Clinical nurse specialists
ESC	5	11-9032.00	Education administrators, elementary and secondary school
Conventional–Enterprising–Social			
CES	3	13-2081.00	Tax examiners and collectors and revenue agents
CES	3	13-2082.00	Tax preparers
CES	4	13-2072.00	Loan officers
Conventional–Social–Enterprising			
CSE	3	25-4031.00	Library technicians
CSE	4	21-1093.00	Social and human service assistants
CSE	5	25-4021.00	Librarians
Enterprising–Conventional–Investigative			
ECI	4	11-3021.00	Computer and information systems managers
ECI	4	13-2061.00	Financial examiners
ECI	4	15-1199.09	Information technology project managers
ECI	4	11-9199.10	Wind energy project managers
ECI	5	11-1011.03	Chief sustainability officers
ECI	5	11-9039.01	Distance learning coordinators
Enterprising–Investigative–Conventional			
EIC	4	11-9199.11	Brownfield redevelopment specialists and site managers
EIC	4	13-1199.04	Business continuity planners
EIC	4	11-9121.01	Clinical research coordinators
EIC	4	13-2099.04	Fraud examiners, investigators, and analysts
EIC	4	15-1199.10	Search marketing strategists
Investigative–Enterprising–Conventional			
IEC	4	13-1161.00	Market research analysts and marketing specialists
IEC	4	11-9121.02	Water resource specialists

Note. C = Conventional; E = Enterprising; I = Investigative; S = Social.
Data from Standard Occupational Classification number from the Bureau of Labor Statistics (see https://www.Bls.gov/soc/2018/soc_2018_user_guide.pdf).

only considering occupations with the requirement of a college degree. For the full list of occupations that matched the interests, see the O*NET.

Overall, the client's expressed and measured interests were quite congruent with his current occupational pursuits. He expressed satisfaction with his past positions though he regretted the entrepreneurial venture. The challenge for the client was being able to return to positions similar to the ones he had left behind.

Case 10. Linda's Conventional Interest Profile

Linda was assessed as part of an assessment center of accountants in an industrial selection project for a West Coast company. She had earned a college degree in accounting and business after starting work, going back to school on a part-time basis. She left her organization to work for a government agency that made use of her accounting skills but ultimately returned to her current manufacturing organization in an accounting management role. She was well respected in her current position and generally viewed by nonaccounting managers as being someone who had good advancement potential.

At the time of her assessment, she listed no occupational daydreams on the SDS (J. L. Holland, 1985), which is not uncommon when using the measures in the selection context. Note that some of the assessment information was used for career development feedback but not in the assessment for selection. Her occupation as an accounting manager or industrial accountant would most likely be coded as Conventional–Enterprising or Enterprising–Conventional. Her measured interest profiles are shown in Table 4.20.

On all parts of the Strong, Linda had 17% "like" responses, 21% "indifferent," and 62% "dislike," reflecting either guardedness in the context of a work assessment, a clear perception of what she did or did not like, or possibly a naysaying tendency.

TABLE 4.20. Linda's Conventional Interest Profile (Case 10)

	Self-Directed Search	Vocational Preference Inventory	Strong Interest Inventory
Realistic	7	0	30
Investigative	21	0	37
Artistic	3	0	34
Social	28	0	32
Enterprising	26	1	43
Conventional	39	5	57
Interest code	CSE	CE	CEI

Note. C = Conventional; E = Enterprising; I = Investigative; S = Social. Self-Directed Search and Vocational Preference scores are raw scores; Strong Interest Inventory scores are standardized scores (mean = 50, general population norms).

Her interests across three different measures of interests were highest on the Conventional interest scales. Consistent with the Conventional interest pattern, she endorsed a rather narrow range of occupational interests. It is a bit unusual, on the VPI, to have so few occupations endorsed, but her score on the VPI's Self-Control scale was quite high (13). Similarly, on the Strong, only the Conventional interests were in the average range compared with general population norms. Given that the assessee was working in a highly Realistic manufacturing organization, the rather low Realistic interests might cause Linda to see herself more as a specialist in accounting rather than as a generic manager.

With interest patterns like these it is important not to overinterpret the secondary and tertiary codes when, as in the case of the Enterprising score of 1 on the VPI, they may not have much meaning, particularly when a similar result is not found on other measures. Common across all three of the client's top endorsed interests were Conventional and Enterprising, with Social and Investigative, respectively, in the top three on one of the measures. The secondary and tertiary codes on the SDS and Strong were only high relative to the other scales. This pattern was consistent with an accountant's profile on the Conventional side, and it is possible that she simply has well-defined interests that are very focalized. On the other hand, to the extent that she aspires to higher level work in an organization, she may need to broaden her perspectives. Otherwise, she may need to be in a large enough organization where it is possible to move up as a specialist in accounting roles.

The client's highest occupational scales on the Strong and the occupational matches on the O*NET are shown in Table 4.21. Her most highly endorsed Basic Interest Scales on the Strong included office practices (49), business management (48), and mathematics (48). The O*NET's occupational matches for her interests are shown in Table 4.21 for Conventional–Enterprising, Enterprising–Conventional, and for Conventional–Social–Enterprising interest patterns for Job Zones 4 and 5.

Summarizing, the client's interests were well suited to her current position as an accounting manager. She also fit the general patterns found among those expressing highest interest patterns in Conventional.

SUMMARY AND CONCLUSIONS

Occupational interests are well-established individual difference variables that are, without question, important in career assessment. They provide an excellent starting point in career assessment for orienting the assessor to the client and for helping to understand and contextualize ability and personality findings. The career assessor needs to be familiar both with the theories and research on interests and with the practical realities of interest measurement. Considerable care is needed in interpreting interest assessment results, particularly when there is disagreement across multiple measures of the same constructs.

Interests, of course, are only one of the three major domains covered in this book, and in the next section abilities are introduced, followed by personality. Then, the final section focuses on combining across domains and contextualizing interests with other findings.

TABLE 4.21. Linda's Case, Strong Interest Inventory and O*NET Interest Matches (Case 10)

STRONG INTEREST INVENTORY MEASURE HIGHEST OCCUPATIONAL MATCHES

Occupation	Strong standard score/code	O*NET code
Marketing executive	62/EI	EC (marketing manager)
Banker	61/C	ECS (financial manager)
Investments manager	59/ESR	EC (investment fund manager)
Accountant	55/CRE	CEI

Note. C = Conventional; E = Enterprising; I=Investigative; R = Realistic; S = Social. Strong scores are standard scores for same sex norms. Strong scores are standard scores for same sex norms. Occupational codes are from the O*NET (https://www.onetonline.org/find/).

O*NET INTEREST MATCHES

Interest code	Job zone	BLS number[a]	Occupation
Conventional–Enterprising			
CE	4	13-2011.01	Accountants
CE	4	15-2011.00	Actuaries
CE	4	25-9011.00	Audio-visual and multimedia collections specialists
CE	4	13-2011.02	Auditors
CE	4	15-2041.02	Clinical data managers
CE	4	11-9199.02	Compliance managers
CE	4	13-1051.00	Cost estimators
CE	4	15-1141.00	Database administrators
CE	4	15-1199.12	Document management specialists
CE	4	13-1041.01	Environmental compliance inspectors
CE	4	13-2051.00	Financial analysts
CE	4	19-4041.01	Geophysical data technicians
CE	4	15-1122.00	Information security analysts
CE	4	13-1081.02	Logistics analysts
CE	4	13-1041.07	Regulatory affairs specialists
CE	4	13-2099.02	Risk management specialists
CE	4	41-4012.00	Sales representatives, wholesale and manufacturing, except technical and scientific products
CE	4	21-1093.00	Social and human service assistants

(*continues*)

TABLE 4.21. Linda's Case, Strong Interest Inventory and O*NET Interest Matches (Case 10) (*Continued*)

Interest code	Job zone	BLS number[a]	Occupation
CE	4	43-9111.00	Statistical assistants
CE	4	15-1199.03	Web administrators
Enterprising–Conventional			
EC	5	25-4011.00	Archivists
EC	5	19-1029.01	Bioinformatics scientists
EC	5	15-2041.01	Biostatisticians
EC	5	11-1011.00	Chief executives
EC	5	11-1011.03	Chief sustainability officers
EC	5	25-4012.00	Curators
EC	5	11-9039.01	Distance learning coordinators
EC	5	19-3011.00	Economists
EC	5	11-9033.00	Education administrators, postsecondary
EC	5	13-2099.01	Financial quantitative analysts
EC	5	11-9199.03	Investment fund managers
EC	5	23-1012.00	Judicial law clerks
EC	5	25-4021.00	Librarians
EC	5	15-2021.00	Mathematicians
EC	5	11-9111.00	Medical and health services managers
EC	5	15-2031.00	Operations research analysts
EC	5	29-1051.00	Pharmacists
EC	5	15-2041.00	Statisticians
EC	5	19-3022.00	Survey Researchers
EC	5	11-3031.01	Treasurers and controllers
Conventional–Social–Enterprising			
CSE	4	21-1093.00	Social and human service assistants
CSE	5	25-4021.00	Librarians

Note. C = Conventional; E = Enterprising; S = Social.
[a]Standard Occupational Classification number from the Bureau of Labor Statistics (see https://www.Bls.gov/soc/2018/soc_2018_user_guide.pdf).
Data from https://www.onetonline.org/explore/interests/Conventional/Enterprising/ and https://www.onetonline.org/explore/interests/Conventional/Social/Enterprising/

II

ASSESSING CAREER-RELATED ABILITIES

5

Career-Related Abilities
Conceptual Issues and General Intelligence

And from the look on his face I could see he was one of the lucky ones, one of those people who like doing what they're good at. That's rare. When you see it in a person, you can't miss it.
—THE STORY OF EDGAR SAWTELLE (WROBLEWSKI, 2008, P. 416)

Abilities speak to capacity, in this case to learn and to do particular kinds of work. If vocational interests speak to motivation, abilities concern whether one can adequately perform (or learn to perform) the job duties associated with particular careers.

In the field of career assessment, the term *aptitudes* is sometimes used for the construct covered here. That word aims to capture the idea of potential, whereas *abilities*, the term that will generally be used here, may imply already acquired capabilities. Preckel et al. (2020) demonstrated that there are complicated processes that have to occur in order for an aptitude to be translated into a corresponding competency or achievement. Another definitional issue is whether the goal is to measure maximal performance in a particular ability domain or the possession of sufficient levels of an ability to be able to learn, or to succeed, in careers.

The goal of this chapter and Chapters 6–12 that follow is to identify and discuss a wide range of abilities, including general intelligence, that have demonstrated consistent positive associations with work or career outcomes. Recognizing that career assessments identify performance at a particular point in time, it is still the case that many abilities are relatively stable over time. In fact,

---

https://doi.org/10.1037/0000254-006
Career Assessment: Integrating Interests, Abilities, and Personality, by R. L. Lowman
Copyright © 2022 by the American Psychological Association. All rights reserved.

there is emerging evidence in a number of abilities of a strong genetic component that would, potentially, influence stability. Because different types of careers call for different abilities, the goal in general career assessment is to measure across a range of career-relevant abilities to identify areas of relative strength and weakness in the context of possible career options.

Although the literature in psychology has not emphasized abilities for some time, the fields of industrial–organizational (I–O) psychology and, to some extent, of educational assessment have developed expansive research bases on a number of the abilities discussed in this chapter. Another important resource that will be used extensively in these chapters is the U.S. Department of Labor's Occupational Information Network, or O*NET (https://www.onetonline.org). This remarkable, free-to-anyone, online database contains a wealth of information about abilities related to specific occupations.

The O*NET also differentiates between abilities and skills, which are defined, respectively, as "enduring attributes of the individual that influence performance" (National Center for O*NET Development, 2018a) and "developed capacities that facilitate learning or the more rapid acquisition of knowledge" (National Center for O*NET Development, 2018d). The O*NET's abilities category includes cognitive, physical, psychomotor, and sensory abilities, each of which has its own "elements" or facets.

The definition of abilities used by the O*NET matches the concept of the term used here, though the term aptitudes is also used with the same intended meaning. And although there are a number of technical issues associated with this issue, the preference here is to measure best, not typical, performance, since the goal is to identify and differentiate among relative strengths and relative weaknesses.

ABOUT THIS CHAPTER AND WHY ABILITIES MATTER

This is a long section. There is much to cover and a lot of it is technical. You may be inclined to skim it or to skip it. If you do, you'll be like too many career assessors who seem to think that abilities do not matter for career choice or change, and that it is sufficient to measure the more readily accessible interest and personality variables or to rely on simple (but neither comprehensive nor well-validated) measures. This is problematic since all three domains are relevant (and sometimes other domains and variables as well). When it comes to careers, however, abilities matter. Always.

Yet, it also needs to be said at the outset of this chapter that the field of vocational guidance has had, and still has, a very checkered and ambivalent relationship with abilities. Dawis (2002) observed that Parsons's (1909) approach to vocational guidance is still the basis of many contemporary approaches to career assessment and counseling. As Parsons (1909) put it,

> In the wise choice of a vocation there are three broad factors: (1) a clear understanding of . . . aptitudes, abilities, interests, ambitions, resources, limitations,

and their causes; (2) a knowledge of the requirements and conditions of success, advantages and disadvantages, compensation, opportunities, and prospects in different lines of work; (3) true reasoning on the relations of these two groups of facts. (p. 5)

However, Dawis (2002) noted that although Parsons had known what was needed for effective vocational guidance, when he went looking for instruments in the cupboards of the psychological laboratories of the day, he found that they were bare.

From a more recent vantage point, and with a more full cupboard, H. J. Kell and Lubinski (2015), and Lowman (1993c) before that, put the matter more strongly. They suggested that, in vocational assessment, ignoring, not measuring, or relying solely on self-estimates of abilities was seriously problematic. As H. J. Kell and Lubinski (2015) concluded,

> There is little doubt that vocational psychologists and career counselors are obliged to incorporate cognitive ability constructs and measures into their practice, research, and theorizing about choice, performance after choice, and persistence in learning and work environments. . . . Neglecting this important domain of human psychological diversity would be like biologists trying to better understand life, while disregarding carbon atoms. (p. 316)

Contemplating *why* abilities have been neglected, Austin and Hanisch (1990) observed,

> Vocational and counseling psychologists may have neglected abilities and focused more on interests than is warranted by our findings. We speculate that interest scales provide more opportunity for the provision of positive feedback to those being counseled, whereas ability scales may not allow such interpretations. In addition, there may be a greater potential for bias in interpreting the results of gender-typed interest scales. (p. 83)

Despite what has been characterized as relative neglect of abilities by career assessors, the scientific measurement of abilities exemplifies one of the ways in which psychology has defined its identity and contributed to the study of human behavior. By combining psychometric sophistication with the measurement of real-world problems (such as the appropriate placement of children with mental disability or hiring the best-qualified candidates for a particular job), psychologists have made much progress both in advancing knowledge and in addressing practical problems. Indeed, since early in the twentieth century, assessment tools have been created that have improved the development, remediation, and placement of people with varied psychological needs (Embretson, 2004; R. J. Gregory, 2004). At the same time, work on applications for job and school placement has helped to clarify the nature of abilities (see, e.g., Farr & Tippins, 2017).

Perhaps because the measurement of abilities has had obvious practical applications, it was developed early and extensively in the history of psychology. In many respects, however, important early developments (including the formulation of ability taxonomies and of what, at the time, were sophisticated measuring approaches) have not always been sustained as the field has progressed. Embretson's (2004) vision for the second century of ability testing (including shorter, continually updated items generated by artificial intelligence methods), while possibly the norm for certain well-funded, widely used measures for particular selection tasks, has not diffused to many of the ability tests that may be available to career assessment practitioners.

This situation may partly reflect the reality of corporatization of the testing market, with a few large corporations (four, actually) controlling many of the available measures of ability, particularly in the educational assessment arena (see M. A. Roberts, 2015; "The Testing Industry's Big Four," n.d.). Additionally, rapid early progress often slows as stubborn problems of conceptualization and measurement emerge and as inertia in using "known" measures causes them to persist. Finally, relative neglect of ability measurement by many career assessors and counselors may result in lowered demand that, in turn, might serve to lessen the willingness of test publishers to invest in improved measures of abilities.

Even when dated or outmoded tests continue to be used past their prime, there is still the need to assure that at least the norms for the tests are updated and reflective of the populations being assessed and that validity evidence for the intended uses is sufficient to justify continuing to use the assessment measure. Even if spatial or musical abilities today, for example, were conceptually identical to the constructs measured in the 1940s (which is probably not the case—there is much new knowledge to consider), norms and validity coefficients would still need to be reasonably current. Also, some types of instruments periodically need to be updated in content to reflect cultural and societal changes. New or improved measures with robust validity and reliability evidence, as well as those accessible electronically and at lower costs, are particularly useful.

Of similar concern for practitioners is the substantial divergence between new theoretical developments and applied measuring devices. Alternative approaches to conceptualizing intelligence (e.g., emotional intelligence: Goleman, 1995; the theory of multiple intelligences: Gardner, 1983/2011, 1999; Sternberg's triarchic intelligence: Sternberg, 1997b; managerial intelligence: Sternberg, 1997a) will be discussed in this chapter. These theories of ability have potential implications for measurement but have not always been easy to incorporate into career assessment practice. This is either because the theories have not always been fully developed or because well-validated measures of the constructs do not yet exist. Also, some new measures, although promising, may be too long to incorporate in the context of a larger battery, or the costs of using the instruments may be prohibitively expensive. A promising development is the growth of open-source ability measures such as the International Cognitive Ability Resource (https://www.ICAR-project.com; Revelle et al., 2020), but these are currently intended primarily for use by researchers.

These are real concerns but probably not the largest one. The most significant neglect in career assessment, I suggest, continues to be failing to measure abilities at all, relying exclusively on self-ratings of ability, or relying on a single measure of overall intelligence often developed for purposes other than career assessment. Presumably, no one would argue that it would be appropriate in career assessment to ignore or not measure occupational interests, but the equivalent treatment of abilities can lead to significant omissions and less-than-useful career guidance (see L. S. Gottfredson, 2003; Kell & Lubinski, 2015).

CONCEPTUAL ISSUES

Applied practice requires an understanding of conceptually complex theoretical models of abilities as well as practical measurement techniques. For many career assessors, considerable study and supervised practice may be needed to learn about the measurement of abilities. Otherwise, assessment measures may be chosen without proper understanding of the theoretical rationale and purpose of assessing each variable. Although these ability chapters therefore adopt a structural and theoretical approach that is variable and research driven rather than a "which test to use" one, it can only provide an abbreviated review of current theories of intelligence (see, E. Hunt, 2010, for a summary of recent advances in this area). Nor do I review or attempt to integrate all of the neuropsychological findings relevant to the academic study of abilities, though some of them are referenced. Research identifying the neurological situs of a particular ability (e.g., whether musical perception is primarily centered in a particular part of the brain) or the consequences of neurological disabilities (e.g., whether someone with a right posterior lesion is likely to be unable to navigate around a room) may seem distant from career choice or change but in some cases can be relevant and important. Overall, this review is focused mostly on the needs of the career assessor, who must be concerned with such applied problems as the minimal aptitude level needed for successful performance as a surgeon, a truck driver, an artist, or an engineer. Assessors must also help their clients sort out the unique pattern of abilities they possess or can develop and how they choose to invest those gifts.

In these chapters, then, I will discuss a number of human abilities that are important for the career assessor to understand conceptually and to know how to measure. For convenience of discussion, I present abilities in an order that roughly corresponds to Holland's structure of vocational interests (see Chapters 2–3) in that certain abilities are more likely to be associated with occupations associated with particular interest types. Of course, an exact, one-to-one match is not possible, and many abilities (e.g., spatial and intellectual) are applicable not just to one, but to several of Holland's interest categories. Still there is evidence for a factor structure of abilities paralleling interests (see Lowman et al., 1985).

I will first differentiate between general intelligence and more circumscribed abilities, such as musical and mechanical abilities. By all accounts, general intelligence belongs in its own category since it can be used in a wide variety of occupational pursuits. *Primary abilities* (the name often used for them in the literature) are those that apply to a fairly narrow range of work performances and that do not usually generalize across a wide range of work applications in the same way that general intelligence does. Primary abilities are important in career profiles and can assist clients in considering a range of strengths beyond general intelligence (see Kell & Lubinski, 2015; Prediger, 1989). This chapter focuses on general cognitive ability. The following chapters (6–12) then consider primary ones.

GENERAL INTELLIGENCE

General intelligence ("g") is perhaps the single most important variable for determining job and career success in a variety of occupational pursuits (E. Hunt, 2010; Schmidt & Hunter, 1998). As Ones et al. (2017) put it,

> The question of whether cognitive ability tests are useful predictors of performance in occupational settings has been definitely answered: yes, they are excellent predictors of training performance and job performance. In fact, no other predictor construct in employee selection produces as high validities, as consistently, as does cognitive ability. (p. 258)

In this section I identify some of the major issues arising in the use of general intelligence in career assessments (see S. Goldstein et al., 2015, and Sternberg & Kaufman, 2011). In personnel selection research, the question is usually not whether alternative predictors of job performance work better than cognitive abilities but rather whether alternative ability and other abilities or personality and interest measures add incremental validity beyond g. That said, the purposes of career assessment (helping clients with career choice and satisfaction) are different, and somewhat less well researched, than the vast literature on job performance prediction. The purpose of assessing abilities in career assessment is to predict whether people are likely to be successful and satisfied in particular occupations. Whether the profile of abilities is consistent with people already working successfully in occupations under consideration helps advise this. Still, cognitive abilities affect the kind of careers one can pursue educationally and how effectively people will be able to perform in a particular occupation.

Although intelligence is unquestionably important in career-related abilities assessment, by no means is it exclusively important. As Pawlik (1966) appropriately cautioned, "For too many practicing psychologists . . . important issues begin and end with the king of abilities–intelligence" (p. 552).

Curiously, a universally, or even a commonly agreed-upon, definition of the intelligence construct still does not exist. Wechsler (1975), who developed some of the still most widely used intelligence measures in the practice of clinical psychology, grappled with the alternative definitions of intelligence then prominent, including the pragmatic view that intelligence is what tests of intelligence measure, and, in an article based on a Distinguished Professional Contribution address to the American Psychological Association, concluded that what we measure with tests is not what tests measure—not information, not spatial perception, not reasoning ability. These are only means to an end. What intelligence tests measure, what we hope they measure, is something much more important: the capacity of an individual to understand the world about him and his resourcefulness to cope with its challenges. (Boring, 1923, p. 139)

Yet, after reviewing several serious efforts by psychologists to define the term "intelligence," Arthur Jensen, another major researcher in intelligence, concluded that "the overall picture remains almost as chaotic as it was in 1921. . . . [I am convinced] that psychologists are incapable of reaching a consensus on its definition. It has proved to be a hopeless quest. Therefore, the term 'intelligence' should be discarded altogether in scientific psychology" (Jensen, 1988, p. 48). He proposed, instead, substituting scientifically relevant, operationally defined constructs such as "ability" and "proficiency," particularly at the item and factor levels, all tied to psychometric evidence.

Theoretical and Conceptual Issues

The nature of intelligence (still using that widely used name for a construct on whose definition psychologists apparently still cannot agree but also cannot abandon) remains one of the most widely researched areas in psychology and education. Not surprisingly, there are many models of intelligence established for different purposes, and therefore the criteria for evaluating them may differ.

From the perspective of psychometric studies, most researchers today would agree that there is a general factor of intelligence (J. P. Guilford's, 1985, Structure-of-Intellect [SOI] model did offer the view that there was not a general factor, but it was widely rejected; see Jensen, 1998). The general factor of intelligence dates back to Spearman (1904, 1927; see also Jensen, 1998, and Thorndike, 1985). This general factor has been viewed as being both overarching and multifaceted and has been celebrated for its power, at the group level, to predict career, work, and life achievements. It is also relatively stable over time (partly due to a strong genetic component; see, e.g., Lyons et al., 2017). However, this stability can be misinterpreted. The quantity and content of what is known and learned is not stable, just the rank of an individual in comparison to similarly aged peers on similar measures (Neisser et al., 1996). Academic, work, and life achievement is tied not just to raw capacity but also to the use of that talent to learn and adapt (see Schmidt, 2015).

In addition to general intelligence, however, a number of researchers dating back to Thurstone (J. P. Guilford, 1972; Gulliksen, 1968; Thurstone, 1938, 1948) have also identified focal areas of abilities initially called "primary mental abilities" that went beyond g. (An interesting factoid about Thurstone is that after completing his undergraduate degree in engineering at Cornell University and before he went to graduate school in psychology at the University of Chicago, he served as a research assistant to famed inventor Thomas Edison; Guilford, 1957b). In a 1936 publication, Thurstone reduced a large set of 59 primary abilities to seven particularly important ones: visual imagery (spatial visualization), perceptual speed and memory (associative memory), word fluency, number facility, induction (reasoning), and verbal relations (verbal comprehension). These facets, or more narrow and circumscribed abilities, were also analogous to Spearman's initial model in having identified both general ("g") and specific ("s") areas of intelligence.

In recent decades, the concept of intelligence itself has been under revision and extensive review as to its implications for both individuals and the larger society. Efforts by a variety of researchers have been moving concepts of intellectual functioning, such as its stability and changeability, in new directions. Here are brief summaries of some of the major, not exactly competing, but elaborative models of intelligence.

Cattell-Horn-Carroll—Three Stratum Model

Cattell, a student of Spearman, and Horn, who was a student of Cattell, some time ago differentiated fluid and crystallized intelligences (Horn & Cattell, 1966). Fluid intelligence requires the use of general reasoning methods to solve cognitive problems—or "the capacity to figure out novel problems," according to Jensen (1998, p. 123)—whereas crystallized intelligence measures problem solving using already-acquired content knowledge (E. Hunt, 2010)—or the "consolidation of knowledge" (Jensen, 1998, p. 123). Evidence shows that these two types of intelligence, on average, decline over time at different rates, with peak fluid intelligence maturing earlier and declining more rapidly than crystallized (McDonough et al., 2016). From a career assessment perspective, this supports the importance of knowing what type of cognitive test is being used and whether age-specific norms were employed. Later, Cattell and Horn partnered with Carroll, and over time they added additional second stratum variables (including auditory skills) and a tertiary level, which, essentially, was analogous to Spearman's g (H. A. Carroll, 1993). Note that crystallized intelligence is not primarily dependent on genes or inherent capacity. Motivation, good education, and persistence can help people learn what they need to know to be successful in a career, provided they have at least the minimal cognitive levels needed for content mastery of their respective fields. Additionally, since crystallized intelligence declines less rapidly than fluid intelligence (Zaval et al., 2015) maintaining and expanding it appears to provide some protection against cognitive decline associated with aging (Opdebeeck et al., 2016). Finally, crystallized intelligence speaks to motivation to learn in particular areas that may reflect likely interest in particular careers.

Sternberg's Triarchic (Successful Intelligence) Theory

Sternberg (1982a) proposed a "triarchic" theory of intelligence (not without critics; see Neisser, 1983) that included analytical (componential), creative (experiential), and practical (contextual) as the model's three aspects of intelligence. Of special importance in Sternberg's componential approach to intellectual development was a metaconstruct described as the ability to recognize the nature of the problem to be solved (a construct akin to Pawlik's, 1966, sensitivity to problems factor) and to then select a strategy and methodology for solving it. Some problems provide lower level, routine components to be solved, whereas others demand higher level organization and strategizing. Sternberg also explored the intelligence required to solve practical, real-world problems and noted that, because solutions are often culturally specific, the context in which the problem is presented must be considered (see Sternberg, 2004; Sternberg & Wagner, 1986). Another implication suggested by this model is the importance, for some assessees, of measuring creative potential and practical problem-solving ability versus sheer abstract conceptual knowledge, often the focus of traditional measures of intelligence.

Johnson and Bouchard's Verbal-Perceptual-Image Rotation Model of Intelligence

W. Johnson and Bouchard (2005) compared the fluid-crystallized, verbal-perceptual, and Carroll's three strata using the Twins Reared Apart database. Bouchard has been an important investigator of genetic versus environmental influences on abilities, including intelligence, using the paradigm of comparing responses of identical twins raised together or apart versus nonidentical twins similarly raised and nontwin siblings. Respondents completed a large number of tests (42) including several widely used measures of general intelligence. Each subtest was considered to be a separate test. Johnson and Bouchard then considered whether several widely used models of intelligence better fit their data. They found the best fit to be Vernon's (1950, 1961/2014) model (with some modifications):

> [Vernon] stressed the importance of general intelligence in contributing to all mental abilities, but observed that, once a general intelligence factor is extracted from any collection of ability tests, the correlations among the residuals fall into two main groups. He labeled one of these v:ed to refer to verbal and educational abilities, and the other k:m to refer to spatial, practical, and mechanical abilities. The v:ed group, he noted, generally consists of verbal fluency and divergent thinking, as well as verbal scholastic knowledge and numerical abilities. The k:m group generally consists of perceptual speed, and psychomotor and physical abilities such as proprioception in addition to spatial and mechanical abilities. (W. Johnson and Bouchard, 2005, p. 395)

Concerning abilities, most researchers including these suggest g is unquestionably important, but that there is more to consider after that. This model essentially creates two broader sub-g factors, whereas the model presented here treats separately each of the primary abilities in a way that potentially has career relevance.

Gardner's Theory of Multiple Intelligences

Different in kind and in the pervasiveness of its influence is Gardner's (1999, 1983/2011) popular theory of multiple intelligences. This approach was not primarily test (psychometric) based and did not encompass a general factor of intelligence. Instead, it identified multiple "intelligences." The approach was intended to be far more than a listing of facets of intelligence. In Gardner's model, before something could be defined as an "intelligence," which he conceptualized as *"a biopsychological potential to process information that can be activated in a cultural setting to solve problems or create products that are of value in a culture"* (Gardner, 1999, pp. 32–33; italics in original), it had to meet eight criteria:

1. It has a biological basis that can be isolated by brain damage;

2. There is an evolutionary history and rationale;

3. It is associated with an identifiable set of operations;

4. It uses a particular encoding or symbol system;

5. It is associated with a developmental pattern and "end-state" performances on which experts can agree;

6. Mono-savants or prodigies exhibit high levels of the intelligence;

7. Experimental psychological tasks support its existence; and

8. It is supported by psychometric findings (Gardner, 1999, pp. 36–38).

Of these criteria, the last one has been used the least in research about the model since it has been tested largely using data based on case studies both of highly gifted exemplars of an identified intelligence and using neuropsychological evidence of deficits resulting from brain damage to identified areas of the brain. Gardner and his colleagues at Project Zero at Harvard University, the epicenter of this approach, identified six intelligences in the original statement of the model (see Gardner, 1983/2011). These were linguistic, musical, logical-mathematical, spatial, bodily-kinesthetic, and two personal intelligences: intrapersonal and interpersonal. The original book-length treatment of his model (Gardner, 1983/2011) was called *Frames of Mind: The Theory of Multiple Intelligences* and was highly popular, particularly among educators and educational advocates who found approaches to general intelligence as being overly restrictive, constituting a sort of intellectual hegemony. As Gardner put it in his own critique of the theory, "In its strong form, multiple intelligence theory posits a small set of human intellectual potentials, perhaps as few as seven in number, of which all individuals are capable by virtue of their membership in the human species" (Gardner, 1983/2011, p. 278). Still, there remains to this point few empirical tests of the model using traditional well-validated measures of the respective intelligences.

One such study (Visser et al., 2006) included two measures for each of the intelligences in Gardner's model. Reviewing this study, E. Hunt (2010) noted that it favored positive results for the theory in that the model was based on the abilities of a diverse group of people of above average intelligence was selected and that such groups are more likely to have special abilities beyond g. In this study, measures of cognitive ability (linguistic, logical-mathematical) loaded highly on a general intelligence factor. They reported that, after controlling for g, the correlations across the two measures of each intelligence were not particularly high. Results that were most separable from cognitive abilities were those involving physical (sensory and motor) abilities and those where personality influences were stronger. E. Hunt (2010), while supportive of some of the general purposes of broadening how and what schools teach, noted that overall, "There is virtually no objective evidence for the [multiple intelligences] theory" (p. 119).

One does not have to ignore the limitations of the empirical evidence to date to appreciate the potential contributions of the theory of multiple intelligences for career assessment. Nor does one have to use the term "intelligences," with all the baggage that term entails, to benefit from the respect for the diversity of human talents that this theory has highlighted. Indeed, if the theory were called "multiple abilities," it might have been easier to contextualize it in existing research. But even a well-articulated model of abilities cannot, in effect, ignore g.

Some Questions About General Intelligence

It is clear from the literature that no single theory of general intelligence is universally embraced. Still, there is widespread acceptance of the finding of a general factor of intelligence. Even though this general factor is not sufficient for career assessment purposes, it cannot be ignored. Here are some common questions that arise about general intelligence and very brief summaries of the known literature.

Do All Theories of Intelligence Include a General Mental Ability Factor?

Virtually all contemporary intelligence theories (and most of the historical ones) that have relied on psychometric tests of intelligence include a general factor of intelligence. Of course, depending on the specific assessment measures used, other factors beyond g have also been identified that may add incremental variance when predicting job performance. A number of studies have also considered the work implications of general mental ability (GMA), and some have examined career implications, finding substantial predictive power of GMA to work outcomes (Ones et al., 2017).

Is Intelligence Largely Inherited? Can It Change?

Among those researchers who have studied the heritability of intelligence using twin studies, a sizeable genetic component of intelligence has been demonstrated, though it is by no means the sole component (Bouchard, 1998; Bouchard et al., 1990). This suggests that certain career assessees will be advantaged by genetic makeup and others disadvantaged. However, there is no question that intelligence can change over time. It can increase and it can decrease. This is true at both the individual and societal level. The Flynn effect (Trahan et al., 2014) has demonstrated that intelligence can and does change in societies over time. Research evidence shows that intelligence averages have been increasing over a number of generations as factors such as diet, education, and parental concern with children's learning have all improved or increased. S. J. Ritchie and Tucker-Drob (2018) conducted a meta-analysis of the role of education in improving intelligence and concluded that "the beneficial effects of education on cognitive abilities [are] approximately 1 to 5 IQ points for each additional year of education" (p. 1358). So yes, there is a genetic component to intelligence and, as it develops, to at least some of the primary abilities. But no, intelligence is not, at either the individual or societal level, a fixed component of ability, dooming or privileging people to a particular position. This also suggests that intelligence norms can become obsolescent over time with implications for test score interpretation.

Conversely, and largely ignored by the career assessment literature, there is substantial evidence that intelligence can, and likely will, decline with age. Specifically, fluid intelligence slowly but steadily declines with age, and crystallized intelligence, while decreasing more slowly, does ultimately decrease (E. Hunt, 2010; McDonough et al., 2016). Additionally, there are a number of sequelae of health conditions (strokes, Alzheimer's disease, Parkinson's disease, attention-deficit/hyperactivity disorder, Asperger's spectrum disorder, etc.) that have known effects on cognitive ability. When conducting career-relevant assessments of intelligence, it is important to know whether the measure used is able to provide reliable and valid inferences related to g (along, hopefully, with verbal and nonverbal intelligence), and how age or health status may have affected the result. But to assume that even when using a well-established measure of general intelligence that the result will persist over the lifespan is a flawed assumption. Intelligence (and intelligence scores) can go up, and with some degree of certainty among those who live long enough, it can and likely will decline. Knowing where the assessee is in the life cycle, medical status, and many other variables are important in interpreting cognitive ability test results.

Are There Multiple Factors Within or Additional to General Intelligence?

Many, if not most, of those studying g and its factors (e.g., Benbow et al., 1983; Hakstian & Bennet, 1977, 1978; Irvine & Berry, 1988; Pawlik, 1966; Thurstone, 1938) have included in their models and factor structures a verbal factor (loading, e.g., on tests of verbal comprehension and verbal reasoning) and a nonverbal factor (loading on visual-perceptual, nonverbal reasoning, and, sometimes, spatial tests). The verbal factor generally assesses understanding of words or verbally expressed ideas (verbal comprehension) and logical thinking with words (verbal reasoning). Verbal skills are typically measured by reading comprehension, vocabulary, synonyms, proverbs, and analogy tests. In the verbal reasoning area, Pawlik (1966) tentatively identified three verbal reasoning factors in addition to the verbal comprehension factors: Deduction, applying a rule or a general principle to a specific case; Induction, discovering a rule or a principle from case examples; and General Reasoning, whose exact meaning is somewhat ambiguous.

Broadly focused cognitive ability tests generally have included both verbal and nonverbal ability factors (e.g., R. C. Johnson & Nagoshi, 1985; W. Johnson & Bouchard, 2005; Weiss et al., 2010). Note that what factors are found interacts with how intelligence is measured. Most measures of intelligence involve language and words, so it is not surprising that a "verbal factor" would commonly emerge. As Pawlik (1966) long ago noted, "Verbal Comprehension (V) . . . [is one] the best confirmed of all aptitude factors known" (pp. 546–547). Pawlik also noted that a Verbal Comprehension factor had been found in virtually all factor-analytic studies (over 50 to that point) in which verbal tests were included. The Kit of Factor Referenced Cognitive Tests (Ekstrom et al., 1976) included several cognitive aptitude factors in a model of primary abilities. These included five markers of Verbal Comprehension, four of Logical Reasoning, three of General Reasoning, and four of Numerical Abilities. Verbal abilities have generally shown high intertest correlations, such that a single factor or a small number of verbal ability factors are typically found (for an alternate view, see Sincoff & Sternberg, 1987). Gardner's (e.g., 1982, 1983/2011) theory of multiple intelligence also included linguistic intelligence as a separate intelligence domain. Applied measures of intelligence (e.g., the widely used Wechsler scales; Holdnack, 2019) often include subtests that are primarily verbal and others that are thought to be primarily nonverbal, including those associated with perceptual processing.

Although there is considerable evidence in the literature about verbal comprehension aspects of intelligence, there is less consensus on what constitutes nonverbal intelligence. Often it is defined by what it is not, for example, cognitive capacities not relying on verbal stimuli or verbal processing brain modalities, but that is not an adequate definition. As Naglieri, the author of a major K–12 nonverbal intelligence test, put it in noting such tests' lesser dependence on school and class-influenced abilities, "The purpose of a nonverbal measure of general ability is to measure 'ability' with tests that do not require verbal, social, and quantitative knowledge" (Naglieri & Ford, 2015, p. 235).

Nonverbal intelligence (or, abilities) can be differentiated from verbal intelligence in that it is typically based on the primary use of cognitive skills that make use of understanding and reasoning using visual processing functions, nonverbal reasoning ability, and nonverbal communication (e.g., perception of facial expressions, voice tones, and other social cues). Some models would also consider Spatial Abilities to be an aspect of nonverbal intelligence, but with current knowledge, it may belong in its own category and is therefore discussed in its own section of this chapter.

Differentiating nonverbal and verbal intelligence does not imply that both are not necessary in complex tasks (see W. Johnson & Bouchard, 2005). However, trait-like differences in these abilities may be important in career assessment.

How Do Verbal and Nonverbal Intelligence Matter for Career Assessment?

When considering broad samples of test scores of people with normal-range abilities, verbal and nonverbal intelligence are usually moderately to highly correlated. As Margolis et al. (2013) noted, "The intercorrelation of performance on IQ subtests, shared variance, accounts for 50% of the total variance in performance. Roughly 70% of this shared variance represents g. The remaining 30% of variance is captured by factors representing domain-specific abilities" (p. 14135).

At the individual level, differences in verbal and nonverbal intelligence (arguably both measures of g) may be significant in identifying career-relevant strengths and limitations, so it is important to differentiate these abilities routinely, especially when there is a question about differences in verbal versus nonverbal performance either in terms of relative strengths or deficits.

Persons scoring higher on nonverbal intelligence measures greater than on comparable verbal intelligence measures have been found with greater incidence among those with certain autism spectrum disorders (Ankenman et al., 2014; F. Chen et al., 2010; Chiang et al., 2014), learning disabilities (including dyslexia and hyperactivity; Everatt et al., 2007; Fiorello et al., 2001), school underachievement (Whittington, 1988), among those with high levels of high performance in STEM occupations (Park et al., 2007; Wai et al., 2009, 2010).

Causes of differences in verbal and nonverbal ability may vary. These include preferences for one type of activity or another such that different parts of the brain are used more than others, brain disease or dysfunction, hearing impairment, working or studying in a second, not fully mastered, language, and hemispheric asymmetries. Such differences may also be associated with morphological or structural differences in persons with normal brain functioning (see Margolis et al., 2013; Naglieri, 2003; Ryan et al., 2009).

Does General Mental Ability Differentiate Occupations?

Considerable research examining the relationship of general intelligence to occupational performance has persistently found that occupations differ systematically on their demand for general intelligence and that, within occupations, it predicts to differential job performance (L. S. Gottfredson, 1986a, 1986c; Hunter, 1986). This position has repeatedly been supported by large-scale studies using measures such as the General Aptitude Test Battery (GATB; Hammond, 1984; U.S. Department of Labor, 1970, 1979) or military selection measures such as the Armed Services Vocational Aptitude Battery (ASVAB; Kass et al., 1983; Talboy, 2011; Wall, 2018). However, job performance, while highly correlated with g when predicting to speed of learning (training criteria), and to many aspects of performance in the work role, can also be associated with other factors (including amount of experience and measures of personality such as conscientiousness). As E. Hunt (2010) noted, "The influence of intelligence is undoubtedly mediated in part by education. This is especially true across fields, for the vast majority of the more lucrative occupations have, as an entry requirement, at least a college education" (p. 342).

Does General Mental Ability Predict Work Performance?

The predictive validity literature for job performance, primarily conducted in the field of I–O psychology, has shown time after time and study after study that g is a robust predictor of work outcomes across a range of occupations and career achievements (see, e.g., E. Hunt, 2010; Ones et al., 2017; Schmidt & Hunter, 1998, 2004). Additionally, intelligence (in particular, g) is closely related to occupational level (the higher the intelligence, the higher the occupational level attained; see E. Hunt, 2010; Jensen, 1998). The professions (e.g., medicine, law, accounting), for example, attract and require, on average, a higher level of intelligence and persistence (and of education) than do nonprofessional occupations. This of course does not mean that every member of such professions is at the high end of intelligence; there are other strategies for success, including persistence and skill in applications. However, there is probably a level of cognitive ability below which it will be difficult to succeed in a profession. Additionally, professional and graduate school training programs typically include high-end cognitive screening measures that narrow the range of abilities among trainees, particularly in high-demand programs.

Intelligence differentiates both across and within occupations. Among those in specific careers, intelligence is often correlated with higher job performance and greater likelihood of being promoted to higher levels, which generally involve more complex work duties (Schmidt, 2015; see also A. Howard & Bray, 1988; Wilk et al., 1995). Although some have argued that, in managerial roles at least, intelligence only up to a certain level is predictive of job performance and thereafter does not differentiate among high and low performance (see Antonakis et al., 2017), other researchers (e.g., Coward & Sackett, 1990; Schmidt, 2015) have challenged this view and noted that the empirical literature does not support such a conclusion. They found instead at all levels a linear relationship between g and job performance. As Schmidt (2015) put it,

> It has also been shown that over their careers people gradually move into jobs that are consistent with their level of GMA. . . . That is, a process that sorts people on GMA takes place gradually over time in everyday life. People whose GMA exceeds their job level tend to move up to more complex jobs; and people whose GMA is below their job level tend to move down. (p. 5)

This is not to suggest that non-g abilities do not matter for career preferences and performance (about which, more later) but rather to acknowledge that g is unquestionably important in career ability assessment. Again, from E. Hunt (2010), "Intelligence predicts a person's job status and income better than any other trait that has been studied. This leaves us with two questions: why does this association exist, and why is that association so widely denied by people who have not studied the topic?" (p. 342). The question of "why" this might be so is indeed important. Schmidt (2015) provided useful suggestions:

> The major direct determinant of job performance is not GMA but job knowledge. People who do not know how to do a job cannot perform that job well. . . . The simplest model of job performance is this: GMA causes job knowledge, which in turn causes job performance. But this model is a little too simple: there is also a causal path directly from GMA to job performance, independent of job

knowledge. That is, even when workers have equal job knowledge, the more intelligent workers have higher job performance. This is because there are problems that come up on the job that are not covered by previous job knowledge, and GMA is used directly on the job to solve these problems. (p. 5)

All this said, individual-level prediction should be differentiated from group-level prediction. When working at the individual level of individuals choosing careers rather than when evaluating candidates for hiring or promotion, the same caveats that apply to averaged vocational interest data (see Chapter 2) also apply to averaged ability data. Averages disguise important differences among members of the same profession. Sheer intelligence in the general intellectual sense may help to explain achievement, underachievement, or boredom, but alone it is insufficient to explain many aspects of career behavior, much less to help clients understand why they are unhappy, misguided, or unfulfilled in their current line of work or study. Members of an occupation also differ systematically on abilities other than intelligence. It seems unlikely, for example, that intellectual abilities alone predict differential success among professional athletes, garbage collectors, artists, and musicians or why equally bright individuals do not succeed equally well even in the same occupation and organization.

Does General Mental Ability Predict Career Outcomes?
From the perspective of career assessment, the outcome criterion is not always work performance alone. Rather, it often includes goodness of fit of person with possible occupations and, to some extent, satisfaction not with jobs but more generally with career choice, typically over an extended period of time. Although there is an expansive literature on job satisfaction and work outcomes (see, e.g., Bowling, 2007; Judge et al., 2001), there is far less research on career satisfaction, particularly over time (see Gonzalez-Mulé et al., 2017; C. I. S. G. Lee et al., 2017). Gonzalez-Mulé et al. (2017), for example, found rather small positive relationships between GMA and job (not career) and life satisfaction. And of course people seeking career counseling can be highly productive and valued at work and yet be quite unhappy in career or job choice.

Should Measures of Cognitive Ability Be Included in Career Assessment Ability Batteries?
Standardized tests of intelligence do have a place in career assessment, especially because so many career choices are influenced by intellectual ability levels. From the career standpoint, many standard measures of intelligence with adequate reliability and validity evidence for their intended inferences can be used to determine the degree of intellectual ability possessed by the client at the time of the assessment. Care should be taken to assure that the measure is robust and reasonably up-to-date. Short, sometimes dated, measures of verbal comprehension and numerical fluency are sometimes employed in career assessment as the sole measures of intellect, but this approach has limitations.

Consideration should also be given to the client's estimated intelligence as suggested by educational achievement before deciding on which tests to use in career assessment. For someone with an advanced graduate or professional degree, measures relevant for differentiating at high levels of ability may be needed. Measures of overall intelligence that are individually administered and normed by age, though sometimes useful, may have ceiling effects that fail to differentiate clients at superior levels of functioning. Conversely, someone with below-average estimated cognitive abilities might be frustrated by a measure that is perceived as being too difficult. Nonverbal measures of intelligence may also provide better estimates of cognitive ability when verbal intelligence is impaired or when nonverbal abilities are likely to be higher than verbal ones.

Why Not Just Measure General Mental Ability?
Although g is unquestionably important to measure in most career assessments, it is insufficient when a client's anticipated career directions include those for which specific (primary) abilities are likely to be needed. Although GMA does give clients the ability to apply that capacity in many different directions, it is insufficient to differentiate fitness for a number of career paths (see, e.g., Prediger, 1989a). As is elaborated in the rest of this chapter, there are a number of specific abilities that have career implications.

Conclusion and Recommendations
Summarizing, general intelligence matters for a number of outcome variables in life, of which career is decidedly not an exception. Although it does include a genetic component, that is not determinative of all career outcomes. Across groups of individuals, intelligence is stable in the short to medium run, and, concerning relative position, in the long run. However, intelligence does change over time, increasing in youth and, for most people, decreasing over the lifespan, particularly in fluid intelligence. Crystallized intelligence can compensate for relative losses in fluid intelligence to a certain point, but that too will decline in later life for most people. Important as general intelligence is in career-related abilities, however, it is not all-powerful, as the rest of this chapter shows.

Assessment of GMA is important to include in most career assessment batteries when the referral questions include those related to abilities. The specific measures of intelligence to use will vary depending on whether one is assessing high-level ability individuals or those in the average or below range. Assessing using measures that can differentiate verbal and nonverbal intelligence is also recommended.

SPECIFIC CAREER-RELEVANT ABILITIES

There is more to career assessment than general intelligence. The sheer volume of literature on the relationship of cognitive abilities (in particular, general intelligence) to work should not result in the conclusion that nothing else matters in career assessment. As famed I–O psychologist Joseph Tiffin (1947) said,

> For several reasons, we shall consider tests of mental ability before we consider tests in such areas as mechanical aptitude, dexterity, or trade ability. It is hoped, however, that such prior consideration of the field of mental ability will not give

a wrong impression of the relative importance of mental ability tests. We do not consider intelligence tests first because they are more important than other tests, nor because most jobs demand persons of high intelligence. [Rather] we consider [intelligence] first because probably no other area of psychological testing has been so thoroughly explored. (p. 82)

Stenquist (1928, as quoted in T. Hunt, 1936) put it this way:

The question of "what knowledge is of most worth" will probably never be finally answered to the satisfaction of all. But it seems certain that as life becomes more and more complex, the world's tasks become more varied, and group inter-dependence increases, there is constant need for broader conceptions of what constitutes worthwhile mental ability. We should recall that the history of the past century . . . could well be written in terms of the achievement of applied science and applied mechanical genius. Inventions of hitherto undreamed of significance, which have revolutionized or at least profoundly influenced the life of every nation on the globe, have sprung from this field of knowledge. And while the attempts to measure the mental abilities back of these forces represent but crude beginnings, the importance of the task is stoutly maintained. Indeed, to explore, measure and adequately capitalize these capacities seems at least as important as doing the same for the more abstract type of intelligence required in academic school subjects. The discovery of special abilities has a two-fold significance. . . . It not only opens the door of new promise to pupils, many of whom have been labelled as failures, but in doing so, it leads toward further contributions to society. (p. 89)

Supporting the notion that g is not everything when it comes to predicting work outcomes, Prediger (1989a) criticized some of the then-published articles and noted 34 studies that had challenged g's limitations. Measures of job knowledge and work task proficiency were often better than g in predicting to job performance. He then presented results of a study in which expert raters assigned nine cognitive abilities and six noncognitive ones to each of six job clusters (business contact, business operations, technical, scientific, arts, and social service; roughly analogous to Holland's RIASEC types) into which each job in the 12,099 positions from the *Dictionary of Occupational Titles* was classified. The researchers found that specific abilities showed more promise than did g alone in predicting to job performance since there was a greater rationale for why the ability would predict. Prediger classified some abilities (e.g., leadership/management, helping people, sales) as noncognitive that, in today's context, seem problematic. However, this study still provides a good introduction to the next section, in which we discuss in detail specific abilities with career relevance based on evidence as well as theory.

SUMMARY AND CONCLUSIONS

Abilities are extremely important in career choice and change. Abilities are different in their organization from that of either interests or personality. They are hierarchically organized such that general cognitive ability (intelligence) assumes particular importance even though other abilities are also important.

It has by far the best track record of predicting many work-relevant outcome measures. For that reason, this chapter went into considerable detail on various approaches to general intelligence.

General intelligence, however, is not the only ability measure that is important in career assessment work. In the next chapters (6–11), specific abilities (s's) are identified and discussed. In Chapter 12, applied cases are presented.

6

Mechanical and Physical Abilities

The ability to think mechanically, especially relevant for Realistic-interest occupations and some Investigative ones, requires understanding principles about the physical world and about how machines work and operate. Practical applications of mechanical ability also require the ability to work with one's hands and to translate knowledge about things to specific applications. The major research work on mechanical abilities and aptitudes was completed between the 1920s and the 1940s (see Harrell, 1937, 1940; Patterson et al., 1930). The United States at the time was transforming from an agricultural to an industrial base, and the valid selection of people with mechanical abilities was of great societal importance. With the exporting of manufacturing to other countries there are fewer opportunities in the United States for hands-on work, but there are still many jobs and careers in this area, and career assessors should clearly be competent when working in this space.

One of the most significant treatises on mechanical abilities remains that of Patterson et al. (1930), which summarized work on an impressive mechanical test battery developed and validated in the 1920s. These authors defined mechanical ability as "the ability to succeed in work of a mechanical nature . . . that which enables a person to work with tools and machinery and the materials of the physical world . . . that which enables a person to succeed in a . . . restricted range of vocational and trade school courses" (Patterson et al., 1930, pp. 6–7). An interesting study published by Brody (1937) examined the genetic basis of mechanical ability using pairs of mono- and dizygotic twin pairs. Although the measure was one emphasizing spatial abilities, the author provided evidence

https://doi.org/10.1037/0000254-007
Career Assessment: Integrating Interests, Abilities, and Personality, by R. L. Lowman
Copyright © 2022 by the American Psychological Association. All rights reserved.

that the measure was appropriate to use as a mechanical ability test. He found evidence for a sizable contribution of genetics in that the scores of monozygotic twin pairs were much more closely related than those of dizygotic pairs.

Additional research was completed in the 1940s, and special attention was directed during World War II toward developing efficient selection batteries for such war-related occupations as mechanics, welders, and pilots. Since then, there have been relatively few studies in the professional literature on mechanical abilities, and no significant or "revolutionary" tests have been published in the ensuing years to measure mechanical abilities or strengths.

Unlike spatial abilities, in which controversy over sex differences has generated considerable research in the last few decades, work on sex differences in mechanical abilities has been relatively quiescent. Few substantively different conclusions can be drawn today compared with those put forth in the early days of mechanical ability test development and research as to the nature of the ability or how to measure it. An exception has been recent work in examining the causes of the frequently found differences in men versus women (higher scores on average for men) on measures of mechanical ability. In an interesting approach not commonly used in career ability studies, Berenbaum et al. (2012) examined whether individuals with congenital adrenal hyperplasia (CAH), a medical condition which exposes children prenatally to higher than normal androgen levels, but who were raised as their respective biological sex had higher scores on mechanical and spatial tests than did their siblings without CAH. For women, but not for men, that was the case. Such hormone exposure differs in its effects for men and women in that very high levels of prenatal androgen increases mechanical/spatial abilities for women but lowers them for men. Beltz et al. (2011) also found that women who had CAH had greater occupational interests in working with things rather than with people. These studies reflect the increasing interest in considering, when relevant, the physiological basis for various abilities.

As a practical matter, the measurement of mechanical abilities for the type of career assessment emphasized in this book apply especially to assessments of individuals interested in blue-collar work or, at the higher educational level, to those interested in college majors like engineering, science, or technology. Prada and Urzúa (2017) found that persons with high mechanical abilities were less likely to attend 4-year colleges, so they may need career assessment and counseling that differs from those attending, or planning to attend, college. People whose skills are most appropriate for skilled labor or lower level mechanical applications are unlikely to seek out the type of individualized assessment and counseling that is presented here. Employers may use mechanical or physical ability measures to screen large applicant groups, but typically the emphasis is on measuring only one or, at most, a few abilities rather than a complex combination of ability, interest, and personality data (or integrity testing).

There have been some controversies about whether mechanical abilities represent a distinct category of ability or a combination and integration of other primary abilities (Super & Crites, 1962). Muchinsky (2004) noted the tendency to lump mechanical and spatial abilities together, stating,

The union of these two assessments is more a product of their similarity of use in personnel selection than the similarity of their conceptual origins or content. There may be some manifestations of spatial abilities in selected items assessing mechanical aptitude, but in most cases the respective item domains are distinct. (p. 21)

Whether distinct or integrated, the ability to function successfully in occupations for which mechanical skills are needed is generally associated with a competency in real-world, thing-oriented activities. At the higher levels (skilled mechanics, engineers, and certain types of scientists), this involves understanding principles about the physical world and about how machines work and operate. In lower level Realistic occupations, physical abilities (rather than abstract ones) may assume greater emphasis. Thus, an engineer might examine a structure and, using mechanical principles, logic, and other abilities, determine a method to improve structural stability, whereas a riveter may help build or repair the structure. Realistic vocational interests may figure prominently in the interest patterns of both, but the engineer may have conceptual and mathematical skills without necessarily having skills in manual dexterity or mechanical ability, the presumed province of skilled laborers.

In terms of career assessment, Super and Crites's (1962) excellent but quite dated book *Appraising Vocational Fitness* devoted an entire chapter to mechanical aptitude. However, they stated that "the title of this chapter, indeed the writing of a separate chapter on this subject, are a concession to practical considerations and to popular usage, rather than an organization of materials dictated by the nature of aptitudes" (Super & Crites, 1962, p. 219). The chapter included a detailed summary of the research that had been done to that point, demonstrating that, whatever mechanical ability tests were measuring, they did predict well to real-world outcomes. More recently, Lowman and Ng (2010), examining the performance of two groups defined by having endorsed Realistic interests most highly (and well above general population averages), found a measure of mechanical reasoning to be the highest area of performance. They also found that the samples scored significantly higher on nonverbal than on verbal intelligence. Of note, however, the spatial scores were not elevated, suggesting that mechanical ability profiles may differ from mechanical–spatial ones. The scores found by Lowman and Ng (2010) on the Bennett Mechanical Comprehension Test (Bennett & Cruikshank, 1942) were slightly higher than results from the same measure used in a validation study by Muchinsky (1993). He reported that the mechanical ability test exceeded or equaled all other predictors of relevant outcome criteria in two settings.

DIMENSIONALITY OF MECHANICAL ABILITIES

The factor structure of mechanical ability and related constructs was mostly examined early in the history of abilities. Harrell (1940) factor-analyzed 37 variables from a variety of mechanical tests including the Minnesota Mechanical Ability Tests, the MacQuarrie tests (Goodman, 1947; MacQuarrie, 1927), Stenquist's Picture Matching Test, and scores on O'Connor's Wiggly Blocks

(J. O'Connor, 1927, 1943). The factors they identified included ones labeled: Perceptual, Manual Agility, Spatial, and Verbal. Harrell noted that mechanical ability variables loaded primarily on spatial and perceptual factors. Harrell's (1937) study of the mechanical abilities of cotton mill machine fixers (aged 19–51) showed that two primary factors resulted from mechanical tests administered in a 7-hour test battery: perceptual and spatial. Super and Crites (1962) concluded that mechanical ability has factors of Spatial, Perceptual, and Mechanical Knowledge (the latter, presumably trainable). R. B. Cattell (1987) identified mechanical aptitude as a separate primary mental ability and included a measure of it in the Comprehensive Ability Battery (Hakstian et al., 1982; Nichols, 1985; K. R. White, 1985; see also the Kit of Factor-Referenced Cognitive Tests: Ekstrom et al., 1976). Goodman (1947) found three factors: space, controlled manual movement, and something concluded in another study to be visual inspection.

Conceptually, at least two types of job-related mechanical abilities especially useful in career assessment can be identified: (a) understanding the principles of how mechanical objects function and (b) translating that understanding into practical, concrete action (e.g., repairing objects or using tools to get some task accomplished). In actuality, many Realistic jobs require the use of one's hands without demanding specialized knowledge of mechanical issues (e.g., a line worker who assembles car parts day after day, performing the same motions repetitively). Patterson et al. (1930) identified two aspects of mechanical abilities: the manipulation of tools and materials and the ability to secure information about tools, materials, and their uses. Depending on what measures are included in a factor analysis, other specific abilities may also cluster, but most empirical studies in this area have included mechanical, spatial, and, when measured, physical abilities (see, e.g., Benbow et al., 1983; Bowd, 1973; Vernon, 1961/2014).

Studies also have found that mechanical abilities are likely not to be associated with verbal ones. Although spatial abilities show a correlation with mechanical abilities and are likely to overlap, mechanical abilities alone versus mechanical-spatial elevations may point to different patterns of application.

The O*NET (https://www.onetonline.org) provides a measure of mechanical ability. Its advantage is its availability for nonselection purposes without cost. Here is a list of the O*NET's top 20 occupations said to make use of this ability (National Center for O*NET Development, 2018b)[1]:

- mechanical engineering technologists
- control & valve installers & repairers
- mechanical drafters
- mechanical engineers

---

[1] Reprinted from *Search results for "mechanical abilities,"* by National Center for O*NET Development, 2018 (https://www.mynextmove.org/find/search?s=mechanical+abilities). CC BY 4.0.

- mechanical engineering technicians
- mechanical door repairers
- insulation workers, mechanical
- electro-mechanical technicians
- mobile heavy equipment mechanics
- sailors & marine oilers
- motorboat mechanics & service technicians
- maintenance & repair workers, general
- bus & truck mechanics & diesel engine specialists
- mechatronics engineers
- automotive master mechanics
- aircraft mechanics & service technicians
- stationary engineers & boiler operators
- industrial machinery mechanics
- machinists
- first-line supervisors of mechanics, installers, & repairers

These occupations seem likely to call for mechanical abilities, but it is clearly a very small list in comparison with the number of occupations that would also likely require these abilities.

MEASUREMENT ISSUES

Because career assessment that solely makes use of cognitive ability measures (in particular, g) may not play to the strengths of assessees with Realistic-related abilities, mechanical ability measures are recommended for routine inclusion in career assessment batteries, especially when working with those with Realistic interests. This recommendation acknowledges that many widely used paper-and-pencil (or computer-administered) tests of mechanical abilities measure the understanding of mechanical principles more than the ability to use this understanding in practical applications, including those involving one's hands, so physical ability assessment may also be relevant. Additionally, in some but not all applications of mechanical ability, spatial abilities may also be needed (about which, there is more to come later in this chapter and in Chapter 7).

Most of the currently available measures of mechanical abilities are paper-and-pencil and can be used with group administrations. The Armed Services Vocational Assessment Battery (ASVAB; Wall, 2018) includes a measure of mechanical ability, called "mechanical comprehension," that "measures knowledge of mechanical and physical principles, and ability to visualize how illustrated objects work" (Wall, 2018, p. 47). The measure's usefulness in career counseling (vs. selection into the armed services) includes specific abilities versus the overall g equivalent. The ASVAB mechanical test was grouped with the spatial, manual, and organization tests, constituting what was labeled a technical jobs cluster (Prediger & Swaney, 1999). Many broad brush measures of ability, such as the Differential Aptitude tests, also include a measure of mechanical reasoning.

Sex difference in mechanical abilities in favor of men has been reported, creating potential adverse impact issues when such measures are used in selection (see Lemos et al., 2013; Stricker et al., 2001), although component parts of mechanical ability, including perceptual skills, have shown a sex difference in favor of women (Anastasi, 1982). Accordingly, scores on measures of mechanical ability should be compared with same-sex as well as opposite-sex norms when sex-specific norms are available. Scores on measures of mechanical ability, especially assembly tasks, appear to increase with age and experience; scores on mechanical ability tests by older subjects who have worked in mechanical jobs may therefore be elevated compared with scores of those without such experience (R. B. Cattell, 1987; Mayberry & Carey, 1997).

Scores on many of the tests of mechanical ability have been validated against relevant job criteria. Most commonly, measures tapping mechanical abilities have been validated in populations of youth against such criteria as grades in shop courses or against worker outcomes in specific Realistic occupations. Because scores on measures of mechanical ability appear to increase with age and experience (and particularly with exposure to mechanical tasks), adult and/or occupation specific normative data should be used. For occupations in which mechanical abilities are relevant, profiles still need to be developed that distinguish the relative importance of mechanical, spatial, perceptual, and intellectual abilities. New, updated norms are needed for many of the presently available measures of mechanical ability. Age distributions across the adult span, as well as expanded occupational norms, are also needed.

PHYSICAL ABILITIES

Physical abilities, especially important in Realistic- and some Conventional-interest occupations, can include the ability to work effectively with one's hands, limbs, and body. J. Hogan and Quigley (1999) noted that,

> although national demographic data indicate that American business is moving from traditional manufacturing toward service industries, this trend will not completely eliminate physically demanding work. Instead, jobs requiring substantial physical effort will be with us well into the 21st century. (p. 85)

Consistent with that prescient prediction, Baker and Gebhardt (2017) cited Bureau of Labor statistics in noting that 28% of the U.S. workforce perform physically demanding jobs.

There is a relatively extensive literature on physical abilities especially to the early work of Edwin Fleishman and his colleagues. Fleishman's important and lifelong work (e.g., Fleishman, 1954, 1957, 1964; Fleishman & Quaintance, 1984) developing and researching a taxonomy of physical abilities as well as an index of effort (Fleishman et al., 1984) identified several types of physical ability. In one study of 38 tests of various aspects of psychomotor ability (Fleishman, 1954), multiple factors were identified, including Wrist-Finger Speed, Finger Dexterity, Rate of Arm Movement (speed with which gross rapid arm movements can be made), Aiming (ability to perform quick and precise movements requiring eye-hand coordination), Arm-Hand Steadiness, Reaction Time, Manual Dexterity (arm-hand movement skill), Psychomotor Speed, Psychomotor Coordination, and factors labeled Spatial Relations and Postural Discrimination. (See also subsequent work, e.g., Fleishman, 1957, 1964; Fleishman & Hempel, 1956; Fleishman & Quaintance, 1984; Howell & Fleishman, 1981.) Fleishman and colleagues also created methods for categorizing the physical characteristics or demands of jobs (e.g., Fleishman & Quaintance, 1984; B. Schneider & Schmitt, 1986).

More recently, in a review chapter, Baker and Gebhardt (2017) summarized a seven-factor model of physical abilities that included the following:

1. Muscular Strength

2. Muscular Endurance

3. Aerobic Capacity

4. Anaerobic Power

5. Flexibility

6. Equilibrium

7. Coordination

ASSESSMENT ISSUES

There are limits to the use of physical ability assessment in the context of career assessment. Because physical abilities do not generalize readily from one area of physical ability to another (e.g., fine motor skill and trunk strength show low correlations), there is no g equivalent in the physical ability area. Also, Fleishman's work, and that of other researchers in this area, primarily focused on the use of physical abilities in personnel selection where jobs, but not people, were given. Further, studies and applications have often relied on specially devised mechanical measures (or job-specific methods) that have not yet been standardized so that assessors can easily adopt them to measure individuals in the context of career assessment.

For these reasons, it is unlikely that career assessors working with individuals at the college level or above will routinely administer a comprehensive physical ability battery as part of a standard assessment, except, perhaps, for clients who have a special interest in work that is primarily physical (e.g., many blue-collar jobs) or unless a preliminary screening suggests that physical abilities may be the areas of greatest strength. The cost and time investment of administering a lengthy battery of physical ability measures and the lack of available instruments are also factors in minimizing their routine usage. However, physical ability assessment may be quite relevant for personnel selection when there is a well-defined job for which specific physical ability requirements can be determined and an appropriate screening battery can be developed. Additionally, for those who work primarily with people in the context of jobs and careers that require physical work, or those who work with people experiencing physical problems potentially affecting their clients' work, assessment and attention to physical abilities may well be needed. For those working primarily with blue-collar workers or assessing vocational abilities of those who have been injured, it may also be desirable to have this capability.

SUMMARY AND CONCLUSIONS

Mechanical abilities are extremely important in much of the world's work that involves understanding and working with machines, equipment, and one's hands. Assessing mechanical abilities is especially important when working with persons in blue-collar careers, those in mechanical or engineering areas, and those with interest in technical jobs, and when Realistic (and some Investigative and Conventional) occupations are among those being considered by clients. Physical abilities assessment should be considered for measurement when assessing individuals in the context of occupations involving physical work.

7

Spatial Abilities

Research in spatial abilities began early (e.g., Thurstone, 1938; Vernon, 1961/2014) but has also been persistent and prolific over time. Vernon (1961/2014) and El Kousy (1935) labeled spatial abilities as the K factor, whereas R. B. Cattell (1987) referred to such abilities as Universal Index (UI) Number 3 (also designated by the subscript index letter "s" and more generally as S). Although the construct has been defined (when formally defined at all) in a fairly similar way from one ability study to the next (usually as the ability to visualize or mentally manipulate two- or three-dimensional objects), the early theorists did not determine exactly what was included and excluded in the construct and did not always evaluate the multidimensionality of spatial abilities in the context of occupational preferences or settings. A consensus panel on cognitive abilities convened by the National Academy of Sciences defined spatial abilities as "the capacity to unravel, understand, and remember the spatial relationships among objects" (National Research Council, 2015, p. 65). Moreover, marker variables (specific measures) that have been used to assess spatial abilities have varied widely from one researcher to another, and surprisingly few studies have examined the correlations among the alternative measures of spatial abilities to determine both the factorial structure of spatial abilities and the extent to which the alternative measures in fact assess similar abilities or constructs. Still, of the primary mental abilities (with the possible exception of verbal abilities), spatial abilities have been studied the most extensively, with much research directed to the persistent question of whether there are sex differences in favor of men (see, e.g., L. J.

---

https://doi.org/10.1037/0000254-008
Career Assessment: Integrating Interests, Abilities, and Personality, by R. L. Lowman
Copyright © 2022 by the American Psychological Association. All rights reserved.

Harris, 1981; Jeng & Liu, 2016), to the neuropsychology of spatial abilities and dysfunctions (Benton, 1982; Portegal, 1982; Ratcliffe, 1982; Sheehan & Smith, 1986; Spelke, 2005), and to the genetic and hormonal mechanisms that lead to spatial and other ability differences (Christiansen & Knussmann, 1987; Diamond et al., 1983; Geschwind & Galaburda, 1985a, 1985b; Jacklin et al., 1988; Puts et al., 2008; S. M. Resnick et al., 1986).

Although not without controversy (see, e.g., Berfield et al., 1986), researchers have generally found a consistent difference between men on average and women on average on tasks that are typically used to measure spatial abilities (Hegarty, 2018; Maccoby & Jacklin, 1974; Vandenberg & Kuse, 1979). However, this interacts with the way in which spatial abilities are measured (see Spelke, 2005). Rotational spatial tasks are more likely to show a sex difference in favor of men. Although the question of sex differences in spatial abilities is very important for the psychology of individual differences, for cognitive science, and for understanding possible patterns of sex differences in abilities, it is somewhat less important in individualized assessments. where the focus is on relative strengths and weaknesses.

The consensus report previously referenced (National Research Council, 2015) stated that spatial abilities were generally not acquired by formal instruction, but rather are obtained incidentally to other activities (p. 65). Even if skill acquisition in spatial abilities can be enhanced by nonclassroom activities (e.g., by playing certain sports and video games), there are still predispositional factors influencing them. Both genetic (e.g., Rimfeld et al., 2017; Tosto et al., 2014) and early (neonatal) hormonal influences (see Geschwind & Galaburda, 1985a, 1985b; L. J. Harris, 1981; Jacklin et al., 1988; Spritzer et al., 2011) have been shown to influence spatial abilities. Puts et al.'s (2008) meta-analysis concluded that, for women, prenatal exposure to high levels of androgen (e.g., among those with congenital adrenal hyperplasia [CAH]) increased spatial abilities compared with controls (while, for men, very high levels of prenatal androgens associated with CAH lowered it). Sexual orientation or sex role preferences have also been reported to be associated with spatial abilities (greater femininity being associated in some studies with lower spatial scores; see Rahman et al., 2017). An extensive literature also considers spatial abilities as a function of lateralization of brain functioning. Although spatial abilities have generally been viewed historically as being primarily right-brain-centered functions, Vogel et al.'s (2003) meta-analysis of cerebral lateralization of spatial abilities found more complex patterns. In particular, spatial abilities varied as to specific hemispheric involvement in patterns associated both with sex and handedness (handedness is the preference most people have for dominant use of the right or the left hand). Concerning sex, many women were found to be less lateralized in the distribution of the parts of the brain that are involved with spatial problem solving as compared with men in general. This would suggest that women (and others who are less lateralized) may solve spatial problems differently from those who are highly lateralized, that is, those whose spatial ability is primarily associated with one side of the brain.

Differing patterns of brain lateralization and spatial abilities have implications for how they are assessed. Research has suggested that those with less brain lateralization for spatial abilities tend to rely on both verbal and visual strategies in solving spatial problems. Tests (or subtests) relying primarily on visual rotation or on geometric orientation generally show a sex difference in favor of men, whereas others that rely on navigational or landmark strategies or those that can be solved with both verbal and visual skills may favor women (see Spelke, 2005).

Past studies have also found that earlier and ultimately more specialized, right-hemisphere development to be associated with higher spatial abilities. Handedness has also been studied as an indicator of spatial abilities. Sanders et al. (1982) found that sex interacted with handedness and ethnicity in predicting spatial abilities. Strongly left-handed men in this study had higher spatial abilities than did strongly right-handed men, whereas women had the opposite pattern. However, in the context of mathematics and handedness, research has reported limitations of either extreme of handedness (which can be measured on a continuum, not just dichotomously), but under some circumstances, left-handedness has been associated with high mathematical ability, which also has been linked to spatial abilities. Sala et al. (2017), who reached this and other conclusions in a series of studies, also noted an important limitation of this finding, stating, "Nonetheless, it seems reasonable that mathematical ability in children is based on their overall level of cognitive skill, and not only on their spatial ability" (p. 10).

Brain lateralization has also been associated with other ability patterns. Those whose brains are less lateralized (i.e., whose language functions are well represented in both hemispheres) have typically shown superiority of verbal over spatial and other nonverbal ability functions (e.g., Geschwind & Galaburda, 1985a; S. M. Resnick et al., 1986). However, this may not mean that they are disadvantaged compared with those with more lateralized brain patterns, just that they may use different mechanisms to solve spatial problems. Hence care must be taken in interpreting spatial abilities results to consider how the type of spatial measure used might have affected the results.

Some cultural differences have also been noted on spatial abilities. Lynn and Hampson (1987) found that Japanese children (aged 4–6 years) were superior to other ethnic groups on measures of spatial and numerical ability. Nagoshi and Johnson (1987) reported that a difference between subjects of Caucasian and Japanese ancestry remained even when general intelligence was partialed out of the cognitive ability factors. After this partialing, participants of Japanese ancestry scored higher than those of Caucasian ancestry on spatial and perceptual speed factors. Flaherty (2005) found country differences on a visual rotational task among samples, with Irish and Japanese samples scoring higher than Ecuadorians. A persistent sex difference was found, however, across all three cultures in favor of men. Interest in traditional male activities was also correlated positively with spatial abilities for both boys and girls. In a study of spatial abilities in a Hazdan mobile forager group in Tanzania (Cashdan et al.,

2012) and with an isolated Yucatec Maya group (Cashdan et al., 2016) found sex differences in spatial cognition. In the first study, men were higher than women on three different spatial tasks. They also were stronger on an object location memory task (in which women often excel compared to men). Most of the women who were strong on spatial tasks were older, suggesting a possible hormonal factor for the increased abilities. In the second study, the researchers found that women expressed more anxiety about navigating in novel areas, but that for both men and women, the distance covered in their foraging activities was similar before marriage but decreased for women and increased for men after marriage, suggesting that martital roles may also affect abilities related to spatial ability.

Spatial abilities generally increase with age from youth to young adulthood for both men and women (Sneider et al., 2015) and also increase with training, although sex differences persist even after training (Uttal et al., 2013). Scores on spatial abilities tests are also affected by practice, and by sustained attention to spatial tasks (Eliot, 1987; Embretson, 1987; Stericker & LeVesconte, 1982; Uttal et al., 2013). Moreover, different patterns of spatial abilities may require changing the instructional sets provided in order to improve performance (see, e.g., Casey et al., 1986). It appears that a substantial amount of effort may be required to obtain even modest increments in the ability (Ericsson & Faivre, 1988). Lord (1985), Dorval and Pépin (1986), A. S. Wolff and Frey (1984–1985), and others have reported the positive effects of training and video game playing on spatial visualization ability. However, even though Embretson (1987) found substantial improvement in test results when spatial aptitude training preceded measurement, a sex difference still was found after the training.

Such studies usually do not take interest into account. It is likely that individuals choose to practice those skills in which they have prior interest and ability. Thus, although spatial abilities scores apparently can be affected by practice, whether such practice can translate into occupationally relevant changes has not been well studied nor is there much evidence on the amount of practice needed to affect spatial abilities over time. That said, if spatial abilities are enhanced by playing video games and if children and adolescents are spending many hours a day engaged in those activities, it would not be surprising that spatial abilities are raised over time among those whose interests involve video games. Whether such games will be sought out by girls and young women depends on the appeal of the content.

DIMENSIONALITY OF THE CONSTRUCT

Factor-analytic studies of abilities have been conducted for many decades (see, e.g., McGee, 1979; National Research Council, 2015) yet they remain surprisingly inconclusive about the structure of spatial abilities. This was (and is) partly accounted for by the diversity of measures that have been used to assess spatial abilities. I. M. Smith (1964), for example, identified 60 spatial measures, the most recent of which had a 1960 publication date. Many new spatial measures have appeared since that volume was published.

Not surprisingly, with so many different instruments being used, there are often inconsistent results from one study of spatial abilities to the next. McGee (1979) reviewed the various factor-analytic studies conducted to that point and concluded that there was convincing evidence for at least two factors of spatial abilities. The first one, perhaps most important in occupational and educational applications, was a spatial visualization factor which was defined by Ekstrom et al. (1976) as "the ability to manipulate or transform the image of spatial patterns into other arrangements" (p. 173) and by McGee as "the ability to mentally manipulate, rotate, twist, or invert a pictorially presented stimulus object" (p. 19; see also Marmor & Zaback, 1976). This typically large factor appears in most factor studies of the structure of spatial abilities (e.g., Poltrock & Brown, 1984). The second factor was a spatial orientation factor, defined by Ekstrom et al. as "the ability to perceive spatial patterns or to maintain orientation with respect of objects in space" (p. 149) and by McGee as "the comprehension of the arrangement of elements within a visual stimulus pattern and the aptitude for remaining unconfused by the changing orientation in which a spatial configuration may be presented" (p. 19). Pawlik (1966) noted that spatial orientation's chief markers are similar to those used in navigating an airplane.

More recent research suggests that factors such as spatial visualization may have subfactors (see Yoon, 2011). Burton and Fogarty (2003), using a test battery composed of 41 types of measures, including a number of spatial tasks, found some support for Carroll's idea that there was a separate spatial factor (or facet) called Independent Imagery (IM) by which people are able (or not) to visualize objects and mentally manipulate them. They also identified five oblique (correlated) factors of spatial abilities: Visualization, Speeded Rotation, Speed of Closure, Visual Memory, and a combined Perceptual Speed–Closure Flexibility factor. Principal axis factor analysis of the visual imagery data set identified three first-order IM factors labeled IM Quality (defined by accuracy measures), IM Self-Report, and IM Speed (defined by latency measures).

Still other researchers have reported additional factors. Vernon (1961/2014), for example, long ago cited evidence that suggested a possible subfactor of memory for shapes versus imaginative manipulation of objects. Lohman (1979) differentiated between major (Spatial Relations, Spatial Orientation, and Visualization) and minor (Closure Speed, Serial Integration, Visual Memory, etc.) factors in spatial abilities. H. A. Carroll (1993) identified six spatial factors: Visual Memory, Spatial Scanning, Perceptual Speed, Serial Integration, Closure Speed, and Kinesthetic factors. Uttal et al. (2013) differentiated between two major "families" of spatial factors: intrinsic versus extrinsic (associated with mental rotation of objects, so-called small-scale tasks thought to be centered in the parietal part of the brain) and static versus dynamic ("large-scale tasks," such as way finding and navigation, thought to be centered in the hippocampus and medial lobes; see also National Research Council, 2015; L. Wang et al., 2014).

Although the factor structure of spatial abilities has been actively researched for many decades, there remains a paucity of research studies translating various models of factor structure into practice. This possibly reflects a field still sorting out the conceptual and structural issues of this ability. Clearly, at the factorial level, spatial is a still-emerging area of research and translating the current factor structure research into practical career assessment strategies is not yet easily done. This is not to suggest that it is unimportant to measure spatial abilities. Just the opposite is true since spatial abilities are important in many occupations and career-relevant tests are available.

RELATION TO OTHER ABILITIES

Ample evidence exists that spatial abilities can be differentiated from general intellectual ability, even though it has shown positive correlations with intelligence (see, e.g., Hakstian & Cattell, 1974, 1978a, 1978b; Super & Crites, 1962). Measures of spatial abilities can be more or less dependent on cognitive ability, depending on how the construct is measured. For example, in some studies, the marker for spatial abilities has been performance on measures such as the Block Design subtest of the Wechsler Adult Intelligence Scale-Revised (WAIS-R; e.g., Gormly & Gormly, 1986; MacLeod et al., 1986) or the Raven's Progressive Matrices Test (e.g., Lynn & Gault, 1986; Raven et al., 1992, 1994). Although the Block Design subtest may be an effective measure of nonverbal intellectual ability, it is unclear whether it is also a good measure of spatial abilities. In any case, such a measure would be expected to be highly correlated with intellectual ability. Similarly, Raven's test is primarily a measure of nonverbal general intellectual ability or of reasoning ability, not of spatial abilities (see Court, 1983). Conclusions about spatial abilities drawn on the basis of measures such as these are therefore likely to suggest that spatial and intellectual abilities are more closely related than would conclusions based on other, less intellectually dominated tests. Clearly, how the ability is measured will have implications for its overlap with cognitive ability since some measures of spatial abilities are more complex and presumably draw more on g than do others.

Beyond g, spatial abilities are also moderately correlated with mechanical abilities (see Chapter 6). Additionally, spatial and mechanical abilities tend to cluster together in cross-ability profiles such as in engineering and skilled trade occupations (see Chapter 6). Finally, in visual arts, spatial abilities cluster with aesthetic abilities and reproductive drawing abilities.

CAREER IMPLICATIONS

From a career perspective, many of the proposed taxonomies of spatial abilities conclude or imply that high spatial abilities (although there are no exact rules for determining what level of elevation constitutes "high") are related to greater likelihood of success in a variety of occupations primarily related to technical jobs and those in science, engineering, and the visual arts. Conversely, low levels of spatial abilities (say, below the 25th percentile on general population norms) probably point to less likelihood of success in occupations requiring spatial ability. In the case of midrange scores attention should also be given to occupational interests when clients are considering occupations in which spatial abilities are necessary for success in careers under consideration.

Here is a list of the top 20 occupations identified by the O*NET as requiring use of spatial abilities[1]:

- geospatial information scientists & technologists
- cartographers & photogrammetrists
- geographers
- geographic information systems technicians
- sailors & marine oilers
- architects
- biochemists & biophysicists
- precision agriculture technicians
- geography teachers, postsecondary
- mates- ship, boat, & barge
- fine artists, including painters, sculptors, and illustrators
- air traffic controllers
- landscape architects
- interior designers
- welders, cutters, & welder fitters
- construction managers
- tool and die makers
- choreographers
- motorcycle mechanics
- electronics engineers

All of these occupations required use of one or more spatial ability, for example, the O*NET's Visualization variable. Note that spatial ability may be important in both occupations requiring high levels of education or not. The bulk of the sample occupations listed are associated with the Realistic, Investigative, and Artistic areas.

---

[1]Reprinted from *Search results for "spatial abilities"*, by National Center for O*NET Development, 2018 (https://www.mynextmove.org/find/search?s=spatial+abilities). CC BY 4.0.

A number of studies that have suggested that spatial ability is related to successful occupational performance have focused on predictive validity research paradigms (see McGee, 1979, pp. 23–38; National Research Council, 2015) using measures of spatial ability whose factor loadings have not always been adequately determined. Other often-cited studies (e.g., U.S. Employment Service, 1957), on close scrutiny, were simply presumptions about the need for spatial abilities. Even in contemporary listings on the O*NET, it is difficult to know whether it is spatial orientation, spatial visualization, imagery visualization, or some other ability or combination of abilities that accounts for observed occupational differences.

Spatial abilities have been widely researched in the ability patterns of precocious high-ability youth (Webb et al., 2007) and performance in STEM occupations (Park et al., 2007; Wai et al., 2009), especially mathematics (see Tosto et al., 2014). In the context of career assessment, spatial abilities more generally would be expected to be important in some but not all Realistic occupations, in many Investigative occupations (particularly in STEM careers and in some medical specialties), in physics (Pallrand & Seeber, 1984), and in some Artistic occupations (specifically in the visual arts and architecture).

Indeed, there is a fair amount of evidence in support of the relation between spatial ability and artistic talent (Bryan, 1942; Hermelin & O'Connor, 1986; Jain et al., 2017; Lowman et al., 1985; Sadana et al., 2017) and architecture (Peterson & Lansky, 1980). J. O'Connor (1941, 1943) reported that surgeons, scientists, architects, engineers, draftsmen, and mechanics scored high on measures of structural visualization, whereas people in the more verbally oriented occupations (e. g., law, accounting, teaching) tended, he argued, not to make use of the ability and, on average, to score lower on measures of it. This view was supported by research on academically gifted youth whose careers were followed longitudinally. High spatial scores, measured in youth, were found (along with general cognitive ability) to predict successful careers in STEM occupations but not in the humanities or more verbally oriented occupations (Wai et al., 2009, 2010). Research evidence suggests a relation between spatial abilities and math (Benbow, 1988), especially for women (Ethington & Wolfle, 1984; Fennema & Tartre, 1985; Solan, 1987), and physics (Pallrand & Seeber, 1984). Spelke (2005), however, identified five cognitive systems involved in mathematical thinking, noting that even if spatial abilities are implicated in mathematics, it may be in combination with other abilities.

Spatial abilities would be expected to be particularly important when working with the world of things and, to some degree, ideas, and to be less important in people and data applications such as those often needed in Social, Enterprising, and Conventional occupations. The role of spatial abilities in Enterprising (managerial) occupations, typically viewed as being more verbal- than thing-oriented, may vary with the type of organization or enterprise being managed. In Realistic-oriented companies (e.g., manufacturing), spatial ability may be desirable in managerial roles such as production oversight or planning. The mechanical ability domain has been most closely associated with the spatial domain, and some researchers (see Bennett & Cruikshank, 1942; Bennett et al., 1989; and Chapter 6, this volume, on mechanical abilities) posited a spatial-mechanical factor as being important in a number of blue-collar occupations.

A frequently quoted listing of occupations that were said to require scores in the top 10% on measures of spatial ability was published by the U.S. Employment Service (1957). Although most of the occupations listed have received at least some support from other literature, it is often overlooked that the list was composed largely without empirical data (I. M. Smith, 1964). Still, it is interesting that the overwhelming majority of the occupations listed fell into Holland's (1985a) Realistic, Investigative, and Artistic categories (in that order). Interestingly, the Armed Services Vocational Aptitude Battery (ASVAB), used in U.S. military recruiting and placement, has included since 2002 a measure of spatial ability: the Assembling Objects (AO) test. A major validation effort of the ASVAB test was the Joint-Service Job Measurement Project (National Research Council [2015]). The ASVAB is required to be taken by all U.S. enlisted military personnel.

Many engineering students (typically Realistic/Investigative interest occupations) do well on measures of spatial ability (W. V. D. Bingham, 1937; Likert & Quasha, 1970; Wai et al., 2009, 2010). I. M. Smith's (1964) early review of the literature on how spatial ability related to school performance showed that spatial aptitude predicted higher performance in shop and industrial design courses, in math (especially geometry), and in university-level engineering courses. Higher science grades were also correlated with spatial ability. Spatial ability has also shown good power for predicting dental school success (C. E. Thompson, 1942). W. V. D. Bingham (1937) argued that spatial ability was important to both medicine and dentistry. Airplane pilots generally score highly on measures of spatial ability (J. F. Johnson et al., 2017).

J. P. Guilford (1948) identified three spatial factors relevant for flying ability: Perceptual Speed, Visualization, and Length Estimation. However, there were high correlations among the three dimensions. H. W. Gordon and Leighty's (1988) study of tests used to predict training success in a sample of 600 naval student aviators found that two aspects of spatial skills (mental rotation and locating points in space) were especially discriminating of those aviators who graduated and those who dropped out of flight training. In another study, H. W. Gordon et al. (1982) found that fighter pilots were more likely than bomber pilots, navigators, and helicopter pilots to score high on a measure of spatial ability and to show a pattern of right-brain lateralization. Fighter pilots performed in a superior manner on spatial abilities and scored significantly higher than other occupational groups and a normal comparison group. Performance on those measures was positively associated with success in the pilot training program. Among other findings of this study is the need to examine occupational subgroup differences: All flying personnel, for example, may not require spatial ability to the same degree. Perhaps career assessors can use spatial ability test results to help clients in professional training programs for pilots or engineers, among others, select an appropriate area of specialization. This is particularly true as aspects of flying become increasingly computerized. The differential influence of spatial ability in other occupational subspecialties has not been adequately studied empirically.

Diverse occupations that include areas of specialization (e.g., medicine, engineering, law, psychology) may require separate ability and interest profiles for each area of specialization. Note, for example, that industrial psychologists are included in the U.S. Employment Service's (1957) and the O*NET's similar lists of occupations requiring a high degree of spatial ability, whereas other applied psychology specialties do not appear on the list. Although Realistic (technical and engineering) and Investigative (medical, dental, and scientific) occupations are especially likely to show an association between spatial ability and occupational success, particularly among trainees (e.g., Schlickum et al., 2016; Wanzel et al., 2003), they are not the only areas in which spatial abilities are relevant.

Spatial ability has also been found important in some of the Artistic professions. Although some of the Artistic professions have an obvious need for spatial ability (e.g., sculptors), reproductive and visual artists also require spatial ability, a long-recognized finding (D. W. Barrett, 1945; H. O. Barrett, 1949; Bryan, 1942). Goldsmith et al. (2016) examined the effects of studying visual arts on youth (vs. those in theater). They found that, over three data collection points, the visual art students improved more in geometric reasoning (which relies on spatial ability) than did those in theater, suggesting that, when spatial ability is required, the skill itself improves with practice. Further, those visual arts students who accurately spatially represented a still life scene had higher scores on the geometric reasoning measure. Architecture, which combines engineering and art (see MacKinnon, 1962, 1970), also requires spatial ability (see Peterson & Lansky, 1980). Gardner (1983/2011) argued that music also requires a kind of spatial ability, an idea that has been supported by others (Lynn & Gault, 1986; see also the music ability section that follows in Chapter 8).

To summarize, three somewhat distinct occupational clusters appear most consistently to make use of spatial ability: engineering and technical (Holland's, 1985a, Realistic and Investigative groupings), scientific (Investigative), and visual arts (Artistic interests). It is presently unclear whether the same type or quantity of spatial ability is called for in all three occupational clusters or whether some spatial factors better account for a pattern of occupational or educational success. Interests presumably interact with abilities to determine whether the same spatial aptitude would be directed toward art, music, engineering, or science (note, e.g., the Lowman et al., 1985, finding that spatial and artistic abilities clustered together in a sample of college women). Whether interests precede and direct abilities or are directed by them cannot be answered by the existing literature.

MEASUREMENT ISSUES

What are the best measures of spatial ability? There is no one answer to that question. For career assessment and counseling purposes, the greatest research need is for measures of spatial ability to be updated (at least in the last decade) with adult normative data for the general population, grouped by age (as with IQ tests) and by occupation. In addition, there is a need for multidimensional assessment of spatial ability to be examined in occupational contexts. Such studies will help to determine whether spatial factors such as orientation, visualization, and memory relate differentially to career and occupational outcomes. Finally, more work is needed on the interactions between spatial ability, other types of ability, (e.g., general intelligence), and personality constructs.

As for specific measures, spatial ability has been measured in a wide variety of ways over a considerable time period (e.g., National Research Council, 2015; Estes, 1942). No currently available single test meets all of the criteria recommended for use in career assessment (U.S. Department of Labor, 1970, 1979). The spatial subtests of the Differential Aptitude Test (Bennett et al., 1989) and the General Aptitude Test Battery (GATB) have some utility, but occupational norms may not be available to the individual practitioner, and the GATB is still unavailable outside of the government, except to nonprofit institutions. Although its norms are somewhat outdated, the Minnesota Paper Form Board (Likert & Quasha, 1970), among currently published measures, still provides one of the broadest ranges of occupational normative data in a commercially available test and therefore holds a slight advantage over many of its competitors in the paper-and-pencil measures of spatial ability. Individually administered measures, such as the O'Connor Wiggly Block Test (J. O'Connor, 1927, 1943), appear to offer no particular advantage over the paper-and-pencil measures to justify their time and expense. Other measures (e.g., the Kit of Factor Referenced Cognitive Test's spatial subtest; Eliot et al., 1987) was well-designed but lacked norms and was not recommended for applied use by its authors (Ekstrom et al., 1976).

As noted, the O*NET and also the ASVAB include measures of spatial abilities aimed at the general population. Of these two measures, only the O*NET is available for use by assessors, although unlike the O*NET's interest profiler, the materials for its ability profiler are more difficult to find and make use of, and it appears to make accessible only an administrative manual, not a technical one.

Embretson (1987) advocated a dynamic testing approach in which spatial test-taking skills are first trained and then measured. Her Spatial Learning Ability Test (Embretson, 1994) made use of a novel design approach and purported to be a "pure" measure of spatial ability (with minimum intrusion of verbal factors). A fairly recently updated spatial ability test is the Revised Purdue Spatial Visualization Test (Yoon, 2011).

For reasons already discussed, career assessors must be cautious about drawing sweeping conclusions about the occupational implications of a single test. If a career assessee unambiguously scores low or very low on a psychometrically sound measure of spatial ability with evidence for career relevance predictions, and if the person has no special interests or other aptitudes necessary for spatially related occupations, then a single measure may be sufficient. However, if an individual scores marginally high on a spatial measure and aspires to an occupation that presumably requires the ability, then the assessor may need to administer additional tests to assess consistency of performance or ability in spatial subareas.

Other measurement factors must also be considered. Speed and age at the time of assessment (e.g., Dziurawiec & Deregowski, 1986; Embretson, 1987) must be taken into account in interpreting the results of spatial tests. Spatial ability has been reported to decline with age (Flicker et al., 1984; Meudell & Greenhalgh, 1987; Moore et al., 1984; Puglisi & Morrell, 1986; H. L. Swanson, 2017; Zagar et al., 1984), but, though this may be a real phenomenon (all abilities decline at some point for those living long enough), this apparent decline may possibly be influenced by slowed reaction time, not just by deterioration of the underlying ability. Because most standard measures of spatial ability do have a significant speeded component (indeed, some researchers believe that the ability to solve spatial problems rapidly and correctly actually defines the ability), it may be necessary in testing older clients to consider both a "speeded" and a "power" (no significant time limit) score. In such cases, it may be necessary to allow clients to finish a timed measure to determine whether low or marginal scores are primarily due to the time factor (Tinker, 1944, described a methodology for this type of administration). Since handedness may also affect performance on spatial tasks (Burnett et al., 1982; Schacter & Galaburda, 1986; Sheehan & Smith, 1986), the assessor should routinely collect information on handedness, preferably using a measure such as the Edinburgh Handedness Inventory (Oldfield, 1971). However, there is conflicting evidence in the literature on the relation between spatial ability, handedness, and the extent of hand preferences (see Burnett et al., 1982; Casey et al., 1986; Shettel-Neuber & O'Reilly, 1983). Sex differences should also be considered in interpreting test results. Because women as a group characteristically score lower than men on spatial ability measures, a woman who scores high compared with both own-sex and opposite-sex norms on spatial ability measures should probably be encouraged to consider professions for which the ability is needed. Other factors possibly important for interpreting test results include a history of alcohol misuse, which has been demonstrated to lower spatial ability (Clifford, 1986). The assessor should also inquire whether the client is taking medications at the time of assessment, because performance on spatial measures can be lowered or otherwise affected by medication (Helmes & Fekken, 1986; J. Taylor et al., 1987). Occupational history (e.g., exposure to toxic fumes) may also lower performance on spatial tasks (Arlien-Søborg, 1984).

SUMMARY AND CONCLUSIONS

Spatial abilities have received much greater attention in recent decades as a large and growing literature has demonstrated their importance in a number of occupational applications. Particularly relevant in many Realistic and Investigative occupations, they also are needed in the visual arts and can be useful in some types of leadership roles. Spatial ability is recommended for inclusion as part of standard or specialized assessment batteries. This is especially true as these abilities have been demonstrated to predict performance incrementally over g. Consideration should be given to the modality of assessment, since the persistent sex differences in favor of men may be lessened by the choice of measures used.

8

Artistic and Creative Abilities

At the general level, there are common themes that are associated with artistic ability. As Zaidel (2016), a neuropsychologist who has written extensively on artistic abilities and brain dysfunction, put it, "There seems to be a consensus that art is a human-made creation that communicates ideas, concepts, meanings, and emotions, and in this regard it has a social anchor; that art represents human-unique talent, skill, and creativity; and that art gives rise to aesthetic response" (p. 3). Although J. L. Holland's (1985a) interest model groups almost all of the artistic/creative professions into a single primary interest category, there are important differences in the talents, skills, and abilities associated with such creative pursuits as art, music, dance, and fiction writing. Indeed, the Artistic interest group of occupations encompasses considerable diversity and call for different abilities.

Even within a single Artistic-interest-related occupation, such as music, there are various types of talent. Composers, musicians, and music critics may all have musical talent, but each occupational subgroup may have a unique constellation of abilities. Although J. L. Holland (1985a) maintained that Artistic-interest types are generally "creative" (an ability, but with associated personality characteristics), in fact, people may have Artistic vocational interests and score high on artistic-related ability tests yet not be particularly creative in the sense of making something that did not previously exist or putting existing pieces together in novel ways. Illustrative, at one extreme, is the musical talent expressed by autistic savants (Gardner, 1983/2011; Minogue, 1923; Viscott, 1970), individuals of otherwise limited cognitive abilities who have a

https://doi.org/10.1037/0000254-009
Career Assessment: Integrating Interests, Abilities, and Personality, by R. L. Lowman
Copyright © 2022 by the American Psychological Association. All rights reserved.

distinctive capacity to memorize and repeat music, yet whose "creativity" may be minimal. At the other extreme, exemplifying creativity in this domain, are musical composers who create music that did not previously exist.

Clearly there is a difference in roles between musicians and orchestra leaders and, to take another example, between directors and actors. Actor turned director Paul Dano put it this way in an interview with National Public Radio's Terry Gross (2018):

> I think that, for me, acting is just a bit more lonely [than directing] because you do so much of the work on your own. And then you arrive kind of hopefully full, so to speak. And then you're with your scene partners and your director . . . but directing is so collaborative. It's more like, you know, playing in an orchestra or something, and maybe . . . you're the leader. . . . And I don't mean that arrogantly. I just mean that's the job. . . .
>
> And, honestly, one of the hard things for me [in directing] was that I didn't have any alone time. . . . Somebody is always asking you a question. . . . You have to make a million decisions a day. But I loved that feeling of collaboration with every little bit of the crew and sort of just helping to create . . . a space where we could all kind of go to work together. And you're almost, like, parenting. Like, you're just trying to get the best out of everybody.

Conversely, it should not be overlooked that creative talent is not limited to those in the Holland Artistic interest categories. Doubtless, there are creative engineers, teachers, financial analysts, and therapists. As Zaidel (2016) noted,

> Because creativity is more obvious in art than in other fields, we have come to commonly associate the two terms. However, the neuroanatomical and neurophysiological underpinnings of artistic creativity need not be wholly different from creativity in other human endeavors. (p. 13)

A biological or genetic basis for some aspects of creativity is suggested by neuropsychological studies of those with brain impairments affecting creativity and from evidence of musical savants. Neuropsychological evidence from creative persons with brain impairments is associated with decreased artistic performance and persistence even among highly talented artists. That some, presumably rare, individuals with no prior artistic talent suddenly develop such skills after brain damage, or as a side effect of certain medications, suggests that brain functions can be very complex, especially in trying to understand the underlying structural basis for creativity. Studies of musical savants, who have a specific, often isolated, ability in music, may imply that talent interacts complexly with biological factors.[1]

Genetics may also play a strong role in some of the Artistic abilities, as is discussed later. But it cannot be assumed that simply because there is a genetic disposition underlying certain abilities that they will translate into career-related abilities.

It is not possible to cover in detail all of the abilities involved in specific areas of creative performance. However, in this section I highlight some of the major

---

[1] However, McLeish and Higgs (1982) noted that most individuals with intellectual impairment are also musically impaired, so autistic savants are not the norm among those who are intellectually limited (see also Farnsworth, 1958).

artistic-related abilities for which career-assessment measures of ability have been developed. Many of the better-established measures are not new and often have not been updated.

MUSICAL ABILITIES

Theorists and factor analysts of intelligence have generally included musical ability among the primary mental abilities (R. B. Cattell, 1987; Vernon, 1961/2014). Gardner (1983/2011; Walters & Gardner, 1986) included music as one of seven major "intelligences," arguing that musical talent has evolutionary value and that there was an identified neuropsychological situs for musical ability. However, possibly because of the expense of testing and the relatively narrow distribution of the talent in the context of people making a living in it, most standard ability batteries such as the Differential Aptitude Test, the General Aptitude Test Battery (GATB), and the O*NET abilities measure do not include assessments of musical talent.

Age affects the development and expression of musical talent, which is thought to mature early (Shuter-Dyson & Gabriel, 1981), possibly implying a strong genetic component. Carl Seashore (1915), himself one of the major early researchers on musical talent, suggested as much, stating,

> Musical talent, like all other talent, is a gift of nature inherited, not acquired; in so far as a musician has natural ability in music, he has been born with it. . . . The measurement of musical capacity, therefore, concerns itself chiefly with inborn psycho-physic and mental capacities as distinguished from skill acquired in training. (p. 129)

A growing body of modern scientific evidence supports that contention, suggesting that music talent does benefit from genetic factors. Indeed, in a cleverly titled article, "Practice Does Not Make Perfect," Mosing et al. (2014) found in a study of 10,500 pairs of Swedish twins that music ability was 40% to 70% heritable and that, among monozygotic twins, when genetics were controlled for, there was very little association between practice and ability. The authors suggested the intriguing hypothesis that ability levels may affect *inclination* to practice rather than practice affecting abilities. In a review of 21 empirical studies of the role of genes in music ability, Tan et al. (2014) found evidence from mostly small sample studies of specific gene locations for various aspects of music ability. However, Tsay's research (Tsay & Banji, 2011) demonstrated that, among raters of musical performers, when people performed about the same, those characterized as having natural talent ("naturals") were rated more highly than those not being perceived to have it ("strivers"). This has been called the "talent bias." Further, when musical competition performances were rated by both novices and experts who either listened to videotaped performances or watched a videotaped performance without sound, only the latter group reliably predicted the performance winners. This suggests that there can be many biases needing to be avoided when making judgements about musical performances.

Even though there may be genetic components to some musical abilities, age and training may affect the measured abilities. Psychoacoustical perceptual discrimination abilities, for example, are believed to increase with age as short-term memory skills improve (Zenatti, 1985). Also, musical training has clearly been demonstrated to affect musical skills and brain processes associated with music. Habibit et al. (2016) found no pretest differences in a group of children age 6 to 7 matched on socioeconomic status (SES) who received weekly musical training, a comparison group whose members engaged in sports training rather than music, and a control group. After two years of music training, however, the experimental group showed accelerated development of auditory cortical potentials and greater ability to detect pitch changes. Conversely, contrary to some claims, the evidence that children's music training improves their cognitive abilities is limited (see Sala & Gobet, 2017).

Further evidence on presumably inherited predispositional brain structures was provided by Norton et al. (2005). They considered whether there were preexisting neural, cognitive, or motoric markers for musical ability by examining young children's (5- to 7-year-olds) abilities and brain structures. Using two small sample groups, one of which was to receive string instrument music lessons and the other not, tests were administered on cognitive ability, including spatial ability and MRIs. No differences were found between the two groups on the various markers, but correlations were found between music perceptual skills and both nonverbal reasoning and phonemic awareness. The researchers noted that "such pre-existing correlations suggest similarities in auditory and visual pattern recognition [and] a sharing of the neural substrates for language and music processing, most likely due to innate abilities or implicit learning during early development" (Norton et al., 2005, p. 124).

Still another example of the possible role of genetics in music ability is the relative rarity of absolute pitch (AP), defined as "the ability to name or produce a note of a given pitch in the absence of a reference note" (Deutsch, 2013a, p. 141). This is differentiated from the more widely distributed relative pitch, in which notes are perceived and identified in relationship to other notes. Wilson's review reported that AP was influenced by genes on chromosome 8q; music perception by genes on chromosome 4, 8q, and 12q; music memory by those on 17q and 12q; choir participation by those on 17; and music listening by those on 12q. This line of research suggests that genetic effects of musical ability may be complex, that various genes may be involved, and that combinations of somewhat narrow abilities may differentially be present and account for music outcomes. Seesjärvi et al. (2016) conducted a study of the musical abilities of monozygotic and dizygotic twins raised together or apart. In musical tasks that involved simple comparison of melodies that differed in pitch and tone (common in many music ability tests), genetics played a greater role than in tasks that required use of acquired musical knowledge. The authors concluded that genetics plays a role in some types of music tasks, but environment and learning play a role in others.

Deutsch (2013) estimated that only around one in 10,000 in the general population has AP. She noted, however, that AP is overrepresented in eminent composers and performers. (In contrast, AP is more common in other species such as songbirds, while relative pitch is not; Patel & Demorest, 2013.) Specifically, AP has been reported to be more common among Asians and Asian Americans in comparison to other ethnic groups (Gregersen et al., 1999). Although there is evidence of a genetic component in AP, research suggests that it is overrepresented among those who started musical training early (i.e., before 4 years of age; Baharloo et al., 1998). Indeed, Takeuchi and Hulse's (1993) comprehensive review of the AP literature found that there was variability among those designated as having AP and that to some extent it could be learned, particularly when training was undertaken before the age of 5. These authors also noted that AP is likely mediated by verbal approaches in which a name or word is attached to a particular note. This suggested that it was not a sound that was being identified on its own but rather the pairing of a specific pitch and a word by which it is designated. Even with training, which improved the ability to recognize pitches, the groups identified as having AP still on average did better on pitch discrimination tasks than did those who had been trained but did not have it.

Even though musical talent may mature early, this does not necessarily mean that those whose abilities are identified early will be consistently high performers over time. For example, musical prodigies may experience a breakdown in performance as they move from adolescence to adulthood (Bamberger, 1982), and many, perhaps the majority, of talented musicians do not make their living at it due to the highly competitive nature of the field. This raises the question of the number of students and jobs in music, since those with musical talent and interests not infrequently find that they cannot make a living at it.

E. E. Gordon (1965, 1986a, 1986b, 1989), a prominent musical researcher, and others (e.g., Wing, 1968) have noted that musical ability is normally distributed. As E. E. Gordon (1989) put it, "Musical aptitude, like all other aptitudes, is normally distributed. . . . Everyone has at least some music aptitude. Most persons have average music aptitude. Relatively few persons have a very high level or a very low level of music aptitude" (p. 10). Still, musical talent at high levels is likely required for those who make a career in musical performance.

Dimensionality of Musical Abilities

Schellenberg and Weiss (2013) referred to musical abilities as "musical cognition" and defined musical aptitude as "natural music abilities or the innate potential to succeed as a musician." This definition belies the reality that succeeding in music may also depend on many different nonability factors. In any case, many of the musical ability measures that have been used as the basis of factor analyses were designed for practical applied purposes, namely, the measurement of musical abilities in the context of training or, to a lesser extent, selection.

There is a long history of psychologists studying and assessing musical abilities, if not for purposes of career assessment, at least for musical education and student selection purposes. There is also a growing recent literature approaching musical abilities from a cognitive psychology perspective. Most of the measures of underlying (presumably primary) abilities in music make use of psychoacoustical measures. Examples of historical interest include the Kwalwasser-Dykema music tests (Whitley, 1932) and Lundin's (1949) measures of musical ability, which included five subtests: Interval Discrimination, Melodic Transposition, Mode Discrimination, Melodic Sequences, and Rhythmic Sequences. As described by Schellenberg and Weiss (2013),

> The typical task on tests of musical aptitude involves presenting two short melodies (or two short rhythms) on each trial. Listeners are asked whether the second melody (or rhythm) is the same as or different from the first. After several trials, a score is calculated separately for each test. An aggregate score can also be calculated by averaging across tests. (p. 500)

Carl Seashore was one of the pioneers in the scientific study of musical abilities and developed a test of musical abilities that was used for many years. Of Swedish birth, he was raised on a farm in Iowa, but received, in 1895, the first PhD in psychology conferred by Yale University. Subsequently, he developed a thriving program of grants, funded by AT&T, for the scientific study of music at the University of Iowa (Gjerdingen, 2018). Seashore's (1939) well-known (but not without controversy; see Henson & Wyke, 1982) Seashore Measures of Musical Talent (SMMT) assessed six dimensions. The three best-validated of these were Rhythm, Pitch, and Tonal Memory. The remaining three were Loudness, Timbre, and Time. There is relatively little contemporary evidence of the measure's validity, and it appears no longer to be marketed or much used.

Another well-known measure of musical ability that was widely used in the past was Wing's (1960) Standardised Tests of Musical Intelligence. Factorial study of Wing's (1941) musical ability battery revealed three major factors: a large general factor, a factor related to the perception and discrimination of sound qualities, and a factor related to judgment of the quality or goodness of music (see also Vernon, 1961/2014).

There have been several factor studies of some of the major or commonly used measures of musical ability over the years. In contrast to other areas of ability, however, the factor-analytic study of musical talents remains rather inconclusive.

R. M. Drake (1939) factor-analyzed all then-published musical measures that had reliabilities greater than 0.31 (a rather low criterion) and found one general factor and three specific factors of musical ability. Farnsworth (1958) reviewed the early factor studies and noted anywhere from one general musical factor to eight highly specific factors (e.g., pitch, memory). In a Swedish study by Franklin (as cited in Farnsworth, 1958) in which the Wing, the Seashore, and other, nonmusical, tests were administered to the same participants, two factors emerged, a factor labeled as "mechanical-acoustical" (on which loaded such measures as pitch, timbre, time, and loudness) and a "judicious-musical factor" (essentially, an aesthetic factor), which pertained to the ability to make judgments about the quality of music.

Other factor structures have also been suggested. Teplov hypothesized three basic musical aptitudes, including

> Tonality, the ability to sense the tonal relationships of the notes of a melody and the emotions expressed by melodic movement . . . closely connected with pitch discrimination; the ability to reproduce a tune when heard by ear (which is presumably related to tonal memory); and the ability to feel and reproduce rhythmic movement. (as cited in Shuter, 1968, pp. 237–238)

Stankov and Horn (1980), using a sample of 240 men, examined the factor structure of 44 auditory and nonauditory tasks. This research identified seven factors. As summarized by Carson (1998b), these included (a) listening verbal comprehension (Va), (b) auditory immediate memory (MSa), (c) temporal tracking (Tc), (d) auditory cognition of relationships (ACoR), (e) discrimination among sound patterns (DASP), (f) speech perception under distraction/distortion (SPUD), and (g) maintaining and judging rhythm (MaJR). Carson (1998b) also noted that

> Va, MSa, ACoR, and SPUD appeared similar to previously identified auditory ability factors and none were especially identified with musical abilities. The remaining three factors—Tc, DASP, and MaJR—were argued to have unique variance [differing] from previous factor-analytic studies of ability, and all three suggest abilities with particular importance for the musical domain. MaJR suggests a rhythm maintenance factor, which I will call "simple rhythm"; measures of simple rhythm have long been included in test batteries used in music education programs. DASP, while relating broadly to pattern recognition, relates strongly to traditional measures of tonal memory. Stankov and Horn suggested that the Tc factor related to temporal integration of stimuli, and that "no factor of temporal integration had been identified in previous research." (p. 42)

Carson (1989b) singled out Tc, DASP, and MaJR as being particularly relevant to musical abilities. He also noted, correctly, that "there is a richness to Stankov and Horn's factors that may not be required in career assessment, and there exists no data bearing on the question of which of these specific factors predict vocationally relevant outcomes" (p. 319), suggesting a work in progress that is not easily applied to career assessment practice.

Naoumenko (1982) postulated a hierarchical system comprising both general musical abilities (emotional imaginative, rational, reproductive) and specific musical talents (rhythm, creative imagination, and "sense of closure"). Karma (1985) also proposed an alternative way of conceptualizing musical talent that differed from the psychoacoustical approaches such as that of the Seashore tests. Specifically, Karma (1985) instead focused on a cognitive processes model of musical ability, which encompassed such musical abilities as recognizing patterns, understanding timing, and analyzing internal structures. E. E. Gordon (1986) performed factor analyses using his Measures of Music Audiation (MMA) and Musical Aptitude Profile (MAP), his family of measures of music ability. His factors differentiated between stabilized and developmental (accomplished versus potential) music ability. For adults and older youth, Gordon's Advanced Measures of Music Audiation (AMMA) include two subtests: pitch and rhythm. Bregman (1990) suggested yet another possibly auditory/acoustical factor in that sound may contribute to spatial perception in a way additive to, or possibly differentiated from, visual perception.

The use of the voice, rather than the ability to play a musical instrument, calls for still other factors. Lundin's (1967) review of the factors that make for singing ability identified the following as relevant: pitch intonation and control, vibrato ("a rapid series of pulsations in the tonal stimulus, most commonly in its pitch, but . . . frequently also accompanied by pulsations in loudness and timbre"; p. 272), tonal intensity (greater intensity is more desirable, often associated with the physiological characteristics of the throat), resonance (at both low and high points), and stability of tone intensity.

Clearly there have been many different approaches to musical aptitude and ability measurement. Because each of the measures discussed has used a slightly (or very) different approach, generating more or fewer studies, conclusions about a universal factor structure of musical talents remain difficult to sort out at this time.

Carson (1998b) summarized a state of affairs that is as relevant today as when he wrote it: "There is as yet no consensus as to the factorial structure of musical and auditory aptitudes and their relations to other abilities, although musical aptitudes do appear to exist that are distinct from most other major abilities" (p. 317). He did identify a preliminary model that included M1 and M2, respectively, the mechanical acoustical and aesthetic factors of Franklin (Farnsworth, 1958) and the three "unique" factors from Stankov and Horn (1980) of Tc, DASP, and MaJR. Unfortunately, Carson's model seems not to have inspired much research, and the characterization of lack of consensus on the factor structure of musical abilities remains.

Relation to Other Abilities

Nonmusical factors also appear to be important in musical talent, especially when the demands of playing an instrument are considered. As Wan and Shlaug (2013) noted,

> Neuroimaging studies have confirmed that playing music relies on a strong coupling of perception and action mediated by sensory, motor, and multimodal integration regions distributed throughout the brain. . . . For example, to play the violin competently requires a host of complex skills, including visual analysis of musical notations and translation into motor acts, coordination of multisensory information with bimanual motor activity, development of fine motor skills coupled with metric precision and auditory feedback to fine-tune a performance. (p. 565)

Depending at least partially on the specific musical talent (e.g., composing vs. performing) and on the instrument played, other relevant abilities may include finger dexterity, access to emotions (presumably Gardner's, 1983/2011, social intelligences), and linguistic skills (Judd, 1988; Karma, 1983; Super & Crites, 1962). Mastery of a symbol set and language are also required for those who read music (which not all musicians do). Memory factors captured partially by tonal memory measures are also relevant.

A number of studies have considered whether music abilities are associated with other abilities and, if so, whether there was evidence of causality in either direction. This is not a new topic of research. Morrow (1938) found little relation between musical talents (as measured by the problematic Kwalwasser-Dykema Music Tests) and mechanical and aesthetic judgment abilities. Wing (1941) reported a slight relation between musical abilities and scores on intelligence measures, a result confirmed by others reviewing this literature (see Hobbs, 1985; Lundin, 1967); this may partially be artifactual to the specific measures used. For example, little relation has been shown between the Seashore musical measures and intelligence, whereas a stronger relation with intelligence has been shown when other criteria of musical ability are used (Mursell, 1939; see also Shuter-Dyson & Gabriel, 1981, pp. 295–301). This may suggest that when aspects of music involve multiple components or higher level tasks, intelligence may be important.

Spatial abilities have also been associated with different aspects of musical talent. Hassler and Birbaumer (1985) examined the relationship between musical talents and visual-spatial abilities in a longitudinal study of youths. They examined whether male and female musically talented students compared with those in a control group scored highly on a measure of musical ability and one of creative musical ability (music composition and improvisation), as well as a measure of visual-spatial ability. Compared with controls, both sexes who were in the musical groups and who excelled at musical composition scored higher on a measure of spatial orientation. For the male students, but not the female students, they also scored higher on a measure of spatial-visualization. These researchers also found that spatial ability changed over time as to its representation for the male musical students in comparison to the female and nonmusical controls. Specifically, spatial ability was represented bilaterally rather than primarily in the right hemisphere.

Other studies have been reported in this area. Lynn and Gault (1986) found a positive relation between intelligence as measured by the Raven's Standard Progressive Matrices (RSPM; a nonverbal measure; Raven et al., 1994) and the Wing music measures, especially pitch change and pitch memory. Moreover, as Anastasi (1982) noted, the absence of a relation between scores on measures of music and intelligence does not mean that intelligence is not needed for success as a musician, because different research paradigms than those commonly used may be needed to establish the connection. This may also be relevant for understanding an apparent relation reported between scientific (especially mathematical) abilities and musical talents (Arenson, 1983; Révész, 1953; Shuter-Dyson & Gabriel, 1981; Vernon, 1961/2014, as cited in Shuter, 1968).

More recently, Schellenberg and Weiss's (2013) excellent chapter on musical and cognitive abilities did find a relationship between general cognitive ability and musical ability. They noted exceptions, such as persons of normal intelligence scoring poorly on tests of music aptitude because of pitch perception deficits and others of low intelligence who had high levels of music ability. They also noted associations of music abilities and math and spatial skills.

Helmbold et al. (2005) examined primary abilities in a criterion group of German musicians versus one of German nonmusicians (the average age for both groups was in their early 20s). Across an assortment of primary abilities (including, among others, verbal comprehension, word fluency, space [mental rotation], flexibility of closure, perceptual speed, verbal memory, and spatial memory), there were group differences only in flexibility of closure and perceptual speed. Other studies (e.g., Talamini et al. 2016) also found an advantage for working memory among musicians compared with nonmusicians.

Career Implications

Concerning those employed in music-related jobs, the Bureau of Labor Statistics (BLS) of the U.S. Department of Labor (BLS, 2018b) estimated that, in 2016, there were 74,800 music directors and composers and 172,400 musicians and singers (BLS, 2018c) in the United States. This compares with the overall U.S. population, at this writing, of around 330,000,000 people. There is also a narrow geographic distribution of where most of these jobs are located, primarily in New York, California, Tennessee, Florida, and Illinois (BLS, 2018a).

These numbers are believed to be underestimates because they excluded self-employed individuals. K. Thomson (2012) attempted to address this omission by considering organizational membership data from performance rights organizations like the American Society of Composers, Authors, and Publishers (ASCAP), the Broadcast Music Inc. (BMI), and unions such as the American Federation of Musicians (AFM) and the American Federation of Television and Radio Artists (AFTRA). (Note that musical composers and certainly musical managers and agents may have different talent profiles, so such data must be further parsed to be sure they include only those needing to make use of musical talent to do their work.) It is also highly likely that many more people who have music talent perform in local, often unpaid, venues (churches and the like) and are not in any trade or professional association, so clearly more information is needed to establish a meaningful baseline for artistic talent. Nevertheless, when including those in self-employment, the number of individuals who presumably have sufficient talent to make a living at music, the national BLS statistics would appear to underestimate occupational data for those working in musical careers. Adding in estimates of self-employed individuals would bring the numbers to well over a million (if not more). (Even with this addition, these figures would still be relatively low in a country as wealthy and large as the United States.) By comparison, the National Institute for Occupational Health and Safety (2017) reported that there were over 17 million people in the United States employed in health care, which did not include unpaid home health care providers. Nor did the reported statistics of those in musical work consider or report the number of individuals who began a career in music but later abandoned it either due to there being too few opportunities or the salary levels being too low.

Most tests of musical ability were designed to assess instructional needs in schools or for music school admissions purposes. However, the validation criteria used (e.g., R. M. Drake, 1933; C. S. Harrison, 1987a) often correlated scores on musical ability measures with instructor ratings or grades in music courses, which can be highly subjective,rather than those related to ultimate success as musicians.

These challenges in establishing criterion validity evidence have been longstanding. Highsmith (1929) reported high correlations between scores on the Seashore measures and course grades (although intelligence was a better predictor of academic music courses); however, the reliability of the Seashore measures was low. When professional musicians have been the subject of investigation, questions have been raised about the reliability and validity in predicting (concurrently) successful posttraining performance on these measures because the professional musicians do not always perform well on such tests (Henson & Wyke, 1982). Of course, the motivation of professional musicians and of students or job candidates may differ.

Shuter's (1968) review of the Wing tests noted that the Chord Analysis test successfully differentiated among a carefully selected group of music students (all presumably musically talented) at the prestigious Eastman School of Music, although the Pitch Change and Memory tests, which were highly associated with a general musical factor, were not as differentiating of overall music student competency. On the other hand, these two subtests may be good at identifying less talented musical students. Shuter (1968) noted that the appreciation subtests of the Wing measures were not useful with very young children but did discriminate between average and weak music students. Other evidence suggests that the Appreciation of Phrasing test, which required judgment as well as perception, may be useful for differentiating between groups with and without musical ability. In another validity paradigm, C. S. Harrison (1987a) published a 5-year follow-up study of 135 college freshmen who had completed the MAP. With grades in music theory and applied theory as a criterion, the best validity coefficients were obtained with the Tonal Imagery, Rhythm Imagery, and Composite scores.

Measurement Issues

As discussed, a variety of measures of musical ability have been developed over the years, some no longer commercially available and many with problems of reliability or technical inadequacy (e.g., Carson, 1998b; Mills, 1984). Schellenberg and Weiss (2013) concluded that such measures have generally been found to be correlated, that the criterion measures used for validation evidence have varied from one measure to the next, and that "no test of music aptitude ... is considered to be the 'gold standard'" (p. 500). The variations among tests, they further note, likely account for some of the disparities across findings. Although not constituting a "gold standard," the Gordon measures of musical ability may win the "last test standing" award, since most of the others are no longer commercially available. (A relatively recent measure is also mentioned in this section, but its evidence of validity and reliability is not yet extensive.)

Here we briefly review some of the measures that have been widely used, at least historically, to assess musical talent: the SMMT (Seashore et al., 1960), the Wing Standardised Tests of Musical Intelligence (Wing, 1941, 1960, 1968), and the various versions of the MMA test (E. E. Gordon, 1965, 1989; Harrison, 1987a, 1987b). Another, more recent measure not yet with a large research database is the Profile of Music Perception Skills (PROMS; Law & Zentner, 2012). This measure includes subtests of the following musical abilities or factors: Tonal (melody, pitch), Qualitative (timbre, tuning), Temporal (rhythm, rhythm-to-melody, accent, tempo), and Dynamic (loudness).

Early reviews of tests were provided by R. M. Drake (1933), Farnsworth (1958), Lehman (1968), Shuter (1968), and Wing (1968) and more recently, if primarily indirectly, by Schellenberg and Weiss (2013). J. Hanson (2019) reviewed the literature on the Gordon family of measures and was generally favorable about those tests' predictive power.

Tests have taken varying approaches to assessing musical abilities. For example, the once popular Seashore tests were developed as a test of acoustical perception using artificially created tones on the premise that the sounds should be relatively independent of training influences and should reflect basic, fundamental aspects of musical talent. However, as Schellenberg and Weiss (2013) demonstrated in their review, there are positive and significant correlations between so-called music aptitude and music training, so it is not clear that there is a "pure" measure of musical ability that is both independent of training and predictive of later career success in this field.

Critics (well summarized by Lehman, 1968; Wing, 1968) had a variety of criticisms of the Seashore measure and have challenged its reliability and mixed pattern of validity evidence as well the test's approach to measuring musical abilities. Moreover, Wing (1968) argued that the degree of perceptual precision embedded in the Seashore measures exceeds what may be needed even by exceptionally accomplished musicians. Shuter (1968) therefore argued that searching for cutoff scores when using the Seashore may be more promising than accepting the assumption that higher scores are better.

The SMMT subtests may also differentially apply to success with different instruments and in different cultures. Stringed instruments, for example, require a great deal of sensitivity to pitch (Shuter, 1968); others may not. Farnsworth (1931) noted that music from Eastern cultures was less pitch sensitive than that of Western cultures. Three SMMT subtests have had the best reliability and validity evidence: Rhythm, Tonal Memory, and Pitch. R. M. Drake (1933), for example, found the Pitch subtest to be the best of the Seashore measures in predicting musical academic criteria (exam and school principal's ratings). Similarly, Highsmith (1929) found the best reliabilities on an earlier version of the Seashore for the Pitch and Tonal Memory subtests. The interpretation of performance on the Seashore measures is not uncomplicated. What is desired is not that the person being evaluated scores at the top of the various Seashore scales but that some minimally acceptable level of basic psychoacoustical skills be demonstrated. Seashore himself, according to Brennan (1926), believed that scoring at the 50th percentile demonstrated sufficient musical skills (as measured by his tests) for musical performance. Unfortunately, no validated cutoff scores were found that could be used for career advising purposes and the test manual was not helpful for this purpose.

The Wing measures, developed in the United Kingdom used only piano music and consisted of subtests, several of which were otherwise similar to Seashore's. They also included subtests for chord analysis (requiring the participant to identify the number of pitches present in various chords), a memory test (judging whether notes in two series were the same or different), and pitch change (judging whether chords are the same or different), along with rhythmic accent, harmony, intensity, and phrasing (measuring musical acuity and preferences for different types of music). The Wing measures, if used as a whole, are long (60 minutes) and are not readily accessible in the United States, and may have limited usefulness in non-British cultures (Lehman, 1968; Rudocy & Boyle, 1979).

E. E. Gordon's (1965, 1989) MAP evolved from a long (three sessions of 50 minutes each) but potentially valuable measure of musical abilities. It is particularly useful for students with identified musical talent. The subtests on this measure included Tonal Imagery (Melody and Harmony), Rhythm Imagery (Tempo and Meter), and Musical Sensitivity (Phrasing, Balance, and Style). Gordon's MAP used actual musical instruments rather than specially generated sounds. It incorporated several stringed instruments and also made use of professionally trained musicians to play the notes. Reported reliabilities for the combined scores were fairly high, and the measure has shown reasonably good validity evidence (Lehman, 1968).

The MAP evolved to become the Measures of Music Audiation (MMA; E. E. Gordon, 1989) and was offered at three levels: the PMMA ("P" for primary) for students in pre-K to Grade 3, the IMMA ("I" for intermediate) for Grades 3 to 6, and the AMMA ("A" for advanced) test for Grade 6 to adult. It produces scores in Tonal Imagery, Rhythm Imagery, and a Composite score. Unlike many of the others, this test is currently available for computer administration from GIA Music Assessment (https://www.GIAMusicAssessment.com). The reliability and validity evidence for the MMA suite of tests was considered in a recent meta-analysis by J. Hanson (2019).

Table 8.1 provides a comparison of the scales associated with several of the most widely used musical ability measures. This review suggests that the career assessor should be clear on the specific goals of assessment and the needs of the client when measuring musical ability. Identifying the presence of musical ability is a different task from differentiating among the gradations of talent for those already identified as musically gifted. As part of a "standard" abilities battery (about which, more later), inclusion of a test such as the Gordon AMMA with adults or youth can be helpful in assessing basic abilities in music. A more elaborate (and sometimes customized) battery may be needed when assessing individuals who have known musical talents.

TABLE 8.1. Comparison of Seashore, Wing, and Gordon Musical Tests

Component	Seashore	Wing	Gordon
Rhythm	Rhythm Are two series of notes the same or different? If different, which is preferred?	Rhythmic accent Are two series of notes the same? If different, which is preferred?	Rhythm imagery Tempo: Is the tempo in two passages of music the same or different? Meter: Are the accents the same or different in two passages of music?
Tone	Tonal memory Which note in the second of two sets has been changed?	Memory test Are 30 pairs of melodies the same or different? If different, which note was changed?	Tonal imagery Melody: Is a second passage with added notes the same or different from the first if the added notes were removed? Harmony: Similar to tonal imagery melody except that bass as well as melody present. If added notes in second playing were removed, would the lower voice be the same?
Pitch	Pitch Is a second note higher or lower in pitch than the first?	Pitch change Are two chords the same, or is the second pitched higher or lower?	
Chord Analysis		Chord analysis How many notes are present in a series of chords?	
Loudness	Loudness Which of two notes is loudest?	Intensity Are two series of notes equally loud? If not, which is preferred?	
Timbre	Timbre Are two tones the same or different in tonal quality?	Harmony Are two series of notes harmonized the same? If not, which is preferred?	
Timing	Time Is the second tone longer or shorter than the first?		
Phrasing		Phrasing Rhythmic, accent, harmony, intensity and phrasing. (All have an evaluative and aesthetic component.)	Musical sensitivity Style: Which of two tempos is best? Phrasing: Which of two endings is more desirable? Balance: Which of two endings to a passage is more desirable?

It remains true, however, that musical talent in a particular application (e.g., playing the flute or singing) may still need to be evaluated for admission to music schools by including portfolios of actual performances. Therefore, if the career assessor determines that musical talent is the assessee's special talent and interest, trained professionals could be used to review samples of the person's performance. However, people with musical or other artistic talents often seek out career counseling not so much to determine whether they have the talent but because they need to know what other options they might have, given the intensely competitive nature of the performing arts and the limited number of musicians and artists who are able to support themselves through their artistic efforts.

VISUAL ARTS ABILITIES

There are a diversity of visual arts occupations and identifying the relevant abilities may include abilities beyond those specific to the visual arts. A search of the O*NET for "visual artists" resulted in 254 occupations, including the 20 listed in Table 8.2.

Note that the Table 8.2 list and the longer list of "visual artistic" occupations includes many occupations that would clearly call on visual arts abilities (e.g., fine artists, graphic designers, craft artists). However, others (e.g., arts managers, librarians, and special education teachers) would appear to fall into different occupational categories, not necessarily needing visual artistic abilities to do that work. It should also be noted that the O*NET does not include visual arts abilities as a separate category. It does, however, identify some cognitive abilities (e.g., spatial) that have relevance, and several sensory abilities that would appear related to art. These included depth perception and visual color discrimination (see National Center for O*NET Development, 2019b).

Visual artistic performance and its origins have been studied by many researchers using a variety of research paradigms (see Winner, 1997). Some of this research is not recent, often focused on very high levels of artistic talent/giftedness or on well-established, eminent artists, and has generally been based on small samples. Those limitations aside, some of the research about visual artistic talent provides evidence for an artistic ability profile that, to some extent, appears to cut across novices and well-established artists. Still, much of the currently available research has focused primarily on fine artists, reproductive drawing ability, and art teaching, leaving many occupations presumably requiring visual-artistic talents (as in the O*NET list) unstudied.

Some of the more interesting research on artistic abilities has focused on what can be learned from the neuropsychology of accomplished, well-functioning artists (e.g., Chatterjee, 2004, 2015; Solso, 2000) and those functioning less well, including those artists who have experienced brain damage (e.g., Chiarello & Schweiger, 1985). There have also been some cases in which individuals who were previously not artistically talented suffered brain damage and

TABLE 8.2. Visual Artists O*NET Interest Matches

Code	Occupation
27-1013.00	Fine Artists, Including Painters, Sculptors, and Illustrators
25-9011.00	Audio-Visual and Multimedia Collections Specialists
27-1014.00	Multimedia Artists and Animators
27-1019.00	Artists and Related Workers, All Other
27-1011.00	Art Directors
25-1121.00	Art, Drama, and Music Teachers, Postsecondary
13-1011.00	Agents and Business Managers of Artists, Performers, and Athletes
29-1122.01	Low Vision Therapists, Orientation and Mobility Specialists, and Vision Rehabilitation Therapists
27-4032.00	Film and Video Editors
25-2032.00	Career/Technical Education Teachers, Secondary School
27-1024.00	Graphic Designers
27-1026.00	Merchandise Displayers and Window Trimmers
25-2022.00	Middle School Teachers, Except Special and Career/Technical Education
25-2031.00	Secondary School Teachers, Except Special and Career/Technical Education
25-4021.00	Librarians
25-4031.00	Library Technicians
27-1012.00	Craft Artists
25-2052.00	Special Education Teachers, Kindergarten and Elementary School
27-4011.00	Audio and Video Equipment Technicians
39-5091.00	Makeup Artists, Theatrical and Performance

Note. Reprinted from *Search Results for "Visual Artists,"* by National Center for O*NET Development, 2019a (https://www.onetonline.org/find/quick?s=visual+artists). CC BY 4.0.

then developed new expertise in the visual arts (see, e.g., Midorikawa & Kawamura, 2015; B. L. Miller et al., 1998). Studying individual cases of accomplished artists with known brain disorders (e.g., the sequelae from a stroke affecting right hemisphere functions) can help localize what specific brain structures or functions are involved with visual arts work. Also making important contributions to understanding artistic abilities are studies with children that differentiate the artistic abilities of normal children (for whom art is of near-universal interest) from the approach and skills of those children who are precocious in art. Finally, there are many studies and reported cases of artistic savants, especially those with autism spectrum disorders (A. W. Snyder & Thomas, 1997; Zaidel, 2016).

Reproductive drawing ability is important for visual artists. Talented young artists come naturally to it and generally have that capability even if they go on to become abstract artists. But even that ability appears to be different from creative artistry such that strong reproductive drawing skill may not be sufficient to be a creative artist. Getzels's and Csikszentmihalyi's (1976) still-noteworthy study of art students identified the importance of differentiating between those able to do well with a presented problem (e.g., creating a graphic illustration for marketing a product) and being able to devise a new solution to an artistic task. For the latter, they noted the importance of "problem finding," which requires the artist to define the problem to be worked on as well as its solution. This may imply that different abilities (or additional ones) are required for artistic "re-creation" versus art that is novel and judged to be creative or innovative.

Although current thinking about the laterality of brain functioning is changing from a static view to a more dynamic one (see, e.g., Geschwind & Galaburda, 1985b), success in art may be associated with relatively superior visual thinking ability (normatively, but not exclusively, likely to be associated with right-hemisphere functions). Also of note, several studies have reported that left-handedness is overrepresented among visual artists. Peterson (1979) reported a tendency for students in design, art, and architecture (and, to a lesser extent, engineering) to exceed the expected rate of left-handedness and (Peterson & Lansky, 1980) for left-handed architecture students to be overrepresented among highly rated students. Mebert and Michel (1980) also found a group of art students to have higher-than-expected rates of left-handedness, both compared with the general population and to a comparison group of similarly aged nonartists. Left-handedness appeared in this study to be associated with greater "visual thinking" ability, contrasted with those students whose approach was more "cognitive-conceptual." Other studies have not found support for left-handedness being overrepresented in particular occupations (see Cosenza & Mingoti, 1993). These differences may be part of a larger pattern that left-handedness may be associated with higher levels of spatial than verbal abilities (see, e.g., Natsopoulos et al., 1992).

Artistic talents, like many, manifest early. Meier (1942), who developed an early and widely used measure of artistic talent (the Meier Art Judgment Test), noted that in his study of 40 artists "of significance," all had been producing art at an early age. Winner (1996), one of the major contemporary researchers of artistic talent, along with her colleagues, have similarly found the early emergence of artistic talent. J. E. Drake and Winner (2012) identified several characteristics of youth who were highly talented in the visual arts. They noted that they have particularly strong observational and perceptual skills. They are

> able to just see the shapes of things, including the distortions that occur as objects recede into depth and diminish in size. A typical child might see a road as having parallel sides because she knows that a road's edges are parallel, whereas an artistically gifted child overrides her knowledge about the road and sees its sides converging in the distance. (J. E. Drake & Winner, 2012, para. 12)

J. E. Drake and Winner (2012) also found that those gifted in art as children (who may or may not become recognized domain experts or "game changers" as adults) typically demonstrated self-taught early abilities to draw realistically, were very focused on art, and had an intense drive to master artistic performance.

Most such children who showed early achievement in arts, talented though they might be, do not persist into adult careers as notable artists. Those who become domain creative as adults, in addition to being highly independent and driven to do art, are high risk takers and more susceptible to stress and mood disorders. As Winner (1996) put it in differentiating youthful art prodigies and impactful domain artists, "You don't have to want to be gifted. You either are or you are not. You do have to want to be creative [as an adult]. You have to be motivated to want to leave your mark on a domain" (p. 13).

Dimensionality of the Construct

Gardner (1983/2011), himself a well-recognized researcher on the development of artistic abilities (see Gardner, 1973, 1982a), did not identify artistic ability as a separate "intelligence" in his model of multiple intelligences, although he did address artistic talents in discussing his concept of "spatial intelligence."

A number of early abilities researchers did address the visual arts (see Dreps, 1933). Vernon (1961/2014) grouped visual artistic abilities under the category of aesthetic discrimination. R. B. Cattell (1987; Hakstian & Cattell, 1978b; Hakstian et al., 1982) identified both aesthetic judgment ability (the ability to "detect examples of adherence to basic principles of good art or designing"; Hakstian et al., 1982, p. 7) and representational drawing ability ("the ability to draw accurate reproductions of stimulus figures"; Hakstian et al., 1982, p. 8) as separable primary abilities. Interestingly, the representational drawing ability loaded on a Visualization Capacity factor, whereas aesthetic judgment ability had its highest loading on a factor labeled General Retrieval Capacity and was described as the "capacity for the retrieval of concepts or items from long-term memory storage" (Hakstian & Cattell, 1978b, p. 663). Pawlik (1966) did not specifically identify art abilities in his model of cognition and aptitudes but did identify a "visual thinking" cluster of aptitude variables that were associated with speed of perception, spatial visualization, and gestalt perception. Similarly, Cattell's constructs refer to the capacity for re-creative art or drawing, not necessarily the ability to create new works of art that will be recognized as substantial or significant.

As with the early music studies, much of this work was done at what is now Iowa State University. Meier (1939, 1942) led these efforts. Six factors were suggested from the work of Meier and his colleagues: aesthetic intelligence (an aggregation of other primary abilities), aesthetic judgment, creative imagination, perceptual facility (the ability to observe and recall sensory experiences), manual skill, and finally, energy output and perseveration.

Dewar's (1938) early analysis of the factor structure associated with a number of art ability measures (e.g., the Meier-Seashore, the McAdory Art Test, and the Bulley and Burt "postcards" of art judgment [Bulley, 1933]) reported only a single artistic factor in a sample of high school women. However, Meier (1939, 1942) and most subsequent investigators have reported a number of dimensions believed to be important in artistic production. These included aesthetic judgment ("probably the most important single factor"; Meier, 1942, p. 156), creative imagination, perceptual facility (sensitivity to the visual world), greater absorption and retention of visual materials, drawing skills, manual and motor skills, at least average intelligence, perseverance, and high levels of energy and persistence. Meier's "aesthetic judgment" (or aesthetic sensitivity) has been identified by several researchers as being important (see, e.g., Dreps, 1933). Meier (1928) defined the construct as

> the ability to recognize compositional excellence in representative art-situations, or the ability to sense quality in an aesthetic organization. It is the ability which . . . artists manifest, to arrange, to re-arrange, and to select, the arrangement superior in organization; also to know when a composition has in it too much or too little, when the light and shade relations are correct, and when its elements are in conformity with the principles of aesthetic structure. (p. 185)

Getzels's and Csikszentmihalyi's (1976) work also suggested that artistic ability encompasses a number of dimensions, including aesthetics, problem finding and solution, as well as spatial skill in perceiving and manipulating objects. Getzels and Csikszentmihalyi's study also confirmed that there are differences among those who specialize in one aspect of art or another (e.g., graphic art vs. fine arts). Hermelin and O'Connor (1986), in a small-sample study, found that 12- to 14-year-old participants gifted in art or mathematics had superior visual recognition memory compared with IQ-matched subjects and that the artistic youth were especially good at constructive imagination, given very few cues, whereas the mathematical youth exceeded all groups in solving verbally presented spatial problems. Rosenblatt and Winner (1988) examined the importance of visual memory for artists and nonartists. They also found that artistically able students had better incidental visual memory (i.e., the capacity to recall visual information when that was not part of the instructional task) for two-dimensional (although not for three-dimensional) tasks. They also noted that visually gifted children (for whom art would be one manner of directing the ability) possess a variety of skills, including focused attention, visual-motor mastery allowing for representational accuracy, aesthetic abilities, and creativity allowing unusual compositions to be produced.

A different approach to identifying the components of visual artistic performance was used by J. E. Drake and Winner (2012, 2013). These researchers identified several characteristics associated with precocious visual artists. These included (a) well-developed reproductive drawing ability usually manifested before age two; (b) intense interest in art; (c) ability to use decorative and colorful expression in art; (d) well-developed perceptual skills and attention to the parts, not just to the whole (so-called local processing); (e) a great drive to create and be original; and (f) intrinsic motivation with what the authors labeled as a "rage to master." These characteristics may predict to those who become outstanding artists as adults, but of course there are many artistic pursuits that do not require such high-level skills. Whether people have manifested some (or all) of these characteristics in youth does not necessarily mean they can become artists as adults. Clearly, this listing crosses both personality and ability measures but suggests some of the specific abilities that may be entailed in visual arts abilities and, by implication, speak to relevant artistic ability dimensions.

Relation to Other Abilities

Artistic ability has consistently been demonstrated to be related to spatial abilities (Gardner, 1983/2011; Getzels and Csikszentmihalyi, 1976; Lowman et al., 1985). More recent findings are consistent in finding a relationship between artistic and spatial-perceptual ability, but Chamberlain et al. (2018) found that the particular approaches to the measurement of perceptual abilities mattered. In this study, experts' ratings of artistic drawings were correlated with nonverbal intelligence, mental rotations spatial ability, and a cognitive styles (field dependence/independence) measure.

The relation between artistic ability and general intelligence has also been considered. Although some studies (e.g., Bryan, 1942; Farnsworth & Issei, 1931; Tiebout & Meier, 1936; see also J. E. Drake & Winner, 2012) found little relationship between art abilities and intelligence, other studies (Parvathi & Natarajan, 1985) have found such a relationship. In seeking to explain why competing results have been obtained, it may matter who is being tested (children vs. adults), which measure of intelligence is being used (verbal vs. nonverbal), which particular visual arts tests were used, and the particular sample from which participants have been drawn. Furnham and Chamorro-Premuzic (2004) found that art judgment was correlated with intelligence but not art experience (consisting of interests, activities, and knowledge). That artistic ability can be independent of general intellectual abilities is illustrated by the finding of artistic savants, that is, those with highly developed artistic ability but seriously impaired intellectual abilities, including those with virtually no language skills. N. O'Connor and Hermelin (1987), for example, found that in small samples of persons with normal and subnormal intelligence compared with matched groups who did and did not have artistic drawing ability, cognitive ability mattered for pattern recognition and matching tasks, but not for drawing. The artistic work of savants on the autistic spectrum, however, is often characterized as being technically adequate or even distinguished but not innovative. As Zaidel (2016) noted, "Their works are spatially correct but there is not much to see by way of creativity" (p. 215).

In the case of persons with dementia or Alzheimer's disease, research has demonstrated severe deterioration of artistic ability in some well-established artists (e.g., J. L. Cummings & Zarit, 1987; B. L. Miller & Hou, 2004). Conversely, case studies (Chakravarty, 2011) have noted the sudden expression of artistic abilities among patients who prior to the disease had manifested neither evidence of artistic talent or interest. Some cases (e.g., Miller et al., 1998) experienced a freeing up of established artists' work despite major deterioration in language and other cognitive functions (Mell et al., 2003). These findings suggest complex patterns of artistic talent among people with brain disease and potentially will help to identify more about the biological and neurological bases of artistic abilities.

Occupational Applications

Because people with artistic abilities are often selected for training, jobs, or assignments on the basis of work samples, abilitiy and interest measures may best be used as a preliminary screen of artistic talents but are probably not a good substitute for work samples. Predictive validity studies of some of the major measures of art ability are variable as to the quality, sufficiency, or recency. Carroll (1933), for example, found reasonably high correlations between Meier Art Judgment Test (MAJT; then called the Meier Seashore Art Judgment test) scores and art teacher ratings and found that this measure was superior to the McAdory Art Test on this criterion. H. O. Barrett (1949) found the MAJT to have some value in predicting to the criterion of expert evaluation of actual artwork but to have less value in this prediction than school grades. Meier's (1928) original research on the measure revealed that it differentiated appropriately among criterion groups, with art faculty scoring the highest. A weighted battery of tests was recommended, including aesthetic judgment, values, spatial ability, and interests.

Artistic performance, as with music, likely encompasses a number of specific abilities. G. Clark and Zimmerman's (1983; see also G. Clark & Zimmerman, 1984) review of 70 years of studies on the identification of artistic talent concluded that no single ability factor is associated with artistic talent and that measurement of diverse characteristics must therefore be made. As Zaidel (2016) wrote,

> When Monet painted the same object under varying degrees of sunlight, it is hard to see how his understanding, analysis, and talent of execution of those effects were critically dependent on good spatial perception and mentation. Placing a dab of one color here and another color there to deliberatively connote the interaction of light and object may only mildly require the use of spatial relationship skills. Similarly, mixing of colors on a painter's palette to obtain just the desired pigment is not necessarily related to spatial knowledge. Other features in Monet's paintings do indeed depend on spatial skills; the use of convergence and linear perspective would reflect such dependence. (p. 214)

The exact nature of which specific abilities matter and for what specific type of visual arts are not yet well settled, but there are some general trends. This is partly because there is little agreement on what measures to use to identify abilities in the visual arts. What can be said with some consensus concerning the abilities themselves is that, in the visual arts, the following have been demonstrated to be relevant: perceptual and observational skills, aesthetic judgement, spatial abilities, field independence, and visual memory skills. Visual reasoning ability, which calls on both perceptual and cognitive abilities, may include geometric reasoning ability. Whether specific abilities alone are sufficient for artistic performance or are rather part of a profile that must also include interests and personality is further discussed later in the book.

Measurement Issues

Measurement issues in the visual arts are complex. The first question needing to be considered is once again the purpose of the career assessment. An assessor working in the context of evaluating prospective or current art students has a different task than one who is working in a general career assessment context. For the assessment of individuals with known, or likely, talent in the visual arts, more sophisticated assessments will be needed than for a general assessment population.

As with assessment of musical talent, testing for visual arts talent generated considerable interest in the first half of the 20th century and then fell off. Most of the early efforts at visual arts talent assessment did not fare well when scientifically validated, and others were not kept up. As G. Clark and Zimmerman (1984) noted,

> The 1920s, 1930s, and 1940s . . . [were] a period of active test developing in the visual arts. Standardized and idiosyncratic tests designed by researchers became available for research about visual arts abilities. . . . None of [these tests] however, has been shown to be satisfactory as a test for aptitude or ability in the visual arts . . . by the end of the 1940s aptitude and ability tests in the visual arts had come to a halt. (p. 322)

The Barron-Welsh Art Scale (BWAS; Barron & Welsh, 1952), which consists of a series of black-and-white figures, each of which the respondent is simply asked to indicate liking or disliking, is still available and used. Barron was a major contributor to the study of creativity and art (see, e.g., Barron, 1972). A number of studies have appeared over the years using the BWAS. Rosen (1955), for example, administered the test to a group of art students at a university, established artists, and nonartists. Although the scores did not differentiate between established artists and those in training, they did differentiate both groups from nonartists. Additionally, test scores for the art students were moderately (0.40) correlated with faculty ratings of a single work of art by each student.

The question of whether a preference for complex versus simpler drawings reflects artistic talent is not settled. Using a male student sample, Eysenck and Castle (1970) concluded that greater complexity of stimuli was not the sole differentiator between artistic/creative individuals and those who were not, and that high scorers' results may reflect a rejection of conventionality rather than the presence of originality. However, in a comprehensive review of 40 years of research on the BWAS, Gough et al. (1996) did find that high scorers tended to choose complex and asymmetrical designs. Further, persons with high scores on the test tended to have a personality profile often associated with creativity. Correlates included "imaginativeness, unconventionality, independence, intuitiveness, and ego strength, along with impulsivity, rebelliousness, and touchiness" (Gough et al., 1996, p. 280). Accessibility to primary, unconscious processes versus logical and reality-bound ones also differentiated higher versus lower BWAS scorers. Although this test is not necessarily an appropriate measure for all types of creativity, its relevance for assessing aesthetic judgment does make it appropriate for inclusion in visual arts abilities.

Other measures of artistic ability are also available, particularly in research contexts. Clark's Drawing Abilities Test (G. Clark, 1989; G. Clark & Wilson, 1991) was developed over an extensive period primarily for use in evaluating prospective art students in gifted/talented programs. This test involves respondents making actual drawings with written instructions (e.g., drawing a picture of an interesting house from the perspective of viewing it from across the street) that are then scored against standardized criteria. It is viewed by its author as being a measure of art achievement and therefore it may be less suitable to use as part of a general career assessment battery. Although not specific to measurement in the visual arts, a special issue (Barbot & Reiter-Palmon, 2019) of the *Psychology of Aesthetics, Creativity, and the Arts* journal focused on the challenges and some solutions to the difficult problems associated with creativity assessment (particularly when measuring creative products). The issue is mostly relevant for research purposes but raises important issues relevant for assessment in any area of creativity.

In a general career assessment battery, abilities in the visual arts can best be assessed by using several ability measures. These include spatial ability, nonverbal intelligence, and some perceptual measures (such as flexibility of closure), aesthetic judgement (such as measured with the BWAS), and some type of reproductive drawing ability (such as with Clark's Drawing Ability Test). Such measures are also relevant for evaluating visual arts abilities for school-related or avocational arts activities (see Diedrich, Jauk, et al., 2018). Because creative careers in fine visual arts can be highly competitive, pursuit of such occupations may also depend on motivation and ambition, so personality measures would also be relevant (see Chapters 13–16).

OTHER ARTISTIC-RELATED ABILITIES

Briefly identified here are some other artistic/creative abilities associated with certain occupations.

Writing

Writing requires an assortment of abilities including general mental ability (GMA), verbal fluency, logical reasoning, verbal expression, and independent judgement. Creative writing also calls for social acuity (empathy, understanding others' motives), imagination, and access to unconscious processes. As a group, writers are often rated near the top of various lists of the average intelligence scores found among members of occupational groups (R. B. Cattell, 1987; Matarazzo, 1972; see also Wallace & Walberg, 1987; S. W. Williams et al., 1938). However, although high levels of intelligence would be an expected characteristic of writers, studies supporting such conclusions are limited.

Moreover, one would expect to find within-groups occupational differences among different types of writers. Groups of writers, for example, whose job involves both extensive social contact and writing (e.g., journalists), may have a different profile than writers whose job involves highly independent, solitary activities. The O*NET grouped together poets, lyricists, and creative writers (National Center for O*NET Development, 2019h). Identified abilities for this group included written expression, fluency of ideas, originality, written comprehension, and near vision. Editors had a very similar list except for adding oral comprehension and oral expression and, curiously, omitting near vision. (National Center for O*NET Development, 2019g). The ability profile for journalists and correspondents was also similar to editors but added speech clarity (National Center for O*NET Development, 2019f).

Other ability factors expected to relate to writing include planning and goal-directedness (Ackerman & Smith, 1988; J. R. Hayes & Flower, 1986; Wallace & Walberg, 1987). Expert writers incorporate abilities involving the creation of prose and those of an internal "critic" that enables them to shape and direct what is written (Townsend, 1986). For nonfiction writers at least, so-called domain knowledge (i.e., content knowledge) is also relevant and can be differentiated from being able to express this knowledge in understandable words (McCutchen, 1986); the latter implicitly makes use of knowledge of writing or textual structure (see Englert et al., 1988). This factor and its complexity are noted by writer Annie Dillard (1989):

> Every book has an intrinsic impossibility, which its writer discovers as soon as his first excitement dwindles. The problem is structural; it is insoluble. . . . Complex stories, essays and poems have this problem, too—the prohibitive structural defect the writer wishes he had never noticed. [The writer] writes it in spite of that . . . [finding] ways to minimize the difficulty; . . . [strengthening] other virtues; . . . cantilever[ing] the whole narrative out of this air and it holds. (p. 23)

Nonability factors associated with writing include tolerance of working conditions that often include isolation. For many occupations involving writing, there is a need for self-direction, self-discipline, and being able to work for long hours on one's own (see Chapters 13–16).

Dance

On the ability side, a high level of several physical and kinesthetic primary abilities is clearly required for dance, but as discussed in the physical abilities section, few standardized assessment measures are available that are specific to this type of work. The O*NET identifies the following abilities as being associated with dance: (a) gross body coordination, defined as "the ability to coordinate the movement of your arms, legs, and torso together when the whole body is in motion"; (b) extent flexibility, "the ability to bend, stretch, twist, or reach with your body, arms, and/or legs"; (c) stamina, "the ability to exert yourself physically over long periods of time without getting winded or out of breath"; (d) dynamic strength, "the ability to exert muscle force repeatedly or continuously over time . . . [involving] endurance and resistance to muscle fatigue"; and (e) gross body equilibrium, "the ability to keep or regain your body balance or stay upright when in an unstable position" (National Center for O*NET Development, 2019e, Abilities section). It is unlikely that an evaluation of this extensive list of physical abilities could be incorporated into a general career assessment protocol.

In addition to kinesthetic and physical abilities, dancers have been reported to be unusually sensitive to the perception of movement and oriented toward feeling and intuition (Kincel & Murray, 1984). Other relevant abilities include memory skills, including for movements (Kogan, 2002), and spatial and temporal processing abilities (Ladda et al., 2020). These contribute to their ability to coordinate movement with music.

Dancers face particular challenges over time. Their careers are typically short (Pickman, 1987) and injury prone (Nilsson et al., 2001). Nevertheless, they tend to see themselves as participating in an important undertaking with a likely early demise (Kogan, 2002). On the negative side, many dancers are preoccupied with weight, body condition, and food, may have experienced delayed menarche, amenorrhea, anorexic disturbances, and preoccupation with food commonly reported in the literature (Arcelus et al., 2014; Braisted et al., 1985; Brooks-Gunn et al., 1987; Hincapié & Cassidy, 2010; Lowenkopf & Vincent, 1982). Taken collectively, these factors identify a stressful, physically and emotionally demanding occupation that nonetheless attracts far more people than can be accommodated in it.

Acting

The essence of acting involves publicly assuming the identity of someone else and making that character believable and engaging to others (Barron, 1972). This calls for high levels of empathy in relating to a character by assuming the character's thoughts, feelings, and actions. According to the O*NET, the abilities associated with acting include oral expression, oral comprehension, memorization, speech clarity, and written comprehension, in other words verbal intelligence and memory along with speaking abilities (National Center for O*NET Development, 2019d). All of these abilities seem reasonable but would not appear to constitute a comprehensive list. As with dance, physical abilities are required for many actors in that they use their bodies as an important part of their work. They are required to capture and communicate the essence of a character, using all parts of themselves, including their bodies, feelings, and voices. Actors, as a group, also have demonstrated generally high levels of empathy (see discussion of social abilities in Chapter 9). In a chapter related to the effects of practice versus inherent talent in acting, T. Noice and Noice (2013) discussed aspects both similar to those mentioned and additional to them. They identified the concept of "being fully present in the moment" as being "the heart of great theater" (T. Noice & Noice, 2013, p. 315). The component parts of this skill went beyond memory, unquestionably an important element. For example, they described what they called "embodied cognition" to describe actors' needed ability to integrate language, thought, memory, and motor/sensory abilities. Actors need to take written text, lines from a script, to make a character come alive and be believable. One relevant ability involves the actor's ability to experience and to convey the mental-emotional-physical aspects of a character (T. Noice & Noice, 2013). As they noted, "The art of acting has been defined as the ability to live truthfully under imaginary circumstances" (H. Noice & Noice, 2006, p. 14).

Although this is more an issue of personality than ability (see Chapter 14), neuroticism is commonly found among actors (Nettle, 2006a). It is difficult to know the extent to which the acting process per se attracts those with preexisting emotional maladjustment or whether the continual unemployment and underemployment so commonly found in the profession contribute to the creation of anxiety and other psychological difficulties. More generally, contextual variables with which actors must often cope include the willingness and capacity to manage chronic employment uncertainty; long, often evening work hours when employed; and, on average, low wages. This means that acting for many will never be a full-time job and additional work will likely be required to survive financially. T. Noice and Noice (2013) noted the paucity of success even among talented actors by citing a highly experienced professor at a well-respected university theater program who estimated that only about 1% of the graduates of that program had the talent to be able to compete with well-established actors.

Miscellaneous Areas

Scant but incipient psychological research attention has been aimed at abilities associated with other performing arts, such as comedy (Fisher & Fisher, 1981; Greengross & Miller, 2009; Sheppard, 1985) and specialized artistic talents such as sculpting, pottery making, graphic design, and so forth, or with subtypes of artistic talent (e.g., poets vs. nonfiction writers). That there are important differences among various subgroups of artistic occupations is suggested by the research of Helson (1978). She found important personality differences among writers and critics of children's books. The critics were found to be more socially ascendant and conventional, whereas the writers were less conventional and more in touch with alternative states of consciousness.

Few primary abilities are uniquely relevant to nonmusical and nonartistic areas of creative performance. Although Mumford and Gustafson (1988) made a valuable effort to identify a "creativity syndrome" that would cut across multiple types of creativity, their emphasis was more on characteristics of personality that influenced creativity than on abilities per se. In activities such as creative writing, acting, and dance, with the latter two being illustrative of the performing arts, there are probably unique abilities that are necessary for successful performance in each profession. Such abilities have been largely unidentified and unexamined, however, and certainly popular and widely studied primary abilities (e.g., spatial, verbal reasoning) have yet to be applied systematically to these areas.

From a career assessment perspective, work in many creative occupations raises complicated issues. Although many aspire to such fields, few will succeed (see, e.g., Kogan, 1990; P. Thomson & Jaque, 2016). Additionally, compared with other occupational groups, it is more difficult to obtain representative samples because there are relatively fewer individuals in the performing artist domain (see L. S. Gottfredson, 1980), suggesting that some research findings have to be conservatively interpreted. Another factor is geographic. Many who make a living with creative abilities must often reside in large metropolitan areas sometimes quite distant from the assessee's current location. It is necessary to consider practical factors when considering "best fit" creative occupations.

Moreover, as with architecture, performing arts professions may combine at least two major and somewhat divergent types of abilities, as well as personality and interest factors. Thus, what may differentiate a dancer from a professional athlete may not so much be the exact physical abilities required (which may, at least for certain types of athletics, not be dissimilar from those needed in dance) but rather the artistic interests and a pattern of what is termed here, for lack of clarifying literature, a personality characteristic (see Chapter 5). In some cases the personality characteristic becomes like an ability. For example, actors may need the self-centered, somewhat narcissistic capacity to rely on one's self as the medium to translate a creative "problem" into an artistic expression or solution (see Csikszentmihalyi, 1996). MacKinnon (1962) differentiated scientific and artistic creativity. The former involves translating and integrating knowledge associated with externally defined reality, whereas many types of artistic creativity requires using one's self to create a new reality. Thus, a quasi-ability (in fact, a hybrid ability-personality construct) potentially differentiating many performing artistic ability patterns may be the intense focus on self as the means for creating.

Csikszentimhalyi (1996, 1997) also contributed to the literature the concept of "optimal" or "flow" experiences, involving intense focusing on something to the exclusion of most other things. Other characteristics (again posited in the interspace between abilities and personality characteristics to be discussed in more detail in Chapter 13) include (a) tolerance of ambiguity; (b) psychological openness to new experience (often appearing, for men, as elevations on measures of psychological femininity; see Chapter 15); (c) independence; and (d) an intrinsic motivation pattern (Amabile, 1983; Arieti, 1976; Barron, 1972; J. P. Guilford, 1950, 1959; Roe, 1946; Torrance, 1965), although sometimes the effects of intrinsic rewards are moderated by extrinsic ones (Fischer et al., 2019; Prabhu et al., 2008).

Concerning relevant nonability factors (especially affective disorders, including bipolar and major depression), psychopathology is not uncommonly found among creatively talented people, especially eminent ones (see Chapter 15; Andreasen & Canter, 1974; Andreasen & Powers, 1975; F. K. Goodwin & Jamison, 2007). To this list of common characteristics or working conditions of creative individuals can be added persistence, including in the face of known conditions of unemployment throughout what is often a brief career (see Kogan, 1990).

SUMMARY AND CONCLUSIONS

There are a variety of types of artistic performance, and the ability profile will vary depending on the particular type of creative performance. This chapter has identified abilities related to several areas of artistic performance, including musical, visual arts, writing, dance, and acting. Assessment of artistic-related abilities are recommended for inclusion as part of specialized assessment batteries, at least when working with clients with artistic interests and possible talents. For others they can be included if time and money permit. Clients typically enjoy taking these measures. Artistic abilities are domain specific, however, and other assessment approaches may be needed. Even when expanded artistic ability measures cannot be included, a generalized measure of aesthetic judgement and a short measure of verbal fluency could still be included as part of a standardized ability battery.

9

Social Abilities

Social and Emotional Intelligence

Social intelligence (SI; and its later iterations, including emotional intelligence [EI]) has been studied starting in the early 20th century. In a widely cited article called "Intelligence and Its Use" that appeared not in a journal but in *Harper's Magazine*, psychologist Edward Lee Thorndike (1920) used the term "social intelligence" to describe "the ability to understand and manage men and women, boys and girls, to act wisely in human relations" (p. 228). E. L. Thorndike suggested that SI could be differentiated from mechanical and abstract intelligence (Landy, 2005). In particular, R. L. Thorndike (1936; see also Thurstone, 1963) differentiated among three types of intelligence: abstract, cognitive intellectual abilities; practical abilities, especially those abilities relevant in working with mechanical objects; and abilities used in working with other people (the "social intelligence" construct). This would not be Edward Thorndike's only foray into the popular media. Later titles he published in *Harper's Magazine* included "The Psychology of the Half-Educated Man" (1920), "The Psychology of Labor" (1922), and "The Psychology of the Profit Motive" (1936). SI, however, was not a major interest of E. L. Thorndike, who was an influential animal and learning research psychologist at Columbia University. Among his many other contributions in that role was the "law of effect," a classic environmentalist position which held that any behavior that is followed by positive consequences is likely to be repeated, and any behavior followed by adverse consequences is likely to be stopped. But beyond the widely cited *Harper's Magazine* general audience article, E. L. Thorndike did not really study SI. As Landy (2005) put it, "To say that 'social

https://doi.org/10.1037/0000254-010
Career Assessment: Integrating Interests, Abilities, and Personality, by R. L. Lowman
Copyright © 2022 by the American Psychological Association. All rights reserved.

intelligence' was central to E. L. Thorndike's view of intellectual ability would be akin to saying that Italian food is central to the Pope's view on social justice" (p. 414).

There was indeed a Thorndike who conducted empirical research on SI, but his name was Robert Ladd (R. L.) Thorndike, Edward Thorndike's son. R. L. Thorndike had been a professor at George Washington University (GWU) for 2 years before moving on to his father's university, Columbia, where, like his father, he also received his PhD in psychology). While at GWU, R. L. Thorndike published research on a measure called the Social Intelligence Test (Moss et al., 1930) and later, in its second edition, the George Washington University Test of Social Intelligence (T. Hunt et al., 1955). This test included subtests of Social Judgement, Recognition of Mental States, Observation of Human Behavior, Memory for Names and Faces, and Sense of Humor (T. Hunt, 1928). However, when factor analyzed along with cognitive ability subtests (e.g., Vocabulary and General Intelligence), it was highly saturated with cognitive ability (see Strang, 1930a, 1930b; R. L. Thorndike, 1936; R. L. Thorndike & Stein, 1937), and R. L Thorndike appears to have gone on to other areas of interest.

There continued to be intermittent but persistent interest in SI for several decades after this somewhat shaky start but rather little systematic study. O'Sullivan and Guilford (1966) developed a four-factor measure of SI. It was also believed by many clinicians that the Picture Arrangement subtest of the widely used Wechsler intelligence tests (Sipps et al., 1987; Zimmerman et al., 1973) was a good measure of social abilities, though that assumption has been challenged (e.g., J. M. Campbell & McCord, 1996; Nobo & Evans, 1986). Some scattered research was also published on other SI tests including the Social Participation Scale (Chapin, 1939) and the Social Insight Scale (Chapin, 1942). A revised measure, the Tests of Social Intelligence, measured Guilford's six factors of behavioral cognition (O'Sullivan & Guilford, 1975). Another method differentiated between knowledge of normative behavior and ability to predict peoples' behavior across situations (Sechrest & Jackson, 1961). Hoffman (1981) distinguished between how people understand things and how they understand other people; the latter (which Hoffman considered to be an innate ability) developed on the basis of affect, which, through empathy, allows one to understand what other people are feeling. Getter and Nowinski (1981) developed a measure of social abilities focused on self-reported behavior. Respondents on the Interpersonal Problem Solving Ability Test (IPSAT) were presented a series of scenarios that were inherently conflictual and for which they had to identify as many ways that they could think of to handle the situation and then to designate the one response that they would actually do in response to the situation. The responses chosen as being most likely to actually do were scored using a set of objective criteria as to whether they were effective, avoidant, dependent, inappropriate, or unscorable. There were also studies (e.g., Tenopyr, 1967) in this period exploring criterion validity evidence for some of the SI measures. None of these measures really caught on and it was not until the 1980s and beyond that the constructs related to SI really became of widespread interest.

Given the role that Thondike's foray into the popular literature played in generating research in SI, it is ironic that contemporary sustained interest in research and applications of SI were jump-started by two major publishing events that led to the explosion of popular and research interest in the modern instantiations of the construct.

In 1983, Gardner's book on multiple intelligences was published (Gardner, 1983/2011). It included among its list of "intelligences" the "personal intelligences" that were described as including both intrapersonal and interpersonal aspects. The former allows people to have access to, and awareness of, their internal affects or emotions and the latter describing an external facing aspect by which people can discern feelings and reactions in others. Gardner's work became wildly popular, though it has not yet inspired much empirical assessment using traditional psychometric measures.

A second major influential event was the publication in 1995 of Goleman's best-selling book *Emotional Intelligence: Why It Can Matter More Than IQ*. Goleman is a psychologist and social science journalist, and, as the book's title suggests, his book was directed to a general audience, rather than to a technical or research one. That it remained on the *New York Times* best seller list for a year and a half speaks to the popular interest the book engendered. (Ironically, as the scientific field has moved from SI to EI, Goleman later wrote another popular trade book called *Social Intelligence: The New Science of Human Relationships* [Goleman, 2006], whose cover touted "Beyond IQ, Beyond Emotional Intelligence" and "The Revolutionary New Science of Human Relations.")

Since this renewed attention to what were not new concepts, both research and applied interest—and particularly applications—have exploded. One does not have to go far on the internet to find vendors with outsized promises, for example, "The 3-Second Trick to Improve your EQ"; "Test Your Emotional Intelligence, Free EQ Quiz, EI Test"; "High EQ People Are Happier | Meditation Can Boost Your EQ"; and "Emotional Intelligence Classes | Transform Your Life with EQ."

In addition to all the popular hype, there have been some rigorous research studies on competing ways to define and measure the focal EI constructs and to assess their relevance for work and careers. This research has typically been conducted in the context of predicting work-related outcomes and addressing the question of whether EI adds incremental predictive power to general intelligence (and other clearly cognitive variables) in predicting job performance. With the growing interest of researchers, particularly in industrial–organizational (I–O) psychology, a robust—but by no means final—literature has emerged, though results are necessarily dependent on which conceptual approach and which measures are used.

THEORETICAL AND CONCEPTUAL ISSUES

The early literature on EI/SI had been criticized for (a) the failure to define the constructs consistently across studies, (b) an overreliance on paper-and-pencil measures, and (c) a relative absence of external criteria to demonstrate validity. O'Sullivan and Guilford (1976), reviewing then-available literature, concluded that "no 'social-intelligence' measure currently has the status to serve as a calibrator for any other" (O'Sullivan & Guilford, 1976, p. 13). Although this conclusion has relevance today, it is for different reasons.

Unlike in the 1970s, there are now multiple measures of EI/SI and a burgeoning literature that is generally more sophisticated but no more conclusive as related to competing models. However, a number of issues need sorting out.

One basic issue concerns whether the intent is to address social abilities or social disabilities (Lowman & Leeman, 1988). Social deficits can arise among persons who fail to develop even the minimally acceptable social skills needed for basic social intercourse (deficits in "social competence"; Hartup, 1989; see also Cartledge, 1987; Kihlstrom & Cantor, 2011). For people on the autistic spectrum, for example, which includes a number of people who work in technical positions (Grandin & Panek, 2013), social skills deficits are one of the defining characteristics of the disorder (A. S. Carter et al., 2005). An important but relatively neglected area is the career assessment of persons with such difficulties.

It should also be noted that those who have had normal or even superior interpersonal skills can later experience certain medical conditions that are associated with difficulties in social interactions. People with Alzheimer's disease may have serious social deficits accompanying their memory and other cognitive impairments. Affective disorders (including depression or bipolar disorders) can also be associated with social deficits and behavioral abnormalities (see Lowman, 1993a, 1993b).

Social abilities, even within normal ranges, can be complex. A pattern of apparent strengths may mask limitations since social abilities are not a unidimensional construct. For example, managers might be quite successful at work due to their ability to channel their hard-driving personalities into sales or to the oversight of others toward a common goal. However, they may at the same time be deficient in some of their social skills in that they are sociopathic, narcissistic, or otherwise lack empathy. Whether such deficits are simply the flip polarities of positive traits or different in kind is not fully settled, but it does seem likely that there are multiple social abilities, not a single one.

Gardner's (1983/2011; Walters & Gardner, 1986) concept of personal intelligences, emphasizing intrapersonal and interpersonal, provides a useful beginning to studying contemporary approaches to SI. He defined intrapersonal intelligences as those focusing on

> access to one's own feeling life—one's range of affects or emotions: the capacity instantly to effect discriminations among these feelings and, eventually, to label them, to enmesh them in symbolic codes, to draw upon them as a means of understanding and guiding one's behavior. (Gardner, 1983/2011, p. 239)

Interpersonal intelligence, in contrast, he stated, was "the ability to notice and make distinctions among other individuals and, in particular, among their moods, temperaments, motivations, and intentions" (italics in original removed; Gardner, 1983/2011, p. 239).

Another way to consider Gardner's approach is that these might be two dimensions of a larger social abilities construct. Psychotherapists, for example, who must be able to discern the feelings and moods of others (interpersonal) also benefit from being able to discern their own feelings and moods (intrapersonal). Aderman and Berkowitz (1983) demonstrated that the willingness to be helpful was related to self-concern: Those who were the most preoccupied with themselves were the least likely to be helpful to another in an experimental situation. This may help to explain how an unusually perceptive novelist or salesperson, whose focus is on how observed behavior relates to a personal goal or need (to write books, to make a sale), might be socially perceptive but not interpersonally adept. Nor may these be the only occupationally important dimensions of social skills. For example, Gardner's (1983/2011; Walters & Gardner, 1986) interpersonal intelligence encompasses both cognition (understanding social dynamics) and action (doing something about that knowledge). Although there may be a high correlation between knowing what to do and being able to do it, there is no reason to believe that sensitivity to others' reactions and ability to act on that sensitivity are necessarily related.

As discussed, a common criticism of all of Gardner's "intelligences" is that they have not been examined with rigorous empirical research protocols using psychometric measures (an approach to which Gardner takes objection, believing that a more qualitative approach is needed to demonstrate and understand the multiple intelligences constructs). When the concepts have been examined using quantitative methods, support for the model has, at best, been mixed (E. Hunt, 2010). Further, Gardner and his followers have tended to present more in words than in symbol sets (i.e., quantitative empirical data) so they have provided little evidence about the empirical relationship between intra- and interpersonal intelligences. Even Gardner, however, acknowledged overlap between these two personal intelligences.

The resurgence of contemporary interest in social abilities has especially been fueled by popular, general audience books but has also generated an expanding empirical literature (Hartup, 1989). The term "emotional intelligence," popularized by Goleman's (1995) book, has become widely used. But as with SI, definitions of EI have varied widely from one researcher to another. One of the largest differences has been between the conceptualization of EI/SI as a circumscribed ability to be measured like other abilities, using measures that have right-or-wrong answers, and as a broader variable crossing domains such as abilities and personality (Mayer et al., 2008).

Each of these approaches to SI/EI has both advocates and empirical measures. The former approach is typified by the Mayer–Salovey–Caruso Emotional Intelligence Test (MSCEIT; Mayer et al., 2003) and the latter by Bar-On's model of emotional-social intelligence (ESI) and its 133-item self-report measure called the EQ-i (Bar-On, 2006). Yet another approach, that of Goleman and Boyatzis (S. B. Wolff, 2005), resulted in the creation of the Emotional and

Social Competence Inventory (ECI), which was built on social competencies. "Competencies" were defined by Boyatzis (2011) as "a set of related but different sets of behavior organized around an underlying construct called the 'intent'. The behaviors are alternate manifestations of the intent, as appropriate in various situations or times" (p. 92).

These newer measures of EI/SI have helped advance understanding of these constructs and provided a basis for evaluating their effectiveness. But the validity evidence for some of these is not as robust as advocates for the respective instruments might suggest (e.g., for the MSCEIT, see Rossen et al., 2008, and Wilhelm, 2005; for the EQ-i, see Conte, 2005; and for the ECI, see Watson & Watson, 2014).

Despite these advances (summarized in Lievens & Chan, 2017), studies have found considerable overlap of these measures either with cognitive abilities (when EI is measured using an ability model) or with personality (when measured as a combination of ability and personality). Partly, the methodology employed influences obtained results. Self-ratings of EI have inherent limitations (E. Hunt, 2010). Additionally, advocates for particular measures cannot always be relied on for objective, critical reviews of their own research on their own measure versus competing ones. For example, J. D. Mayer et al. (2011) in responding to the question "What Does Emotional Intelligence Predict?" excluded any mixed-model measures and offered only a few "examples" of EI research findings, making their review, at best, selective.

Then there are those who find the entire construct problematic. Jensen (1998) rejected the construct of EI altogether, stating,

> The term "emotional intelligence" has gained momentary popularity, but it is something of a misnomer, as it is not a cognitive variable at all. It actually comprises several relatively uncorrelated personality traits, mainly management of feelings (low neuroticism), motivation, zeal, and persistence of optimism and effort in the face of obstacles and setbacks, empathy for others and the ability to read their unspoken feelings, self-awareness, and social skills. . . . What has been termed "social intelligence" is better termed social competence, or the tendency to act wisely in human relations. It is not a unitary dimension of personality, but is analyzable into a number of distinct factors (seven, in the most comprehensive study), each of which is correlated with a number of well-known personality factors. (p. 576)

E. Hunt (2010), while critical of much of the EI research to date, concluded,

> There is a good case for the existence of emotional intelligence. . . . Despite the present record [of research on EI] . . . I would not dismiss the potential contribution that [EI] may make to the study of intelligence. I suggest that these contributions will be greatest when we examine "will do" rather than "can do" performance, over a fairly long period of time, and when the performance being evaluated requires interpersonal interaction in face-to-face situations. (pp. 136, 138)

Overall, EI/SI is an area in which professional practice currently exceeds research. We cannot draw many definitive conclusions at this point as to the dimensionality of "the construct" until there is agreement on what the construct is (or, what the constructs are). Perhaps a single definition will not suffice at this point to identify the career-relevant aspects of EI/SI. The various approaches currently in use are simply not using the same concepts.

Interestingly the O*NET does not include any EI/SI abilities in its current listings. However, it does include several items under its "social skills" category (defined as "developed capacities used to work with people to achieve goals"; National Center for O*NET Development, 2018e, Skills section), which included coordinating, instructing, negotiating, persuasion, service orientation, and social perceptiveness. Under abilities, for some of the more obviously social or helping jobs like counselor, the O*NET included the following: oral and written comprehension, problem sensitivity, oral expression, and inductive reasoning. The O*NET's distinction between abilities and skills mirrors some of the variations in the currently popular ways of measuring SI/EI. In career assessment, the goal is to measure abilities (in the O*NET sense) in that these are stable characteristics of individuals that are likely to be important in career choice. Yet, the O*NET's not including EI/SI-related abilities needs to be kept in mind means that it will be necessary to drop down to the skills level to find jobs where social-interpersonal abilities are required.

DIMENSIONALITY OF THE CONSTRUCT

The question of dimensions of EI/SI speaks to the heart of what SI or EI is intending to measure or actually is measuring. Clearly, this is not a new issue. R. L. Thorndike (1936a) found very little variance unique to SI dimensions after accounting for general intelligence. Woodrow (1939), in a factor analysis of 52 ability measures, including SI abilities, found that the SI abilities primarily loaded on verbal abilities. J. P. Guilford's (1967) multidimensional model of intelligence postulated 30 different components of SI, although only four measures were ever published in a form that could be researched or used in practice (O'Sullivan & Guilford, 1976). Interestingly, those four (reduced from six; see Hendricks et al., 1969; O'Sullivan & Guilford, 1976) published measures of SI (Expression Grouping, Missing Cartoons, Social Translations, and Cartoon Predictions, which are subtests of the Social Intelligence Test) based on J. P. Guilford's models all related to the ability "to recognize or understand behavioral units, classes, relations, systems, transformations, and implications" (O'Sullivan & Guilford, 1976, p. 1) and would be expected to overlap considerably with general intelligence.

As identified in the previous section, contemporary approaches have reconceptualized and expanded older models of SI/EI but not in a consistent way. The number of factors found not surprisingly varies depending on how SI/EI is conceptualized and measured. The question of dimensionality of the construct(s) in this area is, arguably, premature until there is greater consensus on the nature of the construct(s) in EI/SI to be measured and until there is more consistency in outcome criteria (preferably behavioral ones) and in the research paradigms used to gather and evaluate validity evidence.

OCCUPATIONAL APPLICATIONS

Perhaps the most that can be concluded at this point is that there is little consensus about (a) what constitutes EI/SI; (b) whether it is sufficiently differentiated from cognitive ability or personality variables to merit separate measurement in the context of career assessment; (c) which, if any, of the popularly used and top-selling measures is an appropriate "criterion" measure to use in comparing across measures; and (d) how best to balance the competing goals of time and money of assessing in this area versus the sometimes small incremental explanatory power added by the EI/SI measures. Yet assessors may still need to measure in this area when social skills and abilities are germane to the assessment issues and important to the career path in either a positive or negative way (social abilities vs. social disabilities). In the former case, social abilities may be an (or the most) important strength. However, when a person has social skill deficits in an otherwise well-fitting career that requires interpersonal abilities for success, EI/SI assessment may be important.

Of course, occupations also may differ in the type of social abilities required. As E. Hunt (2010) noted, "A salesperson taking orders in a telephone call center for a ready-made clothing store does not have to have high [EI]; a salesperson in an expensive clothing boutique does" (p. 138). Yet this statement assumes there is just one type of EI/SI, whereas in careers the range of social skills and abilities is wide, and the models and measures offered to date do not address that diversity. Managers, ministers, and counselors, for example, need social abilities to facilitate their work, to make a sale, or to motivate others. Types of social interactions with others might include, in order of increasing complexity, talking with people face-to-face and exhibiting positive, prosocial behavior (e.g., a pleasant and efficient receptionist); assessing the reactions of others and attempting to influence those reactions (e.g., a productive salesperson); matching one's own reactions to the needs manifested by others (e.g., a teacher); and creatively influencing others by assessing their behavior, engaging others in "relationships," and transforming the behavior of others by one's own actions (e.g., a manager or salesperson). Matching the type of social skills needed in a career is a challenge still needing further research attention. Table 9.1 provides a metric for considering the types of social abilities that may be needed in particular occupations.

MEASUREMENT ISSUES

When *The Clinical Practice of Career Assessment: Interests, Abilities, and Personality* was published, it was appropriate to state that "despite a wealth of psychological literature, no tangible product suitable for routine . . . application has resulted" (Lowman, 1991, p. 106). Today, despite there being a number of popularly used measures of EI/SI, with much more validity evidence about them, none can be considered the gold standard by which others should be judged or calibrated. The ideal measure of social and interpersonal ability would overlap modestly with

TABLE 9.1. Hypothetical Taxonomy of Social Demands of Jobs

Degree of social involvement	Social job dimensions and abilities	Examples
+ + +	Interact with people > 50% of time on job; perform therapeutic, educative, or managing roles; abilities include social perception and socially appropriate behavior	Business manager, nurse, psychotherapist
+ +	Interact with people 25%–50% of time on job; although significant time is spent with others on job, the contact may be more incidental than primary	College professor, social science researcher
+	Interact with people less than 25% of time on job but in manner requiring social facilitation	High level executive
−	Interact with people in some job duties, but do so in a manner in which recognition of and manipulation of people's feelings and reactions is insignificant	Clerk in discount department store
− −	Very limited interaction with people on job; no requirement for therapeutic or influencing roles	Theoretical physicist who does not teach, novelist
− − −	Adequate social functioning is not only not required, but work setting or group is anti- or unsociable	Computer technician

general intelligence and would measure behavioral as well as cognitive and emotional aspects of EI/SI. Its validity evidence would reveal a clear pattern of differentiating between those occupational groups that, on average, score higher and lower in social skills (e.g., teachers vs. engineers) and, within an occupational group, would differentiate between groups rated high and low on social skills by competent evaluators of social abilities. A sex difference in favor of women would also be expected (e.g., Bronfenbrenner et al., 1958). The measure would identify these who can act competently in social settings, not just those who can identify the "right" thing to do in a theoretical sense. And it would differentiate between trait-like aspects of the ability and those that are trainable.

Each of the currently available—and widely used—measures of SI/EI includes positive aspects and limitations. Here, three of these are briefly reviewed.

The Mayer-Salovey-Caruso Emotional Intelligence Test (MSCEIT) approaches EI as a set of abilities in four major areas: "The ability to perceive emotions in oneself and others; to use emotions in the service of thinking and problem solving; to understand emotions and the relations among them; and to manage emotions in oneself and others" (Kihlstrom & Cantor, 2011, p. 572). This approach overlaps conceptually with Gardner's two SI "intelligences" but, unlike Gardner's, has been measured psychometrically. Issues have been raised about the general utility of the MSCEIT (e.g., Rossen et al., 2008, and Wilhelm, 2005) given the conceptual and other concerns already discussed.

Bar-On's EI instrument was based on the following conceptual model: "Emotional-social intelligence is a cross-section of interrelated emotional and social competencies, skills and facilitators that determine how effectively we understand and express ourselves, understand others and relate with them, and cope with daily demands" (Bar-On, 2006, p. 3). The EQ-i includes five factors: Intrapersonal, Interpersonal, Stress Management, Adaptability, and General Mood.

In Goleman and Boyatzis's (S. B. Wolff, 2005) original ECI, 18 competencies were identified. These were Self-Awareness (Emotional Self-Awareness, Accurate Self-Assessment, Self-Confidence), Self-Management (Emotional Self-Control, Transparency, Adaptability, Achievement, Initiative, Optimism), Social Awareness (Empathy, Organizational Awareness, Service Orientation), and Relationship Management (Developing Others, Inspirational Leadership, Influence, Change Catalyst, Conflict Management, and Collaboration). The ECI instrument, clearly based on a mixed model of EI, was primarily designed for use in personnel selection and development applications for managers and leaders. This instrument raised psychometric concerns (Watson & Watson, 2014), in that several of its scales were significantly correlated with personality variables. Currently the ECI is published by KornFerry, a large consulting firm, and requires training (at a cost to test users) before assessors are able to use the instrument, which now includes 12 scales (https://www.kornferry.com/capabilities/leadership-professional-development/training-certification/esci-emotional-and-social-competency-inventory).

There may be situations in which it is worth the time and money entailed in using one of the commercially available EI/SI tests, but those costs are not trivial in a broad brush battery. Career assessors should also look for at least suggestive evidence in other measures, even in personality tests, that they are using anyway. Part III of this book addresses personality variables and measures, but EI/SI is one of those areas in which the cross between personality and ability may provide additional, or alternative, ways to measure an ability that might otherwise go unmeasured.

SUMMARY AND CONCLUSIONS

Assessment of social abilities is particularly important in working with persons with Social and Enterprising interests and sometimes in other areas as well. Unfortunately, existing measures of EI/SI social abilities tend to be long, expensive, and not without limitations, including a lack of consensus about the best way to measure these constructs. As of this writing, no EI/SI measure can be recommended for routine inclusion in a standard assessment battery for all or most assessees. This may change as shorter, less expensive measures emerge for versions of SI/EI not overly confounded with general intelligence or with personality measures. Depending on testing circumstances, assessment center exercises and some measures classified as personality may provide useful information relevant to social abilities. Still, there may be times also when a longer measure of social abilities might be appropriate.

10

Managerial and Leadership Abilities

There is a large literature on the predictors of success in management and leadership (see, e.g., Farr & Tippins, 2017), but it often covers variables that cross multiple domains (personality, abilities, and interests) and, within the ability area, the variables identified have often been more focused on general cognitive abilities than on aspects specific to management. This is not to detract from the literature on intelligence, but there is no need to reprise that literature here. As with other work domains, general mental ability (GMA) does matter and is related to a number of important work and career outcomes. Beyond g, however, there are other ability variables and other assessment modalities beyond traditional psychometric testing that have been used to assess managers. These include assessment centers (see Gaugler & Rosenthal, 1987; Hunter & Hunter, 1984; Klimoski & Brickner, 1987; Kuncel & Sackett, 2014; Thornton et al., 2015) that simulate a "live" managerial experience, but these are complicated and can be expensive to administer. They may also focus more on narrow skills than broad-brush abilities. Additionally, specific abilities such as prioritizing, persuasion, and getting things done working with and through other people are all part of most managers' jobs. Social abilities are also important parts of many managers' work including abilities associated with exercising authority over others and coordinating various resources to help organizations achieve common objectives.

https://doi.org/10.1037/0000254-011
Career Assessment: Integrating Interests, Abilities, and Personality, by R. L. Lowman
Copyright © 2022 by the American Psychological Association. All rights reserved.

THEORETICAL AND CONCEPTUAL ISSUES

Because managerial talents are important to society, they are generally well compensated, and employers are willing to pay for assessing candidates' abilities and fitness for particular jobs. Industrial–organizational (I–O) psychologists have focused much of their attention on profiles and behavior of this career group; a large and relatively deep literature is available. Necessarily, the present summary is abbreviated both because of the large number of studies but also because a lot of the literature focuses on interests and personality more than abilities per se. Moreover, the modal successful manager fits a pattern suggestive of a relatively narrow distribution of abilities, abilities not unique to managerial work but useful in addressing the variety of issues that arise in the course of management.

Because managerial and leadership skills do not typically require a lengthy educational preparation and because multiple paths are possible to succeed in management, some might assume that anybody can be a manager and that managers' comparatively high compensation levels are unearned. That belies the reality that the skill set that is required for high-level managerial performance is considerable and, conversely, that the consequences of having ineffective leaders can be substantial.

Buckingham (2005), writing in the *Harvard Business Review* on the topic of "What Great Managers Do," opined,

> Great managers don't try to change a person's style. They never try to push a knight to move in the same way as a bishop. They know that their employees will differ in how they think, how they build relationships, how altruistic they are, how patient they can be, how much of an expert they need to be, how prepared they need to feel, what drives them, what challenges them, and what their goals are. These differences of trait and talent are like blood types: They cut across the superficial variations of race, sex, and age and capture the essential uniqueness of each individual.
>
> Like blood types, the majority of these differences are enduring and resistant to change. A manager's most precious resource is time, and great managers know that the most effective way to invest their time is to identify exactly how each employee is different and then to figure out how best to incorporate those enduring idiosyncrasies into the overall plan. To excel at managing others, you must bring that insight to your actions and interactions. Always remember that great managing is about release, not transformation. It's about constantly tweaking your environment so that the unique contribution, the unique needs, and the unique style of each employee can be given free rein. Your success as a manager will depend almost entirely on your ability to do this. (p. 79)

JOB DUTIES

A variety of definitions of the managerial job have been put forth over the years. J. P. Campbell et al. (1970), for example, defined the managerial job as being any set of actions believed to be optimal for identifying, assimilating, and utilizing both internal and external resources toward sustaining over the long term, the functioning of the organizational unit for which a manager has some degree of responsibility. The effective manager is . . . an optimizer in utilizing all available and potential resources. (p. 105)

More recently, the O*NET listed many specific types of managers, including chief executives, yet job duties for all were fairly similar to the category of "General and Operations Managers" (11-1021.00), for which the following work tasks (job duties) were identified:

- Making Decisions and Solving Problems—Analyzing information and evaluating results to choose the best solution and solve problems.

- Communicating with Supervisors, Peers, or Subordinates—Providing information to supervisors, co-workers, and subordinates by telephone, in written form, e-mail, or in person.

- Getting Information—Observing, receiving, and otherwise obtaining information from all relevant sources.

- Coordinating the Work and Activities of Others—Getting members of a group to work together to accomplish tasks.

- Guiding, Directing, and Motivating Subordinates—Providing guidance and direction to subordinates, including setting performance standards and monitoring performance.

- Identifying Objects, Actions, and Events—Identifying information by categorizing, estimating, recognizing differences or similarities, and detecting changes in circumstances or events.

- Interacting With Computers—Using computers and computer systems (including hardware and software) to program, write software, set up functions, enter data, or process information.

- Judging the Qualities of Things, Services, or People—Assessing the value, importance, or quality of things or people.

- Monitor Processes, Materials, or Surroundings—Monitoring and reviewing information from materials, events, or the environment, to detect or assess problems.

- Organizing, Planning, and Prioritizing Work—Developing specific goals and plans to prioritize, organize, and accomplish your work.

- Developing and Building Teams—Encouraging and building mutual trust, respect, and cooperation among team members.

- Evaluating Information to Determine Compliance with Standards—Using relevant information and individual judgment to determine whether events or processes comply with laws, regulations, or standards.

- Establishing and Maintaining Interpersonal Relationships—Developing constructive and cooperative working relationships with others, and maintaining them over time.
- Processing Information—Compiling, coding, categorizing, calculating, tabulating, auditing, or verifying information or data.
- Scheduling Work and Activities—Scheduling events, programs, and activities, as well as the work of others.
- Training and Teaching Others—Identifying the educational needs of others, developing formal educational or training programs or classes, and teaching or instructing others.
- Coaching and Developing Others—Identifying the developmental needs of others and coaching, mentoring, or otherwise helping others to improve their knowledge or skills.
- Communicating with Persons Outside Organization—Communicating with people outside the organization, representing the organization to customers, the public, government, and other external sources. This information can be exchanged in person, in writing, or by telephone or e-mail.
- Resolving Conflicts and Negotiating with Others—Handling complaints, settling disputes, and resolving grievances and conflicts, or otherwise negotiating with others.
- Performing for or Working Directly with the Public—Performing for people or dealing directly with the public. This includes serving customers in restaurants and stores, and receiving clients or guests.
- Monitoring and Controlling Resources—Monitoring and controlling resources and overseeing the spending of money.
- Analyzing Data or Information—Identifying the underlying principles, reasons, or facts of information by breaking down information or data into separate parts.
- Developing Objectives and Strategies—Establishing long-range objectives and specifying the strategies and actions to achieve them.
- Documenting/Recording Information—Entering, transcribing, recording, storing, or maintaining information in written or electronic/magnetic form.
- Updating and Using Relevant Knowledge—Keeping up-to-date technically and applying new knowledge to your job.
- Estimating the Quantifiable Characteristics of Products, Events, or Information—Estimating sizes, distances, and quantities; or determining time, costs, resources, or materials needed to perform a work activity.
- Selling or Influencing Others—Convincing others to buy merchandise/goods or to otherwise change their minds or actions.

- Interpreting the Meaning of Information for Others—Translating or explaining what information means and how it can be used.

- Performing Administrative Activities—Performing day-to-day administrative tasks such as maintaining information files and processing paperwork.

- Staffing Organizational Units—Recruiting, interviewing, selecting, hiring, and promoting employees in an organization.

- Inspecting Equipment, Structures, or Material—Inspecting equipment, structures, or materials to identify the cause of errors or other problems or defects.

- Thinking Creatively—Developing, designing, or creating new applications, ideas, relationships, systems, or products, including artistic contributions.

- Provide Consultation and Advice to Others—Providing guidance and expert advice to management or other groups on technical, systems-, or process-related topics.
(National Center for O*NET Development, 2019c, Work Activities section[1])

Even a casual review of the various approaches to identifying the job duties of managers and, in some cases, related abilities suggests considerable consistency in the dimensions of the manager's job. Managers' work requires them to make happen things that are needed to help organizations or departments run successfully and to help contribute to the successful achievement of the purposes which the organizations or business units exist to serve. Although the O*NET job duties appear to be based on midlevel rather than higher level managers, they reflect the kind of skill sets needed by managers at many organizational levels. Senior executives are generally required to address very complex issues, but their purpose is still focused on managing resources—including people—to get jobs done, usually in organizational contexts, and they do so largely in the context of the work duties shown here. Not captured in this list is the fact that managerial work has to be done under pressures of time and in a managerial and political system, typically hierarchical, in which actors have different amounts of power and influence.

ABILITIES AND SKILLS

What abilities and skills are needed to successfully perform these work roles? So many researchers and theorists have examined the duties and personal characteristics of successful managers that it is impossible to adequately review this literature in detail. However, a brief review of some of the major findings is helpful in identifying cross-cutting personal characteristics, mostly abilities,

---

[1]Reprinted from *Summary Report for: 11-1021.00—General and Operations Managers*, by National Center for O*NET Development, 2019 (https://www.onetonline.org/link/summary/11-1021.00). CC BY 4.0.

that have been identified as being important in managerial work and leadership roles.

Ghiselli (1963), whose writings on human abilities remain valuable long after their original appearance, described the managerial job as requiring (a) the ability to direct the activities of others, (b) intelligence, (c) self-assurance, (d) identification with high occupational levels, and (e) initiative. Ghiselli elaborated,

> Management perhaps does not represent the very highest levels of abstract thinking, but it does involve the capacity to see and develop novel solutions to problems. While not synonymous with leadership, managerial talent does manifest itself in the effective direction of others . . . it implies a willingness to depend on oneself coupled with a self-generated impetus to activity and a striving for and a willingness to accept the authority and responsibility which goes with high level positions in organizations. (p. 640)

Similarly, Miner (1978), in summarizing 20 years of role prescription theory (in which people's behavior in work is defined by the nature of the position or job that they occupy), noted the following essential characteristics of successful managers: (a) a positive attitude toward authority, (b) wanting to compete, (c) a desire to exercise power, (d) being willing to stand out, and (e) being willing to perform routine administrative duties (attend meetings, prepare budgets, etc.). Klemp and McClelland (1986) also identified sets of requisite competencies found among senior managers in two broad categories: intellectual abilities and ability to influence others. Intellectual competencies included (a) planning and causal thinking, (b) diagnostic information seeking, and (c) conceptualization and synthetic thinking. Influencing competencies included (a) need for power (see McClelland & Burnham, 1976); (b) exercising power within groups; and (c) "symbolic influence," essentially, personal power by example. A final identified competency (or possibly a personality variable) was self-confidence (Klemp & McClelland, 1986).

Note that, taken alone, many of these variables could describe the modal incumbent of a variety of occupational groups. Medical students are competitive, actors like to stand out, and accountants suffer routine gladly. It is the constellation of these traits, taken as an aggregate (particularly the attitude toward authority and toward the exercise of power), and a specific but somewhat generalist ability profile that appear to differentiate this profile from that of other career paths.

Sternberg (Sternberg & Wagner, 1986) suggested the construct of "managerial intelligence" to address the unique ability patterns of people in executive and managerial occupations. In many respects, the managerial intelligence construct appears to be an extension of Sternberg's (1982, 1997a) metaconstruct of "practical intelligence," one of three major components of his triarchic intelligence theory (see Chapter 5) being the ability to recognize the nature of the problem to be solved and select an appropriate strategy to solve the problem address it. Conceptually, the term builds on Sternberg's concepts of problem definition, tacit knowledge ("action-oriented knowledge, acquired without direct help from others, that allows individuals to achieve goals they personally value"; Sternberg & Wagner, 1983, p. 483), and selective comparison (identifying, comparing, and deciding upon alternative courses of action).

This approach is conceptually useful in its suggestion that traditional measures of GMA miss aspects of pragmatic applications of intelligence. Sternberg (1997a) provided as an illustration of the approach in the following example:

> It is your second year as a midlevel manager in a company in the communications industry. You head a department of about thirty people. The evaluation of your first year on the job has been generally favorable. Performance ratings for your department are at least as good as they were before you took over, and perhaps even a little better. You have two assistants. One is quite capable. The other just seems to go through the motions but to be of little help. You believe that although you are well liked, there is little that would distinguish you in the eyes of your superiors from the nine other managers at a comparable level in the company. Your goal is rapid promotion to the top of the company. The following is a list of things you are considering doing in the next two months. You obviously cannot do them all. Rate the importance of each by its priority as a means of reaching your goal.
>
> a. Find a way to get rid of the "dead wood" (e.g., the less helpful assistant and three or four others).
> b. Participate in a series of panel discussions to be shown on the local public television station.
> c. Find ways to make sure your superiors are aware of your important accomplishments.
> d. Make an effort to better match the work to be done with the strengths and weaknesses of individual employees.
> e. Write an article on productivity for the company newsletter. (p. 484)

Expert raters were used to determine what were the "right answers" to this prompt.

Unfortunately, the managerial intelligence approach has not generated very much literature or empirical evidence, and it was not well anchored in the massive literature on predicting managerial performance. Such a model must also consider the role of general cognitive ability in the measurement. Does this approach add incremental explanatory power in predicting managerial performance over and above GM? The model is conceptually useful in helping frame managerial-related abilities in the practical reality in which they are applied and in identifying potential components of tacit knowledge (such as problem definition and selective comparison) that perhaps can be measured in a way that is not overly concrete. E. Hunt (2010) noted that Sternberg's practical intelligence tests are similar to job knowledge tests and that they essentially are ways of measuring crystallized intelligence in a particular content knowledge area or domain.

For the Enterprising (or managerial) group of occupations, the abilities that predict managerial success are generally not ones unique to the Enterprising area (although ultimately some may be found) but rather are a combination of abilities that are shared with other occupational groups. Of course, a major thesis of this book is that cross domain (interdomain) variables must be examined in career assessment. Entereprising-related abilities illustrate the inevitable artificiality of firmly separating variables into interests, abilities, and personality characteristics as if there were no overlap or patterns among them. This partly reflects the still-developing nature of social and interpersonal abilities (see Chapter 9), which are often important in managerial work. And, as R. B. Cattell (1987) noted, personality variables can sometimes function like ability variables (see also Harrell & Harrell, 1973; J. D. Mayer et al., 1989; Megargee & Carbonell, 1988). For example, managers as a group tend to score high on personality measures of dominance (Gough, 1996). This may in turn cause them to be attracted to work in which they can assert control over others (interests). And in such roles, they use these characteristics to lead others to get work accomplished (an ability). Is dominance then an ability? Perhaps not (it may be a mediator or moderator), but at the least an intricate overlap across the domains is suggested.

For these reasons, I will deviate briefly from the usual structure of this section of the book to present the ability-personality profile of the typical manager rather than limit the focus to abilities alone. I will also differentiate between subcategories of managerial/leadership talent (e.g., managers vs. leaders, managers vs. entrepreneurs). First is a review of the general job duties associated with managerial roles.

There are a few classic empirical studies and some more recent ones (e.g., Dunn et al., 1995; Marcus et al., 2007) that are particularly relevant. Some of the most valuable studies on managerial talent to appear in the literature are the longitudinal studies conducted in (the former version of) American Telephone & Telegraph (AT&T; Bray et al., 1974; A. Howard & Bray, 1988; see also Rychlak, 1982) and the research on Sears executives (Bentz, 1985). A now-outdated but still important book (J. P. Campbell et al., 1970) provided a good summary of early research literature on the abilities (and personality characteristics) of managers, including studies done at Exxon, at the University of Minnesota, and by the American Chamber of Commerce. Studies such as those of AT&T (Bray et al., 1974; A. Howard & Bray, 1988) and Sears (Bentz, 1985) managers and executives have examined predictors of the future success of would-be executives using psychological measures of ability, interests, and personality. Of course, there is no assurance that what constitutes success in large, bureaucratic organizations such as Sears or the former, pre-deregulation version of AT&T will constitute success in smaller organizations.

Careful examination of these studies points to a consistent picture of the successful corporate executive (more qualitative, clinical descriptions of the managerial "type" can be found in Kofodimos et al., 1986; Kotter, 1982; Mintzberg, 1973). Men (more about women managers later) who perform better in managerial positions tend to be bright (in an applied rather than academic sense), generally well-educated, "take charge" individuals who, from an early age, excelled in competitive activities such as sports and grades and who naturally gravitated (and have done so throughout their lives) to roles in which they could lead others or be in charge. Successful managers also appeared able to sacrifice individual needs to those of the corporation and able to present themselves and their organizations positively, both in word and in personal appearance (Nykodym & Simonetti, 1987). The modal executive has moderately high to high general levels of intelligence and education (e.g., Bentz, 1985; J. P. Campbell et al., 1970; Gakhar, 1986; Ghiselli, 1963, 1966; A. Howard & Bray, 1988; Jaskolka et al., 1985). There is some evidence that general intellectual ability predicts how far one will rise within a managerial hierarchy (see Korman, 1968). As Klimoski and Brickner (1987) put it, "There seems to be no doubt that intelligence is important for managerial effectiveness" (p. 251). The type of intelligence used by managers, however, is applied rather than theoretical (see Sternberg, 1997; R. K. Wagner & Sternberg, 1985; see also Klimoski & Brickner, 1987).

Personality factors (see Chapters 13 and 14) have also shown relevance for predicting success in managerial occupations (e.g., Ansari, 1984; Ghiselli, 1968, 1969; Maitra, 1983; Olson & Bosserman, 1984; Ones et al., 2007; see also Chapters 13 and 14, this volume). The importance of positive relationships with others (arguably both a personality and ability construct) apparently lessens as one rises in the hierarchy (see A. Howard & Bray, 1988) although a balance between tough-mindedness and cordiality is apparently important. Other promising personality variables include need for achievement (Hough et al., 2015; McClelland, 1961; Rainey, 2000) and power, especially at lower organizational levels (Erez & Shneorson, 1980; McClelland & Boyatzis, 1982). Stress tolerance, particularly of the role overload variety (too much to do in too little time), is also needed for many managerial jobs (Boyd & Gumpert, 1983). Managers and executives also typically have outgoing personality styles (extraversion) and good interpersonal relations (Deb, 1983) as well as interests and skills in overseeing the activities of others to get a job done (J. S. Brown et al., 1981; Megargee & Carbonell, 1988). Moderately high levels of what psychologists might term sociopathy may also help advance careers (see Harrell & Harrell, 1973; Lowman, 1989).

To the extent that these summaries describe a generic managerial profile, it becomes clearer why cognitive abilities alone may not predict as well as when used in combination with other dimensions (e.g., Korman, 1968). Assuming authority over others, interacting with subordinates in a controlling manner, tolerance for routine, competitiveness, needs for power and achievement—these may be at least as much be influenced by characteristics of personality as they are by ability. In addition, as with social intelligence, measurement of the interpersonal skills related to these factors can be difficult to measure.

As I noted in describing managerial job duties, the O*NET does not have a single category for managers but identified the following abilities for "General and Operations Managers" (11-1021.00):

- Oral Comprehension—The ability to listen to and understand information and ideas presented through spoken words and sentences.

- Oral Expression—The ability to communicate information and ideas in speaking so others will understand.

- Problem Sensitivity—The ability to tell when something is wrong or is likely to go wrong. It does not involve solving the problem, only recognizing there is a problem.

- Speech Clarity—The ability to speak clearly so others can understand you.

- Written Comprehension—The ability to read and understand information and ideas presented in writing.
(National Center for O*NET Development, 2019c, Abilities section[2])

The following O*NET skills are listed for this occupation:

- Active Listening—Giving full attention to what other people are saying, taking time to understand the points being made, asking questions as appropriate, and not interrupting at inappropriate times.

- Coordination—Adjusting actions in relation to others' actions.

- Monitoring—Monitoring/Assessing performance of yourself, other individuals, or organizations to make improvements or take corrective action.

- Social Perceptiveness—Being aware of others' reactions and understanding why they react as they do.

- Speaking—Talking to others to convey information effectively.
(National Center for O*NET Development, 2019c, Skills section[3])

These O*NET-identified skills and abilities are thought to be needed by managers but it would be difficult to measure all of them in a career assessment process. Fortunately, it is not always necessary to measure every skill needed by managers when more overarching abilities combined with interests and personality assessment can be sufficient to identify likely fit with managerial careers.

When assessing for higher level positions, where the success or failure of the organization may hinge on making good selection decisions (a somewhat different task from career assessment), a more situation-specific job analysis may be required. Thus, in comparing several high level candidates, each of which has excellent qualifications, the question of "fit" may become more fine-tuned. Among highly successful executives, does the situation call for a turnaround artist, someone to hold the ship steady, someone proven in entrepreneurial leadership, someone who can get along with an autocratic board, or some other particular characteristics? Blankenship (2021) identified some of the approaches that can be used in such assessments when assessing high level leaders.

Subtypes of managers and leaders have also been identified. Some types of managers such as in marketing or finance may have profiles that differentiate

---

[2]Reprinted from *Summary Report for: 11-1021.00—General and Operations Managers*, by National Center for O*NET Development, 2019 (https://www.onetonline.org/link/summary/11-1021.00). CC BY 4.0.

[3]Reprinted from *Summary Report for: 11-1021.00—General and Operations Managers*, by National Center for O*NET Development, 2019 (https://www.onetonline.org/link/summary/11-1021.00). CC BY 4.0.

them from the generic managerial profile. Managers in public-sector organizations, for example, may differ systematically from those in private-sector organizations (Homberg et al., 2015; D. J. Houston, 2000; Warrier, 1982). Two well-studied types of managers that can be differentiated are managers versus leaders and managers versus entrepreneurs.

MANAGERIAL VERSUS LEADERSHIP ABILITIES

Since the publication of Zaleznik's (1974, 1977, 1989) still-important papers differentiating managers from leaders, there has been recognition that managers differ in important ways from leaders, though many of the same job duties apply. In contrast to managers, leaders tend to be idiosyncratic, future-focused high risk takers, good at seeing the bigger picture, often psychologically conflicted and complex (Kets de Vries, 1985) while managers emerge as "company men and women" more conforming and achieving along well-defined tracks. As Katz and Kahn (1978) appropriately noted, much literature on leadership describes a psychology of managing and leading within existing structures rather than creating new ones. In Zaleznik's terms, that is a psychology of managers, not leaders. Zaleznik (1974) also differentiated leaders who manage others on a charismatic versus a consensus basis and noted the psychological characteristics that claimed to differentiate the two groups. Specifically, Zaleznik argued that charismatic leaders are inner directed, heavily influenced by their relationships with their family of origin, and behaviorally complex (mixing passivity and assertiveness), possessing the ability to inspire their followers on an affectively charged basis. In contrast, Zaleznik portrayed consensus leaders as being more extraverted people who tend to follow opinion rather than lead it, who emphasize the past rather than the future, and who do not as easily develop an emotional attachment with their followers. Buckingham (2005) put it this way:

> Great leaders discover what is universal and capitalize on it. Their job is to rally people toward a better future. Leaders can succeed in this only when they can cut through differences of race, sex, age, nationality, and personality and, using stories and celebrating heroes, tap into those very few needs we all share. The job of a manager, meanwhile, is to turn one person's particular talent into performance. Managers will succeed only when they can identify and deploy the differences among people, challenging each employee to excel in his or her own way. This doesn't mean a leader can't be a manager or vice versa. But to excel at one or both, you must be aware of the very different skills each role requires. (p. 72)

MANAGERIAL VERSUS SALES ABILITIES

People in sales share in common with many managers a focus on achieving goals and working with others. But whereas managers have considerable real and implied power in working with others to get things done, those in sales must rely on persuasion and knowledge of product and of prospective customers' motivations. In many sales contexts, a success rate of 1% to 10% would be common. Put another way, "failure" (i.e., not making sales) occurs often at a rate of over 90%. If a manager "failed" at a similar rate it is unlikely they would be kept in the role for very long.

A meta-analysis of the determinants of sales performance by Churchill et al. (1985) showed personal factors, including aptitude, to be important in predicting sales performance. Vinchur et al. (1998) found that cognitive ability predicted positively to supervisory ratings of people in sales but near-zero (.04) to objective sales outcomes. Sales abilities (primarily job knowledge tests) predicted both ratings and objective sales (as did certain personality and interest measures). Verbeke et al. (2011) also found job knowledge tests predictive of sales performance. The interaction between abilities and personality is suggested by a number of studies. D. M. Mayer and Greenberg (1964), for example, identified two essential psychological components for success in sales: empathy and complex ego strength such that failure to make a sale (such failures are common) is taken personally enough to be an inspiration for new effort but not enough to devastate the individual or cause renewed efforts to cease (the ego characteristic is labeled by D. M. Mayer and Greenberg as high ego drive). Empathy, in sales, the ability to correctly identify the psychological orientation of the sales prospect, and emotional intelligence (EI) have also been identified by other researchers (e.g., K. B. Clark, 1980; Deeter-Schmelz & Sojka, 2003; T. V. Rao, 1981) as being ability constructs related to sales success.

MANAGERIAL VERSUS ENTREPRENEURIAL ABILITIES

Much recent attention, especially in popular literature, has been focused on the psychology of entrepreneurs (those who found and manage their own companies, sometimes within a larger organizational context, e.g., Goleman, 1986; Markman, 2007). This is not just due to the glamorization of certain spectacularly successful entrepreneurs, the few but sometimes awe-inspiring individuals who took ideas from garage start-ups to "richest in the world" successes, but also the large numbers of entrepreneurs—some 25 million as of 2016—and those are just the ones in the United States alone who own or start their own enterprises, the vast majority of which will not reach historically noteworthy wealth (https://www.Babson.edu/news-events/babson-news/Pages/2017-global-entrepreneurship-monitor-united-states-report.aspx).

Most of the literature on personal characteristics of entrepreneurs has focused on personality rather than ability characteristics (see, e.g., Zhao & Seibert, 2006; see also Chapters 13–16, this volume). In this chapter, however, the focus is on abilities.

The study of the cognitive abilities of entrepreneurs is still young. Baron and Ensley (2006) identified pattern (opportunity) recognition, a cognitive ability in their view, that they defined as "the cognitive process through which individuals identify meaningful patterns in complex arrays of events or trends" (p. 1331). This, they argued, enables them to find new business opportunities that others may miss. In a similar vein, Levine et al. (2017) referred to "strategic intelligence," which was defined as the ability to anticipate competitors' behaviors and preempt it, which, along with analytical and abstract thinking abilities, was identified as being an important factor in entrepreneurial thinking. Of course it is easy to object to yet another "intelligence" being proffered but the idea does suggest that cognition may need to be used in different ways in some managerial/entrepreneurial tasks versus others.

Markman (2007) also added to this view, stating,

> Entrepreneurs must have an ability to collect, process, apply, and disseminate tacit and explicit knowledge regarding undervalued resources and to deploy and exploit these resources to create new wealth. . . . Ability as an entrepreneur's competency . . . is the aptitude to combine assets and resources (including knowledge) in new ways to deploy them to meet customers' needs while maintaining profitability. (p. 79)

This conceptualization appears to meld abilities and their expression in particular contexts and would be difficult to measure predictively with today's assessment tools.

Although research is still emerging on entrepreneurs versus managers, for now it does seem that managers work more often within existing structures rather than creating new ones. To the extent innovations in management require the creation of new products or processes and an ability to identify innovative solutions to existing problems or needs, entrepreneurs may be able to be differentiated from managers. But when entrepreneurs have to work within existing structures, to develop and oversee teams of people, to hold them accountable and to assure they accomplish complex outcomes on a tight timetable, entrepreneurship and management will overlap and presumably call for a common set (or subset) of abilities.

DIMENSIONALITY OF THE CONSTRUCT

In terms of the job duties, perhaps no other career area has been studied in so much behavioral detail as "leadership" (more accurately, "management" since, as noted, leaders do not always have the same profile as managers). Because the job of managers has typically been studied by psychometrically sophisticated psychologists (primarily I–O psychologists), extensive factor analyses have been reported for over 30 years. No matter how measured, however, these studies have consistently shown that two factors emerge with regularity: a structural variable, typically (and inappropriately) labeled initiation of structure (IS), and an interpersonal variable, typically labeled consideration (C). Managers are appropriately known as "doers," and what they characteristically do best is providing direction and order, reaching objectives (often set by others), and, above all, working with and through other people in pursuit of goals.

Coordinating the work of others as a vehicle for achieving tasks is a central feature of the business management role. Personal needs and objectives must be consistent with and generally subordinated to the needs of the organization. Unlike artistic enterprises, in which the emphasis is on a unique product, in management roles the typical emphasis is on sustained production of a product or service. In a fast food restaurant, for example, the task is assurance that a large number of individual employees will deliver what is qualitatively the same burger in thousands of locations. At the corporate level, however, there are very high-level tasks that are associated with supplying the food, quality control in the supply and delivery chain, system-wide marketing, and brand positioning in a highly competitive and international context. Conformity to prescribed behavioral rules has obvious survival value at the individual business unit level in such settings. It is valued not just as a control mechanism of interest in itself but as a means of assuring consistency and quality.

Determining the dimensions of managerial abilities is complicated by the finding that multiple abilities are called for. If primary attention is given to GMA, then arguably there is only one factor or perhaps a verbal and nonverbal intelligence factor. However, approaches that also include abilities like prioritizing, interpersonal, and political expertise point to a more complex model of managerial abilities. From the perspective of career assessment, I argue that assessing more broadly rather than more narrowly is preferable, particularly when it is known through interests and personal history that a business or managerial career is clearly relevant to a client. On the other hand, there are practical limitations in terms of available instrumentation, time, and cost that can affect the range of managerial abilities that can be assessed. When assessing individuals one at a time, it may be difficult to include simulations that involve group participation. Online assessments may permit assessors to combine managers in different locations for group simulations.

MEASUREMENT ISSUES

As this review suggests, within the managerial abilities domain, it is important at least to measure general intellectual ability, organizing ability, social and interpersonal abilities and interests, and, within the personality domain, such characteristics as dominance, need for achievement, and toughmindedness. Assessment center methodologies, in which multiple candidates are evaluated on a variety of dimensions, including their ability to interact with others in group activities, continue to show evidence of validity (see Klimoski & Brickner, 1987; Kuncel & Sackett, 2014; Thornton et al., 2015) and have the added advantage of being better received as job relevant than cognitive ability tests sometimes are. However, such methods are expensive and may be difficult for the clinician to undertake in a small practice setting. Most assessment center studies have shown that the overall rating of the candidate (in which data from a variety of sources are assembled clinically into a single or a small number of ratings) indicates superior validity to any single component of the assessment exercise. Components of the typical assessment center include group discussion exercises, paper-and-pencil tests, and job simulation exercises such as the in-basket test (see Bray et al., 1974; Frederiksen, 1962; Frederiksen et al., 1957; Hakstian et al., 1986; Thorton et al., 2015). However, these may not be commercially available or adequately validated. Other managerial assessment methodologies have also been reported (e.g., Childs & Klimoski, 1986; King, 1985; Miner, 1985; Weekley & Gier, 1987), and measures for specific Enterprising occupational groups have also been published (e.g., the Diamond Sales Aptitude Test; Oda, 1982, 1983).

Sex differences in the aptitude and personality patterns (which, in management, sometimes act similarly to abilities) associated with successful managerial performance appear to be minimal and have been decreasing over time (e.g., Eagly et al., 2020; Hopkins & Bilimoria, 2008; R. J. Ritchie & Moses, 1983; Steinberg & Shapiro, 1982), and, contrary to times past where there were significant differences in the numbers of men and women in MBA programs and in managerial jobs, those differences have greatly lessened as barriers to entry have been removed. Indeed, according to the Bureau of Labor Statistics (Torpey, 2017), in 2016, slightly less than 40% of all management positions in the United States are now held by women. However, in a number of managerial positions (e.g., human resource management, medical and health service, and educational administrators), women were in the majority. At top level business schools, the female:male ratios are now over 0.40, a significant change (Byrne, 2017). However, women continue to be underrepresented at the higher levels of management (Barreto et al., 2009).

Both age (see especially A. Howard & Bray, 1988) and level within the managerial hierarchy (Thornton et al., 2017) should be taken into account in deciding which variables to measure and in interpreting results. Superior levels of intellectual functioning may be required for higher levels of executive talent but may be problematic for positions in which there is little opportunity for upward mobility. Characteristics of the organization must also be considered. Companies that reward upward mobility (where much of the selection literature has been conducted) may differ from those that reward status quo. Career aspirants should take into account the reward structure of the organization and whom it "really" wants to hire; in some companies, this may be discrepant with its espoused desires. As for age, heavily timed tests may put older candidates at a disadvantage compared with younger ones. For purposes of career assessment, it is desirable to have age-based norms as well as more general population ones. Additionally, including measures that build more on crystallized rather than fluid intelligence may provide a clearer understanding of how an older assessee's performance has been affected by the aging process.

Clearly, what is being measured in managerial abilities interacts with how the work of management is defined. To the extent that management fundamentally involves achieving goal-directed results typically in an organizational context involving working with and through other people, there are elements both of understanding what it is that needs to be done (and why) and then helping to make that happen. Differentiating managers and leaders and managers and entrepreneurs may also need to be considered, and entrepreneurial work may call for additional competencies not well measured by right-or-wrong answer type tests as they currently exist.

As this review suggests, general intellectual ability is an important component of managerial abilities, and it will in part identify the complexity of management tasks that can be taken on and may well predict how far someone who is otherwise well-suited to managing will be likely to rise. In most managerial roles, interpersonal abilities will also be needed, since the work usually involves overseeing and collaborating with other people, including those who have backgrounds that differ from their own. Being able to focus on goal achievement is also important because the activities entail subordinating personal preferences or wishes to the current needs of the organization. Being able to learn applied and technical information in detail, to make decisions while taking a broad number of factors into account, and being able to work effectively in often-politicized and highly interactive environments are also called for in this work.

From a career perspective, there are those who have always gravitated to being in charge and who clearly have strong needs to oversee others and to be the boss. Others, however, never aspired to oversee others but find themselves having opportunities to move from research or service delivery roles into management ones. For them, the question may be, should they pursue those higher paying jobs and the greater demands on their time that will entail or should they remain in nonmanagerial roles?

SUMMARY AND CONCLUSIONS

To date, the "gold standard" that typically accounts for the largest amount of variance of managerial behavior remains g. However, it does not explain all performance variance among managers. An alternative (or additional) approach has been to utilize content-specific measures that are based on tasks that managers need to master to be effective. This approach may identify not just capacity to learn in a particular domain (management) but also the ability to function effectively in specific applications. This methodology, whether applied using assessment centers or in tacit ability measures of so-called managerial intelligence (Sternberg, 1997a; R. K. Wagner & Sternberg, 1985) is similar to situational judgement tests (SJTs) sometimes used in selection or development assessments (Lievens & Chan, 2017). Additionally, interests (see Chapters 2–4) and personality variables (see Chapters 13–16) help to provide a profile that better identifies the degree of match with prototypical ability-interest-personality patterns. Integration across domains are discussed in Chapters 17 and 18.

11

Perceptual, Computational, and Other Abilities

Occupations that have Conventional as the highest endorsed interest code largely involve clerical, numerical, and data-related duties. Typical occupations include accountants, bookkeepers, computer programmers, data processing employees, and billing clerks. Many such jobs involve attention to detail; applying rules, especially to data; and facility in working with numbers, or computational math. Attention to detail, accuracy, consistency, and speed are relevant to many lower level conventional jobs, while those with more complexity will have high cognitive ability demands. In this section the focus is on perceptual speed and accuracy (PSA) and computational (vs. higher order) mathematics.

PERCEPTUAL SPEED AND ACCURACY

A research project at the University of Michigan's Institute of Social Research, where I worked early in my career, included, among other sites, one of the Internal Revenue Service's tax processing centers. The large, cavernous building housing the facility included work stations with computers that, at peak tax submission time, housed thousands of lower level civil service employees whose job it was to enter data from physical tax returns into the computer. Each return was entered by two different people, and any discrepancies were flagged by the computer and the errors corrected. There were strict standards of speed and accuracy. Thinking about this work (and other such jobs like that of entering zip codes on mail when the sender did not provide one) call for accuracy and speed, an ability that has been identified and studied for a number of decades.

The O*NET includes Perceptual Speed among its abilities. It defines it as

> the ability to quickly and accurately compare similarities and differences among sets of letters, numbers, objects, pictures, or patterns. The things to be compared may be presented at the same time or one after the other. This ability also includes comparing a presented object with a remembered object. (National Center for O*NET Development, 2021c)

This definition well describes the basis for many perceptual speed and accuracy tests.

Theoretical and Conceptual Issues

PSA has long been recognized as an important variable with career and work implications (Blair, 1951). Hakstian and Cattell (1974) defined it as the ability "to rapidly [assess] . . . visual stimuli, usually to determine the sameness or difference of the members in pairs of such stimuli" (p. 174). Pawlik's (1966) work included a Perceptual Speed factor, J. P. Guilford's (1967) had a Figural Identification component, and Ekstrom et al.'s (1976) Kit of Factor Referenced Cognitive Tests contained a Perceptual Speed factor. All appear to be referring to similar constructs. Pawlik (1966) identified the essential characteristic of his factor P (Speed of Perception) as being "fast speed in comparing visual configurations" (p. 542).

This construct has also been studied for decades in the context of what has typically been called clerical aptitude (see Super & Crites, 1962). There is not that much variability (or new developments other than computerization) in such measures, but their validity evidence in supporting prediction to clerical and nonmanagerial administrative jobs has been sustained. Indeed, Whetzel et al.'s (2011) meta-analysis of predictors of clerical job performance building on the work of Pearlman et al. (1980) was titled "Meta-Analysis of Clerical Performance Predictors: Still Stable After All These Years" and well stated the findings of many studies.

Although the perceptual speed validity coefficients were stable over time in their ability to predict clerical job performance, the authors noted that, due to the increased complexity of clerical jobs, general cognitive ability had become more important, such that cognitive ability and PSA together better predicted work-related outcomes. This is an important finding for the stability of perceptual speed, but also for the suggestion that when jobs change, the needed abilities may also change, either in importance or magnitude. It is also consistent with Super and Crites's (1962) conclusion: "When appraising clerical promise it is well . . . to use tests of both perceptual speed and intelligence" (p. 178).

Dimensionality of the Construct

An early factor analysis of clerical aptitude tests, including 17 clerical aptitude tests and a measure of general intelligence, showed three major factors: perceptual analysis (accuracy), speed, and verbal ability; these factors accounted, respectively, for 17%, 14%, and 11% of the variance, collectively accounting for less than half of the variance (Bair, 1951). R. C. Johnson and Nagoshi's (1985) study of abilities in a large, cross-ethnic sample also showed that perceptual speed and accuracy were separate factors.

How such tests are constructed and scored can influence the factors that emerge. The perceptual speed factor includes measures requiring the comparison of two numbers or names to determine if they are the same or different. Measures such as the Minnesota Clerical Test (Andrew et al., 1979) include subtests for verbal material (names) and quantitative material (numbers), and although such subtest scores have generally been highly correlated, working with words versus numbers may result in different outcomes.

McGue et al. (1984) reported in a sample of monozygotic and dizygotic twins and triplets that there was a relation between some of the measures of PSA and speed of spatial processing and speed of information processing. More generally, Lindley et al. (1988) raised important considerations about the relation between timed paper-and-pencil tests and psychometric intelligence. P. L. Ackerman et al. (2002) considered PSA in relationship to other variables including various cognitive and working memory tests. They found a strong relationship between PSA and working memory. To the extent a "pure" measure of PSA is desired, it should be as free as possible from other factors, including general mental ability (GMA).

Career Implications

The O*NET's listing of occupations that make high use of PSA are shown in Table 11.1.

Many of these occupations are associated with Realistic, Investigative, and/or Conventional interests. They would all appear to require attention to detail and monitoring of data, often having to take actions in response to particular readings on what is being monitored.

Ghiselli's (1966) work on the ability patterns of occupational groups examined validity coefficients for clerical occupations. Training criteria (outcome measures collected at the end of instructional programs), not unexpectedly, were generally better predicted by general intelligence measures than by primary abilities. More recently, Mount et al. (2008) found that with warehouse workers' task performance, PSA was correlated with the number correct score (NC), and the number wrong score (NW) was negatively correlated with rule compliance. (They also found that a personality variable, conscientiousness [see Chapter 13], provided incremental predictive power for both task performance and rules compliance.) P. L. Ackerman and Beier (2007) reviewed some

TABLE 11.1. O*NET Occupations Using Perceptual Speed Ability

Code	Occupation
53-2021.00	Air Traffic Controllers
53-2011.00	Airline Pilots, Copilots, and Flight Engineers
19-4051.00	Nuclear Technicians
51-8011.00	Nuclear Power Reactor Operators
51-8093.00	Petroleum Pump System Operators, Refinery Operators, and Gaugers
53-2012.00	Commercial Pilots
51-8092.00	Gas Plant Operators
29-1211.00	Anesthesiologists
51-9041.00	Extruding, Forming, Pressing, and Compacting Machine Setters, Operators, and Tenders
53-4011.00	Locomotive Engineers
29-1071.01	Anesthesiologist Assistants
51-9012.00	Separating, Filtering, Clarifying, Precipitating, and Still Machine Setters, Operators, and Tenders
53-5011.00	Sailors and Marine Oilers
51-9162.00	Computer Numerically Controlled Tool Programmers Bright
49-9099.01	Geothermal Technicians
11-3051.06	Hydroelectric Production Managers
53-7072.00	Pump Operators, Except Wellhead Pumpers
13-1041.01	Environmental Compliance Inspectors, Government Property Inspectors
19-4051.02	Nuclear Monitoring Technicians
43-9031.00	Desktop Publishers
53-7121.00	Tank Car, Truck, and Ship Loaders
29-1141.03	Critical Care Nurses
51-8091.00	Chemical Plant and System Operators
17-2051.00	Civil Engineers
29-1217.00	Neurologists

Note: Reprinted from *Abilities: Perceptual Speed*, by the National Center for O*NET Development, 2021b (https://www.onetonline.org/find/descriptor/result/1.A.1.e.3?a=1). CC BY 4.0.

of the literature on the types of jobs for which PSA tests had successfully predicted work outcomes. These included census enumerators, hand transcribers, sewing machine operators, navigators, and air traffic controllers (ATCs). With respect to ATCs, P. L. Ackerman and Cianciolo (2000) found that PSA could be incorporated into computer-based assessment measures designed to assess job-related skill mastery at various levels.

Measurement Issues

PSA can be measured by a variety of speeded perceptual tasks. A venerable test, still widely used, is the Minnesota Clerical Test (D. M. Andrew et al., 1979), which, typical of the genre, involves the comparison of pairs of numbers and names (or symbols) to determine whether they are the same or different. The Differential Aptitude Tests (DAT), Comprehensive Ability Battery (CAB), and Armed Services Vocational Aptitude Battery (ASVAB) also contain relevant subtests for this ability.

Most of these tests rely on both speed and accuracy. Presumably, if given unlimited time and assuming normal vision and absence of any impediments such as depression or other health problems, most people could complete the task with high accuracy. However, for workplace applications the goal is to complete the tasks both accurately and swiftly.

P. L. Ackerman and Beier (2007) designed PSA tests that could be administered on a computer. They reviewed evidence concerning reliability and validity of paper-and-pencil versus computer-administered cognitive and PSA tests and noted that the validity coefficients were higher for cognitive than for PSA or other speeded tests. This led them to create a touch sensitive platform for administering PSA (and also motor) tests. The reliability and validity evidence was promising, but it is not clear whether the measures are commercially available.

Concerning group differences, women (and homosexual men) tended, on average, to score better on these tests than did heterosexual men (Giffard et al., 2012), and younger people tended to respond at a faster rate than did older people (Salthouse, 1996). Sex- and age-specific norms may therefore be needed when using these tests in career assessment contexts. Additionally, when assessment is being done in the context of more complex careers (e.g., high-level administrative positions, computer programmers, or accountants), cognitive ability tests will also be relevant.

NUMERICAL COMPUTATIONAL ABILITIES

Most models of cognitive abilities include aspects relating to mathematics. Pawlik (1966) found numerical fluency in 40 studies and noted that it was one of the two "best confirmed . . . aptitude factors known" (pp. 546–547). Numerical fluency, the term then used, generally encompasses skill in performing rule-driven calculations with numbers and is to be distinguished from higher level mathematical reasoning, which requires more complex cognitive abilities. Gardner (1983/2011) similarly differentiated isolated, very high ability in numerical calculations (e.g., autistic savants with great computational skills but below normal intelligence; see L. K. Miller, 1999; P. A. White, 1988) from abstract mathematical ability. Computational math ability (numerical ability), here termed numerical computational ability (NCA; essentially equivalent to Cattell's, 1987, Number Facilitation [N, or UI2]), refers to facility with basic mathematical processes, especially addition, subtraction, multiplication, and division. The O*NET identified an ability called Number Facility, defined as "the ability to add, subtract, multiply, or divide quickly and correctly," and Mathematical Reasoning, defined as "the ability to choose the right mathematical methods or formulas to solve a problem" (National Center for O*NET Development, 2021c). Number Facility would appear to be required primarily for low level math computational work and Mathematical Reasoning for cognitively complex work involving numbers.

As E. Hunt (2010) noted,

> It is important . . . to distinguish between arithmetical calculation and doing mathematics. Calculation is a tool for mathematics, distinct from any distinct understanding of mathematics. It is hard to imagine a mathematician who could not calculate. On the other hand, there are numerous cases of calculating prodigies who had little mathematical talent. (p. 305)

Hunt (2010) went on to note that there are specific brain areas associated with math calculations and simple mathematics. R. E. Mayer (2011) similarly differentiated between computation and problem solving, which was identified as "being able to solve arithmetic word problems" (p. 744).

The particular type of mathematics competency that will be needed varies with the type of work. When duties are limited to oversight of numbers, as in bookkeeping or simple math computations, the ability would be of the type discussed in this section. Some jobs (especially in science and engineering) require logical reasoning using symbol systems that are at the highest level of abstraction. In between are occupations like accounting, which involve intensive work with numbers but often in the context of applying formulae and rules to numbers.

Dimensionality of the Construct

NCA is well represented in the factor-analytic studies of primary abilities (e.g., the Number Aptitude factor in Ekstrom et al.'s, 1976, Kit of Factor Referenced Cognitive Tests). Computational mathematical abilities appear to emerge naturally, independently of schooling, and are affected by practice and memorization (L. B. Resnick, 1989). NCA is also not reduced to subfactors in most common measures of the ability, although a variety of mathematical processes have been identified (see, e.g., L. B. Resnick, 1989). Resnick noted that the preferred adult strategy for solving computational math problems is automaticity or retrieval, which is a low-effort, rapid-response methodology. Osborn

(1983) found that a test developed to measure math ability resulted in a four-component factor solution, including a computational factor and a pattern recognition factor.

Relation to Other Abilities

Riggio and Sotoodeh (1987) found an arithmetic test to correlate with measures of finger dexterity in predicting the performance ratings of microassemblers. Hakstian and Cattell (1978b), in a study of 20 primary ability variables (all measured solely with tests from the authors' own CAB; see Hakstian et al., 1982; Hakstian & Gale, 1979), found no relation between PSA (their "I" variable) and verbal ability ($r_{xy} = .01$) but found sizable correlations between P and NCA (their "C") and spatial ability (correlations of .40 and .42, respectively) in a Canadian high school sample. Their P and C variables loaded on the the same factor, one that was also associated with spatial and mechanical abilities. Lowman et al. (1985) found, in a sample of 149 college-level women, that PSA, as measured by the Minnesota Clerical Test, loaded on a factor separate from computational abilities, as measured by the Wide Range Achievement Test-Arithmetic (the latter loaded more with the intellectual ability measures). Speed of information processing, McGue et al. (1984) noted, generally shows a high and negative correlation with intelligence when the task to be done is simple and a high and positive correlation with intelligence when mental transformations are required rather than simple tasks such as copying numbers (or, presumably, the Digit Symbol subtest of the Wechsler scales). Thus, perceptual speed may need to be considered in relation to intelligence in evaluating career implications.

Career Implications

The occupations listed by the O*NET that require Number Facility are shown in Table 11.2.

Despite the O*NET's definition of this ability as being primarily computational math abilities, and some of the occupations listed would make use of such skills, others would make use of math skills at a much higher level of ability, namely Mathematical Reasoning ability.

Most of these occupations would appear relevant for higher level mathematical reasoning as an important part of the work. Judgement is needed in differentiating careers requiring higher versus lower level abilities in working with numbers.

Concerning predictive validity, several studies used both PSA and NCA to predict to job performance of people in positions like clerks and administrative support. Not many studies were found examining the sole use of computational ability to predict to job outcomes. Arithmetic (i.e., number facility) predicted best for most types of clerks, especially against training criteria. Gael et al. (1975) examined predictive validity of minority and nonminority clerks

TABLE 11.2. O*NET Occupations Using Number Facility Ability

Code	Occupation
19-2012.00	Physicists
15-2021.00	Mathematicians
15-2041.00	Statisticians
15-2011.00	Actuaries
15-2031.00	Operations Research Analysts
25-1022.00	Mathematical Science Teachers, Postsecondary
13-2099.01	Financial Quantitative Analysts
43-9111.00	Statistical Assistants
13-2031.00	Budget Analysts
13-1051.00	Cost Estimators
19-2011.00	Astronomers
17-1022.01	Geodetic Surveyors
13-2011.00	Accountants and Auditors
19-3022.00	Survey Researchers
19-3011.01	Environmental Economists
17-1022.00	Surveyors
43-3071.00	Tellers
17-2112.03	Manufacturing Engineers
17-2051.00	Civil Engineers
13-2041.00	Credit Analysts
13-2052.00	Personal Financial Advisors
11-3031.01	Treasurers and Controllers
17-2041.00	Chemical Engineers
17-2051.02	Water/Wastewater Engineers
13-1081.01	Logistics Engineers
43-3041.00	Gambling Cage Workers
19-1029.01	Bioinformatics Scientists
15-2041.01	Biostatisticians
11-3031.03	Investment Fund Managers
17-2141.00	Mechanical Engineers

Note: Reprinted from *Abilities: Number Facility*, by the National Center for O*NET Development, 2021a (https://www.onetonline.org/find/descriptor/result/1.A.1.c.2). CC BY 4.0.

using work sample criteria. Extensive analyses have been made of the occupational skills utilized in typewriting and word processing (see Glencross & Bluhm, 1986; Grudin, 1983; Salthouse, 1984, 1986a, 1986b), which are surprisingly complex abilities requiring perceptual, motoric, and cognitive skills in "chunking" together information. As usual, it is the combination of abilities that will determine specific occupational fit. Those people, for example, who score high on PSA but lower on NCA and intelligence may be best suited for routine clerical positions, whereas those who combine intelligence with NCA and rapid information-processing skills may do best in higher level clerical or computer applications. The higher level Conventional occupations such as accounting and computer technology necessitate high levels of general intelligence and reasoning ability.

Changing environmental conditions must also be considered. With the automation of clerical and simple computational tasks becoming the norm even in small offices, many Conventional occupations have been redefined or eliminated. Presumably, with a lower demand for routine and low-level clerical tasks, those people with predominantly Conventional interests and abilities may have more difficulty finding outlets for these skills unless they are also able to use intelligence and reasoning to make sense of numbers. Analytical abilities that combine a preference for information-processing activities with the ability to determine and make sense of patterns of data will presumably become more important in the emerging workplace.

Research Needs

More studies are needed examining the relation between PSA and NCA, particularly using measures of NCA that are minimally "contaminated" with higher level mathematical skills. More work is also needed to be able to differentiate occupations that call for computational math abilities without complex mathematical reasoning. Accountants, for example, involve the use of numbers without (typically) needing to apply higher level math skills. Even so, general intelligence is likely important in such occupations.

Measurement Issues

Most widely used measures of math ability in workplace applications do not require high-level math. They are measuring ability to do simple computational math or problems requiring low-level algebra. This type of test appears to predict well when it is computerized, even though paper-and-pencil measures are also common (Silver & Bennett, 1987). The Wide Range Achievement Test series (e.g., Wilkinson & Robertson, 2017) includes a measure of computatioal and lower level math with relevant normative data. In the first half of the adult form, which measures primarily computational skills, N. C. Beck et al. (1989) reported that an advanced computational ability factor was found in a factor analysis of 409 psychiatric patients' test scores using the Wechsler Adult Intelligence Scale-Revised. In contrast, the Quantitative Thinking subtest (Test Q) of the Iowa Tests of Educational Development (Ansley et al., 1989) has been reported to be a relatively pure measure of math problem-solving ability rather than computational skills. It is important to determine whether computational or higher level math skills are needed for a particular career assessment.

OTHER ABILITIES

The coverage of abilities in this chapter is necessarily incomplete. In this section I briefly identify some additional abilities that are necessary for success in some careers. Memory is required in a number of careers, including acting, servers in restaurants, medical service personnel and many others. Creativity in non-artistic areas is also discussed.

Memory

Memory (called Memorization by the O*NET and defined as "the ability to remember information such as words, numbers, pictures, and procedures"; National Center for O*NET Development, 2021c) is an important cognitive skill needed in a variety of types of work, from a server taking an order to a supervisor giving directions on how to run a machine. Although there is a very large literature on memory and deterioration of memory with certain health problems, memory has not yet been well studied concerning its relevance to career assessment. However, there are a number of studies from the cognitive sciences that have studied memory mechanisms in particular occupational groups exhibiting special memory expertise. These include actors (H. Noice & Noice, 2006), London cab drivers (Woollett & Maguire, 2009), simultaneous translators (Hiltunen et al., 2016), and musicians (Talamini et al., 2017, 2016).

Well-developed memory skills that are required for acquisition and retention of information that includes unrelated strings of numbers or made-up words sometimes found on memory tests are different in a number of ways from the skills used by those who must remember large amounts of information within a content area of expertise. In work applications, the content of memory used is often embedded in tasks that allows incidental memory acquisition to occur (Ericsson, 2018; Ericsson & Moxley, 2014; Ericsson & Staszewski, 1989). In other words, individuals (experts, anyway) learn material less by rote memorization than by practicing the skill in actual situations requiring it (such as by playing chess or driving a cab). As H. Noice and Noice (2006) noted about actors, "Actors themselves rarely consider memorization a defining skill. Rather they are concerned about giving honest, spontaneous performances, ones that focus on communicating the meanings underlying the literal words" (p. 14). This would be consistent with the idea of the approach to acting that is based not on rote memorization but rather on incidental learning.

Although there may be some crossover from memory skills in one cognitively complex domain to another (e.g., Sala & Gobet, 2017), the depth and specificity of knowledge in complex areas of learning may limit the extent of the crossover. It has also been demonstrated that expertise in one area may come at the expense of learning in another. The case of London cab drivers is illustrative. Licensed cab drivers in London must pass a very difficult series of exams that require expansive knowledge demonstrating their ability from memory to travel to and from any two or more points in the vast and complex London metropolitan area consisting of 25,000 streets. Several studies (see Maguire et al., 2006) have documented that these cab drivers, compared with matched controls, have greater gray matter volume in the midposterior hippocampus region of the brain but also that they have less gray matter volume in the anterior hippocampus. As for real-life differences, the taxi drivers, compared with the controls, were significantly more knowledgeable about London landmarks and their spatial relationships but were significantly less good at forming and retaining new associations involving visual information (Woollett & Maguire, 2009). There were no differences in other memory skills such as recognizing objects, retrograde memory, or perceptual and executive functions. Such studies may suggest that development of memory skills related to one area of the brain may come at the expense of skills related to another area. Additionally, memory may grow from the experience of having to use it in one's work, so a one-time measure of memory may not clearly predict later expertise in work requiring use of memory.

The relevance of assessing memory in career assessment depends on the purposes of assessment. When assessments are done in the context of physical or mental impairments, there may well be a need to assess retained memory in the context of specific work duties since memory impairments may be associated both with aging (Adams et al., 2013) and with a variety of physical and mental disorders, including, as examples, major depression (H. R. Snyder, 2013), insomnia (Fortier-Brochu et al., 2012), and preclinical Alzheimer's disease (Bäckman et al., 2005). However, when administered as part of a career assessment, most currently available measures of memory concern short-term memory or working memory skills, and are often measured using meaningless material that may provide little information about work-related memory.

Creative Abilities in Areas Not Associated With Artistic Interests

Because creativity is domain-specific, it must be evaluated in the context of a specific area or areas of performance. People are not likely to be creative in particular areas such as art, music, writing, helping others, or architecture if they have not mastered the basics of the abilities and skills needed for that particular career. If anything, however, creatively talented individuals tend to have abilities that cross multiple domains. Indeed, creativity often is associated with pulling together knowledge and abilities from diverse areas. Still, there are general characteristics that tend to be found among creatively talented individuals, but these include both ability and personality characteristics. In Chapters 13 through 16 we consider some of these factors.

SUMMARY AND CONCLUSIONS

This chapter has focused on abilities typically made use of in Conventional interest areas. The focus has been on PSA and numerical computational abilities. Each of these areas can be measured in a relatively straightforward way, and they do not add much time or cost when included in a standard career assessment battery. Brief attention was also given to memory abilities and abilities in creative pursuits in non-Artistic occupations. As noted, creativity can be found among people in any career, but some ability patterns in creativity (such as having knowledge and skills that transcend areas) are common among many creatively talented individuals.

12

Case Illustrations of Ability Profiles

In this section, I present the ability profiles for Cases 5 to 10 introduced in Chapter 4. Each of these individuals was assessed on a number of abilities that have been discussed in this chapter. The case information illustrates test measures and results in applied work.

The individuals whose data are presented in the cases were assessed because they were self-referred or referred by an employer. (Details of the reasons for the referral context were provided in Chapter 4.) Although there are several measures that all of the assessees completed, some were specific to a particular assessment context.

Each of the cases will briefly be discussed, identifying strengths and weaknesses in their ability profiles. Additionally, as appropriate, information about the process itself will be noted in terms of the value added by the various measures.

SAM'S REALISTIC ABILITIES PROFILE (CASE 5)

Sam was assessed as a candidate for a new job within his company that entailed teamwork in a technically advanced operation. As discussed in Chapter 2, Realistic individuals tend to be practical, more oriented to things than to people or ideas, and, in many cases, to enjoy working with their hands. His ability profile includes some interesting features and illustrates why more, rather than less, assessment can be important in understanding people's strengths.

---

https://doi.org/10.1037/0000254-013
Career Assessment: Integrating Interests, Abilities, and Personality, by R. L. Lowman
Copyright © 2022 by the American Psychological Association. All rights reserved.

Table 12.1 presents this assessee's ability results. Many of the measures used in the assessment process included strong cognitive components (as noted, intelligence is still a powerful predictor of job performance for most jobs) and it might be expected that a strongly Realistic person would not, on average, excel on such measures. Rather, such individuals would be expected to do better on practical applied measures, especially related to working with things.

TABLE 12.1. Sam's Realistic Interests Ability Profile (Case 5)

Mechanical Reasoning

Normative groups	Percentile
Bennett Mechanical Comprehension Test—56	
Grade 12 technical high school	90
Industrial sample	81
Mechanical employees sample	80
Development Laboratories career assessment sample	82
DAT Mechanical Reasoning Test—41	
Grade 12 high school	85
Industrial sample	81
Development Laboratories career assessment sample	83

Spatial Ability—Minnesota Paper Form Board, AA series—27

Normative groups	Percentile
Grade 12 males	3
Engineering students	1
Industrial sample	11
Development Laboratories career assessment sample	5

General Intelligence—Multidimensional Aptitude Battery (MAB)

Overall standard scores and norms

	Standard scores	General population average/median/mode	Development Laboratories career assessment norms (percentile)
Verbal	440	500	10
Performance	593	500	74
Full Scale	507	500	30

Overall standard scores and norms

Subtest standard scores

Information	52	Digit Symbol	60
Comprehension	43	Picture Completion	56
Arithmetic	51	Spatial	58
Similarities	45	Picure Arrangement	52
Vocabulary	40	Object Assembly	49

Note. Scores are standardized where 500 is average/median on total summary scores and 50 is average/median on the subtest scores.

Nonverbal Reasoning Ability—Raven's Standard Progressive Matrices—46

Normative groups	Percentile
Test normative sample	25
Development Laboratories career assessment sample	45

Verbal Reasoning Ability—Wesman Personnel Classification Test (Verbal)—9

Normative groups	Percentile
Production supervisor	5
Shop supervisor	3
Industrial norms	11
Development Laboratories career assessment sample	5

Managerial Abilities—Development Laboratories In-basket

	Raw scores and percent correct		Norms (percentile)	
	Client's	Group averages	Managerial sample	Development career assessment norms
Prioritizing*	70	60	46	45
Managerial judgment	11/21	12/21	59	59

*Lower scores are better, that is, less discrepant with the criterion group's answers.

(*continues*)

TABLE 12.1. Sam's Realistic Interests Ability Profile (Case 5)   (*Continued*)

Negotiating Skills—Development Laboratories Negotiating Exercise—3.2/5.0

Normative groups	Percentile
Industrial sample	27.3

Reading Comprehension—Gates McGinitie—17 (48 possible)

Normative groups	Individual score	Group average
Industrial sample	4.7th grade equivalent	Post high school grade equivalent

Numerical Reasoning—Wesman Personnel Classification Test—8

Normative groups	Percentile
Production supervisor	33
Shop supervisors	26
Industrial sample	67
Development Laboratories career assessment sample	47

Reviewing this ability profile, there are some possibly expected results and some surprises. Although he scored well on mechanical measures (definite areas of relative strength), he scored less well on a measure of spatial abilities. Strong Realistic interests paired with strong mechanical abilities but lower spatial ability may make an individual enjoy and do well with hands-on activities but have less interest or ability in more abstract work as an electrician or engineer. But while the assumption might be made that verbal ability at the average level or below would be a potential problem for him in a supervisory role, it is important to understand this client's broader range of abilities. Beyond his mechanical ability strengths, two features stand out. One important finding in understanding his abilities results show a large difference between verbal and nonverbal intelligence on the measure of general intelligence. His nonverbal intelligence suggested general intelligence in the high average to superior range. The low average to average scores in verbal intelligence may therefore underestimate his cognitive abilities. (Many assessment approaches use a single, usually brief, often verbal, measure of cognitive ability and would have missed out on this information.) Another important finding that may help put the results in context is Sam's reading ability test result. His score on that measure was typical of students at the fourth grade. Therefore, his ability results on the verbal side may be underestimates. Sam was working successfully with his current abilities, but it is possible he would be effective in the position under consideration by using his oral rather than written skills. In this respect, assessment center exercises provide information on how people would be expected to work in real-life contexts. On the Negotiating exercise, he performed at the average or above level compared with others in his industrial sector. Overall, Sam had very strong mechanical abilities, excellent nonverbal intelligence, average or above results on supervisory skills, but lower scores on verbal than nonverbal intelligence.

TREVOR'S INVESTIGATIVE ABILITY PROFILE (CASE 6)

This profile (Table 12.2) presents the ability results of a PhD scientist who was trying to decide between a bench scientist career or seeking out options in management. (His interests were presented in Chapter 4.) Trevor had concluded that he would never become a world-class scientific innovator and did not feel that he had the patience needed to be an academic. Additionally, he wanted more work-life balance than he saw those in basic research experiencing. Still, he had invested a significant number of years in rigorous training in science, and he was not considering going into a totally different field. He was essentially trying to decide between a managerial position in science or continuing in his current track as a bench scientist. Within management, he viewed himself as being a good "number two," playing a solid support role for executing plans but not necessarily the one to create them.

TABLE 12.2. Trevor's Investigative Interests Ability Profile (Case 6)

Mechanical Reasoning—Bennett Mechanical Comprehension Test—62

Normative groups	Percentile
Grade 12 academic high school norms	99
Grade 12 technical high school	99
Industrial sample	99
Mechanical jobs, aviation company (applicants)	97
Development Laboratories career assessment sample	95

Spatial Ability—Minnesota Paper Form Board, AA series—64

Normative groups	Percentile
Grade 12 males	99
Engineering students	99
Industrial sample	99
Development Laboratories career assessment sample	99

(continues)

TABLE 12.2. Trevor's Investigative Interests Ability Profile (Case 6) (*Continued*)

General Intelligence—Multidimensional Aptitude Battery (MAB)

Overall standard scores and norms

	Standard scores	General population average/median/mode	Development Laboratories career assessment norms (percentile)
Verbal	693	500	98
Performance	673	500	84
Full Scale	700	500	99

Subtest standard scores

Information	63	Digit Symbol	66
Comprehension	63	Similarities	64
Arithmetic	79	Spatial	59
Picture Completion	62	Picture Arrangement	56
Vocabulary	64	Object Assembly	58

Note. Scores are standardized where 500 is average/median on total summary scores and 50 is average/median on the subtest scores.

Nonverbal Reasoning Ability—Raven's Advanced Progressive Matrices—31

Normative groups	Percentile
Test normative sample	93
Highly selective university sample	81
Development Laboratories career assessment sample	98

Verbal Reasoning Ability—Watson-Glaser Critical Thinking Appraisal—70

Normative groups	Percentile
Freshmen, 4-year college	97
Upper division 4-year college students	90
MBA students	70
3rd year medical students	65
Development Laboratories career assessment sample	93

Aesthetic Judgment—Meier Art Judgment Test—93

Normative groups	Percentile
High school students	25
College art students	15
Development Laboratories career assessment sample	37

Musical Aptitudes and Abilities

Subtest	Raw score	Normative sample (percentile)	Development Laboratories career assessment sample (percentile)
Pitch	47	92	84
Rhythm	25	28	26
Tonal Memory	28	72	69

Artistic Drawing Ability—Comprehensive Ability Test Reproductive Drawing Test—32

Normative groups	Percentile
High school students (male)	87
Development Laboratories career assessment sample	77

Verbal Fluency

Development Laboratories Verbal Fluency Measure—330

Normative groups	Percentile
Development Laboratories career assessment sample	95

CAB Fi (Ideational Fluency)—24

Normative groups	Percentile
High school students (males)	55
College students (males)	27
Development Laboratories career assessment sample	34

Creative Imagination (Things)—The CAB-O (Original Uses)—7

Normative groups	Percentile
High school students (males)	28
College students (males)	5
Development Laboratories career assessment sample	26

(*continues*)

242 Career Assessment

TABLE 12.2. Trevor's Investigative Interests Ability Profile (Case 6) *(Continued)*

Social Judgment—Interpersonal Problem Solving Assessment Technique

	Raw scores*		Norms (percentile)
	Client's scores	College students	Development Laboratories career assessment sample
Effective responses	18	13	91
Avoidant responses	2	4	74
Inappropriate responses	2	4	30
Dependent responses	0	1	70
Unscorable responses	0	1	47

*Responses client said he would actually do

Managerial Abilities—Development Laboratories In-basket

	Raw scores and percent correct		Norms (percentile)
	Client's	Group averages	Development career assessment norms
Prioritizing*	54	60	87
Managerial judgment	11/21 (52%)	12/21 (57%)	59

*Lower scores are better, that is, less discrepant with the criterion group's answers.

Perceptual Speed and Accuracy—Minnesota Clerical Test (Numbers, 118; Names 123)

Normative groups	Percentile	
	Names	Numbers
Male clerks	70	85
Female tellers	45	60
Development Laboratories career assessment sample	60	63

Computational Math Ability—Arithmetic subtest, Wide Range Achievement Test-Revised—44

Normative groups	Percentile
Same-age general population norms	86
Development Laboratories career assessment sample	90

The results of this assessment present a pattern of very high ability on all of the cognitive ability measures. There were slight differences, mostly not significant, between verbal and nonverbal abilities (in favor of verbal). When someone has as many high abilities as this client they could, potentially, apply abilities in many different areas. High general intelligence is very versatile in its applications. Interests and personality can help focus such abilities.

In this case, however, the question was not about the client's decision to be a scientist. He wanted a less grueling schedule and one that would allow him to progress. He was considering moving from medical research to a corporate setting in a managerial role. On the managerial in-basket he scored very well, suggesting a good sense of prioritizing and managerial judgment. He also performed well on the social skills measure.

On the creative measures, the client scored well on one of the verbal fluency measures but less well on a second, more structured one. He also did not score highly on a task (Comprehensive Ability Battery—Original Uses measure [CAB-O]) involving innovative uses for two seemingly unlike objects. He scored well on a perceptual checking task (the Minnesota Clerical Test [MCT]) that involved rapid attention to detail.

Overall, the client clearly was a very high performer on almost all of the cognitive measures. As related to the reasons for which help was sought, he also demonstrated relative strengths in managerial assessments. Given his preference for a role as a manager, probably in a corporate setting such as a pharmaceutical company, his abilities would be consistent with that goal as long as it involved technical/scientific management.

ELIZABETH'S ARTISTIC ABILITY PROFILE (CASE 7)

Not atypical of people with high Artistic interests, there was complexity in this client's ability profile (see Table 12.3). The client was currently working as a paralegal, an occupation fairly discrepant with her measured interests (see Chapter 4) but one that was providing a good income. At the same time, she was considering the possibility of working in an arts area, possibly in interior design.

Although her overall scores on the MAB were in the average range, there was a slight difference in favor of nonverbal abilities. There was also unevenness on the subtests for both verbal and nonverbal subtests. Her highest score was on the Digit Symbol subtest (which paralleled her perceptual speed and accuracy test result). This profile demonstrates how, possibly through sheer persistence and high motivation, people with average abilities can complete college. Still, she might have had an easier and more enjoyable time than she reported had she chosen a major that was more aligned with her abilities.

Considering that most of her occupational daydreams were in the arts, as were her interests, the question arises as to whether she also had strong test scores in those areas. In the visual arts, the expected profile would include

TABLE 12.3. Elizabeth's Artistic Interests Ability Profile (Case 7)

Mechanical Reasoning—Bennett Mechanical Comprehension Test—33

Normative groups	Percentile
Grade 12 academic high school norms	40
Mechanical jobs, aviation company (applicants)	10
Skilled jobs, auto company	10
Development Laboratories career assessment sample	26

Spatial Ability—Minnesota Paper Form Board, AA series—48

Normative groups	Percentile
Grade 12 females	75
Engineering students	40
Draftsmen	40
Engineers and scientists, R&D	40
Development Laboratories career assessment sample	78

General Intelligence—Multidimensional Aptitude Battery (MAB)

Overall standard scores and norms

	Standard scores	General population average/median/mode	Development Laboratories career assessment norms (percentile)
Verbal	490	500	21
Performance	510	500	27
Full Scale	505	500	21

Subtest standard scores

Information	50	Digit Symbol	60
Comprehension	55	Picture Completion	55
Arithmetic	55	Spatial	55
Similarities	50	Picture Arrangement	40
Vocabulary	50	Object assembly	65

Note. Scores are standardized where 500 is average/median on total summary scores and 50 is average/median on the subtest scores.

Nonverbal Reasoning Ability—Raven's Advanced Progressive Matrices—20

Normative groups	Percentile
Test normative sample	50
Select university sample	11
Development Laboratories career assessment sample	32

Verbal Reasoning Ability—Watson-Glaser Critical Thinking Appraisal—57

Normative groups	Percentile
Freshmen, 4-year college	65
Upper division 4-year college students	40
MBA students	15
3rd year medical students	10
Development Laboratories career assessment sample	32

Aesthetic Judgment—Meier Art Judgment Test—109

Normative groups	Percentile
High school students	86
College art students	73
Development Laboratories career assessment sample	92

Musical Aptitudes and Abilities

Subtest	Raw score	Normative sample (percentile)	Development Laboratories career assessment sample (percentile)
Pitch	29	8	12
Rhythm	27	55	46
Tonal Memory	23	29	26

Artistic Drawing Ability—Comprehensive Ability Test Reproductive Drawing Test—30

Normative groups	Percentile
High school students (female)	76
Development Laboratories career assessment sample	59

(continues)

TABLE 12.3. Elizabeth's Artistic Interests Ability Profile (Case 7) (*Continued*)

Verbal Fluency

Development Laboratories Verbal Fluency Measure—237

Normative groups	Percentile
Development Laboratories career assessment sample	71

CAB Fi (Ideational Fluency)—16

Normative groups	Percentile
High school students (females)	17
College students (females)	4
Development Laboratories career assessment sample	8

Creative Imagination (Things)—The CAB-O (Original Uses)—9

Normative groups	Percentile
High school students (females)	53
College students (females)	18
Development Laboratories career assessment sample	34

Social Judgment—Interpersonal Problem Solving Assessment Technique

	Raw scores*		Norms (percentile)
	Client's scores	College students	Development Laboratories career assessment sample
Effective responses	14	13	45
Avoidant responses	6	4	20
Inappropriate responses	2	4	30
Dependent responses	0	1	70
Unscorable responses	0	1	47

*Responses client said she would actually do.

Perceptual Speed and Accuracy—Minnesota Clerical Test (Numbers, 143; Names, 159)

	Percentile	
Normative groups	Names	Numbers
Female clerks	95	90
Female tellers	90	85
Development Laboratories career assessment sample	90	80

Computational Math Ability—Arithmetic subtest, Wide Range Achievement Test-Revised—37

Normative groups	Percentile
Same-age general population norms	47
Development Laboratories career assessment sample	37

strengths in both aesthetic judgment and spatial ability. Her test results in these areas were strong. Recognizing that on the spatial ability measure (the Minnesota Paper Form Board) the occupational groups to which she was compared were ones expected to be high on spatial ability, her midrange scores when compared with those groups were strong, since the standard was high with such samples. The score was also strong in comparison to the general population. She also scored above average to high on the other creative measures related to visual fluency and to the arts. It is not expected that someone strong in the visual arts would be strong in all creative areas, so the relatively low musical ability scores are not surprising.

Also of note was the client's strong score on the Perceptual Speed and Accuracy test. Although the client did not have corresponding interests in Conventional occupations, this skill set probably proved useful in her current occupation, which required her to be highly attentive to detail. People with artistic interests and abilities often need a "day job," and her current arrangement might work well so long as the creative interests and abilities find other outlets. However, in this client's case, that was not happening, though she had some feedback from the marketplace of a talent in interior design. The question was, what was keeping her from pursuing that career possibility? Chapters 13 through 16 on personality provide useful information relevant to that question.

SARAH'S SOCIAL ABILITIES PROFILE (CASE 8)

In this case, the purpose of the assessment, initiated by the client's parents, was to help the young woman identify a college major and career path fitting with her profile. As demonstrated in Chapter 4, her interests were highly Social and she expressed interest in working with helping people. This illustrates how interests may sometimes drive career choice even when abilities are quite strong across a number of areas. The client could well pursue science, medicine, and other areas. At the same time, a high school or college student is still developing and career choices may change or sharpen in college. Her ability results are shown in Table 12.4.

Despite the client's presenting fairly unsophisticated understanding of careers, many of her interests and avocational activities were in Social areas. Yet, her abilities, if anything, were higher in the nonverbal than verbal side. There was a significant difference between her nonverbal and verbal scores on the general intelligence measure in favor of the nonverbal. She also scored highly on measures of spatial ability, and on a difficult measure of nonverbal

TABLE 12.4. Sarah's Social Interests Ability Profile (Case 8)

Mechanical Reasoning—DAT Mechanical Reasoning Test—45

Normative groups	Percentile
Grade 12 academic high school norms (female)	90
Grade 12 combined sex norms	75
Development Laboratories career assessment sample	38

Spatial Ability—Minnesota Paper Form Board, AA series—56

Normative groups	Percentile
Grade 12 females	95
Engineering students	90
Draftsmen	80
Development Laboratories career assessment sample	98

Field Dependence—CAB Flexibility of Closure (Cf) Test—11

Normative groups	Percentile
High school (females)	83
College freshmen (females)	71
Development Laboratories career assessment sample	79

Note. Higher scores are in the field independent direction.

General Intelligence—Multidimensional Aptitude Battery (MAB)

Overall standard scores and norms

	Standard scores	General population average/median/mode	Development Laboratories career assessment norms (percentile)
Verbal	593	500	81
Performance	634	500	76
Full Scale	621	500	84

Subtest standard scores

Information	57	Digit Symbol	80
Comprehension	58	Picture Completion	60
Arithmetic	61	Spatial	63
Similarities	64	Picture Arrangement	40
Vocabulary	55	Object assembly	65

Note. Scores are standardized where 500 is average/median on total summary scores and 50 is average/median on the subtest scores.

Nonverbal Reasoning Ability—Raven's Advanced Progressive Matrices—28

Normative groups	Percentile
Test normative sample	83
Select university sample	57
Development Laboratories career assessment sample	89

Verbal Reasoning Ability

Watson-Glaser Critical Thinking Appraisal—64

Normative groups	Percentile
Freshmen, 4-year college	85
Upper division 4-year college students	70
MBA students	40
3rd year medical students	30
Development Laboratories career assessment sample	77

Wesman Personnel Classification Test (Numerical)—29

Normative groups	Percentile
Salaried workers	84
High level executives	46
White collar employees	51
Development Laboratories career assessment sample	93

Aesthetic Judgment

Meier Art Judgment Test—84

Normative groups	Percentile
High school students	<9
College art students	<5
Development Laboratories career assessment sample	14

Welsh Figure Preference Test

Scale	Client's scores	Mean scores, creative artists	Career assessment sample (percentile)
Original art scale	36	40.0	76
Revised art scale	37	37.6	70
Origence	45	61.9	60

(continues)

TABLE 12.4. Sarah's Social Interests Ability Profile (Case 8) *(Continued)*

Musical Aptitudes and Abilities

Subtest	Raw score	Normative sample (percentile)	Development Laboratories career assessment sample (percentile)
Pitch	47	92	84
Rhythm	27	55	50
Tonal Memory	20	16	15

Artistic Drawing Ability—Comprehensive Ability Test Reproductive Drawing Test—36

Normative groups	Percentile
High school students (male)	97
Development Laboratories career assessment sample	92

Verbal Fluency

Development Laboratories Verbal Fluency Measure—366

Normative groups	Percentile
Development Laboratories career assessment sample	98

CAB Fi (Ideational Fluency)—41

Normative groups	Percentile
High school students (females)	89
College students (females)	97
Development Laboratories career assessment sample	90

Creative Imagination (Things)—The CAB-O (Original Uses)—10

Normative groups	Percentile
High school students (females)	60
College students (females)	60
Development Laboratories career assessment sample	28

Social Judgment—Interpersonal Problem Solving Assessment Technique

	Raw scores*		Norms (percentile)
	Client's scores	College students	Development Laboratories career assessment sample
Effective responses	9	13	10
Avoidant responses	6	4	5

	Raw scores*		Norms (percentile)
	Client's scores	College students	Development Laboratories career assessment sample
Inappropriate responses	5	4	2
Dependent responses	2	1	2
Unscorable responses	0	1	47

*Responses client said she would actually do.

Managerial Abilities—Development Laboratories In-basket

	Raw scores and percent correct		Norms (percentile)
	Client's	Group averages	Development career assessment norms
Prioritizing*	82	60	33
Managerial judgment	11	12	59

*Lower scores are better, that is, less discrepant with the criterion group's answers.

Perceptual Speed and Accuracy—Minnesota Clerical Test (Numbers, 200; Names, 196)

Normative groups	Percentile	
	Names	Numbers
Male clerks	99	99
Female tellers	99	99
Development Laboratories career assessment sample	99	99

Computational Math Ability

Arithmetic subtest, Wide Range Achievement Test-Revised—46

Normative groups	Percentile
Same-age general population norms	98
Development Laboratories career assessment sample	92

Wesman Personnel Classification Test (Numerical)—17

Normative groups	Percentile
Salaried workers	91
High level executives	66

(*continues*)

TABLE 12.4. Sarah's Social Interests Ability Profile (Case 8)   (*Continued*)

Normative groups	Percentile
White collar employees	71
Development Laboratories career assessment sample	99

Arithmetic subtest, Multidimensional Aptitude Battery—60

Normative groups	Percentile
Development Laboratories career assessment sample	88

reasoning. On an ability measure of field dependence, she scored in the field independent direction. Additionally, on the social ability test in use at the time of her assessment, her scores were relatively low. It is possible that her social abilities were still maturing at the time of the assessment. However, from the perspective of abilities, these results would be consistent with a science profile, although she did have other strengths including a very high score on the Perceptual Speed and Accuracy measure and a very high score on the Digit Symbol subtest of the Multidimensional Aptitude Battery (MAB).

The client's interests would likely favor a career in the helping and people-oriented occupations. But what is sometimes overlooked when it comes to science careers are those in the social sciences. Such occupations combine working with people with scientific methods. That the client had very low Investigative interests on all but one of the measures might predispose her to different occupations, but possibly she would want to take some courses in the social sciences (psychology, sociology, anthropology, and the like) to see if those were appealing to her.

STAN'S ENTERPRISING ABILITIES PROFILE (CASE 9)

This case illustrates people of different ages may seek out career assessment and counseling. When someone in their 50s undertakes the process it would often be for purposes of retirement planning. In this situation the questions were raised by someone who was rather urgently in need of finding employment. He was working with a job finding coach but sought out career assessment to try to better understand his areas of strength and relative weakness. The client's ability results are shown in Table 12.5.

TABLE 12.5. Stan's Enterprising Interests Ability Profile (Case 9)

Mechanical Reasoning—DAT Mechanical Comprehension Test—54

Normative groups	Percentile
Grade 12 high school (males)	91
Grade 12 high school (combined sex)	97
Development Laboratories career assessment sample	79

Spatial Ability—Minnesota Paper Form Board, AA series—43

Normative groups	Percentile
Grade 12 males	50
Engineering students	20
Draftsmen	30
Customer service engineers	25
Development Laboratories career assessment sample	56

Field Dependence—CAB Flexibility of Closure (Cf) Test—12

Normative groups	Percentile
High school (males)	99
College freshmen (males)	78
Development Laboratories career assessment sample	99

Note. Higher scores are in the field independent direction.

General Intelligence—Multidimensional Aptitude Battery (MAB)

Overall standard scores and norms

	Standard scores	General population average/median/mode	Development Laboratories career assessment norms (percentile)
Verbal	594	500	82
Performance	564	500	57
Full Scale	579	500	73

Subtest standard scores

Information	57	Digit Symbol	57
Comprehension	61	Picture Completion	57
Arithmetic	58	Spatial	61
Similarities	55	Picture Arrangement	49
Vocabulary	65	Object assembly	58

Note. Scores are standardized where 500 is average/median on total summary scores and 50 is average/median on the subtest scores.

Nonverbal Reasoning Ability—Raven's Advanced Progressive Matrices—15

Normative groups	Percentile
Test normative sample	36
Select university sample	3
Development Laboratories career assessment sample	45

(continues)

TABLE 12.5. Stan's Enterprising Interests Ability Profile (Case 9) *(Continued)*

Verbal Reasoning Ability—Watson-Glaser Critical Thinking Appraisal—63

Normative groups	Percentile
Freshmen, 4-year college	85
Upper division 4-year college students	65
MBA students	35
3rd year medical students	25
Development Laboratories career assessment sample	67

Aesthetic Judgment—Welsh Figure Preference Test

Scale	Client's scores	Mean scores, creative artists	Career assessment sample (percentile)
Original art scale	27	40.0	55
Revised art scale	37	37.6	70
Origence	45	61.9	60

Musical Aptitudes and Abilities

Subtest	Raw score	Normative sample (percentile)	Development Laboratories career assessment sample (percentile)
Pitch	16	1	<1
Rhythm	28	73	67
Tonal Memory	6	1	<1

Artistic Drawing Ability—Comprehensive Ability Test Reproductive Drawing Test—39

Normative groups	Percentile
High school students (male)	99
Development Laboratories career assessment sample	96

Verbal Fluency

Development Laboratories Verbal Fluency Measure—288

Normative groups	Percentile
Development Laboratories career assessment sample	85

CAB Fi (Ideational Fluency)—20

Normative groups	Percentile
High school students (males)	38

Normative groups	Percentile
College students (males)	10
Development Laboratories career assessment sample	26

Creative Imagination (Things)—The CAB-O (Original Uses)—8

Normative groups	Percentile
High school students (males)	26
College students (males)	38
Development Laboratories career assessment sample	10

Social Judgment—Interpersonal Problem Solving Assessment Technique

	Raw scores*		Norms (percentile)
	Client's scores	College students	Development Laboratories career assessment sample
Effective responses	17	13	81
Avoidant responses	4	4	56
Inappropriate responses	1	4	47
Dependent responses	0	1	70
Unscorable responses	0	1	70

*Responses client said he would actually do.

Managerial Abilities—Development Laboratories In-basket

	Raw scores and percent correct		Norms (percentile)
	Client's	Group averages	Development career assessment norms
Prioritizing*	20	18	41
Managerial judgment	9/21	15/21	31

*Lower scores are better, that is, less discrepant with the criterion group's answers.

Perceptual Speed and Accuracy—Minnesota Clerical Test (Numbers, 145; Names 115)

	Percentile	
Normative groups	Names	Numbers
Male clerks	95	75

(continues)

TABLE 12.5. Stan's Enterprising Interests Ability Profile (Case 9) (*Continued*)

	Percentile	
Normative groups	Names	Numbers
Female tellers	45	60
Development Laboratories career assessment sample	81	54

Computational Math Ability

Arithmetic subtest, Wide Range Achievement Test-Revised—45

Normative groups	Percentile
Same-age general population norms	84
Development Laboratories career assessment sample	66

Arithmetic subtest, Multidimensional Aptitude Battery—58

Normative groups	Percentile
Same-age general population norms	84
Development Laboratories career assessment sample	66

Earlier in this book the decline in fluid abilities (vs. crystallized) with age was discussed. Crystallized abilities are stable over the lifespan, but they also eventually decline for most people though at a slower rate than fluid. At the individual level, however, it is difficult to reliably know whether abilities are stable or declining absent a baseline from prior testing with which to compare the client's abilities. However, were the same profile found in an assessee in his 20s, the abilities would certainly be sufficiently high for many careers in business and management.

There is a slight tendency in this profile for verbal abilities to be higher than nonverbal ones, consistent with many managerial profiles. Concerning general intelligence, his overall verbal score was in the high average to superior range. His nonverbal abilities were in the high average range. Both are typical scores for college graduates and for those in business management careers. He scored below average on the managerial in-basket, completing a version that was created for financial and accounting management, an area of his specialization in management. He scored in the field-independent direction, suggesting the ability to consider a situation outside the context in which it is embedded. He scored highly on verbal fluency but generally lower on measures of creativity. One of his stronger scores compared with norms were on the Perceptual Speed and Accuracy test, a common finding among individuals with finance and accounting work experience.

Overall, the abilities, with some exceptions, were consistent with his chosen profession in business. Although probably closer to the end than the beginning of his career, he still had strong abilities relevant for work in his chosen occupation. However, he would probably do better in his areas of primary expertise—business finance roles—than in an entrepreneurial one. His brief foray into starting a business franchise had not gone well.

LINDA'S CONVENTIONAL ABILITY PROFILE (CASE 10)

In reviewing this client's ability profile (see Table 12.6), it should be noted that she started out her career as a high school graduate in a clerical position, went to college at night to complete her college degree in accounting, left her initial employer to work in a large government agency involving work with financial data, and subsequently returned to her original employer at a managerial level. Linda was assessed as part of a selection and development project at her company.

TABLE 12.6. Linda's Conventional Interests Ability Profile (Case 10)

General Intelligence—Multidimensional Aptitude Battery (MAB)

Overall standard scores and norms

	Standard scores	General population average/median/mode	Development Laboratories career assessment norms (percentile)
Verbal	620	500	92
Performance	594	500	52
Full Scale	620	500	85

Subtest standard scores

Information	73	Digit Symbol	64
Comprehension	67	Picture Completion	58
Arithmetic	60	Spatial	60
Similarities	53	Picture Arrangement	62
Vocabulary	63	Object Assembly	58

Note. Scores are standardized where 500 is average/median on total summary scores and 50 is average/median on the subtest scores.

Nonverbal Reasoning Ability—Raven's Advanced Progressive Matrices—22

Normative groups	Percentile
Test normative sample	61
Select university sample	18
Industrial sample	84
Development Laboratories career assessment sample	51

(continues)

TABLE 12.6. Linda's Conventional Interests Ability Profile (Case 10) *(Continued)*

Verbal Reasoning Ability—Watson-Glaser Critical Thinking Appraisal—70

Normative groups	Percentile
Freshmen, 4-year college	97
Upper division 4-year college students	70
MBA students	35
3rd-year medical students	25
Industrial sample	98
Development Laboratories career assessment sample	89

Verbal Fluency—Development Laboratories Verbal Fluency Measure—140

Normative groups	Percentile
Development Laboratories career assessment sample	35

Accounting Managerial Abilities—Development Laboratories In-basket

	Raw scores and percent correct		Norms (percentile)	
	Client's	Group averages	Industrial accounting sample	General accounting sample
Prioritizing*	20	18/24	55	69
Managerial judgment	18/22 (82%)	15/22 (57%)	99	99

*Higher scores on this scale indicate higher prioritizing ability. The individual was also assessed with a number of assessment center exercises. She scored well above average in a speaking presentation, and in a leaderless group discussion in which she was a less verbally active, but still quite effective, participant. Her score on a negotiating exercise is shown below.

Negotiating Skills—Development Laboratories Negotiating Exercise—4.4/5.0

Normative groups	Percentile
Industrial sample	98
Development Laboratories career assessment sample	95

Perceptual Speed and Accuracy—Minnesota Clerical Test (Names, 178; Numbers, 198)

	Percentile	
Normative groups	Names	Numbers
Female clerks	99	99
Retail sample	99	99
Industrial sample	99	99
Development Laboratories career assessment sample	99	99

Computational Math Ability—Arithmetic subtest, Wide Range Achievement Test-Revised—10

Normative groups	Percentile
Same-age general population norms	84
Development Laboratories career assessment sample	66

Numerical Reasoning

Wesman Personnel Classification Test (Numerical)—10

Normative groups	Percentile
High school seniors	67
Office supervisor	34
Executives	12
Industrial sample	67
Development Laboratories career assessment sample	82

DAT Numerical Ability Test—24

Normative groups	Percentile
Grade 12 norms	95
Industrial sample	95

Arithmetic subtest, Multidimensional Aptitude Battery—60 (standard score; mean, 50)

Normative groups	Percentile
Same-age general population norms	96
Development Laboratories career assessment sample	70

Field Dependence—CAB Flexibility of Closure (Cf) Test—6

Normative groups	Percentile
High school (females)	33
College freshmen (females)	8
Development Laboratories career assessment sample	42

Note. Higher scores are in the field independent direction.

Linda's pattern of abilities included very strong general cognitive abilities (in the superior to very superior range on verbal intelligence and in the superior range on nonverbal). Her pattern was generally higher on the verbal than on the nonverbal measures. She scored in the field dependent direction on CAB-CF measure. Her scores on the Perceptual Speed and Accuracy test were near-perfect on the Numbers subtest and very high on the Names subtest. She scored similarly to the group of accountants with whom she was assessed on one measure of math ability and above the group average on another. Her scores on the managerial in-basket (accounting management version) were at or above the accounting group's performance level. She also performed well on a negotiating simulation measure. Overall, she had particular strengths in business, math, and general intelligence. She had proven herself in a variety of work roles and would be well-suited for higher levels of management, particularly in accounting areas.

SUMMARY AND CONCLUSIONS

This part (Chapters 5–12) has covered a lot of ground in assessing abilities that have demonstrated career relevance. The importance of general mental ability was recognized, as was the importance of a variety of other ability variables that are relevant for particular careers. The chapter has also identified and discussed measurement issues to be considered when selecting ability assessment measures. These include characteristics both of tests and of people. For example, age matters significantly when measuring abilities of adults, and gender and multicultural issues, including language, may also be important to consider in some testing applications. When a person coming from a limited educational background is being assessed, the nonverbal abilities may be a better guide to overall potential.

Career assessment is appropriate for a variety of people and situations. Sometimes the question involves choice of a college major; sometimes it concerns unhappiness in a career; sometimes the question is what work options exist for someone who has suffered a physical or mental impairment. Criteria used for selecting ability measures vary with the particular assessment situation. Someone attending or having graduated from an elite university will likely need a different assessment battery from someone who is struggling to complete high school or suffering early signs of dementia. Reading difficulties may also confound verbal ability measurement.

Ability profile interpretation methods and guidelines are still emerging. Research on profile analysis of abilities is still in its infancy. Although general intelligence remains an important variable in ability assessment, the chapter has introduced a number of other career-relevant abilities. Examples were provided of how ability results look and of some of the complexities in interpreting the results across measures.

ABC

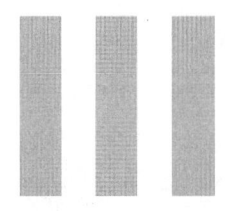

ASSESSING CAREER-RELATED PERSONALITY CHARACTERISTICS

13

Conceptual and Measurement Issues of Career-Related Personality

The personality of the artist, at first a cry or a cadence or a mood and then a fluid and lambent narrative, finally refines itself out of existence, impersonalizes itself so to speak. . . . The artist, like the God of the creation, remains within or behind or beyond or above his handiwork, invisible, refined out of existence, indifferent, paring his fingernails.
—JOYCE, 1947, P. 483

The third of the three major career assessment domains, personality, is the focus on this and the two following chapters. In the first section of this chapter, the nature of personality is considered along with efforts to define it. Emerging research on personality factors is then taken up, followed by an overview of issues important in the measurement of personality.

PERSONALITY DEFINITIONS

What is personality? Here is how the American Psychological Association (APA) defined the term:

> *Personality* refers to individual differences in characteristic patterns of thinking, feeling and behaving. The study of personality focuses on two broad areas: One is understanding individual differences in particular personality characteristics, such as sociability or irritability. The other is understanding how the various parts of a person come together as a whole (as cited in APA, n.d., para.1).

---

https://doi.org/10.1037/0000254-014
Career Assessment: Integrating Interests, Abilities, and Personality, by R. L. Lowman
Copyright © 2022 by the American Psychological Association. All rights reserved.

Here is another such definition, from a textbook of personality psychology:

> Personality is the set of psychological traits and mechanisms within the individual that are organized and relatively enduring and that influence his or her interactions with, and adaptations to, the intrapsychic, physical, and social environments. (Larsen & Buss, 2008, p. 4)

Saucier (2008) noted that among the various definitions of personality that have been found in the research literature, "Personality is defined either as (a) a set of attributes characterizing an individual, or as (b) the underlying system that generates the set of attributes" (p. 29).

As it relates to work and careers, the measurement of personality has greatly expanded in recent decades. In the past, the literature on personality in the work context (B. Schneider, 1987) was generally unpersuasive as to its importance in predicting career success. It is useful to consider why personality, so important in other applications of psychology, had been considered to be of so little importance in career and work applications.

First, early empirical research (see, e.g., Ghiselli & Barthol, 1953; Guion & Gottier, 1965; Kinslinger, 1966) applying personality characteristics to personnel selection led to the conclusion (premature, as it developed) that these variables were not very predictive of job or career performance. Influential industrial–organizational (I–O) psychologists also saw little use for personality in work-related assessments. They argued that the small predictive power that was added over cognitive abilities in predicting job performance was trivial and that the personality variables were in any case unimportant.

Second, the existing research itself related to personality and work was criticized on a variety of grounds, both as to volume and content. For example, Guion (1987) wrote that his earlier (mostly negative) review of personality and work (Guion & Gottier, 1965) had not been updated "because the reported use of such measures since the mid-1960s has not been large enough to merit the summary" (Guion, 1987, p. 200). Yet, later studies (see, e.g., Bernardin & Bownas, 1985; Miner, 1985) showed that the conclusions had been far too negative, sweeping, and premature, based as they were on few, and often not very robust, studies.

Third, several of the measures used in personnel selection studies (many of which were reviewed in Burbeck & Furnham, 1985; Guion & Gottier, 1965; Hargrave & Berner, 1984; Lowman, 1989) typically assessed how measures of *psychopathology* rather than normal personality characteristics predicted job performance. An obvious limitation of such an approach is that most work performance relates more to variations of normal, than to abnormal, personality. Although in some occupations, particularly in the creative arts, psychopathology may be commonly encountered, especially among highly successful creators (Jamison, 1996; Lowman, 1989), creative work is not of primary concern to many occupational psychologists. (A later section of this chapter will discuss why psychological dysfunction is, in some cases, important for career assessors to be able to address.)

Still other factors also influenced the comparative neglect of personality in vocational applications. Many "normal" personality variables (e.g., achievement motivation, dominance, introversion/extraversion) had not been adequately evaluated as to their ability to predict career-relevant outcomes, although there were promising starts (see Bernardin & Bownas, 1985; Ghiselli, 1971; J. S. Guilford et al., 1976, Chapter 17; A. Howard & Bray, 1988; Miner, 1985; see also R. B. Cattell, 1987, Chapter 12). Many early studies relied on personality assessment devices that were not designed for occupational choice or personnel selection, instead repurposing existing measures or scales for new uses. There were exceptions, of course, including the Miner Sentence Completion Scale (Miner, 1978) and the more recently developed (and now widely used) Hogan Personnel Selection Series (R. Hogan & Hogan, 2007). Still, vocational applications have typically come after the development of the test rather than before. When personality variables are work-relevant and appropriately measured, some of these tests have proven to be useful in career and work assessment.

Although a deficit had previously existed in studies on the use of personality variables in predicting to work outcomes, that is not the case now (Barrick & Mount, 2012; Schmitt, 2014). In the past few decades, there has been a robust and still-growing literature on personality, and the findings, as shown in this chapter, suggest an important place for personality in the career and work domain. Illustrative of more recent approaches, Denissen et al. (2018) had experts determine the personality requirements of particular German jobs. They then examined degree of personality fit to the "ideal personality of job holders" and salaries. They found that there was a "fit bonus" attributable to personality but that excessive amounts of some personality variables versus the ideal were not always valued.

Personality variables do not replace abilities (or, for that matter, interests) in career assessment, but their assessment provides much valuable information at both the group and individual levels concerning career choice and change.

EMERGING RESEARCH FINDINGS ON PERSONALITY VARIABLES

After the multidecade dry period in which not much research about the relationship of normal personality and work and careers was occurring, the "rediscovery" of personality—both normal and not—began to emerge in the 1990s and ultimately has resulted in a large, growing, and robust literature. As Hough and Dilchert (2017) put it, "Greater recognition of the role personality plays in individual, group, and organizational outcomes has resulted in more sophisticated thinking about personality variables and their role as determinants (predictors) of individual, team, and organizational outcomes" (p. 298). Much of the focus was associated with reducing the rather large number of individual variables that were reflected in broad-brush measures of personality to five more robust dimensions. The popularization by researchers and practitioners of the five-factor model (FFM) of personality facilitated that work. Ironically, this was not a new focus among personality researchers. Digman (1990) well summarized the early and emerging efforts at identifying structural factors in measures of personality, particularly normal personality. As Digman (1996) noted in describing the "curious history" of the FFM, there were a number of researchers who had identified overarching factors long before the FFM came along. Indeed, Norman (1963; see also McCrae & Costa, 1985b) had identified five factors that closely paralleled the current factor terminology. Specifically, Norman's labels (except for Conscientious, borrowed from Tupes and Christal, 1961, who worked in this same research space even earlier) were Extraversion or Surgency, Agreeableness, Conscientiousness, Emotional Stability, and Culture (today's "Openness"). And before these researchers was R. B. Cattell (1946), who also considered personality factors as related to work. Table 13.1 shows some of the major early models of such factors.

At this writing, the FFM dominates the literature on personality and work, but it does have limitations and omissions. Costa and McCrae's (1995) development of a popular personality measure based on the FFM with facet scales for each of the five major factors helped to popularize the FFM among applied assessors. Some find limits to the current FFM and have reported better outcomes when predicting some job-related variables from facets rather than factors (Bergner et al., 2010; Judge et al., 2013). Hough and Dilchert (2017) concluded in a review that the FFM

> is an inadequate taxonomy of personality variables for I–O psychology to build knowledge and understand the determinants of work behavior and performance . . . the FFM is not comprehensive, combines variables into factors that are too heterogeneous, and is method-bound, dependent upon factor analysis. (p. 301)

In addition to identifying variables and facets omitted by many FFM approaches, they drew attention to an alternative model, K. Lee and Ashton's (2004a, 2004b) HEXACO six-factor model (see also Zettler et al., 2020). Hough and Dilchert (2017) also noted the value of compound variables (two or more factors being aggregated in predicting to work-related outcomes). Stanek and Ones (2018) described compound or blended traits as ones that draw from

TABLE 13.1. Alternative Models and Labels for "Big Five" Structural Personality Variables

Tupes and Christal[a]	Cattell[b]	Costa and McCrae[c]	Hogan and Hogan[d]
Surgency	Extraversion	Extraversion	Sociability
Dependability	Self-Control	Conscientiousness	Prudence
Culture	Openness	Independence	Inquisitive
Emotional Stability	Anxiety	Neuroticism	Adjustment
Agreeableness	Independence	Agreeableness	Interpersonal Sensitivity

[a]Tupes and Christal (1961); Norman (1963), in a similar approach used the term Conscientiousness rather than Dependability.
[b]Cattell (1957); Cattell initially referred to Self-Control as Superego strength.
[c]Costa and McCrae (1985).
[d]Hogan and Hogan (2007); this model includes two other factors not related to most FFM models, Ambition and Learning Approach.

multiple so-called pure personality facets and factors, noting, as an example, that "Ambition is a compound trait that draws variance from both Conscientiousness and Extraversion" (p. 382). Much of this literature is just emerging and is more suggestive than well-established, though it is very promising in its potential ability to predict career and work outcomes.

Compound traits are not new. Cattell (e.g., R. B. Cattell et al., 1970) statistically identified the following composites used for his second-order factors: (a) Extraversion (.3A + .3F + .2H − .3N − .3Q2 + 4.4), (b) Anxiety (−.4C + .3L + .4O + .4Q4 + 1.65), (c) Self-Control (−.2F + .4G − .3M + .4Q3 + 3.85), (d) Independence (.6E + .3H + .2L + .3Q1 − 2.2), and (e) Tough-Mindedness (−.2A − .5I − .3M − .5Q1 + 13.75). Gough's (1996) California Psychological Inventory (CPI) manual also identified a number of compound traits including the structural vectors (v.1 and v.2) and also special scales integrating cross-scale items such as those measuring Managerial Potential, Work Orientation, and Creative Temperament.

Another important idea that has emerged in recent years is the idea of trait activation by characteristics of the work (or of situations; Tett et al., 2013). This is particularly important for career assessment applications. Rather than viewing characteristics of people as fixed and static, trait activation theory considers personality to be a latent trait, characteristics of which are displayed in response to certain aspects of work-related situations. Thus, personality may have very little correlation with job when the job duties do not call on the particular personality variables. Extraversion may correlate well with criterion measures when the nature of the job requires intense interpersonal contact but, in a job that does not, may show little association.

DESIRABLE CHARACTERISTICS OF CAREER-RELEVANT PERSONALITY VARIABLES

In evaluating the relevance of personality variables for career assessment, criteria similar to those recommended for evaluating ability measures can be used. A career-relevant personality variable will ideally be one with demonstrated theoretical and empirical evidence whose measures offer norms for various occupational groups that are of sufficient size and diversity. The variable will also demonstrate a pattern in which the scores differentially predict to career satisfaction and job performance. For example, if the work duties call for outgoing social behavior, extraverts would perform better than will introverts. In addition, the variable will demonstrate inter- and intra-occupational differences in a manner consistent with the construct. In an occupation whose job duties include close and persistent interactions with others, higher levels of extroversion than introversion would be expected. However, to determine how high one will rise in a particular occupation (for which a good fit has been suggested by other measures), intra-occupational personality patterns may also be relevant. Profiles in technical sales, which require mastery of complex product knowledge, may be different from those in nontechnical sales. Finally, evidence as to whether the variable measures change with age is important to consider when personality variables may, on average, vary as a function of age (see Grupp et al., 1968; A. Howard & Bray, 1988; Martin et al., 1981) such that age-specific norms may be needed.

In Chapters 14 and 15, personality variables with theoretical or empirical relevance to occupational assessment are examined in detail. I review the variables one at a time, even though, as the case examples in Chapter 16 demonstrate, it is the integration of personality data that is particularly important in the practice of individual-level career assessment. Nevertheless, the assessor must first understand the nature of each personality variable and the research literature suggesting career relevance before attempting the more complex task of integration.

The literature on personality and work is now large and complex. This chapter attempts to navigate some of these findings. Then, in Chapter 14, each of the FFM factors are reviewed, including a brief summary of the current literature findings related to work, the dimensionality and facets of the factors, how different measures have approached the factors and facets, and career and work applications. Additional personality variables beyond the FFM are considered in Chapter 15.

Some general issues can be identified that arise across the various personality models, variables, and measures.

First, there is no consensual agreement among experts about the definitions of the various personality factors, much less the number and nature of associated facets and subdimensions (aspects). The implications of this for measurement of real people grappling with real career decisions are not trivial. Connelly et al. (2018) noted that narrower traits (facets) do not always align uniquely with a single factor. Rather, they may load on multiple broad factors. This suggests that facets, if career relevant, need to be thought of less as dimensions of a particular broad-brush factor, and more as variables of interest on their own merits.

Other researchers have also argued for examining personality variables beyond the FFM ones when predicting to work performance. These included Hough and Dilchert (2017), Rothstein and Goffin (2006), and Tett and Christiansen (2008). Mussel et al. (2011), for example, showed in the case of Openness (Openness to Experience) that combinations of facets better predicted work performance than did the overall personality factor.

Although the general consensus had been that the global personality traits were better predictors of job performance than were the narrower facet traits, an important study by Judge et al. (2013) reported evidence that facets are sometimes better predictors of job outcomes than are the global traits. DeYoung et al. (2007a) provided an alternative view to the idea that each of the FFM factors have six facets with a model they termed the 6-2-1 model, in which each of the FFM factors have two newly defined facets, which are themselves aligned with three of the six original Costa and McCrae facets. As an example, in the DeYoung et al. (2007a, 2007b, 2009) 6-2-1 model, Conscientiousness is the "1," the two introduced aspects of Industriousness and Orderliness are the "2," and the two groups of three subfacets are the "6." Achievement, Competence, and Self-Discipline were associated with the Industriousness aspect, and Deliberation, Dutifulness, and Order were associated with Orderliness.

Recognizing the challenge of having to use a large number of items to measure each of these constructs, De Young et al. (2007a) suggested using briefer measures to make the approach practical. They provided evidence that this hierarchical structure works better in predicting work-related personality than does the sole use of the broad FFM variables. Although this may be a promising approach to sorting out some of the considerable messiness still associated with personality measurement, there is much more work to be done, particularly in the context of career assessment. This point was well made by Stanek and Ones (2018), who noted that "more research needs to be done to understand how each facet is related to each aspect" (p. 381).

A second major issue is that assessing and interpreting at the individual level is different from working at the aggregated level. Massive cross-study data sets are useful for meta-analysis and for examining general trends, but they mask individual differences. Additionally, outcome literature tends to focus on grouped rather than individual data, whereas career assessment is usually about individuals. Assuming the person, but not the job or career, is the given requires a different perspective, although literature findings can and should still help to guide interpretations. Put another way, meta-analyses are typically based on very large sample sizes, but work with individuals is based on a sample size of one. Career assessors are largely working with clients one at a time, and this means there will be considerable variation in patterns needing interpretation at the individual level. Understanding people in their complexity is the goal, using assessment data to help them better understand themselves and to make better career choices than they might otherwise make.

Thirdly, although the FFM is usually labeled from the perspective of only one end of a spectrum (e.g., extraversion or agreeableness vs. introversion and disagreeableness), career assessors should be careful not to "privilege" one part of a factor (e.g., extraversion vs. introversion). This is a problem because many approaches to identifying trait or predispositional tendencies focus primarily on one end of a continuum (typically the one considered "positive") and look negatively, if at all, on the other polarity, usually saying very little about those scoring in the middle. For that reason, each of the major factors or variables is discussed with the premise that there is no single "desired" place to be for persons in particular careers, though some personality types may have an easier time of it than others. Additionally, for those otherwise well suited by virtue of abilities and interests to particular careers, work roles may be executed differently depending on personality dimensions. Even with the personality factor rather pejoratively labeled "Neuroticism" in some models, scoring in the less-well-adjusted direction is not necessarily a deficit or even atypical. At the group level, scores on the Adjustment factor in the less-well-adjusted area may be a predictor of work-related difficulties. However, there are certain occupations in which neuroticism is typically found and may actually be adaptive. Additionally, too much of a "good thing" can also be maladaptive. N. T. Carter et al. (2018), for example, noted ways in which each of the "positive" side FFM factors (e.g., high Conscientiousness and high Emotional Stability) can be problematic. Obsessive-compulsive personality disorder may be found among those scoring very high on Conscientiousness, and those too high in Emotional Stability may fail to experience anxiety that may be an appropriate signal to take action in response to a threatening situation or may also be more closed when greater openness may be called for.

Fourth, personality can change over time. It is true that there is solid evidence that certain personality characteristics are trait-like and have a genetic component (Polderman et al., 2015), but even with 40% to 50% contribution from genetics, there is much variance (50%–60%) that is subject to environmental influences. There are also findings, however, that certain personality variables do, on average, change over time. For example, in longitudinal studies of managers by A. Howard and Bray (1988), average Achievement Motivation declined over time. Several studies (some cross-sectional, some longitudinal) found patterns of decreasing Extraversion and Openness, and increasing Agreeableness and Conscientiousness (although in some studies Conscientiousness declined in later years; Donnellan & Lucas, 2008; Lucas & Donnellan, 2011; Wortman et al., 2012). Helson and Stewart (1994) summarized research on creative individuals and found reduced impulsiveness and flexibility over time. As they noted, "Careers and creative products change character at different points in the life course" (p. 204). Additionally, variables like Neuroticism/Adjustment can definitely be changed by exposure to stress in one's personal or work life. Such organizational factors as toxic work environments or occupational stress can have direct impact on individuals (Harms et al., 2017; Lowman, 1993). Similarly, youth experiencing long-term health problems demonstrated increased external (vs. internal) locus of control (Elkins et al., 2017).

GENERIC MEASUREMENT ISSUES

Assessors will need to select personality measures appropriate for the intended career-related inferences. In practice, however, it is not unusual for queries to begin with the question of which test(s), rather than which variables, to use in conducting career assessments. In career assessment practice, it is not unusual for queries to begin with the question of which test(s), rather than which variables, to consider when conducting career assessments. The focus of this chapter, however, is not on "which personality test to use" but rather on which personality variables to measure. Each of the FFM variables and additional ones that have shown career relevance are reviewed here in some detail.

As for specific tests, there are a number on the commercial market and additional ones available for research that are in the public domain. Table 13.2

Conceptual and Measurement Issues of Career-Related Personality   271

shows a comparison of some of the major factors and facet scales (or variables) on several measures of personality widely used in career assessment. Although contemporary measures often are built around some version of the Big Five model, others pre-dated that approach. Even for broad-brush measures such as the CPI, the scales can be translated into the Big Five factors (see, e.g., McCrae et al., 1993; Soto & John, 2009).

TABLE 13.2. Comparison of Second-Order and Facets/Variables on Four Commonly Used Measures of Normal Personality Tests[a]

CPI	16PF	NEO-Revised	HPI
Second-order factors including Big Five			
v.1 Internality/Externality	Extraversion (E)	Extraversion (E)	Sociability (SY)
v.2 Norm Favoring/Questioning	Self-Control (SC)	Conscientiousness (C)	Prudence (PR)
v.3 Self-Realization	Anxiety (A)	Neuroticism (N)	Adjustment (ADJ)
	Tough Poise (TP)	Openness (O)	Inquisitiveness (INQ)
	Independence (IN)	Agreeableness (A)	Interpersonal Sensitivity (IS)
			Ambition (AMB)
			Learning Approach (LA)
CPI scale groupings			
Group 1: Interpersonal Style and Orientation			
Group 2: Normative Orientation and Values			
Group 3: Cognitive and Intellectual			
Group 4: Role and Personal Style			
Facets, variables, or HICs[b]			
	Warmth (A)	Warmth (E1)	Likes People (IS)
Sociability (Sy; Group 1)		Gregariousness (E2)	Likes Parties (SY)
			Likes Crowds (SY)
Dominance (Do; Group 1)	Dominance (E)	Assertiveness (E3)	
	Boldness (H)		
Social presence (Group 1)			No Social Anxiety (AMB)
	Shrewdness (N)		
		Activity (E4)	

(continues)

TABLE 13.2. Comparison of Second-Order and Facets/Variables on Four Commonly Used Measures of Normal Personality (*Continued*)

CPI	16PF	NEO-Revised	HPI
		Excitement-Seeking (E5)	Experience Seeking (SY)
			Exhibitionistic (SY)
		Competence (C1)	Mastery (PR)
		Order (C2)	
Responsibility (Re; Group 2)		Dutifulness (C3)	Virtuous (PR)
Socialization (So; Group 2)			Not Autonomous (PR)
			Moralistic (PR)
Self-Control (Sc; Group 2)	Self-Discipline (Q3)	Self-Discipline (C5)	Impulse Control (PR)
Good Impression (Gi; Group 2)			
Communality (Cm; Group 2)	Conformity (G)	Dutifulness (C6)	
		Compliance (A4)	
Tolerance (To; Group 2)			
Flexibility (Fx; Group 4)	Radicalism (Q1)		Not Spontaneous (PR)
		Fantasy (O1)	
		Aesthetics (O2)	
		Feelings (O3)	
		Actions (O4)	
	Imagination (M)	Ideas (O5)	Generates Ideas (INQ)
		Values (O6)	Culture (INQ)
			Avoids Trouble (PR)
			Curiosity (INQ)
			Thrill Seeking (INQ)
			Intellectual Games (INQ)
Femininity/ Masculinity (Fe; Group 4)			
	Emotional Stability (C)		
	Tension (Q4)	Anxiety (N1)	Not Anxious (ADJ)
		Angry Hostility (N2)	

CPI	16PF	NEO-Revised	HPI
		Depression (N3)	
Self-acceptance (Sa; Group 1)		Self-Consciousness (N4)	Calmness (ADJ)
	Impulsivity (F)	Impulsiveness (N5)	
			Even Tempered (ADJ)
	Insecurity (O)	Vulnerability (N6)	
Well-being (Wb; Group 2)		Positive Emotions (E6)	
			No Complaints (ADJ)
			Trusting (ADJ)
			Good Attachment (ADJ)
	Suspiciousness (L)		
	Sensitivity (I)	Sympathy/Tender-Mindedness (A6)	Sensitive (IS)
			No Guilt (ADJ)
		Trust (A1)	Easy to Live With (IS)
		Straightforwardness (A2)	
		Altruism (A3)	Caring (IS)
			No Hostility (IS)
		Modesty (A5)	
Empathy (Em; Group 1)			Empathy (ADJ)
Capacity for Status (Cs; Group 1)			
			Competitive (AMB)
			Self-Confidence (AMB)
Achievement via conformance (Ac; Group 3)		Achievement Striving (C4)	Accomplishment (AMB)
			Leadership (AMB)
			Identity (AMB)
			No Social Anxiety (AMB)
Independence (In; Group 1)	Self-Sufficiency (Q2)		
Achievement via independence (Ai; Group 3)			

(continues)

TABLE 13.2. Comparison of Second-Order and Facets/Variables on Four Commonly Used Measures of Normal Personality (*Continued*)

CPI	16PF	NEO-Revised	HPI
Intellectual efficiency (Ie; Group 3)			
	Abstract Thinking (B)		Education (LA)
			Math Ability (LA)
			Good Memory (LA)
			Reading (LA)
			Science (INQ)

Note. This table illustrates the diversity of factors and variables/HICs across four widely used measures of normal personality. The focus is across, not within, tests. The comparable factors and variables across measures are shown on the same row. Ones that do not appear to be measuring comparable constructs are listed on their own lines. There is not a robust literature comparing empirically across these measures so a comparison of the content said to be measured was used as the basis for the listings. The major point is that normal personality measures cannot be used interchangeably.
[a]CPI = California Psychological Inventory (Gough, 1996); 16PF = Sixteen Personality Factor (Cattell & Mead, 2008); NEO-Revised (Costa & McCrae, 1992); HPI = Hogan Personality Inventory (Hogan & Hogan, 2007).
[b]HICs = homogeneous item clusters.

This book does not advocate for or against the use of any particular measure but it does identify strengths and limitations of some of the more commonly used ones. The goal rather is to help equip the reader with a roadmap of which personality variables are relevant for career assessment and to identify some of the challenges encountered in measurement. There are also differences among measures in the facet scales (subscales, essentially) associated with the more overarching factors or variables.

A particular challenge in personality assessment is that a number of measures were developed for purposes other than career and work assessment. It is not necessarily problematic to repurpose measures developed for new uses, but the relevance and utility of the measure for career assessment purposes must still be established. As the *Standards for Educational and Psychological Testing* (American Educational Research Association [AERA], APA, and National Council on Measurement and Evaluation [NCME], 2014) noted,

> Standard 1.4. If a test score is interpreted for a given use in a way that has not been validated, it is incumbent on the user to justify the new interpretation for that use, providing a rationale and collecting new evidence, if necessary. (p. 24)

> Standard 9.4. When a test is to be used for a purpose for which little or no validity evidence is available, the user is responsible for documenting the rationale for the selection of the test and obtaining evidence of the reliability/precision of the test scores and the validity of the interpretations supporting the use of the scores for this purpose. (p. 143)

Taking just two of the better-developed and most widely used measures of so-called normal personality this section illustrates the value and limitations of repurposing tests. Both the CPI (Gough, 1996) and the Sixteen Personality Factor Questionnaire (16PF; R. B. Cattell et al., 1970) were carefully developed and widely researched and are commonly used measures of normal personality. Each has limitations, but also relevance, for career assessment as briefly discussed here.

The CPI (Gough, 1996), originally created over 60 years ago partly from a subset of the items on the Minnesota Multiphasic Personality Inventory, was developed as a measure of "normal" personality measurement. More specifically, in identifying the purposes of the CPI, its author, Harrison Gough (1996), stated,

> The primary purpose of Form 434 of the CPI is the same as that of earlier versions . . . namely, to furnish information to the interpreter from which a veridical (true-to-life) and useful picture may be drawn of the person taking the test. The portrait should be recognizable as accurate by friends and acquaintances, and should also provide a good starting point for predicting future behavior and for understanding prior actions. (p. 1)

The 16PF (R. B. Cattell et al., 1970) began its life as a psychometric experiment to find the "elements of personality" (H. E. P. Cattell & Schuerger, 2003). Both of these measures demonstrate some of the issues involved when applying other-purposed personality measures to career and work. These two venerable tests have been widely used in work and career counseling contexts, and there is some career-oriented literature available for both instruments. Neither measure, however, was specifically designed for vocational or personnel selection purposes, neither is particularly theory-based, and some scales were validated against criterion groups not particularly relevant for work issues, at least not without further research. For example, the CPI Socialization (So) scale was initially validated against a criterion of juvenile delinquency and inappropriate rebelliousness. It is certainly possible, and perhaps likely, that people who score in the same direction as the behaviorally problematic youth sample will be poor employment risks or ill-suited for an occupation demanding social conformity. However, it is also possible that they actually will be, in certain occupational settings and contexts, an asset to the organization (e.g., entrepreneurs, who tend to challenge current thinking rather than fit in, vs. traditional managers, who work within well-defined parameters rather than question them).

Studies in career and personnel selection contexts are necessary to reach appropriate conclusions about the uses and limitations of a particular personality scale. A positive feature of both the CPI and the 16PF is that they do provide occupational norms. Indeed, the manuals for the 16PF (Conn & Rieke, 1994) and the CPI (Gough, 1996) included occupational profiles for several groups, such as accountants, airline pilots, musicians, and sales personnel. Unfortunately, the sample sizes for the profiled groups were generally small, the samples highly selective (not necessarily representative), and the interpretations somewhat enthusiastic compared with the results, particularly concerning the interoccupational differences, which sometimes did not occur in the predicted direction. For example, Gough's (1996) CPI test manual included norms for occupational samples (18 male and 11 female normative groups; p. 181) and for a number of educational samples, many grouped by college major, but the results did not always conform to expectations about the prototypical characteristics associated with the various professions. Illustrative of these issues are two work-specific CPI scales: Managerial Potential (Mp) and Work Orientation (Wo). If there is a conceptual reason explaining why male research scientists (generally not known for managerial prowess) scored the highest among the occupational samples on the Mp scale (above sales managers and business executives), it is not articulated in the test's manual.

Neither of these still widely used measures were designed specifically for career or occupational applications as their primary purpose, though they continue to be used in such contexts. Both, however, have generated considerable research and each included not only an individual personality variables but also a smaller number of empirically derived second-order factors thought to identify the measure's underlying structure and presumably able to predict more robustly across situations. This work paralleled and to some degree preceded the revolution in personality assessment that reduced focus to a smaller number of such factors, the so-called Big Five (or FFM; Digman, 1996; Goldberg, 1981) discussed later.

For the CPI, structural vectors were identified that derived from the folk concept scales that form the heart of that instrument. The first, v.1, was labeled Internality; the second, v.2, Norm-Favoring; and the third, v.3, Self-Realization. Two of the CPI's second-order variable scores (internality–externality and norm favoring–norm questioning) are used to place respondents into one of four personality types: Alpha (prosocial, traditional, achievement oriented), Beta (norm facing, introverted, inwardly focused), Gamma (norm questioning but active and engaged), and Delta (norm questioning but withdrawn; Gough, 1987, p. 34). The v.3 variable is intended to assess the level of adjustment within the basic personality orientation (the highest level being self-fulfilled and the lowest being poorly adjusted and less self-efficacious).

The CPI's occupational samples were grouped into the four structural types (Alpha, Beta, Gamma, Delta) and the percentage of the occupational samples falling into particular categories was reported. For example, among a large sample of male West Point cadets, 64% were Alphas (a perfectly reasonable finding), 22% were Betas, 10% Gammas, and only 2% Deltas. Taking it the other way, Alpha-dominant occupational groups included both business executives (male), a reasonable finding, but also anesthesiologists (male and female), a somewhat counterintuitive one. There were few modal Betas, but they included mathematicians and pharmacy students (male) and university clerical personnel (female). Modal Gammas included artists and children's book critics (male and female). Modal Deltas, few in number, included prison inmates (male and female) and psychiatric patients (male). Looking across the occupational and educational groups, some strange bedfellows emerged. Modal Gammas included male architecture students (reasonable), male and female juvenile delinquents (curious), psychology graduate students (perhaps apt), and San Francisco area residents (Gough, 1996, pp. 37–38). Clearly, there is a strong need for criterion-based, theory-contextualized approach to personality, and for further study of the intra-occupational differences in occupations.

These findings also point to the challenges of applying interpretations of personality variables to an occupational group as a whole. Consider, for example, the need for achievement (Achievement Motivation) variable. Would differences be expected between a group of physicians and a group of construction workers on this variable? Does scoring highly on an Achievement Motivation measure imply that one is best suited for a particular occupation? Is it possible to experience job satisfaction in a low-status job while scoring consistently high on an Achievement Motivation measure? Might Achievement Motivation be patterned differently among people in various occupations? For example, ambitious members of artistic occupations might score low on typical measures of Achievement Motivation in that creative types tend to reject conventional societal norms of advancement and of getting ahead, yet they may be still be highly ambitious in wanting recognition and financial success for their particular oeuvre. Another possibility is that certain personality variables such as Achievement Motivation may differentially predict job success only when the "fit" within an occupation has been established on the basis of other measures. Thus, scores on a measure of Achievement Motivation, to continue the example, are unlikely to determine alone whether a person would make a good physician or an engineer. To the extent that high energy and ambition are necessary to complete strenuous training programs, Achievement Motivation may differentiate among individuals otherwise well suited to a career. In other words, personality variables alone may not effectively determine or identify appropriate career choices, but within members of an occupation there may be differential patterns in which some are more success-oriented than others.

Turning to the 16PF, a still widely used measure intended to assess normal personality, it too has second-order factors that integrate across the more discrete variables. The 16PF's five second factors are Extraversion, Anxiety/Neuroticism, Tough-Mindedness, Independence, and Self-Control. These closely parallel the currently popular FFM variables. Third-order factors resulted in two overarching, structural factors: Factor 1, dealing with external focus, pro-active, self-efficacious actions and absence of neuroticism (vs. the opposite), and Factor 2, dealing with self-restraint versus impulsivity, and low anxiety. These factors, arguably, roughly parallel the two structural factors of the CPI.

There are, of course, other widely used measures of normal personality. One such measure (rather, measures) is the NEO (e.g., Costa & McCrae, 1992), actually a suite of personality instruments. This was among the first commercial measures to be built on the FFM. Most of the NEO measures include FFM scales to measure Neuroticism, Extraversion, Openness, Conscientiousness, and Agreeableness. Some NEO versions exclude the Neuroticism scale. Many also include an assortment of facet scale scores associated with each of the five broad factors. Still another measure primarily developed for selection and development of managers was the Hogan Personality Inventory (HPI; R. Hogan & Hogan, 2007). The HPI includes similar, but differently named, scales as the FFM. Here are their names and in parenthesis the FFM factor they seem designed to measure: Prudence (Conscientiousness), Adjustment (Neuroticism), Sociability (Introversion/Extraversion), Interpersonal Sensitivity (Agreeableness), and Inquisitive (Openness). Additionally, as with the 16PF, the HPI includes a cognitive/ability variable labeled as Learning Approach.

Like all such measures, the NEO and the HPI have their advantages and limitations. The HPI has been widely used in personnel selection and development contexts, especially with managers, but does not have a wide database for use outside of managerial applications. The NEO's possibly excessive transparency and lack of a test-taking orientation or validity scales other than a few entirely obvious questions, is a concern when perceptual distortions might be expected.

SUMMARY AND CONCLUSIONS

This chapter introduced the last of the three major domains: personality. It focused on defining what personality is, discussing some of the emerging finding in personality research related to work and careers, and identifying structural issues of how personality variables are related to each other. Then, measurement issues were discussed, including preferred characteristics of personality measures. Chapter 14 discusses the widely used FFM, followed by consideration of other personality variables important in career and work assessment (see Chapter 15). The final chapter in Part III, Chapter 16, presents personality profiles of the six cases being followed in this book.

14

The Five-Factor Model of Personality

Because of their ubiquity, the factors of the five-factor personality model (FFM), which still dominates much of the current personality literature in work applications, are reviewed next. Other personality variables are presented in Chapter 15. In this chapter, each of the FFM factors is introduced and discussed, one at a time. Various definitions of the underlying construct are presented, along with conceptual and foundational issues. Then, the dimensionality and facets of the factor are identified, and career and occupational and measurement aspects reviewed.

INTROVERSION/EXTRAVERSION PERSONALITY FACTOR

Dating at least to Carl Jung, psychologists have differentiated between extraversion and introversion. The differences have been popularized and also have been widely misunderstood. Glib characterizations in the popular press do not always translate to career-relevant guidance. One does not, for example, have to be highly extraverted to be successful in sales or highly introverted to succeed in a technical position. Assuming the requisite interests and abilities are present, persons at different ends of this personality dimension may approach the same roles differently. Of course, some careers are likely to be better fits than others depending on the personality profile. As an example, U.S. actor Sara Gilbert, a producer of two different television shows at the time of an interview in the *New York Times*, stated, "I'm an introvert who's energized by work" (Itzkoff, 2019,

---

https://doi.org/10.1037/0000254-015
Career Assessment: Integrating Interests, Abilities, and Personality, by R. L. Lowman
Copyright © 2022 by the American Psychological Association. All rights reserved.

para. 6). She went on to say that she was not interested in "getting under people's skin" and noted that her "style in life is not very provocative. . . . It's more like: What's the reasonable way to look at this? Is there another side to things?" (Itzkoff, 2019, paras. 4–5), suggesting that there is more than one way to interact with others when job duties call for managing others.

Conceptual Issues

Introversion/Extraversion is well established in the literature, and it has at least some evidence of occupational relevance. From Heymanns to C. G. Jung (1921/1971) to H. J. Eysenck (e.g., 1953) to Cattell (e.g., R. B. Cattell & Kline, 1977) to today, researchers and theorists have posited Extraversion/Introversion (or "exvia-invia," in the case of Cattell) as an individual difference variable (see Wilt & Revelle, 2009). Yet, specific definitions (and even the labels attached to the concepts) of introversion/extraversion are not yet universally agreed upon. Frieder et al. (2018), in a well-regarded journal, asserted, "Extraversion describes an individual's tendency to gain power and status" (p. 326), not much of a definition and certainly not an inclusive one. H. E. P. Cattell and Mead (2008), in a chapter on the Sixteen Personality Factor Questionnaire (16PF), like many authors, used a technical approach, noting that the 16PF's "Extraversion/Introversion global factor was defined by the convergence of the five primary scales that represent basic human motivations for moving toward versus away from social interaction" (p. 139).

Jung himself defined extraversion as follows:

> Extraversion is characterized by interest in the external object, responsiveness, and a ready acceptance of external happenings, a desire to influence and be influenced by events, a need to join in and get "with it," the capacity to endure bustle and noise of every kind, and actually find them enjoyable, constant attention to the surrounding world, the cultivation of friends and acquaintances, none too carefully selected, and finally by the great importance attached to the figure one cuts. (C. G. Jung, 1921/1971, CW6, para. 972)

As for introversion, Jung stated,

> The introverted type is characterized by the fact that he applies his horme [energy] chiefly to himself i.e. he finds the Unconditioned Values within himself, but the extraverted type applies his horme to the external world, to the object, the Non-Ego, i.e. he finds the unconditioned value outside himself. The introverted considers everything under the aspect of the values of his own Ego; the extraverted depends upon the value of his object. (as cited in Geyer, 2012, p. 2)

Stanek and Ones (2018) defined extraversion as referring

> to a domain of traits characterized by behavioral engagement with the external world, particularly in the interpersonal arena. Global Extraversion describes individual differences in liking and feeling comfortable amidst larger groups, being outgoing, active, and assertive as well as cheerful. Extraverted individuals are described as talkative, high-energy, sociable, fun-loving, and seekers of external stimulation. (p. 390)

Gough's (1996) California Psychological Inventory (CPI) includes Introversion/Extraversion as one of its vector, or structural, dimensions and placed extraversion and introversion at opposite poles, with introversion anchored by need for privacy and detachment and extraversion by involvement with others and participation. Using adjectival descriptions from peers, spouses, and staff members, the introverted groups were more likely to be described as being quiet, cautious, and shy, and extraverts as being talkative, outgoing, and ambitious. Scarr (1969, p. 823) similarly identified Introversion/Extraversion as including sociability, social anxiety, friendliness to strangers, and social spontaneity. The polarity anchors included, in Scarr's formulation, shy, introspective, anxious withdrawal (introversion) versus friendly, extraverted, self-confident engagement with the interpersonal environment (extraversion).

None of these definitions is by itself sufficient and many focus primarily on one side of the polarity, defining (typically) extraversion and not Extraversion/Introversion. Collectively, however, these definitions identify useful aspects of extraversion and introversion. Of particular interest to career assessors is the need to understand that, although some people fit at the extremes of introversion or extraversion polarities, many, if not the majority, do not. Career assessors need particularly to be aware of, and responsive to the needs of, those in between introversion and extraversion—ambiverts—people who score neither clearly introverted nor extraverted. Although Jung has been criticized for placing people into one of two distinct, generally dichotomous categories of extraverts versus introverts, in an interview conducted toward the last part of his life, he modified his position:

> There is no such thing as a pure extravert or a pure introvert. Such a man [person] would be in the lunatic asylum. Those are only terms to designate a certain penchant, a certain tendency. For instance, the tendency to be more influenced by environmental influences, or more influenced by the subjective fact—that's all. There are people who are fairly well-balanced who are just as much influenced from within as from without, or just as little. And so with all the definite classifications . . . they are only a sort of point to refer to, points for orientation. (Evans, 2018, p. 23)

This particular personality trait (Introversion/Extraversion), even if not yet consistently defined, has been researched and theorized upon for many decades, and if early theoretical and anecdotal sources of evidence are considered, for centuries. The emerging consensus is that this is a meaningful and empirically established dimension of personality that remains fairly constant over time. There is also a substantial heritable component to this trait (Scarr, 1969), and introverts and extraverts are differentiated by their response to stimuli and to rewards. Introverts and extraverts have been reported to differ in their degree of social inhibition, in their level of arousal, and, by implication, in their preference for external world arousal reduction (introverts, who are higher in cortical arousal) or stimulation (extraverts, who tend to be lower; L. W. Morris, 1979). This is not a new finding. Eysenck's (1967) arousal theory of Introversion/Extraversion held that introverts had lower arousal thresholds than extraverts such that extraverts were more likely to seek out stimulation and to respond well in high arousal situations and introverts, the opposite. Gray (1970) found that extraverts experience more positive affect than introverts and are more quickly conditioned to stimuli with positive reward valences (Wilt and Revelle, 2009). Several studies (e.g., Diener et al., 1992) have reported that extraverts report greater subjective well-being (happiness) than do introverts. What does seem clear is that extraverts are more likely to take much of their rewards from social interaction, to enjoy and seek out social contact including in large groups, to have a relatively positive view of the world, and seek out external stimulation, especially through people (Wilt & Revelle, 2009).

Costa and McCrae (1986, 1992) described extraverts as generally being more sociable, active, cheerful, energetic, and optimistic than introverts. In contrast, introverts were characterized as being reserved, submissive, and even-paced. That grouping of characteristics, not atypically, attributes more socially desirable characteristics to extraverts and more negative ones to introverts. Indeed, the trait itself is often labeled just as extraversion, ignoring the other type. But the story is more complex than that, and introverts are not simply the poor cousins of extraverts.

As with other personality variables, like Agreeableness and Adjustment, care should be taken not to privilege the so-called positive ends of the polarities. Neither extraversion nor introversion should be viewed as being more or less desirable. Career assessors need to know as much about introversion as they do about extraversion. Unfortunately, however, too much of the literature has been more focused on the extraverted side of the polarity, with introversion considered, often negatively, from an ancillary or contrast perspective. As Frieder et al. (2018) stated, "Compared to introverts who are drained by interactions with others and prefer impersonal work environments, extraverts are outgoing, gregarious, ambitious, and characterized by sociability and dominance. . . . Extraverts desire to get ahead and attain attention and rewards/power" (p. 326). This "dichotomous" mentality is unfortunate because much of the literature suggests that Introversion/Extraversion is a trait or temperament variable, a dimension of personality that is established early in life and appears to be relatively immutable, with strong genetic influences (Jiménez et al., 2017; Scarr, 1969; Wilt & Revelle, 2009) so that even if one wanted to change, at least at a structural level, it is not likely possible. In contrast to these perspectives and characterizations, Cain (2013), in a popular trade book called *Quiet: The Power of Introverts in a World That Can't Stop Talking*, provided a positive overview of introversion, its advantages, and ways to work around certain challenging situations. (Additionally, contrast group studies tend to focus on the extremes, not giving much attention to those who score in between the two polarities, the so-called ambiverts.)

If work can be divided very roughly into occupations that emphasize work with data, people, and things, introverts would be expected to be at an advantage in work involving the first and third and extraverts, the second. Costa et al. (1977), for example, compared scores on the Strong Vocational Interest

Blank (SVIB) and Introversion/Extraversion factors. People who preferred "task-oriented" occupations (e.g., engineer, chemist, artist, dentist) over socially oriented occupations (e.g., YMCA secretary, social worker) were more likely to be introverted. This does not of course mean that extraverts cannot successfully perform work involving intense concentration or that introverts cannot have careers in people occupations, but the question for career assessment is whether careers primarily play to individuals' strengths and preferences or call for excessive working around relative weaknesses and are contrary to preferences.

Relationships between Introversion/Extraversion and other personality variables have been reported. L. W. Morris (1979) found correlations between Introversion/Extraversion and field dependence-independence, impulsiveness, and sociability. In Cattell's 16PF, the Extraversion second-order factor was especially associated with warmth (A+), impulsivity (F+), boldness (H+), and group dependence (Q2−), with Introversion associated with those scales being in the opposite direction (Krug, 1981). Stanek and Ones (2018) identified a number of what were termed compound personality traits that were associated with each of the FFM factors. Examples include Emotional Intelligence, Generalized Self-Efficacy, Innovation, Passive Aggressiveness, and Borderline Personality Disorder. All of these were thought to be positively associated with Extraversion except for Passive Aggressiveness, which was inversely correlated (i.e., it was positively associated with Introversion).

Dimensionality and Facets

The dimensionality of Introversion/Extraversion has been examined by researchers, but not exactly with consensus. Judge et al.'s (2013) 6-2-1 model made use of DeYoung et al.'s (2007a) aspects (subtraits or facets) of enthusiasm and assertiveness. These were in turn populated by facets (or subfacets), more narrow aspects of personality that sometimes are better predictors of the overarching trait. However, there is no consensus across measures and models on facets, either their number, content, or which are the most relevant for inclusion in career-related assessment. Costa and McCrae's (1986, 1992, and 2008) models and measures encompassed six facets for their Extraversion dimension: warmth, gregariousness, assertiveness, the tendency to experience positive emotions, activity, excitement seeking, and assertiveness. Stanek and Ones (2018), while identifying assertiveness and enthusiasm as the two "aspects" (higher order components) of the trait, also labeled their facets slightly differently: activity, dominance, lack of anhedonia, positive emotionality, sensation seeking, sociability, and social withdrawal. Hogan's Personality Inventory (HPI; R. Hogan & Hogan, 2009) model differed in using a seven-factor model, and it would appear that two of their factors were related to Introversion/Extraversion: Sociability and Ambition. Facets on Sociability (defined as "the degree to which a person seems to need and/or enjoy interactions with others"; R. Hogan and Hogan, 2007, p. 25) are the following: likes parties, likes crowds, experience-seeking, exhibitionistic, and entertaining. For the Ambition factor (defined as "the degree to which a person seems socially self-confident, leader-like, competitive, and energetic"; R. Hogan and Hogan, 2007, p. 25), facets included competitive, self-confident, accomplishment, leadership, lack of social anxiety, and identity (essentially self-acceptance or satisfaction with one's life). Suggesting some overlap, the two HPI factors correlated 0.41 (R. Hogan & Hogan, 2007).

Other Introversion/Extraversion facets have also been offered. L. W. Morris (1979) identified the following Introversion/Extraversion dimensions: social activity (time spent in social and interpersonal activities, talkativeness), social facility (dominance, leadership, and social skills), risk taking and adventuresomeness (vs. restraint and inhibition), and action orientation (vs. preference for introspective, abstract intellectual pursuits). The broad-brush 16PF (R. B. Cattell et al., 1970) included several variables (arguably, facets) related to Introversion/Extraversion: A (warmth), E (dominance), F (liveliness), H (social boldness), and Q2 (self-reliance). Gough's (1996) CPI measures include these variables that measure aspects of Introversion/Extraversion: Sociability (Sy), Dominance (Do), Self-Acceptance (Sa), Empathy (Em; a scale developed as part of Robert Hogan's doctoral dissertation), and Social Presence.

Although there is overlap across some of the models of dimensions and facets, there are also inconsistencies. Although dominance is sometimes categorized as a facet of Introversion/Extraversion, in this book it is viewed as a variable of value in its own right. A separate section of this chapter is therefore directed to the construct.

Career and Work Issues

There appear to be differences in the relative prevalence of people scoring in the introverted and extraverted direction in various occupational groupings.[1] Using the census approach (tabulating the number of respondents in each of the personality measure groupings), Myers et al. (1998) reported on the results of Myers-Briggs Type Indicator (MBTI) Introversion/Extraversion scores. Applying a dichotomous split on the Introversion/Extraversion scale of the MBTI (a measure not without problems, including its practice of using ipsative scoring on dichotomous rather than continuous scales), more extraverts were found in business and industry occupational groups, whereas engineers, physicians, librarians, and various technical groups more commonly scored in the introverted direction.

---

[1] The percentages of the general population who are introverts, ambiverts, and extraverts are not reliably known. Using a dichotomous measure of extraverts and introverts, for example, the MBTI, in a U.S. national representative study, Hammer and Mitchelle (1996), found 54% of the respondents were introverted and 46% extraverted. In an international study, Bhargava et al. (2015) found 26% to be extraverts, 15% introverts, and 59% ambiverts. Cain (2012) estimated that 33% to 50% of the population were introverted. Clearly, dichotomous measures cannot be used to estimate ambiverts, and the types of measures used will affect classification.

In almost every occupational group dominated by one polarity (introversion vs. extraversion) there will be many people who do not score on Introversion/Extraversion tests in the same direction as the majority, suggesting that there is considerable diversity on this variable within occupations. Additionally, the census approach does not usually measure against a criterion, so it does not by itself address whether one type of personality was more successful than another. Additionally, dichotomous splits do not usually consider the large group in the middle who may actually have more successful work outcomes in certain occupations than those at the extremes (see, e.g., A. M. Grant, 2013).

L. W. Morris (1979) reviewed literature on the occupational implications of Introversion/Extraversion and concluded that a variety of studies had shown scores on this personality dimension were associated with preferences for particular types of work. Since most careers will be facilitated by having particular combinations of interest, abilities, and personality characteristics, not too much should be made of any single variable or factor outside of the broader assessment profile. Still, it was suggested that introverts often gravitate to occupations demanding concentration and intellectual mastery. Indeed, a general tendency has been reported in the literature for introversion to be associated with higher grades in school after early adolescence and for higher performance in a variety of professions requiring mastery of complex, intellectually demanding material (see R. B. Cattell & Kline, 1977; L. W. Morris, 1979). R. B. Cattell et al. (1970) also noted that the 16PF and the Clinical Analysis Questionnaire (CAQ) differentiated people on the basis of their occupational preferences for working alone or with others. They reported that people scoring high on Factor A (A+, i.e., those more oriented toward others) tended to prefer working with other people, whereas those scoring low (A–) preferred working with things and ideas rather than with other people. Artists, electricians, and research scientists scored in the A– direction, whereas the results of social workers and business executives were in the A+ direction.

Concerning the relationship of Introversion/Extraversion and job performance, a robust literature, primarily in industrial–organizational (I–O) and vocational psychology, has emerged, starting roughly in 1991 with the publication of Barrick and Mount's important meta-analysis concerning the FFM of personality and work outcomes. Examining the relationship of FFM factors with job and training criteria, and with personnel data such as salary level, turnover, status change, and position tenure (most data were available for only some of the samples included in the study), they found that extraversion predicted to positive outcomes, especially for the two people-oriented occupational groups: sales and management. Extraversion also predicted to training criteria across all the occupations. Connelly et al. (2018) noted that because extraverts are more sensitive to rewards, Extraversion may also be associated with job satisfaction and well-being. However, the highest and most robust correlations were associated with Conscientiousness rather than Extraversion.

Considering the purpose of the career assessment, the client will likely need assistance in better understanding (and correcting any misconceptions) of the nature of introversion and extraversion. Introverts in particular may need help in understanding and possibly in destigmatizing their trait orientation.

The context for helping clients understand their orientation are the careers and jobs being considered, as suggested by the client or the assessor. Their trait orientation may be a better fit for some career directions than others, but clients also need to understand that they can learn skills (e.g., for introverts, self-presentation in groups; for extraverts, listening skills) if they are otherwise a good fit with a particular career direction. Understanding the client's self-identity on this factor in the context of the test results is also important. Introverts may tend to see themselves as selectively social and feel more engaged with others than they are perceived to be. When test results suggest that a client is highly introverted, is this finding consistent with their view of themselves and is it viewed as being problematic or desirable? For those strongly extraverted, are they able to accept that there may be limitations to this orientation in particular career applications? Or, if they are considering a career that requires high amounts of working alone and intense work with data or ideas versus people, how would they imagine their preference for working with people to find expression?

Measurement Issues

There are many persuasive reasons to include Introversion/Extraversion as part of any standard career assessment battery. For those clients scoring strongly in one polarity direction versus the other, the impact of this variable on career choice and satisfaction may be high. Those scoring in-between, however, present a less compelling argument for a particular career and more opportunities to pursue alternative careers while training or adapting to the areas of potential misfit. In considering whether the variable is particularly important for contemplated career choices, it is important to examine whether those choices are strongly oriented to social-interpersonal duties or to those requiring intensive independent work. These job duties will more likely match, respectively, with extraversion and introversion.

Many broad-brush personality measures typically include Introversion/Extraversion scales, either as first- or second-order scales or factors. These include the 16PF, which includes Extraversion/Introversion as a second-order, or global, factor that is loaded on by the test's Warm–Reserved (A), Lively–Serious (F), Bold–Shy (H), Private–Forthright (N), and Self-Reliant–Group-Oriented (Q2) facet scales (H. E. P. Cattell & Mead, 2008). When there is a career-relevant reason to administer the Minnesota Multiphasic Personality Inventory (MMPI; Tellegen & Ben-Porath, 2011), the test includes a Social Introversion scale, Scale 0, that aims to measure Introversion/Extraversion. Virtually all of the widely used FFM measures, including the NEO Personality Inventory (Costa & McCrae, 1988, 1992; 2008) and the HPI (R. Hogan & Hogan, 2007), include Introversion/Extraversion factors. Other widely used measures include the MBTI (Introversion/Extraversion scale) and the SVIB's "Occupational Introversion" scale (Donnay et al.,

2004; Hansen, 2000). Each of these measures has advantages and disadvantages, but broad-brush measures take considerable time to administer, and the quality of the scales must be evaluated in the context of administration time, cost, and of course the other scales provided on such measures. Care must also be taken in interpreting facet scales since there is not yet consensus on which facets are better than others for predicting career choice. There is much disagreement on the specific facets included across various measures, and in some cases there are questions about their validity.

CONSCIENTIOUSNESS PERSONALITY FACTOR

To date, the research evidence has generally found that the personality factor with the highest level of predictive power for job performance in most (but not all) work areas has been Conscientiousness, but the results do vary depending on the specific criterion that is being predicted (Dudley et al., 2006).

Conceptual Issues

As with Introversion/Extraversion, researchers do not agree on a single definition of this construct. They range from Digman's (1990) emphasis on willfulness and achievement to R. Hogan and Hogan's (2007) description: "The degree to which a person seems conscientious, conforming, and dependable" (p. 19), a definition that obviously can be challenged on several points ("seems"; "conscientiousness" being used as both the term to be defined and the definition; and "conforming" not having been defined). A more elaborated and useful definition was provided by B. W. Roberts et al. (2009): "The propensity to follow socially prescribed norms for impulse control, to be goal directed, to plan, and to be able to delay gratification" (p. 369). Stanek and Ones (2018) provided this definition for trait Conscientiousness: "A domain of personality traits that describe the ways in which individuals self-regulate impulses to follow socially prescribed norms . . . Conscientiousness describes individual differences in being disciplined, focused, tenacious, organized, and responsible" (p. 388).

However defined, persons scoring high on Conscientiousness generally tend to be perceived (and self-perceived) as being reliable, dependable, planful, goal-oriented, fairly conforming, high on self- and impulse control, able to pursue long-range goals, and accepting of constraints (Dudley et al., 2006). Persons scoring low on measures of Conscientiousness, in contrast, are likely to exhibit the reverse of those behaviors, including the tendency to have lower impulse control, to be less planful in achieving goals (and less likely to set long-term goals), and to be less conforming in meeting the expectations of others. In terms of career issues, low scores on Conscientiousness might seem to portend poor outcomes, and this may indeed be a concern. However, in other cases, particularly with persons with Artistic interests, low scores on this factor may simply reflect a creative orientation, not wanting to conform to the views of others about appropriate behavior, or a desire to work on one's own. Conversely, "too much" Conscientiousness (presumably expressed by overly high scores on particular personality Conscientiousness measures) may also be problematic. N. T. Carter et al. (2018) noted that the "positive" aspects of this trait's behavior may, at higher levels, be associated with excessive intensity and rigidity and can be associated with obsessive-compulsive personality disorder. Although it is important not to stereotype low Conscientiousness scores as necessarily being associated with undesirable outcomes, there is still considerable evidence not to be ignored that this scoring direction, on average, is associated with poorer work performance and that at the least the behavioral tendencies need to be understood and managed.

There is evidence (e.g., Mischel, 2014) that persons with low Conscientiousness scores on average tend to be less successful in their careers, to suffer from poorer health outcomes, and even to live less long (Kern et al., 2009). Kern et al. (2009) found that among men who had been in the Terman longitudinal gifted study (Terman, 1925), all of whom were very bright and who had been followed for 65 years, childhood-measured Conscientiousness predicted shorter lifespans, but only for those who had had limited career success. In other words, there was a relationship between career success and longevity that was moderated by Conscientiousness as measured in youth. Those low on both Conscientiousness and on career success were most likely among those in the sample to die sooner.

Why might this be? A career is typically a long-term undertaking that requires completion of relevant education and training and applying specialized knowledge, skills, abilities, and other characteristics for some productive purpose. Success in careers and work is therefore likely to be enhanced by being goal-focused, planful, and by being able to control immediate impulses in favor of longer term objectives (see Duckworth et al., 2012).

Of course, not all work or career patterns require linearity, and in any case there may be multiple explanations for low Conscientiousness scores. As an example, the late Walter Mischel's (2014) famous "marshmallow test," in which young children were incentivized to delay eating a treat (marshmallows, cookies, etc.) if they waited, provides interesting evidence about the value of having impulse control. Long-term follow-up of the early participants in this research, originally conducted at Stanford University, showed that those who as children had not delayed gratification were less likely to complete college, were less successful in their careers, and were more likely to have been divorced. (The study has received various interpretations and attempts at replication or refinement, e.g., Watts et al., 2018, but the central finding has held up.) Interviewed a few years before his death, Mischel noted that it is important to understand why children who "failed" the "marshmallow test" chose not to wait and the factors affecting adults who also do not delay gratification:

> People experience willpower fatigue and plain old fatigue and exhaustion. What we do when we get tired is heavily influenced by the self-standards we develop and that in turn is strongly influenced by the models we have. . . . Confusion

about these kinds of behaviors [tremendous willpower in one situation, but not another] is erased when you realize self-control involves cognitive skills. You can have the skills and not use them. If your kid waits for the marshmallow, [then you know] she is able to do it. But if she doesn't, you don't know why. She may have decided she doesn't want to. (as cited in Urist, 2014, para. 16)

Concerning work and careers, this suggests that aspects of Conscientiousness, such as self-control, may at least to some degree be situationally specific and, by implication, trainable. Still, there is considerable stability in Conscientiousness over time when grouped data are considered with high stability coefficients in longitudinal studies. However, there is some evidence that Conscientiousness may, on average, change over time as a function of age. Elkins et al. (2017), for example, found that Conscientiousness scores increased in a 4-year period from adolescence to young adulthood. At the other end of the age spectrum, a cross-sectional but partially longitudinal, national sample study of persons 50 years and older found that both general Conscientiousness and some of its facets changed with age. In particular, Conscientiousness and two facets (Industriousness and Orderliness) peaked at age 70 and declined somewhat thereafter, whereas Traditionalism and Virtue facets increased (Chopik, 2016).

Dimensionality and Facets

An additional aspect of Conscientiousness concerns its dimensionality and, by implication, its measurement. When it comes to facet scales (narrower variables offered by test publishers as being components of the broader Conscientiousness factor), there is neither consensus on what the appropriate variables are nor agreement as to how best to measure them. There are even questions about whether, and how well, they predict to work performance.

Costa and McCrae's (1986, 1992) six facets in the NEO's Conscientiousness factor included achievement striving, competence, self-discipline, deliberation, dutifulness, and order. Judge et al.'s (2013) 6-2-1 model applied to Conscientiousness made use of DeYoung et al.'s (2007a) subtraits of Industriousness (hard-working, disciplined, and purposeful) and Orderliness (organized and oriented to dutifulness). Stanek and Ones's (2018) facets for the same two "aspects" (higher order components of the trait) were labeled achievement, avoidance of distraction, cautiousness, dependability, order, persistence, and procrastination avoidance. R. Hogan and Hogan's (2009) HPI Prudence factor (defined as "the degree to which a person is conscientious, conforming, and dependable"; p. 25) encompassed seven HICs (homogeneous item clusters, or facets): moralistic, mastery, virtuous, not autonomous, not spontaneous, impulse control, and avoids trouble.

The 16PF (H. E. P. Cattell & Mead, 2008) includes a Self-Control versus Lack of Restraint global factor, also called Conscientiousness. At the variable level, the following are particularly relevant: F (lively vs. serious), G (rule consciousness vs. expediency), M (abstract vs. practical), and Q3 (perfectionism vs. tolerance of disorder). As H. E. P. Cattell and Mead (2008) put it, "Higher levels of Self-Control/conscientiousness are related to lower levels of openness/Receptivity: Thus, highly conscientious, self-controlled people also tend to be tough-minded and less open to emotions and new ideas" (p. 140).

In Gough's (1996) CPI, two overarching factors (vector v.2), Norm Favoring versus Norm Questioning, would be expected to be associated with Conscientiousness. Among the CPI scales (variables), Responsibility (Re), Socialization (So), and Self-Control (Sc) are related constructs. Ac (Achievement through Conformity) would also be relevant. In the four types personality model, Alphas would be particularly likely to be high on Conscientiousness, or to present themselves that way.

There appears to be considerable diversity among the various Conscientiousness facet scales (and the models from which they derive). Some researchers have looked at overarching subfactors in a way that may help integrate the differences. Connelly et al. (2018) identified two thematic aspects that have shown promise in the Conscientiousness factor: Industriousness (focusing on longer term vs. shorter term goals and being motivated to achieve) and Orderliness (willingness to be attentive to, and to follow, rules). And Dudley et al. (2006) found that Conscientiousness facets did explain variance incrementally over broad trait Conscientiousness but primarily for certain jobs and certain criteria. They found that Dependability and Achievement were particularly additive but that Cautiousness was not. The results varied by type of incumbent (skilled and semiskilled vs. managerial). These dimensions tended to additively predict job performance for the former and contextual performance for the latter.

Thus, although there is some overlap in constructs among Conscientiousness facets on alternative personality measures, there is considerable diversity as well. There is no single set of facets that is consensually agreed upon as the preferred set. Caution is therefore urged in choosing a measure and then assuming that facet scales can be interpreted as meaningful aspects of personality as related to career and work issues.

Career and Work Issues

Conscientiousness is an important personality factor to measure because it has such a good track record in predicting, at the group level, job performance and other positive life outcomes. Persons with high scores are likely have an easier time sticking with tasks and achieving long-term goals, whereas low scorers experience more difficulty in their work and personal lives. In general, positive and significant validity coefficients have consistently been found for the main Conscientiousness factor (Barrick & Mount, 1991, 2005, 2012; Hurtz & Donovan, 2000). The same, however, cannot be said for the facets in predicting work outcome criteria (Harari et al., 2014; Salgado et al., 2013). Although there is evidence in support of some but not all of the many facets found on the various Conscientiousness measures (see Dudley et al., 2006), care must be taken to know which variables are being measured on which test and on how strong the validity evidence is for the intended inferences. In particular, Dudley et al.'s (2006) meta-analysis suggested that facets (rather than factors) are sometimes more predictive of occupational performance in some types of occupations, but not in others. This may imply that specific career directions matter in interpreting personality results in the context of career assessment practice.

If Conscientiousness-related behavior is important for career success, and if those scoring low on it are at risk for impulsivity and poor performance, this may be a needed focus of career assessment and counseling. In such cases assessors can consider behavioral patterns and help the client better understand the issues. But low scores alone on this variable would not preclude pursuit of particular occupations, provided there is a plan for working around low Conscientiousness scores.

Additionally, although most studies have found that Conscientiousness predicts to positive work outcomes, the relationship between Conscientiousness and work may be more complicated when studied over time. George et al. (2011) examined a longitudinal sample of women who had graduated from Mills College in the 1960s and were followed for over 50 years. Mills College at the time the students matriculated was an elite all-women's school, the first all-women's college in the United States west of the Rockies, and it attracted bright, often creative, women when there were few such educational opportunities for them. The study considered the impact over the participants' lives and careers of three personality variables: Introversion/Extraversion, Openness, and Conscientiousness. Conscientiousness predicted both work and personal outcomes. In the period following graduation, Conscientiousness was associated with a commitment to wife and mother roles (consistent with expectations of the day), but during midlife and later, Conscientiousness was a strong predictor of commitment to work roles and was negatively associated with an interest in early retirement. Conscientiousness was also inversely associated with early divorce but, in contrast to Openness, had little association with creative pursuits and careers.

At the individual level, medium and low scores on trait Conscientiousness may have different meanings than when found in the context of selection. Although low scores may be cause for concern or applicant rejection in selection, at the individual level they are not necessarily the equivalent of a career death sentence. In artistic and creative profiles, low Conscientiousness scores may simply reflect a rejection of conventional approaches to work and life. On the other hand, creatively talented individuals may be less disciplined than they need to be to succeed in highly competitive careers. In these and other cases, it is important to help clients understand the personality findings and learn how to work around some areas that might pose challenges. The context and behavioral evidence matter. Some individuals otherwise well suited to managerial roles with low Conscientiousness scores may reject the behavioral conformity expected in some types of work roles and organizations but thrive on work in fast-changing and short-term contexts such as in consulting, start-ups, turnarounds, and those involving creativity. Conversely, those who score "too high" on Conscientiousness scales may be overly rigid and inflexible. This too may need consulting about the challenges to their orientation and ways to behave more flexibly when that is needed to be successful in a work role.

As for career assessment work, the use of well-validated facet scales whose construct and criterion validity for career assessment have been demonstrated is appropriate. At the same time, an assessor does not have to use all facet (or, for that matter, trait) scales on a broad-brush measure of personality just because they are there.

Measurement Issues

Some version of a Conscientiousness factor or variable is included in most of the current widely used measures of personality. These include the NEO suite of measures, Hogan's HPI, the CPI, 16PF, and many other contemporary measures of "normal" personality. Another such broad-brush measure is Tellegen's Multidimensional Personality Questionnaire (MPQ; Tellegen & Waller, 2008), which includes a Control versus Impulsivity scale as well as a higher order factor of Constraint on which loaded factor scales of Social Potency (negative) Control, Harm-Avoidance, and Traditionalism. Overall, there is no shortage of measures from which to choose for this factor and related facets, although the specific characteristics of each measure need to be understood and considered in the context of the assessment purposes.

Because Conscientiousness is often measured as part of broad-brush personality tests, the task is not usually choosing a stand-alone measure of it. Even though most of the broad (vs. facet) measures have reasonably high correlations with each other, the assessor must still understand the particular characteristics of the specific scale used to measure this trait. The conceptualization and method of measuring Conscientiousness may affect its interpretation.

Even more care must still be taken in the use and interpretation of facet scores. Simply choosing and interpreting the scores of tests with facet scales based on their labels is problematic, even when they are similarly named. Rather, the assessor should choose tests with facets for which there is validity evidence for the intended inferences, paying particular attention to facets that are measuring dependability, achievement, and order.

NEUROTICISM/ADJUSTMENT PERSONALITY FACTOR

This personality factor is a complicated one. Despite FFM models presenting themselves as being measures of normal personality, this factor is often labeled Neuroticism or, on the positive side, Emotional Adjustment. By any standard the term Neuroticism has a pejorative connotation. As A. Weiss and Deary (2020) noted, "People with higher levels of neuroticism seem to have drawn the short straw of personality" (p. 92). Clearly, one polarity of this factor has the potential to cross the line into diagnosable psychopathology and therefore can raise concerns when used as part of personnel selection.

Conceptual Issues

Variously labeled as Neuroticism (the "N" of the OCEAN acronym widely used to abbreviate the FFM factors), this factor has also, less pejoratively, been referred to as Emotional Stability or Adjustment. Whatever the term used (and this book labels the factor Neuroticism/Adjustment to anchor the name not just on the negatively perceived polarity), this factor and its constituent facets or subdimensions have a long history of research and application.

Although the FFM factors have always and intentionally been associated with the so-called normal range of personality, some scoring in the less-well-adjusted direction of this factor will have diagnosable forms of psychological disorder. There is no distinct line of separation between low adjustment and psychopathology. Clearly, there are low scorers on Neuroticism/Adjustment scales who, at the time of assessment, are also experiencing diagnosable psychopathology (see Samuel & Widiger, 2008) and, at the other polarity, those who score in the well-adjustment direction on FFM measures but who have character pathology or a denial/fake good test taking orientation that masks or misrepresents their actual levels of adjustment. Further, high levels of neuroticism may reflect a trait (chronic) or state (temporary, stress-related) condition, suggesting either a transitory condition (possibly deriving from work/career issues) or a longer term condition that needs to be taken into account in career assessment.

Even though some aspects of neuroticism are trait-like (Weiss & Deary, 2020), it would be a mistake to assume that a one-time assessment of Neuroticism/Adjustment reflects a condition that will necessarily be long-lasting. Indeed, it is useful to contextualize Neuroticism/Adjustment by considering national statistics on mental disorders. The U.S. National Institute of Mental Health (NIMH) defined the term "any mental illness" (AMI) as the presence of any "mental, behavioral, or emotional disorder" (NIMH, 2017, Definitions section) and reported that, among those in the United States aged 18 or older, in 2017, there were 46.6 million, or 18.9%, of all U.S. adults meeting diagnostic criteria. These figures estimated the number of individual adults affected by AMI during a single year, whereas other statistics focus on the lifetime prevalence, that is, the number of people who at any time during their lives have experienced particular disorders. Steel et al. (2014) aggregated global studies of both one year and lifetime prevalence of selected mental disorders. Whereas the NIMH data were from the United States only, Steel et al.'s data came from studies done around the world. However, they considered only common mental disorders. These usually include affective, anxiety, and substance misuse disorders, which are the most frequently occurring. Across countries in their aggregated studies, an average of 17.6% of adults experienced these mental disorders. The lifetime prevalence identifies those who have experienced one or more of the defined common mental disorders at any point in their lifetimes. That figure was 29.2%. This and other research (Bagalman & Cornell, 2018; Kessler et al., 2007; Kessler, Berglund, et al., 2005; Kessler, Chiu, et al., 2005) suggest that diagnosable mental illness is rather common and that those who may not be experiencing it at one point may well do so at another point and vice versa. And these figures do not include those with subclinical psychological dysfunctions who do not currently meet a diagnostic criterion.

Another psychological condition that is difficult to measure reliably, especially in work contexts, concerns what are called personality (or character) disorders. Some of these, particularly antisocial personality disorder, are often associated with the tendency to exhibit positive self-presentation and to deny personal pathology or the experience of anxiety. Therefore, individuals experiencing these disorders may well be identified on commonly used measures of normal personality as not having psychological problems or concerns. This population is not trivial in numbers, as suggested by the findings of a large study ($n = 36,309$) by R. B. Goldstein et al. (2017), who used a face-to-face interview methodology and standardized protocol, the Alcohol Use Disorder and Associated Disabilities Interview Schedule-5, in a large U.S. epidemiological survey. Prevalence of two conditions, antisocial personality disorder and adult antisocial behavior without conduct disorder before age 15, was 4.3% and 20.3%, respectively. People with these two classifications were found to be at risk (both at 12 months after the study and in lifetime prevalence estimates) for a variety of other disorders, including substance misuse, depressive disorders, posttraumatic stress, and disabilities.

The assessment of FFM Neuroticism/Adjustment clearly raises questions about the relationships between personality and psychopathology. Many of the FFM measures lay claim to being measures of normal personality. This contention may relate to a theoretical model but also to the Americans with Disabilities Act of 1990 (ADA, 1990) which protects mental and physical disabilities from being considered until after postconditional offers of employment and, even then, only when job relevant. Yet the Neuroticism/Adjustment factor names, descriptions, and evidence clearly suggest the possibility they have measured variables associated with, or predicting to, psychological disorders.

Various definitions of this factor have been offered over the years. Preceding the FFM personality model, Eysenck (1967; Eysenck & Eysenck, 1976), a pioneer in personality measurement whose approaches bridged normal and abnormal variants, developed the influential three-factor PEN (Psychoticism, Extraversion, and Neuroticism) model of personality. Each of these factors was considered to be a "super factor" that had other variables underlying it. Psychoticism was the factor least congruent with contemporary FFM models. High scorers were thought to exhibit impulsiveness, lack of cooperation, oral pessimism, rigidity, low superego controls, low social sensitivity, low persistence, lack of anxiety, and lack of feelings of inferiority (Howarth, 1986). If anything, that list appears to be related more to sociopathy or other character disorders or to be a factor overlapping several in the FFM. The PEN model has had its share of criticism (see, e.g., Goldberg & Rosolack, 1994) contradicting Eysenck's contention that the PEN factors were "super factors" and generally demonstrating the concordance of P and N of the PEN model with the Neuroticism/Adjustment and E with the Introversion/Extraversion FFM factors. Similarly, McCrae and Costa's (1985a) Neuroticism variable of the NEO Personality Inventory correlated with the N factor of the Eysenck Personality Inventory but the Psychoticism factor did not. Compared with the FFM and other more recent models, PEN appears not to be in wide use now, either theoretically or for the measurement of normal personality in career contexts.

Another early model of the Neuroticism/Adjustment trait was Cattell's Factor C (Emotional Stability) on the 16PF (R. B. Cattell et al., 1970). Cattell considered C to be a measure of stress tolerance. High scorers were thought generally able to handle stress well and low scorers to have fewer resources with which to meet day-to-day challenges. Gough (1996) also incorporated several aspects of adjustment into the CPI. The v.3 variable was designed to measure Self-Realization, the extent to which test respondents had fulfilled their potential. The Wb (Well-Being) scale also identified the extent that CPI test-takers were presenting themselves in a well-adjusted, versus not-well-adjusted, manner. This scale, when low, can reflect personal distress but also can serve as a possible indicator of dissimulation among clients trying to simulate psychological disorder.

Costa and McCrae have published widely on their NEO FFM measure, but it is surprisingly difficult to find in their work a coherent definition of their version of the Neuroticism construct. In an early article (Costa & McCrae, 1985), they defined the construct in terms of its facets: "Neuroticism consists of these specific traits: anxiety, hostility, depression, self-consciousness, impulsiveness, and vulnerability" (Costa & McCrae, 1985, p. 712). Partly, this reflects the use by these researchers of what is called a lexical approach, that is, using vocabulary words commonly used by the general population.

Stanek and Ones (2018) defined Neuroticism as follows:

> A domain of traits relating to tendencies to experience negative emotions . . . individuals scoring high on this Big Five factor are easily frustrated, stress intolerant, and emotionally reactive. Global Neuroticism describes the degree of emotional dysregulation and maladjustment experienced by the individual. (p. 386)

Widiger (2009) defined the construct of Neuroticism as being "a fundamental trait of general personality, [referring] to an enduring tendency or disposition to experience negative emotional states" (p. 129).

Dimensionality and Facets

The currently used models and approaches to measuring Neuroticism/Adjustment have some commonalities and some differences. Starting with earlier approaches, R. B. Cattell et al. (1970) identified a global or second-order factor labeled Anxiety (low vs. high). Associated with the Anxiety Global Factor were four 16PF primary factors (in this model, analogous to facets), of C (Neuroticism/Adjustment), L (Trusting vs. Vigilant), O (Self-assured vs. Apprehensive), and Q4 (Relaxed vs. Tense; H. E. P. Cattell & Mead, 2008). People scoring high in C and O tended to have high ego strength and to differ from those scoring lower in being more emotionally mature, showing restraint in behavior, and separating the demands of a situation from their own emotional needs. Low scorers tended to show a pattern of emotional instability and ego weakness and were also prone to worry and to being easily disturbed. The 16PF's Q4 factor was thought to represent a generalized energy that, in high scorers, exceeded the capacity of the ego strength to integrate it, and may have converted it to less well-adjusted responses. These and other 16PF factors are combined to make a generic factor, Anxiety (Ax; high vs. low anxiety), and two adjustment scales, Psychoticism (P; well-integrated vs. disorganized) and Neuroticism (N; well-adjusted vs. unstable). The 16PF (H. E. P. Cattell & Mead, 2008) included an Anxiety/Neuroticism global factor. At the subfactor or facet level, the following are particularly relevant: C (Neuroticism/Adjustment), L (vigilance), O (apprehension), and Q4 (tension).

Gough's (1996) CPI did not include a Neuroticism scale per se but did have some scales and factors for Neuroticism/Adjustment. However, the 1996 revision of the instrument was partly aimed at removing items that were potentially problematic from the perspective of the ADA, which protected mental conditions from preemployment offer consideration. The 1996 version of the measure was focused less on emotional dysfunction than on emotional well-being. It included a substantially revised scale for a factor called the Well-Being scale (Wb) that was partly a test-taking orientation scale. Indeed, very low scores (raw scores of 20 and below) were potentially indicators of intentional exaggeration of symptoms of mental or physical ill health. Nevertheless, when spouses, peers, and staff members completed adjective check lists of individuals who had taken the CPI, those who had received low scores on the Wb scale were more likely to be described as "anxious," "complaining," "worrying," and the like than to be described as adaptable, cheerful, or self-confident. Thus the Wb scale likely measures at least correlates of anxiety and negative emotions, as well as, for high scorers, positive emotions and well-being. The CPI also contain what are called vectors (analogous to second-order factors) to classify people on three overarching dimensions. The third of these, v.3, was intended to assess a continuum of "self-realization, or psychological competence, or ego integration" (Gough, 1996, p. 29). In the context of Neuroticism/Adjustment, it appears to measure positive emotionality at the high end and the opposite at the lower end. Finally, the v.1 and v.2 vectors (externality/internality and norm favoring/norm questioning, respectively) were combined to classify those completing the instrument into four groups: Alpha, Beta, Gamma, and Delta. The Deltas (higher on internality and moving away from others) were particularly likely to experience emotional and behavioral maladjustment. The "modal Deltas" included, for both men and women, high school disciplinary problem students, psychiatric patients, and adult prison inmates; for men, but not women, young prison inmates; but also, for women, writers of children's books and creative writers. The CPI's Good Impression (Gi) scale, a test-taking orientation scale and validity indicator, may also be relevant for this factor in that persons with some personality patterns tend to deny difficulties and present themselves in an overly positive light. Finally, special scales were developed using CPI items to measure anxiety (the Leventhal Scale for Anxiety; Leventhal, 1966), narcissism, and other character pathology (e.g., the Wink-Gough Scale for Narcissism, Wink & Gough, 1990; Gough, 1996). Other personality measures also include a Well-Being factor. The MPQ's, e.g., related to having a "cheerful, happy disposition," being positive and optimistic versus (for lower scorers) the opposite, including seldom being happy, excited, or having fun in life (Tellegen & Waller, 2008, p. 273). Additionally, the MPQ found a higher order (overarching) factor of Positive Emotionality (PEM) and another one of Negative Emotionality (NEM).

As has been shown with other FFM variables, various facets have been associated with the Neuroticism/Adjustment factor. Widiger (2009, p. 130) provided a good summary of facet scales across various Neuroticism/Adjustment measures. Three of the six measures he compared included those focused on anxiety (a fourth included a measure labeled "fear of uncertainty"). Most of the other facets were not consistent across the measures.

Judge et al.'s (2013) 6-2-1 model applied to Neuroticism/Adjustment made use of DeYoung et al.'s (2007a) subtraits ("aspects") of Neuroticism/Adjustment, Volatility, and Withdrawal. They included Costa and McCrae's (1986, 1992) six Neuroticism/Adjustment facets: Angry Hostility, Impulsiveness, Anxiety, Depression, Self-Consciousness, and Vulnerability. Stanek and Ones's (2018) facets for the same two "aspects" (higher order components of the trait) were slightly different: Anxiety, Depression, Negative Affect, Perseveration, Somatic Complaints, Suspiciousness, and Uneven Temper.

The HPI model's Adjustment factor, defined as "the degree to which a person appears calm and self-accepting" (R. Hogan & Hogan, 2009, p. 25) currently includes eight HICs: Empathy, Not Anxious, No Guilt, Calmness, Even Tempered, No Complaints, Trusting, and Good Attachment.

Clearly, the various measures conceptualize Neuroticism/Adjustment differently both at the factor and at the facet or aspect (subdimension) level. Neuroticism/Adjustment does appear to be an important variable associated with so-called normal personality (and overlapping psychopathology), but until there is more consensus on the facets, care should be taken in interpreting facet scales that happen to be on a particular test.

Career and Work Issues

It is generally assumed, with supporting evidence, that high levels of Adjustment are associated with positive performance on the job or, put another way, that Neuroticism is associated with poorer performance on the job (Widiger & Oltmanns, 2017). High neuroticism is also associated with being more prone to stress, being less happy, and experiencing less life satisfaction (A. Weiss & Deary, 2020). The biggest challenge to such a conclusion, however, is the quite large prevalence of mental disorders across the life spectrum. For these reasons, correlations between one-time measured Neuroticism/Adjustment and outcomes may be misleading since those scoring low on Neuroticism/Adjustment at one point in time may not do so at the next. They can also be misleading because mental problems are typically stigmatized, causing people to deny symptoms when completing personality measures (Link & Phelan, 2013), particularly in work-related contexts.

The base rate of the experience of psychological dysfunction in particular occupations must also be taken into account in making sense of career assessment results. Managers, for example, tend to deny the experience of "negative emotions," so they will be more likely to appear well-adjusted on Neuroticism/ Adjustment scales independent of distress they may actually experience. In contrast, in certain occupations, especially in the creative arts, there are higher-than-average levels of psychological dysfunction and perhaps a greater willingness to acknowledge the experience of a full range of emotions. J. P. Guilford et al. (1976), in the test manual for the Guilford Zimmerman Temperament Survey (GZTS), reported occupational group averages for the various test scales. Those groups scoring in the less well-adjusted direction on the measure's Neuroticism/Adjustment scale, with the sole exceptions of female telephone operators and religious trainees, were all found in artistic/creative occupations.

The association of creative pursuits (or at least particular kinds of creative occupations) with lower levels of psychological adjustment has been reported in a number of studies (see F. K. Goodwin & Jamison, 2007). Jamison's (1989) study of creative artists found high levels of affective and mood disorders, suicide, and attempted suicide among people in these occupations, particularly among eminent individuals. Higher-than-average substance misuse, a type of diagnosable mental disorder, has also been reported in certain creative occupational groups, particularly writers (Andreasen & Canter, 1974; Andreasen & Powers, 1975; Dardis, 1989; D. W. Goodwin, 1988; Hayter, 1988; Helson, 1978; Jamison, 1989).

Within-occupation differences have also been reported on this dimension. Getzels and Csikszentmihalyi's (1976) important study of visual artists found different profiles of successful male and female art students, with the highest-rated male students experiencing higher levels of sensitivity and social isolation. Wills (1984) found personality differences among professional musicians based on the instrument of choice: trumpeters had the lowest Neuroticism scores on the Eysenck Personality Questionnaire (EPQ), while guitarists had the highest scores on both the P and N scales. Among writers, for example, certain types of writers (e.g., poets and fiction writers) have been reported to be more at risk of psychological disturbance than others (e.g., nonfiction writers). J. C. Kaufman (2001) found a high rate of mental illness and alcoholism among prize-winning authors, including a group winning the Nobel Prize.

As for how to make sense of these findings, there have been many theories. The creative process may call for access to affect but also be associated with certain protective mechanisms. Rhoads (2013), in a study of visual artists, found that although there was overall more mood dysfunction than in a control group, there was also a higher level of hardiness. This might enable artists with affective or other mood disorders to work effectively in spite of having psychological disorders. Piechowski and Cunningham (1985) reported five patterns of overexcitability found in a small sample of artists: psychomotor, emotional, sensual, intellectual, and imaginational. Restlessness, emotional vulnerability, and conflict between balance and integration were found to characterize the artists, suggesting that what may be perceived as psychopathology may actually (or additionally) be an essential component of the creative process.

Not all studies have supported the findings of creativity being associated with greater mental illness. Knudsen et al., (2019) found little evidence for diagnosable or self-reported past mental illness in a sample of highly creative visual artists and scientists but did find, particularly with the visual artists, higher levels of subclinical schizotypal characteristics. J. C. Kaufman (2014) published an edited book on creativity and mental illness that included the finding that psychological disorder and creative performance may primarily be in the area of affective disorders rather than in other types of mental illness or psychopathology.

Thus, for certain occupations, or subgroups of occupations, psychopathology or personality dysfunction might be quite common. As Proust put it (no doubt, too extremely), "Without nervous disorder there can be no great artist" (as cited in Coles, 1989, p. 30). That does not of course mean that all of those with Artistic interests or abilities will also score highly on measures of Neuroticism. But when that pattern is found, it is not particularly unusual.

Within other occupational groups, especially managers (Bentz, 1985; A. Howard & Bray, 1988), teachers, and other people-oriented professions (J. S. Guilford et al., 1976), emotional stability is generally the expected and reported condition found. Bentz (1985), whose research was done when Sears was the United States' largest retailer, found that its executives scored very high on measures of adjustment and emotional control. Bartram and Dale (1982) reported that lower N scores were associated with success in training for a group of 607 male pilots and trainee pilots. Stewart and Latham (1986) found that high Neuroticism/Adjustment were negatively correlated with leadership performance ratings.

Finally, from a career assessment standpoint, it should also be noted that a client with any interests-abilities-personality profile can experience neuroticism or other, sometimes career-relevant, psychological disorders. Work dysfunctions can cause psychological dysfunction, and psychological disorders can cause problems on the job. Fortunately, the adverse effects of neuroticism are responsive to treatment both by psychopharmaceutic (Widiger & Oltmanns, 2017) and behavioral (Barlow et al., 2014) interventions. Depending on the particular situation, referral for assessment and treatment of the mental health condition may be needed.

Measurement Issues

A number of objective personality measures assess Neuroticism/Adjustment. Neuroticism was one of the three original and primary variables on Costa and

McCrae's (1986, 1992) NEO Personality Inventory and along with psychoticism was also one of the primary variables of the Eysenck Personality Inventory. The GZTS (J. S. Guilford et al., 1976) also included a Neuroticism/Adjustment factor. The 16PF (R. B. Cattell et al., 1970) included Neuroticism/Adjustment-related variables at both the trait and variable level. The CPI (Gough, 1996), as discussed, included several variables relevant to Neuroticism/Adjustment. More recently, the Hogan measures (R. Hogan & Hogan, 2007) have included both Neuroticism/Adjustment and "dark side" variables. There are also, of course, a number of measures (such as the MMPI-2-RF) of psychopathology.

The measures of Neuroticism/Adjustment in "normal" populations are not interchangeable, though the major Neuroticism/Adjustment factors are typically correlated with one another and also with facets that are measuring comparable constructs. In considering which test to use for which purpose, it is important to determine whether measures of adjustment or neuroticism were conceptualized and validated using samples representative of the larger population, those with psychopathology, or both. Measures normed and validated on the general population are usually more appropriate for career assessment, but there can still be times when norms for a specific population are needed. When preliminary results suggest the presence of psychopathology that may be job dysfunctional, the assessor may wish to conduct or suggest a formal assessment of psychopathology. (For a more detailed discussion of the issues involved in the career-related assessment of psychopathology, see Lowman, 1989, 1993a.)

Clearly, when conducting career assessments, assumptions cannot be made that either high or low Neuroticism/Adjustment scores will persist over time. Career assessors will be gathering test evidence on personality variables that are generally stable over time (J. Wagner et al., 2019) and those that are not. High Neuroticism/Adjustment scores may suggest a character-like trait that will persist over time, a pattern of denial, or something that will change with exposure to high stress situations. Conversely, low Neuroticism/Adjustment scores may reflect trait anxiety or depression or an acute state that in a month or a year may look quite different. It is important to further explore low scores with clients and to determine whether there are career choice or change implications to the personality test findings. When persistent or more serious forms of psychopathology are encountered, assessment using measures designed for that purpose may be needed by those trained in their administration and interpretation.

Finally, the stigma associated with psychological dysfunction should not be exacerbated by the assessor. Low Neuroticism/Adjustment (high N) scores are not unusual in certain occupations, particularly in the arts. Understanding ways in which low Neuroticism/Adjustment can be functional or adaptive in certain career paths is important. Without underestimating the real work and career problems sometimes faced by those with diagnosable psychopathology, assessors need to understand that career assessees can experience both psychological dysfunction and successful work performance.

AGREEABLENESS PERSONALITY FACTOR

Agreeableness is one of the FFM factors that has a less stellar record in predicting overall work performance but has been demonstrated to predict certain aspects of work. Agreeableness (or the absence of Disagreeableness) would be expected to be relevant in a number of careers involving active social interaction and particularly in helping roles. Agreeableness has been shown to be particularly related, positively, to Organizational Citizenship Behavior (OCB) and inversely to Counterproductive Workplace Behavior (CWB; Chirumbolo, 2017). But understanding what this factor is about goes beyond its label. How the construct is defined matters in terms of whether Agreeableness is even the right label to put to this factor.

Conceptual Issues

There are some commonalities in the definitions or conceptualizations of the Agreeableness factor but also some differences, and consensus on the trait, if that is what it is, is not yet established. Carlo et al. (2014) described Agreeableness as being "characteristic of individuals who are sympathetic, compassionate, warm, and kind" (p. 287). Graziano and Tobin (2009) stated that Agreeableness

> describes individual differences in being likeable, pleasant, and harmonious in relations with others. Research shows that persons who are described by others as "kind" are also described as "considerate" and "warm," implicating a superordinate dimension that is relatively stable over time and related to a wide range of thoughts, feelings, and social behaviors. (p. 46)

Using a different approach, the Cybernetic Big 5 Theory (CB5T) model, Connelly et al. (2018) noted that

> Agreeableness captures variation in individuals' willingness to coordinate goals with others. At the low levels of the trait, disagreeable individuals are most likely to pursue their own self-interests over concern for others and may be willing to manipulate others to achieve their own goals. (p. 326)

Stanek and Ones (2018) defined Agreeableness as "a domain of personality traits that describe behavioral tendencies in getting along with others . . . [being] likable, friendly, nurturing, interpersonally sensitive, sincere, eager to be liked by others and to fit in" (p. 387). Graziano and Tobin (2009) noted that "Agreeableness is an abstract, higher level summary term for a set of relations among connected lower level characteristics . . . [describing] individual differences in being likeable, pleasant, and harmonious in relations with others" (p. 46). And, in still another model, K. Lee and Ashton (2014b) described the trait as follows:

> *Agreeableness (vs. Anger)*: Persons with very high scores on the Agreeableness scale forgive the wrongs that they suffered, are lenient in judging others, are willing to compromise and cooperate with others, and can easily control their temper. Conversely, persons with very low scores on this scale hold grudges

against those who have harmed them, are rather critical of others' shortcomings, are stubborn in defending their point of view, and feel anger readily in response to mistreatment. (para. 4)

Many of these descriptions overlap and focus on the positive polarity and define the opposite polarity quite negatively. This approach not only has measurement implications (particularly when using self-assessments) but also theoretical ones.

Dimensionality and Facets

As has been shown with other FFM variables, here too there are differing facets associated with the Agreeableness factor. Judge et al.'s (2013) 6-2-1 model applied to Agreeableness made use of DeYoung et al.'s (2007a) subtraits of Compassion and Politeness. Stanek and Ones's (2018) facets for the same two "aspects" of Compassion and Politeness were Cooperation, Lack of Aggression, Modesty, Non-Manipulative, Nurturance, Not Outspoken, and Tender-Minded. Curiously, three of these facets (e.g., not being outspoken) were defined or at least labeled in terms of what they were not. The overall theme of those six facets is of honesty, good behavior, and authenticity, but also, arguably, passivity.

Costa and McCrae's (1992, 1995) facets for Agreeableness were Trust, Straightforwardness, Altruism, Compliance, Modesty, and Tender-Mindedness. Hogan's (R. Hogan & Hogan, 2009) HPI includes an Interpersonal Sensitivity factor (defined as "the degree to which a person is seen as perceptive, tactful, and socially sensitive"; p. 25) that encompassed five HICs: Easy to Live With, Sensitive, Caring, Likes People, and No Hostility.

In comparing Raymond Cattell's model to FFM models, H. E. P. Cattell and Mead (2008) presented as an analogue of Agreeableness the 16PF's factor of Independence versus Accommodation. Relevant facets they placed here were D (dominance vs. being deferential), H (bold vs. shy), L (vigilant vs. trusting), and Q1 (open to change vs. traditional). Gough's CPI (Gough, 1996) included the v.1 (internality/externality) vector. Scales of variables in the CPI's first factor grouping including Sociability (Sy), Dominance (Do), Social Presence (Sp), and Empathy (Em) are particularly relevant and suggest another way to measure Agreeableness.

Other models, facet variables, and names have also been put forth. For example, Ashton and Lee's (2009) HEXACO model, which added an Honesty-Humility factor to the FFM factors, included the following facets for its Agreeableness factor: Forgiveness, Gentleness, Flexibility, Patience, and Altruism (vs. Antagonism). Clearly, there is more work to be done to sort out these various models and approaches.

Career and Work Issues

As noted, the Agreeableness factor has had a somewhat mixed record when it comes to adding incremental power in predicting work and career outcomes.

Unlike other personality measures such as Conscientiousness that predict across a wide range of job duties, Agreeableness predicts especially to jobs that require abilities to deal effectively with others (Connelly et al., 2018). It is certainly reasonable that this variable would predict best when the job duties require customer service or an empathetic orientation to others. However, there are also conceptual differences in how the polarities of the factor are conceptualized that may account for some of the results.

Agreeableness has been defined and conceptualized by various researchers and test developers in different ways. Some, as suggested by the first definitions presented above, conceptualize the construct as measuring "Agreeableness versus Disagreeableness." To others, "Submissiveness versus Independence" is the salient issue underlying this factor. In the former approach, Agreeableness stems from warmth and pleasantness and eagerness to please others (or their absence). In an alternative approach, submissiveness and desire to please versus preferring to work on one's own and to achieve one's own goals instead of those of others are the opposite ends of the scale. Jung expressed a similar construct in describing introverts when he noted that "always . . . [they have] to prove that everything . . . [they do] rests on [their] own decisions and convictions, and never because . . . [they are] influenced by anyone, or desires to please or conciliate some person or opinion" (C. G. Jung, 1971/1921, CW 6, para. 893). One does not have to be an introvert to be independent, but interventions (and feedback) might differ if someone is indifferent to the reactions of others due to independence rather than from being a generally disagreeable person who may wish others harm.

Measurement Issues

There are some important implications for career assessment associated with these alternative conceptual approaches to the Agreeableness factor. First, one end of the Agreeable/Disagreeable model is highly socially desirable and the other not. The literature is mixed as to the extent to which social desirability (SD) affects Agreeableness measures (Connelly & Chang, 2016). Paulhus et al. (1995) differentiated between intentional motivation (IM), in which respondents were attempting consciously to present themselves in a positive way or to deny negative attributes, and self-deception (SD) components of SD in which respondents were unaware of their self-enhancement bias. He recommended correcting for the former but not the latter. Connelly and Chang (2016), in a meta-analytic study designed to sort out issues related to high SD responses (typically measured by "unlikely virtues" scales in which high scorers tend to deny deficiencies that most people would endorse) found important areas of concern. First, they found that those who presented themselves more favorably than the estimation coming from their peers were at risk for poorer performance, both in school and on the job. As they put it, "Given that self-report response styles were associated with substantial losses in validity for predicting academic and job performance, assessing response styles may be especially important" (Connelly & Chang, 2016, p. 329). Secondly, however, they also concluded that there were strong correlations between the SD responses and three personality factors: Conscientiousness, Neuroticism/Adjustment, and Agreeableness. Thus, corrections for SD themselves may improve validity in predicting to outcomes but also change scores on these three dimensions, making the question of whether or not to correct for SD a complicated one. These authors noted that correcting results based on SD scales was not recommended and pointed to alternative, emerging approaches.

As a practical matter, some personality assessment measures (e.g., the CPI) have well-developed "good impression" measures and others (e.g., the NEO measures) have a very simple, nonsubtle, approach to SD measurement. In career assessment at the individual level, the test-taking orientation can be addressed in the feedback process. Because it is not the career assessor's job to make decisions based on the data but rather to help the client make informed decisions on the basis of the data, it may be sufficient to help those with high SD responses better to understand their implications.

Another issue with Agreeableness scores is what to do when low scores on Agreeableness are found. In using an Agreeableness/Disagreeableness model of the Agreeableness construct, presenting feedback to people that suggests that they are "disagreeable," especially to people who truly are so, may not be a particularly constructive experience, though it may be a necessary one. Conversely, the polarity of Autonomy versus Submissiveness conceptualization in effect may make it easier for people scoring low on Agreeableness to understand and accept their scores as both having positive characteristics—or at least not inherently negative ones—and to recognize the special risks that they may be prone to when trying to get things done in a social context.

Additionally, career assessors need to be aware of the potential negative aspects of feedback provided to those scoring highly in the Agreeable direction. Willingness to respond positively and to interact well with others are, after all, socially desirable characteristics, though if they derive from excessive submissiveness or conflict avoidance, they have their limits. If people are too quick to agree with others when the job or career calls for rigorous debate or inherent skepticism (e.g., in law and science), that may be problematic. Conversely, certain jobs and occupations will benefit from high autonomy skills (e.g., entrepreneurs and highly trained technicians), but some social skills may still be needed to be effective in the job. Still, conceptualizing low Agreeableness scores as a potential excess of autonomy or very high Agreeableness scores as perhaps reflecting a potential deficit of assertiveness may be a useful way to help test scores be easier to accept and to understand how some aspects of their behavior, if not managed, may interfere with career or job success.

As for measuring at the facet level of Agreeableness, although some of the identified facets likely overlap or measure parts of the same concepts, others do not, and assessors should take care not to assume that a single list of facets that happens to come with a particular test has consensual agreement or similar psychometric results. Care should therefore be taken not to overinterpret facet scales on a particular personality measure without careful review of research evidence associated with that variable and its pattern of correlations with other relevant variables and outcome measures. Too much can be made about "highs and lows" on an array of facet variables presented in an attractive feedback format. Most important is the need to focus on the major themes and polarities of the overarching factor and the particular conceptualization on which it is based. Of course, there is no single "right answer" (interpersonal orientation and pleasantness, "good"; independence, "bad"), and the strengths and challenges potentially associated with being too far out on either polarity need to be considered in the context of the individual assessee's career goals and ambitions.

OPENNESS PERSONALITY FACTOR

The last factor to be reviewed in the FFM model, Openness to Experience (here called Openness except when otherwise labeled by particular models or measures) is included in most FFM models. Those scoring in the open direction are likely to be seen as being imaginative, receptive to new ideas, and behaviorally and intellectually flexible in contrast to those scoring in the less flexible direction, who are more likely to resist change and innovation and to prefer known and traditional approaches (McCrae & Sutin, 2009). This was the last of the five factors to be added to the FFM, and some researchers have questioned whether it is a facet or a major factor of personality.

Conceptual Issues

Although now included in most FFM models, concerns were raised early and still persist about whether Openness was separable from more cognitively influenced characteristics such as Intellectance (Connelly et al., 2018; S. B. Kaufman et al., 2016). McCrae and Sutin's (2009) chapter called "Openness to Experience" was, to the chagrin of the authors, placed in a section of the *Handbook of Individual Differences in Social Behavior* called "Cognitive Dispositions." As they noted, "[Openness to Experience] is not a cognitive disposition, nor is it a dimension of social behavior.... [It is] fundamentally an intrapsychic variable" (p. 257).

Yet the concept of Openness to Experience was not new. Carl Rogers (1959) described it as an aspect of people (closest, seemingly, to personality) by which people can accept experiences in a minimally defensive way. As he put it,

> When [individuals are] in no way threatened, then [they are] open to [their] experience[s]. To be open to experience is the polar opposite of defensiveness. The term may be used in regard to some area of experience or in regard to the total experience of the organism. It signifies that every stimulus, whether originating within the organism or in the environment, is freely relayed through the nervous system without being distorted or channeled off by any defensive mechanism. There is no need of the mechanism of "subception" whereby the organism is forewarned of experiences threatening to the self. On the contrary,

whether the stimulus is the impact of a configuration of form, color, or sound in the environment on the sensory nerves, or a memory trace from the past, or a visceral sensation of fear, pleasure, or disgust, it is completely available to the individual's awareness. In the hypothetical person who is completely open to his experience, his concept of self would be a symbolization in awareness which would be completely congruent with his experience. There would therefore be no possibility of threat. (p. 206)

Rogers's concept of being open to experience was essentially an idealized model of psychological functioning, whereas the contemporary models of openness, though not necessarily incompatible with Rogers's ideas, describe an individual difference variable that is associated with relatively fixed aspects of personality and that constitutes a basic orientation to the external world. It is possible that Rogers's Openness to Experience was a subset of a larger construct in which persons high on this dimension not only can accept their own experiences but also those of others and of the larger world as well.

Other, indeed most, contemporary approaches have defined the Openness construct fairly broadly. Schwaba et al. (2018) described this construct as reflecting

the breadth and depth of an individual's consciousness and reflection ... [reflecting their] intellectual curiosity, imagination, and aesthetic sensitivity.... People high on openness are likely to experience chills when encountering something that is aesthetically pleasing ... tend to daydream ... and [to] hold liberal political views. (p. 119)

In a generally similar vein, McCrae and Sutin (2009) described the polarities of Openness:

Highly open people are ... seen as [being] imaginative, sensitive to art and beauty, emotionally differentiated, behaviorally flexible, intellectually curious, and liberal in values. Closed people are down-to-earth, uninterested in art, shallow in affect, set in their ways, lacking curiosity and traditional in values. (p. 259)

The HPI's (Hogan & Hogan, 2009, p. 25) Inquisitive factor was defined as "the degree to which a person is perceived as bright, creative, and interested in intellectual matters" (p. 19), which raises questions about the overlap between this concept of Openness and intellect. In prior HPI models (Hogan & Hogan, 1992) this factor was labeled Intellectance, suggesting a confound with intelligence (McCrae & Sutin, 2009).

Although, at a general level, there would appear to be many commonalities associated with these conceptualizations, they also suggest alternative ways in which people may be open and particular interests (such as in aesthetic and artistic areas) that potentially mask the consistency of the overall definition of a construct in which specific content areas of interest may apply. McCrae (1994) encouraged the use of the Openness to Experience (vs. terms involving intellect) because it was

a broader construct that implies both receptivity to many varieties of experience and a fluid and permeable structure of consciousness. The construct of Openness can be transported across geographical and cultural boundaries to function as a universal dimension of personality structure. (p. 251)

Dimensionality and Facets

Compared with the other four FFM factors, Openness was late in being added, and arguably has been less well, or at least less consistently, developed. The basic construct has been represented in many established measures of personality, including those that pre-dated the FFM. Cattell's 16PF (R. B. Cattell et al., 1970) included two factors of special relevance: Factor M and Factor Q1. The M factor was originally called Praxernia for the low scorers and Autia for the higher ones (Cattell et al., 1970). It was later referred to, much more accessibly, as "Practical v. Imaginative" (Institute for Personality and Ability Testing Staff [IPAT], 1986). The term "Abstractedness" was also used for high M scorers (H. E. P. Cattell & Mead, 2008). The M factor differentiated those who were seen as being "down to earth," pragmatic and unimaginative in their approach to life versus those who were more likely to be focused on ideas, interested in the arts, highly imaginative, and fanciful. Slightly different anchors were identified with factor Q1 originally labeled "conservatism of temperament versus radicalism" (R. B. Cattell et al., 1970) and later called "Conservative v. Experimenting" (IPAT Staff, 1986). H. E. P. Cattell and Mead (2008), in a more recent publication, labeled Q1 as "Openness to Change."

Gough's CPI included a scale called Flexibility (vs. rigidity) and a second-order factor, v.2, was labeled Norm Favoring versus Norm Questioning (Gough, 1996). Those scoring in the norm doubting and in the high flexibility direction would be expected to score in the high Openness direction in the FFM model and those at the other extreme in the closed direction. In the CPI's occupational census data for the v.2 higher order factor, less flexible scorers included, among others, West Point cadets (male), Catholic priests, best citizen nominees, and education students (female). More flexible groups included art students, psychology graduate students, and juvenile delinquents (both male and female; Gough, 1996).

On the HPI, the Openness factor is called Intellect/Openness to Experience (labeled by these authors as "Inquisitive"). They defined it as "the degree to which a person is perceived as bright, creative, and interested in intellectual matters" (R. Hogan & Hogan, 2007, p 25). This suggests a potential confound of intelligence and Openness, a concern raised by McCrae and Sutin (2009).

Although the measure has been widely criticized on psychometric grounds (e.g., Hicks, 1984; Pittenger, 2005), the MBTI (Myers, 1980, 1987; Myers et al. 1998) is among the most widely used personality tests in the world. Its variable for Openness is labeled Intuitive (N) versus Sensing (S), harkening back to Jung's typology. Those more open to experience on this measure generally have higher N than S scores and those less so, the opposite. The problem with dichotomization of people into one of two categories (either N or S) remains. Those with slight differentiations among types are probably different in kind than those who are at the extremes, and bimodal scales are employed in this measure as if they were two single scales, which they are not (Hicks, 1984).

As has been shown with other FFM variables, here too there are differing facets associated with the Openness factor in the various models and measures. Judge et al.'s (2013) 6-2-1 model applied to Openness to Experience made use of DeYoung et al.'s (2007a) subtraits of Intellect and Aesthetic Openness. Costa and McCrae's (1986, 1992) six facets involving Openness to Experience were Ideas, Actions, Aesthetics, Fantasy, Feelings, and Values, suggesting an approach in which people may be differentially open. Stanek and Ones's (2018) facets for their two "aspects" of Intellect and Experiencing were Aesthetics, Curiosity, Fantasy, Ideas, Introspection, Need For Cognition, Being Non-Traditional, and Variety Seeking. The HPI's (R. Hogan & Hogan, 2007) Inquisitive factor encompassed six HICs: Science Ability, Curiosity, Thrill Seeking, Intellectual Games, Generates Ideas, and Culture. The inclusion of a facet labeled as an ability in a measure of personality raises concerns as to its being a personality, ability, or interest HIC. The remainder seem to assess specific areas of openness, personality characteristics (e.g., thrill seeking), or particular areas of application (e.g., generates ideas) These facets do not overall seem to be consistent either in concept or in content across these measures or models and that creates measurement concerns.

Career and Work Issues

Although Openness has been part of most contemporary FFM models and those that preceded them, Openness has had a somewhat spotty record in predicting to job performance (e.g., Barrick et al., 2001; Ones et al., 2007). Mussel et al. (2011) accurately noted that part of this outcome may be associated with the lack of consistency in what is included in the Openness measures, especially in the facet scales. They provided evidence that, when two subfactor groupings, which they labeled perceptual (fantasy, aesthetics, and feelings) versus epistemic (openness to ideas, flexibility, and creativity), are considered, only the latter, and, in particular, openness to ideas, was associated with work-related outcomes.

Concerning careers, neither Openness, nor its converse, being closed, is universally better or more desirable than the other, but each is a better fit for some occupations and, within an occupation, to specific occupational roles more than others. For example, managers as a group tend to score in the more closed than open direction (see Gough, 1996). Management (vs., say, entrepreneurial activities) is generally about working to achieve particular outcomes and organizing groups of diverse people to be disciplined in working toward common goals. Conversely, start-ups often call for new and creative ideas, and those who are successful are generally more open to seeing opportunities where others do not. Although creative individuals may well be higher on openness than noncreative ones (McCrae, 1987), a person does not have to be creative to be open.

Clearly, Openness is more advantageous in some careers and work roles than in others. Thus, some occupations or jobs persistently call for creativity and openness to new ideas. Gough's technical manual for the CPI (Gough, 1987, 1996), for example, reported the following higher average occupational scores on the Flexibility scale for those in psychology, social welfare, writing, and artists, versus lower average scores for bankers, police, and probation officers. There can of course be within-occupational differences. For example, higher level managers or executives, in contrast to lower level ones, may benefit from higher Openness because they have responsibility for imagining the future, not just dealing with the present or past (H. E. P. Cattell & Mead, 2008).

Measurement Issues

Although there are fairly high correlations across various measures of Openness (McCrae & Sutin, 2009), the conceptualizations of the construct differ from one assessment measure to the next, as do the facets. Some, for example, the Big Five Aspects Scale (DeYoung et al., 2007a, 2007b, 2009), clearly focused on both intellectual interests and aesthetics/cultural interests. Others place more emphasis on aesthetic interests, and still others emphasize openness to feelings. Theoretically, there might be a single, broader factor that underlies a number of different possible areas to which an individual can be open.

Care should therefore be taken to assure that there is clarity in what is being measured by the Openness scales and that not too much is made of facet scales absent compelling evidence in support of a particular approach. Whether Openness is primarily conceptualized as being oriented to a preference for cognitive pursuits, curiosity, thrill seeking, aesthetics, imagination, culture, intellectualism, or science abilities/interests will affect what research questions are asked and what interpretations are given in applied measurement. Thus, the various Openness measures cannot be used interchangeably, particularly at the facet level.

Depending on one's perspective, the extremes of Openness may seem to paint high openness favorably and low openness less so. Although this reaction may vary depending on whose eyes are doing the beholding, it is important not to privilege one extreme or the other of this (or any other) personality factor. In fact, there are potential assets and potential deficits with any orientation. For example, highly open people can be too receptive to new ideas, neglecting the development of any of them. Individuals more closed to experience and the like, in contrast, may stick to a particular idea or career pursuit long after it is clear that alternative paths are likely to be better for them.

SUMMARY AND CONCLUSIONS

Judging from the breadth and depth of its literature, the FFM has been widely used in a variety of applications, including in the career and work areas. Each of the factors was reviewed, and a sampling of the literature relevant to career and work applications was presented. Clearly, several of the FFM factors have proven their worth, but some have not, and there are inevitable flaws and limitations in applying this model to careers and work. In the next chapter, additional personality variables that have relevance for career and work are presented.

15

Other Career-Relevant Personality Characteristics

In many respects, the popularity and dominance of the five-factor personality model (FFM) in the personality literature, particularly as it relates to work and careers, has masked its limitations and critics (e.g., Livneh & Livneh, 1989) and has taken focus off other variables that may also be important for career assessment issues (Ashton & Lee, 2009; Hough & Dilchert, 2017; Hough et al., 2015; K. Lee & Ashton, 2004a, 2004b). Some of the broad-brush instruments designed around the FFM or other conceptual models include facet scales or other variables that may be career relevant. For this reason, and without taking a stand on whether these are or are not "merely" facets, a few additional variables are identified here for further discussion.

LOCUS OF CONTROL AND CAREER-RELATED SELF-EFFICACY

Certain generic variables have complicated relationships with career and work issues in that they may both derive from personality traits but also interact with work or school experience. There is an extensive literature on Locus of Control (LOC) and a still-emerging one on career-related Self-Efficacy. Both of these characteristics identify the extent to which an individual believes that there is a relationship between their actions and desired career-related outcomes. Clearly, regardless of their etiology, feelings that one's efforts will not result in desired career-related outcomes put people at a disadvantage in pursuing—and sometimes even in being aware of—their career goals. Those who have had difficult

---

https://doi.org/10.1037/0000254-016
Career Assessment: Integrating Interests, Abilities, and Personality, by R. L. Lowman
Copyright © 2022 by the American Psychological Association. All rights reserved.

upbringings, abusive parents or caretakers, or impoverished childhoods may underestimate their abilities or the ways in which they can succeed or advance themselves. Career assessors may have a different issue to consider when clients present with a generalized lack of self-determination.

Conceptual Issues

The concept of LOC, an attribution style, was introduced by Rotter (1966) in the context of contingencies of reinforcement. LOC refers to the assumptions that people make about whether they control their fate (internal LOC, or ILOC) or are controlled by others (external LOC, or ELOC). Furnham (2009) defined LOC as "the belief that a behavioral response will or will not influence the attainment of reinforcement" (p. 275). Furnham also cited Rotter's (1966) earlier definition of LOC:

> When a reinforcement is perceived . . . as following some action of . . . [one's] own but not being entirely contingent upon . . . [one's own] action, then, in our culture, it is typically perceived as the result of luck, chance, fate, as under the control of powerful others, or as unpredictable because of the great complexity of the forces surrounding him . . . we have labeled this a belief in external control. If the person perceives that the event is contingent upon his own behavior or . . . [upon one's] own relatively permanent characteristics, we have termed this a belief in internal control. (as cited in Furnham, 2009, p. 275)

Although generally conceptualized as a relatively fixed individual differences variable, LOC can also be influenced by the larger environment. Twenge et al. (2004) provided evidence showing that youth had (between 1960 and 2002) grown, on average, more external in their LOC and had increased in cynicism. Furnham's review chapter (2009) noted that both ILOC and ELOC can be either stable or unstable and global (generalized) or specific to a particular performance. Judge and Bono (2001) identified LOC as a component variable or facet of a proposed higher order factor of core self-evaluation. Many studies have found a direct relationship between LOC and various job- and life-related outcomes but it has also been identified as a moderator variable (Turnipseed, 2018).

Dimensionality and Facets

As with the FFM model, LOC was established as being a hierarchical factor. General LOC was seen as an overall tendency to attribute rewards to one's own behavior rather than to external causes (e.g., institutions, good or bad luck). More narrow versions of LOC, below the main factor, include several specific areas of application in particular domains, including general well-being; health, including mental health; marital happiness (Ng et al., 2006; Q. Wang et al., 2010); and openness to change (J. Chen & Wang, 2007).

Whether Self-Efficacy/LOC is influenced by other personality variables was considered by Stajkovic et al. (2018). Using multiple student populations, they considered whether any of the FFM factors would mediate the relationship between Self-Efficacy and academic performance. This study found that Self-Efficacy was positively associated with academic outcomes across all the samples. However, only Conscientiousness and Emotional Stability related to the criterion measure and to Self-Efficacy.

Career and Work Issues

The relationship of LOC to work has generally found adverse outcomes to be associated with external attributions/LOC and positive ones with internal attribution/LOC (Ng et al., 2006). Specifically, positive correlations have been reported between ILOC and task performance, job satisfaction, and self-efficacy. Ng et al. (2006) also noted that LOC is based on a cognitive process influenced by three major psychological aspects: (a) self-evaluation (with ILOC individuals having a positive self-evaluation and high self-esteem), (b) motivation (for ILOC, involving high expectations of achieving their goals given their efforts), and (c) the continual presence of behavioral control.

Furnham's (2009) review cited a variety of studies that identified more positive outcomes associated with ILOC. Evidence has shown people with attribution styles that focused on things they considered to be uncontrollable by them tended to fare much worse than those who did not. In a well-known study by Seligman and Schulman (1986), life insurance sales agents who had more positive and optimistic explanatory styles (presumably higher ILOC) were more likely to initiate calls and to succeed. There was also a relationship between explanatory style and job satisfaction and work motivation (Furnham, 2009).

Measurement Issues

A number of tests have been developed for the measurement of LOC and attribution style. Many of these have been used primarily in research. However, Q. Wang et al. (2010) found that work-related LOC was a better predictor of work outcomes than general LOC and suggesting choosing, or adapting, measures of LOC to workplace issues. Ng et al. (2006) also found a small effect for the instruments used to measure LOC. Specifically, the Spector and Rotter measures had higher relationships with the outcome measures than did others.

Concerning interpretation, once again the evidence points to positive results associated with one polarity and negative, or worse, relationships associated with the other. This views ELOC, essentially, as a deficit. From the perspective of career assessment, clients scoring unambiguously in ELOC need to understand the construct and what they can do to change, or at least lessen, the impact of it on career choice and change issues. To the extent that people perceive their work and career as being controlled by fate or luck there will be less likelihood of taking the necessary steps that may be needed to pursue a change of career directions. In such cases, understanding the source of the ILOC assumptions may be needed. Are parents or others in the assessee's environment putting pressure on an individual to proceed in a particular direction?

Have there been many career and work failures or perceived failures that have contributed to passivity or attribution of causality to others? In what aspects of the client's life is there more of a sense of self-efficacy and why in those areas and not in career pursuits? Is the person from a disadvantaged background where they have not seen much connection between pursuing one's own career goals and outcomes? How firmly are those assumptions held? In well-entrenched cases, referral for coaching or counseling may be needed to help the person identify and change the assumptions that they are making about the role of their own behavior in obtaining desired career outcomes.

ACHIEVEMENT MOTIVATION

The Achievement Motivation factor (or facet; also known as Need for Achievement) is particularly relevant for assessments in the context of work that is demanding and offers advancement opportunities or that requires completion of a lengthy educational preparation program. Recognizing that talent development and actual achievement require far more than motivation to achieve (see Preckel et al., 2020), this factor has generated considerable research attention. Recognizing at the outset that not everyone will be high on this dimension, the positive end of the polarity is not "better" than the other, and this dimension is still relevant for providing career assessment advice. Achievement Motivation is relevant for both those with high-level career ambitions and those for whom a career is more of a job than something that overshadows other personal identities. Conversely, when assessees aim for a happy, balanced life where work is just one aspect of their lives, average or lower levels of the construct may be more appropriate.

Conceptual Issues

Achievement Motivation (or orientation) generally refers to a liking for goal-directed activities and a persistent striving to accomplish tasks successfully and to avoid failure. For some people, this includes a preference for competitive activities in which success is defined in terms of how one performs in comparison to others. For others, the preference is for competing against a standard of excellence. Spence and Helmreich (1983), who conducted a number of studies in this area, defined achievement orientation (motivation) as "task-oriented behavior that allows the individual's performance to be evaluated according to some internally or externally imposed criterion, that involves the individual in competing with others, or that otherwise involves some standard of excellence" (p. 12).

Much of the early research literature on Achievement Motivation (then known primarily as Need for Achievement or nAch) was conducted or inspired by the theories and research of David McClelland (e.g., 1961), John Atkinson (Atkinson & Feather, 1966), and their associates. McClelland considered Achievement Motivation to have both individual-based (personological) and social-context-based (sociological) aspects. With his associates, McClelland developed a measurement approach based on projective testing, assessing what today would be called implicit motives. Building on Murray's (1938, 1943) work, respondents were asked to make up stories about what was depicted in pictures from the Thematic Apperception Test (TAT). Motives were scored using an explicit coding system.

McClelland's work was quite influential and, in an era in which psychologists sought to address important societal problems, he and his colleagues considered the societal, not just the individual, level. Some societies were noted to be more achievement-oriented than others. Societies that value achievement, McClelland argued, have transmitted the importance of getting ahead and the need for a strong work ethic in many ways through the culture, including in children's literature. Using this methodology, differences across cultures were associated with this variable. Western societies tended to identify strongly with advancement, whereas in other cultures, particularly non-Western, there was less single-minded focus on work and success. This theory was not without its critics and revisionists (e.g., Frey, 1984). The coding systems were sometimes problematic, and concerns were raised about the stimuli in terms of which ones would be expected to elicit achievement motives. Although new stimuli and coding systems were devised, there remained poor correlations between implicit and explicit measurement approaches. However, implicit and explicit motives were not measuring the same aspects of the construct (Conroy et al., 2009).

Many decades of research has continued on Achievement Motivation after the initial focus, with a variety of more traditional assessment measures being used. Some of the recent approaches to this dimension have reconceptualized Achievement Motivation to focus more on achievement and competence. Nicholls (1984) defined Achievement Motivation as "behavior directed at developing or demonstrating high rather than low ability" (p. 328). Conroy et al. (2009) noted that "achievement motivation theories seek to explain the processes that energize, direct, and sustain efforts to be competent" (p. 382). Conroy et al.'s definition reflects a motive- and goal-focused approach to Achievement Motivation in which behavior is undertaken to fulfill certain positive states (such as pride) and to avoid certain negative ones (such as shame). This is in keeping with many of the contemporary approaches to the construct.

The presence of a sex difference on Achievement Motivation has been considered by several researchers (Lipman-Blumen et al., 1980; see also Deaux, 1985). Chusmir and Hood (1988) reported a sex difference for men and women on Achievement Motivation as it related to Type A and Type B behavior patterns. Specifically, the Achievement Motivation predicted the Type A behavior pattern for women but not for men. Schroth (1987) found that college men scored higher than women on Achievement Motivation (and dominance), whereas women scored higher on need for affiliation. These results held for both the TAT, a projective test, and the Edwards Personal Preference Schedule (EPPS), an objective one. S. Rao and Murthy (1984) also reported a sex difference in favor of men on ILOC and higher levels of Achievement Motivation. Elder and MacInnis (1983) noted that women assessed in their youth could be classified into two motivational groupings in a sample whose members were first assessed in 1932. Those who were grouped in the social-marital path had lower initially rated levels of Achievement Motivation, whereas those in the worklife-career path were more likely to finish school, marry, and have children later and were more oriented toward a career over the lifespan. However, other studies measuring Achievement Motivation in different ways and with different samples have disputed a sex difference. Chusmir (1985), for example, examined a group of male and female managers and found the women to have higher scores on Achievement Motivation and need for power and that there were no sex differences on need for affiliation. Chusmir (1984) also noted that these findings run counter to the views of personnel administrators, who believed that male and female personnel administrators were about equal in Achievement Motivation but viewed women as being higher in need for affiliation and men as being higher in need for power. However, people who become managers are presumably selected, both by employers and by themselves, on the basis of their personality characteristics. Schroth and Andrew (1987) reported that in a Hawaiian college student sample, men and women differed on subscales of an Achievement Motivation measure. Specifically, men scored higher on the Competitiveness scale, women on the Work Dimension scale. A third subscale, Mastery, showed no sex difference. Faver (1984) also noted that age may interact with sex such that younger women high in Achievement Motivation are more likely to pursue a career than older women.

Achievement Motivation levels can change. Levels can also moderate as the result of psychological intervention (Craig & Olson, 1988; McClelland & Winter, 1969) or the passage of time. Several researchers (e.g., A. Howard & Bray, 1988; McClelland, 1961) have reported that Achievement Motivation tends to decline with age. This may occur as people come to terms with their actual levels of accomplishment and accept the lowered possibilities of mobility as they rise within an occupational or organizational hierarchy. Because the number of vacancies at the higher levels is small, with age comes a greater recognition that continued advancement may not be likely. Achievement Motivation may change differentially over time for the sexes. Jenkins (1987), for example, measured Achievement Motivation in a sample of 117 female college seniors and again 14 years later. She found on follow-up that Need for Achievement predicted being in careers that were congruent with achievement and high status jobs where standards of excellence could be met. The highest increases in Achievement Motivation were found among those who became professors and those in business. Faver (1984) reported that there were cross-sectional differences in the likelihood of pursuing a career; younger women were more likely than older women to express Achievement Motivation by pursuing a career.

Dimensionality and Facets

There is considerable evidence that achievement orientation is not unidimensional and also that there are relationships with other variables and constructs.

Researchers examining the dimensionality of the Achievement Motivation variable have identified multiple factors, including competitiveness, status aspirations, dominance, and striving (Bendig, 1963, 1964; Bendig & Martin, 1962; Jackson et al., 1976). Gough's (1996) California Psychological Inventory (CPI) differentiated Achievement through Conformity and Achievement through Independence with the idea that the former concerned Achievement Motivation in the context of well-established parameters and the latter concerned achieving on one's own terms. Derman et al. (1978) identified factors reflecting both a desire to get ahead and a liking of competition; however, not all agree on the latter as a necessary component of Achievement Motivation (see Lipman-Blumen et al., 1983). Supporting the multidimensional conception of Achievement Motivation is the finding of an association between the Achievement Motivation and authoritarianism (Teevan et al., 1988).

Still more models of dimensions have been identified. Spence and Helmreich (1983) identified at least three dimensions of achievement orientation: work orientation (high in those with elevated Achievement Motivation scores), need for mastery (also high), and interpersonal competitiveness (generally low in the most successful). Elaborating on the interpersonal aspects of achievement orientation, Lipman-Blumen et al. (1983) identified three styles used to achieve goals: direct, in which one uses one's own efforts to accomplish goals; instrumental, in which others may also be used to accomplish goals; and relational, in which one contributes actively or passively to the accomplishment of others' goals.

Some researchers and some models (e.g., Costa & McCrae, 1995; Stanek & Ones, 2018) have integrated this concept into a facet scale of Conscientiousness. In doing so, definitions have been offered that conceptualize the dimension as one form of a broader factor. Stanek and Ones (2018) differentiated two Aspects of Conscientiousness: Industriousness and Orderliness. Achievement was a facet described as "individual differences in having high aspiration levels and working hard to achieve goals. . . . [High scorers] work hard and derive satisfaction from accomplishing challenging goals" (p. 389). Achievement Motivation does not need to be enmeshed in the unresolved controversies surrounding FFM personality facets to be considered important to be included in career assessment test batteries.

Complex relationships have been suggested between Achievement Motivation and other variables. R. B. Cattell and Kline (1977) objected not so much to the construct of Achievement Motivation as to its isolation as a distinct measure of personality. They conceptualized Achievement Motivation as an amalgam of self-assertion, career orientation, and self-sentiment. Reeve et al. (1987) found complex relations among Achievement Motivation, the experience of success and failure, and LOC. They noted that Achievement Motivation is affected both by individual difference variables and by the results one achieves (or thinks one has achieved) on a task. Using a sample of women, Schroth (1987) reported relations not just between Achievement Motivation on the TAT and the EPPS but also on other variables such as need for affiliation and need for power on the TAT.

Career Relevance

Relatively few studies have been published examining the effects of the variable in specific occupational groups, especially among nonbusiness occupations. Within entrepreneurial and managerial occupations, Achievement Motivation has received research support for its ability to predict level of management reached (e.g., Orpen, 1983), and there is evidence that individuals who rate themselves as having high Achievement Motivation value advancement and promotion more than pay (e.g., Terpstra, 1983). Ghiselli (1971) published data showing that a need for occupational achievement differentiated between managers, supervisors, and workers, with the managerial sample scoring significantly higher, on average, than the other two groups. McClelland (1961) suggested that individuals high in Achievement Motivation find particularly good outlets for it in business and entrepreneurial occupations, which might partially explain why much of the Achievement Motivation literature has been conducted with people in, or aspiring to be in, managerial careers.

Other researchers have also noted the importance of Achievement Motivation in managerial occupations (e.g., D. L. Grant et al., 1967). However, the interaction of variables mattered in many of these studies. Stahl (1983) found that in a variety of occupational and student samples, high Achievement Motivation paired with high need for power predicted higher levels of managerial performance. McClelland and Boyatzis (1982) reported that the so-called leadership motive pattern (elevated needs for power, lower needs for affiliation, high inhibition of activity) predicted long-term managerial success and that Achievement Motivation without the other variables predicted only lower levels of success within management. (These results held only for nontechnical managers.) D. Miller and Droge (1986) reported data that suggested that CEOs who were high in Achievement Motivation may structure their organizations differently from those low in the dimension. Schilit (1986) found that middle-level managers with a high Achievement Motivation (and those with a high need for power or those scoring in the internal direction on a LOC measure) had more influence on their superiors in the organizations than did those scoring in the opposite direction on these variables. Kernan and Lord (1988) reported, for an undergraduate sample, that Achievement Motivation moderated the relation between work motivation and type of goal setting (participatory vs. assigned). Those high on Achievement Motivation performed better when they participated in setting the goals; low Achievement Motivation subjects did best when the goals were assigned. Bretz et al. (1989) examined the relation between need structures (including achievement, power, and affiliation) and preference for a particular type of organization in which to work.

Although some differences were noted in occupational choice, the intervention was so weak (deciding which of two companies college students would want to work for after viewing a videotape staged to represent different organizational reward structures) that it severely limited generalizability. W. H. Cooper (1983) reported data suggesting that Achievement Motivation (defined as the desire to approach success and to avoid failure) was associated with several other variables, including initial task choice, persistence, performance, value attached to success and failure, and task difficulty estimates. Other research has examined the relation between Achievement Motivation and productivity among nonbusiness professions.

Spence and Helmreich's (1983) Achievement Motivation instrument demonstrated some interoccupational differences consistent with presumed occupational differences. They also reported correlations between salary earned among business professionals and Achievement Motivation and, for scientists, between scientific publications and Achievement Motivation. However, for both groups, Achievement Motivation interacted with competitiveness. Those who had high needs for mastery and high work motivation did better than those who also had high interpersonal competitiveness. Other studies have been less positive, reporting little relation between Achievement Motivation and workplace effectiveness (Mohan & Brar, 1986). Mehta and Agrawal (1986) also found no relation between Achievement Motivation and job satisfaction.

Measurement Issues

The conceptualizations of Achievement Motivation discussed here have moved from a simple high–low dichotomization to a more complex and nuanced approach. The assessor may therefore need to be sensitive to the varieties of Achievement Motivation that can be manifested by the same individual. Many omnibus measures of personality (e.g., the EPPS, CPI, Sixteen Personality Factor Questionnaire [16PF]) include scales relevant to achievement needs. McClelland's use of the TAT measures for need for achievement have also been widely used.

A number of objective measures of achievement need have been developed. Sid and Lindgren (1982) reported a 30-item questionnaire for differentiating between Achievement Motivation and Need for Affiliation. Questionnaire measures of achievement were developed and used by Spence, Helmreich, and their associates, including the Work and Family Orientation Questionnaire (see Spence & Helmreich, 1983). The L-BLA Achieving Styles Inventory (Lipman-Blumen et al., 1980) is based on a multidimensional model of type of achievement behavior (relational, direct, and instrumental) and on subtypes within each major grouping. Tellegen's Multidimensional Personality Questionnaire (MPQ; Tellegen & Waller, 2008) also includes an Achievement factor. Theirs focuses on working hard, embracing difficult and demanding tasks, persistence, being ambitious, holding high standards, and being perfectionistic versus the opposite (including working no harder than necessary and avoiding difficult projects; Tellegen & Waller, 2008, p. 273). Stahl and Harrell (1982) reported a behavioral measure of needs for achievement, affiliation, and power.

A second approach has been widely used in the measurement of Achievement Motivation. The projective approach (Blais & Baity, 2008) made popular by McClelland coded Achievement Motivation as expressed in stories generated in response to the TAT (Murray, 1943) cards to establish Achievement Motivation motives. Objective measures, in contrast to projective ones, use written questions similar to those on most measures of personality. Spangler (1992) compared these two methodological approaches in a meta-analysis and found that scores from both were associated with outcome measures when the situations employed in the projective measures pulled for the variable. Correlations between the two types of measures were generally low, however, suggesting the two types of measures differ. Projective measures generally outperformed the objective measures against the criteria employed in the studies. Although a number of criticisms of the TAT have been raised, particularly concerning rating consistency, Reuman (1982) noted that TAT projective measures of Achievement Motivation may demonstrate construct validity, even in the absence of high internal consistency.

The fact that Achievement Motivation can change over time has measurement implications. Howard and Bray's (1988) important longitudinal study of managers at the prebreakup version of AT&T, when it was one of the most important and largest corporations in the world, found that managers' Achievement Motivation scores declined across time even for the most successful groups. It also declined for those who had reached a plateau in their careers beyond which level they were unlikely to go. This suggests that age and sex-based norms would be useful in interpreting the results. Additionally, Achievement Motivation has been reported to be trainable (McClelland & Winter, 1969) and thus subject to change. This provides an important perspective when there is a discrepancy between the espoused career ambitions and scores on the Achievement Motivation score. By helping clients who may not understand the commitment it may take to succeed at ambitious career plans, it is possible they will raise their expectations and self-efficacy and in turn become more motivated to achievement. Conversely, when someone is not high on achievement needs and is satisfied with that, or when Achievement Motivation naturally declines later in a career, processing that information and its implication can be a useful part of the assessment feedback.

Indeed, like any other such variable where there may be a socially desirable polarity, for the client there is no single "right direction" in which to score. Mount et al.'s (2005) meta-analysis of the relationships of interests and personality (see Chapter 5) found three major dimensions, one of which was Striving for Accomplishment versus Striving for Personal Growth. This differentiation may help to identify those, at the extremes at least, who will primarily be motivated by personal growth versus by accomplishment. Additionally, just as it is possible to have "too little" achievement orientation for career ambitions, it is also possible to be "too high" on achievement focus. This is particularly true when the desire to succeed in demanding work roles exceeds abilities to do so or when career success is associated with high stress and at the expense of nonwork and family lives. Persons who place higher value on nonwork activities (e.g., having a happy family life) may not score highly on such a measure, and that is important to know in providing career guidance and in interpreting test results.

"DARK SIDE" PERSONALITY AND PERSONALITY DISORDERS

The FFM model of personality, as noted, is essentially focused on normal personality. Yet, recent career- and work-related research has begun to study personality dysfunction, characteristics that, particularly under stress, can result in problematic interactions with others.

Conceptual Issues

The widely used distinction popularized in work contexts by R. Hogan and Hogan (2009) distinguished between "bright side" and "dark side" personality characteristics. To differentiate these two terms, bright side aspects of personality refer to "positive" FFM scores (e.g., high scores on Conscientiousness and Agreeableness and scoring in the extraverted direction on the Introversion/Extraversion factor) while "dark side" ones refer to aspects of individuals' personality that are more likely to predict to people's failure rather than success and that refer to behavior such as self-focus, being overly aggressive, and lacking concern for the feelings and rights of others (see R. Hogan & Hogan, 2007, 2009). The evidence is still emerging on some of the dark side variables.

The question arises as to whether dark side personality characteristics cross over into psychopathology. Kaiser et al. (2015) asserted that dark side syndromes (as they termed them) were not "clinical personality disorders because they do not impair significant life functioning as required for a clinical diagnosis . . . although they can interfere with relationships and judgment" (p. 58). However, the thread linking dark side characteristics (or possibly traits) only to normal personality variations is thin, especially since the very premise of such taxonomies and measures is that the measured conditions do indeed impair, or can impair, a significant life function, namely, work.

It is useful to consider why what seems like a somewhat arbitrary separation (between dark side behavior on measures of "normal" personality and personality disorders) would be made. One aim of such separations of "dark side characteristics" and personality disorders in selection contexts might be to avoid people being assessed as having conditions that are protected by the Americans with Disabilities Act (ADA, 1990). This is because such conditions, in selection contexts, can only be assessed postconditional offers of employment. It is also possible that a goal of such distinctions might be to avoid test users running afoul of professional training and licensure requirements. Assessment of certain mental disorders may require a particular license, and many of those using the measures of normal personality do not have such licenses. Such motives, although understandable, are arguably not really a sufficient basis for concluding that these conditions do not, essentially or potentially, overlap with personality disorders or other diagnosable psychological conditions.

This is not to ignore that current personality disorder taxonomies are not without problems. Widiger and other researchers (Sleep et al., 2018; Widiger, 2011, 2017; Widiger & Trull, 1992, 2007) have challenged the *Diagnostic and Statistical Manual of Mental Disorders* (*DSM*)-based personality disorder diagnostic taxonomy, criticizing the categorization of people as either having or not having a personality disorder. (Of course, the idea that dark side "syndromes" are independent of personality disorders is itself a problematic dichotomization.)

Rather than dichotomizing "normal" and "abnormal" personality, Widiger (2011) made this differentiation: "Personality is the characteristic manner in which one thinks, feels, behaves, and relates to others. Mental disorders are clinically significant impairments in one or more areas of psychological functioning" (p. 103). Clearly, in that model, there is room for overlap between dark side characteristics and personality disorders. Widiger further noted three kinds of relationships that can exist between these personality disorders and psychopathology: pathoplastic, spectrum, and causal. In pathoplastic relationships, the two areas work together to affect how the characteristic is expressed. Spectrum relationships, in his model, are those having a common etiology, and in causal relationships, one is the source, or cause, of the other.

Assuredly, more research is needed to sort these issues out, but caution is urged when using assessment instruments that classify persons with dark side characteristics as if there were a definitive border between "dark side" syndromes and personality disorders. Clearly, some individuals with elevations on "dark side" measures will not have personality disorders while others will have both elevations on dark side measures and also meet diagnostic criteria for personality disorders.

Dimensionality and Facets

The literature on dark side personality syndromes is still emerging, and much of the work-related literature to date has been based on use of particular measures such as the Hogan Developmental Survey (HDS; R. Hogan & Hogan, 2009). The HDS instrument's approach to the dark side characteristics was derived from Karen Horney's model of "moving away, moving against, and moving toward" types of personality styles, which are described by the HDS as "behavioral tendencies" particularly likely to emerge under stress (R. Hogan & Hogan, 2009). The 11 scales on the HPS include, to take one example, "excitable," said to be related to the *DSM-IV-TR* personality disorder of borderline personality and defined as being "moody and hard to please, with intense but short-lived enthusiasms for people and projects. High scorers are sensitive to criticism, volatile, and unable to generate respect from subordinates due to frequent emotional displays" (R. Hogan & Hogan, 2009, p. 7).

A particular combination of dark side variables has received both research and applied attention. The so-called dark triad grouping, however, emerged not from study of normal personality but rather from research on people who exhibited some, but not all, and generally subclinically elevated scores on certain personality disorder scales. Paulhus and Williams (2002) described the key components of this triad as including what they considered to be the particularly pathological combination of Machiavellianism (using and exploiting others to serve personal ends; Christie & Geis, 1979), Narcissism (grandiosity, entitlement, superiority, and dominance over others; Raskin et al., 1991), and Psychopathy (high impulsivity and thrill-seeking, low empathy and anxiety; Hare, 1985). The common characteristics across the triad, Paulhus and Williams noted, were that "all three entail a socially malevolent character with behavior tendencies toward self-promotion, emotional coldness, duplicity, and aggressiveness" (p. 557). Additionally, all involved aversive interpersonal behaviors or, as Kowalski (2001) put it in the title of an article, ones that were "annoying, thoughtless, and mean."

O'Boyle et al. (2015) conducted a meta-analysis of studies on the dark triad and its relationship to FFM factors. They found a number of relationships to FFM factors that were somewhat predictable. Both Machiavellianism and Psychopathy were negatively correlated with Agreeableness and Conscientiousness and positively with Neuroticism. Psychopathy scores were also positively correlated with Extraversion and Neuroticism, but the size of the correlations were quite small. Narcissism was positively correlated with Extraversion (highest), Openness, and Conscientiousness (lowest), and negatively with Agreeableness (highest) and Neuroticism (less so).

As for the dimensionality of "dark side" characteristics, depending on how they are conceptualized and their assumed relationship (or lack of relationship) to personality disorders, diagnostic manuals present a number of different diagnosable personality disorders, and measures of subclinical "dark side" personality characteristics invoke their own taxonomies, or borrow those from the personality literature. However, the research in this area is relatively new and is not yet associated with a commonly agreed upon factor structure. And unlike the case of Neuroticism, in which there is some suggestion of a common factor of negative emotions, personality disorders seem to have more distinctiveness across different syndromes or disorders.

Career and Work Issues

Dark side personality characteristics in the work context to date have mostly been found to be associated with negative work outcomes, including counterproductive work behaviors (CWBs) and, except for some aspects of narcissism, performance deficits (Grijalva & Newman, 2015; O'Boyle et al., 2012). When all three components were examined as a whole, these authors found the relationship with performance to be statistically significant but trivial (1% or less) in explaining performance deficits, but substantial (26.7%) in explaining CWBs. Concerning the latter, Narcissism was the largest contributor (18.9%) of the three components and Machiavellianism the second largest (5.3%). Psychopathy actually had a negative effect, likely the result of a statistical artifact (O'Boyle et al., 2012). Grijalva and Newman's (2015) meta-analysis included those in the O'Boyle et al. study plus an additional 9 studies. They found a smaller relationship of $\hat{\rho} = .23$ (corrected correlations and omitting one outlier study) and that the relationship between CWB and narcissism was moderated by ingroup collectivist cultures (those emphasizing loyalty and cohesiveness), which served to lower the relationship.

Not all evidence finds that dark side characteristics are associated with negative outcomes. Furnham (2015), for example, found both dark and bright side personality characteristics as predictors of a measure of divergent thinking (DT). Using Hogan's HDS and several other measures, they found incremental predictive power (4%–9%) associated with some, but not all, dark side characteristics. In particular, Imaginative (schizotypal) and Colorful (histrionic) scores were best positive predictors in contrast to diligent (obsessive-compulsive) and skeptical (paranoid), which were negatively associated with DT measures.

An interesting theory about the complexity of narcissism in the work context was suggested by Grapsas et al. (2020), who proposed a self-regulation model of what they termed grandiose narcissism. In this approach, persons high on this dimension seek social status. They find and engage with situations in which they can enhance their self-esteem either by raising it or by lowering the status of others. One approach focuses on self-promotion and the other on what they call "other-derogation." And the particular approach used will in turn influence how others assess the behavior and react to the person.

That all dark side behavior is not viewed equally negatively is suggested by a study by S. Harrison et al. (2018) that considered how adult raters would view working with or for various individuals with what they termed "subclinical personality disorders." Using vignettes that incorporated personality syndromes that were based on Hogan's HDS model, they reported that respondents were most favorably inclined to "moving toward," next to "avoidant," and least to the "moving against" categories of personality.

Managers have been the target of particular attention in the study of dark side characteristics and in the popular press such as in the book *Snakes in Suits: When Psychopaths Go to Work* (Babiak & Hare, 2006). The question arises: If dark side characteristics are generally considered to be negative, why would such managers be hired? Those with narcissistic personality characteristics (W. K. Campbell & Miller, 2011; Zajenkowski & Dufner, 2020), to take one example, are often good at arousing support and engagement. When such characteristics are well-matched with the particular managerial tasks or organizational needs of the moment, the match may work, but the long-term consequences of such leaders are often negative (Boddy, 2010).

Dark side personality characteristics have also been implicated in managerial derailers (personal characteristics or behaviors likely to cause negative disruption in ones' career). These are aspects of people that, whatever their initial successes, can ultimately be associated with job problems of sufficient severity that job loss or demotion might occur. Although the construct of managerial derailers has received a lot of media attention, its anchoring in the peer-reviewed empirical literature is somewhat limited. Some of the early research on this topic included a qualitative study by McCall and Lombardo (1983) and the AT&T study by A. Howard and Bray (1988). J. Hogan et al. (2011), in a chapter on managerial derailment, cited evidence suggesting that the mean level of failure among managers was around 50%. Others have suggested even higher rates (e.g., 75% or more; see Dalal & Nolan, 2009). However, most of the evidence on which such estimates were made appears not to have been very scientifically rigorous nor was personality the only reason for derailing.

Additionally, the concept of managerial derailment places "blame" primarily on the individual, not the supervisors of the manager or the degree of fit of the person with their work. Of course managers can "fail"—if by failure is meant they leave a particular position or underperform—for a number of reasons that may have little to do with the leader as when a company is merged and only one of the CEOs survive or a new leader comes in and wants their own people and so fires all the current managers. Even when individual level characteristics are responsible for managerial failure, dark side behavior is only one reason for this outcome. Ability deficits and being misfit with the needs of a particular position likely account for a lot of so-called derailment.

Measurement Issues

The Hogan Development Survey (R. Hogan & Hogan, 2009) was created as a commercial measure of 11 "dysfunctional personality syndromes" (p. 1). Elsewhere the HDS scales have been described as "behavioral tendencies" and "forms of interpersonal behavior." The 11 HDS syndromes (e.g., Excitable, Cynical, Cautious) were also tied directly to formal personality disorders (e.g., Excitable to borderline personality disorder), while still viewing them as being different in kind from the formal personality disorders. Elevations on the scales were viewed as potential employment derailers. The same characteristics, they argued, when properly channeled, could also be potential strengths (see Hogan Assessment Systems Inc., 2018).

Kaiser et al. (2015) used a different approach to conceptualizing "at risk" dark side personality characteristics. They worked within the Hogan Development Survey (HDS)'s model and also employed the Hogan Personality Inventory (HPI)'s adjustment scale. The approach was based on the assumption that dark side behavior was not simply "more is worse" but that both too much and too little of certain personality variables would be problematic. A criterion measure called the Leadership Versatility Index was completed by peers, superiors, and subordinates using the "too much" to "too little" scaling approach for behaviors in four managerial areas: forcefulness, enabling, and strategic and operational areas. The "other" ratings were aggregated. The researchers found that high, but also low, scores of HDS scores were associated with more problematic behaviors and that low Emotion Stability exacerbated (moderated) the negative outcomes. This again points to variables acting in combination, rather than in isolation. Simply scoring highly on a particular component of dark side personality may not be sufficient to predict problematic performance.

In still another approach, Wu and LeBreton (2011) suggested that selected facets were likely better dark side measures than were FFM factors. They generated a number of interesting hypotheses in their review article—for example, "When unable to achieve their goal(s), high Machs are more likely to engage in subtle or covert forms of verbal CWBs (e.g., spreading rumors, gossiping) than low Machs" (p. 608). They also noted that, in addition to the HDS measure, those measures that were developed specifically for the three component parts of the "dark triad," such as Christie and Geiss's (1970) Mach-1V, may be useful for work-related assessment.

Finally, some studies have compared multiple approaches. Moscoso and Salgado (2004) compared the relationship of dark side characteristics and mental-health related personality disorders in a predictive validity paradigm of new hires. They administered to job applicants a Spanish-language instrument assessing dysfunctional personality characteristics. Most of the instrument's scales were related to diagnostic criteria for personality disorder assessment. The authors found that dysfunctional "personality styles" they labeled "suspicious, shy, sad, pessimistic, sufferer, eccentric, and risky" were generally negatively related to supervisor-rated task, contextual, and overall job performance. What they termed the "egocentric personality style" negatively predicted only contextual performance (supporting colleagues and taking initiative). The "egoistic" scores were associated with lower contextual, but not lower job or overall performance criteria. One interpretation of the findings is that personality disorders do have relevance for work outcomes and that the distinction between dark side characteristics and personality disorders needs further assessment, since it is far from clear that dark side characteristics are different in kind from personality disorders.

Morey et al. (2012) conducted a longitudinal study of the power of alternative measures to predict to long-term adjustment of people who at baseline had met diagnostic criteria for at least one of four personality disorders (avoidant, borderline, obsessive-compulsive, or schizotypal) or for the diagnosis of major depression without personality disorder. The authors compared the various assessment approaches. These were NEO-measured FFM factor and facet scores, categorical *DSM* personality disorder diagnoses, and the Schedule for Nonadaptive and Adaptive Personality (SNAP; L. A. Clark, 1993). Although they found predictive validity for all the approaches, the diagnostic and facets approaches did least well in predicting to the outcome measures, and the best predictive ability was found for the SNAP, which was built to measure both normal and pathological traits. This may suggest that, at least for some criteria, a combined approach using both normal personality and pathological traits may be most effective.

GENDER IDENTITY/MASCULINITY-FEMININITY

Gender, or sex role, identity, sometimes reflected on personality tests as a Masculinity/Femininity variable, may seem to be an unusual factor to consider in a book on career assessment. After all, the occupational world, in many countries, has been trying to move away from gender-related impediments to careers. Yet, there is persistent evidence that gender identity influences choices of careers and work preferences, especially with respect to interests, which in turn have impact on liking of particular careers or work. Here we will focus on the career implications for Gender Identity.

Conceptual Issues

Gender Identity was described by Wood and Eagly (2009) as the self-definitions of masculine and feminine associated with gender, which they defined as "the cultural meanings ascribed to male and female social categories in society" (p. 109). They noted that there are three components of masculinity and femininity: gender-typed or expected personality traits, approach to relationships to others, and societally defined concepts of women or men. Differentiating aspects of Gender Identity center around a preference, among those with feminine identity, for highly engaged interpersonal relationships (communality and interdependence), sensitivity to the needs of others, and a collective and helping identity versus, among those with masculine identity, a more self-reliant, "agentic" (action- and goal-oriented) approach. As G. N. Powell and Greenhaus (2010) put it, "Individuals who see themselves as high in femininity display an interdependent self-construal . . . in which others (e.g., family members) are considered part of the self, as opposed to an independent self-construal in which others are seen as separate from the self" (p. 1030). These differences especially affect long-term career goals in how men and women often envision their desired goals, which can vary among those with different gender identities (Evans & Diekman, 2009).

The extensive literature on this construct and related (but separable) ones such as role identities and gender stereotypes has raised many issues. However, studies and various versions of the gender identity constructs have used widely differing measurement approaches (Constantinople, 1973), alternative conceptualizations, and varying interpretations of aspects defined as being trait-like characteristics. Recent research has suggested, however, that apparent sex differences on key components of Gender Identity may relate not so much to inherent, trait-like sex differences, but rather to alternative ways of expressing the same underlying need. In the case of one of these elements, prosocial behavior, for example, Eagly (2009) argued that although prosocial behavior may be universal (see also Dahl & Brownell, 2019) and that the often-noted differences between men and women on this dimension may stem in part from differences in how such behavior is expressed. Men's prosocial helping behavior, she argued, tends to place more emphasis on being action-oriented and women's to be more interpersonally engaged, such as in direct helping roles.

People can have gender identities that are congruent or incongruent with their personal identities. For example, female engineers or male nurses may feel perfectly at ease with their respective choices of occupations. However, gender identities also interact with, and in turn are influenced by, the broader environment. If a person's culture or subculture communicates that contemplated or actual career choices are gender-role-inappropriate, or if society punishes or prohibits the preferred choice as being inappropriate or a disallowed one, internal and/or external conflicts may arise. Additionally, gender role conflicts can arise at various stages of the career process. G. N. Powell and Greenhaus (2010) identified three types of decisions—those made at role entry, how to participate in the workplace, and at exit—that can be influenced by gender roles and role identity.

Dimensionality of the Construct

Gender Identity is complicated when it comes to its dimensionality. Whether it is a bipolar unidimensional construct, a two-factor one, or one with many factors and facets will depend in part on its definition, conceptualization, and the particular measures used. At the simplest level, Gender Identity has two factors (or one bipolar one)—femininity and masculinity—but complications arise. Are femininity or masculinity flip sides of the same underlying factors, for example, high versus low social engagement, or are they different in kind? Or it may be that aspects of Gender Identity are themselves multidimensional, reflecting interrelatedness or aggression as separate dimensions on which men and women might differ.

In an empirical study done in the context of marketing research, Palan et al. (1999) administered the Bem Sex-Role Inventory (BSRI), the Personal Attributes Questionnaire (PAQ; Spence & Helmreich, 1978), and the Sexual Identity Scale (SIS; Stern et al., 1987) to a group of undergraduate respondents. The measures differed in their factors, and the authors concluded,

> Taken together, these results suggest that the measurement of gender identity is more complex now than it was 25 years ago. Although further research is encouraged, at a minimum, the results of this study suggest that researchers should examine what we have typically defined as "masculine" traits as at least two separate dimensions of instrumentality and autonomy, and "femininity" as expressiveness. The presence of an additional "feminine" dimension, emotionality, and an additional "masculine" dimension, composure, is also indicated in this study. (Palan et al., 1999, p. 375)

Twenge's (1997) meta-analysis using 63 data sets also found that masculinity and femininity had changed in that women's scores on the masculine scales had increased over time. The effect sizes for male/female differences also decreased over time. Men's low endorsement of femininity characteristics measured by these scales continued over time.

Egan and Perry (2001), using a different approach and working with school children, considered three aspects of gender: whether respondents (a) felt psychologically compatible with their gender and were satisfied with their biological sex, (b) experienced pressure to conform to gender stereotypes, and (c) felt their sex was superior to the other. Felt gender compatibility correlated positively with psychosocial adjustment, but, interestingly, felt pressure and intergroup bias were negatively correlated with it.

Career and Work Issues

Gender Identity (or Masculinity/Femininity) remains an important variable for career assessment consideration because sex differences, sometimes very large ones, in preferences for various occupations continue to exist and to influence career choices (Feather & Said, 1983; Lippa, 2005, 2006).

Unquestionably, there has been extensive growth in the number and percentages of women participating in the U.S. labor force in the 50-year period from 1950 to 2000. Among women, the percentage in the workforce went from 34% to 60% (from 18 million to 66 million, an annual growth rate of 2.6%) and the percentage of women versus men in the work force went from 30% in 1950 to 47% in 2000 (Toossi, 2002). Nonetheless, there remain a number of occupations with substantial differences in the relative percentage of women and men in them, and these tend to parallel sex-related interest differences. Among engineers and architects in the United States in 2016, only 14% were women (Bureau of Labor Statistics, 2017d), and among nurses in 2011, around 9% were men (U.S. Census Bureau, 2013). Many of these different preferences between the sexes start early in life (A. R. Hayes et al., 2018) and persist, particularly when the occupations are depicted, as they often are, as being dominated by, or a career primarily for, one sex.

Why do such sex-specific differences in particular careers arise or persist? Certainly, there are societal factors that discourage or forbid members of one sex, typically women, from participating in certain occupations. Governments, cultures, and families can set up barriers to preferred career choices. In the more extreme version, in some geopolitical contexts, women are simply not allowed to pursue particular occupations or even to attend school. Conversely, men may perceive social or peer/family disapproval if they express interest in career choices thought to be feminine and then avoid pursuit of what might otherwise have been a well-matched career.

That there are group differences in Gender Identity (or related constructs) among men and women in particular occupations has been of interest in empirical studies for some time. In a study of teachers, K. E. Smith (1986) reported that male preschool teachers (who are still greatly outnumbered by women) scored higher on femininity than male high school teachers and that female high school teachers (who are outnumbered by male high school teachers) scored more masculine than did female preschool teachers. People in creative occupations also tend to score in the more feminine direction. Roe's (1946) early study of the personality of 20 leading American painters (all men living in New York) found a feminization among male painters. She reported that these painters were markedly nonaggressive in their general personality structure, exhibiting more feminine than masculine qualities. J. S. Guilford et al.'s (1976) Guilford-Zimmerman Temperament Survey (GZTS) included a Masculinity/Femininity scale. Most of the occupational groups reported in the test's manual scored at about the average compared with general population norms on the scale. However, male artist and musician samples tended to score in the feminine direction, whereas female artists scored slightly in the masculine direction. Ghiselli (1971) found that on the Masculinity/Femininity scale of his Self-Description Inventory adjective checklist, there were small differences among managers, line supervisors, and rank-and-file workers, in the order listed, with managers scoring highest in the masculine direction. Gough (1996) reported results from the CPI with a variety of occupational samples on the measure's Masculinity/Femininity scale, on which higher scores are in the feminine direction. Occupational groups scoring in the feminine direction (i.e., above the 50th percentile on the CPI's Mf scale) included architects, mathematicians, and Catholic priests. Among the lower (i.e., more "masculine") groups were bankers, correctional officers, and military officers.

Gender differences emerge early and can be stable over time. Biological, neurobiological, and/or genetic factors may account for some of people's gender identities (Roselli, 2018), but Eagly and Wood (2017) noted the interactive effects of nature and nurture. Teig and Susskind (2008) examined children's perceptions of three samples of young children ranging in age from 6 to 12. Girls preferred feminine to masculine occupations, but those "masculine" occupations that were also high status were also positively regarded. The boys considered both masculine and feminine occupations but for the older (9–12 years old) boys, they were more influenced by status than gender relevance.

Looking at overall career-related patterns, it would appear that achievement and career-oriented women (vs. those less oriented to career advancement), somewhat independently of occupation and the measuring device used, are more likely to score in the "masculine" direction on Masculinity/Femininity measures (F. T. Waddell, 1983; M. T. Westbrook & Nordholm 1984; Wong et al., 1985). These results are likely to be present from childhood (Metzler-Brennan et al., 1985; S. W. Williams & McCullers, 1983). Women high on femininity are likely to choose traditional female-dominated occupations (S. W. Williams & McCullers, 1983). Men, on average, are more likely to express a preference for gender-congruent occupations and to reject femininity (Feather & Said, 1983; Kilianski, 2003; D. M. Mayer, 2018; Storms, 1978), whereas femininity scores are likely to be elevated for men in creative occupations and who are in female-dominated occupations.

Measurement Issues

The history of measuring Gender Identity as an overall construct is long but fraught with controversy. By today's standards, these measures were problematic in that test authors tended to choose items for such measures that exaggerated differences in a sometimes-stereotypical way (Constantinople, 1973; Palan et al., 1999). A widely used measure of Gender Identity, the BSRI (Bem, 1974) was based on items that were found to be highly desired, rather than more typical, characteristics of masculinity or femininity or that were maximally differentiating (Wood & Eagly, 2009). In later versions, this measure added the construct of psychological androgyny (Lubinski et al., 1983) as an idealized and preferred approach. Although often used in Gender Identity research, the flaws in the measure were significant (see Deaux, 1985). Still another measure of Masculinity/Femininity was Spence, Helmreich, and Stapp's Personal Attributes Questionnaire (Spence & Helmreich, 1978).

A Femininity/Masculinity (F/M) scale is included on the CPI (Gough, 1996). Recalling that the CPI was built on measuring "folk notions" of personality, the F/M scale was based on "culturally universal perceptions of what is feminine, and what is masculine" (p. 146). The scale items were selected based on those that differentated men in general from women in general. Most of the items on the scale were associated with traditional concepts of masculinity (e.g., aggressive, determined, robust) versus femininity (e.g., gentle, sentimental, warm). The scale was designed such that higher scores were in the feminine direction and separate norms were provided for men and women. High F/M scorers were described on adjective checklists as being genuine, complaining, high-strung, and sensitive. In contrast, low scores on F/M were associated with adjectives such as aggressive, confident, boastful, independent, and forceful. For high F/M, women associated adjectives included feminine, dependent, and emotional. Lower F/M scores were associated with adjectives like self-confident, strong, and aggressive. Of note, the ratings varied by whether the raters were spouses, peers, or staff members. Higher F/M scores were found among women in nursing, selected other health-related occupations and writing while lower scores were found among police officer applicants and juvenile delinquents. For men, low scorers were found in respondents from engineering, military, and police while higher scorers were found among nurses, mathematicians, and children's book authors. Most of the occupational samples were small, as were the group differences, and overall, they were rather dated. Of perhaps greatest importance were Gough's (1996) correlations of the F/M scale and scores on the Strong RIASEC scales. For both sexes, F/M scores were negatively correlated with Realistic, Enterprising, and Conventional interests. For women, there was a negative correlation of F/M scores with Investigative interests, whereas for men there was a positive correlation with Artistic Interests. These correlations were not always very high and there were over twice as many men as women in the samples used. Overall, these data may indicate that low F/M scores for women suggest strong career identity and self-confidence, but, for men, high F/M scores may suggest dysphoria or, alternatively, more creative interests.

Some of the vocational interest measures (e.g., the Vocational Preference Inventory; J. L. Holland, 1985c) have a Masculinity/Femininity scale. The widely used Strong Interest Inventory (Harmon et al., 1994; Herk & Thompson, 2012) recognizes that preferences for many occupations and scales differ by sex but it aims to help respondents consider a wide range of career possibilities. In the case of Realistic and Social interests, for example, there is a gender difference on average, with men's Realistic interests and women's Social interests being respectively higher than the other gender's. The test therefore provides General Reference Sample (GRS) norms as well as those specific to gender (male, female) for both the Basic Interest Scales (BISs) and General Occupational Themes (GOTs) and for the specific occupations for which normative groups and normative interest data are provided. In this manner, a female respondent could understand that although her overall GRS normative scores on, say, Realistic were only average, the same scores on female norms were high. The goal is to encourage those taking the instrument to carefully consider all relevant possibilities and not just to reject certain occupations as being more appropriate to the other gender.

In general, career assessors who include Gender Identity or Masculinity/Femininity variables in career assessment contexts should examine what the scales they will use are measuring and the recency of its validation and norming data to assure that it is reflective of current views in this rapidly changing area of study. Measures based on outmoded constructs of male- or female-appropriate behavior may result in inappropriate conclusions about the occupational profiles of career assessees. Even when gender identity is not explicitly measured, the related scales and data from personality and interest measures should be reviewed and integrated into the feedback process.

As to why certain occupations are perceived as being "feminine" and others as "masculine" stems from an interaction of Gender Identity and societal factors. To the extent that certain careers call for helping roles, social interaction, or for minimizing the expression of aggressive, self-promoting behavior in favor of the collective, they may attract more women and more men and women high on femininity and fewer who are higher on masculinity. The job duties matter (and can be the source of misinformation or imagined career stereotypes) as does the comparative gender distribution, and the perception that the occupation calls more for helping and interpersonal sensitivity than agentic, aggressive, and action-oriented behaviors.

At the individual level, the context for understanding career-related gender identity issues needs to be anchored in the purposes of the career assessment. Congruence (or lack thereof) of gender identity with culturally specific occupational expectations or limitations may need to be explored as an issue in helping clients sort through issues of career choice and change. In a number of industrialized democracies, including in the United States, career options have broadened such that there are fewer perceived barriers associated with sex. For clients in other countries, or subcultures in more open ones, there may be considerable gender identity concerns and cultural expectations that are at issue.

DOMINANCE

Dominance appears as a facet scale in some FFM models but not in others. Because it is important to measure in career assessment independent of its inclusion or exclusion in particular structural personality models, this section provides an overview of this construct.

Humans are not alone in being differentiated on levels of Dominance. It turns out that Dominance (along with some of the FFM factors) is particularly important among some animals' personality characteristics. A. Weiss et al. (2000) studied dominance and FFM personality characteristics in chimpanzees. They found Dominance to be a "big one" factor while the FFM factors did emerge but were of secondary importance compared with Dominance. Additionally, Dominance was the only one of the six personality factors that, in the chimpanzee populations studied, had a demonstrable genetic component.

A hormonal factor may also be relevant for humans. Sherman et al. (2016) found an interesting interaction in male executives between testosterone and cortisol blood levels. Endogenous testosterone levels (which tend to be associated with dominance and status seeking) were associated with the number of people supervised among male executives, but only for those who were low in endogenous cortisol levels (the latter being associated with lower stress levels).

Conceptual Issues

Stanek and Ones (2018) placed Dominance as a facet of Extraversion and conceptualized it as describing "individual differences in being dominant, forceful, and socially ascendant/potent" (p. 390). By anchoring the concept in Extraversion, they further emphasized that it was associated with self-assurance, being active in groups, and preferring leadership rather than followership roles. Gough's (1996) CPI included, in their folk concepts of personality, a Dominance scale meant to differentiate those who are confident, assertive, and task-oriented from those who are cautious, quiet, and hesitant to take initiative. On the other hand, in Gough's system of quadrants, Alphas, who are norm-favoring but also externally oriented, on average scored high on Dominance. Adjective descriptors chosen for this group includes productivity, assertion, high aspiration, and social poise/presence.

H. E. P. Cattell and Mead (2008), however, noted that Dominance (Factor E on the 16PF) has been one of the central dimensions of personality for some time and that the FFM models do not sufficiently recognize this dimension. In Cattell and Mead's model, Dominance was not tied specifically to having *social* dominance but rather, on the dominant side of the polarity, identifying characteristics of being dominant, forceful, and assertive versus being deferential, cooperative, and conflict avoidant (H. E. P. Cattell & Mead, 2008, p. 236). In fact, Factor E loaded not on the 16PF's Extraversion/Introversion global factor but rather on a global factor named Independence/Accommodation. In addition to Dominance (Factor E), this global factor was also loaded onto by Factor H (Bold/Shy), Factor L (Vigilant/Trusting), and Factor Q1 (Open-to-Change/Traditional). Cattell and Mead also provided profiles for several occupational groups and found E scores to be elevated (along with Independence) among managers and leaders, entrepreneurs, and creative individuals.

Here then are two alternative models of dominance that overlap but also are differentiated. In the FFM approach, Dominance is, at most, a facet scale of Extraversion/Introversion, arguably relegating it to lesser significance both conceptually and in its measurement and interpretation in comparison to the larger factors. In Cattell's model and, to some degree, Gough's, what emerges is Dominance as an important factor in its own right but also as part of a larger, global factor of Independence. In this approach, then, people can be forceful, dominant, and intent on influencing others for purposes other than having social influence over others, such as to promote a particular idea, product, or point of view.

Dimensionality and Facets

Although there is scant literature examining the overlapping relationship between dominance and need for power, a fair amount of literature has been published on the need for power variable, and it is reasonable to believe that the two variables do overlap. Winter (1973) and McClelland (1975) have provided the most definitive statements on the power motive. Winter defined social power as "the ability or capacity of [one person] to produce (consciously or unconsciously) intended effects on the behavior or emotions of another person" (p. 5). McClelland, who was somewhat better at describing the experience than defining the concept, depicted power as an individual difference variable associated with having impact on others (p. 7). People scoring high on need for power seek outlets in activities such as accumulating possessions, joining clubs and organizations (especially seeking or holding officer positions in them), and participating in competitive interactions with others (McClelland & Burnham, 1976). The Derman et al. (1978) dominance construct shows strong similarity to the need for power construct. They hypothesized three Dominance subscales: Do1, wants power over others versus being submissive; Do2, pushes own ideas versus respecting others' ideas; and Do3, being conscious of one's own rights versus being tolerant. However, these subscales did not factor in the predicted direction, so no marker scales were included in these researchers' personality measures (Derman et al., 1978). M. A. Bouchard et al. (1988), on the other hand, found a correlation between assertiveness and extraversion and between peer-rated assertiveness and Agreeableness and Conscientiousness, suggesting that dominance is not an isolated personality characteristic. Concerning sex differences in the power and assertiveness motives, a variety of studies (e.g., Maccoby & Jacklin, 1974) have shown sex differences on aggression (a form of dominance) in favor of men. Schroth (1987) found that college men scored higher than women on need for dominance. Other researchers have indicated that this difference extends to the occupational setting (e.g., Radecki & Jennings, 1980). More recent analyses have shown the sex difference to be less influential than sometimes assumed (see Deaux, 1985). The power motive can be experimentally manipulated, which implies that it is able to be changed. Increases in the expression of power have been associated with threat perception and with feeling inhibited even by symbols that connote power (e.g., uniforms and titles; House & Singh, 1987).

Career and Work Issues

Winter (1973) provided data from an elite college sample (Wesleyan undergraduates) showing different need for power scores among people indicating a preference for different occupations. Specifically, people indicating a preference for people-oriented occupations (teaching, psychology, clergy, and business) tended to have the highest need for power scores. Aspirants to jobs in medicine, the creative arts, architecture, and (surprisingly) government and politics scored relatively low on the expressed need for power. In a group of Harvard students whose actual (rather than preferential) career choices were charted, similar patterns were noted, and the findings have been replicated with other occupational groups. Jenkins (1994) found that for women who were high on assessed power needs as college seniors, need for power predicted career progression but only for those in power-oriented careers. Those high in this dimension versus those lower also reported both more power-related job satisfaction and dissatisfaction.

Managers scored very high on the Ascendance scale of the GZTS (J. P. Guilford et al., 1976) variable; people in the creative arts, especially men, scored low. Other occupational groups have also been studied. Jacobs and Dunlap (1976; see also Kumar & Mutha, 1985) suggested that teachers of young elementary school students generally represent a nondominant group, whereas teachers of the older grades need a certain amount of dominance to be able to sell the subject (and, it is today presumed, to maintain order and discipline). Helson (1978) found important personality differences among writers and critics of children's books. The critics were found to be more socially ascendant and conventional, whereas the writers were less conventional, less dominant, and more in touch with alternative states of consciousness. Chusmir (1984) reported that need for power was found for almost every position in a police force. Chusmir claimed that the desired profile for most police positions would include a high need for power, a moderately high Achievement Motivation, and a low need for affiliation. R. B. Cattell and Kline (1977, p. 306) reported average scores on the Dominance (E) scale of the 16PF for a variety of occupational groups. Although many of the findings are understandable (e.g., nurses and physicians scored low on the E scale; police, high), others are not. For example, a sample of writers had the highest score on the E scale of all of the occupational groups, and business executives were actually lower than a group of male elementary school teachers. These results are of course limited by reliance on only one measure of dominance and, in some cases, by small and possibly nonrepresentative samples. More literature has been published on the occupational implications of the need for power related to managerial occupations. McClelland (1975) suggested that the essence of the managerial job is influence over others and that the modal manager scores high on need for power (as well as on Achievement Motivation). Jackson et al. (1987) reported that personnel executives (especially women) scored much higher than the normative population on a dominance measure. Sedge (1985) found dominance to be one of the factors that differentiated a group of engineer managers from practicing engineers. Cornelius and Lane (1984), however, assessed the need for power, along with needs for achievement and affiliation. They found that for first-line supervisors in a for-profit foreign-language instruction organization, need for affiliation more than need for power or achievement predicted job performance and (not surprisingly) favorable attitudes of subordinates. However, the so-called leadership motive profile (above-average need for power, higher need for power than need for affiliation, and at least moderate levels of action inhibition [constraints on the expression of power needs]) predicted only whether subjects were in a high-status office, not job performance or subordinate morale. Cornelius and Lane noted that foreign-language instructors and administrators may be more similar to technical than to generic managers. House and Singh's study presented a more favorable review of the leadership motive pattern (McClelland, 1985) and concluded that need for power is a promising construct in organizational assessment and research. It is especially relevant for positions in which social and interpersonal managerial skills (rather than technical expertise) are demanded.

A variety of studies have demonstrated that various measures of ascendance or dominance relate differentially to job outcomes. Generally, there is a positive association between scores on personality measures of dominance and ascendance and success on the job, at least for occupational groups in which dominance is a modal characteristic. Bentz (1985), for example, found that a dominance-masculine scale was the best predictor of several personality variables of success in the managerial ranks. The need for power relates positively to certain managerial outcomes, but the projective measures (especially the TAT and the Miner Sentence Completion Scale) have not found it to predict technical (vs. bureaucratic) managerial positions (House & Singh, 1987). The GZTS (J. S. Guilford et al., 1976), for example, has yielded some of the most extensive data on the role of the Ascendance scale (its dominance factor) in career and occupational issues. In several occupational samples, vocations in the Enterprising area (especially managers and sales personnel) scored, on average, considerably above the mean on the Ascendance scale. Moreover, the Ascendance scale was often an effective predictor for differentiating high-achieving managers from low-achieving ones. Other occupational groups (e.g., artists, dentists, scientists, counselors, and engineers) tended to score at or below average on this scale. When nonmanagerial occupations were considered, Dominance sometimes predicted career success. For example, although scores for a particular occupational group may be average on the Ascendance scale compared with other groups, scores on the measure may still differentiate more and less successful career paths, especially for women (J. S. Guilford et al., 1976). However, within some occupational groups, the opposite relation holds. For example, among people in training for the clergy, several studies have shown that people scoring higher on the Ascendance scale have tended to be more likely to leave the training program. Dominant individuals have been reported to be more decisive about career choice (S. E. Cooper et al., 1984). Phillips and Bruch (1988) found that shyness (presumably the antithesis of at least interpersonal dominance) was associated with less career information seeking, an avoidance of less interpersonally oriented career fields, and a lack of understanding about how appearing assertive in employment interviews might enhance the likelihood of a favorable outcome. Wiener and Vaitenas (1977) provided evidence that a group of 45 midcareer job changers scored lower on ascendancy and dominance (along with endurance and order) than a group of vocationally stable individuals. The extent to which needs for control and dominance are primarily wired in by genetics or influenced by environment is not settled. A study by Ispa et al. (1984) found that childrearing attitudes of persons in occupations oriented to things or technical issues versus those oriented to people (helping relationships and the like) found that the former had more control-oriented parenting styles than the latter. If dominance styles of parents influence dominance needs of children, occupation may play a role.

Measurement Issues

Most broad-brush personality measures include some measure of dominance or ascendance. Gough's (1987) CPI includes a well-validated measure of dominance, the EPPS has a Need for Dominance scale, the NEO Personality Inventory includes Assertiveness as a facet scale under the Extraversion category, and the GZTS includes an Ascendance scale. R. B. Cattell's 16PF and Clinical Analysis Questionnaire (CAQ; R. B. Cattell et al., 1970; Krug, 1981) include a factor (E) that measures the tendency to be dominant versus submissive. R. B. Cattell and Horn's (1964) Motivation Analysis Test (MAT) also includes an assertion scale. Another widely used (and not infrequently criticized) measure in career and work contexts, the Fundamental Interpersonal Relations Orientation-Behavior (FIRO-B; Furnham, 2008; Schutz, 1978) contains scales having to do with wanting control over others versus wanting control from others. McClelland and Winter's (see Winter, 1973) adaptation of the TAT is probably the most widely used projective measure of the need for power construct. The relation between the various measures of ascendance and dominance is not well established empirically and is badly in need of examination. M. A. Bouchard et al. (1988) found poor convergence among self-reported, laboratory role-played, self-observed, and peer-rated measures of assertiveness, implying that behavioral and paper-and-pencil measures of the construct may yield different results. It should also be noted that ascendance scales may be influenced by one's test-taking orientation so that the desire to "fake good" (especially in the prosocial, controlling manner that generally characterizes managers) must be evaluated when considering individual scores. Concerning the fake good issue, J. S. Guilford et al. (1976) reported that the Ascendance (A) scale on the GZTS was easily faked. Under normal conditions, fewer than 50% of test takers would be expected to have elevated A scale scores. However, when given instructions to "fake good," more than 50% had elevations on this scale. This implies that measuring assertiveness, ascendance, or need for power under conditions in which a positive test-taking orientation would be expected (e.g., in personnel selection contexts), assertiveness and need for power or ascendance will need to be confirmed by means other than paper-and-pencil tests.

WHICH PERSONALITY VARIABLES TO MEASURE?

Given the complexity of the personality domain, which variables should the practicing career assessor measure? No easy or well-validated universal answers emerge, but there are promising leads. Ideally, career assessors would work with clearly defined variables appropriate for the specific purposes of each occupational assessment. Practically, however, many are likely to measure personality with broad-brush instruments originally designed for noncareer purposes. That said, there is a need to reduce data from such measures to a relatively small set of well-established, occupationally relevant personality variables and to be especially careful when interpreting test results that have demonstrated limited occupational relevance.

From the perspective of career satisfaction and work performance, focusing on a combination of broad factors (e.g., the FFM or HEXACO models), coupled with the overarching structural (second-order) factors (e.g., v.1, v.2, & v.3 on the CPI) and selected narrower facet variables (e.g., Self-Efficacy, Achievement Motivation, Dominance, Independence), is recommended. It is generally helpful, when possible, to have more than one measure of the particularly important variables. As discussed in Chapter 18, a sequential approach is recommended such that interests and abilities are considered prior to examining personality. Again, the context is goodness of fit to careers, not relative fit compared with others competing for the same job. However, the results of personality measures must also be interpreted in the light of career and avocational information and behavioral evidence in support of, or inconsistent with, the assessed results.

SUMMARY AND RECOMMENDATIONS

This chapter aimed to move beyond the FFM. Reviews were provided on LOC, Achievement Motivation, dark side personality characteristics, Gender Identity/Masculinity-Femininity, and Dominance. Some would argue that some or all of these variables are simply facets of one or another of the FFM factors, but there is little consensus about the facets, and these personality factors are important for many career assessment applications. Chapter 16 presents six personality profiles to illustrate the value and complexities of personality assessment.

16

Applications
Case Illustrations of Personality Profiles

This chapter presents the personality test results for six cases. The interest and ability results are found, respectively, in Chapters 4 and 12. The particular measures used varied somewhat from one case to another because the specific purposes of the assessments differed or a longer or shorter assessment was employed. The results are presented in the following order: (a) test-taking orientation (evidence from the validity indicators for tests providing them), (b) selected second-order scale scores, and (c) results across tests for the particular personality dimensions and constructs measured. Not all data were included from broad-brush measures of personality in these summaries. Rather, the focus is on those variables with career relevance that have been presented in Chapters 13 through 15. Conversely, in two cases whose data were collected as part of a selection process, results are presented from broad-brush personality measures that would not have been used in the workplace assessment.

In the aggregated summaries provided in this chapter, the process of personality test interpretation is only briefly addressed. In practice, assessors would need to carefully review as part of the process of test interpretation specific information about particular tests. For example, when using the California Psychological Inventory (CPI) there are specific steps that would be taken to examine test-taking orientation and the profile's validity (see Gough, 1996), scores across the major factors, and then specific patterns and profiles that may be found. Depending on the particular careers being considered, the assessor could

---

https://doi.org/10.1037/0000254-017
Career Assessment: Integrating Interests, Abilities, and Personality, by R. L. Lowman
Copyright © 2022 by the American Psychological Association. All rights reserved.

also use some of the occupation-specific personality profiles available in the CPI's test manual (Gough, 1996) or in other literature sources.

Here, the results of similar personality variables on different tests have been included to demonstrate consistency or inconsistency in results of similar constructs across alternative measures. For more information on the variables and constructs measured by the various tests, see Chapters 14 and 15. As with interests, results of alternative measures of personality are not always consistent with one another and are not always measuring exactly the same constructs. When that occurs, further work with a client may be needed to help the client understand differences across measures and to sort out the discrepancies. It is also important to note that some of the measures (e.g., the Sixteen Personality Factor Questionnaire [16PF] and the CPI) were not designed specifically to measure the Big Five factors, although the groupings are made based on scales measuring comparable constructs (see Chapter 15).

Summarizing, the six tables include information about test-taking orientation, scores across the various measures on Big Five personality factors, and scores on other personality variables that have demonstrated relevance in career assessment. A brief aggregated summary of the client's personality testing results is provided in the text.

SAM'S REALISTIC PERSONALITY PROFILE (CASE 5)

Sam had strong interests in the Realistic area (see Chapter 4) and related abilities (see Chapter 12). Although he had been assessed in the context of job selection, only some of the normal personality variables were used for that purpose. Here we present a broader selection of personality data and focus not on his relevance for a particular job but rather on the context of career development. The personality results are shown in Table 16.1.

TABLE 16.1. Sam's Realistic Interests Personality Profile (Case 5)

Test-taking orientation	
California Psychological Inventory	
Reliability indicators	Valid profile; all items completed
Good Impression (Gi)	60 (above average to high)
Communality (Cm)	58 (gave typical replies to commonly agreed upon items)
NEO PI-R	
Reliability indicators	Profile validity indicators normal

Sixteen Personality Factor Questionnaire (16PF)	
Reliability indicators	Valid profile; all items completed
Fake Good	7 (above average)
Fake Bad	5 (average)

Second-order personality factors

California Psychological Inventory (CPI)	
Type	Alpha (level 4)

NEO

See Big Five dimensions below

Sixteen Personality Factor Questionnaire (16PF)	
Anxiety (Ax)	3.3 (low)
Extraversion (Ex)	7.1 (extraverted)
Independence (In)	5.6 (average)
Self-Control (Superego Strength; Se)	7.6 (high)
Tough Poise (Ct)	7.8 (high)

Big Five dimensions

Introversion/Extraversion

CPI	Internality/Externality (v.1)	48	Midrange
NEO PI-R	Extraversion	69	Extraverted
16PF	Extraversion	7.1	Extraverted
Strong Interest Inventory	Introversion/Extroversion (Work Orientation)	68	Introverted

Conscientiousness

CPI	Responsibility (Re)	59	High
CPI	Self-Control (Sc)	54	Average
NEO PI-R	Conscientiousness	51	Average
16PF	Expedient vs. Conscientious (G)	9	Conscientious
16PF	Self-Control (Superego Strength; Se)	7.6	High
16PF	Self-Discipline (Q3)	6	Average

(*continues*)

TABLE 16.1. Sam's Realistic Interests Personality Profile (Case 5) (*Continued*)

Openness			
CPI	Flexibility (Fx)	45	Average to closed
CPI	Norm favoring (v.2)	67	Norm favoring
NEO PI-R	Openness	45	Average to closed
NEO PI-R	O4 (Openness to Actions)	73	Very high
NEO PI-R	O5 (Openness to Ideas)	46	Average
16PF	Imaginative vs. Practical (M)	6	Average
16PF	Openness to Change (Q1)	7	High
Adjustment/Emotional Stability			
CPI	Realization (v.3; level 4)	52	Average
CPI	Well Being (Wb)	64	High
NEO PI-R	Neuroticism	36	Low
16PF	Anxiety (Ax)	3.3	Low
16PF	Emotional Stability (C)	6	Average
16PF	Suspiciousness (L)	4	Low
16PF	Tension (Q4)	3	Low
Agreeableness			
CPI	Empathy (Em)	51	Average
CPI	Sociability (Sy)	60	High
NEO PI-R	Agreeableness	55	Average to high
NEO PI-R	Trust	69	Very high
16PF	Reserved vs. Warm (A)	5	Average

Note. CPI = California Psychological Inventory; NEO PI-R = NEO Personality Inventory-Revised; 16PF = Sixteen Personality Factor Questionnaire.

Other personality variables/factors			
Dominance			
CPI	Dominance (Do)	67	High
FIRO-B	Expressed Control	2	Low
FIRO-B	Wanted Control	2	Low
NEO	Assertiveness (E3)	54	Average
16PF	Dominance (E)	6	Average

Independence			
CPI	Independence (In)	58	High
16PF	Independence (In)	5.6	Average
16PF	Self Sufficiency (Q2)	3	Low
Tough Mindedness			
NEO	Tender Minded (A6)	53	Average
16PF	Tough-Minded (I)	3	Tough-minded
16PF	Tough Poise (Ct)	7.8	Tough-minded
Achievement			
CPI	Achievement via Conformance (Ac)	55	Average to high
CPI	Achievement via Independence (Ai)	44	Average to low
CPI	Capacity for Status (Cs)	44	Average to low
NEO	Achievement Striving (C4)	59	High

Note. CPI = California Psychological Inventory; FIRO-B = Fundamental Interpersonal Relations Orientation-Behavior; 16PF = Sixteen Personality Factor Questionnaire. All scores are standardized (adult norms) except for the FIRO-B, which uses raw scores.

Concerning test-taking orientation, the "fake good" scale of the 16PF scale was elevated. Because the assessment was completed in an industrial selection context, it is not unusual for a positive test-taking orientation to be found. The CPI test results also include test-taking orientation scale scores, but they were indicated to be within normal limits by the automated scoring service used. Nevertheless, it is noteworthy that the Good Impression (Gi) scale was elevated, possibly suggesting a positive self-presentation orientation. However, the Communality scale was high. This is a measure of the extent to which the test taker answered questions that are typically answered in a similar manner. He also answered all or almost all the questions on each of the measures. When a positive self-presentation is found, it is important to understand whether the test-taking context was the likely cause of this orientation or if it reflects a broader tendency to present oneself in a positive light. Typically, in the selection context for leadership roles, there is a tendency for people to present themselves as being more sociable and outgoing than they may actually be and to deny any psychological dysfunction (e.g., anxiety or negative emotions and the like) when completing self-report personality measures. In this case there was behavioral evidence to support that the individual assessed was more sociable than many in the male-dominated job in which he worked.

The client's second-order type on the CPI was Alpha. This type is typically found among people who are proactive and norm-adherent, liking to make things happen in a traditional way. The structural components of this type are v.1 (Internality/Externality), on which he scored in the Extraverted direction, and v.2 (Norm Favoring/Questioning), in which he scored in the norm favoring direction. On the v.3 variable, Realization, his standard score of 52 was in the average range, suggesting average initiative and self-confidence and the potential (and perhaps need) to grow further.

The 16PF measure also has second-order factors. These include Extraversion, Tough Poise, Independence, and Neuroticism. Sam scored in the Extraverted direction on several of the measures except for the midrange score on the CPI's second-order IE factor and the introverted score on the Strong interest measure. In interpreting why the latter measure was inconsistent with the other measures of extraversion, consider that the purpose of that instrument is to help people identify their interests. One of the underlying dimensions of interests includes having preferences for working with things versus with people, which is what that scale primarily considers. Since realistic jobs typically involve more work with things than with people it is not surprising to find that those with Realistic interests on the Strong measure often also score in the introverted direction on that test's scale. However, in Sam's case, he also had secondary or tertiary interests in the Social area, reflecting people-oriented interests. To the extent the test scores accurately represent his personality, he is likely to enjoy contact with people in addition to his skills and interests relating to things. The paradox in this case is that Sam is reasonably extraverted but his occupation involves working with things. For someone who might assume a quasisupervisory role in a highly Realistic work environment, the combination of interest in things and personality dimensions that orient him to enjoy interacting with people could be an effective one.

Concerning the other Big Five personality factors, data were available from three major personality measures: the 16PF, the CPI, and a version of the NEO. All three of the broad-brush measures were well established and included many relevant scales. His scores were in the extraverted direction on all but one of the measures. However, his needs for control came out in mixed direction, on one measure very low, on another, average, and on a third, high. Further exploration would be needed to understand his preferences and whether he would enjoy having supervisory influence over others. His Openness scores were in the average level, as were his measures of Conscientiousness. He presented himself in the well-adjusted direction. His Agreeableness scores were in the average to higher direction.

Considering his other personality scores, Sam scored average on Independence and low on Neuroticism. He scored relatively highly on the Tough Poise factor, suggesting a tendency to process information in an objective, logical way rather than in a subjective or sensitive one. The discrepancies across some of the measures illustrate the need for using multiple measures of the same (or similar) constructs. Generally, when the test results on personality measures are discrepant with one another, it would be important to note the general trends and to consider whether there were aspects of the specific measures that were discrepant with one another that might offer hypotheses about the inconsistencies. In high-stakes testing, such as when used in the context of selection, people's tendency to positively present themselves (exaggerating sociability, reliability, and minimizing stress) is understandable. Comparing test results to behavioral evidence can be helpful. For example, when test results suggest a highly extraverted individual but they are quiet and reserved throughout the assessor's contact and the avocational activities all point to a preference for solitary activities, the discrepancies can be presented to the career assessment client during the feedback, arming the client with information and processes that can be used to try to clarify the findings in the real-world context.

In Sam's case, if the personality measure results matched his behavior, the client would be suggested to be well adjusted, pleasant to deal with, and enjoying working with others rather than strictly on his own. Depending on the interest and ability assessments results, he could have supervisory or leadership potential.

TREVOR'S INVESTIGATIVE PERSONALITY PROFILE (CASE 6)

This client was assessed in his mid-30s while working in a highly complex area of science. He sought help in deciding whether to pursue a bench scientist career versus one in lab management (see Chapter 4). His personality results are shown in Table 16.2.

TABLE 16.2. Trevor's Investigative Interests Personality Profile (Case 6)

Test-taking orientation

California Psychological Inventory (CPI)	
Reliability indicators	Valid profile; all items completed
Good Impression (Gi)	65 (high)
Communality (Cm)	58 (gave typical replies to commonly agreed upon items)

Sixteen Personality Factor Questionnaire (16PF)	
Reliability indicators	Valid profile; all items completed
Fake Good	7 (above average)
Fake Bad	1 (low)

Second-order personality factors

California Psychological Inventory (CPI)	
Type	Beta (level 6)

(continues)

TABLE 16.2. Trevor's Investigative Interests Personality Profile (Case 6) (*Continued*)

Sixteen Personality Factor Questionnaire (16PF)	
Anxiety	4.7 (average)
Extraversion (Ex)	6.2 (midrange)
Independence (In)	4.0 (low)
Self-Control (Superego Strength; Se)	9.3 (high)
Tough Poise (Ct)	8.2 (high)

Big Five dimensions

Introversion/Extraversion

CPI	Internality/Externality (v.1)	22	Internality
16PF	Extraversion	6.2	Midrange to extraverted
Strong Interest Inventory	Introversion/Extroversion (Work Orientation)	66	Introverted

Conscientiousness

CPI	Responsibility (Re)	68	High
CPI	Self-Control (Sc)	65	High
16PF	Expedient vs. Conscientious (G)	8	Conscientious
16PF	Self-Control (Superego Strength; Se)	9.3	High
16PF	Self-Discipline (Q3)	10	Very high

Openness

CPI	Flexibility (Fx)	31	Low
CPI	Norm favoring (v.2) [raw score]	34	Norm favoring
16PF	Openness to Change (Q1)	4	Low
16PF	Imaginative vs. Practical (M)	5	Average

Adjustment/Emotional Stability

CPI	Realization (v.3; level 6)	48	High
CPI	Well Being (Wb)	60	High
16PF	Anxiety (Ax)	4.7	Average
16PF	Emotional Stability (C)	5	Average
16PF	Suspiciousness (L)	4	Low
16PF	Tension (Q4)	4	Low

Agreeableness

CPI	Empathy (Em)	51	Average
CPI	Sociability (Sy)	47	Average
16PF	Reserved vs. Warm (A)	6	Average

Note. CPI = California Psychological Inventory; 16PF = Sixteen Personality Factor Questionnaire.

Other personality variables/factors

Dominance

CPI	Dominance (Do)	53	Average
FIRO-B	Expressed Control	1	Low
FIRO-B	Wanted Control	6	High
16PF	Dominance (E)	6	Average

Independence

CPI	Independence (In)	47	Average
16PF	Independent (In)	4.0	Low
16PF	Self Sufficiency (Q2)	4	Low

Tough Mindedness

16PF	Tough-Minded (I)	3	Tough-minded
16PF	Tough Poise (Ct)	8.2	Tough-minded

Achievement

CPI	Achievement via Conformance (Ac)	64	High
CPI	Achievement via Independence (Ai)	60	High
CPI	Capacity for Status (Cs)	61	High

Note. CPI = California Psychological Inventory; FIRO-B = Fundamental Interpersonal Relations Orientation-Behavior; 16PF = Sixteen Personality Factor Questionnaire. All scores are standardized (adult norms) except for the FIRO-B, which uses raw scores.

The validity indicators on Trevor's personality measures were generally within normal limits. His very low score on the Fake Bad measure of the 16PF suggested the possibility of denying any psychological difficulties and was generally consistent with his high score on the Good Impression score on the CPI. Such results are typically found among those in managerial positions.

On the CPI, the client's score on the v.2 (Norm Favoring/Questioning) second-order variable was very high on norm favoring, suggesting an order-seeking, conservative, and preservative approach. His above average score on v.2 (Internality/Externality) was in the internality, or introverted, direction.

Together these placed Trevor in the Beta quadrant, suggesting an orientation to stability and predictability, preserving the existing order, and being comfortable working within it. Such characteristics can be useful in well-defined work roles and in highly structured organizations. They may be less helpful when innovation and change are needed. His v.3 (Realization) score was at Level 6 (out of 7), suggesting a high level of self-actualization.

On the 16PF second-order factors he scored in the average range on Extraversion and Anxiety factors. He scored high on the 16PF's Tough Poise factor and scale. He scored low on the Independence factor. The score of 47 on the CPI's Independence scale was just below the general population median and mean of 50, and the 16PF Independence factor was below average. Considering that the client was a scientist, and that the training in this field is highly structured and that he was in his 30s at the time of his assessment, it is difficult to know how these scores, which could be interpreted as not being particularly strong on self-sufficiency versus dependency, would affect his career choice concern. Perhaps lab scientists would need to chart their own course in independently overseeing a lab, whereas a research manager might need to fit into a framework, including goals that are established by others.

Trevor presented himself on the various personality measures as being introverted to midrange, relatively closed and inflexible on the Openness factor, high to very high on Conscientiousness, midrange to low on Agreeableness, and midrange to high on Well Being (low on Neuroticism). His very high scores on the Responsibility and Self-Control scales of the CPI suggest strong superego controls (high persistence, reliability, and work-orientation), consistent with what would be expected of a highly trained scientist. He also scored in the tough-minded direction on the 16PF Sensitivity/Tough Poise measures. Also of note were his strong needs for achievement, slightly higher in the traditional versus independent direction.

Although the client did not present himself as being particularly social or engaged with others, there was some evidence of his being able to work with others as part of his job. His needs for control over others were average (CPI-Do) to low (wanted Control on the Fundamental Interpersonal Relations Orientation-Behavior [FIRO-B] measure). Since Trevor was contemplating a position as a manager, these findings might need further exploration. However, in areas such as science leadership roles (or academic administration) where research degrees are often required, managerial duties may also require technical knowledge and competencies. Also, on some of the personality measures, some change may be expected as he moves from his 30s and has more job and personal life experiences.

ELIZABETH'S ARTISTIC PERSONALITY PROFILE (CASE 7)

This client sought help with her career directions after experiencing personal distress in her life and finding herself less than fulfilled in her work (see Chapter 4). Her personality results are shown in Table 16.3.

TABLE 16.3. Elizabeth's Artistic Interests Personality Profile (Case 7)

Test-taking orientation

California Psychological Inventory (CPI)

Reliability indicators	Valid profile; all items completed
Good Impression (Gi)	46 (average to below average)
Communality (Cm)	60 (gave typical replies to commonly agreed upon items)

Sixteen Personality Factor Questionnaire (16PF)/Clinical Analysis Questionnaire (CAQ)

Reliability indicators	16PF/CAQ validity indicator: 1 (valid profile; all items completed)

Second-order personality factors

California Psychological Inventory (CPI)

Type	Delta (level 4)

Sixteen Personality Factor Questionnaire (16PF)

Anxiety (Ax)	8.3 (high)
Extraversion (Ex)	4.3 (introverted)
Independence (In)	6.5 (average to high)
Self-Control (Superego Strength; Se)	5.7 (average)
Tough Poise (Ct)	6 (average)

Big Five dimensions

Introversion/Extraversion

CPI	Internality/Externality (v.1)	26	Internality
16PF	Extraversion	4.3	Introverted
Strong Interest Inventory	Introversion/Extraversion (Work Orientation)	53	Slightly introverted

Conscientiousness

CPI	Responsibility (Re)	50	Average
CPI	Self-Control (Sc)	54	Average
16PF	Expedient vs. Conscientious (G)	4	More expedient
16PF	Superego Strength (Se)	5.7	Average
16PF	Self-Discipline (Q3)	6	Average

(continues)

TABLE 16.3. Elizabeth's Artistic Interests Personality Profile (Case 7) (*Continued*)

Openness			
CPI	Flexibility (Fx)	46	Average
CPI	Norm favoring (v.2) [raw score]	19	Norm questioning
16PF	Imaginative vs. Practical (M)	5	Average
16PF	Openness to Change (Q1)	7	High
Adjustment/Emotional Stability			
CPI	Realization (v.3; level 4) [raw score]	40	Average
CPI	Well Being (Wb)	52	Average
16PF	Anxiety (Ax)	8.3	High
16PF	Emotional Stability (C)	3	Low
16PF	Suspiciousness (L)	9	High
16PF	Tension (Q4)	8	High
16PF (CAQ)	Low Energy Depression (D5)	7	High
16PF (CAQ)	Neuroticism (Ne)	8.4	High
Agreeableness			
CPI	Empathy (Em)	50	Average
CPI	Sociability (Sy)	44	Average
16PF	Reserved vs. Warm (A)	4	Reserved

Note. CPI = California Psychological Inventory; 16PF = Sixteen Personality Factor Questionnaire; CAQ = Clinical Analysis Questionnaire version of the 16PF.

Other personality variables/factors			
Dominance			
CPI	Dominance (Do)	42	Average to low
FIRO-B	Expressed Control	0	Very low
FIRO-B	Wanted Control	1	Low
16PF	Dominance (E)	6	Average
Independence			
CPI	Independence (In)	48	Average
16PF	Independence (In)	6.5	Average to independent
16PF	Self Sufficiency (Q2)	6	Average

Tough Mindedness			
16PF	Tough-Minded (I)	6	Average
16PF	Tough Poise (Ct)	6.0	Average
Achievement			
CPI	Achievement via Conformance (Ac)	55	Average to high
CPI	Achievement via Independence (Ai)	55	Average to high
CPI	Capacity for Status (Cs)	52	Average

Note. CPI = California Psychological Inventory; FIRO-B= Fundamental Interpersonal Relations Orientation-Behavior; 16PF = Sixteen Personality Factor Questionnaire. All scores are standardized (adult norms) except for the FIRO-B, which uses raw scores.

The validity indicators on Elizabeth's personality measures were generally within normal limits. There were no missing items on the various personality measures completed. Her validity scale score on the 16PF (Clinical Analysis Questionnaire [CAQ]) was within normal limits. Her score on the Communality scale of the CPI suggested that she was not responding to the instrument items in an atypical manner. However, her slightly below average score on the Good Impression (Gi) and average score on the Well Being (Wb) scale score suggested she may have been experiencing some distress at the time of the assessment that could have affected how she responded to some of the items.

On the CPI, the client's scores on the v.2 (Norm Favoring/Questioning) second-order variable were in the norm questioning direction (typical of those with Artistic interests). Her v.2 (Internality/Externality) score was in the internal, or introverted, direction. She scored at the lowest level (1) on the Realization score. Her scores placed her in the Delta quadrant. The Delta group can use their sensitivity and self-focus to creative advantage, but they can also be self-defeating and overly focused on areas of unhappiness. The very low level on the Realization scale suggests someone who is in distress and may need ongoing counseling or therapy.

Elizabeth presented herself on the various Big Five personality measures as being midrange (average) on Openness (not typical of artists, but that can vary depending on the specific type of creative talent), average to below average on Conscientiousness, midrange to low on Agreeableness, and midrange to mostly low on Well Being (i.e., high on neuroticism and anxiety). Her midrange scores on measures of the Responsibility and Self-Control scales of the CPI contrasted with the low score on the 16PF's G scale. The latter findings might be expected with someone with strong Artistic interests, but here there seems to be a mix of conformity and reliability versus a less controlled side (perhaps one that is seeking to find expression). This may represent an area of conflict for her. She also scored in the midrange on tough-minded versus sensitivity scale. She obtained relatively high scores on needs for achievement and expressed relatively low needs for control over others and did not particularly look for others to control her.

There were significant elevations on the anxiety and some of the depression scales of the CAQ. These results suggest that she may need counseling assistance even as she works on some of her career concerns. It is difficult to know whether these elevations reflect situational concerns or are part of a more persistent pattern. The fact that her highest interests do not seem to be finding an outlet, especially when considered in the context of her high achievement needs, may be contributing to some of her current difficulties.

Overall, the pattern is not a consistent one, which may help explain some of the career conflicts Elizabeth is experiencing. A tension for her may be between feeling her environment is impinging on her in a way over which she feels little control (CPI Delta level 4). It is not possible to know from these data alone whether the anxiety she acknowledged feeling is the consequence or the cause of her work concerns, but that could be explored in individual work with her. Possibly she would be more effective if she could channel her career or avocational work in a direction consistent with her interests and abilities.

SARAH'S SOCIAL PERSONALITY PROFILE (CASE 8)

Sarah, in her early 20s and in college at the time of her assessment, was introduced in Chapter 4 and her ability profile was presented in Chapter 12. Her personality results are presented in Table 16.4.

TABLE 16.4. Sarah's Social Interests Personality Profile (Case 8)

Test-taking orientation

California Psychological Inventory (CPI)	
Reliability indicators	Valid profile; all items completed
Good Impression (Gi)	42 (low)
Communality (Cm)	48 (gave average number of similar replies to commonly agreed upon items)

Sixteen Personality Factor Questionnaire (16PF)/Clinical Analysis Questionnaire (CAQ)	
Reliability indicators	16PF/CAQ validity indicator: 5 (atypical response set; care in interpreting results is recommended)
Fake Good	6 (average)
Fake Bad	3 (low)

Second-order personality factors

California Psychological Inventory (CPI)

Type	Beta (level 3)

Sixteen Personality Factor Questionnaire (16PF)

Anxiety (Ax)	2.2 (low)
Extraversion (Ex)	6.6 (extraverted)
Independence (In)	3.7 (low)
Self-Control (Superego Strength; Se)	7.5 (high)
Tough Poise (Ct)	6.0 (average)

Big Five dimensions

Introversion/Extraversion

CPI	Internality/Externality (v.1)	22	Slightly introverted
16PF	Extraversion	6.6	Extraverted
Strong Interest Inventory	Introversion/Extraversion (Work Orientation)	52	Midrange

Conscientiousness

CPI	Responsibility (Re)	44	Average to low
CPI	Self-Control (Sc)	44	Average to low
16PF	Expedient vs. Conscientious (G)	7	Conscientious
16PF	Self-Control (Superego Strength; Se)	7.5	High
16PF	Self-Discipline (Q3)	7	High

Openness

CPI	Flexibility (Fx)	50	Average
CPI	Norm favoring (v.2) [raw score]	25	Norm favoring
16PF	Imaginative v. Practical (M)	4	Not imaginative
16PF	Openness to Change (Q1)	6	Average

Adjustment/Emotional Stability

CPI	Realization (v.3; level 3)	3	Low
CPI	Well Being (Wb)	40	Low
16PF	Anxiety (Ax)	2.2	Low
16PF	Emotional Stability (C)	4	Low

(*continues*)

TABLE 16.4. Sarah's Social Interests Personality Profile (Case 8) (*Continued*)

	Adjustment/Emotional Stability		
16PF	Suspiciousness (L)	6	Average
16PF	Tension (Q4)	6	Average
16PF (CAQ)	Low Energy Depression (D5)	6	Average
16PF (CAQ)	Neuroticism (Ne)	5.8	Average
Agreeableness			
CPI	Empathy (Em)	52	Average
CPI	Sociability (Sy)	52	Average
16PF	Reserved vs. Warm (A)	8	Warm, personable

Note. CPI = California Psychological Inventory; 16PF = Sixteen Personality Factor Questionnaire; CAQ = Clinical Analysis Questionnaire version of the 16PF.

Other personality variables/factors

Dominance			
CPI	Dominance (Do)	38	Low
FIRO-B	Expressed Control	1	Low
FIRO-B	Wanted Control	9	High
16PF	Dominance (E)	6	Average
Independence			
CPI	Independence (In)	28	Very low
16PF	Independence (In)	3.7	Low
16PF	Self Sufficiency (Q2)	4	Low
Tough-Mindedness			
16PF	Tough-Minded (I)	6	Average
16PF	Tough Poise (Ct)	6	Average
Achievement			
CPI	Achievement via Conformance (Ac)	48	Average
CPI	Achievement via Independence (Ai)	49	Average
CPI	Capacity for Status (Cs)	44	Average to low

Note. CPI = California Psychological Inventory; FIRO-B= Fundamental Interpersonal Relations Orientation-Behavior; 16PF = Sixteen Personality Factor Questionnaire. All scores are standardized (adult norms) except for the FIRO-B, which uses raw scores. College female norms were used for the 16PF and adult norms for the other measures.

Sarah's test-taking orientation scales on the 16PF measures did not show evidence of "fake good" or "fake bad." However, a measure of atypical test taking was elevated. Her CPI Good Impression (Gi) scale score was below-average, suggesting personal stress that may have affected her responses on the test or a disinterest in the reactions or opinions of others. However, the Communality scale was in the average range, suggesting that she generally answered in a manner consistent with the normative group's responses. She also answered all or almost all the questions on each of the measures.

The client's second-order type on the CPI was Beta. This type of result is typically found among people who are norm-adherent, who accept and try to work within accepted values and rules. They tend to be seen as conventional and aiming to preserve things as they are. This orientation may explain her liking of traditional female roles (see Chapter 4) and not being particularly career oriented. On the structural components of this type, she scored slightly in the internality direction on the v.1 variable (Internality/Externality). On the v.2 (Norm Favoring/Questioning) component, she scored in the norm favoring direction. On the v.3 variable, Realization, her standard score of 31 was at Level 3, suggesting a relatively low level of self-realization. This may not be surprising given the age at which she completed these measures.

On the Big Five measures of personality, Sarah scored slightly in the Extraverted direction on the 16PF second-order factor, but also slightly in the introversive direction on the CPI v.1 variable. This may reflect someone who is an ambivert, that is, having characteristics of both types (see the discussion in Chapter 14 on Introversion/Extraversion). Or it may be that the use of college female norms for the 16PF versus adult norms for the CPI accounted for the discrepancies. Sarah's scores on Conscientiousness were mixed with low scores on two of the variables included here and high on another. Conscientiousness generally increases with age, and this variable may change or become more consistent as she progresses through college. Openness scores were in the average to less flexible direction. She may also have been under some stress and anxiety at the time of the assessment. She did score in the average to above average range on Agreeableness markers, which would be expected of someone with strong Social interests.

The client scored fairly low on measures of Dominance and on Independence. She had a striking difference on the FIRO-B between wanting to exert control over others (a very low score of 1) and wanting control to come from others (a quite high score of 9). Her need for Achievement scores were relatively low, possibly reflecting greater interest in relationships with others than in a career. This was consistent with some of the interview data, which suggested a person who was less oriented to career than to other aspects of life, including romantic relationships and relationships with friends. As noted in Chapter 4, it was her parents' idea for her to be assessed, although she was agreeable to doing so.

Sarah's personality results provide some areas of fit and misfit with the rest of her assessment profile but are not necessarily fixed in time. As she proceeds in her college work and beyond, some of the seeming contradictions may be resolved. Should further clarification be needed, retesting on some of the personality measures when she is older may be appropriate.

STAN'S ENTERPRISING PERSONALITY PROFILE (CASE 9)

This case was introduced in Chapter 4 and concerns an individual who, relatively late in his career, lost his job and sought career assessment not for job finding help but rather to better understand possible career paths that might be relevant for him. His interests were in the Enterprising area, and his career had mostly been spent in the for-profit world.

Stan's personality results are shown in Table 16.5. The validity indicators of the NEO were generally suggestive of reliable and valid responses. This is arguably the least subtle of the broad-brush measures, and he had the highest elevations on scales that tend to be affected by positive impression management factors. However, on the 16PF, his score on the Impression Management score was at the 6th percentile, suggesting rather atypical responses, a pattern sometimes found among people experiencing personal distress. This test-taking orientation should be kept in mind when interpreting his results on that measure. The CPI showed no evidence of invalidity. He did leave eight items blank on the CPI, but his Good Impression (Gi) and Communality (Cm) scores on the CPI were in the average range; his Gi score was lower than those typically found among managers and those in business occupations.

TABLE 16.5. Stan's Enterprising Interests Personality Profile (Case 9)

Test-taking orientation

California Psychological Inventory (CPI)	
Reliability indicators	Valid profile; left 8 items blank
Good Impression (Gi)	53 (average)
Communality (Cm)	54 (average in giving typical replies to commonly agreed upon items)

NEO-4	
Reliability indicators	Profile valid

Sixteen Personality Factor Questionnaire (16PF)/Clinical Analysis Questionnaire (CAQ)	
Reliability indicators	16PF/CAQ validity indicator: 6 (atypical response set; care in interpreting results is recommended)
Fake Good	4 (average)
Fake Bad	1 (low)

Second-order personality factors

California Psychological Inventory (CPI)

Type	Alpha (level 4)

NEO

See Big Five Dimensions below

Sixteen Personality Factor Questionnaire (16PF)

Anxiety (Ax)	6.4 (midrange to high)
Extraversion (Ex)	5.8 (midrange)

Sixteen Personality Factor Questionnaire (16PF)

Independence (In)	5.3 (midrange)
Self-control (Superego Strength; Se)	6.3 (midrange)
Tough Poise (Ct)	5.6 (midrange)

Big Five dimensions

Introversion/Extraversion

CPI	Internality/Externality (v.1)	35	Extraverted
NEO-4	Extraversion	70	Highly extraverted
16PF	Extraversion	5.8	Midrange
Strong Interest Inventory	Introversion/Extraversion (Work Orientation)	52	Midrange

Conscientiousness

CPI	Responsibility (Re)	61	High
CPI	Self-Control (Sc)	57	High
NEO-4	Conscientiousness	69	Very high
16PF	Expedient vs. Conscientious (G)	6	Midrange
16PF	Self-Control (Superego Strength; Se)	6.3	Average
16PF	Self-Discipline (Q3)	6	Midrange

Openness

CPI	Flexibility (Fx)	35	Inflexible
CPI	Norm Favoring (v.2)	65	Norm favoring
NEO-4	Openness	53	Average
NEO-4	Openness to Actions (O4)	47	Average
NEO-4	Openness to Ideas (O5)	48	Average
16PF	Imaginative vs. Practical (M)	5	Average
16PF	Openness to Change (Q1)	5	Average

(continues)

TABLE 16.5. Stan's Enterprising Interests Personality Profile (Case 9) (*Continued*)

Adjustment/Emotional Stability			
CPI	Realization (v.3; level 4)	52	Average
CPI	Well Being (Wb)	46	Midrange
16PF	Anxiety (Ax)	6.4	Midrange to high
16PF	Emotional Stability (C)	5	Midrange
Adjustment/Emotional Stability			
16PF	Suspiciousness (L)	6	Midrange
16PF	Tension (Q4)	6	Midrange
16PF (CAQ)	Low Energy Depression (D5)	6	Average
16PF (CAQ)	Neuroticism (Ne)	5.3	Average
Agreeableness			
CPI	Empathy (Em)	60	High
CPI	Sociability (Sy)	55	High
NEO-4	Agreeableness	36	Low
NEO-4	Trust	40	Low
16PF	Reserved vs. Warm (A)	7	Warm

Note. CPI = California Psychological Inventory; 16PF = Sixteen Personality Factor Questionnaire; CAQ = Clinical Analysis Questionnaire version of the 16PF.

Other personality variables/factors

Dominance			
CPI	Dominance (Do)	72	Very high
FIRO-B	Expressed Control	9	High
FIRO-B	Wanted Control	2	Low
NEO-4	Assertiveness (E3)	63	High
16PF	Dominance (E)	7	High
Independence			
CPI	Independence (In)	63	High
16PF	Independence (In)	5.3	Average
16PF	Self-Sufficiency (Q2)	5	Average

Tough-Mindedness			
NEO-4	Tender Minded (A6)	46	Average to low
16PF	Tough-Mindedness (I)	6	Average
16PF	Tough Poise (Ct)	5.6	Average
Achievement			
CPI	Achievement via Conformance (Ac)	63	High
Achievement			
CPI	Achievement via Independence (Ai)	55	Average to high
CPI	Capacity for Status (Cs)	54	Average
NEO-4	Achievement Striving (C4)	74	Very high

Note. CPI = California Psychological Inventory; FIRO-B = Fundamental Interpersonal Relations Orientation-Behavior; 16PF = Sixteen Personality Factor Questionnaire. All scores were standardized (using adult norms) except for the FIRO-B, which uses raw scores. Also note that the NEO-4 does not include the Neuroticism (N) scales.

As with many Enterprising interest types, his CPI type was Alpha, reflecting an extraverted personality orientation and belief that he can be successful in influencing the external world. However, his v.3 (Realization) variable on the CPI was only at Level 4 (and at the low end of that), suggesting that he was not feeling that he had reached as much of his potential as he might have hoped by his fifth decade.

On the Big Five measures, Stan presented himself in the midrange to extraverted direction on most of the measures. He scored high on most the 16PF Conscientiousness-related scales. He presented himself as being less flexible and more norm-conforming than open to new ideas or actions, a pattern consistent with many managers. Concerning Adjustment, he scored slightly below the median on the Well Being (Wb) scale of the CPI and somewhat elevated on the Anxiety factor of the 16PF, suggesting he was possibly experiencing stress at the time of the assessment. Further evaluation of his psychological reactions to his current unemployment might need attention. His Agreeableness scores were mixed, scoring low on the NEO-4 measure but in the warm, involved direction on others. His scores on the Tough Poise variables were slightly lower than might have been expected of someone in management.

On other scales, his needs for dominance and control were very high. The discrepancy on the FIRO-B between expressed control (very high) and wanted control (low), along with the quite high Dominance score on the CPI, along with the high assertiveness score on the NEO-4, suggested a possible tendency to be insensitive to his impact on others when he expresses his authority. His needs for achievement were quite high—higher in the conforming than independent direction. His strong needs for dominance and control on the personality measures, coupled with high achievement needs, could be a source of stress to someone currently unemployed.

Overall, the personality results identify some general trends that need to be taken into account in interpreting Stan's overall profile. Acute stress reactions to job loss can be expected, particularly for those whose identity is primarily tied up in their work. Despite affecting certain personality variables, stress may have little impact on stable, character-like personality traits. The personality results identified for this client, although generally compatible with his career choices to date, suggest he may be at risk from an overly controlling style of relating to others. Also, he may be better suited for work that requires working within well-defined parameters rather than those that require working with limited structure.

LINDA'S CONVENTIONAL PERSONALITY PROFILE (CASE 10)

This case was initially described in Chapter 4. The client's interests and abilities were consistent with her career to date, and she was being assessed as part of a workplace evaluation and development. Only a few of the normal personality variables were used in her job-related assessment results. Here we present the larger collection of data and focus not on her relevance for a particular job but on using the results for career development. Her personality results are shown in Table 16.6.

TABLE 16.6. Linda's Conventional Interests Personality Profile (Case 10)

Test-taking orientation

California Psychological Inventory (CPI)	
Reliability indicators	Some profile validity concerns; all items completed
Good Impression (Gi)	63 (high)
Communality (Cm)	62 (gave a high number of typical replies to commonly agreed upon items)

Hogan Personality Inventory	
Reliability indicators	14 (valid and interpretable profile)

Sixteen Personality Factor Questionnaire (16PF)	
Reliability indicators	All items completed. Fake Good orientation quite high and results should be cautiously interpreted.

Sixteen Personality Factor Questionnaire (16PF)	
Fake Good	10 (very high)
Fake Bad	6 (average)

Second-order personality factors

California Psychological Inventory (CPI)	
Type	Alpha (level 5)

Sixteen Personality Factor Questionnaire (16PF)	
Anxiety (Ax)	2.9 (low)
Extraversion (Ex)	8.1 (extraverted)
Independence (In)	6.1 (average)
Self-control (Superego Strength; Se)	6.4 (midrange)
Tough Poise (Ct)	6.0 (average)

Big Five dimensions

Introversion/Extraversion			
CPI	Internality/Externality (v.1)	42	Externality
16PF	Extraversion	8.1	Extraverted
Strong Interest Inventory	Introversion/Extraversion (Work Orientation)	68	Introverted

Conscientiousness			
CPI	Responsibility (Re)	65	High
CPI	Self-Control (Sc)	61	High
HPI	Prudence	80	Very high
16PF	Expedient vs. Conscientious (G)	6	Midrange
16PF	Self-Control (Superego Strength; Se)	6.4	Midrange
16PF	Self-Discipline (Q3)	7	High average

Openness			
CPI	Flexibility (Fx)	35	Low
CPI	Norm favoring (v.2)	64	Norm favoring
HPI	Intellectance (Inquisitive)	72	Above average
16PF	Imaginative vs. Practical (M)	8	Imaginative
16PF	Openness to Change (Q1)	6	Average

Adjustment/Emotional Stability			
CPI	Realization (v.3; level 5)	58	Average
CPI	Well Being (Wb)	60	High
HPI	Adjustment	66	Well-adjusted

(*continues*)

TABLE 16.6. Linda's Conventional Interests Personality Profile (Case 10) (*Continued*)

Adjustment/Emotional Stability (continued)

16PF	Anxiety	2.9	Low
16PF	Emotional Stability (C)	6	Average
16PF	Suspiciousness (L)	6	Average
16PF	Tension (Q4)	3	Low

Agreeableness

CPI	Empathy (Em)	50	Average
CPI	Sociability (Sy)	58	High
HPI	Likeability	37	Average to low
16PF	Reserved vs. Warm (A)	7	Average to warm

Note. CPI = California Psychological Inventory; 16PF = Sixteen Personality Factor Questionnaire; HPI = Hogan Personality Inventory.

Other personality variables/factors

Dominance

CPI	Dominance (Do)	70	Very high
FIRO-B	Expressed Control	9	High
FIRO-B	Wanted Control	0	Very low
16PF	Dominance (E)	5	Average

Independence

CPI	Independence (In)	48	Average
16PF	Independence (In)	6.1	Average
16PF	Self-Sufficient (Q2)	5	Average

Tough-Mindedness

16PF	Tough-minded (I)	4	Average to low
16PF	Tough Poise (Ct)	6.0	Average

Achievement

CPI	Achievement via Conformance (Ac)	63	High
CPI	Achievement via Independence (Ai)	59	High

Achievement			
CPI	Capacity for Status (Cs)	64	High
HPI	Ambition	67	Midrange to high

Note. CPI = California Psychological Inventory; FIRO-B= Fundamental Interpersonal Relations Orientation-Behavior; 16PF = Sixteen Personality Factor Questionnaire; HPI = Hogan Personality Inventory. All scores were standardized (using adult norms) except for the FIRO-B, which uses raw scores, and HPI scores, which are percentiles.

As is common for assessments done in work contexts, her test-taking orientation was in the Fake Good direction, suggesting that she aimed to present herself in a favorable light. The validity scales for the CPI and the Hogan Personality Inventory were within normal limits. However, Linda's Good Impression (Gi), Well-being (Wb), and Communality (Cm) scales were all high, suggesting a tendency to present herself in a positive way, as would be expected in this type of assessment. Similarly, the 16PF was very high in the "fake good" direction. For these reasons it is important to conservatively interpret the results. People scoring in this manner may tend to present themselves as being more extraverted than they may sometimes be and tend to deny presence of stress or emotional difficulty.

On the CPI, she scored in the norm favoring (v.2) and externality (v.1) directions, placing her in the Alpha personality grouping. Alphas tend to be extraverted, proactive, and like to have influence on others. The extent to which she presented herself in a more prosocial, assertive way than she might actually be needs to be considered in light of the context in which the assessment took place. On the 16PF second-order factors, she presented herself as being involved with others and well adjusted, indicating little experience of psychological stress.

On the Big Five factors, Linda consistently presented herself as being extraverted, with the exception of the vocational interest measure, which can be confounded by the particular interests endorsed. She also presented herself as being highly conscientious, agreeable, and emotionally stable. She scored midrange on the Openness factor; as a group, managers and accountants tend to score in the less open, less flexible directions on such measures. She presented herself on other scales or factors as being high on Dominance. On the FIRO-B, she presented herself as being much higher on wanting to control others than to be controlled by them. She scored quite high on measures of ambition and achievement orientation.

Overall, the personality results suggest an individual who was very motivated to obtain the job for which she was being considered. When the purpose turns to using the personality test results for career counseling, the assessor would need to review the findings in the context of her other results (including behavior in the ability assessment center exercises that involved interpersonal interactions). Helping her sort her needs for control over others (the results of which have to be interpreted in the context of her also presenting herself as being likable and agreeable) would be part of the process of her better understanding what is of greatest importance to her and how best to deal with the apparent contradictions in some of the results.

SUMMARY AND CONCLUSIONS

This chapter presented six personality profiles of people whose interests and abilities were presented earlier in the book. Each illustrated the type of personality results that are obtained in career assessment work. These real-life data show that there can be inconsistencies across multiple measures of the same constructs. Personal results add depth and dimension to interest and ability results. The next chapter introduces the relationships across interest-ability-personality domains and how data across domains can be integrated.

IV

APPLYING THE INTERDIMENSIONAL MODEL

17

Relationships Across Interest, Ability, and Personality Domains

A foundational premise of this book is the value of assessing—and then combining—interest, ability, and personality data to arrive at a more comprehensive understanding of clients in the context of the reasons for which assessment was sought. In Chapters 2 through 16 of this book, evidence was presented concerning the career and work relevance of each of the three major focal areas as separate domains and on their own merits. The book has examined major themes in the literature that speak to the validity and inferential relevance for career and work issues of the major factors and variables within these domains. This chapter focuses on how these domains relate to each other and how the cross-domain relationships contribute to a more coherent understanding of clients.

The first task of this chapter is to examine the literature on interdomain (interest-ability-personality) relationships. This evidence is important because there are overlaps between these domains that have to be taken into account in understanding and interpreting results. Additionally, some empirically established profiles have been found to be commonly associated with particular occupations. These include, for example, among scientists, Investigative interests, high General Cognitive and Spatial abilities, and Openness (see Wai et al., 2010) and, among men with Realistic interests, elevated Mechanical abilities, Nonverbal Intelligence, and personality tendencies to be masculine and closed rather than open (Lowman & Ng, 2010). Then, in Chapter 18, practical guidance is offered in the context of the still-emerging research about assessment interpretation and communication of interdomain findings.

---

https://doi.org/10.1037/0000254-018
Career Assessment: Integrating Interests, Abilities, and Personality, by R. L. Lowman
Copyright © 2022 by the American Psychological Association. All rights reserved.

Interdomain relationships include those between and among (a) interests and personality; (b) interests and abilities; (c) abilities and personality; and, most complexly, (d) interests, abilities, and personality. As will become clear, much of the literature reviewed in this chapter is a work in progress. Although, as earlier chapters of this book have demonstrated, there is a rich and diverse literature on the nature, structure, and occupational applications of the various within-domain factors and variables, the interdomain literature is still in early stages. Despite a growing literature, however, much more research is needed before stable conclusions can be drawn and comprehensive translations to practice reliably made.

Except for some early, more qualitative writings on the subject (e.g., Blatt & Allison, 1981; Murray, 1938), little systematic attention had been given to the interdomain relationships, despite a large literature on the three individual domains and variables (see Super & Crites, 1962). Some of the pioneering early work in the interdomain work included that of R. B. Cattell (e.g., 1987) and his associates (especially Horn, 1976a), who examined ability-personality connections. Interest-personality relationships have also been widely researched. Ward, Cunningham, and Wakefield (1976), e.g., examined the relationship between the Vocational Preference Inventory (VPI) and the Sixteen Personality Factor Questionnaire (16PF). Very few early studies, however, set out to measure interests, abilities, and personality at the same time. Even now interest-ability-personality studies are fairly scarce.

In the next sections of this chapter, research evidence from each of the four types of interdomain relationships is in turn presented and summarized, starting with interest-personality relationships. The studies cited vary considerably in their methodologies and samples, making it often difficult to aggregate across them. For that reason, some of the studies will be discussed in detail to provide a clearer understanding of the types of research approaches that so far have been used.

INTEREST-PERSONALITY RELATIONSHIPS

J. L. Holland's (1997a) RIASEC interests model (see Chapter 2) remains the most widely applied and studied interests model. The popularity of Holland's theory and the existence of widely used assessment instruments for measuring interests (usually employing the RIASEC variables) has resulted in a number of research studies focused on the intersection of interests and personality variables (especially ones based on, or incorporating, the five-factor personality model [FFM] factors; see Chapter 4).

More than the relative ease of measurement accounts for the attention paid to interest-personality research. J. L. Holland (1985a) himself viewed vocational interests as being measures of personality; therefore, cross-domain relations between personality and RIASEC interest variables were implied by the theory almost from its inception. But most researchers would agree that although there is overlap between interests and personality variables, they are not measuring the same constructs.

A study by Costa et al. (1984) is illustrative of the early studies in comparing FFM factors and facet scores (in this case, three of the five FFM factors: Neuroticism, Enterprising, and Openness) with the Self-Directed Search (SDS) RIASEC interest factor. Atypically of this genre of study, both self-ratings and spouse ratings were included for both the personality and interest measures. The authors also examined the results separately for men and for women, and by age, and included a wide range of participants from ages 25 to 89.

This study illustrated that how personality is measured can also affect obtained interest-personality results. In examining the correlations between self-rated interests (using Holland's SDS) and self-rated personality (using one of Costa and McCrae's NEO measures), the highest correlations for both men and women were between Investigative and Artistic with Openness, and Extraversion (here, and unless otherwise noted, elsewhere in the chapter, high scores were in the extraverted direction) with Social and Enterprising interests. When comparing the spousal ratings of personality to interests, however, the results were somewhat different and, in some cases, more consistent with Holland's theory. For men, Realistic and Investigative interest scores were correlated negatively with Extraversion (i.e., introversion scores were positively correlated); for both men and women, Openness was positively correlated with Artistic vocational interests and negatively correlated with Conventional interests and (for men but not for women) with Realistic interests. Also for men (but not, contrary to the theory, for women) spousal ratings of Introversion/Extraversion were positively correlated with Social and Enterprising interests. Overall, these finding suggested some commonalities between the two domains in a way that Holland's interest theory would predict but also provided early evidence that how personality was measured (self- vs. other-ratings) can moderate the results.

In a variation of this approach, Peraino and Willerman (1983) classified occupations and people on RIASEC interest dimensions separately. Participants' occupations (rather than their measured interests) were first classified by assigning high point interests to study participants' jobs using Holland's *Occupations Finder* (J. L. Holland, 1985a; see also G. D. Gottfredson & Holland, 1996) and were further classified by raters, using the Socioeconomic Index (SEI), as to the status level of the occupation. The researchers then analyzed personality data that had been collected from the participants as part of an adoptive parent evaluation. (Artistic and Conventional occupational groups were not represented by the jobs included in the sample.) Those employed in job groups classified as Enterprising and Social had the highest mean scores on Extraversion, with Investigative next and Realistic last. Investigative and Enterprising interest occupational groups scored highest on Tough Poise (and lowest on Social), whereas on the Field Independence scores, men in the Investigative and Enterprising occupations were higher (more field independent) than were those in the Social and Realistic occupations. The authors also found that those in the lower status Social interest occupational groups scored higher on Introversion/Extraversion (higher scores were in the extraverted direction) and lower on reported Anxiety (higher scores were in the anxious direction). The authors concluded that individuals in low status, high Social occupation groups may be better suited for direct care roles than for higher level positions in that group of occupations. Put another way, that finding suggested that there may be important moderators of relationships between interests and personality and that persons in the same broad occupational groups are likely not homogeneous. The study was limited by not having measured interests at the individual level and by use of what may well have been a nonrepresentative sample.

Gottfredson et al. (1993) conducted a study of VPI interests and NEO personality factor (and facet) scores with a sample of male and female U.S. Navy recruits. In separate analyses, they also integrated other studies to examine trends. The results were complicated because in the main study, male and female respondents differed somewhat in their results. In particular, for the combined sex sample there were four significant canonical correlations between interests and personality variables. These included Openness with Artistic and Investigative interests, Extraversion with Social and Enterprising interests, and Conscientiousness with Conventional interests. However, the canonical factors varied by sex.

In examining the correlations across the reported study and two other relevant studies, the authors calculated median correlations between RIASEC interests and FFM personality. The highest median correlations were between Extraversion and both Enterprising (.38) and Social (.26); between Control (Conscientiousness) and Conventional (.18); between Intellectance (a version of Openness) and Investigative (.20), Social (.12), and Artistic (.10); and between Likability (Agreeableness) and Social (.11), Artistic (.10), Investigative (.10), and negatively correlated with Enterprising interests (−.09). Except for the small positive correlation (.05) with Artistic scores, the correlations for Neuroticism and RIASEC variables were all negative (the highest, with Social, was −.18). These correlations were small to medium, and the authors concluded it was still necessary to measure both interests and personality, a conclusion reached by others (e.g., Waller et al., 1995).

Another type of study has considered the genetic basis of the interaction between interests and personality. Kandler et al. (2011), working with a German mono- and dizygotic twin population, examined the genetic links between FFM factors and interests using a German measure of interests that appeared to combine work and leisure interests. The authors interpreted their seven interest factors in terms of the six-factor RIASEC model. A noteworthy feature of the study was the inclusion both self- and other-ratings of both personality and interests. The relationships between the German version of interests they employed and the RIASEC model variables was inexact. In particular, the stimuli items used were not just work-related, and the interpretations put on some of these scales (e.g., Hedonistic-Enterprising, Domestic-Manual, Artistic-Creative, and Cultural-Intellectual) make it difficult to interpret the results in the context of other studies. Clearly, however, Openness was highly correlated with both of the Artistic factors (Cultural-Intellectual, .61; Artistic-Creative, .50), and, to a lesser extent with Technical-Logistic (.20) and Investigative-Scientific (.18). Also found was a high correlation (.35) with Extraversion and Hedonistic-Enterprising and, to a lesser degree, Social-Educational (.17). The correlations between Conscientiousness and the interest scores were relatively low (highest, .12, with Domestic-Manual) and, similarly, the highest correlation of Neuroticism was −.11, with Investigative-Scientific. The authors did consider the genetic and environmental overlap, finding that about a third of the genetic variance and a tenth of the environmental variance in interests was explained by personality, especially by Openness. Other studies of interests and personality in twins (e.g., Waller et al., 1995) also concluded that these domains were essentially separable and both needed to be measured.

A number of researchers (e.g., Dietrich, 2007, 2014; Knudsen et al., 2019) have challenged some of the conclusions or the approach to research connecting creativity and psychopathology. They found fault with samples (elite eminent creators may be different than others with creative interests), the criteria for creativity, and the manner in which mental illness was defined or determined. Recent studies have tried to work around some of these challenges. C. Waddell (1998) and more recently Lauronen et al. (2004) conducted literature reviews of studies finding a link between mental illness and creativity. Removing studies that lacked control groups or that were not well designed, they still found a statistical link between the two areas.

Wiernik et al. (2016) used criterion profile analysis to examine interest-personality relationships among 19 creative samples. They found Investigative and Artistic interests both to be associated with Openness. However, the respective profiles differed thereafter, with Investigative interests being associated with high Conscientiousness and Emotional Stability, and Artistic interests being associated with lower scores on both of those personality dimensions. Investigative interest profiles were also associated with lower scores on Extraversion and Agreeableness, and Artistic interest profiles were also associated with lower scores on Assertiveness. These findings were persistent across the personality measures used and suggested that it was the profile pattern that drove the results, not individual variables.

Other studies examined specific personality variables and specific interests. Witkin et al. (1977) found an association between field independence (which can be considered as both a measure of personality and of ability) and expressed interests in the Realistic and Investigative areas and, among field-dependent people, increased expression of Social and Enterprising interests. This is in keeping with the idea that field dependence may be better for fitting in with and understanding the context of other people, whereas Realistic and Investigative occupations more often require an externalized, objective perspective.

Several other interest-personality studies are reported in the literature (e.g., Bolton, 1985; De Fruyt & Mervielde, 1997; G. D. Gottfredson et al., 1993), most with a similar methodology at least as far as comparing Holland's RIASEC types and self-reported scores on personality measures.

De Fruyt and Merivelde (1997) compared RIASEC interests and NEO FFM variables in the context of predicting postcollege employment in a European sample. Examining only the zero order correlations, they found a rather high correlation (.54) between Openness and Artistic interest scores. Openness was also highly correlated with Social interests (.42). High Artistic interests were negatively correlated with Conscientiousness (−.20). Realistic interests were correlated negatively with Introversion/Extraversion (−.12) and with Neuroticism (here, and unless otherwise noted, high scores were in the less-well-adjusted direction; −.14). Investigative interests correlated only with Neuroticism (−.32), but the usual association was found between Introversion/Extraversion and Social (.26) and Enterprising (.44) interests. The research also found correlations between Conventional interests and Conscientiousness (.44) and Neuroticism (−.26).

The study went on to compare personality and interests in predicting job finding. Among the FFM variables, only Conscientiousness and Extraversion predicted having a job a year after graduation, while the interest variables did not add incremental variance. Interests did predict, however, better than did personality variables to a job classification system reflecting the types of activities required in the job. In examining the personality variable differences between the employed and the much smaller unemployed group (335 vs. 66), the two groups on which the not-yet-employed and the employed differed significantly were, in order, Conscientiousness, Introversion/Extraversion, Neuroticism, and Openness. The employed group had a three letter Holland code of Investigative–Enterprising–Social and the unemployed, Investigative–Social–Enterprising. Overall, the authors concluded that personality variables were more effective at predicting to employer-related variables, and interests to employee-related ones.

P. L. Ackerman and Heggestad (1997) used a somewhat different methodology to examine relationships between interests and personality variables (they also focused on abilities, and on aggregation across the groups of three variable types, which is discussed later in this chapter). Interests and personality in this review article were somewhat less of a focus than the ability-personality and ability-interests relationships, but the authors did note positive correlations between Social and Enterprising interests and Introversion/Extraversion and Openness. They also reported from their cross-study analyses a positive correlation of Openness and Investigative interests. Negative correlations were reported between Artistic Interests and Traditionalism. Conscientiousness, Traditionalism, and Control, they found, were correlated with Conventional interests. Their conclusion that neither Agreeableness nor Neuroticism were associated with any of the six RIASEC types was not consistent with some of the studies reviewed here, and they found Realistic interests were not correlated with any personality variables. Interestingly, they also found well-being, probably a facet scale of Neuroticism/Adjustment (or a reverse-scored Neuroticism scale), to be associated with Social and Enterprising interests. Finally, they identified a variable they labeled harm-avoidance, which was used to describe those prone to excessive worrying and fearfulness (likely a facet scale of Neuroticism). Scores on harm-avoidance had negative correlations with Artistic interests. In a subsequent study using the Ackerman and Heggestad's interdomain model, the Multidimensional Personality Questionnaire (MPQ), to measure personality and the Strong Interest Inventory to measure interests, Staggs et al. (2007) reported slightly different findings within the four trait complexes that had been identified in the earlier study.

Larson et al. (2002) noted the lack of interest-personality studies in their meta-analysis/theory development study. They conducted a meta-analysis of 24 samples that employed three popularly used measures of the RIASEC interests and the Revised NEO Personality Inventory. The findings that were common to women and men and across all the interest measures were associations between Artistic and Investigative interests with Openness, Enterprising and Social interests with Extraversion, and Social interests with Agreeableness. Of course, the study limited the variance by relying on studies that used only one FFM measure.

An important meta-analysis by Barrick et al. (2003) considered the then-extant studies examining interest-personality relationships. Using primarily studies that had employed self-ratings of both interests and personality, they examined a series of hypotheses about the relationship of interests and personality. These included predictions that Social and Enterprising interests would be correlated with Extraversion, Agreeableness with Social interests, and Openness with Artistic and Investigative interests. Some hypotheses (e.g., that Conscientiousness would be especially related to Conventional interests) were less persuasive since Conscientiousness has shown such broad predictive power across occupations; see Chapter 14 of this book). Barrick et al. (2003) included the results of 21 studies (only 13 of which had been published in peer-reviewed journals) with 41 independent samples. Curiously omitted from their meta-analysis were peer-reviewed studies that focused on the relations between and among interests, personality, and abilities (e.g., Carless, 1999; Lowman et al., 1985), since such studies also included data on interest-personality relationships.

The authors' hypotheses were generally confirmed, especially for Extraversion and Enterprising and Social interests, and for Openness with Artistic and Investigative interests. There were small to moderate correlations (using rho [ρ] as the aggregated correlation across studies when correcting for sample size and unreliability). Specifically, $\rho = .29$ and .41 for the correlations with Extraversion and Social, respectively; $\rho = .25$ and .39, respectively, for Openness and Investigative and Openness and Artistic; $\rho = .15$ between Agreeableness and Social; and $\rho = .19$ between Conscientiousness and Conventional. There was also a small association ($\rho = .12$) between Emotional Stability and Investigative. Significant moderators were found for working versus student status (with being employed rather than being a student increasing the magnitude of the interest-personality relationship especially for Enterprising-Openness). They also found a small moderator effect for use of Holland-based RIASEC measures and for use of personality variables other than the FFM factors. Other potential moderators were considered. These included sex and whether or not an ipsative measurement approach (removing a generalized response taking variable before analyzing the relationships) was used. Both of these variables were found to moderate the interest-personality relationships. Additionally, the use of FFM rather than facet scales were reported to moderate the magnitude of the associations, with FFM variables having higher relationships with interests than did facet scales.

Overall, these results suggest promising overlap between interests and personality, mostly in the hypothesized directions. In most cases the magnitude of the significant hypothesized relationships were moderate, not high, suggesting that, although there are some predictable relationships between interests and personality variables, each of these domains needs to be separately measured.

Mount et al. (2005) examined the relationship between FFM personality traits and RIASEC types in a complicated, but important, meta-analytic study of the interaction not just between interests and personality at the factor or variable level but rather at the structural, or higher-order, level. This research is difficult to summarize briefly, but several important findings can be noted.

Specifically, Mount et al. (2005) employed cluster analysis and multidimensional scaling methods using 46 independent samples and 12,433 individuals to identify what they called the "higher-order structure" of interests and personality. They included data sets, not all of which were in each of the analyses, that used a variety of RIASEC interest measures (VPI, SDS, Strong, Career Assessment Inventory [CAI], and Unisex Edition of the ACT Interest Inventory [UNIACT]; see Chapter 2) and, on the personality side, by the FFM (as measured by the NEO Personality Inventory [NEO-PI], the Hogan Personality Inventory, and two other personality measures).

Although their primary focus was on the higher-order factors, these authors also provided meta-analytic correlations (rho $[\rho]$) between and among interest and personality factors taken two at a time. The strongest associations within interests were found between Enterprising and Conventional (.53), Social and Enterprising (.51), Realistic and Investigative (.45), Artistic and Social (.39), and Investigative and Artistic (.36). Among the personality factors, the strongest relationships were between Emotional Stability (labeled Stability) and Conscientiousness (.52) and Extraversion with Openness (.45). Across the two domains, Realistic interests were not significantly correlated with personality factors. However, Artistic (.41) and Investigative (.25) interests were associated with Openness, Social (.29) and Enterprising (.40) with Extraversion, and Conventional (.19) interests with Conscientiousness.

They identified three higher-order dimensions from their analyses. The first higher-order factor, labeled γ (gamma), was loaded on by the six interest factors clustered together in a way consistent with the RIASEC theory and separable from personality. There were, however, two, not one, personality dimensions that the authors interpreted as being consistent with Digman's (1997) work that identified two higher-order personality factors, summarized by Mount et al. (2005) as follows:

> [Digman] found support for two—and only two—higher-order factors. Factor α [alpha] consisted of the FFM factors of Conscientiousness, Emotional Stability, and Agreeableness, whereas Factor β [beta] consisted of the FFM factors of Extraversion and Openness to Experience. According to Digman (1997) Factor α pertains to impulse restraint, conscience, low hostility and aggression, and neurotic defense. Factor β refers to actualization of the self, venturesome encounters with life, openness to new experiences, and use of one's intellect. (p. 451)

Mount et al. (2005) found that the personality dimensions were separable from interests and that the shared variance across all interests represented "the desire to engage in activities that are liked and to avoid those that are disliked" (p. 468). Concerning personality, they identified two higher-order personality factors that they interpreted as being similar to Digman's Factor α and Factor β. They described α, which was loaded on by Conscientiousness, Emotional Stability, and (secondarily) Agreeableness, as representing impulse control and β, loaded on by Extraversion and Openness, as representing an engaged, self-actualizing, prosocial approach to life.

In the attempt to further understand the relationships between interests, the authors used a technique called Property Vector fitting. They identified 16 characteristics or properties thought to be related to interests and personality. Examples include preferences for involvement with data, ideas, things, and/or people; conformity; and having broad preferences. These variables were reduced to 11, eliminating those accounting for insufficiently high variance (R^2). Guided by the vector analyses, the authors refined the interpretation of the three dimensions. The first, interests versus personality traits, was noted to reaffirm the RIASEC six-factor model. The second was interpreted as still reflecting a conformity dimension but also identifying striving for traditional achievement versus for personal growth. The third vector identified a preference for interacting with people versus things. Integrating some of the cluster and vector analysis work, the authors found that the preference for things versus people vector was anchored, respectively, by Investigative and Realistic interests and Emotional Stability for things, and by Social and Enterprising interests and Extraversion for people. Ideas and Abstract preferences were associated with Artistic Interests and Openness and Agreeableness. Opposite Ideas and Abstract were Data, Accomplishment (anchored by Conscientiousness), and Conformity (anchored by Conventional interests).

Since the described meta-analyses, several studies have appeared, some taking new and promising directions. A representative sampling of these studies is presented here.

Burns et al. (2013) examined personality and interest measures as predictors of career indecision (among other variables). They found confirming evidence in some, but not all, cases for the general trends identified in the studies already discussed. In particular, statistically significant relations were found between Extraversion and Social and Enterprising interests, between Openness and Artistic and Investigative interests, and between Agreeableness and Social interests. However, negative correlations were found between Agreeableness with Realistic and Investigative interests, Openness with Conventional interests, and Neuroticism with Realistic, Social, and Enterprising interests but positively with Conventional interests.

Several studies exploring this space have examined the connections between the Holland ("Big Six") interest measures and personality in specific populations (e.g., Duffy et al., 2009), and others have examined the relationship of facets of personality and interests. For example, Larson and Borgen (2002) considered the relationship of 30 facet scales from an NEO measure and 11 primary scales of the MPQ personality measure with the Basic Interest Scales (BISs) of the 1985 Strong Interest Inventory measure in a sample of gifted adolescents. They found that the RIASEC and FFM factors were correlated, as in many of the other studies reported here (Openness was correlated with Artistic and Investigative interests, Extraversion with Enterprising and Social interests, and Agreeableness with Social interests). However, the authors also found that the use of facet-level variables (in particular, the BISs of the Strong and the facets of the personality measures) in some cases was more productive than examining the relationships between the higher level factors. As discussed in Chapter 13, however, there are concerns with the current state of research on facet scales of personality as related to career and work issues (see, e.g., Connelly et al., 2018).

Of course, the degree of relationship between interests and personality will be affected by the particular model of personality (and, for that matter, the model of interests) used. McKay and Tokar (2012) compared the results on the HEXACO personality measure and FFM measures of personality to RIASEC occupational interests. For both sexes, they found several of the somewhat predictable correlations between Openness and Investigative and Artistic interests but also with Social interests. They also found Agreeableness correlated with Social interests. Extraversion was positively correlated with Social interests but otherwise varied by sex. For women, Extraversion was positively associated with Artistic and Enterprising interests, and for men it was positively associated with Investigative interests and negatively correlated with Realistic, Investigative, and Conventional interests. For the two variables that were somewhat differentiated from the FFM, Honesty-Humility and Emotionality, patterns differed by sex. Specifically, for both sexes, Honesty-Humility scores correlated positively with Social interests and negatively with Enterprising ones. For men only, the Honesty-Humility scores also correlated positively with Agreeableness and negatively with Conscientiousness. Emotionality was correlated negatively with Realistic interests for both sexes and, for women, negatively with Investigative interests and, for men, negatively with Conventional interests. Overall, the authors concluded that the HEXACO measure had more, and stronger, correlations between interests and personality variables, but further research is needed examining the HEXACO scales with interest variables.

A recent study by Hoff et al. (2019) was based on longitudinal data measuring interests and personality of Icelandic youth collected over three time periods at ages 16, 18, 22, and 24. Specifically, they administered an Icelandic version of one of the NEO-PI measures and an interest measure developed for use in Iceland, the Icelandic Interest Inventory. The study focused primarily on the stability and change within interest and personality domains, but one interdomain hypothesis was examined. The study was unusual in considering stability and change at both the individual and grouped level and in its inclusion of four waves of both personality and interest measurement.

The participants included in the study were students in randomly selected high schools from across Iceland. The Icelandic Interest Measure (I and II) included 114 items and focused on preferences for school subjects and work activities that were designed to reflect the structure of the Icelandic labor market. The authors provided relatively little information about the validation of the measure, and the two cited references containing validation data about the instrument were in the Icelandic language. Although customizing an interest measure to a particular labor market may make it much more relevant for a particular application, it may also limit its ability to cover the full range of interests. This issue is relevant because, on average, across all four administrations of tests, the profile of the group as a whole showed Artistic and Social interests as the most highly endorsed interests, alternating between Conventional and Investigative as the third most highly endorsed interests, and Realistic interests were on average the lowest endorsed interests. These average characteristics may describe a sample that is more open, creative, and interested in helping roles and less interested in working on mechanical or "hands-on" practical activities.

Concerning interest-personality relationships, the authors had predicted that five pairs of correlations (Extraversion-Social, Extraversion-Enterprising, Openness-Artistic, Openness-Investigative, Conscientiousness-Conventional) would be stronger than correlated changes across general factors and than was the case with the other 25 specific pairings of Big Five traits with RIASEC interests (e.g., Realistic interests with Agreeableness). Despite high correlations between the variables, only Extraversion-Enterprising, Openness-Artistic, and Conscientiousness-Conventional met the criteria associated with the hypothesis of correlated changes. Although Extraversion-Social and Openness-Investigative associations did not exhibit correlated change, the correlations were still high, and the authors interpreted that, in such cases, the changes had likely already occurred by age 16.

As for the 25 other cross-domain relationships that had not been predicted to have correlated changes across the waves of the study, two of these did have high correlated change: Conscientious-Enterprising and Extraversion-Conventional. All of the changes in interest-personality pairs showed positive change over time except for Openness-Realistic and Openness-Conventional. Both pairs showed negative relationships, respectively, of −.37 and −.31.

Of special interest were the findings related to the developmental nature of interests and personality, with the data showing that interests as measured in this study were, on an individual basis, relatively stable over time in the order of endorsement of the six RIASEC factors. However, on average, over time some aspects of personality changed from adolescence to young adulthood, with slight increases in Agreeableness, Openness, and Conscientiousness. The authors also noted that individuals who were at higher levels of interests or abilities at the first data collection point exhibited less change over the study. Overall, however, both personality and interests tended to become more stable over time. The authors covered considerably more ground in this important article, including a model for understanding why specific interests and personality variables may change from youth to adulthood.

The What and the Why

Summarizing the personality-interest interdomain relationships, from a research perspective there are several reliable overlaps of variables across these two domains, some promising possibilities, and other relationships that do not seem to have much in common, at least as currently measured. The most supported correlates to date are Openness with Artistic and Investigative interests (and in some studies to Social interests), Extraversion with Social and (in most studies) Enterprising interests, and Conscientiousness (at least in some studies) with Conventional interests. Although Agreeableness has been one of the least productive variables in FFM outcome research, in some studies it did show a positive relationship with Social interests and in a few, a negative relationship with Enterprising. At the facet level, there are some promising leads, but more research is needed since most studies focused on the FFM and consensus on facets of personality is still lacking. Additionally, when personality and interests are examined at the higher-order level, they are demonstrated to be separable but both important in defining certain second-order vectors. This suggests that interests are different in kind from personality but still overlapping.

These are useful findings because they point to potential ways of integrating data and to knowing what to look for when comparing across these domains. Yet in reviewing the areas of strong overlap, the question arises as to *why* some areas overlap and others do less so. Hoff et al. (2019) carefully considered this question and suggested that there should be overlap when the characteristics associated with an interest area have commonality with the characteristics associated with personality. In particular, they built on Wrzus et al.'s (2016) idea that certain "triggering situations" may provide a potential link between personality and motivational interest measures. For example, Social interests include preferences for activities that involve helping, nurturing, and mentoring, and extraversion tends to place people in situations in which there is contact with other people. Because people repeat activities they like (and avoid the ones they do not like), those situations tend to make use of personality characteristics that are relevant, which may in turn get stronger.

Hoff et al. (2019) also found an association between each of the six RIASEC types and personality except for Realistic, which they characterized as involving, "Working with hands, tools, and materials (farmworker, civil engineer, carpenter)" (p. 2). This reflected the low correlations typically found between Realistic interests and most of the FFM factors, but some did emerge, if not consistently in the studies reviewed here. As discussed in Chapter 14 the FFM does have limitations, but at the same time the question of why there was no personality variable associated with Realistic interests is curious. Do people with realistic interests not experience triggering situations? Are their personalities not relevant for their interests? A possible factor is that personality variables tend to be focused on the positive ends of the personality spectrum and not the opposite polarity. Thus, the triggering situations for Realistic types may be related to positive reactions to activities and situations that are not well addressed by the FFM factors. For example, the usual focus is on the extraverted end of the Introversion/Extraversion scale (even the scale's commonly used name focuses the attention there). But instead of seeing introversion as being the opposite of extraversion (i.e., focusing on introversion as being nonextraversion), it may be that the "triggering situations" draw Realistic types to things and away from people. This, if true, might be associated with negative correlations between Realistic and Extraversion, which have only sometimes been found, but it may also be that different personality variables or alternative measures of social introversion/extraversion are needed to find triggers.

Individual Level Assessment Implications

Interdomain interest-personality research findings can be confirmatory or inconsistent with assessment findings when working at the individual level. At the group level, aggregations of variables may be effective in looking at general trends but have limits when applied at the individual level (see, e.g., Nye et al., 2018). Thus, when a person with, say, strong Social or Enterprising interests scores is clearly extraverted, that is expected and, in these variables at least, consistent with prosocial or managerial career directions. When, on the other hand, Social or Enterprising interest patterns are associated with a high preference for introversion, this pattern needs to be contextualized so that clients understand that such a combination does not necessarily imply the need to avoid pursuit of Social or Enterprising occupations. Rather, the client needs to understand how introversion may need to be taken into account in specific work roles. Teachers in the K–12 grades, for example, are typically in constant contact with students, seemingly a job calling for extraversion. However, those talented in nurturing others and helping them to learn can function perfectly well in the teaching role as long as they can find ways to address their need for time alone, perhaps outside of work.

Similarly, Enterprising types are largely extraverted. Extraversion sometimes predicts to success in managerial roles (see Chapter 10). Yet, someone who has strong Enterprising interests but who is by nature introverted can find many roles in business and management that call for intensive focus on detail and concentration. While not eschewing pursuit of more extraverted aspects of management, a career assessor or counselor can help introverted Enterprising interest individuals understand what introversion is (including that it is not something chosen), how it works, where it will be helpful, and where it needs to be worked around in the accomplishment of work duties. Conversely, they should understand that in many business contexts they will be surrounded by highly extraverted people intent on having influence and keen on sharing their ideas with others (and having them prevail). Learning how to present themselves as being more extraverted than they may feel on the inside may be needed.

As another example of apparent misfits with general trends, the correlation of Artistic interests with Openness is consistently among the highest interest-personality relationships. Yet those with Artistic interests can be both in general open and not particularly open, flexible, or adaptable in some aspects of personality. For example, playing a musical instrument in a symphony may be associated with high Artistic interests but also with the need for rigorous practice and skills development. These may or may not be associated with Openness but would be benefitted by Conscientiousness. In contrast, composers, who create new music, may be different from those who play others' music for their living. Openness may therefore be more complex and nuanced than a simple score on a self-reported measure of personality. Famous creative types may be highly conceptually open to new ideas and at the same time quite rigid when it comes to their particular views, particularly when they are under attack.

Other personality variables that may not correlate highly with interests may still need attention on an individual basis. For example, Conscientiousness has not been shown to correlate very well with interests other than Conventional and, inversely, Artistic. Yet the literature reports this personality factor as one of the ones with the highest correlations with job performance. Artistic interest types scoring low on measures of Conscientiousness may need help in developing Conscientious-related behavior to facilitate transforming their ideas into reality. To succeed, creative types still need self-discipline, and this may be a needed focus of career counseling. Unless they are in the eminent class (e.g., Picasso or Frank Lloyd Wright), most painters and architects are expected to deliver contracted work on time, to show up for meetings, and to be civil to their clients. Of course, persons in other career pursuits may also suffer from deficits in self-discipline or civility, but in many occupations, such as in medicine, the structure of the career and the highly disciplined nature of the work context forces compliance with schedules and service delivery. Conversely, creative individuals with "too high" scores in Conscientiousness may find themselves overly constrained and less likely to generate novel ideas that may be needed to be successful.

In summary, the goal of the career assessor and counselor is to understand an individual in the context of the person's particular career goals and objectives, stage in the career/life cycle, and practical realities. Central trends and mean or modal tendencies are helpful in understanding patterns often encountered, but clients still need to be assessed and understood as individuals whose results may, or may not, match the typical associations.

INTEREST-ABILITY RELATIONSHIPS

Interest-ability relationships have not been as well searched as have those of interests and personality. Even though interests have been studied for over a century, examining their relationship with abilities has not been a major focus even after Holland's work. But occasional studies were published early on and more in the last few decades.

An unusual early study by Tyler (1951) examined the relationship of interests in particular activities with abilities and reputation (personality) among first-grade children in Oregon. Tyler used an empirically derived test of interests that included liking for (a) active outdoor play, (b) indoor play with toys, (c) paper-pencil-crayon activities, and (d) helping adults at work. Arguably, these interests could be related to RIASEC terms as follows: Realistic (active outdoor play), Investigative (indoor play with toys), Artistic (paper-pencil-crayon activities), or Social (helping adults at work) interests. A masculinity-femininity scale was also derived from the male-female differences in preferences. Tyler also compared results of these measured interests—along with peer reputation, which included characteristics like "talkative-silent," "bossy-submissive," "popular-unpopular"—with the results of an age-appropriate ability test, the SRA Primary Mental Abilities Test for children ages 5 and 6 (at the time of the study, the only such test then available for that age group). The SRA ability measure included Verbal, Perceptual, Quantitative, Motor, and Spatial subtests as well as an overall ability score. The results differed for boys and girls. For the girls, there were no statistically significant correlations between the abilities and interests. However, for boys, Verbal test scores correlated positively (.37) with a preference for paper-pencil-crayon activities and negatively (−.28) with helping. Spatial abilities for boys correlated .42 with paper-pencil-crayon preferences and −.33 with helping. The spatial measure also correlated positively (.32) with masculinity. These results, for boys, were mirrored in the overall (aggregated) ability/interest correlations (paperwork, .39; helping, −.39). The author did not make clear whether paper-pencil-crayon activities were primarily drawing or other writing activities. If the former, the results with Spatial ability would parallel findings for interest-ability results found in adults many years later. Of course, this study had limitations for generalizing to adults but it was an innovative and early examination of interest-ability-personality relationships of young children.

Other early studies of interest-ability relationships (e.g., Berdie, 1943; Darley, 1941; R. W. Johnson, 1965; Strong, 1943; for reviews of some of this literature, see L. S. Gottfredson, 1986b; Lowman et al., 1985; Randahl, 1990) also predated the RIASEC vocational interest theory (see Chapter 2). Such studies (and even some of the ones that followed, such as Kelso et al., 1977; R. G. Turner & Hibbs, 1977) tended to find few associations, most small, between interests and abilities. However, those studies have typically been limited in the use of relatively few measures of abilities (primarily variations of measures of intelligence, especially verbal intelligence), male rather than mixed-sex samples, and highly select samples (mostly intellectually able college students). Later studies, however, have corrected some of the deficits of early studies and have extended the literature with new methodologies.

Turning to more recent research, several major studies in the 1980s and 1990s began the trend of assessing across interests, abilities, and personality. In this section, the focus is on the ability-interest findings of these studies.

In a sample of college women, Lowman et al. (1985) examined associations between abilities corresponding to each of the six Holland interest types and vocational interests as measured by the SDS (J. L. Holland, 1979, 1987). These researchers found a similar factor structure between these ability measures and the six-factor interest model, except that (a) no ability factor analogous to the Realistic area emerged in this female sample and (b) there were two ability areas (music and visual arts), rather than one, corresponding to the Artistic area. Common variance across the abilities and the interest variables, however, was relatively low.

Using a different methodology, different tests of ability and interests, and a heterogeneous career assessment sample, Randahl's (1990) dissertation research provided new perspectives on the relation between interests and abilities. In that study, profile analyses rather than correlational and canonical analyses were used, though correlations were also reported. The Strong Vocational Interest Blank/Strong Campbell Interest Inventory (SVIB-SCII; Hansen, 1986) were employed as measures of interests, and the subtests of the General Aptitude Test Battery (GATB; U.S. Department of Labor, 1970, 1979), a test developed for use with the general population, was used as the measure of abilities. The author hypothesized that certain GATB measures of abilities (e.g., verbal, numerical, spatial abilities) would be associated with particular interest types, but she framed her study as a typological approach rather than a correlational one. The study examined the pattern of ability profiles of each of the single six high-point-defined interest groups with selected GATB abilities. In terms of which abilities were correlated with which RIASEC type, Spatial had the highest correlation with Realistic (.34) and Investigative (.27) interests; Verbal with Artistic (.28) and Investigative (.22); Numerical with Investigative (.23) and Conventional (.15); Clerical Perception with Artistic (.13) and, negatively, with Realistic (–.13); Motor Coordination with Artistic (.10) and Social (.10); Manual Dexterity with Realistic (.09); and Form Perception with Investigative (.16) and Realistic (.13). No statistically significant correlations between interests and ability were associated with the GATB Finger Dexterity test. Unfortunately, the author did not report the correlations, or any other data or analyses, between interests and General Learning Ability, the single best measure of general intelligence on the GATB. Not surprisingly, however, the correlation between measures of Verbal and Numerical intelligence (.53) and high correlates of general intelligence with some of the other ability variables suggested that general intelligence was probably a strong factor affecting the results.

Although the patterns of correlations among the variables cannot be ignored, Randahl's (1990) primary purpose was to examine patterns of abilities in their relationship with the so-called typological analyses. She therefore examined mean differences between the average ability scores among the various high point interest groups. For example, in comparing the abilities associated with the Realistic and the Investigative groups, Randahl found the Investigative group to be higher than the Realistic group on the verbal and numerical abilities and the Realistic group to be higher on spatial abilities. Comparing Realistic and Social group ability patterns, the Realistic group scored higher on Spatial and Motor Coordination. The Realistic group was also higher than the Investigative, Social, Enterprising, and Conventional groups on Spatial, and so forth. The rank order profiles for each high point interest group is provided in the article (Table 4, p. 345), and the order of endorsement in many cases was consistent with what would be predicted by Holland's theory (e.g., Conventional and Clerical Perception), but there were several findings that were counter to theory findings (e.g., all groups except Realistic had Clerical Perception as their highest GATB score).

Although this was an important study at the time it was published, it had several limitations. First, it was based on people who had sought assistance from a university's vocational clinic, so the sample may or may not be representative of the general population. Supporting that view were the findings that the sample was higher than average on education level and on test scores on the cognitive abilities Second, interests were defined solely by the highest endorsed interest score, minimizing important individual differences and cross interest patterns (e.g., ability patterns of Realistic-Investigative vs., say, Realistic-Social people). Indeed, in examining the three digit codes of each of the six profile groups for their three, rather than single, highest interest codes (Realistic–Investigative–Artistic, Investigative–Artistic–Realistic, Artistic–Investigative–Enterprising, Social–Artistic–Enterprising, and Conventional–Enterprising–Social), the first three of these codes had Investigative interests either first or second and five of the six groups had Artistic interests in their top three. Third, the study was limited by using the GATB test, which did not include measures that related to specific abilities associated with Artistic, Social, or Enterprising areas. Fourth, the study eliminated from reporting or analyses the measure of general intelligence (a composite of Verbal, Numerical, and, curiously, Spatial Ability), ignoring the general intelligence correlates of the cognitive ability measures.

Other studies of interest-ability overlaps have placed special emphasis on general intelligence, with occasional inclusion of facets (subfactors) of general intelligence such as Nonverbal Intelligence or primary abilities such as Spatial ability. It is still rare, however, to find objective measures of abilities corresponding to all areas of interest including artistic/creative, social, and managerial abilities. Further studies in this area have helped expand the evidence on ability-interest relationships using different methodologies or by examining a selection of interests and/or abilities. These studies are difficult to aggregate because they took very different approaches to variables, measures, and study design. Nevertheless, these studies are of interest.

Austin and Hanisch (1990), in a longitudinal study, examined a composite of abilities and interests with a large sample of Project TALENT youth assessed in 10th grade who were followed into their occupations 11 years after they had graduated from high school. The data used in this study were part of a much larger group of student data gathered some time before this publication. Verbal, math, technical, and spatial/reasoning constituted the ability measure groupings. Interests were organized into 14 scales corresponding to 12 occupational groups (e.g., musical and artistic interests represented fine and performing arts occupations). The interest measures intentionally left out many of what today would be called Realistic interests, and the scales they developed seem to have preceded the RIASEC model. Four factors emerged as important in predicting from the data collected in 10th grade to later occupational pursuits. The first factor was a general ability/verbal intelligence one that had the highest canonical discriminant function, whereas the second factor emphasized mathematical ability as assessed in high school and gender. Only in the third function, which explained 6.3% of the variance, were interests of primary importance. This function was especially associated with physical science, medical, and social service, and women were higher on this function. The final small factor was one associated with nursing and lab tech roles, and again women were more represented than the men. Because of this study's methodology, the interest and ability profiles were combined when creating the 12 occupational categories into which participants' later work fell. The variables that best predicted placement were largely abilities with relatively minor additional contributions from the interests. As the authors put it, "Ability appears to be an overriding force in determining the upper endpoint of an individual's choice of occupation and, as such, is important in career counseling and placement decisions" (Austin & Hanisch, 1990, p. 83).

In a more recent study, Carless and Fallon (2002) compared scores of 880 women and 2,566 men using the Rothwell-Miller Interest Blank interest measure and two ability measures: the Raven's Standard Progressive Matrices and the Australian Council for Educational Research Higher Test ML-MQ (which yielded both quantitative and verbal ability scores). The data appeared to be an Australian convenience sample obtained from a consulting firm, and the interest measure and focused mostly on ranking within a series of occupational titles the ones that were most appealing. The occupations included ones that would correspond roughly to the six RIASEC types (e.g., mechanical paired with Realistic; scientific with Investigative; and musical and literary with Artistic). Overall, there were statistically significant correlations, but modest effect sizes, found between some of the interests and abilities including (for both sexes) between "scientific" and cognitive abilities and between verbal abilities and artistic-related occupational rankings. Realistic interests did not correlate with any of these abilities. Overall, this study had some limitations, including the interest measure used, lack of clarity as to the motivations of the test takers, and a narrow range of abilities, but still provided some useful suggestive information.

Other studies have examined interests and abilities in the context of particular, defined, groups. Lowman and Ng (2010) used a typological approach but focused just on Realistic types, a group for whom interest-ability data have been inconsistent or lacking, providing interesting assessment data. Participants, all male, from two widely separated locations of the same corporation in the paper industry, were evaluated in an assessment center. Almost all of the participants were high school graduates, and all were working at the company at the time of assessment. To be included in the research report, each participant had to have had Realistic interests as their highest endorsed RIASEC interest score. Almost no one was eliminated from the sample because the vast majority of those assessed scored highest on Realistic interests. The abilities showed a similar pattern for both groups. Compared with general population norms, they scored high (combined scores at the 80th percentile and 70th percentile, respectively) on two different measures of mechanical ability but scored low on spatial ability (30th percentile compared with Grade 12 norms on a widely used ability measure). On measures of general cognitive ability, they scored in the average to high average range, but, for both groups, they were higher on nonverbal than for verbal ability (combined sample standardized intelligence scores: 105.6, 112.8, and 108.8 for verbal, nonverbal, and full-scale scores, respectively). On a nonverbal cognitive ability measure, they scored at the 75th percentile and scored slightly lower (70th percentile) on a separate measure of verbal reasoning. Yet, on assessment center type measures of ability (speaking, leaderless group discussion, in-basket, and negotiating exercise), the overall group performance was only in the average range. Summarizing, these two groups of highly Realistic men had quite similar average ability profiles, with clear strengths on mechanical reasoning and nonverbal intelligence, and comparatively lower (but still average) verbal and managerial abilities. An implication of these findings is that studies that include only verbally dominated measures of ability may underestimate Realistic ability patterns. Additionally, a single measure of nonverbal ability (e.g., using only spatial measures, not mechanical ones) may also miss important strengths. High mechanical reasoning, low spatial ability patterns may be different from, say, high spatial, high mechanical ones. Finally, concerning Realistic interest measurements, these two groups were unambiguously highest on Realistic interests (they were after all included in the study on that basis), but otherwise their interest scores were not fully consistent when it came to the secondary and tertiary interest codes both across the groups (RSC for Group 1 and RCS for Group 2; combined samples RCS) and across the two measures (Strong vs. the VPI; RIE for Groups 1, 2, and the combined samples on the VPI). This finding is noteworthy since most studies include only one measure of interests and, particularly when going beyond the high point scores, the differences may matter.

Focusing on social abilities and interests, Wampold et al. (1995) examined self-reported social skills on Riggio's (1989) Social Skills Inventory (SSI) and primary General Occupational Theme (GOT) scores on the Strong Interest Inventory (Hansen & Campbell, 1985) measure of interests in a college student sample. They combined the six scores of the SSI into two categories: social coping skills (emotional expressivity, emotional sensitivity, and social expressivity) and what they termed problem-focused social skills (emotional control, social sensitivity, and social control). They predicted that the scores on social coping skills would be differentiated by high point interest types such that these skills scores would be highest among the group with highest Social interests and adjacent and lower as the circumplex distance between Social interests increased (see Chapter 9). They also predicted that social problem-solving skills would not be differentiated by high point interests scores. These hypotheses were supported. In a second study, a qualitative one, these authors went on to examine social interactions among chemistry lab members, all fully trained professionals or postdocs. Using direct observations and interviews, this study found that the interest patterns and SSI scores were similar as in Study 1 in that these participants were primarily Investigative and Realistic interest types who scored higher on social problem solving than on social coping skills. The observed data matched this pattern with the important finding that the groups were not asocial and in fact engaged in frequent social interaction, both work-related and nonwork-related. However, the nature of their interactions was primarily of the "social problem-solving" type even when addressing areas in which there was conflict. Although this study, like all studies, had its flaws and limitations, it was important in demonstrating that the specific type (or subtype) of ability may matter and that what is found in a college undergraduate study may be replicated in a work setting and describe real-world behavior.

Howland (2015), also working with Social interest-related abilities along with general cognitive ability, in a diverse sample of U.S. and international students and nonstudents, examined the relationships of interests, abilities, and personality, comparing whether two groups of individuals, one high on Social interests and one high on Enterprising interests, differed on a social ability measure (the Mayer-Salovey-Caruso Emotional Intelligence Test [MSCEIT]; Mayer et al., 2002) and a nonverbal measure of General Mental Ability (GMA; the Raven's Advanced Progressive Matrices; Raven, n.d.). These measures, along with a measure of personality, were administered electronically and in different contexts, including with a group of high ability international MBA students, but the MSCEIT scores were correlated significantly only with Realistic, Enterprising, and Conventional interests, in each case negatively. There were statistically significant correlations, all positive, between each interest type except for Social and GMA. The pattern of correlations was counterintuitive in the case of the MSCEIT but somewhat consistent with the theory for the GMA correlations. It is possible that the heterogeneous nature of the sample and the varying motivations for research participation may have affected the results. Additionally, a verbal measure of intelligence would likely have been a better test of cognitive ability with these two interest types than a nonverbal one.

Prediger (1982), using a nationally representative sample of high school seniors ($n = 4,679$), considered the relationship of interests and self-estimates of abilities and occupational choice. Using canonical correlation analyses, interests and abilities were found to correspond with occupational choice. Interests were found to have a higher correspondence to occupational choices than were ability self-estimates. Career certainty, gender, and ethnicity were considered as possible moderators, but only ethnicity was a moderator.

P. L. Ackerman and Heggestad (1997) examined interest and ability relationships as part of a larger meta-analysis of interests, abilities, and personality, which is further discussed in the "Interest-Ability-Personality" section of this chapter. Here, however, it can be noted that this study considered a selection of empirical studies of interest-ability relationships. They reported a relationship between spatial, mechanical, and mathematical abilities with science and engineering interests (Realistic and Investigative interests), though, of note, mechanical abilities more closely associated with Realistic than with Investigative interests. They also reported that literary interests and literary abilities were associated with verbal ability and literature achievement, and that interests in social services were negatively associated with math and spatial abilities. This study drew attention to early work that had found association between general intelligence and depth and breadth of interests. Of the studies they reviewed, however, few included measures related to clerical, social, managerial, or artistic abilities, so their review was primarily of the relationship of (some) cognitive abilities and interests. Additionally, the authors' approach favored the use of typical, versus optimal, intellectual engagement (TIE), a perspective not commonly used, differentiating it from many of the studies they reviewed.

Oswald and Ferstl (1999) examined the "Occupational" items from the Strong Interest Inventory (Hansen & Campbell, 1985) and found that they could be grouped into the four ability clusters (Physical, Bureaucratic, Social and Economic, and Artistic) of L. Gottfredson's Occupational Aptitude Patterns Map. They reported that the ability and interest domains using this method overlapped with each other and were complementary.

Tracey and Hopkins (2001) took a different approach to considering interests and self-rated abilities, working at a higher level of aggregation than the studies so far considered. They employed Prediger's distinction between "things-people" and "data-ideas" to classify interests, abilities, and jobs chosen. Specifically, they considered whether self-rated abilities corresponded to self-rated UNIACT-measured interests (Prediger, 1982) in a large sample of high school seniors and predicted to preferred job choice on the World of Work (Prediger, 2002) inventory. Occupational choice data were focused on students' self-declared "future job choices." Interests, self-rated abilities, and job choices were all placed on the structural bipolar dimensions of data versus ideas and things versus people. Interests (classified only on those dimensions, not on the RIASEC factors), more than self-rated abilities, predicted the occupational choice measures, but self-rated abilities did add some explanatory power. Ethnicity was a moderator of these relationships. Of course, occupational choices as a high school senior are not the same thing as actual occupational choices and variance is reduced by focusing on just underlying structural dimensions.

W. Johnson and Bouchard (2009) examined some interest-ability relationships using an approach called latent class analysis, in which individuals can be categorized and grouped on the basis of their scores on multiple measures with a method that classifies people rather than (as with factor analysis) variables. These groupings are called latent classes. Working with an age-diverse, but perhaps nonrepresentative sample (participants in the Minnesota Study of Twins Reared Apart), the authors used a subset of already-collected data that included scores on a wide range of abilities, interests, and general intelligence to test their models. The model of intelligence from which they worked was called the Verbal-Perceptual-Image Rotation (g-VPR) model (W. Johnson & Bouchard, 2005; see Chapter 5), which, in addition to general intelligence, differentiated three more specific aspects of intelligence: Verbal, Perceptual, and Rotational. Verbal had to do with the usual aspects of verbal intelligence (vocabulary, reasoning with words, and the like), Rotational was a spatial dimension having to do with abstract reasoning involving figures (nonverbal tasks), and Perceptual had to do with focused attention on concrete detail versus being able rapidly to discern patterns and to provide new responses. The authors created eight, which they considered to be a manageable number, of interest/ability groups. These were labeled Leadership, Culture, Science, Administration, Personal Care, Adventure, and Exploration, and these groups were composed of specific participants in the samples. These groups were examined using high point RIASEC codes, and those were generally consistent with expectations (e.g., Leadership with Enterprising-Conventional, Science with Investigative-Artistic, and Personal Care with Social-Conventional).

In summarizing a rather complex methodology briefly, the authors reduced their ability variables to three: rotation versus verbal (RV), focus versus diffusion (FD), and general intelligence (GI). The RV was anchored on the verbal end by high verbal skills and on the rotation end by high spatial ones. The FD was anchored on one end by focused attention on detail and factual knowledge versus, on the other, the ability to glean patterns and to provide rapid, unstructured responses. The eight occupation groups' associated abilities varied in expected ways (e.g., the intelligence levels of the science and leadership groups were highest and those of the personal care group, the lowest). That said, this study was illustrative of a methodological approach but not a basis for immediate translation to practice. Among other things, the groups were far from uniform. For example, the culture group included not just humanities occupations but also medical and social science professions, hardly a homogenous group when it comes to career choice. Additionally, the methodology made use of a lot of assumptions and technical issues (e.g., they removed a "general factor" from vocational interests), and a sample consisting solely of twins may or may not be generalizable no matter where they were raised. Finally, the underlying model of intelligence (g-VPR) is an interesting one, but its use also builds in assumptions in terms of the measures of ability used and how they were analyzed.

Anthoney and Armstrong (2010), using a different approach and a different set of assumptions, built on the Atlas of Individual Differences (Armstrong &

Rounds, 2010) model, which employed a vector analysis methodology to analyze interest-ability relationships. They examined the relationships among self-rated abilities, self-rated skills, and the self-rated RIASEC interests. The O*NET includes both an interest measure and profiles determined to be typical of the many occupations in its expansive database (see Chapters 3 and 4). It also includes abilities and skills profiles thought to be needed in particular occupations. Anthoney and Armstrong used a structural/vector analysis approach using male and female college student data. The study used self-ratings of abilities ($n = 15$). Abilities are described by the O*NET as "enduring attributes of the individual that influence performance" (National Center for O*NET Development, 2018a). They also included self-rated skills ($n = 16$) defined by the O*NET as "developed capacities that facilitate learning or the more rapid acquisition of knowledge" (National Center for O*NET Development, 2018d). Although the authors found vector fit to the RIASEC map between skills and interests than between abilities and interests, skills are more circumscribed than abilities and generalize to fewer occupations.

For the overall sample, 36 of the 90 correlations and 57 of the 96 skills were statistically significant. Many of the correlations were in the moderate or higher range. However, only two abilities were statistically significantly correlated with the Enterprising and Conventional types and only two skills with Conventional interests.

A different pattern emerged when the data were analyzed by sex. For men, only 13 of the 90 possible correlations between the six interest types and the 15 abilities reached statistical significance, and most of those correlations were low. No significant correlations for men between any of the abilities and Realistic, Enterprising, or Conventional interests and abilities were reported. For women, 16 of the ability-interest correlations were statistically and there was at least one significant ability-interest correlation for each of the six interest scales. Concerning skills, 32 of the 96 possible skills correlations with interests, for men, and 29, for women, were statistically significant.

The correlations across the interests in some cases were as might be predicted but in other cases, less so. Examining only the combined sex correlations (Anthoney & Armstrong, 2010, Table 1), teaching was equally correlated with Social and Investigative interests, science skills highest for Investigative but also high with Realistic, spatial orientation highest for Realistic but negatively correlated with Investigative interests, and so on. Additionally, in their complex vector analyses, the authors found that there were no vectors associated with the Conventional interests and only one slightly overlapping with Enterprising interests (Anthoney & Armstrong, 2010, Figure 3). They also found that their approach encompassed the people versus things vector, but only for properties related to the Social and Realistic interest types.

A limitation of this research was its reliance on self-ratings of abilities and skills. As Kell and Lubinski (2015) noted,

> One can make believe that self-reports of cognitive abilities are just fine, but such assessments are soft science at best. To neglect cognitive abilities or objective capabilities in practice and when theorizing about learning, work, and

creativity and to replace them with self-report appraisals constitutes an activity that is far removed from real-world phenomena that clients, educators, employers, and students value most. People can pretend that they are doing important science, but it will not convince people who are informed about the psychological characteristics of the populations with whom they are intimately acquainted. (pp. 316–317)

The study was also limited by only examining the skills, abilities, and interests of college students, most of whom would be expected to have high cognitive abilities. Additionally, the authors did not differentiate between general intelligence and specific abilities. It is likely that many of the ability and skill variables they examined would be correlated with general intelligence. Overall, this research is suggestive and promising for future research, and illustrates a methodology, but does not easily translate into practice (nor was that necessarily a goal for the research).

In still another approach to interest-ability relationships, Pässler et al. (2014) conducted a meta-analysis of RIASEC interests and intelligence. Intelligence is, of course, only one type of ability but certainly an important one (see Chapter 5). The authors limited their meta-analysis to those studies (29 independent samples, 27 studies) that used objective measures of abilities and RIASEC-based measures of interest. They also compared studies that had samples of similar age ranges at the time of data collection so that there were six decade cohorts, ranging from the 1940s to the 1990s. They corrected all correlations for sample size and sampling error and further analyzed age and cohort as possible moderators. Since interests are usually interpreted with the top three RIASEC codes, considering correlations one at a time in comparison to other interests and to abilities will result in finding larger trends, if they are there, but inevitably misses the subtlety associated with pattern analysis. That said, there were statistically significant correlations whose confidence intervals did not cross zero between Realistic and Investigative interests and intelligence, and negative, nonzero correlations that did not cross zero between Social and Enterprising interest scores. The confidence intervals for Artistic and Conventional interests crossed zero, so the correlations were not statistically significant. Age and cohort did moderate these findings, but some of those differences varied by sex.

This study went on to examine non-general-intelligence abilities (what we would called specific or primary abilities) and interests. There were small to moderate positive correlations between Realistic interests and spatial abilities, numerical abilities, and mechanical knowledge. Realistic interests were also related to inductive reasoning. With Investigative interests, positive correlations were found with verbal, numerical, and spatial abilities and, again, a small positive correlation with inductive reasoning and mechanical knowledge. Concerning Artistic interests, there were not enough studies that included measures of abilities of visual art, music, or writing (among others) to analyze, but Artistic interests did overlap with verbal abilities. With both Social and Enterprising interests, predictably, there were negative relationships with mechanical, spatial, and numerical abilities, but, contrary to the authors' hypotheses, there were also small negative relationships with verbal abilities. Finally, the relationship between Conventional interests and numerical abilities was small, and the confidence intervals crossed zero. There was also a small significant relationship between Conventional interests and perceptual speed. Although these relationships were not moderated by gender, the correlations were generally higher for the older than the younger groups for the studies of so-called narrow abilities. There was also a small cohort effect.

Overall, these findings were generally suggestive of a positive relationship between general intelligence and specific abilities and interests that followed the authors' hypotheses. Of most surprise, perhaps, were the low to negative relationships of abilities with both the Social and Enterprising interests. Of note, however, is that only a few studies, insufficient in numbers to meaningfully aggregate, included primary abilities related to social intelligence and to managerial intelligence. Further studies are of course needed to examine these areas. That said, the rather strong overlap of Realistic and Investigative interests and relevant abilities, and the lesser but still significant overlap of verbal abilities with Artistic interests and numerical interests with Conventional interests, were of note.

Research on interdomain relations of interests and abilities is in an exciting, but still developing, period. This is illustrated by Dobrow Riza and Heller's (2015) study of the relationship of "calling" (interests and motivation) in interaction with perceived abilities. They conceptualized this motivation as an intense, meaningful connection ("passion") toward the domain with high internal motivation (Dobrow Riza & Heller, 2015, p. 98). They tested their theory that calling in youth interacted with actual and perceived abilities to determine whether the passion was pursued in an interesting longitudinal sample of musicians. Self-perceived abilities (more than actual abilities, as measured by self-reported prizes received and ratings of ability by experts) actually predicted better to whether the musical career was pursued or abandoned among talented student musicians. Musicians, of course, are in an elite occupation for which many are called and few are chosen, but this research suggests actual abilities interact with peoples' perceptions of their abilities in a complicated way. Perhaps, in a field like music or the other arts, where level of talent needed to succeed is high, self-perceptions of abilities may need to be high to persist. Whether or not this model generalizes to nonelite occupations needs to be examined in further research, but this is a provocative study.

Summary and Practice Implications

What is to be made of all these diverse and complicated studies of the relationships of abilities and interests? Perhaps the best descriptive term is "work in progress." It is, at this writing, very difficult to aggregate across these studies, given that they used quite different approaches (different variables, different measures, different theories, and different samples) to examine interests and abilities. From a "translation to practice" perspective, few findings are as yet fully settled, but some apparent trends are suggested. To begin with, abilities and interests, as a class of variables, are not orthogonal; there are definitely overlaps between the two domains, but the specific overlaps vary by study and sex. Conversely, there is considerable variance unexplained in almost all the studies. This suggests that abilities and interests both need to be measured independently. Patterns may matter as much as individual associations between particular variables and particular interest scores.

As to how to assess abilities, there remain two camps: those who argue strenuously that self-estimates are an acceptable substitute for direct measurement of abilities and those who equally vigorously argue the opposite. (I side with the "measure them directly" group but, in fairness, many studies using self-ratings were done by researchers for researchers, and if the goal is to test out a model early on, that might be a good and less expensive place to begin. Career assessors need to help clients make real decisions about real career choices, and the consequences matter.)

ABILITY-PERSONALITY RELATIONSHIPS

Raymond Cattell (1987), as much as anyone among early researchers, appreciated that personality and ability characteristics were related and that both need to be considered in understanding performance. Cattell's attention to this area is not recent (see R. B. Cattell, 1945a, 1945b). Although his models did not formally integrate contemporary occupational interest theories, they nevertheless addressed the ability-personality interactions, particularly the relation between ability and motivation and, to some degree, interests in the sense of "sentiments" that direct the types of activities that one will find appealing (see R. B. Cattell & Horn, 1964). Even though Cattell's work in this area too frequently relied on his own measures of ability and personality, which are not without problems, he helped to demonstrate that ability and personality can be overlapping constructs (see especially R. B. Cattell, 1987; Hakstian & Cattell, 1978a). Horn (1976b) later concluded, probably overstating, or rather misstating the case, "abilities are traits of personality. They constitute an important part of the total personality and a part that has been studied more thoroughly than most other parts" (p. 164).

The foundational work on the structure of human abilities and to some degree the relationship of intelligence and personality was laid by three pioneers whose theories, collectively, are now called CHC theory (standing for Cattell, Horn, & Carroll; see Chapter 5). These theories and studies, which built on and extended each other's research, laid the groundwork for modern theories of abilities and to some degree explored the interactions of abilities (mostly, intelligence) and personality. Their interest was not particularly focused on career assessment, but some of the work did have career implications.

Industrial–organizational (I–O) psychologists, meanwhile, whose research has tended to focus on selection and work performance outcomes, made major progress over several decades in identifying the role and importance of general intelligence in work effectiveness (see Chapter 5). But that research came at the expense of personality (initially considered to be of little relevance) and interests (not really on the radar screen). Finally, knowledge has progressed over the last several decades by I–O psychologists expanding the studies of Hunter and Schmidt on the major role of general cognitive ability in predicting to work performance, the incremental value of certain personality variables (see Chapter 5), and the relatively recent "re-discovery" of interests. From an initial belief that general intelligence was all important, that view has largely been replaced by one that, while recognizing that general intelligence is unquestionably important, allows that other ability variables (e.g., spatial ability and social intelligence) may also be relevant, and that personality and interests also matter in predicting to career and work outcomes.

Although it is true that there is extensive literature on ability measurement (especially when it comes to "big g," or general intelligence), the literature examining the personality-ability interaction is rather more limited than Horn's (1976b) generalization might suggest. In fact, Horn's review of what he termed suggestive relationships between abilities and certain aspects of personality gives a much less overarching, but more realistic, overview of the then-state of the personality-ability interaction literature than did his conclusion.

The personality variables identified in Cattell and Horn's studies included relations among personality and ability measures of Speed of Closure, Flexibility of Closure (akin to Field Independence-Dependence), verbal and numerical skills, and spatial abilities. People scoring high on Speed of Closure, Horn noted, tended also to score high on personality variables indicating an absence of learned inhibition, whereas those scoring high on Flexibility of Closure tended to be free-thinking, cold and distant in interpersonal relationships, and uninfluenced by others (possibly reflecting characteristics of the Investigative interest type in Holland's RIASEC model). Additionally, high verbal and numerical abilities tended to be associated, the research suggested, with high ego strength and superego development, whereas high Spatial Ability, at least for men, was concluded to be associated with "masculine reticence" (Horn, 1976a). R. B. Cattell's (1987) most recent definitive statement on ability-personality interactions identified similar and additional ability-personality relations. He also suggested that there are personality traits that simulate ability in their behavioral manifestations. These included Field Dependence/Independence, general inhibition factors, and ego strength, among others. Similarly, higher intelligence appeared to be associated, on average, with certain personality characteristics (e.g., conscientiousness, behavioral control, superego strength, persistence, and certain aspects of assertiveness).

R. B. Cattell (1987) suggested other promising personality-ability interactions, including the relation between what today would be called Realistic-related abilities (e.g., mechanical and spatial abilities) and an introverted, tough-minded, "Realistic," nonemotional personality orientation. In contrast, drawing ability (measured, rather primitively, in Cattell's instrumentation) tended to correlate with an intuitive, warm, and extraverted interpersonal nature. Social intelligence was reported by Cattell to be associated with the following personality portrait: high warmth, extraversion, interpersonal ability, high ego strength, low guilt, and high self-sentiment. The "creative" ability-personality profile was characterized by high intelligence, introversion, high dominance (raising the question of whether the 16P might be measuring something other than interpersonal dominance in the California Psychological Inventory [CPI] sense), sensitive (rather than tough-minded), high in imagination, self-sufficient, and radical rather than conservative (R. B. Cattell, 1987; see also Drevdahl & Cattell, 1958). In that similarities of patterns of personality emerge for both creative artists and creative scientists, they felt that this was a "creative personality" profile that could be found in different areas of creativity. These and other findings with potential career assessment implications were reported as being suggestive, not definitive, and Cattell noted, appropriately,

> Achievement is a many-faceted thing, and, except for a few, relatively carefully studied occupations and examination performances . . . the greater number of achievements—from driving fifty years without an accident to raising a family of effective citizens—as yet remain undocumented and experimentally unanalyzed. (R. B. Cattell, 1987, p. 464)

Although Cattell did present some quantitative equations to suggest combinations of personality-ability variables that predicted criteria, such as freedom from accidents and success in sales or as psychiatric technicians, the underlying samples were rather small and the suggested precision of prediction too great to apply the results in routine career assessment practice. Hakstian and Cattell (1978a) also provided a methodology for examining interbattery factor structures.

Although many of the studies on ability-interest have focused on the relationship and common variance across variables in these two domains, others have examined these relationships in the context of outcomes, usually job performance more than career choice.

In important early work, Hough (1990) examined the relation between selected characteristics of ability and personality in a large U.S. Army sample (called Project A). Job performance was influenced (using a predictive validity paradigm) by the following groupings of personality variables: potency (dominance and energy level), achievement (self-esteem and work orientation), dependability (traditional values, nondelinquency, and conscientiousness), and agreeableness (cooperativeness). Hough noted, however, that personality factors were the only variables that added significant predictive validity to the ability measures, in particular, GMA. But the approach was not one of showing that these variables were associated with particular abilities but rather to demonstrate that when they were present, they added to predictive power. Similar findings suggesting that personality may provide additive explanatory power to ability variables in personnel selection contexts had also been reported by Bentz's (1985) work with Sears executives and by A. Howard and Bray's (1988) important longitudinal study of AT&T managers (see Chapters 3 and 10). It is important to again note that the prediction of individual difference variables to career choice or change is not the same focus as selection, but it still provides data potentially useful in career assessment.

Judging from the volume of literature, the relationship between variables in the ability and in the personality domain is, after interest-personality, the second most widely examined interdomain relationship. Yet, in identifying the need for a special issue of the *Journal of Intelligence* on "Ability-Personality Integration," Ziegler et al. (2018) observed,

> There is still little sustained theory and research aimed at integrating both psychological trait foci. In fact, it sometimes appears as if two only slightly overlapping traditions have developed, each using the constructs of the other tradition only as control variables. (para. 2)

Many of these studies have focused on the FFM model and factors and cognitive ability variables. Others have examined facets of personality and a broader range of abilities than just cognitive. Many, like the ones just cited, have focused on predicting to job performance in the context of employee selection.

Relationships Across the Ability and Personality Domains

Because there have been several ability-personality review articles and meta-analyses published (e.g., Judge et al., 2007, 2013; Sackett & Lievens, 2008; Schmitt, 2014), this section focuses on some of the major findings that cut across studies and on some of the conceptual and methodological issues affecting ability-personality studies.

Many ability-personality studies have made use of the FFM model of personality which has both advantages and limitations. Some studies have extended their analyses to facet scales but as discussed in Chapter 13, the personality facets are not well established and differ in content and structure from one measure to the next. And some studies have added non-FFM personality facets or variables. On the ability side, there have been many studies using broad-brush measures of intelligence and cognitive abilities, but few using a wide cross section of objectively measured (vs. self-estimate) career-related abilities. Here are some of the cross-study findings that have emerged to date.

Most of the reviews of the ability-personality literature have reported modest to low correlations across most of the FFM factors and abilities (P. L. Ackerman & Heggestad; 1997; Sackett & Lievens, 2008; Schmitt, 2014). Judge et al. (2007) found that GMA at best was positively correlated .22 with Openness, .20 with Self-Efficacy, and .09 with Emotional Stability but had almost no relationship with Agreeableness, Extraversion, or Conscientiousness. The correlation of GMA with Conscientiousness in this study, though small, was actually negative. Judge et al. (2013) also found that in relating personality variables to work outcome measures, facets often were more effective than the overarching variables. Carretta and Ree's (2018) large sample studies of these variables using data from military recruits (both officer and enlisted) across multiple measures of personality also found rather low correlations across most cognitive variables and personality variables. Overall, these findings suggest statistically significant, but generally low, and often negative, relationships between broad-brush FFM factors and many facet variables and general cognitive abilities. There can be multiple reasons for such findings, including unreliability in the personality variables associated with intentional or other distortion, a not-uncommon issue when the tests were administered in the context of personnel selection, as were many of those studies in the published literature. The specific instruments used also may matter in determining what the obtained relationships are (see Judge et al., 2013). Although there is some common variance between personality and selected abilities, these domains are clearly measuring different constructs (implying the need, in career assessment, to measure both personality and ability variables), but they lend themselves to pattern analysis when there is evidence that there are particular typologies of ability-personality relationships that may be expected in specific careers. Alternatively, when abilities are as expected for a particular profession but personality runs counter to the normative patterns, guidance may be useful about subareas of a career likely to be more satisfying.

Among the FFM factors, there is persistent evidence that Openness correlates positively and strongly (compared with other cross-domain relationships in this area) with general intelligence (Schmitt, 2014) and with creative pursuits within a particular ability domain. Carretta and Ree's (2018) very large sample studies on military recruits, including both officer and enlisted groups and across multiple measures of personality and of abilities, strongly supported this finding. Additionally, atypically for the literature, Carretta and Ree also included a measure of Machiavellianism in some of their samples that was also correlated positively with cognitive abilities.

Negative correlations have also been found between personality and ability variables. Depending on how it is measured, neuroticism (or other nonnormal variations) has been inversely associated with cognitive ability scores (Carretta & Ree, 2018). Mittelstädt et al. (2016) provided data on predictors of those who failed and succeeded in the European Space Agency's astronaut training program. A large group ($n = 902$) of astronaut candidates were screened using interviews and ability tests. Only 46 were chosen for the program. Personality characteristics were analyzed of the 710 individuals who failed the aptitude testing and the 146 who failed in the assessment center and interview process. They found higher Neuroticism scores and lower Agreeableness scores among those who did not move on. In contrast, those chosen were higher on vitality (energy) and achievement scales.

Sorting Out the Complexity of Ability-Personality Criterion-Related Findings

Given the relatively low correlations between abilities and personality, are these two domains more or less orthogonal? It is probably premature to draw such a conclusion.

A number of criterion-related validity studies have demonstrated that personality variables—some of them anyway—improve on the predictive power of abilities—some of them anyway—when used to predict school performance (Bergold & Steinmayr, 2018) and work outcomes (in particular, to job performance; Hough & Dilchert, 2017). In other words, if abilities—particularly cognitive abilities—predict well to work-outcomes in selection paradigms, in at least some cases abilities combined with certain personality variables will do so even better (see Schmitt, 2014). Yet, to date these results have been modest in the incremental variance explained.

Why aren't these correlations higher? The relatively low correlations across abilities and personality could be associated with a number of issues. First, there needs to be a rationale for why personality and ability should be related to work and career outcomes. As P. L. Ackerman (2018) noted, "As yet, there do not appear to be any salient explanations of how intellectual abilities might influence individual differences—in particular, personality traits" (p. 2). Without a rationale as to why these two domains should overlap, simple correlations with broad measures of personality and broad measures of ability are probably not the best way to examine associations. Leutner and Chamorro-Premuzic (2018) noted that

> the validity of personality traits as predictors of career potential—rarely above $r = 0.30$ for individual traits—tends to be underestimated by meta-analyses that fail to match personality traits to relevant career outcomes (e.g., extraversion and sales performance, conscientiousness and methodical task performance, openness and creative jobs, etc.). (p. 2)

These authors went on to note that if there is a curvilinear rather than linear relationship between personality and ability variables, then it is likely that simple correlations may underestimate the degree of relationship between the two domains. Finally, personality facets may work better than high-level personality factors, and specific abilities better than overall cognitive ability in examining such relationships.

To borrow from a related type of study, animal researchers are also considering personality-ability relationships in some studies of how and why animals learn and how personality may matter. Griffin et al. (2015) raised interesting questions, similar to those of human researchers of ability-personality relationships, concerning how personality might affect learning in animals:

> If personality and cognition are related, it is not clear what shape that relationship might take. One possibility is that particular personality traits, and specific personality types within those traits, facilitate or constrain learning. For example, a bolder individual that approaches and explores novel objects more willingly than does a shyer one is likely to encounter new environmental contingencies more quickly. Therefore, boldness, neophilia, activity, and spatial exploration would be behaviors that might correlate positively with learning because those behaviours determine the rate at which animals encounter the environmental contingencies upon which learning depends. (p. 2111)

Summary and Practice Implications

The correlations between abilities and personality are less high than might be expected. The highest one has consistently been that between Openness and GMA. Methodological problems and a diversity of research paradigms have affected the generalizability of some of the relationships so far found between these two domains. More promising approaches have been suggested by using facet scores of personality (not just trait scores) and a broader range of abilities and skills (not just GMA). Additionally, greater attention is needed about the rationale for predicted ability-personality relationships. When job duties call for behavior represented in the personality variables, positive relationships are more likely to be found.

INTEREST-ABILITY-PERSONALITY RELATIONSHIPS

Few studies have considered the relationships across interests, abilities, and personality, but such studies have finally begun to grow in number and diversity of approach. The relative neglect is not surprising since the time and costs associated with lengthy test batteries that validly and reliably collect such data are considerable. In this section, some of the major representative studies, and some of the newer promising ones, that integrated all three domains are reviewed. The literature on interdomain relationship now available is useful, but it is ripe for further expansion.

Much of the predictive interdomain research to date has centered on work outcomes that are of interest to employers (e.g., productivity and job performance). Career assessment adds the important predictive concern of individual "fit" with careers (not just jobs) and consideration of outcome variables of personal satisfaction and productivity in careers. Although such research, particularly that following people over the course of their careers, is not plentiful, we can still identify important threads from existing interest-ability-personality studies that provide guidance and suggestions for further research. These studies are presented in order of their publication.

Butcher (1969) examined the structure of interests, abilities, and personality characteristics in a sample of 1,000 thirteen-year-old Scottish school children who were judged likely to go on to university. The ability measure was primarily a measure of GMA, interests were assessed with the Kuder measure, and personality with Cattell's High School Personality Questionnaire (HSPQ) which included two second-order factors, essentially Anxiety and Extraversion. Ten factors emerged from the data, which tended to differentiate interests, abilities, and personality structurally. Still, the authors were able to identify profiles that were associated with scientific careers, applied science/mechanical work, helping/social work cluster, and literary artistic work orientation.

Lancaster et al. (1994) compared interest-ability-personality data for three applicant groups: bookkeepers, laborers, and secretaries. The interest profiles for the three groups, respectively, were Conventional–Enterprising–Social,

Realistic–Enterprising–Social, and Conventional–Enterprising–Social. On the cognitive ability measure (the Wonderlic), bookkeepers had the highest score; secretaries, next; and laborers, the lowest. On the personality variables, however, those having comparable personality scores did not apply for similar jobs.

Lowman and Leeman (1988) examined the relationships among interests, abilities, and personality related to social intelligence in a sample of college females. They factor analyzed interests, social abilities, and personality and found separate factors for social needs and interests, ability, and knowledge. Each of the variables had low or negative correlations with self-reported GPA. Concerning being in a social college major, only the behavioral measure (the Interpersonal Problem Solving Ability Test (IPSAT; see Chapter 9) had a statistically significant positive relationship with being in a social/helping oriented college major.

P. L. Ackerman and Heggestad's (1997) important study has already been discussed earlier in the chapter, but the focus is on the integration of the data collected from other studies across three domains (interests, abilities, and personality). In analyzing the interest-ability-personality data as a whole, they identified what they called "trait complexes," which were, essentially, typological patterns that were consistent within group and differentiated from the other groups. In this research, they identified four such patterns, which they labeled as (a) Science/Math, (b) Intellectual/Cultural, (c) Social, and (d) Clerical/Conventional. This study provided a promising start to integration across the three focal domains but these would not be sufficient to classify a number of occupational choices. Even within these trait complexes, they were at too broad a level to differentiate subtypes within those they did identify. This is not a criticism of the research, which was intricately tied to studies already published by the time of the meta-analysis. Another group of researchers also liked the idea of trait complexes, stating,

> For career counselors, using . . . trait complexes is appealing. Instead of thinking about a grid involving multiple personality factors, vocational interests, and abilities of the clients, the counselor can hone in on a specific complex that seems most suited to the particular client. (Staggs et al., 2007, p. 426)

It is true that such trait complexes may be appealing but are useful only when (a) there is sufficient confirmatory evidence in support of them, (b) when assessees whose patterns do not fit into those few constellations are offered alternative approaches, and (c) only when assessees are helped to understand what goes into the complex and what to do about missing variables and measured variables for which their findings do not fit well.

Carless (1999) examined the relationships between interests, abilities, and personality in two separate studies. In the first, the SDS, Wechsler Adult Intelligence Scale-Revised (WAIS-R), and NEO-PI were used with a vocational assessment sample ($n = 139$; 91 women, 48 men) who were working either full or part time or in school. Both the overall FFM scales were considered as well as the six facets associated with each of the FFM factors.

Recognizing that, on the ability side, only Verbal, Nonverbal, and General Intelligence scores were gathered in Study 1, only Investigative interests were statistically significantly (positively) correlated with the three ability measures. For women, there were statistically significant positive correlations between all three abilities and Investigative interests. Artistic interests were positively correlated with verbal and overall intelligence and Conventional interests were negatively correlated with verbal intelligence. There were no statistically significant correlations with the remaining interest scales.

Concerning personality-ability correlations in Study 1, there were statistically significant correlations only for Openness and the three intelligence scores for men and for the Verbal and Overall Intelligence scores for women. Interest-personality correlations were statistically significant and positive between Openness and Artistic interests for both sexes, with Investigative interests (for women), and with Social interests for men. Conventional interest were negatively correlated with women's Openness scores. Extraversion scores positively correlated with Social interests and Enterprising interests for both men and women. Neuroticism scores were negatively correlated with Social interests for women. There were no statistically significant correlations with any of the Agreeableness scales for either men or women, but Conscientiousness scores were positively correlated with Social interests for women, with Enterprising interests for both women and men; and with Conventional interests for men but not for women. There were also a number of NEO facet scores that correlated positively with some of the interest scores. The most statistically significant correlations were found between Artistic facets and Openness and between Extraversion and Social interests and Enterprising interests. Facets for other scales had a few isolated significant scores. For example, Achievement facet scores were most highly correlated with Enterprising interests for both sexes and also significantly and positively with Conventional interests for men.

In the second study, the sample consisted of 875 Australian employees (669 men and 206 women) who worked at an international bank. In this study the SDS was used for the interest measure, the personality measure (not without its critics) was the MBTI. The MBTI and NEO personality measures are not strictly comparable, but there is some overlap between Introversion/ Extraversion on the NEO and MBTI Introversion/Extraversion, and between NEO Openness and MBTI Intuitive/Sensing. However, MBTI Thinking/Feeling and Judging/Perceiving scales are probably more comparable to NEO facet scales than to the Agreeableness, Conscientiousness, or Neuroticism factors. The Australian Council of Educational Research Higher Test PL-PQ (Australian Council for Educational Research, 1981) was used as a measure of Verbal and Numeric cognitive ability. The two scores were combined into an overall ability score.

Concerning interest-personality correlations, there were some statistically significant correlations between the personality and interest measures. In the case of Extraversion (low scores indicating the extraverted direction), statistically significant negative relations were found for Social and Enterprising scores for both sexes. For Sensing/Intuition (for which lower scores were in the Sensing direction), positive statistically significant correlations were found with Investigative and Artistic interests and negative ones with Conventional interests, for both sexes. With Thinking/Feeling scores (where low scores were in the Thinking direction), small negative correlations were found with Investigative interests for both sexes and a small positive correlation was found for women's Artistic and Social scores, and small negative correlations were found with Enterprising interests for men. The correlations of the Judging/Perceiving scores (lower scores were in the Judging direction) and the interest scores were nonsignificant for Realistic, Investigative, Artistic, and Enterprising interests. Small, but significant, negative correlations were found with Conventional interests for both sexes and for male Social interests types.

In the case of Personality-Ability relationships, Extraversion correlated with none of the three ability measures. Sensing/Intuition correlated positively with Verbal and Overall Intelligence for both sexes, and positively with Numerical Intelligence for men. Thinking/Feeling had no significant correlations for women, but correlated negatively for men for all three measures. Judging/Perceiving scores did not correlate with any of the three abilities for women but correlated positively with Verbal and Overall Intelligence for men.

Overall, some consistent patterns were found among interest-ability-personality relationships in these two studies. Concerning interests and personality variables, Extraversion correlated with Social and Enterprising interests, as Holland's theory would predict. Openness/Intuition correlated positively for both sexes with Investigative and Artistic interests and negatively with Conventional interests (except for men). Consistent with concerns raised in Chapter 14, Agreeableness had little association with interests. Conscientiousness was positively correlated with Enterprising interests for both sexes (possibly reflecting a positive response bias for persons with these interests), with Social interests for women, and Conventional interests for men. Ability-interest and ability-personality analyses were limited to Verbal, Quantitative, and Overall Intelligence. Significant positive correlations were found for Investigative interests and Openness, and, for women, positive correlations between Verbal and Overall Intelligence and Artistic interests, and negative correlations between those two ability measures and Conventional interests. For men, there were also positive correlations between both Judging and Thinking for the three cognitive ability scores.

There were also differences, however, associated with sex and measures used. Few of these correlations were particularly high, but that reinforces the idea that there is unique variance in each of these domains, supporting the need to assess across all three domains, given that each domain has shown a relationship with career and work outcomes. Additionally, because only intelligence was measured on the ability side, these studies were limited in being able to generalize across the interest-ability domains. Finally, measures may affect the degree and magnitude of the relationships. Some personality facet scales may be more productive than overall factor scores on FFM models. Test-taking orientation may also affect the results.

Other interdomain relationship studies have focused on a narrower range of abilities and on alternative methodologies.

Lowman and Ng (2010) examined interest, ability, and personality characteristics of two geographically diverse industrial samples on their interest-ability-personality profiles. Both groups had highest interest scores on Realistic interests across two different measures. For both groups, the highest ability scores were on measures of mechanical ability. Both groups also had high average scores on Nonverbal (Performance) and average scores on Verbal measures on intelligence. Their scores on managerial and assessment center exercises were in the average range. On personality measures, both groups had high Dominance and Masculinity (Mf) scores and scored low on Flexibility scores.

J. C. Kaufman et al. (2013) identified FFM personality and creativity differences among students enrolled in majors that had been classified as representing one of each interest category, with four analogous to RIASEC interests, except that there were two Investigative subgroups, a STEM group, and a Social Sciences group, and no Conventional majors were included. There are many problems with this approach, since students in majors do not represent a single interest profile, and no independent interest measure was used. Using a college student sample ($n = 3,295$; 2,686 women and 609 men), the ability measures consisted of a self-report rating of creativity and scores on the Compound Remote Associates Task (CRAT), a measure of creativity in which a common word had to be identified that applied to each of three given words. The CRAT measure may be more of a cognitive ability test, however, than one of creativity. The personality measure was based on the FFM. They found that the Realistic major respondents scored higher on Extraversion and Conscientiousness than on the other personality variables. The Investigative majors scored highest on Openness and Agreeableness, Enterprising on Extraversion and Openness, and Artistic on Openness. Consistent with other research, persons in the Investigative and Artistic majors were, on average, higher on Openness than were the Realistic and Social groups, but, inconsistent with many studies, the Investigative group was highest in Agreeableness. The Investigative and Artistic interest college major groups scored highest on the self-reported creativity measure and the Investigative and Enterprising interests, on the CRAT ability measure. Since no independent measure of interests was used, this study depended greatly on the accuracy of interest group classification. The two majors selected to represent Realistic interests, for example, were Criminal Justice and Political Science, which hardly seem to belong in the Realistic category and, of similar concern, Communications, History, English, Liberal Studies, and World Languages were included in Artistic major category. This classification may help explain some of the unexpected findings, including that Realistic group scored, on average, in the extraverted direction.

The Howland (2015) study, already introduced, examined the interest-ability-personality profile of a group of people representing Social and Enterprising careers. Interest-ability-personality profiles were assessed and compared among groups either employed or majoring in two people-oriented areas, one representing Social and one representing Enterprising careers. GMA and emotional intelligence (EI) were the abilities studied. The study also included one interest measure and one FFM measure of personality. Although there were significant differences in interest-ability-personality profiles between the Enterprising and the Social groups, contrary to expectations, a negative correlation was found between Enterprising interests and EI, and no significant correlation was found between Social interests and EI. Because the sample was international and all data collected electronically, it is possible that language or other variables may have affected the results.

A study by Volodina et al. (2015) considered whether abilities, personality, and interests were relevant to satisfaction and intent to quit German apprentice training programs for industrial clerks (mostly female) and technicians (mostly male). The apprentice model included 2 days a week of schooling, with the rest of the time spent in on-the-job training. The technicians' work involved working with tools and equipment, inspecting and fixing technical systems, and knowledge of mechanical and electrical systems. In contrast, the clerks' work was with records and data, using math and accounting and assuring that certain procedures were appropriately followed. The authors noted that the technician job was a Realistic one in the RIASEC model and the industrial clerk position was a Conventional one. Indeed, the average scores on the interest measure for the technicians were Realistic–Enterprising–Investigative and of the industrial clerks were Enterprising–Conventional–Social. The research examined the role of abilities (general cognitive ability and two achievement tests—one in math and one in physics), occupational interests (measured with a German RIASEC measure), and FFM personality variables (measured by a German version of an NEO personality test). They also included two outcome measures: satisfaction with training program and intention to drop out of the program (48% of the combined groups did not express intent to quit, so the variable was dichotomized in some of the analyses). Control variables included socioeconomic status (SES) of families of origin and whether the participants had been in an academic-oriented school prior to joining the apprenticeship training. The cognitive variables were not effective predictors of the outcome measures compared with personality and interests. For both groups, Introversion/Extraversion, Agreeableness, and Conscientiousness personality variables were strongly associated with satisfaction (positively) and with turnover intent (negatively). Neuroticism correlated with these outcome measures in the opposite way (i.e., positively correlated with turnover intent and negatively with satisfaction). Openness had a differential relationship for the two groups in that it was positively associated with satisfaction (and negatively with turnover intent) for the technicians but in the opposite pattern for the industrial clerks (i.e., higher openness for clerks was associated with lower satisfaction and higher intent to leave). Having attended an academic school raised the likelihood for clerks (but not technicians) of thinking about quitting the program. SES of parents did not impact these findings. Since there was considerable common variance between personality and interests, the researchers also examined the effects of interests on the criterion measures when personality was held constant. In this case, interests remained important in that Realistic interests for the technicians, and Conventional for the clerks, were associated with increased satisfaction and decreased intention to leave the program. Overall, this is an interesting and important study, not only for its findings, but also for illustrating the complexity that is involved in doing research in this area.

Diedrich, Neubauer, and Ortner (2018), also working with German (and apparently Austrian) participants in an apprenticeship program *(n = 648)*, considered cognitive abilities (verbal, numerical, and spatial) and some primary abilities (social-emotional, creative, practical), 14 interest scales, and FFM personality scales plus four facet scales of Conscientiousness. They worked with apprentices who were in one of five occupational groups (food service, technical, people-related, office/clerical, and crafts). The two outcome criteria were grades in the program and satisfaction with the program and with the work. The grade criteria was based on grades in school subjects grades that were judged to be related to the work training (e.g., botany grade for a florist apprentice), suggesting that the criterion varied from one participant to another. Additionally, the cognitive measures were highly speeded whereas the primary ability measures were not. Overall, ability scores (general intelligence and the Social Ability measure) and Conscientious best predicted the grade criteria, whereas the other FFM variables and Generalized Self-Efficacy did not add incrementally to the predictions. The satisfaction criteria were predicted by the Conscientious facet scales and, in some cases, by the Social Ability measure (but not by GMA).

Finally, we conclude the literature review with a brief but provocative article by Frank Schmidt (2014). Suggesting a potentially causative mechanism for at least some abilities, interests, and personality dimensions, Schmidt noted possible mechanisms interconnecting abilities, interests, and personality:

> Introversion and fluid intelligence cause interest in general learning (intellectual curiosity), which in turn is a major cause of crystallized intelligence. Certain specific interests and fluid intelligence also contribute to crystallized intelligence. Prenatal testosterone hormone conditioning is postulated to cause sex differences in certain specific interests but not in others. Crystallized intelligence, specific interests, and the personality trait of conscientiousness cause adult academic and occupational performance, whereas crystallized intelligence is the main cause of good mental functioning at older ages. (p. 211)

Summary and Practice Implications

An historic call (Alteneder, 1940) for measuring across ability, interest, and personality domains in career assessment has inched forward on the research side. The interest-ability-personality studies summarized here varied widely in their approaches, methodologies, and samples. Not surprisingly, they also were not always consistent in their findings. Because this kind of research is necessarily complex, it is more difficult to summarize the literature in a way that can be aggregated.

Despite considerable progress, much work remains to further extend and ultimately to be able to generalize from findings. In a newish area like this, there is something to be said in support of diversity of approaches, measures, and aggregation methods used. However, the field will be well served by having more consistency over time in measures and aggregation methods.

This chapter has covered a lot of complicated theory and research regarding integration of interests, abilities, and personality. A summary of the interdomain relationships that have a reasonable amount of consistent support is presented in Table 17.1. Note that in some cases, the evidence is mixed and those findings are put in parentheses. In other cases, the relationship varied by subtypes of the occupational or interest group. For example, some Realistic-interest occupations show elevations in spatial abilities; others do not. Such relationships are indicated in brackets in Table 17.1.

SUMMARY AND CONCLUSIONS

Three conclusions can be drawn from this review: (a) there are reasonably well-established relationships between and among a number of variables and factors in the interests, abilities, and personality domains (contrary to the premature conclusions by some observers, e.g., Carson, 1998a); (b) more research is needed particularly using comparable research paradigms and diverse samples of participants; and (c) none of these relationships are of a sufficient magnitude to suggest that some of the domains do not need to be measured.

A number of studies were reviewed in each of the interdomain areas. The most expansive literature at this writing is in the interest-personality domains; the second most, in the ability-personality areas; and the next most, in ability-interest relationships. Understandably, the fewest studies were found in the most complex area: interests, abilities, and personality considered simultaneously. Even so, certain profiles across all three domains have emerged with some consistency.

As for translating this research into practice, career assessors benefit from knowing which interest, ability, and personality variables tend to cluster together and which do not. At the individual level, matches of assessment findings with interest-ability-personality profiles, such as in science or business, are useful in considering if a family of occupations matches the profile well. However, because career assessors are often dealing with people whose patterns do not fit neatly into profiles, career guidance is needed for interpreting results that may be inconsistent within or across domains (or both). A systematic procedure for conducting cross-domain assessment at the individual level is presented and illustrated in the next chapter.

TABLE 17.1. Summary of Research Findings on Relationships Between Interests, Abilities, and Personality

Interests-Personality	Interests-Abilities	Personality-Abilities
Realistic and	Realistic and	Openness and
Extraversion – [a]	Mechanical Ability	GMA
Openness –	[Spatial Ability]	Writing ability
Field Independence [b]	Nonverbal Intelligence	
	Field Independence [b]	
Investigative and	Investigative and	Extraversion and [a]
Openness	GMA	Managerial abilities
Tough Poise	[Spatial Ability]	Social abilities
Field Independence [b]	Field Independence [b]	
Artistic and	Artistic and	Conscientiousness and
Openness	Spatial, Aesthetic Judgement, Field Independence [b] (Visual arts)	[Job performance] [c]
(Adjustment –)	Music abilities (Pitch, Rhythm, Tonal Memory, [Spatial])	
	GMA (Writing)	
	Others with specific creative performance	
Social and	Social and	Neuroticism/Adjustment and [d]
Extraversion [a]	Social intelligence (awareness, assessment, behavior)	GMA (with Emotional Stability)
Agreeableness		
Tough Poise –	Verbal intelligence	
Field Independence – [b]	Field Independence – [b]	
Enterprising and	Enterprising and	Agreeableness and
Extraversion [a]	Managerial Abilities (prioritizing, judgment)	[Social intelligence]
Tough Poise		
Dominance	GMA	
Likability –		
Field Independence – [b]		
Conventional and	Conventional and	Self-Efficacy and
Conscientiousness	Perceptual Speed and Accuracy	GMA
	Numerical Abilities	

Note. Entries in brackets denote relationships that are found in some subtypes of the occupational group. Entries in parentheses denote a pattern of mixed evidence. All relationships are positive except as noted. Negative relationships are denoted with a "–" after the variable's name. GMA = General Mental Ability.
[a]Extraversion is the term used for Introversion/Extraversion; higher scores are in the extraverted direction. [b]Field Independence/Dependence can be considered as both a personality and an ability variable. Minus sign indicates Field Dependent direction. [c]Job performance is not an ability per se, but this entry is added as a reminder that although few correlations between Conscientiousness and ability measures have been reported, this personality variable persistently has the highest performance. [d]Higher scores on the Neuroticism/Adjustment variables are in the less well-adjusted direction.

18

Applying the Interdomain Model

A Step-by-Step Process for Integrating Career Assessment Data

This chapter addresses ways for combining complex, cross-domain (interests-abilities-personality) psychological assessment data to obtain a more comprehensive understanding of clients' career patterns and potential career paths. People are, after all, not just the results of a single test, much less a single test score, but rather are complicated organisms with specific needs and concerns that caused them to seek career assessment and for which a number of personal characteristics may be relevant. It is the career assessor's job to make evidence-based decisions about which assessment measures to use to address the career assessment's goals and purposes, and then to help clients make sense of the assessment findings. That task is more difficult when, consistent with known findings and literature, there are a variety of traits and other characteristics—some more or less fixed, others changing over the life cycle—that need to be taken into account, and when the reasons for which help was sought can be quite diverse. A further challenge occurs with the wide variety of available instrumentation that is not always consistent, either in underlying theory or in particular scales or facets across measures.

The literature on interdomain research (see Chapter 17) is promising and suggestive but still in its early stages despite considerable research-filled evidence within each of the three domains. Meanwhile, career assessments need to be conducted, data analyzed, interpretations made, and consultation given based on what we now know. This chapter therefore provides a practical step-by-step process deriving from the literature and from many years of professional experience consulting to a wide range of career assessment clients.

https://doi.org/10.1037/0000254-019
Career Assessment: Integrating Interests, Abilities, and Personality, by R. L. Lowman
Copyright © 2022 by the American Psychological Association. All rights reserved.

STEP 1. CAREFULLY CONSIDER THE REASONS, MOTIVATIONS, AND READINESS FOR CAREER ASSESSMENT

Clients seeks career assessment for one or more reasons. Of course, there are some assessments done as part of an exploratory career process open to all people in a particular group, say, high school juniors at a particular school. In such cases all participants will likely complete the same measures, and feedback may well occur as part of a group or with a written summary of findings. For many other clients who seek out career counseling, however, it is because they have not been able on their own to solve a career concern and they have sought out help. In some cases, the question is focused on unhappiness—"I hate my job," or "I'm thinking of switching careers; should I?" Here, the first task is to sort out the source of the perceived unhappiness or of what is prompting the desire to change career directions. Not liking or getting along with a boss is not the same thing as not liking a career choice, though each purpose may need professional help. For others, the choice is whether or not to take one or more years off of work to pursue advanced training or to prepare for enhanced career options. Concern as to whether to invest, say, $100,000 or more plus the opportunity costs associated with not working for a year or two is understandable, as is wanting confirmation that the new direction is consistent with the person's career profile. Whatever the purpose(s) of career assessment, it is important that it, or they, be front and center, both in deciding which assessments to administer and in using the data to help clients make decisions.

How do clients present their own reasons for seeking out help? Here are several examples of what actual career clients have said are their goals for their career assessments:

- "I'm trying to decide on my career path, which way I should be going."
- "Should I stay in my present field or change fields completely?"
- "Help me identify which careers I would be most happy doing or confirm or correct my view of myself."
- "Find some specific options for career path."
- "Help me make a decision to make a change."
- "Help me find a career that will suit me."
- "I hope I will be able to narrow down my choices for a career."
- "To talk with someone who can be a sounding board and help me sort out my own feelings of frustration."
- "To learn what strengths I have that I can transfer to a different line of work."
- "To figure out something to do."

Because the referral questions will anchor the measures used (much as the job analysis does in selection work) and will provide the contextual basis for understanding and feeding back the results, it is important to get it right even when the answer is "I don't know what to do next." Career assessors can add value before the assessment, or rather as the first part of it, by helping to clarify the focal issues. Whatever form the initial session with the client takes (telephone, face-to-face, virtual), one of the major tasks is to understand in detail the client's purpose in pursuing career assessment and whether that purpose matches what career assessment can help with. This process requires a combination of being fully accepting of the client and the client's perceived needs while asking questions and generating possible hypotheses (e.g., "Is it possible that . . . ?") to better understand the goals of the client. This process also involves understanding the career/work/school history of the person, any past career assessments, and how the current request for assistance fits into those experiences.

Career Decision Making and Readiness

In Chapter 1, the topic of readiness for career assessment was introduced. The broader category under which much of the research in this area has been published is called *career decision making*, but a variety of specific terms (including career maturity and career self-efficacy) have been used to describe similar or overlapping concepts. These concern the process side of career assessment versus the content. Whatever benefits come from career assessment, ultimately it is the client who must make the decisions about how to use the information that comes from the career assessment process and what career paths to pursue. So, when there are impediments to decision making or a simple lack of readiness, it is important to know this before proceeding.

Clearly, people are not all at the same place in career readiness for change. (This has implications for outcome research. When participants in career assessment or interventions are not at the same stage of readiness, this may influence the aggregated outcomes.) Gati and Asher (2001) proposed a three-stage model (labeled PIC) for career decision making: prescreening, in-depth exploration, and choice. People do not always fit neatly into models, but this one does identify three aspects of the career search process that are useful for assessors in determining what will be most beneficial for a client. The goal of career assessment is not just to identify well-fitting career choices for the client's consideration, but also to help them become empowered to become "career detectives" to search through options, to better understand their responses to alternative choices, and to know how to initiate the steps that need to be taken to fulfill their goals. If people don't know how to find options or do not feel that they can achieve their goals, that may need to be the first focus of attention.

Considerable literature has developed about readiness for career decision making (also called career decision status or career decidedness; see J. L. Swanson, 2013). This can be useful in considering when career assessment of the type described in this book is something that will benefit the client. The research literature on career decision making has greatly expanded, and a number of measures are available to assess the related concepts. These include the Career-Decision-Making Difficulties Questionnaire (Levin et al., 2020; Osipow & Gati, 1998), the Career Decision Self-Efficacy Scale (Betz & Taylor, 2012), the Career Development Inventory (Savickas, & Hartun, 1996), the Career Maturity Inventory (Busacca & Taber, 2002), the Career Thoughts Inventory (Sampson et al., 1996), the Decisional Process Inventory (Marco et al., 2003), and My Vocational Situation (J. L. Holland et al., 1980). For more information or reviews of some of these measures, see Stoltz and Barclay (2019). Each measure has pluses and minuses, and many of them use different conceptualizations and different factors, but the basic idea of most of them is to attend to readiness to make career decisions and process issues that may impede or enhance career decision making or choice.

Whether done with a formal assessment measure or with an intake interview, it is important to determine the client's motivation and readiness for career assessment, identifying any issues that need attention before (or in place of) career assessment, evaluating the client's skills to conduct career searches, the client's career-related or more general sense of self-efficacy, and many other factors that have been discussed in this book. Career assessments or interventions may need modification for those who are poorly motivated, who are preoccupied with other aspects of their lives or with psychological concerns, or who lack the conviction that their efforts can make a difference in their career choices and life.

Since mental health issues may be present among those referred for, or seeking, career assessment, it is important to consider their relevance as part of the preassessment process. For example, someone may seek career assessment on referral from a therapist who has been treating the client for anxiety and depression. When work and career are intricately tied with those psychological conditions, career assessment may be a valuable aid in addressing those issues. However, for others, when anxiety or depression are themselves the source of the career difficulties, judgement is needed to determine whether or not the assessment is appropriate at that time.

Goals of the Intake/Preassessment Process

From the career intake process the career assessor should have

- established the foundation of a helping relationship with the client;
- developed an understanding of the career-related problems as the client sees them and as the assessor sees them;
- identified whether the current career concerns or unhappiness are associated with reasons that suggest an issue that is career- rather than job-related, such as when people like their career and job but not their employer or supervisor; and

- reached at least an initial understanding of whether career assessment will be appropriate for the client's needs and, if so, whether a general career assessment or a more circumscribed one will be best suited to help the client.

If the needed competencies fall within the training and scope of practice of the assessor, there should also be

- awareness of whether there are mental health problems associated with the career ones and, as relevant, history of past or present interventions, including whether the client is currently receiving personal or mental-health-related counseling;
- an understanding of any health conditions and medications being taken that might be expected to impact the assessment; and
- determination that the client is sufficiently motivated to pursue the assessment.

Types of problems for which career assessment services are likely to be especially relevant include

- unhappiness with current occupation/career/work and considering alternative career directions;
- reaching a point in counseling/therapy in which work issues are relevant, the client is ready to pursue them, and, preferably, where there can be coordination with the counseling service provider;
- considering returning to school or pursuing a particular undergraduate major or graduate/professional degree but wanting to be sure the decision is the right one;
- dissatisfaction with current career prospects or advancement possibilities;
- feeling that important parts of the self are not finding an outlet in the career;
- understanding that a cherished career (say, in the arts) is not going to be possible and needing to find an alternative direction;
- having health or psychological conditions (including learning problems) and needing to find appropriate career possibilities; and
- having an unchosen end to current work (e.g., layoff, reduction in force, termination) that necessitates rethinking the next directions and whether a career, not just a job, change is needed.

Of course, these do not constitute a comprehensive list of presenting concerns, but they are illustrative of the many presenting problems for which career assessment may be useful. Career assessment is less likely to be useful (or unhelpful) when

- the potential client has issues (e.g., patterns of persistent problems dealing with those in authority or chronic procrastination) better addressed by career or personal counseling or psychotherapy;

- the client is questioning career choices as part of a broader problem of questioning everything;

- depression or other behavioral or psychological problems are sufficiently severe that the assessment process may be invalid (e.g., lack of interest in anything; very slow response times, possibly affecting ability test results); and

- the assessment is someone else's idea, and the motivation for change or even assessment is lacking.

Summary

The major points in this section can be combined into an acronym, or memory device, P-A-P-M-O-R-T-R, standing for

- **P**resenting concern(s): What does the client think is the problem? Are there competing hypotheses?

- **A**ppropriateness of career assessment: Are the client's concerns well aligned with the purposes of career assessment, or is something else needed? Is the client ready for career assessment and likely to benefit from it?

- **P**hysical or psychological/behavioral concerns: Are there physical, behavioral health, or substance abuse problems that need to be taken into account in addressing the presenting concerns?

- **M**otivation: How motivated is the client to participate in the process and to make change? Who in the client's life (e.g., parents, spouse) may be motivated to influence the client's choices, and how should such issues be managed?

- **O**penness to change: How flexible is the client's understanding of the causes of the current difficulties, and is there a willingness to try different approaches?

- **R**elationship: Without a relationship with the client that is at its core a helping relationship, the work is unlikely to proceed well. This means that unless the client believes that you are working on their behalf it is unlikely that the experience will be perceived as successful.

- **T**he **R**est: What else is going on that might be affecting the work/career issues? What questions does the client have that they need help in understanding? What other variables need to be considered in this particular assessment? Does the potential client have the energy and persistence to complete the assessment?

STEP 2. DETERMINE WHICH FACTORS AND VARIABLES TO MEASURE

Having concluded that career assessment is appropriate, it is necessary to decide which tests to use for a given assessment. Before that question can be addressed, however, the variables to be measured must first be identified.

The question of which variables should be measured needs to be tied to the assessment/referral questions. The extensiveness of what is to be measured will also depend on the time available and the costs of assessment. Although this book has argued that career assessment should routinely assess interests, abilities, and personality variables, it may be that the client has had prior assessments, the results of which can be used in the current assessment/counseling process. In other cases, time and money will limit the amount of ability testing that can be done. Or, the assessment may be done as a part of a group career exploration, during which everyone will receive the same assessment, which has been predetermined by others. Such factors do not mean that the assessment cannot proceed, but it should be done with full recognition of what is, and what is not, being measured, and the limits that might have for being able to address the referral questions or to help the client.

Even though the specific variables to be measured will vary from one assessment to the next, when the question is about career fit or career change, it is usually preferable to measure interests, abilities, and personality dimensions, since each category of variable has been demonstrated to be relevant to career choice and change. There may be other variables, either within or outside those domains, that may also need to be measured. For example, generalized self-esteem, arguably a measure of personality, might be relevant to assess when there is a discrepancy between actual and perceived abilities or when the client seems to be under-valuing themselves. When psychopathology is identified as part of a screening measure, further assessment may be needed, either by the career assessor (if qualified) or by another professional.

Whatever variables are to be measured, they should be demonstrated to be relevant to the referral questions. The link between the measures chosen and the questions to be addressed should be able to be explicitly identified and justified based on relevant literature. Thought should also be given up front about how the data will be combined and used to address the referral questions.

STEP 3. DETERMINE WHICH ASSESSMENT MEASURES TO USE AND THE MODALITY OF TEST ADMINISTRATION

Having identified the relevant variables, the assessor needs to identify the specific measures to employ in the assessment. The *Standards for Educational and Psychological Testing* (American Educational Research Association [AERA], American Psychological Association [APA], & National Council on Measurement in Education [NCME], 2014) provides important guidance in all aspects of test development and use and represents the best practices that should be incorporated. Concerning the standards for psychological testing and assessment, the following section is relevant:

> The assessment process begins by clarifying as much as possible, the reasons why a test taker will be assessed. Guided by these reasons or other relevant concerns, the tests, inventories, and diagnostic procedures are selected and other sources of information needed to evaluate the test taker are identified. . . . The

professional is responsible for being familiar with the evidence of validity for the intended uses of scores from the tests and inventories selected. . . . Evidence of the reliability/precision of scores, and the availability of applicable normative data in the test's accumulated research literature should be considered during test selection. (AERA, APA, & NCME, 2014, p. 152)

It is understandable, but misguided, to ask, "What's the best test to use?" as if validity and reliability were inherent properties of tests, independent of situation. One measure of interests may be well suited for making inferences about college students' career preferences but less relevant for blue-collar workers. Two personality measures may carry the same variable or factor labels, but one may be more susceptible to perceptual distortion than another. A highly timed measure of abilities may be ill-suited to someone with a learning disability. It is the test user's (i.e., career assessor's) responsibility to make evidence-based judgements on tests to incorporate into a career assessment test battery.

The question also arises about how many tests to give to assess a particular trait or characteristic. Is one enough? Using multiple measures, particularly of self-reports of personality and interests, can result in surprising discrepancies in the findings of one test versus another. For, example, Lowman et al. (2003) found that in comparing RIASEC results across multiple measures of the same constructs taken by the same individuals as part of an assessment process, the results were surprisingly likely to be inconsistent. Having more than one measure of the same interest and personality variables provides consistency evidence when they come up with the same RIASEC results—and a puzzle to be solved when they do not. When two measures of the same constructs do not result in the same high and low scores, it is important to understand whether there are aspects of the tests, such as how they measure the scores (e.g., occupational titles vs. broad brush approaches), that might help to explain the differences. If there are no psychometric reasons to explain the obtained differences, it is not the career assessor's job to make sense of the differences but rather to help the client understand that the differences need to be resolved, since they would take the person in different career directions.

Many personality and interest tests can now be administered electronically whenever and wherever the client is able to complete them. This means that in-person testing time with the client can be used for other purposes. Ability tests in particular need to be administered in person or else under controlled circumstances when done virtually. The order of administration also needs to be carefully planned such that the tests are not overloading the client, potentially affecting the results. Half day testing sessions are particularly well suited for local clients; those visiting the assessor's offices from out-of-town may require an accelerated schedule. Except in group testing administrations, the assessor can follow the client's lead if more or fewer breaks are needed. In a multiple ability assessment, consideration should be given to the order of test administration. For example, it may be preferable to administer ability tests of lesser cognitive demand (e.g., mechanical reasoning tests) before more demanding tests (intelligence, verbal reasoning, nonverbal reasoning, etc.) followed by those that are less cognitively demanding (clerical tests, ones for creative abilities, etc.). Although some people can successfully spend a full day—or multiple days—undergoing ability testing, many if not most cannot without affecting the quality of the results.

The purpose of the testing should be clearly introduced, and the client should be assured that detailed feedback will be provided. It is important that assessees know that they will not likely do equally well or poorly on all ability tests but rather that the purpose is to identify areas of respective strengths and comparative weaknesses. The testing process aims to obtain the client's best effort on each of the measures. Thus, if the assessee does less well on a particular measure it is not because they did not put forth the best effort.

It is also important to obtain clients' reactions to each test. A simple form gathering perceptions of the difficulty level of the test for the client and the degree of enjoyment of it are useful when it comes time for feedback. This process also provides the opportunity for the client to react to the test while it is still fresh. The assessor will find this information useful in interpreting the scores. Was this a difficult measure for the client, and if so, why? If, on the other hand, a client reported that the test was easy when the score was low, that can be explored in the feedback sessions. Was the test easy because limited effort was put forth on it?

STEP 4. ANALYZING THE ASSESSMENT RESULTS ONE DOMAIN AT A TIME

Assuming that data have been collected in each of the three focal domains (interests, abilities, personality), the scores from each domain should first be separately evaluated as if scores from the other domains did not exist. This approach is based on several factors. First, data interpretation is complex and needs to be done in the context of particular measures, norms, and interpretations. Cross-domain findings may or may not be consistent with each other, so it is important first to review and summarize test results in each domain on their own merits and later consider consistencies and inconsistencies across measures and across domains. It is often helpful to summarize the findings test-by-test and scale-by-scale within a particular domain and then to summarize the major cross-test results. These findings should also be evaluated in the context of the particular purpose of the career assessment goals.

For example, in the case of interests, the RIASEC scores (if that is the model on which the interest measures were based) provide a good place to begin the process. Suppose that there are results from three measures of interests, each yielding the familiar RIASEC scores and, in some cases, other interest-related scores as well. The scores on each measure need to be reviewed carefully and analyzed for consistencies and inconsistencies. For example, is the order and relative magnitude of scores on the six scores the same across the three measures? If not, are there major or minor discrepancies? Is the degree of elevation of scores relatively similar across the three measures? Thinking of the occupational choices the client is considering, are the interest codes of those occupations consistent with the measured interests? What do the structural elements (e.g., concern with people vs. data or things) add to the vocational interest understanding? If there are large discrepancies across the measures, does a review of the subparts of the tests provide clues as to the differences? In a measure that relies only on occupational titles, is a particular occupational interest category elevated, whereas when the interests are measured with a multipart test that approaches interests by examining different dimensions of them, including titles, do results more closely match the first measure when only the occupational title reactions are compared? Is there evidence that one versus the other of the interest measures used is a more robust one with more current norms and anchors in the empirical literature? Assuming that there is cross-test consistency in the measured interests, are they compatible with the person's current career pursuits? Or, alternatively, do they suggest that the respondent, at least on the basis of interests, may indeed be ill-suited to the present occupation or educational pursuit? What hypotheses can be generated from the interest data?

A similar approach would be taken in the case of abilities and of personality. In the case of abilities, there may not be multiple measures of each ability. But within a particular ability space, there may be similarities and differences that are noteworthy. For example, measures of cognitive ability or intelligence may have both verbal and nonverbal tests or subtests. Although verbal and nonverbal cognitive abilities at the group level are typically well correlated, and both correlate well with general intelligence (or serve as proxy measures of it), at the individual level there may be a significant discrepancy between verbal and nonverbal strengths, and this difference may have career relevance (and help to explain career and school patterns).

In the case of personality variables, measures can differ significantly in how subtle or overt the items are, such that positive self-presentation may be more likely on one measure than another. To the extent the person has self-presented in a particular way on multiple measures of the same construct (e.g., on introversion/extraversion or openness) then at least tentative conclusions or hypotheses can be generated. Such test findings should be juxtaposed against the behavioral evidence of personality, from both the client's history and interactions with the assessor. Clients who present themselves as being highly extraverted on a test but who have pursued work that is mostly solitary in nature and who are meek and mild in interpersonal interactions during the assessment raise discrepancies that will need clarification.

Hypotheses about the career implications of the data should be generated at each stage of the process. For example, in considering interest data, one would want to know which occupational choices being considered by the client are the most and least compatible with the high-point scores profile. Are there areas of potential conflict within interests or, for abilities, does the client show "too many" abilities such that their integrated expression may be difficult? No effort should be initially made to integrate the domain-specific data at this stage.

Each (tentative) conclusion preferably should be supported by at least two sources of evidence. Because the practice of career assessment and counseling is not an exact science, and some of the measures used may not have much evidence for predicting to long-term career satisfaction or productivity, it is valuable to be able to anchor conclusions and even hypotheses on more than one data source. This is not always possible, of course, because to include two measures of every variable in every case would make a long assessment process even more protracted. However, in some instances, comparable variables moving in a consistent direction provide sufficient basis for drawing conclusions. For example, the Dominance scale of the California Psychological Inventory (CPI), the Dominance (Enterprising) scale of the Sixteen Personality Factor Questionnaire (16PF), and comparable scales on the Hogan Personality Inventory or the NEO tests are all measuring conceptually similar variables, although each scale has been developed and validated differently.

If, for a given client, these scales are all consistent with one another and with behavioral evidence and moving in the opposite direction of scales that are assessing conceptually opposite (such as in the case of dominance and the need for abasement), then there is more solid ground for reaching a conclusion about tendencies toward assertiveness as a general characteristic of personality than if these variables present an inconsistent or situationally variable pattern.

It is not necessary to resolve every source of disagreement or discrepancy in order to draw meaningful conclusions about an assessee. Some data simply raise difficult or inconclusive issues that will require either more data, time, or life experience to understand. It is not the task of the testing and counseling process to resolve all conflicts or inconsistencies. However, the career counselor does have an obligation to help assessees to become aware of sources of potential inconsistency or conflict and to understand how the issues might be worked on or through.

Although method variance may account for some discrepancies in career assessment test results, it is also possible that the obtained differences represent sources of personal or difficult-to-resolve conflicts. For example, Social and Realistic vocational interests are thought to represent theoretically opposing characteristics of personality (J. L. Holland, 1985a, 1987). If present in the same individual, they are a potential source of frustration and conflict because those aspects of the person may be trying to be expressed in ways that are fundamentally incompatible with one another. Similarly, if an individual has skills both in relating to others and in working with mechanical objects, these may be difficult to make use of in one job. Conversely, some difficult-to-resolve issues concern external factors. For example, a would-be fiction writer whose interests, abilities, and personality point to that as a well-fitting career choice may confront the reality of not being able to make a living at that line of work. How they can make use of the profile in related, but somewhat different, work or as part their avocational pursuits may then become the focus. In such cases, it is not the task of the career assessor to solve the issues but rather to make the issue and its dimensions clear to the assessee.

Finally, when considering variables in isolation from one another, a static rather than dynamic understanding of clients' concerns may emerge. Often the research has examined isolated variables (e.g., general cognitive ability) without considering how other variables may interact with it. This individual variable approach to assessment may make for easier research or career counseling but limit understanding, particularly when it comes to real-life applications. For example, people who are temperamentally high on anxiety may successfully manage that trait by throwing their efforts into work and staying busy with activities. Similarly, managers with low cognitive abilities may be able to compensate for this relative weakness by making use of excellent interpersonal skills to build and motivate a team. The important point is that career assessment needs to consider the larger picture, not a few variables taken in isolation.

The career assessor in this model therefore proceeds in the evaluation of each set of data independently, generating hypotheses and issues requiring further clarification and elaboration that can be checked against the findings from other domains. For example, in reviewing a client's vocational interest data, the assessor might note an apparent conflict between managerial and helping (Enterprising and Social) interests and scientific (Investigative) interests. In such instances, the counselor would want to know the nature of the Investigative interests: Are there strong intellectual abilities that might be receiving limited expression in the client's current position? Has the client worked in any managerial or sales position in which intellectual or scientific interests might have been needed (e.g., selling technical products for a computer firm)? Is there some way to clarify whether the interests are more Enterprising than Social or more Social than Enterprising? For example, is there a history of doing volunteer and other helping work? What about the relative conflict between financial and helping interests? These sorts of questions cannot be resolved on the basis of the test scores alone; additional work in career counseling sessions may be needed to help define and clarify these issues.

STEP 5. INTEGRATE THE ASSESSMENT RESULTS: CROSS-DOMAIN ANALYSIS

At the end of the process of examining testing results separately by domain, the assessor will have gathered intradomain findings, made hypotheses about meaning and implications, and identified both consistencies and discrepancies in the data. It will then be time to examine the data on an interdomain basis, looking for what the combined data add up to and considering how the findings relate to the referral questions.

Recognizing that there is much research work still needed in the area of creating reliable profiles and typologies (see Chapter 17), it is still worthwhile to look for cross-domain patterns. When an overall profile is identified from the data that clearly points to a particular typology, the job is made much easier. For example, science and business profiles do have a fair amount of consistency and literature support. But these patterns can be more general than the client's questions need them to be. A "science profile," a general one that at this stage of knowledge does not differentiate between, say, physics and chemistry, or astronomy and biomedicine, nor does it address whether someone should become an administrator of science or an entrepreneur or a bench scientist. Similarly, within a "business profile," there are many subtypes (e.g., accounting vs. management vs. sales/marketing) that call for different interest patterns or skill sets even when the overall profile is generally a good match. And what is to be done when the career directions suggested by the testing results do not match what the client (or those in the client's life, say, parents or spouses) believes should be the preferred career direction?

Career guidance, when it provides overly specific information, down to a particular occupation, can also be too granular, resulting in the client rejecting the guidance and missing the larger points. It is not unusual, in discussions with a client as to whether there has been prior career testing, to be told "I took a test in high school and it told me I should be a [funeral director, kindergarten teacher's aide, circus performer, etc.]," followed by dismissive laughter. Of course, the supposed affinity for an unliked career may have derived from an interest measure that included a number of other occupations with empirical data showing similarity or dissimilarity of a range of client responses to those of people happily working in those occupations. Forgotten, or never provided, was the guidance that those occupations were included to open up individuals to a variety of careers and never offered as "the" occupation to pursue. Clearly, in the example, the client had not been helped because there was no understanding of what led the suggested occupations to have shown up as possibilities for consideration, and because there may have been no way to generalize from the assessment findings to the actual choices of interest to the person.

Still, a plan is needed for the assessor to review the entire profile in a research-informed way. Recognizing that there is overlap across *some* interest, ability, and personality factors and variables, there is also variance that does not overlap, which is why each domain should be interpreted both on its own and also in the context of the others. Guided by the within-domain data review and interpretation, assessors are faced with the job of stitching together the cross-domain findings in a way that is useful to the client.

After hypotheses have been separately generated in each domain, cross-domain comparisons need to be made. One way to begin the process of integrating complex career assessment findings is to generate a table with three separate columns, one each for abilities, interests, and personality (and a fourth, perhaps, for "Other"). The major findings and hypotheses for each domain can then be listed side by side, along with questions that cannot be resolved on the basis of these findings.

For example, in the case of Elizabeth (Case 7), summarized later in the chapter, a portion of these columns might appear as shown in Table 18.1.

TABLE 18.1. Illustration of Summary Findings and Questions, Elizabeth's Case (Case 7)

Domain	Interests	Abilities	Personality
Findings	Highest interests in Artistic, Social, and Investigative. Enterprising second highest on one measure. Better matches to her occupational daydreams than to college major or job.	Strengths in the arts, particularly in the visual arts, including Aesthetic Judgement, Reproductive Drawing ability, and Field Independence. Strength in Perceptual Speed and Accuracy. Absence of strengths in mechanical, cognitive, and managerial areas.	Introversion/Extraversion: Introverted. Conscientiousness: Mixed results; some areas of possible "artistic rebelliousness" and some areas of higher self-control. Agreeableness: Mixed results. Not particularly sociable or oriented to others. Openness: Some areas of inflexibility. Neuroticism/Emotional Stability: Several areas of concern including some anxiety, depression, and possible obsessive-compulsive tendencies. Dominance: Very low; traditional Feminine identity but with strong work identity. Need for Achievement: High.
Questions	Why did she major in business, not seemingly a good fit for her interests? Why did she pursue a job in marketing? Where, if at all, do her Artistic interests find expression? Would avocational expression of her Artistic interests be sufficient? If job change is not possible, are there things she could do to promote her Artistic interests and possibly to prepare for a later job change?	How is the client using her strengths? What strengths and challenges does she experience in her current work? Do her avocational activities make better use of her abilities than her "day job"? Why did she choose her college major given its apparent lack of fit with her abilities?	Would a change of career direction help with the client's anxiety? How can she work around her anxiety and obsessive-compulsive tendencies to consider and act upon alternative career paths? Is there a need for greater assertiveness in seeking her career and work goals? Lower Conscientious scores usually predict to workplace issues. Has this affected her work? Given that such scores are common among people in creative work, would that support transitioning to such careers? The client's high expressed achievement needs create difficulties in that it would be easier to succeed and advance in an area well suited to her abilities and interests. Can she explore this apparent contradiction and take appropriate action? Would coaching/counseling be helpful to sort out her complex pattern of results?

STEP 6. GENERATE INTEGRATIVE CAREER ASSESSMENT HYPOTHESES TIED TO THE REASONS FOR ASSESSMENT

Finally, in this section I make explicit several guidelines, hypotheses really, about the career assessment process in differentiating the relative importance of cross-domain findings. In generating these integrative hypotheses, I begin with a set of assumptions.

Assumption 1. Fit Matters

The career paths most likely to satisfy people and most likely to bring lasting growth and success are those that are reasonably congruent with individual abilities, interests, and personality. When fit varies across the domains, priorities need to be considered (see Assumption 3).

Assumption 2. There Are Usually Several Potentially Well-Fitting Careers

Within most career paths, there are usually multiple directions that an individual can take that are generally consistent with the individual's interdomain profile. For example, two individuals with the same vocational interest pattern (say, Enterprising–Artistic–Social) may both attend and successfully graduate from law school. Both have high inductive reasoning ability and high verbal fluency, but one is extraverted and highly gregarious, whereas the other is shy and reserved. Although both may become excellent attorneys, the former may prefer the on-your-feet engagement of criminal trial law while the other flourishes by specializing in antitrust law, especially doing research.

Assumption 3. Determine How to Prioritize Among the Domains

When there is a conflict between degree of fit to a job (or career), I argue that interests and abilities take precedence over personality characteristics. Interests speak to motivation ("want to do"), abilities to capacity ("can do"), and personality to role implementation ("how to do"). Not all career roles in an occupational group may favor the same personality dimensions. For example, an extraverted scientist can potentially flourish in a scientific manager or sales role. Conversely, an introverted business manager may do well in a technical leadership position, assuming the person's interests and abilities were well-suited to the job.

Assumption 4. Abilities Need to Be Used, and Career Choices in Which They Can Be Used Are Preferred

Abilities, if possessed, benefit from expression at work; if they are not used, this may lead to dissatisfaction with the career or job. When abilities are underutilized either because the career does not call for them or when they are not allowed expression in a particular job, people can feel restless and unhappy. Avocational activities can sometimes be a place for un- or underused abilities to be expressed, but that may be less effective when work is one's central life interest.

Assumption 5. Reality Matters

Real-world options require people to make decisions on career directions in the context of actual, not imagined, circumstances. It is ultimately up to clients to evaluate their assessment results in the context of their own pragmatic needs and preferences. Some may consciously choose a better paying job that is a less good fit with their personal characteristics. Many factors beyond the degree of career fit will influence actual career choices, including earnings potential, availability of jobs in the desired field in one's geographic area, ease of entry (including whether additional training is needed), and financial responsibilities. The career assessor is the coach, but the client is the one who needs to make (hopefully well-informed) career decisions in the context of their own personal situations.

Assumption 6. Further Help May Be Needed

The need for counseling may extend beyond the assessment. For many—perhaps most—career assessees, the process will end when the feedback has been delivered and the report presented. For others, either through referral or in a continuing relationship, they will need additional assistance as they strive to work through the particulars of their career concerns. Career assessors should make clear to the client what to do if further help is needed. Some will find the initial assessment sufficient but will seek help later when they are contemplating additional changes in their work life.

Assumption 7. Agency Matters

Ultimately it is the client's job to make career choices; the assessor is a guide and a coach, not the decision maker. This is not just a quantitative issue ("here's your best-fitting occupation") but a matter of careful and often tedious comparison of relative fits and misfits, likes and dislikes. The assessor can provide very important and sometimes career- and life-changing information, synthesis, and identified choices. Clients, however, are the ones who must use this information (or not) to chart their own career paths. Keeping the responsibility where it belongs is at all times important.

The assessor's goal in this approach is to help clients understand the data and the relevant environmental information and how possible career choices fit into the client's present and longer term career options. The next section provides an example of the process and conclusions.

INTEGRATING ACROSS INTERESTS, ABILITY, AND PERSONALITY— ELIZABETH'S CASE (CASE 7)

Career assessment findings for Case 7 were presented in Chapters 4, 12, and 16. Here we illustrate how the findings can be summarized in each domain and then integrated across the domains.

Interests Analysis and Interpretation

This case was included in the book as an illustration of an Artistic interest profile. The client's interest assessment results are presented in Chapter 4 (Case 7). Interpretive findings are summarized here.

The client's interests were Artistic across all three measures. Her secondary and tertiary RIASEC codes were consistent across two of the measures, being Social and Investigative. The third measure had Enterprising as the second most highly endorsed score, but Investigative score was the tertiary code.

The client had high needs for status (Vocational Preference Inventory [VPI] Status scale) but was not particularly oriented to education (Strong Academic Comfort scale). With the exception of elementary education, physical therapy, and veterinarian, all the client's occupational daydreams (Self-Directed Search) were in the Artistic areas.

The client's current occupation did not match her measured interests. Further exploration is needed about what drew her to that occupation and whether she finds it satisfying. Should she pursue creative avocational interests if she needs to remain in the paralegal position for the money it pays?

The client's interest in professional work with horses might explain her listing veterinarian in her occupational daydreams. However, this was not a good fit with her interests. However, there are matches of some of her occupational daydreams with occupations on the Strong interest measure. Photographer and advertising executive were similar to her daydreams.

The inclusion of Investigative interests as tertiary interests on all three measures may explain some of the appeal of medical areas. Both parents had worked in health care. However, her low Academic Comfort score on the Strong might suggest less interest in an occupation that would require extensive academic preparation.

The client's lowest endorsed scores were Conventional and Realistic. The low Realistic score is not surprising, but aspects of her current occupation include Conventional interests, so it would be important to find out what she dislikes about her current position.

The visual arts were represented in her occupational daydreams list in clothes designer and interior decorator. Both include Enterprising aspects, which was only represented in her highest interest scores on one of the measures. Both of these occupations are fairly competitive to get into.

Except for the VPI scores, Artistic interests were much higher than the next highest interest code. It is likely important that this interest be expressed in her occupation.

On the client's most highly endorsed activities, two were in the arts (including dramatics, matching her occupational daydream of being an actor) and three in medical service or science areas.

Overall, the client's interests were more consistent with her occupational daydreams than with her current occupation. Her abilities and personality results may help to clarify the interest results.

Abilities Analysis and Interpretation

The client's abilities were presented in Chapter 12. Her overall intelligence was in the average range on Verbal Intelligence and in the average to high average range on Nonverbal intelligence. Although the difference between the two types of intelligence was not statistically different, the Nonverbal Intelligence score was lowered by the Picture Arrangement subtest whereas the Verbal subtests had less scatter. The particular subtest that was lower is often associated with social skills. The difference between the Verbal and Nonverbal Intelligence scores may therefore be underestimated.

Concerning the primary and other abilities, she had strengths in the spatial and visual arts areas including in Aesthetic Judgment and Artistic Drawing Ability. She also scored in the field independent direction on a measure of field dependency. She scored quite high on a Perceptual Speed and Accuracy test. She scored high on a measure of verbal fluency but was not high on ideational fluency. Her memory test score was also high. In the music area she scored highest on a Rhythm subtest. She scored in the average level on Social- and Enterprising-related abilities. Her cognitive abilities in verbal reasoning and nonverbal reasoning were lower than might be expected of someone with her educational level.

It would appear that the client's abilities paralleled her interests. They were strongest in the areas of the visual arts. These included Aesthetic Judgement, Spatial Ability, Field Independence, and Artistic Drawing Ability. Her Perceptual Speed and Accuracy Test was also a strength. In contrast, her cognitive results were not particularly high, and her social and managerial abilities did not suggest special strengths in helping or business roles.

Personality Analysis and Interpretation

The client's personality profile (presented in Chapter 16) varied to some degree by measure. On the Fundamental Interpersonal Relations Orientation-Behavior (FIRO-B) results, she had low needs to control others or to be controlled by them. She presented herself instead as having little need for involvement with others. She generally scored in the Introverted direction. Her CPI personality type of Delta resulted from a combination of Internality and Norm Questioning (people with Artistic interests may present themselves as being rebellious or challenging of authority). Her scores on the Conscientiousness measures were at the average or above level. The client's scores on the Agreeableness-related variables suggested modest involvement with others, and she may not relate to others in a particularly sociable way. On the Openness variables, she scored mildly inflexible on the CPI but high on the EPPS need for change variable. Concerning Neuroticism/Adjustment, it would appear that the client was experiencing some distress at the time of the assessment. She appeared to be prone to anxiety and worry, sometimes obsessing about minor details rather than taking action to resolve the issues. Her Self-Acceptance score was quite low, also suggesting an area of concern. She scored low on several measures of Dominance and high on the F/M scale on the CPI, suggesting a traditional orientation to feminine roles.

It would appear that the client is consistent in responding in the introverted direction, not particularly oriented to others, midrange on Conscientiousness, and mixed on her Openness scores. She scored relatively low on adjustment measures with some indication of worry and anxiety. She was low on Dominance and high on a measure of traditional feminine roles.

Integration of Interests, Abilities, and Personality

Major hypotheses for each of the three major domains (interests, abilities, and personality) are shown in Exhibit 18.1. Concerning the reasons for her referral, her current career pursuits do not seem to be meeting her needs. Review of the findings and questions raised by them demonstrate that the client does not appear to working in a career that speaks to her strengths, her interests, or her personality. For people in the arts, having a "day job" is often a necessity, but the client does not seem to have found an outlet for her interests, abilities, and personality. At the same time, it would be important to consider ways in which she could pursue her creative interests (particularly in the visual arts) while keeping her current position. Further exploration is also needed about the impact on her later college and career choices of her physical injuries that blocked her initial career ambitions. Did that loss create a sense of learned helplessness regarding work, careers, and avocational choices? It is possible that her therapist could help her work on some of these issues to facilitate her understanding and to support any career transition.

SUMMARY AND CONCLUSIONS

It is one thing to do research on variables and factors related to career and work assessment. It is another to translate research findings into practice in a way that builds on knowledge but also recognizes the idiosyncrasies of idiographic data.

This chapter reviewed practical ways to proceed in the entire career assessment process, from problem definition, to identifying relevant variables to measure, to administering and interpreting data in order to help real people facing real career problems make decisions about their work and careers. A case example presented earlier in the book was used to illustrate the process of summarizing data, generating hypotheses within a domain, and then combining across them. In the next chapter, issues associated with providing feedback—both oral and written—are addressed.

EXHIBIT 18.1

Conclusions and Hypotheses About Elizabeth's Case (Case 7)

Conclusions and Hypotheses Across and Among the Domains

A. Interests
1. The client's current occupation is not consistent with her interests, nor was her college major.
2. Strong Artistic interests would benefit from expression, preferably in her work, but otherwise in avocational activities.
3. The history of early loss of a cherished anticipated career pursuit may have resulted in unresolved issues and difficulties moving on from that.
4. The tertiary elevation of Investigative interests needs further exploration. One way to combine her interests could be working in medical or scientific illustration. Alternatively, she might combine Investigative and Social interests in a health position as suggested by some of her interest matches. However, the strong Artistic interests do need to find expression.

B. Abilities
5. The client's abilities show greater cognitive strengths in the nonverbal than verbal area. This is the opposite pattern of those modally found among people pursuing her college major but not uncommon in people with strengths in the visual arts.
6. The client's current occupation makes some use of her Conventional-related abilities but does not appear to build on her areas of special strength. One hypothesis is that the work is a "day job" to support herself, but it may also be an important defense. If the latter hypothesis is accurate, a precipitous change of career directions might be problematic.
7. Her abilities and interests are generally consistent with a visual arts profile.
8. Her cognitive ability scores were somewhat lower than might be expected of someone with her educational background. Alternatively, among those with visual arts or Conventional-related abilities, her patterns would not be unusual. Playing to strengths is usually preferable to working around areas of relative weakness.

C. Personality
9. The client's personality results were not particularly consistent with her college major.
10. Her apparent need to conform to others' expectations may be inconsistent with her interests and abilities profile.
11. The relatively strong needs for achievement may create problems for her if she is not pursuing a well-fitting career. These needs may necessitate her working harder and with less satisfaction than if her work makes daily use of her strongest abilities.
12. Her apparent introversion and lack of social presence might be a limitation in pursuing a business of her own; she might be more effective in a visual-arts or similar career in which she is working for others.
13. There were indicators of anxiety, depression, and obsessive-compulsive features associated with the Adjustment dimension. These need to be considered in helping her understand and work with the assessment findings. Because the personality measures used were those designed for use with the normal range of personality, further assessment of psychological functioning may be needed.

D. Interdomain
14. Ideally, the client will find a way to work in a space consistent both with her interests and her abilities. In this case, finding a way to make her Artistic interests and Artistic-related abilities a part of her major work pursuits—or at least an important avocational activity—is recommended.
15. There is not a single career path that will be congruent with the client's interests-abilities-personality characteristics. There are a number of different job families that could fit well with the client's career profile. However, having an understanding of the underlying traits and other factors will help her purposefully and systematically evaluate possible career choices. Additionally, having a plan for exploring alternative careers after the feedback session is something that may need attention.
16. Psychological factors (e.g., anxiety and obsessive-compulsive tendencies) may be affecting the client's apparent suppression of use of her natural strengths and interests and her personality dispositional factors. Such tendencies can affect self-efficacy, in turn interfering with making appropriate career decisions and choices. Conversely, well-matched work in which she can feel good about her achievements may positively affect her sense of self-efficacy and relieve some of her anxiety. When, as in this case, there may be perceived barriers to considering options and insufficient self-efficacy, those issues may need to be approached directly.
17. Anxiety and depression may be derived from her career difficulties or associated with factors separate from them. Career/work issues likely need to be addressed as one aspect of a broader pattern. If they are to be worked on independently of personal counseling, both will benefit from awareness and coordination.
18. Overall, the client may benefit from ongoing counseling/coaching to help her better understand the issues and to make better use of her interests, abilities, and personality factors in workplace applications.

19

Client Feedback and Report Preparation

What information should be fed back to the individual being assessed? In what manner should the results be reported? How should "negative" data be handled? In what form is the feedback most likely to be accepted and assimilated? What about the pragmatics of feedback? How many sessions are needed, who should be in the session, and should follow-up be included as a standard practice?

The issues discussed in this chapter refer both to the oral feedback reviewed with the client at the time of the assessment and the written report, which, if properly prepared, will serve as a lifetime reference document on an individual's career concerns.

PROVIDING IN-PERSON FEEDBACK

Extent and type of feedback to be provided will vary with the particular context and setting. Therefore, there is no one way—but there are some general principles—by which all feedback can be planned.

Varieties of Feedback and Clients

The types of feedback that can be provided will vary by setting. A counselor in a university setting might see, say, eight student clients a day and have only an hour or less with each. In a business setting an assessor might be provided several hours to work with a senior manager. Or the assessor may be called on to meet

---

https://doi.org/10.1037/0000254-020
Career Assessment: Integrating Interests, Abilities, and Personality, by R. L. Lowman
Copyright © 2022 by the American Psychological Association. All rights reserved.

with each candidate who completed an assessment center process—both those selected and the presumably larger number of people who were not. In other settings, the face-to-face feedback will be provided in a group context in which everyone will receive the same information. There may or may not be the possibility of one-on-one follow-up sessions for people wanting them, and even if such sessions are available (often at additional cost), few may choose to pursue them.

Who will be present in individualized feedback sessions may also vary. When parents seek out help for their children, they will likely be part of the feedback session. Indeed, they may be more interested in the findings and recommendations than is the adolescent or young adult who was assessed. It is generally wise to get the permission of the assessee to have third parties be present in a feedback session. Even then, it may be desirable to set aside some time to meet with the individual assessed alone.

There are also situations, such as in a third-party request for services (e.g., assessing an employee's capacity to work after a medical illness), in which the feedback will primarily, or even exclusively, go to a medical or human resources (HR) professional. In the latter cases, assessment was sought for a particular purpose, and the referral sources may want clear, quick answers and a written report they can consult for more information.

Basic Principles of Feedback

Whatever specific feedback format will be used, the principles are similar. The client will likely receive a lot of information in the feedback session and should also receive a written summary of the career assessment findings and recommendations. Although the information must always be technically accurate and consistent with the assessment results, it must also be provided in a way that the client can understand and make good use of. As with a medical consultation, clients seek out the assessor's expertise not for theoretical understanding but for help with a real-life problems or development issues. They neither want nor need to become experts in the vast field of career assessment, yet they still need to have a basic understanding of the assessment process and relevant career theory and research findings. For example, clients need to know that data on particular scores likely fall within a range.

Have a Plan

Assessment is done for specific purposes. How the feedback is provided will influence its effectiveness in helping clients address the reasons for which they sought help. It is a critical part of the process and should be thoughtfully approached and planned for. A useful book to help with the process is J. B. Gregory and Levy's (2015) *Using Feedback in Organizational Consulting*.

Anchor Feedback in the Assessment's Purpose

The reasons for the client's assessment need to be focal in the feedback process. For example, clients may be thinking of changing careers, pursuing school or training, or may just want to know how they can be more effective in their current career. When the assessed individuals are the primary clients, they also may have opinions, sometimes not disclosed to the assessor, about what they should do next.

Reasons for assessment are as varied as the types of clients seeking referral, but typically include such issues as (a) unhappiness in one's present occupation; (b) uncertainty about a contemplated career course; (c) confirmation that a planned career or school direction is an appropriate one; (d) a need to satisfy someone else (typically, a parent or supervisor) who has recommended or insisted that assessment take place; and (e) as a statement to oneself of being ready for change, which not infrequently may have been under consideration for a number of years.

The work to identify the purposes of the assessment should be done on the front end and will hopefully help to guide the assessment. In turn, they should be a central focus of the feedback process. In the feedback, remind the client of the questions for which assistance was sought and determine whether new ones may have arisen during the assessment.

Be Technically Accurate

Career assessment is complicated, particularly when multiple domains are measured. Although the data are complex, the assessor needs to be in full command of it, to be clear on why the identified variables or factors were selected, the measures used, the findings, and how the results relate to the reasons career assessment was sought. That alone calls for considerable expertise—but there is more. The assessor must also be able to translate all this information, including its limitations, to terms the client can understand. When clients are engaged in understanding what was measured, why, what the results suggested, and how to gather more information, they will leave the assessment better empowered to do the hard work that still needs to be done.

It is possible to give both too much and too little information in career feedback. On the one hand, providing overly detailed explanations of every test and procedure will not likely be useful feedback. On the other hand, focusing on conclusions without explanations of procedures used or the limitations of results is also problematic. Too often, career assessors are more likely to gloss over limitations of their methods and to present data in a more conclusive way than may be justified by the findings or the research literature. Clients may also pull for definite answers when they are not there. Clients who, at the end of the process, learn more about themselves, their work preferences, and talents, and who have an understanding of how to use and fine-tune the findings will be empowered to address their immediate concerns and other career issues that may arise in the future.

Be Aware of, and Manage, the Affect

People seek out help for career assessment for a variety of reasons. They may have their heart set on pursuing a particular career, but the findings from the assessment may not be consistent with that. Although the goal of assessment feedback is to enhance understanding and for the client to be better able to make career-related decisions, the process has both cognitive and affective components. This means that the assessor's job in providing feedback includes paying attention to the reactions the client is having to the information and—always—being supportive and understanding, aiming to be helpful.

As a general principle, feedback to individuals on the results of career assessments should match the comprehensiveness of the testing (or other assessment procedures administered) and should emphasize data germane to the reasons for which help was sought. This includes both negative and positive findings. How the results are reported to the client will largely be influenced by the ability of the client to assimilate and make effective use of the findings. The client's psychological defenses must be respected and worked with and around in determining how best to report findings.

Understand and Manage Resistance

The effective career assessor will anchor orally presented and written feedback to the referral questions, even though all collected data may not be directly related to them. Especially in the face-to-face feedback, information needs to be presented to the client in a way that creatively bypasses potential sources of resistance. This means that information must be presented in a manner that is both accurate and able to be accepted by the client, consistent with ethical guidelines and technical standards.

In the typical feedback process, information may be presented to a client about which there will be ready agreement, some that will come as a pleasant surprise, and other information will be disagreed with, including when it is inconsistent with the client's sense of self. Wise assessors know or soon learn that resistance will be encountered not just with so-called negative information or areas of relative weakness. Clients can be just as resistant, if not more so, to accepting positive information that is discrepant with their sense of self. When an assessee has no musical background and does not have a self-perception that includes musical talent, the finding of low scores on a measure of psychoacoustical or musical ability may be readily accepted. On the other hand, if a client has a lifelong self-view of being below average in intellectual ability, it may be surprisingly difficult, even with strong evidence, to facilitate a more positive self-perception.

Reframing information that may be difficult for the client to hear or accept may help. Here is an example. A psychologist with a graduate degree who spent most of his professional time administering intelligence tests in schools was surprised to find that he scored well above average on a measure of intelligence—one that he had never before administered. "No way," he said, when told that his results on that test were in the high average to superior range. It turned out that he had been assessed as a child and, for a variety of reasons, he had scored below average on a verbal measure of intelligence but above average on a nonverbal one. Many years later, that discrepancy had disappeared, and the client's own academic achievements belied the earlier result. It was helpful to have him apply his own understanding of the normal curve to his personal results. Knowing where people with graduate degrees typically scored helped him better understand and accept the results of his assessment.

Conversely, clients may have an exaggerated sense of their own abilities. Aspiring to an occupation that greatly exceeds their average intellectual abilities raises the question of how to feed back this information to the client in a way that can be heard but does not attack self-esteem. It is certainly true that people with average levels of intelligence can, through very high motivation and very hard work, be successful in a demanding career. The odds are against them, however, so it may be useful to understand the source of the ambition and for the client to understand alternative career paths that may provide a better match. People can be successful in a variety of occupations, so it is useful to support the client's ambition while helping them consider careers where it can be put to better use.

In one-on-one feedback sessions, the assessor can also help clients identify the reactions they are having to the information received. Perhaps they are angry with the results, wanting to discuss how unfair a particular test was. Or they may be reacting with superficial agreement that appears to mask anxiety or disappointment. Recognizing reactions, checking them out, contextualizing them, and addressing the source of those reactions is a complicated but important part of the feedback process.

Address Action Plan and Next Steps

Of course, it is not the consultant's job to make decisions for their clients but, rather, to provide relevant information, to raise questions, and to help them make sense of their career paths—past, present, and future. Processing and integrating the findings is not likely to be something completed at the time of the feedback. Clients will need to think through the guidance they have received and incorporate it into their understanding and behavior as they move forward. It is their job to decide what to do with their lives, but the information sought and provided should be helpful. Perhaps it suggests that a planned course of action is not the best one for them to undertake. Or the results may be supportive of a change, but actions that will likely be disruptive are required. Helping the client develop a specific course of action (e.g., exploring particular careers in more depth, finalizing a decision on pursuing further training, or taking classes in a previously not considered area of study) will assist the client in translating sometimes abstract concepts into practical next steps.

WRITTEN REPORT PREPARATION

With few exceptions, it is generally appropriate to provide the assessee with a written report summarizing the results of career assessment. If a third party has contracted for the assessment, then written reports may, with the assessee's permission, need to be provided to the third-party client and a separate report (or other type of feedback) provided to the assessee.

Principles of Report Preparation

Career assessment reports should be customized to the intended audiences. When the client is the individual assessed, providing details on what was assessed and why is useful. When a third party is involved, the purposes of the assessment should dictate the type of report. This book does not cover assessments for purposes of selection since that requires specialized knowledge and expertise and reports need to be prepared with a specific legal context in mind. But when the person requesting the report is a third party, such as in selection or when an employer seeks guidance on managing a disabled worker, different rules may apply. In this book the focus is primarily on assessments commissioned for personal use and goals of development rather than selection.

When individuals go through a career assessment process, it is quite likely to be the only time in their lives they will have such an assessment. They may well retain the report from the assessment and consult it from time to time as career issues arise for them. Additionally, when clients receive verbal feedback on the results of an assessment, it is difficult to fully assimilate all of the data. Even taking notes or recording the feedback session, clients may not go away with a complete or even accurate record of the important points being made or how they might guide future career decisions. For these reasons, the final report of the assessment should be written for posterity and should provide a detailed summary of the purposes of the assessment, the findings, interpretations, and recommendations made. It should also provide sufficient caveats so that the person understands that some things measured will change over time and there is error in almost all assessments. Although the report will need to contain technical information such as names of tests administered, constructs measured, and numerical results and norms, overall, it should be written in language the client can understand (see the American Psychological Association's [APA] Ethical Principle 9.10, Explaining Assessment Results; APA, 2017a).

There are many ways in which career feedback reports can be written, but each report should meet certain minimal standards of accuracy and understandability. These include the following.

The Report Should Be Accurate

The report should not contain false statements or those which, in the context, could potentially be misleading. Here are some examples of problematic statements and more effective ones.

Example: Because your score on the measure of Spatial Abilities was low, you should avoid engineering or architectural careers.

Such a statement is entirely too broad, and the recipient is likely to feel thwarted or inappropriately characterized, especially if it is directed to an assessee who has been planning on a career in architecture.

Better: Your score on the Spatial Abilities test was at the 13th percentile compared with high school female students and at the 2nd percentile when compared with a group of (primarily male) engineers and architects. While this does not rule out such fields as engineering or architecture, they might be more difficult for you to master.

Example: Your score on the measure of verbal reasoning was at the 80th percentile.

This statement is not necessarily inaccurate, but it is insufficient. The client needs both a context for interpreting the result (which level of percentiles are "high," which "low"?) and an explanation of the reference group used to make the normative comparison. The client should also be helped to understand that percentile scores at the middle ranges might still be high when the normative group is one that needs those abilities for their professional work. A score on a cognitive reasoning test at the 40th percentile compared with a sample of Nobel Prize winners would be quite high indeed.

Better: Your score of 66 on the Watson-Glaser Critical Thinking Ability measure was at the 80th percentile compared with a group of upper division students in four-year colleges and was at the 50th percentile compared with a group of MBA students. This score indicates well above-average verbal reasoning ability. Verbal reasoning ability is useful in a variety of occupational pursuits, including . . . [list follows].

Here, the specific name of the test is given (so that a future assessor or career counselor can make use of the data), the normative groups are identified by name, and the general implications of the score in the assessment context noted.

Appropriately Qualify Findings

Caution should be used in drawing conclusions that exceed known facts. Trait-and-factor models may be especially likely to overgeneralize from scores on specific variables on individual psychological tests. Even though many traits are stable over the long run with large populations, they may or may not be at the individual level. Additionally, the measure of the trait almost always contains error variance. Therefore, recognizing likely characteristics associated with a test score should be accompanied by qualifiers as appropriate.

Example: You scored highly on a measure of Need for Dominance. You are quick to express opinions and are seen by others as being overly self-assertive and aggressive. You like to influence others and to get ahead in the world.

Such statements are not necessarily wrong, but they may be unproven in occupational or work settings, may take no account of potential method bias or threats to validity (e.g., "fake good"), and present a very unidimensional view of the person that is likely not based on any specific knowledge of the client.

Better: Need for Dominance refers to your tendency to want to have influence, power, and control over others. On three measures of personality characteristics (the California Psychological Inventory [CPI], the NEO, and the Hogan Personality Inventory [HPI]) you earned scores at or above the 90th percentile on Dominance scales. This suggests consistency in presenting yourself as someone who enjoys having influence and control over others. However, it is also possible to be too high on a measure like this if it results in people avoiding you for being too aggressive. Note also that scores on this measure may change over time, though usually they are fairly stable in the adult working years.

When a measure is experimental, or an internally developed test for which norms are being collected rather than already available, care should be taken not to present the measure as being further along than it really is. It is also desirable to be very clear on what each test has been demonstrated to measure so that readers don't just rely on a scale label to understand the test result.

Labels attached to scales by test developers do not always correspond to what is known about a measure and should not be used as the primary basis for identifying characteristics thought to be associated with high or low scorers. For example, the scale labeled as Psychological Mindedness on the CPI appears more related to intelligence than to introspection (see Gough, 1998; Megargee, 1972). This does not mean it is a bad scale for its intended purposes, but rather that the label, used alone, may mislead the test taker.

The Report Should Be Usable by the Intended Audience and Written in Easily Understood Language

A career assessment report should be able to be read and understood by the recipient audience, the career assessee. It should also, however, be able to be read and understood by a trained professional with whom the assessee may later share a copy of the report when further assessment or help with interpretation may be needed. This requires a careful balance between information that is technically accurate and pragmatically useful. Thus, names of tests, scores, and norms should be presented, but explanatory language may also be needed that the test taker can understand. Some technical information can also be put in footnotes, in parentheses, or in an appendix.

With properly selected career assessment measures, the process can be used with people at varying intellectual and educational levels. The language in the report, however, should be written in a way that clients can understand. Words and phrasing that work for college graduates may be different from those for high school students.

Example: You scored at the 93rd percentile on the CPI's and at the 99th percentile on the NEO's measures of Need for Achievement. The Standard Error of Measurement for the scale did not cross zero.

Though the numbers are accurate, a statement like this is problematic in that it is not reasonable to expect that a person can interpret unanchored normative data accurately, much less complex statistical concepts.

Better: Your score on the CPI's measure of Need for Achievement via Conformance was a standard score of 60 compared with those adult females in the sample on whom the test was normed. You scored similarly high (a standard score of 65 based on adult female norms) on the NEO's Achievement Striving facet scale. Persons scoring in this manner typically have a strong drive to get ahead in the world and are usually highly motivated toward achievement in a variety of occupational and personal activities. Though we are not certain that these scales predict to success in all occupations, persons scoring as you did are thought to be strongly motivated toward high levels of achievement. Measures of Need for Achievement can change over time and, for many people, decline with age.

The Report Should Be Tentative and Hypothetical Rather Than Definitive and Dogmatic

The competent career assessor attempts to guide and assist, to identify areas of conflict and opportunity, but never to cut off avenues for pursuit. Accordingly, statements in the report or in oral feedback should be worded in such a way as to invite further exploration by the client, not as if they were divine and binding pronouncements.

Example: You do not belong in sales. You are ill-suited to management. You would probably make a good teacher.

Obviously, this statement is much too extreme. No assessor can accurately say that a person does not "belong in" a particular occupation. Rather, degrees of fit can be approximated. Even when a candidate seems clearly a poor match with their occupation, the conclusion can be tempered and balanced and made easier for the client to accept.

Better: Your scores on three measures of sales aptitude were all in the 25th percentile or below when compared with successful people in sales. While this may suggest that sales is not the best fit for you, your strong scores on verbal reasoning and analytical abilities (95th percentile or higher on two measures of reasoning ability), combined with your vocational interest scores in helping roles, may suggest a better fit with alternative career paths. These include teaching, counseling, medical, and other helping occupations.

The Report Should Be Customized

Much of a career assessment report can be automated once a template has been developed that is consistent with the suggestions made here. However, there still is a need to customize the report to the specific questions for which help was sought and to provide a written summary of the client-specific recommendations. Standard 9.06, Interpreting Assessment Results, of the APA's Ethics Code (APA, 2017a) is useful:

> When interpreting assessment results, including automated interpretations, psychologists take into account the purpose of the assessment as well as the various test factors, test-taking abilities, and other characteristics of the person being assessed, such as situational, personal, linguistic, and cultural differences, that might affect psychologists' judgments or reduce the accuracy of their interpretations. They indicate any significant limitations of their interpretations. (p. 13)

The career assessor adds value to a report by including specific integrative information about the patterns of the results and how the findings relate to the purposes for seeking assessment.

Reports Should Express Appropriate Cautions

To limit the potential misuse of assessment reports, they should contain relevant cautions. These include not using a report after it (or parts of it) may be reasonably presumed not to be valid, inappropriately concluding that measured characteristics of persons are unchanging or unchangeable, and using the report to draw conclusions about questions for which the collected data were not relevant. Reports prepared for third parties require even greater protection since persons other than the assessee will have access to the report. Despite multiple admonitions to the contrary, the assessors may discover that a report prepared on an assessee became part of the individual's personnel file, was read by inappropriate parties, or was used for purposes other than those originally intended. Cautionary statements in the report can help avoid such problems. For example, an "expiration date" is especially protective when preparing assessment reports for institutional settings or in situations in which persons other than the assessee will have access to the report.

SAMPLE REPORT—ANTONIO'S CASE (CASE 11)

Exhibit 19.1 provides an example of how a career assessment report might be prepared in a manner that is useful for an individual client. The report presented here is a slightly abbreviated version of what would be given to the client. All potentially identifying information has been removed, and some information has been changed to further mask identity.

Case Background: Reason for Referral and Background

Antonio was in his early 20s at the time of assessment. At the suggestion of his family, he had sought career assessment because he was not happy with his planned career directions with his undergraduate degree in engineering or his planned attendance in a graduate business program to which he had been accepted. At the time of the assessment, he was living in a South American country but was temporarily visiting the United States. He was fluent in both English and Spanish (his first language), and his home had been bilingual. Much of his education had been in English. Although he had been moderately successful in his undergraduate major and his family approved of the area of study, he was quite unhappy with it but was not sure what would be a better fit.

Antonio also had had difficulties interacting with others growing up, being somewhat idiosyncratic in his behavior, and in his initial interview he described considerable unhappiness in his school and personal lives. There was some evidence of depression and anxiety. When asked about activities he enjoyed, he described having been successful, and having liked, tutoring others, and he also said he liked to read and had done some writing.

At the time of the assessment, he was being encouraged by his parents to attend a graduate training program into which he had been accepted. The specific area of study would have led him to receive a credential that would likely have meant steady work, including in the family business, but he was clearly ambivalent about proceeding. He was not looking forward to those studies and was wanting to do something else—he just wasn't very clear in his own mind or articulate about describing his preferred options.

Antonio thought the career assessment might be helpful to him and might assist him in dealing with his parents, who were still financially supporting him. A quiet young man, he worked with considerable focus and diligence on each of the assessment measures. Feedback was given in person with follow-up sessions conducted electronically after he had returned to his home country. The referral questions focused on identifying career directions that were consistent with his interests, abilities, and personality and helping him understand his dissatisfaction in his current area of study and planned career. A side issue concerned his social and interpersonal skills.

The client stated that his goals for the assessment were "discovering what would be the right career path to choose, taking into account my strengths, my weaknesses and possibly my interests." He also identified a number of "very serious" or "major or serious" work or school concerns, including "procrastination," "frequently being 'upset' at work," "not finishing work that I start," and "wanting to go to school or college for more training." The assessment report is provided in Exhibit 19.1.

This feedback report identifies which tests were administered in the three domains of interests, abilities, and personality, the results, and how the findings related to the reasons for which career assessment was sought. Recommendations are also provided.

Of course, the feedback report is not a stand-alone document to be provided in a decontextualized manner to clients. Clients also receive a detailed in-person (typically, a half-day) feedback session. This provides the opportunity to go over the results with the client and to address their reactions and any questions they may have.

This sample report is not offered to be blindly emulated (nor are the tests included in assessment presented as "must use" instruments), but rather it provides an example of one way to present the assessment results in keeping with the recommendations made earlier in this chapter. Of course, the specific format must be tailored to the purposes of the career assessment and to the needs of the specific client. Some reports will be shorter and more circumscribed in intent. Different approaches to the career assessment report would also be needed if the assessment were done for a third party, such as a career assessment completed on an employee for an employer. In this case, the report was prepared for the person being assessed who was also the client.

SUMMARY AND CONCLUSIONS

Career assessment data are of most use to clients if the results are provided in a way that is understandable and responsive to the reasons for which career assessment was sought. This chapter presented general principles and a step-by-step approach to preparing for and delivering oral and written feedback. The sample report provides an example of one way in which such a report can be written. It was argued that although technical accuracy is always important, the report should be written in a way that is understandable to the client. Additionally, the goal in feedback—written and oral—is that it will have impact and will help clients effectively address the reasons for which they sought career assessment.

EXHIBIT 19.1

Sample Career Assessment Report for Antonio's Case (Case 11)[1]

Your Results
Issues You Were Concerned About at the Time of This Assessment

You sought career assessment regarding your concerns about your planned graduate school training. You wondered whether there were areas of study or other careers that might be a better fit for you. At the time of this assessment, you were in your early 20s. You were working in an internship role in business and had been accepted into a graduate business program but you had reservations about continuing in this educational and career path.

You indicated on our Work Issues Checklist© that the following areas were of concern to you at the time of your assessment.

Very Severe Concerns
   Procrastination
   Confusion in my thinking at work
   Feeling "stuck" or trapped in my present work
   Frequently being "upset" about my work
   Not fully understanding what is expected of me

Major or Serious Concern
   Feeling that I should be more successful in my work
   Starting too many things
   Not finishing work that I start
   Confusion about what is expected of me in my work
   Dissatisfaction with my chances for getting ahead in my work
   Trouble concentrating when on the job
   Feeling that I do not have the abilities I need to do my work
   Wanting to go to school or college for more training
   "Nervousness" at work, with no apparent explanation
   Lack of confidence in my ability to perform my assigned work
   Wishing my work were more structured
   Thinking about receiving professional help for my career and/or work concerns
   Feeling overly stressed in my work

---

[1]Copyright 2021 by Lowman & Richardson/Consulting Psychologists, PC. Reproduced by permission. All rights reserved. May not be copied or reproduced without permission of the copyright holder.

I. VOCATIONAL INTERESTS

[Brief description on the Holland RIASEC types would go here. See Chapter 2 for detailed descriptions.]

Your Vocational Interest Scores

Four measures of vocational interest were administered: the Strong Interest Blank®, Self-Directed Search®, the O*NET® Interest Profiler and the Vocational Preference Inventory®. On these measures, your highest to lowest scores, along with the summary interest code were as follows.

Strong Interest Inventory® [1]	Self-Directed Search® [2]	O*NET® Interest Profiler [2]	Vocational Preference Inventory® [2]
Artistic (66)	Social (48)	Social (30)	Conventional (11)
Social (65)	Artistic (31)	Investigative (30)	Investigative (9)
Investigative (60)	Investigative (22)	Artistic (29)	Artistic (8)
Realistic (55)	Conventional (21)	Realistic (25)	Social (5)
Conventional (51)	Realistic (19)	Conventional (21)	Realistic (3)
Enterprising (42)	Enterprising (11)	Enterprising (15)	Enterprising (4)
ASI	SAI	S/IA	CIA

[1] Standardized scores, U.S. national norms
[2] Raw scores

Other Strong Interest Inventory® Scores

Work Style (55)—Midrange on preferring working with people versus working alone
Learning Environment (65)—Prefers academic (vs. practical learning environment)
Leadership Style (51)—Midrange on taking charge v. working alone
Risk Taking/Adventure (40)—Dislikes risk taking
Team orientation (48)—Midrange on working on teams v. working independently

Other Vocational Preference Inventory® Scores

Infrequency (13)—High scorers completed the measure in an atypical way and the results of the measure may be questioned. Since your score was very high and the results of the measure inconsistent with the other measures of interest, we suggest focusing more on the interest profiles suggested by the other three measures.
Acquiescence (18)—High scores are associated with endorsing many interests and are commonly found among those who are enthusiastic, cheerful, dominant, and sometimes impulsive. Low scores are associated with having few preferences and self-deprecation. Your score was high. Because this measure can also be associated in some cases with invalidity, the interest profile from this measure should be carefully considered.
Status (10)—High scorers prefer occupations with high prestige and tend to have high self-esteem and self-confidence. Low scores are associated with little concern for prestige and not having the need for upward mobility. Your score was in the midrange.
Self-Control (10)—High scores are indicative of over-control while low scores are associated with impulsiveness and tendency to act out. Your score was in the midrange.

Your Current Occupation's Code:

At the time of your assessment, you had been accepted into a graduate program in business. The typical interest pattern code for this training and related occupations is

Enterprising–Conventional–Social, though it may vary depending on the specific duties. Your undergraduate degree in business would have a similar interest code, but some specializations (e.g., marketing or accounting) would differ from that one.

Issues in Interpreting Your Occupational Preferences:
Your strongest endorsed interest codes were consistently Social, Artistic, and Investigative on three of the four measures. Conventional interests were in the top three on the fourth measure, but we would put less confidence in that due to the possible lack of validity of that measure (see your Infrequency score). Enterprising and Realistic interests appear to be areas of lesser interest and probably Conventional interests as well. The combination of Social, Artistic and Investigative interests is fairly compatible and suggests a pattern in teaching, social sciences, or other helping occupations.

Your "Occupational Daydreams" and Their Interest Codes:
Here are occupations you were considering, or had considered in the past, and their typical interest code profile.

Government teacher, postsecondary	SIA
Secondary teacher [code will vary with subject matter taught]	SAE
Historian	I
Family business specialist	EIC (estimated code)
Journalist [reporters and correspondents]	AEI
Artist/illustrator	AR

Some Occupations Thought to be Consistent With Your Highest Endorsed Interests:
Note that not all of these codes are agreed upon by all experts. Moreover, these represent average codes and will disguise important differences among members of the same occupation. Still, this is a fairly diverse list and further exploration may be needed to understand more about these options. Also, this rather large list of interest patterns could take you in very different directions so try to "fine tune" the list using methods discussed in your feedback session.

SAI/SIA/ISA
- SAI 4 29-1125.00 Recreational Therapists
- SAI 4 21-1011.00 Substance Abuse and Behavioral Disorder Counselors
- SAI 5 25-1121.00 Art, Drama, and Music Teachers, Postsecondary
- SAI 5 25-1122.00 Communications Teachers, Postsecondary
- SAI 5 25-1081.00 Education Teachers, Postsecondary
- SAI 5 25-1123.00 English Language and Literature Teachers, Postsecondary
- SAI 5 25-1124.00 Foreign Language and Literature Teachers, Postsecondary
- SAI 5 21-1013.00 Marriage and Family Therapists
- SAI 5 25-1126.00 Philosophy and Religion Teachers, Postsecondary
- SIA 5 25-1062.00 Area, Ethnic, and Cultural Studies Teachers, Postsecondary
- SIA 5 19-3031.03 Counseling Psychologists
- SIA 5 25-1053.00 Environmental Science Teachers, Postsecondary
- SIA 5 29-9092.00 Genetic Counselors
- SIA 5 25-1125.00 History Teachers, Postsecondary

SIA 5 25-1192.00 Home Economics Teachers, Postsecondary
SIA 5 25-1022.00 Mathematical Science Teachers, Postsecondary
SIA 5 21-1023.00 Mental Health and Substance Abuse Social Workers
SIA 5 21-1014.00 Mental Health Counselors
SIA 5 25-1066.00 Psychology Teachers, Postsecondary
SIA 5 25-1067.00 Sociology Teachers, Postsecondary
SIA 5 29-1127.00 Speech-Language Pathologists
ISA 5 19-3031.02 Clinical Psychologists
ISA 5 19-3039.01 Neuropsychologists and Clinical Neuropsychologists
ISA 5 29-1066.00 Psychiatrists
IAS 5 19-3094.00 Political Scientists
IAS 5 19-3041.00 Sociologists
SAI 4 21-1011.00 Substance Abuse and Behavioral Disorder Counselors
IAS 5 19-3041.00 Sociologists

Consult the *O*NET* (https://www.onetonline.org) for more information on these occupations.

Other Occupations to Consider:

The Strong Interest Inventory® also compares your scores to those of individuals in various professions but does so on a quantitative, empirical basis. You can consult your Strong printout for further listings of occupations on the Strong on which you had similar interests.

Similarity to the interest profiles of persons in these groups may suggest an occupation which is worth further exploration.

Shown here are occupations matching your interests on the Strong Interest Inventory®:

Very Similar
Special Education Teacher (SEA) (60)
Librarian (A) (59)
Translator (AI) (58)
Editor (A) (57)
ESL Instructor (ASI) (56)
English Teacher (ASE) (55)
Sociologist (AI) (55)
Administrative Assistant (CSR) (54)
Arts/Entertainment Manager (A) (54)
Elementary School Teacher (S) (54)
Secondary School Teacher (S) (54)
University Faculty Member (I) (51)

Other occupations that are similar or dissimilar to your interests can be found by reviewing the summary pages of the Strong Interest Inventory® results. We also recommend you consult the O*NET online at the following web address: *https://www.onetonline.org/explore/interests*. At this site, at no charge, you can explore various combinations of your interests.

The Strong Interest Inventory® also lists types of activities which were compatible with your interests. Again, these say nothing about your abilities in these areas, only your interests. Most highly endorsed Basic Interest Scales included:

Teaching and Education (S) (72)
Religion and Spirituality (S) (72)
Social Sciences (S) (70)
Performing Arts (A) (66)
Culinary Arts (A) (64)

II. ABILITIES

You were tested on a number of abilities. These have to do with your capacity or potential ability, as opposed to interest, in doing particular types of activities required in various occupations. Although we have administered a comprehensive battery of tests, there are additional aptitudes and abilities which may be vocationally relevant.

We have grouped your ability results into categories that are relevant to particular vocational interest types. However, interests and abilities are separate constructs that need to be understood independently of each other. We therefore recommend that you consider the results of each test one at a time and that you examine your areas of special strength and of relative weakness.

We believe that abilities at about the 75th percentile or higher compared with general population norms are important to be used in your career choice. (Percentile means the percentage of people who took the test whose scores were lower on the test than were yours.) Aptitude scores below the 25th percentile are sufficiently low that you may want to avoid professions that require strong abilities in those areas. Assuming you have higher areas of ability, scores between the 25th and 75th percentiles may not be high enough to arrange your career around them. However, as you get closer to the 75th percentile and above, you are more likely identifying strengths that can be important to make use of in your work.

Note that in many cases we compare your scores not just to general population norm groups, but also to specialty groups which make use of the ability in their day-to-day work. In the latter cases, you would be expected to have lower percentile scores since the standard of comparison is much higher. For example, if your score on a cognitive ability test is being compared with a group of medical students, that is a high bar because all of those individuals completed undergraduate training and were selected after a very competitive process. If you score at about the 50th percentile or above compared with a relevant, carefully screened normative group in which possession of the ability is needed, this is probably confirmation that you do possess the aptitude or ability in sufficient strength to use it occupationally.

In many cases, multiple norms are listed. Find the comparison group most relevant for you. Note also that in some instances a score will seem high when compared with one group (say, to high school seniors) and lower when compared with another group (say, university students).

Concerning your test-taking approach, you generally were methodical and diligent, sometimes proceeding slowly when speed was called for. This lowered some of your scores on timed measures.

Finally, remember that a test score is just one estimate of your ability in a particular area. Since we can never perfectly measure your abilities, it is best to think of your obtained score as falling within a range of scores, or a "confidence interval" around the actual score you received. Look for the general trends in your results, and do not be too concerned about any one score.

REALISTIC-RELATED ABILITIES

Mechanical Reasoning

This ability concerns one's understanding of mechanical concepts and principles similar to those used by mechanics and others who work with their hands and also by engineers, physicists, or medical specialists.

Your score on the measure employed for this area (the DAT Mechanical Comprehension Test®, PCT version) was 34 out of 45 items on the test. Here is how this score compares with other groups taking the test:

40th percentile, high school (males)
60th percentile, high school (combined sex)
29th percentile, The Development Laboratories® career assessment sample

Here are some average scores on this test for selected groups (these are averages, not percentiles):

ATC trainees, 36
Electrical engineering students, 32
Draftsmen, 37

Your score is below to slightly above average, suggesting this is not an area of special strength.

Physical Abilities

Physical abilities are difficult to measure because they do not appear to generalize very well from one application to another. Three primary dimensions of physical ability have been suggested: a) strength; b) cardiovascular capacity; and c) motor coordination. We measured only the latter. The particular test used, the Minnesota Rate of Manipulation Test® (Two-Hand Turning and Placing Test) required you to rapidly move spheres from one board to another while turning them over. Your score is the total number of seconds it took you to complete four timed trials. Your total score was 169 (standard score and percentile, 55) for the 2-Hand Turning and Placing Test. This was suggested to be an area of average ability.

Spatial Ability

This concept refers to your ability to reason in space, that is, to manipulate three-dimensional objects in your mind. Spatial ability is used by engineers, architects and artists and also by pilots, navigators and the like. Your score was 45 (of 61 items attempted; there are 64 items on this test, the Minnesota Paper Form Board®, AA series). You were given more time to complete the measure and with that additional time you completed the measure and your score increased to 47 (out of 64 attempted). The initial (timed) score and untimed score can be compared to other groups as follows:

55/65th percentile, Grade 12 males
65/74th percentile, The Development Laboratories® career assessment sample
25/35th percentile, Engineers and Scientists, Research and Development
35/40th percentile, Draftsmen
35/45th percentile, IBM Customer Service Engineers
25/35th percentile, Engineering Students

This indicates an area of average to slightly above average ability.

INVESTIGATIVE-RELATED ABILITIES

Nonverbal Reasoning Ability

This area refers to reasoning skills which do not require the use of words. On the test we used to measure this (Raven's Advanced Progressive Matrices®) you had to complete a pattern in which one piece has been removed. You must use logical reasoning ability to do this, but the task is nonverbal. This is a demanding test which we use at the college level and above. Your score on this measure was 27 (of 33 items completed) and is considered high. (You were given more time to complete the measure and your score increased by 1 [to 28] with the 3 additional items attempted.) Here are some normative comparisons:

52nd percentile, Select university sample

79th percentile, The Development Laboratories® career assessment sample

Here are some average (raw scores, not percentiles) scores from other groups for the Advanced version:

Law—20.78	Engineering—25.63
Arts—21.91	Medicine—24.10

Nonverbal reasoning ability can have different applications depending on whether or not spatial abilities are also present. For example, an architect may need both nonverbal reasoning ability and spatial abilities. However, other, more verbally oriented professions also tend to score highly on this measure, such as lawyers and other professionals. Overall, nonverbal reasoning ability would appear to be an area of strength.

Verbal Reasoning Ability

In this area of ability or aptitude we examined your skill in the use of reasoning with words. In the test we used for this area (the Watson-Glaser Critical Thinking Appraisal®), you had to carefully reason with fairly complex and demanding verbal material. You earned a score of 63 out of 80 items on the test (you finished this test on time). Here are some normative comparisons to interpret your scores.

85th percentile, Freshmen, 4-year college

65th percentile, Upper division 4-year college students

35th percentile, MBA students

25th percentile, 3rd-year medical students

67th percentile, The Development Laboratories® career assessment sample

These results suggest that verbal reasoning abilities as measured by this test were an area of relative strength. However, you took the measure in your second language, English, and at the end of a long day of test-taking, which may have lowered your score.

General Intellectual Ability

General intellectual ability is probably the single most important career-related variable. Although general intelligence is grouped with the Investigative ability area, it relates to success in a number of occupations. Some researchers believe that general intelligence is the best predictor of how high one will rise within a particular career. While we would not go that far, we do think general intelligence is very important in a variety of occupational pursuits.

We assessed your general intelligence with the Multidimensional Aptitude Battery® (MAB). Here are your scores (a score of 50 on the subtest scores is average compared with general population norms; a score of 500 on the overall scores is average compared with general population norms):

Information	71	Digit Symbol	60
Comprehension	47	Picture Completion	51
Arithmetic	54	Spatial	64
Similarities	56	Picture Arrangement	69
Vocabulary	57	Object Assembly	72

	Your scores	Overall population average	Overall population norms	Development labs career assessment
Verbal	573	500	76th percentile	70th percentile
Performance	601	500	84th percentile	77th percentile
Full Scale	593	500	82nd percentile	76th percentile

You earned scores in the High Average to Superior range in the Verbal and overall areas of intelligence and in the Superior range on performance (nonverbal) scales. The difference between verbal and performance intelligence scores was suggestive of a small difference between verbal and nonverbal abilities. This overall difference may have been masked somewhat by your very high score on one of the verbal subtests (Information) and by the lower score on a Performance subtest, Picture Completion (which requires English vocabulary).

There was some unevenness on your subtests. All verbal subtests were at or above average. However, the Information subtest was particularly high, and Comprehension lowest. All of your nonverbal subtests were well above average except for Picture Completion. The highest scores were earned on Object Assembly and Spatial, with somewhat lower (but still average) scores earned on the Picture Completion subtest.

Overall, your scores on this measure of intelligence were sufficiently high for you to be able intellectually to pursue a number of areas requiring graduate training.

Field Dependence/Independence
Research suggests that individuals are either field dependent (i.e., rely on primarily on their external environment for cues of how to act) or field independent (i.e., think independently of the environment in which they are functioning). Field dependence/independence is thought to measure your reliance on cues and stimuli from the environment to make judgments and form impressions. Field Dependent individuals tend to be reliant on their environment for cues about appropriate behavior or thoughts, while field independent people tend to exercise their judgment rather separately from the environment in which they find themselves. Scientists, mathematicians, engineers tend, as groups, to field independence while persons with skills in the helping professions and in highly verbal activities are more likely to be field dependent and for that reason we group this concept here with the Investigative-related abilities.

The test we used to assess this dimension (the CAB® Flexibility of Closure test) requires you to find drawings which have been "hidden" in a more complex drawing. Field independent people usually can do this with a high degree of skill while field dependent people usually have trouble with the task. Your score of 4 (field dependent; higher scores are in the field independent direction) compares to others as follows:

    11th percentile, High school males
    2nd percentile, Freshman college males
    7th percentile, The Development Laboratories® career assessment sample

The field dependent pattern is commonly found among writers, artists, helping professions and others, while a field independent cognitive style is more likely to be found in the sciences.

ARTISTIC-RELATED ABILITIES

Aesthetic Judgment

Aesthetic Judgment is thought to relate to a number of different professions in the arts, not just to those requiring drawing ability. Artists, interior decorators, possibly musicians, and other creative groups tend to have aesthetic abilities and would be expected to have an appreciation of things artistic.

For this construct we used the Welsh Figure Preference Test. The Welsh measure requires you to express a preference for a variety of drawings. Your score on the Original Art Scale of this test was 13 (27th percentile, Development Laboratories® norms). Your score compares with average scores earned by the following groups (please note that these are raw score *average* scores, not percentiles):

Group - Average Score

    Artists—40.3
    Artists and Art Students—40.0
    Architects—29.2
    Architects (creative)—37.1
    Creative Scientists—30.7
    Adult Women—18.1
    Adult Men—15.1

A revision of this scale, the Revised Art Scale, was also scored. On this measure, you earned a score of 20 (34th percentile, Development Laboratories® norms). This compares with the following groups (again, these are raw score averages, not percentiles):

Group - Average Score

    Creative Writers—46.4
    Fine Artists—41.7
    Creative Female Artists—37.7
    Creative Male Artists—37.5
    High School Females—35.1
    High School Males—32.1

On still another scale on the Welsh test, Origence, intended to measure creative orientation, you earned a score of 61 (89th percentile, Development Laboratories® norms). This compares with the following groups (again, these are raw score averages, not percentiles):

Group - Average Score

    Art students—61.9
    Architects—48.1
    Psychologists, female—43.2
    Psychologists, males—33.9
    Creative Writing students—55.5
    Acting students—49.2
    Medical students—25.7

Note that the sample sizes for many of the groups listed above were relatively small, but the more artistic the group, the higher the average scores. Your scores would suggest this to be a mixed area. Further assessment might be needed if you were interested in careers in this area.

Musical Abilities

Musical abilities are thought to emerge at a relatively young age and to mature (reach a level at which they can effectively be integrated into important occupational, societal, or life tasks) early. There are a variety of ways to measure musical aptitude. Here are your results from one of the major musical talent measures (the Gordon Musical Aptitude Profile). The specific aspects of musical talent measured by each of these two tests is explained below.

Rhythm: Much of music involves periodicity, that is, the perception and reproduction of notes in certain patterns. In this subtest, your ability to discriminate between different patterns of notes is examined.

Tonal Memory: This refers to the ability to remember a series of musical notes or tones. It is important in many types of musical activities.

You were administered Gordon's Advanced Measures of Music Audiation. Here are your scores on the subtests of this measure. Note that your scores are compared with different groups, including those with demonstrated musical talent.

Subtest	Raw score	Music majors percentile	Nonmusic majors percentile	High school percentile
Tonal	15	<1st percentile	7th percentile	7th percentile
Rhythm	15	<1st percentile	1st percentile	1st percentile
Total	30	<1st percentile	3rd percentile	3rd percentile

These results were low. There are other factors involved in musical talent, including music reading ability, psychomotoric responses in playing some instruments, and the ability to integrate emotion with music.

Artistic Drawing Ability

Artistic drawing ability was measured by a subtest of the Comprehensive Ability Test. On this test you were required to reproduce two drawings. Your score of 23 (CAB®-RD test) compares to normative groups as follows:

    32nd percentile, High school students (male)
    23rd percentile, The Development Laboratories® career assessment sample

This score was relatively low. Of course, being able to reproduce a simple line drawing is not the same thing as being a great painter, but some similarities are shared.

Verbal Fluency

Verbal Fluency reflects the ability to organize thoughts quickly and to express oneself in a clear, coherent manner. In addition, a number of other exercises and personality tests required use of writing to complete unstructured assignments. The actual number of words (395) you produced in the 15-minute time period can be compared as follows:

    97th percentile, The Development Laboratories® career assessment sample

This score was high compared with our normative data (average: 187) for word flow and ideas, which relates to the ability to speak or write fluently in an unstructured situation. Teaching, sales, some aspects of management would be expected to need this skill; in other occupations, such as engineering it might be less important.

A second measure of verbal fluency was administered. On the CAB®-Fi (Ideational Fluency) test, you had to generate as many adjectives to describe certain things as you could think of within a given time period. Your score of 28 compares as follows:

52nd percentile, The Development Laboratories® career assessment sample
71st percentile, High school students (males)
45th percentile, College students (males)

This score was in the average to high average range.

Creative Imagination (Things)

The CAB®-O (Original Uses) subtest of the Comprehensive Ability Battery required you to combine two objects to make one useful thing. Your score of 13 on this measure compares as shown below. This score was in the high average to high range.

80th percentile, The Development Laboratories® career assessment sample
77th percentile, High school students (males)
63rd percentile, College students (males)

Your scores on the creative ability measures were high on two of the three measures, suggesting an area of relative strength.

SOCIAL-RELATED ABILITIES

Social abilities are important in jobs or careers which require that you get along well with others and in which you must work in and through other people. Most of the helping professions would make strong use of these abilities, as would teachers and, to some extent, managers. Unfortunately, our measures of social ability (sometimes called "social intelligence") are not as good as we would like.

You were assessed using a paper-and-pencil measure, the Interpersonal Problem-Solving Assessment Technique. This test was designed to measure your ability to judge the appropriate response in a social situation and to identify the responses you would be most likely to make to a variety of social situations. Because you had to indicate what you thought you would actually do in a given situation, obviously the results of the test will only be as good as the honesty with which you stated what you would actually do in each instance. Here are your scores on this measure:

	Your scores* (raw scores)	Average, college student sample counselees	Percentile, adult career
Effective responses	8	13	6th percentile
Avoidant responses	12	4	2nd percentile
Inappropriate responses	0	4	80th percentile**
Dependent responses	0	4	30th percentile**
Unscorable responses	1	1	14th percentile**

*Responses you said you would actually do
**Percent of people who had less effective scores than you did (higher scores on these measures are in the less effective direction)

These scores suggest mixed abilities in effectively handling social situations, at least as reflected on this type of measure, with a tendency to avoid conflict.

We also administered a second, more sophisticated, test of social abilities, the EQ-i²®, a measure of emotional intelligence. It assesses five dimensions: Self-Perception, Self-Expression, Interpersonal, Decision Making, and Stress Management. It also provides an overall Emotional Intelligence (EI) score.

Here are the dimensions measured and your scores on your EQ-i²®:

Total Emotional Intelligence (EI)	68
Self-Perception Composite	53
Self-Regard (Self-respect and self-confidence)	29
Self-Actualization (Seeks meaning and to improve self)	68
Emotional Self-Awareness (Understands own emotions)	96
Self-Expression Composite	80
Emotional Expression (Constructively expression of emotions)	119
Assertiveness (Nonoffensively communicates feeling & beliefs)	86
Independence (Self-Directed; free from emotional dependency)	38
Interpersonal Composite	98
Interpersonal Relationships (Mutually satisfying relationships)	99
Empathy (Understanding and respecting how others feel)	102
Social Responsibility (Being helpful and socially conscious)	93
Decision Making Composite	65
Problem Solving (Handling emotionally involved problems)	68
Reality Testing (Able to see things as they are; be objective)	73
Impulse control (Delaying or resisting impulse to act)	76
Stress Management Composite	71
Flexibility (Adapting emotions, thoughts, and behaviors)	113
Stress Tolerance (Coping effectively with stressful situations)	71
Optimism (Having a positive attitude and outlook)	43

Source: EQ-i²® Multi-health Systems, Inc.

Scores on this measure are standardized with a mean of 100. In general, these results suggest some areas of comparative strengths and many that were below average. You scored above average on Flexibility and Emotional Expression. You also scored relatively high (compared to your other scores) on Emotional Self-Awareness, Interpersonal Relationships, Empathy, and Social Responsibility. Your overall EI score was well below average, however. Areas of lower scores included Self-Regard, Independence, Self-Actualization, Optimism, and on the Decision Making Composite factors. You also scored low on the overall Self-Perception Composite.

Some work in this area will be needed to build on strengths and to develop areas of relative weakness. Low self-esteem may need attention as you begin to find your place in your career and personal life.

ENTERPRISING-RELATED ABILITIES AND OTHER FACTORS

In this section, we present both abilities and interest and personality data since the modal managerial profile appears to be a composite of these types of factors. The "typical" managerial profile, at least for large companies, for middle level managers and above includes the following:

- Good organizing and prioritizing skills
- High average or above intelligence
- Managerial vocational interests
- Tough-mindedness
- Moderately high needs for power over others
- High need for achievement
- Moderate needs for affiliation
- High levels of adjustment
- Generally positive, optimistic outlook

With regard to interests, your "fit" with business and management would appear to be low.

On all three measures of interests, you endorsed other interest patterns more highly than Enterprising, suggesting interests would not likely propel you to a career in business. Your levels of cognitive ability are generally similar to those found in middle managerial ranks but we don't believe this is the most compatible area in which to apply your intellectual talents. Your personality factors also suggest a marginal fit with the prototypical managerial position.

Concerning organizing and prioritizing skills, a Development Laboratories® in-basket was administered. You did not complete the measure in the allotted time and the scores on both subtests were low. Here is how they compared to norms:

	Your scores	Managerial samples	Development laboratories® samples
Prioritizing*	118	60	6th percentile
Managerial Judgment (untimed)**	2/21 (9.5% correct)	12/21 (57% correct)	<2nd percentile

*Lower scores are better on the Prioritizing scale.
**You completed only the multiple choice items on which this measure was based. You were also asked to provide a rationale for each action selected but you ran out of time to do so.

Your needs for control and dominance were suggested to be lower than are typical for managers. You also scored consistently higher in the introverted rather than extraverted direction in personality, not the usual managerial pattern.

Reported levels of adjustment at the time of this testing were, with some exceptions, atypical of managers. You presented yourself on the various measures of adjustment as being less well-adjusted than the typical manager. You generally scored low in conscientiousness but scored higher on independence than managers often do. Managers tend as a group to score somewhat consistently in the more conscientious/conforming direction. You also scored high on measures of ambition but more in the independent than conforming direction.

On the Managerial Potential scale of the California Psychological Inventory®, you earned a score of 12 (standard score, 41) and a score of 25 (standard score, 32) on the Leadership Potential scale. On the Work Orientation subtest of the same measure, your score was 17 (standard score, 30); executives averaged raw scores of 34. These scores also were generally lower than those of people in business management.

The overall pattern, at least at the time of this testing, suggested low performance in this area. We would not see this as being your primary career "fit."

CONVENTIONAL-RELATED ABILITIES

Perceptual Speed and Accuracy

This measures your ability to rapidly compare numbers and names to determine whether or not they are the same or different. This is thought to be important in many clerical jobs, accounting, bookkeeping and also for reading quickly and accurately. Many other career pursuits involve paperwork and reading of verbal and numerical information.

On the measure we used (the Minnesota Clerical Test®), you had to rapidly determine whether long lists of pairs of figures or letters are the same. Here is how your scores of 115 on the Number Comparison subtest and 125 on the Name Comparison test compared to selected normative groups:

Percentile norms	Numbers	Names
Grade 12 Male	65th percentile	78th percentile
Male Clerks	65th percentile	85th percentile
Female Tellers	40th percentile	65th percentile
The Development Laboratories® career assessment samples	49th percentile	63rd percentile

Your score on the Numbers subtest was average to high average and on the Names subtest was relatively high. This suggests that perceptual speed and accuracy is an area of relative strength for you. These skills are generally used in jobs requiring attention to detail and perceptual speed and accuracy. In our experience, accountants as a group score high on this type of measure.

Computational and Arithmetic Skills

Computational and math skills are important in many clerical jobs, accounting, and, at the higher levels, in many areas of science and engineering. On the measure we used for this purpose, the Arithmetic subtest of the Wide Range Achievement Test - Revised®, your score of 40 compares to normative groups as follows:

57th percentile, The Development Laboratories® career assessment sample
34th percentile, Same-age general population norms

Although this test is utilized in our battery primarily as a measure of computational skills, the more difficult items on this test require mathematical expertise. This score was average to below average.

Other Measures

Memory

On a measure of memory for unrelated material (i.e., nonverbal, "nonsense" material), you earned a score of 12 (out of 14 items) which compares as follows:

    83th percentile, High school students (males)

    80th percentile, College freshmen (males)

    74th percentile, The Development Laboratories® career assessment sample

This was suggested to be a strength.

III. PERSONALITY

The following are the tests you took on which this section is based: 16PF®, California Psychological Inventory® (CPI®), NEO-4®, and the FIRO®-B. You also completed a short version of the NEO®, the Five-Factor Inventory (FFI) Profile, Form S.

Your scores on the various personality tests were discussed with you in your feedback session. Highlights of these results are summarized below.

Several of these measures (but not all of them) have validity scales, indicating your test-taking orientation. The validity indicators on the CPI, NEO, and 16PF/CAQ were within the normal range. This suggests that you presented yourself on the tests in a straightforward way (neither presenting yourself in an overly "positive" or negative manner).

On the FIRO®-B, a measure of need strength in three areas, you had the following scores (raw scores; range of each scale is 1–10):

Need for:	Inclusion	Control	Affection
Expressed	1	1	3
Wanted	8	8	7
Total	9	9	10

These results suggest a consistent pattern of wanting more involvement with others than you may communicate to them. This represents an opportunity for you to develop more relationships with others to get your needs met, also important in many Social occupations.

Here then are your scores on some major dimensions and facets of personality. All of these measures, except for the FIRO®-B, are standardized scores. In the cases of the NEO® and CPI® measures (except for the CPI's v.1, v.2, and level scores), the standard score average is 50 and the standard deviation is 10. In the case of the 16PF®, the scores (called sten scores) were standardized with a mean of 5, a standard deviation of 2, and a range of 1 to 10. The directionality of your results is shown in the descriptors in the far-right column.

Introversion/Extraversion

This dimension reflects a preference for being with people versus needing large amounts of time alone. Most work requiring intense concentration may favor introverted characteristics while extraverts may excel where there is considerable demand for interpersonal contact. It is likely that there is a large genetic component for this personality trait. Both introverts in extravert-favoring careers and extroverts in introvert-favoring careers can be successful and happy in such career choices if the interests and abilities are otherwise present. However, they may approach the role differently. Introverts, for example, when working in a career demanding a great deal of social contact, can be effective but may need time alone after their work ends. Extraverts, on the other hand, in work that does not involve much people contact, may need to find ways to do group projects or to have outside activities that allow more interpersonal contact.

How you scored on scales related to Introversion-Extraversion:

CPI	Internality/Externality (v.1)	54	Slightly higher on Internality
NEO F-FI	Extraversion	55	High average on Extraversion
16PF	Extraversion	6.0	High average on Extraversion
Strong Interest Inventory	Introversion-Extraversion (Work Style)	55	Midrange on preferring to work with people versus working alone

You presented yourself in a fairly consistent manner on these scales. The results suggest a midrange to slightly extroverted tendency. On the CPI measure you scored slightly above the midrange in the internality (or introverted) versus extraversive direction. Overall, you likely have aspects of both Introversion and Extraversion to consider in career and work choices.

Sociability
A related area to Introversion-Extraversion is one's sociability, how much you tend to interact with others and engage well with others. On several measures of this construct, you presented yourself in a somewhat mixed pattern.

Here's how you scored:

CPI	Sociability (Sy)	53	Average
FIRO-B	See above.		High social needs but largely unexpressed
NEO-4	Gregariousness (E2)	45	Midrange
16PF	Warmth (A)	1	Reserved, detached

These results suggest that although you may want to be around others and to work with others, at times you may be perceived as more detached than you actually would like to be. To the extent you prefer to interact with others in your work, you may have to communicate with them in a way that suggests you are interested in being involved with them.

Openness and Imagination
This important dimension of personality has to do with exercise of the free flow of ideas and liking the novel and creative rather than the predictable and routine. People who score low on Openness may prefer structured work activities where there is more routine than innovation. They may have to work harder when change is needed. People who score high on Openness may need to adjust themselves to aspects of a career that are predictable and orderly.

Here's how you scored:

CPI	Flexibility (Fx)	57	High
CPI	Norm favoring (v.2)	54	Norm favoring
NEO FF-I	Openness	72	Very high
NEO-4	O4 (Openness to Fantasy)	67	High
NEO-4	O5 (Openness to Ideas)	75	Very high
16PF	Openness to Change (Q1)	3	Low
16PF	Imaginative vs. Practical (M)	8	High imaginativeness

You generally presented yourself as being high to very high on this dimension, scoring in the more open and flexible direction. You would appear to prefer flexible and changing situations in which you can use your imagination. This personality style may be useful in careers that require creativity, such as in teaching, the arts, or sales.

Conscientiousness

This aspect of personality has to do with being disciplined and reliable versus spontaneous or undisciplined. This factor predicts well to working reliably and predictably. People who are younger at the time of assessment or who have creative and artistic interests may score lower on this characteristic.

How you scored:

CPI	Responsibility (Re)	39	Low
CPI	Self-Control (Sc)	47	Average
CPI	Norm Favoring (v.2)	54	Average to high average
NEO-4	Conscientiousness	21	Very low
NEO-4	Self-Discipline (C5)	< 20	Very low
16PF	Expedient vs. Conscientious (G)	9	Average
16PF	Self-Control (Superego Strength; Se)	5.1	Average
16PF	Self-Discipline (Q3)	4	Low

You generally presented yourself as being average to relatively low on responsibility and self-discipline. This suggests you might need to exercise more discipline as relates to school and work performance. This finding may require attention since it may interfere with pursuit of some of your goals. Note that Conscientiousness scores may well increase as people move from youth into adulthood.

Adjustment

This characteristic has to do with being well-adjusted with little emotional conflict versus having the tendency to experience negative emotions and sometimes to have difficulty handling them.

How you scored:

CPI	Realization (v.3; Level 2)	38	Low
CPI	Well Being (Wb)	23	Very low
NEO F-FI	Neuroticism (N)	75	Very high
16PF	Anxiety (Ax)	7.6	High
16PF	Emotional Stability (C)	3	Low
16PF	Suspiciousness (L)	9	Very high
16PF	Tension (Q4)	7	High

You presented yourself as being in the less-well-adjusted range at the time of the assessment. However, you were considering making major life changes then and were also fairly young at that time. If such issues become problematic for you, counseling or coaching may be needed to work on some of these issues. Note that all of these measures were developed as measures of those in the normal range of personality. Further assessment with other types of psychological measures may be needed if you find yourself experiencing depression or anxiety, particularly if that persists or is recurrent over time.

Agreeableness

Agreeableness refers to whether you present yourself in a manner that others find pleasant and considerate. More research is needed on the extent to which this dimension predicts well to workplace activities. Agreeableness is most relevant when a career clearly calls for interpersonal skills.

How you scored:

CPI	Empathy (Em)	48	Average
CPI	Sociability (Sy)	52	Average
NEO FFI	Agreeableness	56	Average to High
NEO-4	Agreeableness	31	Very Low
16PF	Reserved vs. Warm (A)	5	Average

Overall, you presented yourself in a mixed manner on this dimension. You completed two versions of the NEO® measure, a short version (the F-FI) and a longer one, the NEO® 4. As shown above you scored very low on this dimension on the longer form, but on the shorter form you scored in the average to high range on the same dimension. Most of the scores shown here were in the average range or below however. This is probably an area to further develop if engagement with people is to be a major part of your work.

Authority Minded Versus Norm Questioning

This personality dimension has to do with whether you accept authority of others readily versus questioning it or challenging authority.

CPI	Norm favoring (v.2)	54	Above average
CPI	Socialization (So)	47	Average
NEO-4	Dutifulness (C3)	24	Very low
16PF	Expedient vs. Conscientious (G)	6	Average

On these measures, you presented yourself somewhat inconsistently, generally tending to accept authority and to conform to expectations while also scoring somewhat low on behavioral conformity. However, on the Dutifulness scale, you scored very low. These results may change over time and, like conscientiousness, may increase as you move further into adulthood.

Tough-Mindedness Versus Sensitivity
This personality characteristic involves an orientation to making decisions or expressing views without regard to how they may be received versus being more sensitive to other people's feelings and reactions. Tender-minded people tend to be more sensitive and refined and tend to be more engaged with feelings. In contrast, tough-minded people are more direct, tending to express themselves in a no-nonsense, blunt, and direct manner. Managers or people in law enforcement, for example, as a group tend to score in the tough-minded direction, whereas teachers and counselors more in the tender-minded one.

How you scored:

NEO4	Tender-Mindedness (A6)	60	Low (Tough-minded)
16PF	Tough Poise (Ct)	6.6	Tough-minded
16PF	Tough-Minded (I)	3	Tough-minded

You presented yourself on all three of these measures as being higher in the tough-minded versus sensitive direction. Scientists, engineers, managers and people in business as well as attorneys usually present themselves as being in the more tough-minded direction; teachers, fiction writers, counselors in the opposite direction. At times, people who are high on tough-mindedness may be perceived as being overly realistic, not sensitive enough.

Dominance
This dimension of personality has to do with having the need for control and having influence over others. People high on needs to influence other people may prefer managerial or leadership roles in which they can exercise control over others. Those lower on such needs may prefer working with greater autonomy or in roles in which they are more followers than leaders. Note that people can assert control over others without being highly controlling. For example, teachers need to control a classroom but if they are too assertive in doing that they may be ineffective.

How you scored:

CPI	Dominance (Do)	36	Low
FIRO-B	Expressed Control	1	Low
FIRO-B	Wanted Control	8	Low
NEO4	E3 (Assertiveness)	23	Low
16PF	Dominance (E)	4	Low

You presented yourself on all of these measures as not having high needs to control others. There is no "right or wrong" direction here, but to the extent you experience low dominance in contexts that involve the need to be more assertive, you may need to develop skills to present yourself as more dominant than you may feel on the inside. Although this may change somewhat over time, the results are consistent with your relatively low scores on Enterprising interests and higher scores on Social interests.

Independence

People who are independent like to make decisions on their own. They are less influenced by people around them who might try to persuade them than by their own conclusions. If too independent, people may have trouble engaging with others or in influencing them. If too group oriented or dependent, they may substitute others' ideas and conclusions for their own.

How you scored:

CPI	Independence (In)	34	Low
16PF	Independence (In)	3.3	Low

These results suggested you presented yourself as being low on Independence (i.e., being more oriented to others' judgements than to your own) on the two measures. It may be helpful to pay attention to situations in which you tend to defer to others versus those where it is useful for you to make your own decisions and determine when it is better to use one approach versus the other.

Achievement Needs

These needs have to do with drive to succeed, to advance, to get ahead either through a well-defined career path or on one's own. There is not a single desirable way to live one's life or to pursue a career. Many aspire to a well-adjusted life, well balanced between work and nonwork. Need for achievement tends to peak at a certain point in people's careers and may decline after that.

How you scored:

CPI	Achievement via Conformance (Ac)	45	Midrange
CPI	Achievement via Independence (Ai)	55	High
CPI	Capacity for Status (Cs)	47	Average
NEO4	Achievement Striving (C4)	< 20	Low

Your scores were mixed on the four measures reported here. You scored high on a measure of achievement (Ai) having to do with getting ahead depending primarily on your own efforts. On two other scales (Ac and Cs) your scores were in the midrange to low. On a fourth test, the C4 scale of the NEO, you presented yourself as being low. Thus, there was some inconsistency in how you presented yourself.

***

Summarizing your overall personality results, at the time of the assessment, you presented yourself as being somewhat extraverted, as being highly open and imaginative, somewhat less well adjusted, and somewhat low on conscientiousness. However, you were fairly young at the time of this assessment and some personality patterns may change over time as you become older and have more confidence in yourself and your choice of careers.

You reported some anxiety and stress that may need to be managed as you work on your career concerns. Your high achievement needs (in the more independent than conforming direction) suggest the need to work in a context in which you can have opportunities for growth. However, because of your high level of cognitive abilities and diverse interests, there are multiple options to consider. Nevertheless, specific choices will need to be made about your career. Because of your somewhat high level of anxiety at the time of testing, counseling/coaching may be helpful.

Overall Recommendations

On this career assessment battery your results emphasized Social, Investigative, and Artistic interests. This pattern was generally more consistent with some of the occupations you were considering (occupational daydreams) such as becoming a teacher of government rather than with your planned graduate school training in business. Your abilities were quite strong in areas of general intelligence, imagination/creativity, and memory, but less strong in business-related, science, and engineering areas. Your personality results are summarized above.

Specific recommendations were discussed in detail with you at the time of your feedback session. Some of the highlights include:

1. **Career Choice**—Your pattern of interests suggests that your current career choice, business school (your currently planned next career step), may not be the best fit for your pattern of interests, abilities, and personality. Considering your "occupational daydreams" and other background information, a better fit for you may be in teaching, particularly your daydream of teaching government, a career direction matched in many of your avocational interests and making good use of a number of your strengths. Occupations such as that one may build on your interest pattern, your occupational daydreams, and your abilities and many aspects of personality. There were a number of other specific careers that would be possible for you but most were in the

areas of social science, the humanities, or in some of the helping occupations. Your abilities are generally consistent with careers involving graduate training.

Were you to pursue a teaching and/or research career (e.g., in government, an area in which you appear to have a special interest), the question of the educational level would benefit from further consideration. If, as you described, you like working with children or adolescents, teaching in the middle or high school settings might be a good fit. However, these types of positions involve intensive interactions with children or adolescents. You should consider how you would feel about being in the classroom for most of the day. Teaching at the college level varies with the type of college or university. Instruction in community colleges (2-year post-high school institutions) typically involves more classroom work whereas in four-year universities there may be less teaching but more need to be involved with writing and research. Getting a job as a teacher's aide or as a teaching or research assistant could provide you firsthand experience to help sort out this issue.

Other choices, of course, are also possible. Please carefully review the suggestions from the O*NET that were compatible with your interest scores. For those that are appealing, review the information on the O*NET about employment outlook (geared to the U.S. market), and the skills, abilities, and personality characteristics needed. As you narrow down choices, it is also helpful to meet with people in these occupations to hear first-hand what their work and work settings are like.

2. **Some Career Challenges to Consider**—There are few "perfect matches" for people when it comes to careers. We would expect that under stressful work or school conditions you may experience personal stress and anxiety that will need to be managed. Getting more work experience so that you can learn what is expected of you on the job and gain confidence in your abilities is recommended. Such work can be in your intended career or in any area; learning basic job skills is important for most jobs. However, if you can find a position in an academic setting such as a teacher's aide or assistant (in the middle to high school areas), as a research or teaching assistant in a college or university or working in a library—all of these will give you more exposure to the types of settings in which you might feel most comfortable. However, don't wait for the "perfect job"; at this point many types of work experiences would be of value to you.

Managing your anxiety or depressive feelings as you undertake new work and the inevitable learning curve will take some effort on your part. Having a coach or counselor (especially a cognitive behavioral counselor, psychologist, or coach) to assist should be considered.

3. **Other Issues**—Development of some of your social skills may be needed as you move forward with your training and career choices. Greater sensitivity in social contexts to others' reactions may be an area needing your attention. This may also be an area to work on if you choose to pursue an academic or teaching career.

Note. We hope this assessment has provided you useful information in managing the next phase of your career. Please feel free to contact us if you need additional assistance in understanding or interpreting this report.

Source: Lowman & Richardson/Consulting Psychologists, PC
Copyright 2021. All Rights Reserved.
Reproduced by Permission.

20

Ethical/Legal and Technological Issues

This final chapter identifies ethical/legal and technological matters that arise in doing career assessment work. Some of these topics have already been raised in earlier chapters. Here, however, I provide a broader discussion of these increasingly important issues, illustrating the consensus that exists in what constitutes ethical professional behavior across a range of occupations that work in this space. Finally, the chapter takes up technology issues, as career assessment services have increasingly come to be delivered electronically.

ETHICAL AND LEGAL MATTERS

Professional practice almost always raises concerns about ethical conduct and sources of potential ethical conflict. Legal issues also need to be considered, including in the context of professional licensure.

Professional ethics are established in ethics codes that are tied to particular professions. These codes define what constitutes ethical and unethical behavior for members of a profession. Although there are many professional associations around the world for career-related occupations, their ethics codes tend to be very similar (Leach & Oakland, 2007). Even so, there are many commonalities in the ethical standards across the occupations engaged in this work.

Legal issues can also arise in this work. These include understanding what licenses or certifications may be needed, interjurisdictional practice parameters

---

https://doi.org/10.1037/0000254-021
Career Assessment: Integrating Interests, Abilities, and Personality, by R. L. Lowman
Copyright © 2022 by the American Psychological Association. All rights reserved.

when delivering services electronically or across jurisdictional boundaries, and malpractice matters.

Career assessment typically involves the use of tests—those classified as psychological and those not. Licensing laws may limit the use of particular types of tests to those with specific professional licenses. Complicating matters, in the United States, and to some extent in Canada, the practice of career assessment work is governed at the state or provincial, not national, level. This means the various regulations on practice may vary from one jurisdiction to another. In contrast, in many other countries the license to practice a profession is a national one. Applicable laws can also be tricky to sort out when, thanks to virtual delivery capability, it is possible to administer tests and counsel clients anywhere in the world where there is internet access. In brief, professional ethics codes that may govern career assessment practice and the professions in whose domain the work falls vary from one jurisdiction to another.

Who, then, can provide career assessment and counseling services? Typically, the relevant occupations working in the career assessment and counseling space include various types of psychologists (clinical/counseling, consulting, industrial–organizational, rehabilitation, school), licensed counselors, school counselors, and, in some states, a category called career counselors. This means that any discussion about ethics must be tethered to the code of ethics of particular occupations.

Generally, it is the professional associations of these occupations that promulgate ethics codes that are subsequently incorporated into state or other jurisdictional licensing laws. Examples include the American Counseling Association (ACA, 2014); the American Psychological Association (APA, 2017a); the Canadian Psychological Association (CPA, 2017); the Canadian Counselling and Psychotherapy Association (CCPA, 2020); the National Career Development Association (NCDA, 2015), which is a Division of the ACA and whose ethics code is very similar to the ACA's; and the Vocational Rehabilitation Association of Canada (VRA Canada). This is far from an inclusive list, but it demonstrates the particular ethics standards or principles covered here. As for enforcement, the professional codes of ethics are enforced by the associations and by governments that have issued licenses for the practice of the profession. In some jurisdictions, ethical violations can result in loss of practice licenses and even, in extreme cases, civil and criminal penalties.

Although the particular ethics codes that govern career assessment work vary, this review of specific ethical standards across codes demonstrates that they have more in common than not. Rather than focus on the differences across these professions, in this chapter I focus on the ethical commonalities and consider the general consensus. Complete citations of all potentially relevant codes around the world is not possible here; those wanting to review specific codes can usually download them at no cost from the organizations' websites.

It is also not possible to identify all the ethical considerations that can arise in the professional practice of career assessment. Reviewed here are a number of the most relevant and most significant ethical principles and standards that occur in doing this work. Assuredly, there are others.

Maximizing Good/Minimizing Harm

Applying one of the most fundamental and overarching ethics concepts, most professional codes of ethics requiring avoiding or minimizing harm to their clients and striving to maximize positive benefit. The terms often used for this ethical principle are maleficence and nonmaleficence (see Beauchamp & Childress, 2019).

This nearly universal principle of professional ethics codes is sometimes characterized as requiring professionals to "do no harm," but that is too simplistic and unrealistic a formulation. A physician, for example, whose treatment causes perceived pain in order to help achieve longer term well-being (e.g., chemotherapy for cancer) may nevertheless result in perceived or actual harm en route, hopefully, to a desired outcome (Lowman & Cooper, 2018).

Here are some examples of ethical standards from some of the professions.

> **ACA Code of Ethics**
> **A.4.a. Avoiding Harm.** Counselors act to avoid harming their clients, trainees, and research participants and to minimize or to remedy unavoidable or unanticipated harm. (ACA, 2014, p. 4)
>
> **APA Code of Ethics**
> **3.04 Avoiding Harm**
> (a) Psychologists take reasonable steps to avoid harming their clients/patients, students, supervisees, research participants, organizational clients, and others with whom they work, and to minimize harm where it is foreseeable and unavoidable. (APA, 2017a, p. 6)
>
> **CPA Code of Ethics**
> **Principle II: Responsible Caring Values Statement** . . . A basic ethical expectation of any discipline is that its activities will benefit members of society or, at least, do no harm. Therefore, psychologists demonstrate an active concern for the well-being and best interests of the individuals and groups (e.g., couples, families, groups, communities, peoples) with whom they relate in their role as psychologists. This concern includes both those directly involved and those indirectly involved in their activities. . . . Psychologists define harm and benefit in terms of both physical and psychological dimensions. They are concerned about such factors as: social, family, and community relationships; personal and cultural identity; feelings of self-worth, fear, humiliation, interpersonal trust, and cynicism; self-knowledge and general knowledge; and such factors as physical safety, comfort, pain, and injury. They are concerned about immediate, short-term, and long-term effects. (CPA, 2017, p. 18)
>
> **NCDA Code of Ethics**
> **A.4.a. Avoiding Harm.**
> Career professionals act to avoid harming their clients, trainees, and research participants and to minimize or to remedy unavoidable or unanticipated harm. (NCDA, 2015, p. 14)

VRA Canada Code of Ethics
Vocational Rehabilitation Values
. . . The fundamental spirit of dignity and worth with which the Code is written is based upon six principles of ethical behavior:

Beneficence: To do good to others; to promote the well-being of clients . . .
Nonmaleficence: To do no harm to others . . . (VRA Canada, 2021, p. 8)

Most people would likely agree that causing harm when it is neither necessary, instrumental, nor efficacious is ethically problematic. But consider also what happens when there are multiple choices that are possible to be made in achieving the desired outcomes and when alternative approaches are more or less equal in their efficacy. The ones that are better at minimizing harm, that cost less, and that can be completed more quickly are generally to be preferred. Especially important, when there are both costs (including harm or perceived harm) and benefits, the client needs to be included in the decision of how to proceed (see the discussion of informed consent later in the chapter). This includes explaining in understandable terms the possible harm and benefits of the process and procedures to be used, for example, "Some people will experience fatigue or psychological distress," and the expected positive benefits, for example, "The career assessment process is expected to increase your understanding of your interests, abilities, and personality and to use that information to search for well-fitting career choices."

The purposes of the career assessment help to determine the methods to be used, their potential risks, positive outcomes, and, by implication, the harm or benefits associated with the process. In undertaking a career assessment, as in many types of professional work, there may need to be short-term pain associated with completing measures or with findings that may not be pleasant. For example, a client may be set on a particular career direction that, given the abilities profile, may not be likely to happen. Others may find obtained personality results to be incompatible with their self-perceptions. Or the inconsistency of test results with available school or training options may be frustrating to the client. How the assessor or career counselor deals with these reactions in order to make the feedback and information most useful is something that has ethical implications. Imagine, for example, feedback that races through the results and "data dumps" information on an obviously distressed client whose reactions are being ignored. Ethics questions also arise if a career assessor asks clients to complete measures that, though widely used, have limited evidence of validity for the intended inferences. Or, suppose conclusions about career fit are made on the basis only of interests or personality, ignoring abilities. This too may potentially cause harm in that the client will not have important information to guide the choices to be made. The ethical challenge is always to maximize positive benefit and to avoid or minimize harm.

Competence

Having the skills and competencies to undertake professional work is an ethical requirement for all activities and one that is included in most professions' ethics codes. Competence is one way of assuring compliance with the ethical requirement to maximize benefit and avoid/minimize harm. The ethics codes cited here are all very similar in this area.

Here are some representative ethical standards related to competence.

ACA Code of Ethics—See the NCDA Code, which is nearly identical to the ACA's.

APA Code of Ethics
2.01 Boundaries of Competence
(a) Psychologists provide services, teach, and conduct research with populations and in areas only within the boundaries of their competence, based on their education, training, supervised experience, consultation, study, or professional experience. . . .

(c) Psychologists planning to provide services, teach, or conduct research involving populations, areas, techniques, or technologies new to them undertake relevant education, training, supervised experience, consultation, or study. . . .

(e) In those emerging areas in which generally recognized standards for preparatory training do not yet exist, psychologists nevertheless take reasonable steps to ensure the competence of their work and to protect clients/patients, students, supervisees, research participants, organizational clients, and others from harm. (APA, 2017a, p. 5)

CPA Code of Ethics
Competence and self-knowledge
II.6 Offer or carry out (without supervision) only those activities for which they have established their competence to carry them out to the benefit of others.

II.7 Not delegate activities to individuals or groups not competent to carry them out to the benefit of others.

II.8 Take immediate steps to obtain consultation or supervision, or to refer a primary client to a colleague or other appropriate professional, whichever is more likely to result in providing the primary client with competent service, if it becomes apparent that a primary client's issues or problems are beyond their competence.

II.9 Keep themselves up to date with a broad range of relevant knowledge, research methods, techniques, and technologies, and their impact on individuals and groups (e.g., couples, families, organizations, communities, and peoples), through the reading of relevant literature, peer consultation, and continuing education activities, in order that their practice, teaching, supervision, and research activities will benefit and not harm others. (CPA, 2017, pp. 19–20)

NCDA Code of Ethics
C.2.a. Boundaries of Competence. Career professionals practice only within the boundaries of their competence, based on their education, training, supervised experience, state and national professional credentials, and appropriate professional experience. Whereas multicultural counseling competency is required across all counseling specialties, career professionals gain knowledge, personal awareness, sensitivity, dispositions, and skills pertinent to being a culturally competent career professional.

C.2.b. New Specialty Areas of Practice. Career professionals practice in specialty areas new to them only after obtaining appropriate education, training, and supervised experience. While developing skills in new specialty areas, career professionals take steps to ensure the competence of their work and to protect others from possible harm. (NCDA, 2015, p. 9)

When career assessment and counseling were not part of one's professional training, additional education and supervised practice should precede the work. Having established one's professional competence through training and supervised experience does not mean that there is no further need for learning since competence means continuously updating ones knowledge and skills as new research and better assessment tools emerge. Although it is easy to slip into using the same measures and interpretations over time, the ethical challenge is to stay current in the literature. By analogy, few people would want to go to a medical professional who did not keep up with the latest literature findings both for new and established practices. Career assessment similarly rests on a rapidly expanding research and literature base. Reading journals, attending conferences, and having a professional network of peers with whom to exchange knowledge and information are all ways to keep one's professional practice up-to-date. Finally, when a career assessor or counselor wants to add a new area of specialization or use new approaches or measures, the ethical demand is to properly prepare for these new duties, seeking out appropriate knowledge and skills before incorporating them into one's practice.

Informed Consent

Most professions stipulate that clients have the right to voluntarily choose to participate in career assessment activities and the right also to discontinue such services should they decide to do so. The obligation of the assessor is to clearly explain to the client what is entailed in the career assessment/counseling process, including probable outcomes and any risks. Here are several relevant ethics codes.

ACA Code of Ethics
E.3. Informed Consent in Assessment

E.3.a. Explanation to Clients Prior to assessment, counselors explain the nature and purposes of assessment and the specific use of results by potential recipients. The explanation will be given in terms and language that the client (or other legally authorized person on behalf of the client) can understand.

E.3.b. Recipients of Results Counselors consider the client's and/or examinee's welfare, explicit understandings, and prior agreements in determining who receives the assessment results. Counselors include accurate and appropriate interpretations with any release of individual or group assessment results.

E.4. Release of Data to Qualified Personnel Counselors release assessment data in which the client is identified only with the consent of the client or the client's legal representative. Such data are released only to persons recognized by counselors as qualified to interpret the data. (ACA, 2014, p. 11)

APA Code of Ethics
9.03 Informed Consent in Assessments
(a) Psychologists obtain informed consent for assessments, evaluations, or diagnostic services, as described in Standard 3.10, Informed Consent, except when (1) testing is mandated by law or governmental regulations; (2) informed consent is implied because testing is conducted as a routine educational, institutional, or organizational activity (e.g., when participants voluntarily agree to assessment when applying for a job); or (3) one purpose of the testing is to evaluate decisional capacity. Informed consent includes an explanation of the nature and purpose of the assessment, fees, involvement of third parties, and limits of confidentiality and sufficient opportunity for the client/patient to ask questions and receive answers. (APA, 2017a, p. 13)

CPA Code of Ethics

Informed consent

I.17 Recognize that obtaining informed consent is a process that involves taking time to establish an appropriate trusting relationship and to reach an agreement to work collaboratively, and may need to be obtained more than once (e.g., if significant new information becomes available). . . .

I.23 Provide, in obtaining informed consent, as much information as reasonable or prudent individuals and groups (e.g., couples, families, organizations, communities, peoples) would want to know before making a decision or consenting to the activity. Typically, and as appropriate to the situation and context, this would include: purpose and nature of the activity; mutual responsibilities; whether a team or other collaborators are involved; privacy and confidentiality limitations, risks and protections; likely risks and benefits of the activity, including any particular risks or benefits of the methods or communication modalities used; alternatives available; likely consequences of nonaction; the option to refuse or withdraw at any time, without prejudice; over what period of time the consent applies; and how to rescind consent if desired. . . . Relay the information given in obtaining informed consent in language that the individuals and groups involved understand (including providing translation into another language, if necessary), and take whatever reasonable steps are needed to ensure that the information is, in fact, understood.

I.24 Relay the information given in obtaining informed consent in language that the individuals and groups involved understand (including providing translation into another language, if necessary), and take whatever reasonable steps are needed to ensure that the information is, in fact, understood. (CPA, 2017, pp. 14–15)

NCDA Code of Ethics
A.2.a. Informed Consent
Clients have the freedom to choose whether to enter into or remain in a professional relationship. To make informed choices, clients need adequate information about the working relationship and the career professional. Career professionals have an obligation to review in writing and orally the rights and responsibilities of both the career professional and the recipient of services prior to the beginning of the working relationship. Further, informed consent is an ongoing part of the professional

relationship, and career professionals appropriately document discussions of informed consent throughout the working relationship.

A.2.b. Types of Information Needed
Career professionals clearly explain to clients the nature of all services provided. They inform clients about issues such as, but not limited to, the following: the purposes, goals, techniques, procedures, limitations, potential risks, and benefits of services; the career professional's qualifications, credentials, and relevant experience; the role of technology, continuation of services upon the incapacitation or death of the career professional; and other pertinent information. Career professionals take steps to ensure that clients understand the implications of diagnosis (if applicable), the intended use of tests/assessments and reports, fees, and billing arrangements (including procedures regarding nonpayment of fees). Clients have the right to confidentiality and to be provided with an explanation of its limitations (including how supervisors and/or treatment team professionals are involved); to obtain clear information about their records; to participate in the ongoing career services plans; and to refuse any services or modality change and to be advised of the consequences of such refusal. (NCDA, 2015, pp. 3–4)

It is a basic principle of professional ethics that clients need to be able to agree to the assessment and related services before they are undertaken. As one of the codes noted, obtaining consent is a process, not simply the completion of a form. It entails a complete discussion of the professional services to be provided in a way (and in a language) that is understandable by the client. The assessor needs to explain what feedback will be provided and the likely effectiveness of the services to be delivered. Generally, except in circumstances in which consent is implied, as in group testing in school or work settings, it is desirable to obtain the consent in writing. When, due to unforeseen circumstances, terms of the engagement change, the new terms should be explained and/or negotiated with the client, and the original consent form should be amended to reflect the terms.

Assessment

This is a book on career assessment, so issues of validity and reliability of concepts and tests for their intended purposes has been an important focus throughout. The requirements, however, are not just "best practices"; they are ethical requirements. Most psychology and counseling codes of ethics include specific standards on assessment. Here are some examples.

ACA Code of Ethics
Section E. Evaluation, Assessment, and Interpretation

Introduction
Counselors use assessment as one component of the counseling process, taking into account the clients' personal and cultural context. Counselors promote the well-being of individual clients or groups of clients by devel-

oping and using appropriate educational, mental health, psychological, and career assessments.

E.1.a. Assessment
The primary purpose of educational, mental health, psychological, and career assessment is to gather information regarding the client for a variety of purposes, including, but not limited to, client decision making, treatment planning, and forensic proceedings. Assessment may include both qualitative and quantitative methodologies. (ACA, 2014, p. 11)

APA Code of Ethics

9.01 Bases for Assessments (a) Psychologists base the opinions contained in their recommendations, reports, and diagnostic or evaluative statements, including forensic testimony, on information and techniques sufficient to substantiate their findings. (See also Standard 2.04, Bases for Scientific and Professional Judgments.) . . .

9.02 Use of Assessments
(a) Psychologists administer, adapt, score, interpret, or use assessment techniques, interviews, tests, or instruments in a manner and for purposes that are appropriate in light of the research on or evidence of the usefulness and proper application of the techniques.

(b) Psychologists use assessment instruments whose validity and reliability have been established for use with members of the population tested. When such validity or reliability has not been established, psychologists describe the strengths and limitations of test results and interpretation.

(c) Psychologists use assessment methods that are appropriate to an individual's language preference and competence, unless the use of an alternative language is relevant to the assessment issues. (APA, 2017a, pp. 12–13)

CPA Code of Ethics

Maximize benefit

II.18 Strive to provide and/or obtain the best reasonably accessible service for those seeking psychological services. This may include, but is not limited to, selecting assessment tools . . . that are: (a) relevant and tailored to the needs, characteristics, and contexts of the primary client or contract examinee; and (b) based on the best available evidence in light of those needs, characteristics, and contexts. (CPA, 2017, p. 21)

NCDA Code of Ethics
E.1.a. Assessment
The primary purpose of educational, psychological, and career assessments is to provide measurements that are valid and reliable in either comparative or absolute terms. These include, but are not limited to, measurements of ability, personality, interest, intelligence, achievement, skills, values, and performance. Career professionals recognize the need to interpret the statements in this section as applying to both quantitative and qualitative assessments.

E.1.b. Client Welfare
Career professionals do not misuse assessment results and interpretations, and they take reasonable steps to prevent others from misusing the information these tools provide. They respect the client's right to know the results, the interpretations made, and the bases for career professionals' conclusions and recommendations.

E.2. Competence to Use and Interpret Assessment Instruments

E.2.a. Limits of Competence
Career professionals utilize only those testing and assessment services for which they have been trained and are competent in administering and interpreting. Career professionals using technology-assisted test interpretations are trained in the construct being measured and the specific instrument being used prior to using its technology-based application. Career professionals take reasonable measures to ensure the proper use of psychological and career assessment techniques by persons under their supervision.

E.2.b. Appropriate Use
Career professionals are responsible for the appropriate application, scoring, interpretation, and use of assessment instruments relevant to the needs of the client, whether they score and interpret such assessments themselves or use technology or other services.

E.2.c. Decisions Based on Results
Career professionals responsible for decisions involving individuals or policies that are based on assessment results have a thorough understanding of psychometrics involving educational, psychological, and career measurement, including validation criteria, assessment research, and guidelines for assessment development and use. (NCDA, 2015, p. 13)

This is a representative but necessarily incomplete listing of all the ethical standards regarding assessment. These standards make clear that the ethical requirements for providing assessments are extensive and complicated, consistent with the complexity of assessment itself.

Confidentiality

Every ethics code that might apply to career assessors includes ethical standards relating to maintaining confidentiality. Although each of the following codes expresses it a bit differently, all speak to the need to keep information confidential that was promised to be protected and to let clients know in advance about exceptions to confidentiality.

ACA Code of Ethics—See NCDA Code of Ethics

APA Code of Ethics
4. Privacy And Confidentiality

4.01 Maintaining Confidentiality Psychologists have a primary obligation and take reasonable precautions to protect confidential information obtained through or stored in any medium, recognizing that the extent and limits of confidentiality may be regulated by law or established by institutional rules or professional or scientific relationship. (See also Standard 2.05, Delegation of Work to Others.)

4.02 Discussing the Limits of Confidentiality
(a) Psychologists discuss with persons (including, to the extent feasible, persons who are legally incapable of giving informed consent and their legal representatives) and organizations with whom they establish a scientific or professional relationship (1) the relevant limits of confidentiality and (2) the foreseeable uses of the information generated through their psychological activities. (See also Standard 3.10, Informed Consent.)

(b) Unless it is not feasible or is contraindicated, the discussion of confidentiality occurs at the outset of the relationship and thereafter as new circumstances may warrant. (APA, 2017a, p. 7)

CPA Code of Ethics

Confidentiality

I.43 Be careful not to relay incidental information about colleagues, team members, other collaborators, the primary clients or contract examinees of others, research participants, employees, supervisees, students, or trainees gained in the process of their activities as psychologists, that the psychologist has reason to believe is considered confidential by those individuals or groups, except as required or justified by law. (Also see Standards IV.17 and IV.18.)

I.44 Clarify what measures will be taken to protect privacy and confidentiality, and what responsibilities group members (e.g., couples, families, organizations, communities, peoples) have for the protection of each other's privacy and confidentiality, when engaged in services to or research with groups.

I.45 Share confidential information with others only to the extent reasonably needed for the purpose of sharing, and only with the informed consent of those involved, or in a manner that the individuals and groups (e.g., couples, families, organizations, communities, peoples) involved cannot be identified, except as required or justified by law, or in circumstances of possible imminent serious bodily harm. (CPA, 2017, p. 17)

NCDA Code of Ethics
B.1.b. Respect for Privacy
Career professionals respect client rights to privacy. Career professionals solicit private information from clients only when it is beneficial to the working relationship.

B.1.c. Respect for Confidentiality
Career professionals protect the confidential information of prospective and current clients. Career professionals do not share confidential information without client consent or without sound legal or ethical justification.

B.1.d. Explanation of Limitations
At initiation and throughout the professional relationship, career professionals inform clients of the limitations of confidentiality and seek to

identify foreseeable situations in which confidentiality must be breached. (NCDA, 2015, p. 6)

Note that there are both ethical and legal issues that need to be considered in the confidentiality domain. Clients may or may not have legal rights to confidentiality, and assessors may or may not have privilege such that their communications and data are protected from disclosure. It is important that clients be notified in advance when there are actual or possible exceptions to confidentiality, such as when records might be subpoenaed or abuse allegations would require notification to authorities, since that information might determine what clients would disclose.

Here are a few other ethical issues that frequently arise in doing career assessment and counseling.

Multiple Relationships; Multiple Clients

Typically, career assessments are conducted with an individual client who is able to consent to the process and who will be the recipient of the results of the assessment. However, when working with minors, such as in school settings or when parents contract with the assessor for work, there are often multiple relationships, meaning that the assessor has ethical responsibilities to the person being assessed and to third parties. Similarly, when career assessment is done in institutional settings, the assessor typically has responsibilities both to those being assessed and to the institution. Third parties may dictate specific practices such as using certain measures that the assessor finds problematic.

Here is one (APA's) definition of multiple relations.

3.05 Multiple Relationships
(a) A multiple relationship occurs when a psychologist is in a professional role with a person and (1) at the same time is in another role with the same person, (2) at the same time is in a relationship with a person closely associated with or related to the person with whom the psychologist has the professional relationship, or (3) promises to enter into another relationship in the future with the person or a person closely associated with or related to the person. (APA, 2017a, p. 6)

Multiple relationships have different names in some of the Codes. The VRA Canada Code, for example, uses the term "multiple clients" (VRA Canada, 2021, p. 11). Contrary to some popular beliefs, multiple relationships are not per se unethical. In fact, in many areas of practice (e.g., work, where an organization may be the primary client, in schools, or in forensic settings) multiple relations are common if not the norm. Sticking with the APA Code, here is the ethical guidance provided about when such relationships are unethical and when not.

3.05 Multiple Relationships
(a) . . . A psychologist refrains from entering into a multiple relationship if the multiple relationship could reasonably be expected to impair the psychologist's objectivity, competence, or effectiveness in performing his

or her functions as a psychologist, or otherwise risks exploitation or harm to the person with whom the professional relationship exists. Multiple relationships that would not reasonably be expected to cause impairment or risk exploitation or harm are not unethical. (APA, 2017a, p. 6)

Clearly, there are issues in informed consent that must be addressed when career assessment involves multiple relations or clients. The APA Code of Ethics provides one standard, 3.11, that is particularly helpful in identifying the respective obligations when services are provided in organizational contexts:

3.11 Psychological Services Delivered to or Through Organizations
(a) Psychologists delivering services to or through organizations provide information beforehand to clients and when appropriate those directly affected by the services about (1) the nature and objectives of the services, (2) the intended recipients, (3) which of the individuals are clients, (4) the relationship the psychologist will have with each person and the organization, (5) the probable uses of services provided and information obtained, (6) who will have access to the information, and (7) limits of confidentiality. As soon as feasible, they provide information about the results and conclusions of such services to appropriate persons. (APA, 2017a, p. 7)

Evidence-Based Practice

What is the basis for career assessment practice? Is it acceptable to practice using methods believed, without scientific or research evidence, to be effective, or is there an ethical requirement to make use of the best available evidence from the relevant scientific and professional practice literature?

In general, professions require their members to base their practices on scientific and other research or professional practice evidence from the literature and on the literature or consensus on professional practice applications. Here are two standards related to this issue.

APA Code of Ethics
2.04 Bases for Scientific and Professional Judgments
Psychologists' work is based upon established scientific and professional knowledge of the discipline. (APA, 2017a, p. 5)

CPA Code of Ethics
B. Other terms.
"Best available evidence" refers to the evidence that is the most trustworthy and valid according to a hierarchy of evidence (i.e., a hierarchy that ranks evidence from strongest to weakest), and which is appropriate to the services being delivered. (CPA, 2017, p. 21)

Clearly, practitioners do not have to be scientists or researchers in their respective areas of expertise. But they do need to be aware of, and to keep up with, the professional literature in their areas of practice and be aware of new evidence that becomes available or better approaches that come along. Because career assessment usually involves use of psychological tests, they also need to carefully select measures, to know the literature on the measures they make use of, to know what the major choices are among measures, including new and improved ones, and to be able to justify their particular choices. This book has demonstrated that in some areas (e.g., measurement of interests) there can be inconsistency in obtained results when using one measure or another. Balancing validity and practical issues such as cost and time, assessors may wish to use multiple measures of these very important constructs as one way of addressing inconsistencies. All measures, of course, have limitations, and assessors need to be aware of the ones associated with the particular measures they use and advise clients of any such issues affecting the results when providing feedback.

Multicultural Competence

This book has identified a number of issues that arise in working with multiculturally diverse career assessment clients. These matters not only include age, race, sex, sexual orientation, gender identity, and national origin, but also linguistic minorities. The competencies needed only compound when, thanks to advances in technology, career services can be offered electronically all over the world.

Almost all ethics codes relevant to career assessment and counseling now speak to cultural and multicultural competence. The VRA Canada Code of Ethics, for example, is representative, including, among others, the following ethical standard:

> **1.8 Respecting Diversity.** Vocational rehabilitation professionals demonstrate respect, acceptance, and a willingness to understand different beliefs and client identities that affect their professional activities. Vocational rehabilitation professionals develop and adapt interventions and services to incorporate consideration of client's preferences, and do not discriminate on the basis of age, colour, culture, disability, nationality, ethnicity, gender, race, language preference, religion, spirituality, sexual orientation, marital status, and / or socio- economic status. . . . (VRA Canada, 2021, p. 10)

The APA Code of Ethics further requires knowledge of how diversity factors may affect the particular competencies needed to deliver professional services effectively. The relevant standard (among others) states,

> **2.01 Boundaries of Competence**
> (b) Where scientific or professional knowledge in the discipline of psychology establishes that an understanding of factors associated with age, gender, gender identity, race, ethnicity, culture, national origin, religion, sexual orientation, disability, language, or socioeconomic status is essential for effective implementation of their services or research, psychologists have or obtain the training, experience, consultation, or supervision necessary to ensure the competence of their services, or they make appropriate referrals, except as provided in Standard 2.02, Providing Services in Emergencies. (APA, 2017a, p. 5)

The APA Code, like many, also prohibits unfair discrimination based on specific personal characteristics in its Standard 3.01.

3.01 Unfair Discrimination
In their work-related activities, psychologists do not engage in unfair discrimination based on age, gender, gender identity, race, ethnicity, culture, national origin, religion, sexual orientation, disability, socioeconomic status, or any basis proscribed by law. (APA, 2017a, p. 7)

The NCDA Code is specific about another common issue in career testing: the diversity of the population norms on which the measures were developed.

E.8. Multicultural Issues/Diversity in Assessment
Career professionals use, with caution, assessment techniques that were normed on populations other than that of the client. Career professionals recognize the possible effects of age, color, culture, disability, ethnic group, gender, race, language preference, religion, spirituality, sexual orientation, and socioeconomic status on test administration and interpretation, and place test results in proper perspective with other relevant factors. Career professionals use caution when selecting assessments for culturally diverse populations to avoid the use of instruments that lack appropriate psychometric properties for the client population.

E.9. Scoring and Interpretation of Assessments
E.9.a. When career professionals report assessment results, they consider the client's personal and cultural background, the level of the client's understanding of the results, and the impact of the results on the client. In reporting assessment results, career professionals indicate reservations that exist regarding validity or reliability due to circumstances of the assessment or the inappropriateness of the norms for the person tested. (NCDA, 2015, p. 14)

I end the section on ethics with a case to illustrate the application of ethics in practice.

MARCO'S CASE (CASE 12)

A career counselor met for the first time with a prospective client, Marco, age 22, who was unhappy in his current college major and had uncertainty about whether, as a senior with significant school debt already, he should consider making a change of career directions. He asked to take the "career tests" that a friend had recently completed.

Marco was the first in his family to go to college, and his family has sacrificed a lot to help pay for his college expenses. His parents had hoped he would go into medicine or law so he could have a career where he could do well and help to support the family. He had tried premed and didn't do very well, nor did he like the required science courses. The prelaw courses included an internship at a law firm, but he did not like what he experienced there, especially the backbiting environment. Asked by the career counselor what other areas he was contemplating, he said he enjoyed athletics and coaching, although he knew he was not going to be a professional athlete. However, he thought he would enjoy being a high school coach and was considering changing his major even though it might entail an extra year of college.

The career assessor explored with Marco the issues of family pressure and whether he thought they would support such a move. Marco said his parents always told him that he could do whatever he wanted to do, but when he had suggested he might become a coach and teacher, he thought they were disappointed, though they did not directly say not to do it. The counselor suggested that Marco first explore these concerns in a few counseling sessions and if he still wanted career assessment after that, they would proceed with it.

In the discussions about his career directions, it became clear that Marco was experiencing considerable guilt about changing his major, incurring more debt, and possibly disappointing his family. After those issues had been identified and processed, Marco said he still wanted to complete a career assessment. He signed an amended consent form and a battery of interests, abilities, and personality measures. The results did suggest that careers in a helping profession were well suited to his career profile, and several career options aligned with his profile were identified. Ultimately, he decided to pursue a high school teaching and coaching career with the acceptance, if not exactly the enthusiastic support, of his family. The career counselor offered to meet with him and his parents to review the results, but Marco felt that he could handle those issues himself.

This case illustrates ethical, rather than unethical, behavior in working with a client who initially requested career assessment. The counselor was sensitive to the psychological conflicts Marco was experiencing and postposed career assessment until those could be addressed. He wisely considered the cultural issues experienced by a person from an economically challenged environment trying to decide whether he should prioritize his own or his family's preferences. Although career assessment could have been begun from the outset—after all, that was what the client requested—it was probably more appropriate to do after better understanding the conflicts the client was personally experiencing (issues the career counselor well understood and was competent to address) both in choosing a career and in working through the issues with his family that were important to him to resolve.

USE OF TECHNOLOGY IN TEST ADMINISTRATION AND INTERPRETATION

Among the many advances that have accompanied the digital and internet revolutions has been the technical ability to delivery professional services electronically. With these changes have come a huge expansion in the number of people who potentially can access career assessment services—and a plethora of legal and ethical issues. With the pandemic of the second decade of the 21st century, many barriers to online service delivery have at least temporarily been removed, and licensing boards have been more willing to allow service delivery across geographic boundaries. Accompanying the proliferation of technological advances come both opportunities and concerns. Here I introduce some of the relevant issues associated with the technological revolution as it relates to career assessment.

Advantages of Using Technology in Career Assessment

First the internet itself, and then online assessments, not to mention a variety of apps aimed at enhancing personal decision making, have dramatically transformed many aspects of professional life (Sampson & Osborn, 2015). In the case of career assessments and interventions, routine use is now made of technology (information and communication technology [ICT] is a commonly used term for this) in the form of apps, testing, career interventions, websites and phones, among many others (Venable, 2010). ICT has greatly advanced the practice of career assessment, but it also has limitations and potential challenges.

Increasingly, clients can complete career assessment instruments virtually. Tests and other assessments now have the possibility, when reliable internet service is available, of being administered more precisely and frequently with greater convenience for the person being assessed. The possibilities are also unlimited to design gamification and simulation-based assessments (Hawkes et al., 2018) rather than just traditional written questions and responses (see Drasgow & Olson-Buchanan, 2018). Not without challenges, online profiles and social media postings are also increasingly used to draw conclusions about people's fitness for particular jobs or careers (Jeske & Schultz, 2016; Zickar, 2018). Despite great promise, technological advances have in some cases occurred ahead of validity and reliability.

Long before the current explosion of uses of technology in career assessment, the O*NET (U.S. Department of Labor, n.d.-b) demonstrated that vast quantities of career information with readily accessible data about careers, jobs, and people can be made available to users at no cost to them. This amazing, powerful, and continually updated resource has revolutionized the ease with which such information can be accessed and used for a variety of purposes. Its inclusion of evidence-based classifications of both careers (jobs) and people provides a very powerful tool. And there is good evidence for convergent validity for the RIASEC types of the O*NET's free online interest measure when compared with other well-established interest measures (see Eggerth et al., 2005).

Through electronic delivery methods, career assessors can also provide feedback and counseling services online, saving clients considerable time and the expense of traveling to a physical location. Untimed interest and personality tests can be completed at the client's leisure, resulting in fewer measures having to be taken back-to-back. The global pandemic occurring at the time this book is being finished has demonstrated the potential of moving assessment and counseling/coaching practices to be entirely virtually delivered.

Possibly an advantage, but also with limitations, automated testing and interpretation services are also now widely available. Some of these are in the public domain and offered to anyone without charge. Others charge for the use, but in either case there is usually no personalized contact with a competent career assessor or counselor.

Whereas licensing laws confine practitioners' work to a particular geographic space, with internet availability comes the theoretical possibility of providing career services to anyone, anywhere in the world that there is appropriate internet access. When it is considered that millions to billions of people in the world do not have access to competent career assessment, these developments potentially open service provision to a much larger population. However, they also create potential problems.

Limitations of Technology in Career Assessment

Simply because an assessment can be administered online does not mean that it should be. Gati and Asulin-Peretz (2011) identified challenges with some of the online career assessment measures, particularly those intended for self-assessments. Any assessment measure administered virtually faces the same requirements for validity and reliability evidence as for any measure administered in person. Convenience and ease of access are great assets, but, however delivered, the assessment is still only as good as the measure itself. A poorly validated but easily accessible measure is still a bad measure.

Elaborating, online measures must meet all the usual requirements of validity and reliability for the intended inferences (see American Educational Research Association [AERA], APA, & National Council on Measurement in Education [NCME], 2014), and they must meet an additional standard that the modality of administration does not adversely affect the measurement results. Additionally, the same concerns about standardized administration and protection of the test itself apply to internet-administered assessments, but it is clearly less easy to assure those conditions are met when the assessments are delivered virtually. And just as with in-person test administrations, the test user still has the responsibility to review all the evidence for particular measures, including the effects of electronic delivery of the measures, and then decide which is the best net positive measure for a particular application.

Test security and test administration standardization are also important considerations for deciding whether online test administration is appropriate (see Weiner & Necus, 2018). With ability measures, the use of an online proctor should be considered. Such services, less costly than might be imagined, can monitor the test-taking site and process in the attempt to assure that there are no compromises that might affect the validity and reliability of the obtained information. It might be imagined that test standardization is less important for ability measures administered for career assessment purposes, but that would be incorrect. Test users/administrators not only need reliably obtained information to assure that the results can be accurately interpreted, but they also have an ethical, and sometimes legal, responsibility to ensure that the test's content is not compromised, which can lessen the accuracy and reliability of the test's results for many people, not just one test taker.

Because a number of measures are available online for self-administration, assessees may already have completed some of these measures, including those that lack compelling evidence of validity or reliability. The assessor may then have to explain why the measures used in the current assessment are better and why others are less appropriate to be relied upon, and to clarify any misconceptions about the client's career-related characteristics that derived from unvalidated sources.

Another limitation of worldwide service delivery derives not from the technology itself so much as from the assessor/counselor's need to have competence in the culture and language of the client (see the multicultural sections of the ethics standards presented earlier in this chapter). It is entirely possible for an American or Canadian assessor, say, to administer tests to people in China, Gabon, and Argentina all on the same day. But whether it is appropriate or not to do so will depend in part on the assessor's knowledge of the culture and the language competencies of the client and the assessor. It makes little sense to assess one whose English-language proficiency (if that is the language of the measures being used) is limited. Similarly, even when working with a corporate clientele where English is the common language, assessors may well not understand or appreciate the culture of the assessees. For example, assessors may not understand that in certain cultures, those family members who succeed in getting a good job with a major corporation are expected to keep the position and to keep sending money back home to support the family members left behind. This may limit their willingness to seriously consider alternative career paths, particularly those that pay less than the current career. People from some cultures may also feel that they need to be deferent to those in authority and not necessarily express their true feelings directly. It is also necessary for the assessor to determine whether there is sufficient fluency to proceed with a client whose primary language is not the same as the assessor's language. In my edited book *Internationalizing Multiculturalism: Expanding Professional Competencies in a Globalized World* (Lowman, 2013), the chapter authors demonstrated how in every major commonly used category of diversity (including race/ethnicity, sex/gender, sexual orientation, religion, and national origin), multiculturalism needs to be recrafted, extended, and reconceptualized to more broadly apply when international perspectives are taken into account. That is a tall but necessary order when moving one's services to new cultures, new countries, and new contexts.

There are many other issues that can be considered, but these illustrate some of the challenges in technological applications. A good resource for professionals of many backgrounds is the document *Guidelines for the Practice of Telepsychology* (Joint Task Force for the Development of Telepsychology Guidelines for Psychologists, 2013; available for free download from https://www.apa.org/practice/guidelines/telepsychology). Other useful resources on best practices and guidelines can be found in Coyne and Bartram (2018).

Is it Appropriate to Deliver Career Assessment Services Electronically?

The best answer to this question is neither "no" nor "yes," but rather, "it depends." The career assessor needs first to determine whether the person(s) receiving the assessment services is located in a jurisdiction requiring a license or certification for career assessment service delivery and, if so, whether the practitioner is licensed or certified there. The assessor should also determine from the malpractice insurance carrier whether the policy will cover services that are delivered electronically.

Even when services can technically be delivered electronically, and when they fall within the purview of the provider's license and any governing parameters, there are still a number of other factors that need to be considered before delivering such services. These include the following.

Is the client willing and able to proceed with electronic services? Can clients provide an appropriate noise- and distraction-free setting in which to complete any assessment measures administered electronically? In many parts of the developing world, cell phones are widely available and used but computers are not. Some online assessments can be completed on cell phones; others not.

Is the internet quality a factor in administering the tests reliably? For example, when timed ability measures are being administered, is the person's internet quality sufficiently stable and reliable to obtain a valid result? Do the ability or other measures need to be administered with a virtual or other proctor to assure that the person completing the measures is the intended recipient of the assessment services, and can the proctoring method assure that the client is not accessing any help from others or from other sources, including the internet? Can the intellectual property of the test vendor be protected? Is the assessment a high-stakes one in which people will be selected or rejected based primarily on the results of the testing?

There is a growing literature on internet-based testing, considering with scientific evidence such concerns as test security and intellectual property threats (Addicott & Foster, 2018), cheating (Lowman, 2018), and whether administering tests electronically produces substantially the same results as those administered in person. Although this is a fast moving field of inquiry, a good summary of what is known and not known about technology-enhanced assessment is provided in Scott et al.'s (2018) book *Next Generation Technology-Enhanced Assessment: Global Perspectives on Occupational and Workplace Testing*.

Ethical Standards in Use of Technology in Career Assessment

Some of the ethics codes reviewed earlier in this chapter included standards related to technology's use in career assessment. I end this chapter with a sampling of illustrative ethical standards associated with the use of technology in career assessment. These remind readers that ethical standards apply to all of their work, no matter in what medium or modality the assessments or services are delivered.

ACA Code of Ethics
Section H. Distance Counseling, Technology, and Social Media

H.4.c. Technology-Assisted Services
When providing technology-assisted services, counselors make reasonable efforts to determine that clients are intellectually, emotionally, physi-

cally, linguistically, and functionally capable of using the application and that the application is appropriate for the needs of the client. Counselors verify that clients understand the purpose and operation of technology applications and follow up with clients to correct possible misconceptions, discover appropriate use, and assess subsequent steps.

APA Code of Ethics
4.02 Discussing the Limits of Confidentiality
(c) Psychologists who offer services, products, or information via electronic transmission inform clients/patients of the risks to privacy and limits of confidentiality.

9.02 Use of Assessments
(c) Psychologists use assessment methods that are appropriate to an individual's language preference and competence, unless the use of an alternative language is relevant to the assessment issues. (APA, 2017a, pp. 7, 13)

CCPA Code of Ethics
C5. Technology in Assessment and Evaluation
Counselors/therapists recognize that their ethical responsibilities are not altered, nor in any way diminished, by the use of technology for the administration, scoring, and interpretation of assessment and evaluation instruments. Counsellors/therapists retain their responsibility for the maintenance of the ethical principles of privacy, confidentiality, and responsibility for decisions regardless of the technology used. (See also B2, E8, Section H.) (CCPA, 2020, p. 15)

CPA Code of Ethics
I.41 Collect, record, store, handle, and transfer all private information, whether written or unwritten (e.g., paper or electronic records, e-mail or fax communications, computer files, recordings), in a way that attends to the needs for privacy, confidentiality, and security. This would include protection from loss or unauthorized access, appropriate education of staff or other agents, and having adequate plans in circumstances of one's own serious illness, termination of employment, or death. (CPA, 2017, p. 17)

NCDA Code of Ethics
F.1.a. Knowledge and Competency
Career professionals who engage in providing career services online and using technology and/or social media develop knowledge and skills regarding related technical, ethical, and legal considerations. Career professionals understand and follow the terms of service of any technology or social media platform employed.

F.1.b. Laws and Statutes
Career professionals who engage in providing career services online and using technology and/or social media within their practice understand that they may be subject to laws and regulations of both the career professional's practicing location and the client's place of work/residence. Career professionals ensure that use of technology services with clients is in accordance with all applicable federal, state, local, and/or institutional statutes, laws, regulations, and procedures, particularly when the services are offered via technology across state lines and/or international boundaries. (NCDA, 2015, p. 15)

VRA Canada Code of Ethics
1.21 Technology Used to Communicate with the Client
Vocational rehabilitation professionals ensure technology and/or its applications do not present a barrier to participation in rehabilitation services. Where a barrier exists, the vocational rehabilitation professional ensures the client is provided with alternatives for communication. (VRA Canada, 2021, p. 12)

7.2 Behaviour and Competence
Vocational rehabilitation professionals hold to the same level of expected behaviour and competence as defined by this Code of Ethics, regardless of the technology used (e.g., cellular phones, email, video, audio, audio-visual), or its application (e.g., assessment, research, data storage). They are aware of differences or potential difficulties in communication with clients when using the Internet, and/or methods of electronic communication and the potential misunderstandings arising from the lack of visual cues and voice intonations when communicating electronically. (VRA Canada, 2021, p. 25)

SUMMARY AND CONCLUSIONS

One of the things that distinguishes professionals is that their professions have detailed standards and guidelines and they behave in accord with these standards in their work. In this chapter, a variety of ethics codes and guidelines issued by various professional associations whose members are involved in career assessment activities were introduced. This by no means exhaustive discussion identified a number of ethical standards and guidelines intended to guide career assessment work. Then, a variety of technology issues were introduced that are relevant to the rapid growth in the use of online assessments and virtual delivery of career services. With the accelerated development of technology and electronic service delivery, this coverage was necessarily limited to covering highlights, but they are sufficient to demonstrate some of the advances.

REFERENCES

Abuhamdeh, S., & Csikszentmihalyi, M. (2014). The artistic personality: A systems perspective. In P. McIntyre, J. Fulton, & E. Patton (Eds.) *The systems model of creativity* (pp. 227–237). Springer.

Ackerman, P. L. (2018). The search for personality–intelligence relations: Methodological and conceptual issues. *Journal of Intelligence, 6*(1), 2–12. https://doi.org/10.3390/jintelligence6010002

Ackerman, P. L., & Beier, M. E. (2007). Further explorations of perceptual speed abilities in the context of assessment methods, cognitive abilities, and individual differences during skill acquisition. *Journal of Experimental Psychology: Applied, 13*(4), 249–272. https://doi.org/10.1037/1076-898X.13.4.249

Ackerman, P. L., Beier, M. E., & Boyle, M. D. (2002). Individual differences in working memory within a nomological network of cognitive and perceptual speed abilities. *Journal of Experimental Psychology: General, 131*(4), 567–589. https://doi.org/10.1037/0096-3445.131.4.567

Ackerman, P. L., & Cianciolo, A. T. (2000). Cognitive, perceptual-speed, and psychomotor determinants of individual differences during skill acquisition. *Journal of Experimental Psychology: Applied, 6*(4), 259–290. https://doi.org/10.1037/1076-898X.6.4.259

Ackerman, P. L., & Heggestad, E. D. (1997). Intelligence, personality, and interests: Evidence for overlapping traits. *Psychological Bulletin, 121*(2), 219–245. https://doi.org/10.1037/0033-2909.121.2.219

Ackerman, T. A., & Smith, P. L. (1988). A comparison of the information provided by essay, multiple-choice, and free response writing tests. *Applied Psychological Measurement, 12*(2), 117–128. https://doi.org/10.1177/014662168801200202

Adams, M. L., Deokar, A. J., Anderson, L. A., Edwards, V. J., & Centers for Disease Control and Prevention. (2013). Self-reported increased confusion or memory loss and associated functional difficulties among adults aged ≥ 60 years—21 States, 2011. *MMWR: Morbidity and Mortality Weekly Report, 62*(18), 347–350.

Addicott, S., & Foster, D. (2018). Security of technology-enhanced assessments. In J. C. Scott, D. Bartram, & D. H. Reynolds (Eds.), *Next generation technology-enhanced* assessment: Global perspectives on occupational and workplace testing (pp. 171–192). Cambridge University Press.

Adelmann, P. K. (1989). Occupational gender mix and men's experience of the work role. *Social Behaviour, 4*(4), 225–236.

Aderman, D., & Berkowtiz, L. (1983). Self-concern and the unwillingness to be helpful. *Social Psychology Quarterly, 46,* 293–301.

Alteneder, L. E. (1940). The value of intelligence, personality, and vocational interest tests in a guidance program. *Journal of Educational Psychology, 31*(6), 449–459. https://doi.org/10.1037/h0053686

Amabile, T. M. (1983). *The social psychology of creativity.* Springer Verlag.

American Counseling Association. (2014). *2014 ACA Code of Ethics.* https://www.counseling.org/docs/default-source/default-document-library/2014-code-of-ethics-finaladdress.pdf?sfvrsn=96b532c_2

American Educational Research Association, American Psychological Association, & National Council on Measurement in Education. (2014). *Standards for Educational and Psychological Testing.*

American Psychological Association. (n.d.). *Personality.* https://www.apa.org/topics/personality/

American Psychological Association. (2017a). *Ethical principles of psychologists and code of conduct* (2002, Amended June 1, 2010, and January 1, 2017). http://www.apa.org/ethics/code/ethics-code-2017.pdf

American Psychological Association. (2017b). *Multicultural guidelines: An ecological approach to context, identity, and intersectionality, 2017.* http://www.apa.org/about/policy/multicultural-guidelines.pdf

Americans With Disabilities Act of 1990, Pub. L. No. 101–336, 104 Stat. 328 (1990).

Amerikaner, M., Elliot, D., & Swank, P. (1988). Social interest as a predictor of vocational satisfaction. *Individual Psychology: Journal of Adlerian Theory, Research & Practice, 44*(3), 316–323.

Anastasi, A. (1982). *Psychological testing* (5th ed.). Macmillan.

Anaza, N. A., Inyang, A. E., & Saavedra, J. L. (2018). Empathy and affect in B2B salesperson performance. *Journal of Business & Industrial Marketing, 33*(1), 29–41.

Andreasen, N. J. C., & Canter, A. (1974). The creative writer: Psychiatric symptoms and family history. *Comprehensive Psychiatry, 15*(2), 123–131.

Andreasen, N. J. C., & Powers, P. S. (1975). Creativity and psychosis: An examination of conceptual style. *Archives of General Psychiatry, 32*(1), 70–73.

Andrew, D. M., Paterson, D. G., & Longstaff, H. P. (1979). *Manual for the Minnesota Clerical Test.* Psychological Corporation.

Andrews, H. A. (1975). Beyond the high point code in testing Holland's theory. *Journal of Vocational Behavior, 6*(1), 101–108. https://doi.org/10.1016/0001-8791(75)90025-1

Ankenman, K., Elgin, J., Sullivan, K., Vincent, L., & Bernier, R. (2014). Nonverbal and verbal cognitive discrepancy profiles in autism spectrum disorders: Influence of age and gender. *American Journal on Intellectual and Developmental Disabilities, 119*(1), 84–99. https://doi.org/10.1352/1944-7558-119.1.84

Ansari, M. A. (1984). Psychodynamics of a successful executive. *Managerial Psychology, 5*(1), 25–43.

Ansberry, C. (2003, June 30). A new blue-collar world: Workers now need more skills but get less job security. *Wall Street Journal,* B1.

Ansley, T. N., Spratt, K. F., & Forsyth, R. A. (1989). The effects of using calculators to reduce the computational burden on a standardized test of mathematics problem solving. *Educational and psychological measurement, 49*(1), 277–286. https://doi.org/10.1177/0013164489491031

Anthoney, S. F., & Armstrong, P. I. (2010). Individuals and environments: Linking ability and skill ratings with interests. *Journal of Counseling Psychology, 57*(1), 36–51. https://doi.org/10.1037/a0018067

Antonakis, J., House, R. J., & Simonton, D. K. (2017). Can super smart leaders suffer from too much of a good thing? The curvilinear effect of intelligence on perceived leadership behavior. *Journal of Applied Psychology, 102*(7), 1003–1021. https://doi.org/10.1037/apl0000221

Apostal, R. A. (1991). College students' career interests and sensing-intuition personality. *Journal of College Student Development, 32*(1), 4–7.

Aranya, N., Barak, A., & Amernic, J. (1981). A test of Holland's theory in a population of accountants. *Journal of Vocational Behavior, 19*(1), 15–24. https://doi.org/10.1016/0001-8791(81)90045-2

Aranya, N., & Wheeler, J. T. (1986). Accountants' personality types and their commitment to organization and profession. *Contemporary Accounting Research, 3*(1), 184–189. https://doi.org/10.1111/j.1911-3846.1986.tb00633.x

Arcelus, J., Witcomb, G. L., & Mitchell, A. (2014). Prevalence of eating disorders amongst dancers: A systemic review and meta-analysis. *European Eating Disorders Review, 22*(2), 92–101. https://doi.org/10.1002/erv.2271

Arenson, M. A. (1983, Summer). The validity of certain entrance tests as predictors of grades in music theory and ear training. *Bulletin of the Council for Research in Music Education, 75*, 33–39.

Arieti, S. (1976). *Creativity: The magic synthesis*. Basic.

Arlien-Søborg, P. (1984). Chronic toxic encephalopathy in housepainters. *Acta Neurologica Scandinavica, 69*(S99), 105–113. https://doi.org/10.1111/j.1600-0404.1984.tb05675.x

Armstrong, P., Day, S. X., Mcvay, J. P., & Rounds, J. (2008). Holland's RIASEC model as an integrative framework for individual differences. *Journal of Counseling Psychology, 55*(1), 1–18. https://doi.org/10.1037/0022-0167.55.1.1

Armstrong, P., & Rounds, J. (2010). Integrating individual differences in career assessment: The Atlas Model of Individual Differences and the Strong Ring. *Career Development Quarterly, 59*(2), 143–153. https://doi.org/10.1002/j.2161-0045.2010.tb00058.x

Armstrong-Carter, E., Trejo, S., Hill, L. J. B., Crossley, K. L., Mason, D., & Domingue, B. W. (2020). The earliest origins of genetic nurture: The prenatal environment mediates the association between maternal genetics and child development. *Psychological Science, 31*(7), 781–791. https://doi.org/10.1177/0956797620917209

Arvey, R. D., & Dewhirst, H. D. (1979). Relationships between diversity of interests, age, job satisfaction and job performance. *Journal of Occupational Psychology, 52*(1), 17–23. https://doi.org/10.1111/j.2044-8325.1979.tb00436.x

Ashton, M. C., & Lee, K. (2009). An investigation of personality types within the HEXACO personality framework. *Journal of Individual Differences, 30*(4), 181–187. https://doi.org/10.1027/1614-0001.30.4.181

Atanasoff, G. E., & Slaney, R. B. (1980). Three approaches to counselor-free career exploration among college women. *Journal of Counseling Psychology, 27*, 332–339. https://doi.org/10.1037/0022-0167.27.4.332

Athanasou, J. (1989). Self-reports of vocational interests: Instrumentation and validity. *Australian Psychologist, 24*, 61–69. https://doi.org/10.1080/00050068908259550

Atkinson, J. W., & Feather, N. T. (Eds.). (1966). *A theory of achievement motivation*. Wiley.

Austin, J. T., & Hanisch, K. A. (1990). Occupational attainment as a function of abilities and interests: A longitudinal analysis using project TALENT data. *Journal of Applied Psychology, 75*(1), 77–86. https://doi.org/10.1037/0021-9010.75.1.77

Australian Council for Educational Research. (1981). *ACER higher tests ML-MQ and PL-PQ manual* (2nd ed.).

Babiak, P., & Hare, R. D. (2006). *Snakes in suits: When psychopaths go to work.* HarperCollins.

Bachtold, L. M., & Werner, E. E. (1972). Personality characteristics of women scientists. *Psychological Reports, 31*(2), 391–396. https://doi.org/10.2466/pr0.1972.31.2.391

Bäckman, L., Jones, S., Berger, A.-K., Laukka, E. J., & Small, B. J. (2005). Cognitive impairment in preclinical Alzheimer's disease: A meta-analysis. *Neuropsychology, 19*(4), 520–531. https://doi.org/10.1037/0894-4105.19.4.520

Bagalman, E., & Cornell, A. S. (2018). *Prevalence of mental illness in the United States: Data sources and estimates.* Congressional Research Service. https://fas.org/sgp/crs/misc/R43047.pdf

Baharloo, S., Johnston, P. A., Service, S. K., Gitschier, J., & Freimer, N. B. (1998). Absolute pitch: An approach for identification of genetic and nongenetic components. *American Journal of Human Genetics, 62*(2), 224–231. https://doi.org/10.1086/301704

Bair, J. T. (1951). Factor analysis of clerical aptitude tests. *Journal of Applied Psychology, 35*(4), 245–249. https://doi.org/10.1037/h0059681

Baker, T. A., & Gebhardt, D. L. (2017). Physical ability tests. In J. L., & Tippins, N. T. (Eds.), *Handbook of employee selection* (2nd ed., pp. 277–298). Taylor & Francis.

Bamberger, J. (1982). Growing up prodigies: The midlife crisis. *New Directions for Child Development, 1982*(17), 61–77. https://doi.org/10.1002/cd.23219821707

Bar-On, R. (2006). The Bar-On model of emotional-social intelligence (ESI) 1. *Psicothema, 18*(Suppl.), 13–25. https://reunido.uniovi.es/index.php/PST/article/view/8415

Barak, A. (1982). Vocational interests: A cognitive view. *Journal of Vocational Behavior, 19*(1), 1–14. https://doi.org/10.1016/0001-8791(81)90044-0

Barak, A., Librowsky, I., & Shiloh, S. (1989). Cognitive determinants of interests: An extension of a theoretical model and initial empirical examinations. *Journal of Vocational Behavior, 34*(3), 318–334. https://doi.org/10.1016/0001-8791(89)90023-7

Barak, A., & Meir, E. I. (1974). The predictive validity of a vocational interest inventory-"Ramak": Seven year follow-up. *Journal of Vocational Behavior, 4*(3), 377–387. https://doi.org/10.1016/0001-8791(74)90123-7

Barbot, B., & Reiter-Palmon, R. (2019). Creativity assessment: Pitfalls, solutions, and standards. *Psychology of Aesthetics, Creativity, and the Arts, 13*(2), 131–132. https://doi.org/10.1037/aca0000251

Barlow, D. H., Sauer-Zavala, S., Carl, J. R., Bullis, J. R., & Ellard, K. K. (2014). The nature, diagnosis, and treatment of neuroticism: Back to the future. *Clinical Psychological Science, 2*(3), 344–365. https://doi.org/10.1177/2167702613505532

Baron, R. A., & Ensley, M. D. (2006). Opportunity recognition as the detection of meaningful patterns: Evidence from comparisons of novice and experienced entrepreneurs. *Management Science, 52*(9), 1331–1344. https://doi.org/10.1287/mnsc.1060.0538

Baron-Cohen, S., Wheelwright, S., Skinner, R., Martin, J., & Clubley, E. (2001). The autism-spectrum quotient (AQ): Evidence from Asperger syndrome/high-functioning autism, males and females, scientists and mathematicians. *Journal of Autism and Developmental Disorders, 31*(1), 5–17. https://doi.org/10.1023/A:1005653411471

Barreto, M., Ryan, M. K., & Schmitt, M. T. (Eds.). (2009). *The glass ceiling in the 21st century: Understanding barriers to gender equality.* American Psychological Association. https://doi.org/10.1037/11863-000

Barrett, D. M. (1945). Aptitude and interest patterns of art majors in a liberal arts college. *Journal of Applied Psychology, 29*(6), 483–492. https://doi.org/10.1037/h0062947

Barrett, H. O. (1949). An examination of certain standardized art tests to determine their relation to classroom achievement and to intelligence. *Journal of Educational Research, 42*(5), 398–400. https://doi.org/10.1080/00220671.1949.10881706

Barrick, M. R., & Mount, M. K. (1991). The Big Five personality dimensions and job performance: A meta-analysis. *Personnel Psychology, 44*(1), 1–26. https://doi.org/10.1111/j.1744-6570.1991.tb00688.x

Barrick, M. R., & Mount, M. K. (2005). Yes, personality matters: Moving on to more important matters. *Human Performance, 18*(4), 359–372. https://doi.org/10.1207/s15327043hup1804_3

Barrick, M. R., & Mount, M. K. (2012). Nature and use of personality in selection. In N. Schmitt (Ed.), *The Oxford handbook of personnel assessment and selection* (pp. 225–251). Oxford University Press. https://doi.org/10.1093/oxfordhb/9780199732579.013.0011

Barrick, M. R., Mount, M. K., & Gupta, R. (2003). Meta-analysis of the relationship between the five-factor model of personality and Holland's occupational types. *Personnel Psychology, 56*(1), 45–74. https://doi.org/10.1111/j.1744-6570.2003.tb00143.x

Barrick, M. R., Mount, M. K., & Judge, T. A. (2001). Personality and performance at the beginning of the new millenium: What do we know and where do we go next? *International Journal of Selection and Assessment, 9*(1–2), 9–30. https://doi.org/10.1111/1468-2389.00160

Barron, F. (1972). *Artists in the making*. Seminar Press.

Barron, F., & Welsh, G. S. (1952). Artistic perception as a possible factor in personality style: Its measurement by a figure preferences test. *Journal of Psychology, 33*(2), 199–203. https://doi.org/10.1080/00223980.1952.9712830

Bartling, H. C., & Hood, A. B. (1981). An 11-year follow-up of measured interest and vocational choice. *Journal of Counseling Psychology, 28*(1), 27–35. https://doi.org/10.1037/0022-0167.28.1.27

Bartram, D., & Dale, H. C. (1982). The Eysenck Personality Inventory as a selection test for military pilots. *Journal of Occupational Psychology, 55*(4), 287–296. https://doi.org/10.1111/j.2044-8325.1982.tb00102.x

Batson, C. D., Van Lange, P. A. M., Ahmad, N., & Lishner, D. A. (2007). Altruism and helping behavior. In M. A. Hogg & J. Cooper (Eds.), *The SAGE handbook of social psychology* (pp. 279–295). SAGE Publications.

Beauchamp, T. L., & Childress, J. F. (2019). *Medical ethics* (8th ed.). Oxford University Press.

Beck, E. D., & Jackson, J. J. (2020). Idiographic traits: A return to Allportian approaches to personality. *Current Directions in Psychological Science, 29*(3), 301–308. https://doi.org/10.1177/0963721420915860

Beck, N. C., Tucker, D., Frank, R., Parker, J., Lake, R., Thomas, S., Lichty, W., Horwitz, E., Horwitz, B., & Merritt, F. (1989). The latent factor structure of the WAIS-R: A factor analysis of individual item responses. *Journal of Clinical Psychology, 45*(2), 281–293.

Becker, R. L. (1987). The Reading-Free Vocational Interest Inventory: A typology of vocational clusters. *Mental Retardation, 25*(3), 171–179.

Beltz, A. M., Swanson, J. L., & Berenbaum, S. A. (2011). Gendered occupational interests: Prenatal androgen effects on psychological orientation to Things versus People. *Hormones and Behavior, 60*(4), 313–317. https://doi.org/10.1016/j.yhbeh.2011.06.002

Bem, S. L. (1974). The measurement of psychological androgyny. *Journal of Consulting and Clinical Psychology, 42*(2), 155–162. https://doi.org/10.1037/h0036215

Benbow, C. P. (1988). Neuropsychological perspectives on mathematical talent. In L. K. Obler & D. Fein (Eds.), *The exceptional brain: Neuropsychology of talent and special abilities* (pp. 48–69). Guilford Press.

Benbow, C. P., Stanley, J. C., Kirk, M. K., & Zonderman, A. B. (1983). Structure of intelligence in intellectually precocious children and in their parents. *Intelligence*, 7(2), 129–152. https://doi.org/10.1016/0160-2896(83)90024-7

Bendig, A. W. (1963). The relation of temperament traits of social extraversion and emotionality to vocational interests. *Journal of General Psychology*, 69(2), 311–318. https://doi.org/10.1080/00221309.1963.9920563

Bendig, A. W. (1964). Factor analytic scales of need achievement. *Journal of General Psychology*, 70(1), 59–67. https://doi.org/10.1080/00221309.1964.9920575

Bendig, A. W., & Martin, A. M. (1962). The factor structure and stability of fifteen human needs. *Journal of General Psychology*, 67(2), 229–235. https://doi.org/10.1080/00221309.1962.9711550

Bennett, G. K., & Cruikshank, R. M. (1942). *A summary of manual and mechanical ability tests*. Psychological Corporation. https://doi.org/10.1037/13573-000

Bennett, G. K., Seashore, H. G., & Wesman, A. G. (1989). *Differential aptitude tests for personnel and career assessment: Directions for administration and scoring*. The Psychological Corporation.

Benninger, W. B., & Walsh, W. B. (1980). Holland's theory and non-college-degreed working men and women. *Journal of Vocational Behavior*, 17(1), 81–88. https://doi.org/10.1016/0001-8791(80)90017-2

Benton, A. (1982). Spatial thinking in neurological aspects. In M. Portegal (Ed.), *Spatial abilities: Development and physiological foundations* (pp. 301–331). Academic Press.

Bentz, V. J. (1985). Research findings from personality assessment of executives. In H. J. Bernardin & D. A. Bownas (Eds.), *Personality assessment in organizations* (pp. 82–144). Praeger.

Berdie, R. F. (1943). Factors associated with vocational interests. *Journal of Educational Psychology*, 34(5), 257–277. https://doi.org/10.1037/h0055987

Berenbaum, S. A., Bryk, K. L., & Beltz, A. M. (2012). Early androgen effects on spatial and mechanical abilities: Evidence from congenital adrenal hyperplasia. *Behavioral Neuroscience*, 126(1), 86–96. https://doi.org/10.1037/a0026652

Berfield, K. A., Ray, W. J., & Newcombe, N. (1986). Sex role and spatial ability: An EEG study. *Neuropsychologia*, 24(5), 731–735. https://doi.org/10.1016/0028-3932(86)90013-8

Bergner, S., Neubauer, A. C., & Kreuzthaler, A. (2010) Broad and narrow personality traits for predicting managerial success. *European Journal of Work and Organizational Psychology*, 19(2), 177–199. https://doi.org/10.1080/13594320902819728

Bergold, S., & Steinmayr, R. (2018). Personality and intelligence interact in the prediction of academic achievement. *Journal of Intelligence*, 6(2), 27. https://doi.org/10.3390/jintelligence6020027

Bernardin, H. J., & Bownas, D. A. (Eds.). (1985). *Personality assessment in organizations*. Praeger.

Betz, N. E. (1993). Issues in the use of ability and interest measures with women. *Journal of Career Assessment*, 1(3), 217–232. https://doi.org/10.1177/106907279300100302

Betz, N. E., & Taylor, K. M. (2012). *Career decision self-efficacy scale and short form and manual*. Mind Garden, Inc.

Bhargava, M. A., Semwal, J., Juyal, R., Vyas, S., & Varshney, D. (2015). Assessment of personality types in an urban community of District Dehradun, Uttarakhand using Introversion- Extroversion Inventory. *National Journal of Community Medicine*, 6(4), 466–468.

Bingham, R. P., & Walsh, W. B. (1978). Concurrent validity of Holland's theory for college-degreed Black women. *Journal of Vocational Behavior*, 13(2), 242–250. https://doi.org/10.1016/0001-8791(78)90049-0

Bingham, W. V. D. (1937). *Aptitudes and aptitude testing*. Harper & Brothers.

Blais, M. A., & Baity, M. R. (2008). The projective assessment of personality structure and pathology. In G. J. Boyle, G. Matthews, & D. H. Saklofske (Eds.), *The SAGE handbook of personality theory and assessment: Vol. 2. Personality measurement and testing* (pp. 566–586). SAGE Publications. https://doi.org/10.4135/9781849200479.n27

Blankenship, J. R. (2021). *Assessing CEOs and senior leaders: A primer for consultants.* American Psychological Association.

Blatt, S. J., & Allison, J. (1981). The intelligence test in personality assessment. In A. I. Rabin (Ed.), *Assessment with projective techniques: A concise introduction* (pp. 187–231). Springer.

Boddy, C. R. P. (2010). Corporate sociopaths and organizational types. *Journal of Public Affairs, 10*(4), 300–312. https://doi.org/10.1002/pa.365

Bolton, B. (1985). Discriminant analysis of Holland's occupational types using the Sixteen Personality Factor Questionnaire. *Journal of Vocational Behavior, 27*(2), 210–217. https://doi.org/10.1016/0001-8791(85)90034-X

Bond, S., Bordieri, J., & Musgrave, J. (1989). Tested versus self-estimated aptitudes and interests of vocational evaluation clients. *Vocational Evaluation & Work Adjustment Bulletin, 22*(3), 105–108.

Borgen, F. H. (1986). New approaches to the assessment of interests. In W. B. Walsh & S. H. Osipow (Eds.), *Advances in vocational psychology: Vol. 1. The assessment of interests* (pp. 83–125). Lawrence Erlbaum Associates, Inc.

Borgen, F. H, & Seling, M. J. (1978). Expressed and inventoried interests revisited: Perspicacity in the person. *Journal of Counseling Psychology, 25*(6), 536–543. https://doi.org/10.1037/0022-0167.25.6.536

Boring, E. G. (1923). Intelligence as the tests test it. *New Republic, 35*(6), 35–37.

Bouchard, M. A., Lalonde, F., & Gagnon, M. (1988). The construct validity of assertion: Contributions of four assessment procedures and Norman's personality factors. *Journal of Personality, 56*(4), 763–783. https://doi.org/10.1111/j.1467-6494.1988.tb00476.x

Bouchard, T. J., Jr. (1998). Genetic and environmental influences on adult intelligence and special mental abilities. *Human Biology, 70*(2), 257–279.

Bouchard, T. J., Jr., Lykken, D. T., McGue, M., Segal, N. L., & Tellegen, A. (1990). Sources of human psychological differences: The Minnesota Study of Twins Reared Apart. *Science, 250*(4978), 223–228. https://doi.org/10.1126/science.2218526

Bowd, A. D. (1973). A cross-cultural study of the factorial composition of mechanical aptitude. *Canadian Journal of Behavioural Science / Revue Canadienne des Sciences du Comportement, 5*(1), 13–23. https://doi.org/10.1037/h0082324

Bowling, N. A. (2007). Is the job satisfaction-job performance relationship spurious? A meta- analytic examination. *Journal of Vocational Behavior, 71*(2), 167–185. https://doi.org/10.1016/j.jvb.2007.04.007

Boyatzis, R. E. (1982). *Competent manager: A model for effective performance.* Wiley.

Boyatzis, R. E. (2011). Managerial and leadership competencies: A behavioral approach to emotional, social and cognitive intelligence. *Vision (Basel), 15*(2), 91–100. https://doi.org/10.1177/097226291101500202

Boyd, D. P., & Gumpert, D. E. (1983). Coping with entrepreneurial stress. *Harvard Business Review, 61*(2), 44–51.

Braisted, J. R., Mellin, L., Gong, E. J., & Irwin, C. E.,Jr. (1985). The adolescent ballet dancer: Nutritional practices and characteristics associated with anorexia nervosa. *Journal of Adolescent Health Care, 6*(5), 365–371. https://doi.org/10.1016/S0197-0070(85)80004-8

Bray, D. W., Campbell, R. J., & Grant, D. L. (1974). *Formative years in business. A long-term AT&T study of managerial lives.* Robert E. Krieger Publishing Company.

Bregman, A. S. (1990). *Auditory scene analysis: The perceptual organization of sound.* Massachusetts Institute of Technology. https://doi.org/10.7551/mitpress/1486.001.0001

Brennan, F. M. (1926). The relation between musical capacity and performance. *Psychological Monographs, 36*(1), 190–248. https://doi.org/10.1037/h0093226

Bretz, R. D., Jr., Ash, R. A., & Dreher, G. F. (1989). Do people make the place? An examination of the attraction-selection-attrition hypothesis. *Personnel Psychology, 42*(3), 561–581. https://doi.org/10.1111/j.1744-6570.1989.tb00669.x

Broday, S. F., & Sedgwick, C. (1991). The relationship between the SCII introversion-extroversion scale and occupational scales. *Educational and psychological measurement, 51*(1), 175–179.

Brody, D. (1937). Twin resemblances in mechanical ability, with reference to the effects of practice on performance. *Child Development, 8*(3), 207–217. https://doi.org/10.2307/1125628

Bronfenbrenner, U., Harding, J., & Gallwey, M. (1958). The measurement of skill in social perception. In D. McClelland, A. Baldwin, U. Bronfenbrenner, & F. Strodtbeck (Eds.), *Talent and society: New perspectives in the identification of talent* (pp. 29–111). Van Nostrand.

Brooks, L. (1983). Sexist language in occupational information: Does it make a difference? *Journal of Vocational Behavior, 23*(2), 227–232.

Brooks-Gunn, J., Warren, M. P., & Hamilton, L. H. (1987). The relation of eating problems and amenorrhea in ballet dancers. *Medicine & Science in Sports & Exercise, 19*(1), 41–44. https://doi.org/10.1249/00005768-198702000-00009

Brown, D. (Ed.). (2002). *Career choice and development* (4th ed.). Jossey-Bass.

Brown, S. D., & Gore, P. A., Jr. (1994). An evaluation of interest congruence indices: Distribution characteristics and measurement properties. *Journal of Vocational Behavior, 45*(3), 310–327. https://doi.org/10.1006/jvbe.1994.1038

Brown, S. D., & Watkins, C. E., Jr. (1994). Psychodynamic and personological perspectives on vocational behavior. In M. L. Savickas & R. W. Lent (Eds.), *Convergence in career development theories: Implications for science and practice* (pp. 197–206). Davies-Black Publishing.

Bryan, A. I. (1942). Grades, intelligence, and personality of art school freshmen. *Journal of Educational Psychology, 33*(1), 50–64. https://doi.org/10.1037/h0060928

Bubany, S. T., & Hansen, J. I. C. (2011). Birth cohort change in the vocational interests of female and male college students. *Journal of Vocational Behavior, 78*(1), 59–67. https://doi.org/10.1016/j.jvb.2010.08.002

Buckingham, M. (2005). What great managers do. *Harvard Business Review, 83*(3), 70–79, 148.

Bulley, M. H. (1933). *Have you good taste?* Methuen.

Burbeck, E., & Furnham, A. (1985). Police officer selection: A critical review of the literature. *Journal of Police Science & Administration, 13*(1), 58–69.

Bureau of Labor Statistics, U.S. Department of Labor. (2017a). *Occupational employment and wages, May 2017: 27-2031 Dancers.* Retrieved September 18, 2019, from https://www.bls.gov/oes/2017/may/oes272031.htm

Bureau of Labor Statistics, U.S. Department of Labor. (2017b). *Occupational employment and wages, May 2017: 27-3022 Reporters and correspondents.* Retrieved September 18, 2019, from https://www.bls.gov/oes/2017/may/oes273022.htm

Bureau of Labor Statistics, U.S. Department of Labor. (2017c). *Occupational employment and wages, May 2017: 27-3041 Editors.* Retrieved September 18, 2019, from https://www.bls.gov/oes/2017/may/oes273041.htm

Bureau of Labor Statistics, U.S. Department of Labor. (2017d). Women in architecture and engineering occupations in 2016. *The Economics Daily.* https://www.bls.gov/opub/ted/2017/women-in-architecture-and-engineering-occupations-in-2016.htm

Bureau of Labor Statistics, U.S. Department of Labor. (2018a). *Occupational employment and wages, May 2017: 27-2042 Musicians and singers*. Retrieved March 20, 2018, https://www.bls.gov/oes/current/oes272042.htm

Bureau of Labor Statistics, U.S. Department of Labor. (2018b). *Occupational Outlook Handbook: Music directors and composers*. Retrieved July 2, 2018, from https://www.bls.gov/ooh/entertainment-and-sports/music-directors-and-composers.htm

Bureau of Labor Statistics, U.S. Department of Labor. (2018c). *Occupational Outlook Handbook: Musicians and singers*. Retrieved April 13, 2018, from https://www.bls.gov/ooh/entertainment-and-sports/musicians-and-singers.htm

Bureau of Labor Statistics, U.S. Department of Labor. (2019a). *Occupational employment and wages, May 2019: 27-2001 Actors*. Retrieved September 18, 2019, from https://www.bls.gov/oes/current/oes272011.htm#nat

Bureau of Labor Statistics, U.S. Department of Labor. (2019b). *Occupational employment and wages, May 2019: 27-3031 Public relations specialists*. Retrieved September 18, 2019, from https://www.bls.gov/oes/current/oes273031.htm

Bureau of Labor Statistics, U.S. Department of Labor. (2019c). *Occupational employment and wages, May 2019: 27-3042 Technical writers*. Retrieved September 18, 2019, from https://www.bls.gov/oes/current/oes273042.htm

Bureau of Labor Statistics, U.S. Department of Labor. (2019d). *Occupational employment and wages, May 2019: 27-3043 Writers and authors*. Retrieved September 18, 2019, from https://www.bls.gov/oes/current/oes273043.htm

Bureau of Labor Statistics, U.S. Department of Labor. (2019e). *Occupational Outlook Handbook: Arts and design occupations*. Retrieved September 18, 2019, from https://www.bls.gov/ooh/arts-and-design/home.htm

Bureau of Labor Statistics, U.S. Department of Labor. (2019f). *Occupational Outlook Handbook: Craft and fine artists*. Retrieved September 18, 2019, from https://www.bls.gov/ooh/arts-and-design/craft-and-fine-artists.htm

Bureau of Labor Statistics, U.S. Department of Labor. (2019g). *Occupational Outlook Handbook: Musicians and singers*. Retrieved September 18, 2019, from https://www.bls.gov/ooh/entertainment-and-sports/musicians-and-singers.htm

Burnett, S. A., Lane, D. M., & Dratt, L. M. (1982). Spatial ability and handedness. *Intelligence, 6*(1), 57–68. https://doi.org/10.1016/0160-2896(82)90020-4

Burns, G. N., Morris, M. B., Rousseau, N., & Taylor, J. (2013). Personality, interests, and career indecision: A multidimensional perspective. *Journal of Applied Social Psychology, 43*(10), 2090–2099. https://doi.org/10.1111/jasp.12162

Burton, L. J., & Fogarty, G. J. (2003). The factor structure of visual imagery and spatial abilities. *Intelligence, 31*(3), 289–318. https://doi.org/10.1016/S0160-2896(02)00139-3

Busacca, L. A., & Taber, B. J. (2002). The Career Maturity Inventory-Revised: A preliminary psychometric investigation. *Journal of Career Assessment, 10*(4), 441–455. https://doi.org/10.1177/1069072702238406

Butcher, H. J. (1969). The structure of abilities, interests and personality in 1,000 Scottish school children. *British Journal of Educational Psychology, 39*(2), 154–165. https://doi.org/10.1111/j.2044-8279.1969.tb02058.x

Byrne, J. A. (2017, November 2017). MBA programs edging closer to gender parity. *Poets and Quants*. https://poetsandquants.com/2017/11/29/mba-programs-edging-closer-to-gender-parity/?pq-category=b-schools&pq-category-2=women-in-business-school-2

Cairo, P. C. (1982). Measured interests versus expressed interests as predictors of long-term occupational membership. *Journal of Vocational Behavior, 20*(3), 343–353. https://doi.org/10.1016/0001-8791(82)90021-5

Cain, S. (2013). *Quiet: The power of introverts in a world that can't stop talking*. Broadway Paperbacks (Crown).

Camp, C. C., & Chartrand, J. M. (1992). A comparison and evaluation of interest congruence indices. *Journal of Vocational Behavior, 41*(2), 162–182. https://doi.org/10.1016/0001-8791(92)90018-U

Campbell, D. P. (1994). *Campbell Interest and Skill Survey manual*. National Computer Systems.

Campbell, D. P., & Klein, K. L. (1975). Job satisfaction and vocational interests. *Vocational Guidance Quarterly, 24*(2), 125–131. https://doi.org/10.1002/j.2164-585X.1975.tb00064.x

Campbell, J. M., & McCord, D. M. (1996). The WAIS–R comprehension and picture arrangement subtests as measures of social intelligence: Testing traditional interpretations. *Journal of Psychoeducational Assessment, 14*(3), 240–249. https://doi.org/10.1177/073428299601400305

Campbell, J. P., Dunnette, M. D., Lawler, E. E., III, & Weick, K. E., Jr. (1970). *Managerial behavior, performance, and effectiveness*. McGraw-Hill.

Campbell, W. K., & Miller, J. D. (2011). *The handbook of narcissism and narcissistic personality disorder: Theoretical approaches, empirical findings, and treatments*. John Wiley & Sons. https://doi.org/10.1002/9781118093108

Canby, V. (1990, June 24). Film view; what's art all about? Truth, beauty, unruliness. *The New York Times*. https://www.nytimes.com/1990/06/24/arts/film-view-what-s-art-all-about-truth-beauty-unruliness.html?searchResultPosition=4

Canadian Counselling and Psychotherapy Association. (2020). *Code of ethics*. https://www.ccpa-accp.ca/wp-content/uploads/2020/05/CCPA-2020-Code-of-Ethics-E-Book-EN.pdf

Canadian Psychological Association. (2017). *Canadian Code of Ethics for Psychologists* (4th ed.). https://cpa.ca/aboutcpa/committees/ethics/codeofethics/

Carland, J. A. C., & Carland, J. W. (1991). An empirical investigation into the distinctions between male and female entrepreneurs and managers. *International Small Business Journal, 9*(3), 62–72. https://doi.org/10.1177/026624269100900304C

Carless, S. A. (1999). Career assessment: Holland's vocational interests, personality characteristics, and abilities. *Journal of Career Assessment, 7*(2), 125–144. https://doi.org/10.1177/106907279900700203

Carless, S. A., & Fallon, B. (2002). The relationship between Rothwell-Miller Interest Categories and abilities. *Australian Journal of Career Development, 11*(1), 27–31. https://doi.org/10.1177/103841620201100107

Carlo, G., Knight, G. P., Roesch, S. C., Opal, D., & Davis, A. (2014). Personality across cultures: A critical analysis of Big Five research and current directions. In F. T. L. Leong, L. Comas-Díaz, G. C. Nagayama Hall, V. C. McLoyd, & J. E. Trimble (Eds.), *APA handbook of multicultural psychology*: Vol. 1. Theory and research (pp. 285–298). American Psychological Association. https://doi.org/10.1037/14189-015

Caro, R. A. (1989, November 6). Annals of politics. The Johnson years: A congressman goes to war. *The New Yorker*, 62–125.

Carretta, T. R., & Ree, M. J. (2018). The relations between cognitive ability and personality: Convergent results across measures. *International Journal of Selection and Assessment, 26*(2–4), 133–144. https://doi.org/10.1111/ijsa.12224

Carroll, H. A. (1933). What do the Meier-Seashore and the McAdory Art Tests measure? *Journal of Educational Research, 26*(9), 661–665. https://doi.org/10.1080/00220671.1933.10880360

Carroll, J. B. (1993). *Human cognitive abilities. A survey of factor-analytic studies*. Cambridge U. Press. https://doi.org/10.1017/CBO9780511571312

Carson, A. D. (1998a). The integration of interests, aptitudes, and personality traits: A test of Lowman's matrix. *Journal of Career Assessment, 6*(1), 83–105. https://doi.org/10.1177/106907279800600106

Carson, A. D. (1998b). Why has musical aptitude assessment fallen flat? And what can we do about it? *Journal of Career Assessment, 6*(3), 311–327. https://doi.org/10.1177/106907279800600303

Carter, A. S., Davis, N. O., Klin, A., & Volkmar, F. R. (2005). Social development in autism. In F. R. Volkmar, R. Paul, A. Klin, & D. Cohen (Eds.), *Handbook of autism and pervasive developmental disorders: Vol. 1. Diagnosis, development, neurobiology, and behavior* (3rd ed., pp. 312–334). Wiley.

Carter, H. D. (1932). Twin similarities in occupational interests. *Educational Psychology, 23*(9), 641–655. https://doi.org/10.1037/h0071737

Carter, N. T., Miller, J. D., & Widiger, T. A. (2018). Extreme personalities at work and in life. *Current Directions in Psychological Science, 27*(6), 429–436. https://doi.org/10.1177/0963721418793134

Carter, R. T., & Swanson, J. L. (1990). The validity of the Strong Interest Inventory for Black Americans: A review of the literature. *Journal of Vocational Behavior, 36*(2), 195–209. https://doi.org/10.1016/0001-8791(90)90027-Y

Cartledge, G. (1987). Social skills, learning disabilities, and occupational success. *Journal of Reading, Writing, and Learning Disabilities International, 3*(3), 223–239. https://doi.org/10.1080/0748763870030304

Casey, M. B., Brabeck, M. M., & Ludlow, L. H. (1986). Familial handedness and its relation to spatial ability following strategy instructions. *Intelligence, 10*(4), 389–406. https://doi.org/10.1016/0160-2896(86)90006-1

Cashdan, E., Kramer, K. L., Davis, H. E., Padilla, L., & Greaves, R. D. (2016). Mobility and navigation among the Yucatec Maya: Sex differences reflect parental investment, not mating competition. *Human Nature, 27*(1), 35–50. https://doi.org/10.1007/s12110-015-9250-7

Cashdan, E., Marlowe, F., Crittenden, A. N., Porter, C., & Wood, B. (2012). Sex differences in spatial cognition among Hadza foragers. *Evolution and Human Behavior, 33*, 274–284.

Catalanello, R. F., Wegener, S. M. & Zikmund, W. G. (1978). A career choice experiment, *College Student Journal, 12*, 310–319.

Cattell, H. E. P., & Mead, A. D. (2008). The Sixteen Personality Factor Questionnaire (16PF). In G. J. Boyle, G. Matthews, & D. H. Saklofske (Eds.), *The SAGE handbook of personality theory and assessment: Vol. 2. Personality measurement and testing* (pp. 135–159). SAGE Publications. https://doi.org/10.4135/9781849200479.n7

Cattell, H. E. P., & Schuerger, J. M. (2003). *Essentials of 16PF assessment*. Wiley.

Cattell, R. B. (1945a). Personality traits associated with abilities. I. With intelligence and drawing ability. *Educational and Psychological Measurement, 5*(2), 131–146.

Cattell, R. B. (1945b). Personality traits associated with abilities. II. With verbal and mathematical abilities. *Journal of Educational Psychology, 36*(8), 475–486. https://doi.org/10.1037/h0054618

Cattell, R. B. (1946). *Description and measurement of personality*. World Book Co.

Cattell, R. B. (Ed.). (1987). *Intelligence: Its structure, growth and action* (Revised ed.). North-Holland.

Cattell, R. B., Eber, H. W., & Tatsuoka, M. M. (1970). *Handbook for the Sixteen Personality Factor Questionnaire (16PF)*. Institute for Personality and Ability Testing.

Cattell, R. B., & Horn, J. L. (1964). *Handbook and individual assessment manual for the Motivation Analysis Test (MAT)*. Institute for Personality and Ability Testing.

Cattell, R. B., & Kline, P. (1977). *The scientific analysis of personality and motivation*. Academic Press.

Cegelka, P. T., Omvig, C., & Larimore, D. L. (1974). Effects of aptitude and sex on vocational interests. *Measurement and Evaluation in Guidance, 7*(2), 106–111. https://doi.org/10.1080/00256307.1974.12022628

Chakravarty, A. (2011). De novo development of artistic creativity in Alzheimer's disease. *Annals of Indian Academy of Neurology, 14*(4), 291–294. https://doi.org/10.4103/0972-2327.91953

Chamberlain, R., Drake, J. E., Kozbelt, A., Hickman, R., Siev, J., & Wagemans, J. (2018). Artists as experts in visual cognition: An update. *Psychology of Aesthetics, Creativity, and the Arts*. Advance online publication. https://doi.org/10.1037/aca000015

Chapin, F. S. (1939). Social participation and social intelligence. *American Sociological Review, 4*(2), 157–166.

Chapin, F. S. (1942). Preliminary standardization of a social insight scale. *American Sociological Review, 7*(2), 214–228.

Chatterjee, A. (2004). The neuropsychology of visual artistic production. *Neuropsychologia, 42*(11), 1568–1583.

Chatterjee, A. (2015). The neuropsychology of visual art. In J. P. Huston, M. Nadal, F. Mora, L. F. Agnati, & C. J. Cela-Conde (Eds.), *Art, aesthetics and the brain* (pp. 341–356). Oxford University Press.

Chen, F., Planche, P., & Lemonnier, E. (2010). Superior nonverbal intelligence in children with high-functioning autism or Asperger's syndrome. *Research in Autism Spectrum Disorders, 4*(3), 457–460.

Chen, J., & Wang, L. (2007). Locus of control and the three components of commitment to change. *Personality and Individual Differences, 42*(3), 503–512.

Chiang, H. M., Tsai, L. Y., Cheung, Y. K., Brown, A., & Li, H. (2014). A meta-analysis of differences in IQ profiles between individuals with Asperger's disorder and high-functioning autism. *Journal of Autism and Developmental Disorders, 44*, 1577–1596. https://doi.org/10.1007/s10803-013-2025-2

Chiarello, C., & Schweiger, A. (1985). Harmony of the spheres and the hemispheres: The arts and hemispheric specialization. In D. F. Benson & E. Zaidel (Eds.), *The dual brain: Hemispheric specialization in humans* (pp. 359–373). Guilford Press.

Childs, A., & Klimoski, R. J. (1986). Successfully predicting career success: An application of the biographical inventory. *Journal of Applied Psychology, 71*(1), 3–8. https://doi.org/10.1037/0021-9010.71.1.3

Chirumbolo, A. (2017). Personality and work behavior. In V. Zeigler-Hill & T. K. Schackelford (Eds.), *Encyclopedia of personality and individual differences*. SpringerLink.

Chislett, L. (1978). *Congruence, consistency and differentiation of career interests: A study of construct validity and relationships with achievement, satisfaction and personality adjustment* [Doctoral dissertation, University of Ottawa]. Google Books.

Chopik, W. J. (2016). Age differences in conscientiousness facets in the second half of life: Divergent associations with changes in physical health. *Personality and Individual Differences, 96*, 202–211.

Christiansen, K., & Knussmann, R. (1987). Sex hormones and cognitive functioning in men. *Neuropsychobiology, 18*(1), 27–36.

Christie, R., & Geis, F. L. (1979). *Studies in Machiavellianism*. Academic Press.

Churchill, G. A., Ford, N. M., Harltey, S. W., & Walker, O. C. (1985). The determinants of salesperson performance: A meta-analysis. *Journal of Marketing Research, 22*(2), 103–118.

Chusmir, L. H. (1984). Personnel administrators' perception of sex differences in motivation of managers: Research-based or stereotyped? *International Journal of Women's Studies, 7*(1), 17–23.

Chusmir, L. H. (1985). Motivation of managers: Is gender a factor? *Psychology of Women Quarterly, 9*(1), 153–159.

Chusmir, L. H., & Hood, J. N. (1988). Predictive characteristics of Type A behavior among working men and women. *Journal of Applied Social Psychology, 18*(8), 688–698.

Clark, G. (1989). Screening and identifying students talented in the visual arts: Clark's Drawing Abilities Test. *Gifted Child Quarterly, 33*(3), 98–105.

Clark, G., & Wilson, T. (1991). Screening and identifying gifted/talented students in the visual arts with Clark's Drawing Abilities Test. *Roeper Review, 13*(2), 92–97.

Clark, G., & Zimmerman, E. (1983). At the age of six, I gave up a magnificent career as a painter: Seventy years of research about identifying students with superior abilities in the visual arts. *Gifted Child Quarterly, 27*(4), 180–184. https://doi.org/10.1177/001698628302700407

Clark, G., & Zimmerman, E. (1984). Inquiry about art ability and talent: A remembrance of things past. *Theory Into Practice, 23*(4), 321–329. https://doi.org/10.1080/00405848409543134

Clark, K. B. (1980). Empathy: A neglected topic in psychological research. *American Psychologist, 35*(2), 187–190. https://doi.org/10.1037/0003-066X.35.2.187

Clark, L. A. (1993). *Manual for the Schedule of Nonadaptive and Adaptive Personality*. University of Minnesota Press.

Clifford, J. S. (1986). Neuropsychology: Implications for the treatment of alcoholism. *Journal of Counseling and Development, 65*(1), 31–34. https://doi.org/10.1002/j.1556-6676.1986.tb01225.x

Closs, S. J. (1976). The APU occupational interests guide and the sex discrimination act. *British Journal of Guidance & Counselling, 4*(2), 181–194, https://doi.org/10.1080/03069887608256311

Cobigo, V., Morin, D., & Lachapelle, Y. (2007). Assessing work task preferences among persons with intellectual disabilities: An integrative review of literature. *Education and Training in Developmental Disabilities, 42*(3), 286–300.

Cochran, L. R. (1990). *The sense of vocation: A study of career and life development*. State University of New York Press.

Cole, N. S., Whitney, D. R., & Holland, J. L. (1971). A spatial configuration of occupations. *Journal of Vocational Behavior, 1*(1), 1–9. https://doi.org/10.1016/0001-8791(71)90002-9

Coles, R. (1989, June 18). The gloom and the glory. *New York Times Book Review, 1*, 30–31.

College Music Society. (2015). *Facts and figures concerning music and higher education in the United States*. https://www.music.org/pdf/mihe/facts.pdf

Collins, H. A. (1979). Vocational interests of heroin-dependent patients. *Psychological Reports, 44*(2), 467–470. https://doi.org/10.2466/pr0.1979.44.2.467

Collins, J., Reardon, M., & Waters, L. K. (1980). Occupational interest and perceived personal success: Effects of gender, sex-role orientation, and the sexual composition of the occupation. *Psychological Reports, 47*(3 Suppl.), 1155–1159. https://doi.org/10.2466/pr0.1980.47.3f.1155

Conn, S. R., & Rieke, M. L. (1994). *The 16PF fifth edition technical manual*. Institute for Personality and Ability Testing.

Connelly, B. S., & Chang, L. (2016). A meta-analytic multitrait multirater separation of substance and style in social desirability scales. *Journal of Personality, 84*(3), 319–334. https://doi.org/10.1111/jopy.12161

Connelly, B. S., Ones, D. S., & Hulsherger, U. R. (2018). Personality in industrial, work and organizational psychology: Theory, measurement and application. In D. S. Ones, N. Anderson, C. Viswesvaran, & Sinangil (Eds.), *The Sage handbook of industrial, work and organizational psychology* (2nd ed., pp. 320–365). SAGE Publications.

Conrads, J., Irlenbusch, B., Reggiani, T., Rilke, R., & Sliwka, D. (2016). How to hire helpers? Evidence from a field experiment. *Experimental Economics, 19*(3), 577–594. https://doi.org/10.1007/s10683-015-9455-y

Conroy, D. E., Elliott, A. J., & Thrash, T. M. (2009). Achievement motivation. In M. R. Leary & R. H. Hoyle (Eds.), *Handbook of individual differences in social behavior* (pp. 382–399). Guilford Press.

Constantinople A. (1973). Masculinity-femininity: An exception to a famous dictum? *Psychological Bulletin, 80*(5), 389–407. https://doi.org/10.1037/h0035334

Conte, J. M. (2005). A review and critique of emotional intelligence measures. *Journal of Organizational Behavior, 26*(4), 433–440. https://doi.org/10.1002/job.319

Cooper, S. E., Fuqua, D. R., & Hartman, B. W. (1984). The relationship of trait indecisiveness to vocational uncertainty, career indecision, and interpersonal characteristics. *Journal of College Student Personnel, 25*(4), 353–356.

Cooper, W. H. (1983). An achievement motivation nomological network. *Journal of Personality and Social Psychology, 44*(4), 841–861. https://doi.org/10.1037/0022-3514.44.4.841

Cooper, W. S. (1997, September). *Vocational interests of women who choose careers as professional aviators* (UMI No. 9726348) [Doctoral dissertation, Walden University]. Proquest Dissertations and Theses Global.

Cornelius, E. T., & Lane, F. B. (1984). The power motive and managerial success in a professionally oriented service industry organization. *Journal of Applied Psychology, 69*(1), 32–39. https://doi.org/10.1037/0021-9010.69.1.32

Cosenza, R. M., & Mingoti, S. A. (1993). Career choice and handedness: A survey among university applicants. *Neuropsychologia, 31*(5), 487–497. https://doi.org/10.1016/0028-3932(93)90062-5

Costa, P. T., Jr., Fozard, J. L., & McCrae, R. R. (1977). Personological interpretation of factors from the Strong Vocational Interest Blank scales. *Journal of Vocational Behavior, 10*(2), 231–243. https://doi.org/10.1016/0001-8791(77)90060-4

Costa, P. T., Jr., & McCrae, R. R. (1986). *The NEO Personality Inventory manual. Form S and Form R*. Psychological Assessment Resources, Inc.

Costa, P. T., Jr., & McCrae, R. R. (1988). *The NEO PI/FFI manual* supplement. Psychological Assessment Resources, Inc.

Costa, P. T., Jr., & McCrae, R. R. (1992). *Revised NEO-PI-R Personality Inventory (NEO-PI-R) and NEO-PI-R Five-Factor Inventory (NEO-PIR-FFI) professional manual*. Psychological Assessment Resources.

Costa, P. T., Jr., & McCrae, R. R. (1995). Domains and facets: Hierarchical personality assessment using the revised NEO personality inventory. *Journal of Personality Assessment, 64*(1), 21–50. https://doi.org/10.1207/s15327752jpa6401_2

Costa, P. T., Jr., & McCrae, R. R. (2008). The Revised NEO Personality Inventory (NEO-PI-R). In G. J. Boyle, G. Matthews, & D. H. Saklofske (Eds.), *The SAGE handbook of personality theory and assessment: Vol. 2. Personality measurement and testing* (pp. 179–198). SAGE Publications.

Costa, P. T., Jr., McCrae, R. R., & Holland, J. L. (1984). Personality and vocational interests in an adult sample. *Journal of Applied Psychology, 69*(3), 390–400. https://doi.org/10.1037/0021-9010.69.3.390

Court, J. H. (1983). Sex differences in performance on Raven's Progressive Matrices: A review. *Alberta Journal of Educational Research, 29*(1), 54–74.

Coward, W. M., & Sackett, P. R. (1990). Linearity of ability–performance relationships: A re-confirmation. *Journal of Applied Psychology, 75*(3), 297–300. https://doi.org/10.1037/0021-9010.75.3.297

Coyne, I., & Bartram, D. (2018). Standards and best practices for technology-enhanced assessments. In J. C. Scott, D. Bartram, & D. H. Reynolds (Eds.), *Next generation technology-enhanced assessment: Global perspectives on occupational and workplace testing* (pp. 327–349). Cambridge University Press.

Craig, R. J., & Olson, R. E. (1988). Changes in functional ego states following treatment for drug abuse. *Transactional Analysis Journal, 18*(1), 68–72. https://doi.org/10.1177/036215378801800111

Crandall, J. E. (1981). *Theory and measurement of social interest: Empirical tests of Alfred Adler's concept*. Columbia University Press.

Crites, J. O. (1981). *Career counseling: Models, methods, and materials*. McGraw-Hill.

Crowley, A. D. (1981). Evaluating the impact of a third-year careers education programme. *British Journal of Guidance and Counselling, 9*(2), 207–213.

Csikszentmihalyi, M. (1996). *Creativity: The psychology and discovery of invention*. Harper Collins.

Csikszentmihalyi, M. (1997). *Flow: The psychology of discovery and invention*. Harper & Row.

Cummings, J. L., & Zarit, J. M. (1987). Probable Alzheimer's disease in an artist. *Journal of the American Medical Association, 258*(19), 2731–2734. https://doi.org/10.1001/jama.1987.03400190113039

Cummings, R. W., & Maddux, C. D. (1987). Holland personality types among learning disabled and nonlearning disabled high school students. *Exceptional Children, 54*(2), 167–170. https://doi.org/10.1177/001440298705400210

Cunningham, J. W., Slonaker, D. F., & Riegel, N. B. (1987). Interest factors derived from job analytically based activity preference scales. *Journal of Vocational Behavior, 30*(3), 270–279. https://doi.org/10.1016/0001-8791(87)90005-4

Dahl, A., & Brownell, C. A. (2019). The social origins of human prosociality. *Current Directions in Psychological Science, 28*(3), 274–279. https://doi.org/10.1177/0963721419830386

Dalal, D. K., & Nolan, K. P. (2009). Using dark side personality traits to identify potential failure. *Industrial and Organizational Psychology: Perspectives on Science and Practice, 2*(4), 434–436. https://doi.org/10.1111/j.1754-9434.2009.01169.x

Dardis, T. (1989). *The thirsty muse: Alcohol and the American writer*. Houghton Mifflin.

Darley, J. G. (1941). Counselling on the basis of interest measurement. *Educational and Psychological Measurement, 1*(1), 35–42. https://doi.rg/10.1177/001316444100100103

Darley, J. G., & Hagenah, T. (1955). *Vocational interest measurement: Theory and practice*. University of Minnesota Press.

Davies, A. F. (1952). Prestige of occupations. *British Journal of Sociology, 3*(2), 134–147. https://doi.org/10.2307/587491

Dawis, R. (1991). Vocational interests, values, and preferences. In M. D. Dunnette & L. M. Hough (Eds.), *Handbook of industrial and organizational psychology* (pp. 833–871). Consulting Psychologists Press.

Dawis, R. V. (1992). The individual differences tradition in counseling psychology. *Journal of Counseling Psychology, 39*(1), 7–19. https://doi.org/10.1037/0022-0167.39.1.7

Dawis, R. V. (2002). Person-environment-correspondence theory. In D. Brown & Associate (Eds.), Career choice and development (4th ed., pp. 427–464). Jossey-Bass.

Dawis, R. V. (2005). The Minnesota theory of work adjustment. In S. D. Brown & R. W. Lent (Eds.), *Career development and counseling: Putting theory and research to work* (pp. 3–23). Wiley.

Day, S. X., & Rounds, J. (1998). Universality of vocational interest structure among racial and ethnic minorities. *American Psychologist, 53*(7), 728–736. https://doi.org/10.1037/0003-066X.53.7.728

Day, S. X., Rounds, J., & Swaney, K. (1998). The structure of vocational interests for diverse racial-ethnic groups. *Psychological Science, 9*(1), 40–44. https://doi.org/10.1111/1467-9280.00007

De Fruyt, F., & Mervielde, I. (1997). The five-factor model of personality and Holland's RIASEC interest types. *Personality and Individual Differences, 23*(1), 87–103. https://doi.org/10.1016/S0191-8869(97)00004-4

De Fruyt, F., & Mervielde, I. (1999). RIASEC types and big five traits as predictors of employment status and nature of employment. *Personnel Psychology, 52*(3), 701–727. https://doi.org/10.1111/j.1744-6570.1999.tb00177.x

Deaux, K. (1985). Sex and gender. *Annual Review of Psychology, 36*(1), 49–81. https://doi.org/10.1146/annurev.ps.36.020185.000405

Deb, M. (1983). Sales effectiveness and personality characteristics. *Psychological Research Journal, 7*(2), 59–67.

Deeter-Schmelz, D. R., & Sojka, J. Z. (2003). Developing effective salespeople: Exploring the link between emotional intelligence and sales performance. *International Journal of Organizational Analysis, 11*(3), 211–220. https://doi.org/10.1108/eb028972

Deng, C.-P., Armstrong, I., & Rounds, J. (2007). The fit of Holland's RIASEC model to US occupations. *Journal of Vocational Behavior, 71*(1), 1–22. https://doi.org/10.1016/j.jvb.2007.04.002

Denissen, J. J. A., Bleidorn, W., Hennecke, M., Luhmann, M., Orth, U., Specht, J., & Zimmermann, J. (2018). Uncovering the power of personality to shape income. *Psychological Science, 29*(1), 3–13. https://doi.org/10.1177/0956797617724435

Derman, D., French, J. W., & Harman, H. H. (1978). *Guide to factor referenced temperament scales 1978*. Educational Testing Service.

Deutsch, D. (2013a). Absolute pitch. In D. Deutsch (Ed.), *The psychology of music* (pp. 141–182). Academic Press. https://doi.org/10.1016/B978-0-12-381460-9.00005-5

Deutsch, D. (Ed.). (2013b). *The psychology of music*. Academic Press.

Dewar, H. (1938). A comparison of tests of artistic appreciation. *British Journal of Educational Psychology, 8*(1), 29–49. https://doi.org/10.1111/j.2044-8279.1938.tb03181.x

DeYoung, C. G., Quilty, L. C., & Peterson, J. B. (2007a). Between facets and domains: 10 aspects of the Big Five. *Journal of Personality and Social Psychology, 93*(5), 880–896. https://doi.org/10.1037/0022-3514.93.5.880

DeYoung, C. G., Quilty, L. C., & Peterson, J. B. (2007b). Big Five Aspect Scales. PsycTESTS.

DeYoung, C. G., Shamosh, N. A., Green, A. E., Braver, T. S., & Gray, J. R. (2009). Intellect as distinct from openness: Differences revealed by fMRI of working memory. *Journal of Personality and Social Psychology, 97*(5), 883–892. https://doi.org/10.1037/a0016615

Dharanendriah, A. S. (1989). Occupational interests of physical, natural and social scientists. *Indian Journal of Applied Psychology, 26*, 38–43.

Diamond, R., Carey, S., & Back, K. J. (1983). Genetic influences on the development of spatial skills during early adolescence. *Cognition, 13*(2), 167–185. https://doi.org/10.1016/0010-0277(83)90021-5

Diedrich, J., Jauk, E., Silvia, P. J., Gredlein, J. M., Neubauer, A. C., & Benedek, M. (2018). Assessment of real-life creativity: The Inventory of Creative Activities and Achievements (ICAA). *Psychology of Aesthetics, Creativity, and the Arts, 12*(3), 304–316. https://doi.org/10.1037/aca0000137

Diedrich, J., Neubauer, A. C., & Ortner, A. (2018). The prediction of professional success in apprenticeship: The role of cognitive and non-cognitive abilities, of interests and personality. *International Journal for Research in Vocational Education and Training, 5*(2), 82–110. https://doi.org/10.13152/IJRVET.5.2.1

Diener, E., Sandvik, E., Pavot, W., & Fujita, F. (1992). Extraversion and subjective well-being in a U.S. national probability sample. *Journal of Research in Personality, 26*(3), 205–215. https://doi.org/10.1016/0092-6566(92)90039-7

Dietrich, A. (2007). Who's afraid of a cognitive neuroscience of creativity? *Methods, 42*(1), 22–27. https://doi.org/10.1016/j.ymeth.2006.12.009

Dietrich, A. (2014). The mythconception of the mad genius. *Frontiers in Psychology, 5*, 79. https://doi.org/10.3389/fpsyg.2014.00079

Digman, J. M. (1990). Personality structure: Emergence of the five-factor model. *Annual Review of Psychology, 41*, 417–440.

Digman, J. M. (1996). The curious history of the five-factor model. In J. S. Wiggins (Ed.), *The five-factor model of personality: Theoretical perspectives* (pp. 1–20). Guilford Press.

Digman, J. M. (1997). Higher-order factors of the Big Five. *Journal of Personality and Social Psychology, 73*(6), 1246–1256. https://doi.org/10.1037/0022-3514.73.6.1246

Dik, B. J., & Rottinghaus, P. J. (2013). Assessments of interests. In K. F. Geisinger, B. A. Bracken, J. F. Carlson, J. C. Hansen, N. R. Kuncel, S. P. Reise, & M. C. Rodriguez (Eds.), *APA handbook of testing and assessment in psychology: Vol. 2. Testing and assessment in clinical and counseling psychology* (pp. 325–348). American Psychological Association. https://doi.org/10.1037/14048-019

Dillard, A. (1989, May 28). Write till you drop. *New York Times Book Review*, Section 7, 1–23. https://www.nytimes.com/1989/05/28/books/write-till-you-drop.html

Dipboye, R. L., Zultowski, W. H., Dewhirst, H. D., & Arvey, R. D. (1978). Self-esteem as a moderator of the relationship between scientific interests and the job satisfaction of physicists and engineers. *Journal of Applied Psychology, 63*(3), 289–294. https://doi.org/10.1037/0021-9010.63.3.289

Dobrow Riza, S., & Heller, D. (2015). Follow your heart or your head? A longitudinal study of the facilitating role of calling and ability in the pursuit of a challenging career. *Journal of Applied Psychology, 100*(3), 695–712. https://doi.org/10.1037/a0038011

Donnay, D. A. C., Thompson, R. C., Morris, M. L., & Schaubhut, N. A. (2004). *Technical brief for the newly revised Strong Interest Inventory Assessment: Content, reliability, and validity*. CPP, Inc.

Donnellan, M. B., & Lucas, R. E. (2008). Age differences in the big five across the life span: Evidence from two national samples. *Psychology and Aging, 23*(3), 558–566. https://doi.org/10.1037/a0012897

Donohue, R. (2006). Person-environment congruence in relation to career change and career persistence. *Journal of Vocational Behavior, 68*(3), 504–515. https://doi.org/10.1016/j.jvb.2005.11.002

Dorval, M., & Pépin, M. (1986). Effect of playing a video game on a measure of spatial visualization. *Perceptual and Motor Skills, 62*(1), 159–162. https://doi.org/10.2466/pms.1986.62.1.159

Drake, J. E., & Winner, E. (2012). Predicting artistic brilliance. *Scientific American Mind, 23*(5), 42–48. https://doi.org/10.1038/scientificamericanmind1112-42

Drake, J. E., & Winner, E. (2013). Who will become a super artist? *Psychologist, 26*(10), 730–733.

Drake, R. M. (1933). Validity and reliability of tests of musical talent. *Journal of Applied Psychology, 17*(4), 447–458. https://doi.org/10.1037/h0070351

Drake, R. M. (1939). Factor analysis of music tests. *Psychological Bulletin, 36*, 608–609.

Drasgow, F., & Olson-Buchanan, J. B. (2018). Technology-driven developments in psychometrics. In J. C. Scott, D. Bartram, & D. H. Reynolds (Eds.), *Next generation technology-enhanced assessment: Global perspectives on occupational and workplace testing* (pp. 239–264). Cambridge University Press.

Dreps, H. F. (1933). The psychological capacities and abilities of college art students. *Psychological Monographs, 45*(1), 134–146. https://doi.org/10.1037/h0093309

Drevdahl, J. E., & Cattell, R. B. (1958). Personality and creativity in artists and writers. *Journal of Clinical Psychology, 14*(2), 107–111. https://doi.org/10.1002/1097-4679(195804)14:2<107::AID-JCLP2270140202>3.0.CO;2-T

Droege, R. C., & Hawk, J. (1977). Development of a US Employment Service interest inventory. *Journal of Employment Counseling, 14*, 65–71. https://doi.org/10.1002/j.2161-1920.1977.tb00642.x

Duckworth, A. L., Weir, D., Tsukayama, E., & Kwok, D. (2012). Who does well in life? Conscientious adults excel in both objective and subjective success. *Frontiers in Psychology, 3*, 356. https://doi.org/10.3389/fpsyg.2012.00356

Dudley, N. M., Orvis, K. A., Lebiecki, J. E., & Cortina, J. M. (2006). A meta-analytic investigation of conscientiousness in the prediction of job performance: Examining the intercorrelations and the incremental validity of narrow traits. *Journal of Applied Psychology, 91*(1), 40–57. https://doi.org/10.1037/0021-9010.91.1.40

Duffy, R. D., Borges, N. J., & Hartung, P. J. (2009). Personality, vocational interests, and work values of medical students. *Journal of Career Assessment, 17*(2), 189–200. https://doi.org/10.1177/1069072708329035

Dunn, W. S., Mount, M. K., Barrick, M. R., & Ones, D. S. (1995). Relative importance of personality and general mental ability in managers' judgments of applicant qualifications. *Journal of Applied Psychology, 80*(4), 500–509. https://doi.org/10.1037/0021-9010.80.4.500

Dunnette, M. D. (1957). Vocational interest differences among engineers employed in different functions. *Journal of Applied Psychology, 41*(5), 273–278. https://doi.org/10.1037/h0046985

Dwight, A. H. (1978). Once a blue-collar worker, always a blue-collar worker? *Vocational Guidance Quarterly, 26*(4), 318–325. https://doi.org/10.1002/j.2164-585X.1978.tb01276.x

Dziurawiec, S., & Deregowski, J. B. (1986). Time as a factor in a spatial task. *International Journal of Psychology, 21*(1–4), 177–187. https://doi.org/10.1080/00207598608247583

Eagly, A., & Wood, W. (2017). Gender identity: Nature and nurture working together. *Evolutionary Studies in Imaginative Culture, 1*(1), 59–62. https://doi.org/10.26613/esic/1.1.10

Eagly, A. H. (2009). The his and hers of prosocial behavior: An examination of the social psychology of gender. *American Psychologist, 64*(8), 644–658. https://doi.org/10.1037/0003-066X.64.8.644

Eagly, A. H., Nater, C., Miller, D. I., Kaufmann, M., & Sczesny, S. (2020). Gender stereotypes have changed: A cross-temporal meta-analysis of U.S. public opinion polls from 1946 to 2018. *American Psychologist, 75*(3), 301–315. https://doi.org/10.1037/amp0000494

Egan, S. K., & Perry, D. G. (2001). Gender identity: A multidimensional analysis with implications for psychosocial adjustment. *Developmental Psychology, 37*(4), 451–463. https://doi.org/10.1037/0012-1649.37.4.451

Eggerth, D. E., & Andrew, M. E. (2006). Modifying the C Index for use with Holland codes of unequal length. *Journal of Career Assessment, 14*, 267–275. https://doi.org/10.1177/1069072705283976

Eggerth, D. E., Bowles, S. M., Tunick, R. H., & Andrew, M. E. (2005). Convergent Validity of O*NET Holland Code Classifications. *Journal of Career Assessment, 13*(2), 150–168. https://doi.org/10.1177/1069072704273124

Ekstrom, R. B., French, J. W., & Harman, H. H. (1976). *Manual for kit of factor-referenced cognitive tests*. Educational Testing Service.

Ekstrom, R. B., & Smith, D. K. (Eds.). (2002). *Assessing individuals with disabilities in educational, employment, and counseling settings*. American Psychological Association. https://doi.org/10.1037/10471-000

El Kousy, A. A. H. (1935). An investigation into the factors in tests involving the visual perception of space. *British Journal of Psychology Monograph Supplements, 20*. Cambridge University Press.

Elder, G. H., & MacInnis, D. J. (1983). Achievement imagery in women's lives from adolescence to adulthood. *Journal of Personality and Social Psychology, 45*(2), 394–404. https://doi.org/10.1037/0022-3514.45.2.394

Eliot, J. (1987). *Models of psychological space: Psychometric, developmental, and experimental approaches*. Springer-Verlag. https://doi.org/10.1007/978-1-4612-4788-3

Eliot, J., Medoff, D., & Kimmel, K. (1987). Development of a new spatial test. *Perceptual and Motor Skills, 64*(2), 479–483. https://doi.org/10.2466/pms.1987.64.2.479

Elkins, R. K., Kassenboehmer, S. C., & Schurer, S. (2017). The stability of personality traits in adolescence and young adulthood. *Journal of Economic Psychology, 60*, 37–52. https://doi.org/10.1016/j.joep.2016.12.005

Elton, C. F., & Smart, J. C. (1988). Extrinsic job satisfaction and person-environment congruence. *Journal of Vocational Behavior, 32*(2), 226–238. https://doi.org/10.1016/0001-8791(88)90016-4

Embretson, S. E. (1987). Improving the measurement of spatial aptitude by dynamic testing. *Intelligence, 11*(4), 333–358. https://doi.org/10.1016/0160-2896(87)90016-X

Embretson, S. E. (1994). *Spatial Learning Ability Test (SLAT)* [Database record]. APA PsycTests. https://doi.org/10.1037/t08069-000

Embretson, S. E. (2004). The second century of ability testing: Some predictions and speculations. *Measurement: Interdisciplinary Research and Perspectives, 2*(1), 1–32.

Emery, D. (2019, January 6). *Understanding Mr. Rogers' quote 'look for the helpers' following tragedy* [blog]. https://www.liveabout.com/

Englert, C. S., Stewart, S. R., & Hiebert, E. H. (1988). Young writers' use of text structure in expository text generation. *Journal of Educational Psychology, 80*(2), 143–151. https://doi.org/10.1037/0022-0663.80.2.143

Erez, M., & Shneorson, Z. (1980). Personality types and motivational characteristics of academics versus professionals in the same occupational discipline. *Journal of Vocational Behavior, 17*(1), 95–105. https://doi.org/10.1016/0001-8791(80)90019-6

Ericsson, K. A. (2018). Superior working memory in experts. In K. A. Ericsson, R. R. Hoffman, A. Kozbelt, & A. M. Williams (Eds.), *The Cambridge handbook of expertise and expert performance* (2nd ed., pp. 696–713). Cambridge University Press. https://doi.org/10.1017/9781316480748.036

Ericsson, K. A., & Faivre, I. A. (1988). What's exceptional about exceptional abilities? In L. K. Obler & D. Fein (Eds.), *The exceptional brain: Neuropsychology of talent and special abilities* (pp. 436–473). Guilford Press.

Ericsson, K. A., & Moxley, J. H. (2014). Experts' superior memory: From accumulation of chunks to building memory skills that mediate improved performance and learning. In T. J. Perfect & D. S. Lindsay (Eds.), *The Sage handbook of applied memory* (pp. 404–420). SAGE Publications. https://doi.org/10.4135/9781446294703.n23

Ericsson, K. A., & Staszewski, J. J. (1989). Skilled memory and expertise: Mechanisms of exceptional performance. In D. Klahr & K. Kotovsky (Eds.), *Complex information processing: The impact of Herbert A. Simon* (pp. 235–267). Lawrence Erlbaum.

Escorpizo, R., Brage, S. Homa, D., & Stucki, G. (Eds.). (2015). *Handbook of vocational rehabilitation and disability evaluation: Application and implementation of the ICF*. Springer International.

Estes, S. G. (1942). A study of five tests of 'spatial' ability. *Journal of Psychology, 13*(2), 265–271. https://doi.org/10.1080/00223980.1942.9917094

Estrada-Hernández, N., Wadsworth, J. S., Nietupski, J. A., Warth, J., & Winslow, A. (2008). Employment or economic success: The experience of individuals with disabilities in transition from school to work. *Journal of Employment Counseling, 45*(1), 14–24. https://doi.org/10.1002/j.2161-1920.2008.tb00040.x

Ethington, C. A., & Wolfle, L. M. (1984). Sex differences in a causal model of mathematics achievement. *Journal for Research in Mathematics Education, 15*(5), 361–377. https://doi.org/10.5951/jresematheduc.15.5.0361

Etzel, J. M., Holland, J., & Nagy, G. (2021). The internal and external validity of the latent vocational interest circumplex: Structure, relationships with self-concepts, and robustness against item-order effects. *Journal of Vocational Behavior, 124*, Article 103520. https://doi.org/10.1016/j.jvb.2020.103520

Evans, C. D., & Diekman, D. B. (2009). On motivated role selection: Gender beliefs, distant goals, and career interest. *Psychology of Women Quarterly, 33*(2), 235–249. https://doi.org/10.1111/j.1471-6402.2009.01493.x

Evans, R. I. (1964). *Conversations with Carl Jung and reactions from Ernest Jones*. D. Van Norstrand Reinhold Co.

Everatt, J., Weeks, S., & Brooks, P. (2008). Profiles of strengths and weaknesses in dyslexia and other learning difficulties. *Dyslexia, 14*(1), 16–41.

Eysenck, H. J. (1967). *The biological basis of personality*. Thomas.

Eysenck, H. J., & Castle, M. A. (1970). Factor-analytic study of the Barron-Welsh Art Scale. *Psychological Record, 20*(4), 523–525. https://doi.org/10.1007/BF03393975

Eysenck, H. J., & Eysenck, S. B. G. (1976). *Eysenck personality questionnaire*. Educational and Industrial Testing Service.

Fabry, J., & Poggio, J. P. (1977). The factor compatibility and communality of coded-expressed and inventoried interests. *Measurement and Evaluation in Guidance, 10*(2), 90–97. https://doi.org/10.1080/00256307.1977.12022114

Farnsworth, P. R. (1931). An historical, critical, and experimental study of the Seashore-Kwalwasser test battery. *Genetic Psychology Monographs, 9*, 291–393.

Farnsworth, P. R. (1958). *The social psychology of music*. The Dryden Press.

Farnsworth, P. R., & Issei, M. (1931). Notes on the Meier-Seashore Art Judgment Test. *Journal of Applied Psychology, 15*(4), 418–420. https://doi.org/10.1037/h0074166

Farr, J. L., & Tippins, N. (Eds.). (2017). *Handbook of employee selection* (2nd ed.). Routledge. https://doi.org/10.4324/9781315690193

Farrugia, D. L. (1982). Deaf high school students' vocational interests and attitudes. *American annals of the deaf, 127*(6), 753–762.

Faver, C. A. (1984). Women, achievement and careers: Age variations in attitudes. *Psychology A Quarterly Journal of Human Behavior, 21*, 45–49.

Feather, N. T., & Said, J. A. (1983). Preference for occupations in relation to masculinity, femininity, and gender. *British Journal of Social Psychology, 22*(2), 113–127. https://doi.org/10.1111/j.2044-8309.1983.tb00573.x

Feist, G. J. (1998). A meta-analysis of personality in scientific and artistic creativity. *Personality and Social Psychology Review, 2*(4), 290–309. https://doi.org/10.1207/s15327957pspr0204_5

Fennema, E., & Tartre, L. A. (1985). The use of spatial visualization in mathematics by girls and boys. *Journal for Research in Mathematics Education, 16*(3), 184–206. https://doi.org/10.5951/jresematheduc.16.3.0184

Ferrara, J., Rudrud, E., Wendlegass, P., & Markve, R. A. (1985). Vocational awareness training and job preferences among mentally retarded adults. *Vocational Guidance Quarterly, 33*(4), 305–314. https://doi.org/10.1002/j.2164-585X.1985.tb01324.x

Fiorello, C. A., Hale, J. B., McGrath, M., Ryan, K., & Quinn, S. (2002). IQ interpretation for children with flat and variable test profiles. *Learning and Individual Differences, 13*(2), 115–125. https://doi.org/10.1016/S1041-6080(02)00075-4

Fischer, C., Malcyha, C. P., & Schafmann, E. (2019). The influence of intrinsic motivation and synergistic extrinsic motivators on creativity and innovation. *Frontiers in Psychology, 10*, 1–15. https://doi.org/10.3389/fpsyg.2019.00137

Fisher, S. & Fisher, R. L. (1981). *Pretend the world is funny and forever: A psychological analysis of comedians, clowns, and actors*. Lawrence Erlbaum.

Flaherty, M. (2005). Gender differences in mental rotational ability in three cultures: Ireland, Ecuador, and Japan. *Psychologia, 48*(1), 31–38. https://doi.org/10.2117/psysoc.2005.31

Fleishman, E. A. (1954). Dimensional analysis of psychomotor abilities. *Journal of Experimental Psychology, 48*(6), 437–454. https://doi.org/10.1037/h0058244

Fleishman, E. A. (1957). A comparative study of aptitude patterns in unskilled and skilled psychomotor performances. *Journal of Applied Psychology, 41*(4), 263–272. https://doi.org/10.1037/h0041763

Fleishman, E. A. (1964). *The structure and measurement of physical fitness.* Prentice-Hall.

Fleishman, E. A., Gebhardt, D. L., & Hogan, J. C. (1984). The measurement of effort. *Ergonomics, 27*(9), 947–954. https://doi.org/10.1080/00140138408963573

Fleishman, E. A., & Hempel, W. E., Jr. (1956). Factorial analysis of complex psychomotor performance and related skills. *Journal of Applied Psychology, 40*(2), 96–104. https://doi.org/10.1037/h0045587

Fleishman, E. A., & Quaintance, M. K. (1984). *Taxonomies of human performance: The descriptions of human tasks.* Academic Press.

Fletcher, F. M. (1966). Concepts, curiosity and careers. *Journal of Counseling Psychology, 13*(2), 131–138. https://doi.org/10.1037/h0023416

Flicker, C., Bartus, R. T., Crook, T. H., & Ferris, S. H. (1984). Effects of aging and dementia upon recent visuospatial memory. *Neurobiology of Aging, 5*(4), 275–283. https://doi.org/10.1016/0197-4580(84)90003-4

Fortier-Brochu, E., Beaulieu-Bonneau, S., Ivers, H., & Morin, C. M. (2012). Insomnia and daytime cognitive performance: A meta-analysis. *Sleep Medicine Reviews, 16*(1), 83–94. https://doi.org/10.1016/j.smrv.2011.03.008

Fouad, N. A., Cudeck, R., & Hansen, J.-I. C. (1984). Convergent validity of the Spanish and English forms of the Strong-Campbell Interest Inventory for bilingual Hispanic high school students. *Journal of Counseling Psychology, 31*(3), 339–348. https://doi.org/10.1037/0022-0167.31.3.339

Fouad, N. A., Harmon, L. W., & Borgen, F. H. (1997). Structure of interests in employed male and female members of US racial-ethnic minority and nonminority groups. *Journal of Counseling Psychology, 44*(4), 339–345. https://doi.org/10.1037/0022-0167.44.4.339

Fouad, N. A., & Mohler, C. J. (2004). Cultural validity of Holland's theory and the strong interest inventory for five racial/ethnic groups. *Journal of Career Assessment, 12*(4), 423–439. https://doi.org/10.1177/1069072704267736

Frederiksen, N. (1962). Factors in in-basket performance. *Psychological Monographs: General and Applied, 76*(22, Whole No. 541).

Frederiksen, N., Saunders, D. R., & Wand, B. (1957). The in-basket test. *Psychological Monographs, 71*(9, Whole No. 438).

Freeman, J. (1979). The sex discrimination act and the APU occupational interests guide: A reply to Closs. *British Journal of Guidance and Counselling, 7*(2), 212–217. https://doi.org/10.1080/03069887908258161

Frey, R. S. (1984). Need for achievement, entrepreneurship, and economic growth: A critique of the McClelland thesis. *Social Science Journal, 21*(2), 125–134.

Frieder, R. E., Wang, G., & Oh, I.-S. (2018). Linking job-relevant personality traits, transformational leadership, and job performance via perceived meaningfulness at work: A moderated mediation model. *Journal of Applied Psychology, 103*(3), 324–333. https://doi.org/10.1037/apl0000274

Funk, C., & Parker, K. (2018, January 9). Women and men in STEM often at odds over workplace equity. Pew Research Center. https://www.pewresearch.org/social-trends/2018/01/09/women-and-men-in-stem-often-at-odds-over-workplace-equity/

Furnham, A. (2008). Psychometric correlates of FIRO-B Scores: Locating the FIRO-B scores in personality factor space. *International Journal of Selection and Assessment, 16*(1), 30–45. https://doi.org/10.1111/j.1468-2389.2008.00407.x

Furnham, A. (2009). Locus of control and attributional style. In M. R. Leary & R. H. Hoyle (Eds.), *Handbook of individual differences in social behavior* (pp. 274–287). Guilford Press.

Furnham, A. (2015). The bright and dark side correlates of creativity: Demographic, ability, personality traits and personality disorders associated with divergent thinking. *Creativity Research Journal, 27*(1), 39–46. https://doi.org/10.1080/10400419.2015.992676

Furnham, A., & Chamorro-Premuzic, T. (2004). Personality, intelligence, and art. *Personality and Individual Differences, 36*(3), 705–715. https://doi.org/10.1016/S0191-8869(03)00128-4

Gade, E. M., & Peterson, G. (1977). Intrinsic and extrinsic work values and the vocational maturity of vocational-technical students. *Vocational Guidance Quarterly, 26*(2), 125–130. https://doi.org/10.1002/j.2164-585X.1977.tb00959.x

Gael, S., Grant, D. L., & Ritchie, R. J. (1975). Employment test validation for minority and nonminority clerks with work sample criteria. *Journal of Applied Psychology, 60*(4), 420–426. https://doi.org/10.1037/h0076908

Gakhar, S. C. (1986). Correlational research-individual differences in intelligence, aptitude, personality and achievement among science, commerce and arts students. *Journal of Psychological Researches, 30*(1), 22–29.

Gardner, H. (1973). *The arts and human development: A psychological study of the artistic process*. Wiley.

Gardner, H. (1982). *Art, mind, and brain: A cognitive approach to creativity*. Basic Books.

Gardner, H. (2011). *Frames of mind: The theory of multiple intelligences*. Basic Books. (Original work published 1983)

Gardner, H. (1999). *Intelligence reframed: Multiple intelligences for the 21st century*. Basic Books.

Gasser, C. E., Larson, L. M., & Borgen, F. H. (2007). Concurrent validity of the 2005 Strong Interest Inventory: An examination of gender and major field of study. *Journal of Career Assessment, 15*(1), 23–43.

Gati, I. (1991). The structure of vocational interests. *Psychological Bulletin, 109*(2), 309–324. https://doi.org/10.1037/0033-2909.109.2.309

Gati, I., & Asher, I. (2001). The PIC model for career decision making: Prescreening, in-depth exploration, and choice. In F. T. Leong & A. Barak (Eds.), *Contemporary models in vocational psychology* (pp. 7–54). Erlbaum.

Gati, I., & Asulin-Peretz, L. (2011). Internet-based self-help career assessments and interventions: Challenges and implications for evidence-based career counseling. *Journal of Career Assessment, 19*(3), 259–273. https://doi.org/10.1177/1069072710395533

Gati, I., & Nathan, M. (1986). The role of the perceived structure of occupations in vocational behavior. *Journal of Vocational Behavior, 29*(2), 177–193. https://doi.org/10.1016/0001-8791(86)90002-3

Gati, I., & Winer, D. (1987). The relationship between vocational interests and the location of an ideal occupation in the individual's perceived occupational structure. *Journal of Vocational Behavior, 30*(3), 295–308. https://doi.org/10.1016/0001-8791(87)90007-8

Gaugler, B. B., Rosenthal, D. B., Thornton, G. C., & Bentson, C. (1987). Meta-analysis of assessment center validity. *Journal of Applied Psychology, 72*(3), 493–511. https://doi.org/10.1037/0021-9010.72.3.493

Getter, H., & Nowinski, J. K. (1981). A free response test of interpersonal effectiveness. *Journal of Personality Assessment, 45*(3), 301–308. https://doi.org/10.1207/s15327752jpa4503_12

Getzels, J. W., & Csikszentmihalyi, M. (1976). *The creative vision: A longitudinal study of problem finding in art*. John Wiley.

Geyer, P. (2012). *Extraversion–introversion: What C. G. Jung meant and how contemporaries responded* [Paper presentation]. AusAPT National Conference, Melbourne, Australia. https://www.researchgate.net/publication/264782791_Extraversion_-

Ghiselli, E. E. (1963). Managerial talent. *American Psychologist, 18*(10), 631–642. https://doi.org/10.1037/h0048149

Ghiselli, E. E. (1966). *The validity of occupational aptitude tests*. Wiley.

Ghiselli, E. E. (1968). Some motivational factors in the success of managers. *Personnel Psychology, 21*(4), 431–440. https://doi.org/10.1111/j.1744-6570.1968.tb02043.x

Ghiselli, E. E. (1969). Managerial talent. In D. Wolfle (Ed.), *The discovery of talent* (pp. 212–239). Harvard University Press.

Ghiselli, E. E., & Barthol, R. P. (1953). The validity of personality inventories in selecting employees. *Journal of Applied Psychology, 37*(1), 18–20. https://doi.org/10.1037/h0059438

Greengross, G., & Miller, G. F. (2009). The Big Five personality traits of professional comedians compared to amateur comedians, comedy writers, and college students. *Personality and Individual Differences, 47*(2), 79–83. https://doi.org/10.1016/j.paid.2009.01.045

Greenlee, S. P., Damarin, F. L., & Walsh, W. B. (1988). Congruence and differentiation among Black and White males in two non-college-degreed occupations. *Journal of Vocational Behavior, 32*(3), 298–306. https://doi.org/10.1016/0001-8791(88)90021-8

George, L. G., Helson, R., & John, O. P. (2011). The "CEO" of women's work lives: How Big Five Conscientiousness, Extraversion, and Openness predict 50 years of work experiences in a changing sociocultural context. *Journal of Personality and Social Psychology, 101*(4), 812–830. https://doi.org/10.1037/a0024290

Geschwind, N., & Galaburda, A. M. (1985a). Cerebral lateralization. Biological mechanisms, associations, and pathology: I. A hypothesis and a program for research. *Archives of Neurology, 42*(5), 428–459. https://doi.org/10.1001/archneur.1985.04060050026008

Geschwind, N., & Galaburda, A. M. (1985b). Cerebral lateralization. Biological mechanisms, associations, and pathology: II. A hypothesis and a program for research. *Archives of Neurology, 42*(6), 521–552. https://doi.org/10.1001/archneur.1985.04060060019009

Ghetta, A., Hirschi, A., Herrmann, A., & Rossier, J. (2018). A psychological description of the Swiss labor market from 1991 to 2014: Occupational interest types, sex, salary, and skill level. *Swiss Journal of Psychology, 77*(2), 83–94. https://doi.org/10.1024/1421-0185/a000206

Ghiselli, E. E. (1971). *Explorations in managerial talent*. Goodyear.

Giffard, A., Mullin, C., & Steeves, J. (2012). Sex and sexual orientation differences in perceptual processing. *Journal of Vision, 12*(9), 505–505. https://doi.org/10.1167/12.9.505#

Gjerdingen, R. O. (2018). Psychologists and musicians: Then and now. In I. D. Deutsch (Ed.), *The psychology of music* (pp. 683–705). Academic Press.

Glencross, D., & Bluhm, N. (1986). Intensive computer keyboard training programmes. *Applied ergonomics, 17*(3), 191–194. https://doi.org/10.1016/0003-6870(86)90005-0

Goldberg, L. R. (1981). Language and individual differences: The search for universals in personality lexicons. In L. Wheeler (Ed.), *Review of personality and social psychology* (Vol. 2, pp. 141–165). SAGE Publications.

Goldberg, L. R., & Rosolack, T. K. (1994). The Big Five factor structure as an integrative framework: An empirical comparison with Esyenck's P-E-N model. In C. F. Halverson, Jr., G. A. Kohnstamm, & R. P. Martin (Eds.), *The developing structure of temperament and personality from infancy to adulthood* (pp. 7–35). Psychology Press.

Goldsmith, L. T., Hetland, L., Hoyle, C., & Winner, E. (2016). Visual-spatial thinking in geometry and the visual arts. psychology of aesthetics. *Psychology of Aesthetics, Creativity, and the Arts, 10*(1), 56–71. https://doi.org/10.1037/aca0000027

Goldstein, R. B., Chou, S. P., Saha, T. D., Smith, S. M., Jung, J., Zhang, H., Pickering, R. P., Ruan, W. J., Huang, B., & Grant, B. F. (2017). The epidemiology of antisocial behavioral syndromes in adulthood: Results from the National Epidemiologic Survey on Alcohol and Related Conditions-III. *Journal of Clinical Psychiatry, 78*(1), 90–98. https://doi.org/10.4088/JCP.15m10358

Goldstein, S., Princiotta, D., & Naglieri, J. A. (Eds.). (2015). Handbook of intelligence: Evolutionary theory, historical perspective, and current concepts. Springer Science + Business Media. https://doi.org/10.1007/978-1-4939-1562-0

Goleman, D. (1986, February 2). The psyche of the entrepreneur. *New York Times Magazine*, 30–36.

Goleman, D. (1995). *Emotional intelligence: Why it can matter more than IQ*. Bantam.

Goleman, D. (2006). *Social intelligence: The new science of human relationships*. Bantam Books.

Gonzalez-Mulé, E., Carter, K. M., & Mount, M. K. (2017). Are smarter people happier? Meta-analyses of the relationships between general mental ability and job and life satisfaction. *Journal of Vocational Behavior, 99*, 146–164. https://doi.org/10.1016/j.jvb.2017.01.003

Goodman, C. H. (1947). The MacQuarrie test for mechanical ability; factor analysis. *Journal of Applied Psychology, 31*(2), 150–154. https://doi.org/10.1037/h0056962

Goodwin, D. W. (1988). *Alcohol and the writer*. Andrews and McMeel.

Goodwin, F. K., & Jamison, K. R. (2007). Manic-depressive illness: Bipolar disorders and recurrent depression (2nd ed.). Oxford University Press.

Gordon, E. E. (1965). *Musical Aptitude Profile*. Riverside Publishing Co.

Gordon, E. E. (1986a). A factor analysis of the Musical Aptitude Profile, the Primary Measures of Music Audiation and the Intermediate Measures of Music Audiation. *Bulletin of the Council for Research in Music Education, 87*, 17–25.

Gordon, E. E. (1986b). Final results of a two-year longitudinal predictive validity study of the Instrument Timbre Preference Test and the Musical Aptitude Profile. *Bulletin of the Council for Research in Music Education, 87*, 8–17.

Gordon, E. E. (1989). *Manual for the advanced measures of music audiation*. G.I.A. Publications.

Gordon, H. W., & Leighty, R. (1988). Importance of specialized cognitive function in the selection of military pilots. *Journal of Applied Psychology, 73*(1), 38–45. https://doi.org/10.1037/0021-9010.73.1.38

Gordon, H. W., Silverberg-Shalev, R., & Czernilas, J. (1982). Hemispheric asymmetry in fighter and helicopter pilots. *Acta Psychologica, 52*(1–2), 33–40. https://doi.org/10.1016/0001-6918(82)90024-5

Gormly, J., & Gormly, A. (1986). Social introversion and spatial abilities. *Bulletin of the Psychonomic Society, 24*(4), 273–274. https://doi.org/10.3758/BF03330138

Gottfredson, G. D. (1999). John L. Holland's contributions to vocational psychology: A review and evaluation. *Journal of Vocational Behavior, 55*(1), 15–40. https://doi.org/10.1006/jvbe.1999.1695

Gottfredson, G. D., & Daiger, D. C. (1977). Using a classification of occupations to describe age, sex, and time differences in employment patterns. *Journal of Vocational Behavior, 10*(2), 121–138. https://doi.org/10.1016/0001-8791(77)90049-5

Gottfredson, G. D., & Holland, J. L. (1996). *Dictionary of Holland occupational codes* (3rd ed.). Psychological Assessment Resources.

Gottfredson, G. D., & Johnstun, M. L. (2009). John Holland's contributions: A theory-ridden approach to career assistance. *Career Development Quarterly, 58*(2), 99–107. https://doi.org/10.1002/j.2161-0045.2009.tb00050.x

Gottfredson, G. D., Jones, E. M., & Holland, J. L. (1993). Personality and vocational interests: The relation of Holland's six interest dimensions to five robust dimensions of personality. *Journal of Counseling Psychology, 40*(4), 518–524. https://doi.org/10.1037/0022-0167.40.4.518

Gottfredson, L. S. (1978). An analytical description of employment according to race, sex, prestige, and Holland type of work. *Journal of Vocational Behavior, 13*(2), 210–221.https://doi.org/10.1016/0001-8791(78)90046-5

Gottfredson, L. S. (1980). Construct validity of Holland's occupational typology in terms of prestige, census, Department of Labor, and other classification systems. *Journal of Applied Psychology, 65*(6), 697–714. https://doi.org/10.1037/0021-9010.65.6.697

Gottfredson, L. S. (1986a). The *g* factor in employment. *Journal of Vocational Behavior, 29*(3), 293–296. https://doi.org/10.1016/0001-8791(86)90009-6

Gottfredson, L. S. (1986b). Occupational Aptitude Patterns Map: Development and implications for a theory of job aptitude requirements [Monograph]. *Journal of Vocational Behavior, 29*(2), 254–291. https://doi.org/10.1016/0001-8791(86)90008-4

Gottfredson, L. S. (1986c). Societal consequences of the *g* factor in employment. *Journal of Vocational Behavior, 29*(3), 379–410. https://doi.org/10.1016/0001-8791(86)90015-1

Gottfredson, L. S. (1986d). Special groups and the beneficial use of vocational interest inventories. In W. B. Walsh & S. H. Osipow (Eds.), *Advances in vocational psychology: Vol. I. The assessment of interests* (pp. 127–198). Lawrence Erlbaum.

Gottfredson, L. S. (1999). The nature and nurture of vocational interests. In M. L. Savickas & A. R. Spokane (Eds.), *Vocational interests: Meaning, measurement, and counseling use* (pp. 57–85). Davies-Black Publishing.

Gottfredson, L. S. (2003). The challenge and promise of cognitive career assessment. *Journal of Career Assessment, 11*(2), 115–135. https://doi.org/10.1177/1069072703011002001

Gottheil, E., Exline, R. V., & Winkelmayer, R. (1979). Judging emotions of normal and schizophrenic subjects. *American Journal of Psychiatry, 136*, 1049–1054. https://doi.org/10.1176/ajp.136.8.1049

Gough, H. (1987). *CPI: The California Psychological Inventory administrator's guide.* Consulting Psychologists Press.

Gough, H. G. (1996). *CPI Manual: California Psychological Inventory: Administrator's guide* (3rd ed.). Consulting Psychologists Press.

Gough, H. G., Hall, W. B., & Bradley, P. (1996). Forty years of experience with the Barron-Welsh Art Scale. In A. Mountouri (Ed.), *Unusual associates: A festschrift for Frank Barron* (pp. 252–301). Hampton Press, Inc.

Gough, H. G., & Woodworth, D. G. (1960). Stylistic variations among professional research scientists. *Journal of Psychology, 49*(1), 87–98. https://doi.org/10.1080/00223980.1960.9916387

Grandin, T., & Panek, R. (2013). *The autistic brain: Helping different kinds of minds succeed.* Mariner Books, Houghton Mifflin Harcourt.

Grant, A. M. (2013). Rethinking the extraverted sales ideal: The ambivert advantage. *Psychological Science, 24*(6), 1024–1030. https://doi.org/10.1177/0956797612463706

Grant, D. L., Katkovsky, W., & Bray, D. W. (1967). Contributions of projective techniques to assessment of management potential. *Journal of Applied Psychology, 51*(3), 226–232. https://doi.org/10.1037/h0024661

Grapsas, S., Brummelman, E., Back, M. D., & Denissen, J. J. A. (2020). The "why" and "how" of narcissism: A process model of narcissistic status pursuit. *Perspectives on Psychological Science, 15*(1), 150–172. https://doi.org/10.1177/1745691619873350

Gray, J. A. (1970). The psychophysiological basis of introversion-extraversion. *Behaviour Research and Therapy, 8*(3), 249–266. https://doi.org/10.1016/0005-7967(70)90069-0

Graziano, W. G., & Tobin, R. M. (2002). Agreeableness: Dimension of personality or social desirability artifact? *Journal of Personality, 70*(5), 695–727.

Graziano, W. G., & Tobin, R. M. (2009). Agreeableness. In M. R. Leary & R. H. Hoyle (Eds.), *Handbook of individual differences in social behavior* (pp. 46–61). Guilford Press.

Gregersen, P. K., Kowalsky, E., Kohn, N., & Marvin, E. W. (1999). Absolute pitch: Prevalence, ethnic variation, and estimation of the genetic component. *American Journal of Human Genetics, 65*(3), 911–913. https://doi.org/10.1086/302541

Gregg, C. H., & Dobson, K. (1980). Occupational sex role stereotyping and occupational interests in children. *Elementary School Guidance & Counseling, 15*(1), 66–75.

Gregory, J. B., & Levy, P. E. (2015). *Using feedback in organizational consulting.* American Psychological Association.

Gregory, R. J. (2004). *Psychological testing: History, principles, and applications.* Allyn & Bacon.

Griffin, A. S., Guillette, L. M., & Healy, S. D. (2015). Cognition and personality: An analysis of an emerging field. *Trends in Ecology & Evolution, 30*(4), 207–214. https://doi.org/10.1016/j.tree.2015.01.012

Grijalva, E., & Newman, D. A. (2015). Narcissism and counterproductive work behavior (CWB): Meta-analysis and consideration of collectivist culture, big five personality, and narcissism's facet structure. *Applied Psychology, 64*(1), 93–126. https://doi.org/10.1111/apps.12025

Gross, T. (2018, October 24). *Paul Dano On 'wildlife,' and the different anxieties of acting and directing* [Interview]. NPR. https://www.npr.org/2018/10/24/660168891/paul-dano-on-wildlife-and-the-different-anxieties-of-acting-and-directing

Grotevant, H. D. (1979). Environmental influences on vocational interest development in adolescents from adoptive and biological families. *Child Development, 50*(3), 854–860. https://doi.org/10.2307/1128954

Grotevant, H. D., & Durrett, M. E. (1980). Occupational knowledge and career development in adolescence. *Journal of Vocational Behavior, 17*(2), 171–182. https://doi.org/10.1016/0001-8791(80)90002-0

Grotevant, H. D., Scarr, S., & Weinberg, R. A. (1977). Patterns of interest similarity in adoptive and biological families. *Journal of Personality and Social Psychology, 35*(9), 667–676.

Grudin, J. (1983). Non-hierarchic specification of components in transcription typewriting. *Acta Psychologica, 54*(1–3), 249–262. https://doi.org/10.1016/0001-6918(83)90038-0

Grupp, S., Ramseyer, G., Richardson, J. (1968). The effect of age on four scales of the California Psychological Inventory. *Journal of General Psychology, 78*(2), 183–187. https://doi.org/10.1080/00221309.1968.9710431

Guilford, J. P. (1948). Some lessons from aviation psychology. *American Psychologist, 3*(1), 3–11. https://doi.org/10.1037/h0056736

Guilford, J. P. (1950). Creativity. *American Psychologist, 5*(9), 444–454. https://doi.org/10.1037/h0063487

Guilford, J. P. (1957a). Creative abilities in the arts. *Psychological Review, 64*(2), 110–118. https://doi.org/10.1037/h0048280

Guilford, J. P. (1957b). *Louis Leon Thurstone (1887–1955): A biographical memoir.* National Academy of Sciences. http://www.nasonline.org/publications/biographical-memoirs/memoir-pdfs/thurstone-louis.pdf

Guilford, J. P. (1959). Traits of creativity. In H. H. Anderson (Ed.), *Creativity and its cultivation* (pp. 142–161). Harper and Row.

Guilford, J. P. (1967). *The nature of human intelligence.* McGraw-Hill.

Guilford, J. P. (1972). Thurstone's primary mental abilities and structure-of-intellect abilities. *Psychological Bulletin, 77*(2), 129–143. https://doi.org/10.1037/h0032227

Guilford, J. P. (1985). The structure-of-intellect model. In B. B. Wolman (Ed.), *Handbook of intelligence: Theories, measurements, and applications* (pp. 225–266). Wiley.

Guilford, J. P., Christensen, P. R., Bond, N. A., & Sutton, M. A. (1954). A factor analytic study of human interests. *Psychological Monographs, 68* (4, Whole No. 375).

Guilford, J. S., Zimmerman, W. S., & Guilford, J. P. (1976). *Guilford-Zimmerman Temperament Survey Handbook: Twenty-five years of research and application*. Edits Publishers.

Guion, R. M. (1987). Changing views for personnel selection research. *Personnel Psychology, 40*(2), 199–213. https://doi.org/10.1111/j.1744-6570.1987.tb00601.x

Guion, R. M., & Gottier, R. F. (1965). Validity of personality measures in personnel selection. *Personnel Psychology, 18*(2), 135–164. https://doi.org/10.1111/j.1744-6570.1965.tb00273.x

Gulliksen, H. (1968). Louis Leon Thurstone, experimental and mathematical psychologist. *American Psychologist, 23*(11), 786–802. https://doi.org/10.1037/h0026696

Habibi, A., Rael Cahn, B., Damasio, A., & Damasio, H. (2016). Neural correlates of accelerated auditory processing in children engaged in music training. *Developmental Cognitive Neuroscience, 21*, 1–14. https://doi.org/10.1016/j.dcn.2016.04.003

Hagenah, T., & Darley, J. G. (1955). *Vocational interest measurement: Theory and practice*. University of Minnesota Press.

Hakstian, A. R., & Bennet, R. W. (1977). Validity studies using the Comprehensive Ability Battery (CAB): I. Academic achievement criteria. *Educational and Psychological Measurement, 37*(2), 425–437. https://doi.org/10.1177/001316447703700217

Hakstian, A. R., & Bennet, R. W. (1978). Validity studies using the Comprehensive Ability Battery (CAB): II. Relationships with the DAT and the GATB. *Educational and Psychological Measurement, 38*(4), 1003–1015. https://doi.org/10.1177/001316447803800419

Hakstian, A. R., & Cattell, R. B. (1974). The checking of primary ability structure on a broader basis of performances. *British Journal of Educational Psychology, 44*(2), 140–154. https://doi.org/10.1111/j.2044-8279.1974.tb02281.x

Hakstian, A. R., & Cattell, R. B. (1978a). An examination of inter-domain relationships among some ability and personality traits. *Educational and Psychological Measurement, 38*(2), 275–290. https://doi.org/10.1177/001316447803800209

Hakstian, A. R., & Cattell, R. B. (1978b). Higher stratum ability structures on a basis of twenty primary abilities. *Journal of Educational Psychology, 70*(5), 657–669. https://doi.org/10.1037/0022-0663.70.5.657

Hakstian, A. R., Cattell, R. B., & IPAT Staff. (1982). *Manual for the Comprehensive Ability Battery* [CAB]. Institute for Personality and Ability Testing.

Hakstian, A. R., & Gale, C. A. (1979). Validity studies using the Comprehensive Ability Battery (CAB): III. Performance in conjunction with personality and motivational traits. *Educational and Psychological Measurement, 39*(2), 389–400. https://doi.org/10.1177/001316447903900218

Hakstian, A. R., Woolsey, L. K., & Schroeder, M. L. (1986). Development and application of a quickly-scored in-basket exercise in an organizational setting. *Educational and Psychological Measurement, 46*(2), 385–396. https://doi.org/10.1177/001316448604600212

Hammer, A. L., & Mitchelle, W. D. (1996). The distribution of MBTI types in the US by gender and ethnic group. *Journal of Psychological Type, 37*, 2–15.

Hammond, S. M. (1984). An investigation into the factor structure of the General Aptitude Test Battery. *Journal of Occupational Psychology, 57*, 43–48. https://doi.org/10.1111/j.2044-8325.1984.tb00146.x

Hansen, J.-I. C. (1976). Exploring new directions for Strong-Campbell Interest Inventory occupational scale construction. *Journal of Vocational Behavior, 9*(2), 147–160. https://doi.org/10.1016/0001-8791(76)90073-7

Hansen, J.-I. C. (1986). The Strong Vocational Interest Blank/The Strong Campbell Interest Inventory. In W. B. Walsh & S. H. Osipow (Eds.), *The assessment of interests* (pp. 1–30). Erlbaum.

Hansen, J.-I. C. (1988). Changing interests of women: Myth or reality? *Applied Psychology, 37*, 133–150. https://doi.org/10.1111/j.1464-0597.1988.tb01132.x

Hansen, J.-I. C. (2000). Interpretation the Strong Interest Inventory. In C. E. Watkins, Jr. & V. L. Campbell (Eds.), *Testing and assessment in counseling practice* (pp. 293–262). Erlbaum.

Hansen, J.-I. C., & Campbell, D. P. (1985). *Manual for the Strong Interest Inventory* (4th ed.). Consulting Psychologists Press.

Hansen, J.-I. C., Collins, R. C., Swanson, J. L., & Fouad, N. A. (1993). Gender differences in the structure of interests. *Journal of Vocational Behavior, 42*(2), 200–211. https://doi.org/10.1006/jvbe.1993.1014

Hansen, J.-I. C., Dik, B. J., & Zhou, S. (2008). An examination of the structure of leisure interests of college students, working-age adults, and retirees. *Journal of Counseling Psychology, 55*(2), 133–145. https://doi.org/10.1037/0022-0167.55.2.133

Hansen, J.-I. C., & Neuman, J. L. (1999). Evidence of concurrent prediction of the Campbell Interest and Skill Survey (CISS) for college major selection. *Journal of Career Assessment, 7*(3), 239–247. https://doi.org/10.1177/106907279900700304

Hansen, J.-I. C., Scullard, M. G., & Haviland, M. G. (2000). The interest structures of Native American college students. *Journal of Career Assessment, 8*(2), 159–172. https://doi.org/10.1177/106907270000800205

Hanson, G. R. (1974). Assessing the career interests of college youth: Summary of research and applications. *Research Reports, 67*, 76.

Hanson, G. R., Lamb, R. R., & English, E. (1974). An analysis of Holland's interest types for women: A comparison of the Strong-Holland and the ACT Vocational Interest Profile scales for women. *Journal of Vocational Behavior, 4*(2), 259–269. https://doi.org/10.1016/0001-8791(74)90109-2

Hanson, G. R., & Rayman, J. (1976). Validity of sex-balanced interest inventory scales. *Journal of Vocational Behavior, 9*(3), 279–291. https://doi.org/10.1016/0001-8791(76)90056-7

Hanson, H. A., & Chater, S. (1983). Role selection by nurses: Managerial interests and personal attributes. *Nursing Research, 32*(1), 48–52. https://doi.org/10.1097/00006199-198301000-00010

Hanson, J. (2019). Meta-analytic evidence of the criterion validity of Gordon's music aptitude tests in published music education research. *Journal of Research in Music Education, 67*(2), 193–213. https://doi.org/10.1177/0022429418819165

Harari, M. B., Naemi, B., Viswesvaran, C., Roberts, R. D., & Rodriguez, J. F. (2014). The validity of conscientiousness and its facets: Stable or dynamic across time? *Academy of Management Annual Meeting Proceedings, 2014*(1), 1458–1463. https://doi.org/10.5465/AMBPP.2014.240

Hare, R. D. (1985). Comparison of procedures for the assessment of psychopathy. *Journal of Consulting and Clinical Psychology, 53*(1), 7–16. https://doi.org/10.1037/0022-006X.53.1.7

Hargrave, G. E., & Berner, J. G. (1984). *POST psychological screening manual*. Commission on Peace Officer Standards and Training.

Harmon, L. W., Hansen, J. C., Borgen, F. H., & Hammer, A. C. (1994). *Strong Interest Inventory: Applications and technical guide*. Consulting Psychologists Press.

Harms, P. D., Credé, M., Tynan, M., Leon, M., & Jeung, W. (2017). Leadership and stress: A meta-analytic review. *Leadership Quarterly, 28*(1), 178–194. https://doi.org/10.1016/j.leaqua.2016.10.006

Harrell, T. W. (1937). Validity of certain mechanical ability tests for selecting cotton mill machine fixers. *Journal of Social Psychology, 8*(2), 279–282. https://doi.org/10.1080/00224545.1937.9920008

Harrell, T. W. (1940). A factor analysis of mechanical ability tests. *Psychometrika, 5*(1), 17–33. https://doi.org/10.1007/BF02288557

Harrell, T. W., & Harrell, M. S. (1973). The personality of MBA's who reach general Management early. *Personnel Psychology, 26*(1), 127–134. https://doi.org/10.1111/j.1744-6570.1973.tb01124.x

Harrington, T., & O'Shea, A. (2000). *The Harrington-O'Shea Career Decision-Making System revised*. American Guidance Service.

Harris, J. A., Vernon, V. A., Andrew, M., Johnson, A. M., & Jang, K. L. (2006). Phenotypic and genetic relationships between vocational interests and personality. *Personality and Individual Differences, 40*, 1531–1541. https://doi.org/10.1016/j.paid.2005.11.024

Harris, L. J. (1981). Sex-related variations in spatial skill. In L. S. Liben, A. H. Patterson, & N. Newcombe (Eds.), *Spatial representation across the life span: Theory and application* (pp. 83–125). Academic Press.

Harrison, C. S. (1987a). The long-term predictive validity of the Musical Aptitude Profile relative to criteria of grades in music theory and applied music. *Educational and Psychological Measurement, 47*(4), 1107–1112. https://doi.org/10.1177/0013164487474028

Harrison, C. S. (1987b). The validity of the Musical Aptitude Profile for predicting grades in freshman music theory. *Educational and Psychological Measurement, 47*(2), 477–482. https://doi.org/10.1177/0013164487472021

Harrison, S., Grover, S., & Furnham, A. (2018). The perception of sub-clinical personality disorders by employers, employees and co-workers. *Psychiatry Research, 270*, 1082–1091. https://doi.org/10.1016/j.psychres.2018.05.036

Hartup, W. W. (1989). Social relationships and their developmental significance. *American Psychologist, 44*(2), 120–126. https://doi.org/10.1037/0003-066X.44.2.120

Harvey, D. W., & Whinfield, R. W. (1973). Extending Holland's theory to adult women. *Journal of Vocational Behavior, 3*(2), 115–127. https://doi.org/10.1016/0001-8791(73)90001-8

Hassler, M., & Birbaumer, F. A. (1985). Musical talent and visual-spatial abilities: A longitudinal study. *Psychology of Music, 13*(2), 99–113. https://doi.org/10.1177/0305735685132004

Hawkes, B., Cek, I., & Handler, C. (2018). The gamification of employee selection tools: An exploration of viability, utility, and future directions. In J. C. Scott, D. Bartram, & D. H. Reynolds (Eds.), *Next generation technology-enhanced assessment: Global perspectives on occupational and workplace testing* (pp. 288–313). Cambridge University Press.

Hayes, A. R., Bigler, R. S., & Weisgram, E. S. (2018). Of men and money: Characteristics of occupations that affect the gender differentiation of children's occupational interests. *Sex Roles, 78*(11–12), 775–788. https://doi.org/10.1007/s11199-017-0846-8

Hayes, J. R., & Flower, L. S. (1986). Writing research and the writer. *American Psychologist, 41*(10), 1106–1113. https://doi.org/10.1037/0003-066X.41.10.1106

Hayter, A. (1988). *Opium and the romantic imagination: Addiction and creativity in De Quincey, Coleridge, Baudelaire, and others* (Rev. ed.). Crucible.

Heesacker, M., Elliott, T. R., & Howe, L. A. (1988). Does the Holland code predict job satisfaction and productivity in clothing factory workers? *Journal of Counseling Psychology, 35*(2), 144–148. https://doi.org/10.1037/0022-0167.35.2.144

Hegarty, M. (2018). Ability and sex differences in spatial thinking: What does the mental rotation test really measure? *Psychonomic Bulletin & Review, 25*(3), 1212–1219. https://doi.org/10.3758/s13423-017-1347-z

Heilman, K. M., Nadeau, S. E., & Beversdorf, D. O. (2003). Creative innovation: Possible brain mechanisms. *Neurocase, 9*(5), 369–379. https://doi.org/10.1076/neur.9.5.369.16553

Heilman, M. E. (1979). High school students' occupational interest as a function of projected sex ratios in male-dominated occupations. *Journal of Applied Psychology*, *64*(3), 275–279. https://doi.org/10.1037/0021-9010.64.3.275

Hell, B., & Pässler, K. (2011). Are occupational interests hormonally influenced? The 2D:4D- interest nexus. *Personality and Individual Differences*, *51*(4), 376–380. https://doi.org/10.1016/j.paid.2010.05.033

Helmbold, N., Rammsayer, T., & Altenmüller, E. (2005). Differences in primary mental abilities between musicians and nonmusicians. *Journal of Individual Differences*, *26*(2), 74–85. https://doi.org/10.1027/1614-0001.26.2.74

Helmes, E., & Fekken, G. C. (1986). Effects of psychotropic drugs and psychiatric illness on vocational aptitude and interest assessment. *Journal of Clinical Psychology*, *42*(4), 569–576. https://doi.org/10.1002/1097-4679(198607)42:4<569::AID-JCLP2270420405>3.0.CO;2-H

Helson, R. (1978). Writers and critics: Two types of vocational consciousness in the art system. *Journal of Vocational Behavior*, *12*(3), 351–363. https://doi.org/10.1016/0001-8791(78)90023-4

Helson, R. (1996). In search of the creative personality, *Creativity Research Journal*, *9*(4), 295–306, https://doi.org/10.1207/s15326934crj0904_1

Helson, R., & Stewart, A. (1994). Personality change in adulthood. In T. F. Heatherton & J. L. Weinberger (Eds.), *Can personality change?* (pp. 201–225). American Psychological Association. https://doi.org/10.1037/10143-009

Hendricks, M., Guilford, J. P., & Hoepfner, R. (1969). *Measuring creative social intelligence: Reports from the psychological Laboratory #43*. University of Southern California.

Henson, R. A., & Wyke, M. A. (1982). The performance of professional musicians on the seashore measures of musical talent: An unexpected finding. *Cortex*, *18*(1), 153–157. https://doi.org/10.1016/S0010-9452(82)80026-9

Herk, N. A., & Thompson, R. C. (2012). *Strong Interest Inventory manual update: Occupational Scales Update 2012*. CPP, Inc.

Hermelin, B., & O'Connor, N. (1986). Spatial representations in mathematically and in artistically gifted children. *British Journal of Educational Psychology*, *56*(2), 150–157. https://doi.org/10.1111/j.2044-8279.1986.tb02656.x

Hicks, L. E. (1984). Conceptual and empirical analysis of some assumptions of an explicitly typological theory. *Journal of Personality and Social Psychology*, *46*(5), 1118–1131. https://doi.org/10.1037/0022-3514.46.5.1118

Highsmith, J. A. (1929). Selecting musical talent. *Journal of Applied Psychology*, *13*(5), 486–493. https://doi.org/10.1037/h0072364

Hill, R. E., & Hansen, J.-I. C. (1986). An analysis of vocational interests for female research and development managers. *Journal of Vocational Behavior*, *28*(1), 70–83. https://doi.org/10.1016/0001-8791(86)90041-2

Hiltunen, S., Pääkkönen, R., Gun-Viol Vik, G.-V., & Krause, C. M. (2016). On interpreters' working memory and executive control. *International Journal of Bilingualism*, *20*(3), 297–314. https://doi.org/10.1177/1367006914554406

Hincapié, C. A., & Cassidy, J. D. (2010). Disordered eating, menstrual disturbances, and low bone mineral density in dancers: A systematic review. *Archives of Physical Medicine and Rehabilitation*, *91*(11), 1777–1789. https://doi.org/10.1016/j.apmr.2010.07.230

Hirschi, A., & Läge, D. (2007). Holland's secondary constructs of vocational interests and career choice readiness of secondary students: Measures for related but different constructs. *Journal of Individual Differences*, *28*(4), 205–218. https://doi.org/10.1027/1614-0001.28.4.205

Hobbs, C. (1985). A comparison of the music aptitude, scholastic aptitude, and academic achievement of young children. *Psychology of Music*, *13*(2), 93–98. https://doi.org/10.1177/0305735685132003

Hoff, K. A., Briley, D. A., Wee, C. J. M., & Rounds, J. (2018). Normative changes in interests from adolescence to adulthood: A meta-analysis of longitudinal studies. *Psychological Bulletin, 144*(4), 426–451. https://doi.org/10.1037/bul0000140

Hoff, K. A., Chu, C., Einarsdóttir, S., Briley, D. A., Hanna, A., & Rounds, J. (in press). Adolescent vocational interests predict early career success: Two 12-year longitudinal studies. *Applied Psychology: An International Review.* https://doi.org/10.1111/apps.12311

Hoff, K. A., Song, Q. C., Einarsdóttir, S., Briley, D. A., & Rounds, J. (2019). Developmental structure of personality and interests: A four-wave, 8-year longitudinal study [Supplemental material]. *Journal of Personality and Social Psychology.* https://doi.org/10.1037/pspp0000228.supp

Hoff, K. A., Song, Q. C., Wee, C. J. M., Phan, W. M. J., & Rounds, J. (2020). Interest fit and job satisfaction: A systematic review and meta-analysis. *Journal of Vocational Behavior, 123,* 103503. https://doi.org/10.1016/j.jvb.2020.103503

Hoffman, M. L. (1981). Perspectives on the difference between understanding people and understanding things: The role of affect. In J. H. Flavell & L. Ross (Eds.), *Social cognitive development: Frontiers and possible futures* (pp. 67–81). Cambridge University Press.

Hogan, J., Hogan, R., & Kaiser, R. B. (2011). Management derailment. In S. Zedeck (Ed.), *APA handbook of industrial and organizational psychology: Vol. 3. Maintaining, expanding, and contracting the organization.* (pp. 555–575). American Psychological Association. https://doi.org/10.1037/12171-015

Hogan, J., & Quigley, A. (1994). Effects of preparing for physical ability tests. *Public Personnel Management, 23*(1), 85–104. https://doi.org/10.1177/009102609402300107

Hogan, R., & Hogan, J. (1992). *Hogan Personality Inventory manual* (2nd ed.). Hogan Assessment Systems.

Hogan, R., & Hogan, J. (2007). *Hogan Personality Inventory Form manual* (3rd ed.). Hogan Assessment Systems.

Hogan, R., & Hogan, J. (2009). *Hogan Developmental Survey manual.* Hogan Assessment.

Hogan Assessment Systems Inc. (2018). *Insight: Hogan Development Survey (HDS).* https://237jzd2nbeeb3ocdpdcjau97-wpengine.netdna-ssl.com/wp-content/uploads/2016/10/English_en-HDS-Insight.pdf

Holcomb, W. R., & Anderson, W. P. (1978). Expressed and inventoried vocational interests as predictors of college graduation and vocational choice. *Journal of Vocational Behavior, 12,* 290–296. https://doi.org/10.1016/0001-8791(78)90017-9

Holdnack, J. A. (2019). The development, expansion, and future of the WAIS-IV as a cornerstone in comprehensive cognitive assessments. In G. Goldstein, D. N. Allen and J. DeLuca, (Eds.) *Handbook of psychological assessment* (4th ed., pp. 103–139). Academic Press.

Holland, B. (1989, November 6). Vladimir Horowitz, 86, virtuoso pianist, dies. *New York Times,* A1.

Holland, J. L. (1958). A personality inventory employing occupational titles. *Journal of Applied Psychology, 42*(5), 336–342. https://doi.org/10.1037/h0047330

Holland, J. L. (1959). A theory of vocational choice. *Journal of Counseling Psychology, 6*(1), 35–45. https://doi.org/10.1037/h0040767

Holland, J. L. (1962). Some explorations of a theory of vocational choice: I. One- and two-year longitudinal studies. *Psychological Monographs, 76*(26, Whole No. 545)

Holland, J. L. (1963a). Explorations of a theory of vocational choice: I. Vocational images and choice. *Vocational Guidance Quarterly, 11*(4), 232–239. https://doi.org/10.1002/j.2164-585X.1963.tb00022.x

Holland, J. L. (1963b). Exploration of a theory of vocational choice: II. Self-descriptions and vocational preferences. *Vocational Guidance Quarterly, 12*(1), 17–24. https://doi.org/10.1002/j.2164-585X.1963.tb00620.x

Holland, J. L. (1963c). Explorations of a theory of vocational choice: IV. Vocational daydreams. *Vocational Guidance Quarterly, 12*(2), 93–97. https://doi.org/10.1002/j.2164-585X.1963.tb00637.x

Holland, J. L. (1963d). Explorations of a theory of vocational choice and achievement: II. A four-year prediction study. *Psychological Reports, 12*(2), 547–594. https://doi.org/10.2466/pr0.1963.12.2.547

Holland, J. L. (1966). *The psychology of vocational choice*. Blaisdell.

Holland, J. L. (1968). Explorations of a theory of vocational choice: VI. A longitudinal using a sample of typical college students. *Journal of Applied Psychology, 52*(1, Pt. 2), 1–37. https://doi.org/10.1037/h0025350

Holland, J. L. (1976a). The virtues of the SDS and its associated typology: A second response to Prediger and Hanson. *Journal of Vocational Behavior, 8*(3), 349–358. https://doi.org/10.1016/0001-8791(76)90050-6

Holland, J. L. (1976b). Vocational preferences. In M. D. Dunnette (Ed.), *Handbook of industrial/organizational psychology* (pp. 521–570). Rand McNally.

Holland, J. L. (1979). *Professional manual for the Self-Directed Search*. Consulting Psychologists Press.

Holland, J. L. (1985a). *Making vocational choices. A theory of vocational choices and work environments* (2nd ed.). Prentice-Hall.

Holland, J. L. (1985b). *The Occupations Finder for use with the Self-Directed Search*. Psychological Assessment Resources, Inc.

Holland, J. L. (1985c). *Vocational Preference Inventory (VPI) manual*. Psychological Assessment Resources.

Holland, J. L. (1987). *Manual supplement for the Self-Directed Search*. Psychological Assessment Resources, Inc.

Holland, J. L. (1996). Integrating career theory and practice: The current situation and some potential remedies. In M. L. Savickas & W. B. Walsh (Eds.), *Handbook of career counseling theory and practice* (pp. 1–12). Davies-Black.

Holland, J. L. (1997a). *Making vocational choices: A theory of vocational personalities and work environments* (3rd ed.). Psychological Assessment Resources.

Holland, J. L. (1997b). Why interest inventories are also personality inventories. In M. L. Savickas & A. R. Spokane (Eds.), *Vocational interests: Meaning, measurement, and counseling use* (pp. 87–101). Davies-Black Publishing.

Holland, J. L., Fritzsche, B. A., & Powell, A. B. (1994). *The Self-Directed Search technical manual*. Psychological Assessment Resources.

Holland, J. L., Gottfredson, D. C., & Power, P. G. (1980). Some diagnostic scales for research in decision making and personality: Identity, information, and barriers. *Journal of Personality and Social Psychology, 39*(6), 1191–1200. https://doi.org/10.1037/h0077731

Holland, J. L., Gottfredson, G. D., & Gottfredson, L. S. (1975). Read our reports and examine the data: A response to Prediger and Cole. *Journal of Vocational Behavior, 7*(2), 253–259. https://doi.org/10.1016/0001-8791(75)90065-2

Holland, J. L., Johnston, J. A., Hughey, K. F., & Asama, N. F. (1991). Some explorations of a theory of careers: VII. A replication and some possible extensions. *Journal of Career Development, 18*(2), 91–100. https://doi.org/10.1007/BF01326615

Holland, J. L., Johnston, J. A., & Asama, N. F. (1994). More evidence for the relationship between Holland's personality types and personality variables. *Journal of Career Assessment, 2*(4), 331–340. https://doi.org/10.1177/106907279400200401

Holland, J. L., & Messer, M. A. (2017). *Standard Self-Directed Search* (5th ed.). Psychological Assessment Resources.

Holland, J. L., & Nichols, R. C. (1964a). Explorations of a theory of vocational choice: III. A longitudinal study of change in major field of study. *The Personnel and Guidance Journal, 43*(3), 235–242. https://doi.org/10.1002/j.2164-4918.1964.tb02667.x

Holland, J. L., & Nichols, R. C. (1964b). Prediction of academic and extracurricular achievement in college. *Journal of Educational Psychology, 55*(1), 55–65. https://doi.org/10.1037/h0047977

Holland, J. L., & Rayman, J. R. (1986). The Self-Directed Search. In W. B. Walsh & S. H. Osipow (Eds.), *Advances in vocational psychology: Vol. 1. The assessment of interests* (p. 55–82). Lawrence Erlbaum Associates.

Holland, J. L., Whitney, D. R., Cole, N. S., & Richards, J. M., Jr. (1969). *An empirical occupational classification derived from a theory of personality and intended for practice and research* (ACT Research Report No. 29). The American College Testing Program.

Homberg, F., McCarthy, D., & Tabvuma, V. (2015). A meta-analysis of the relationship between public service motivation and job satisfaction. *Public Administration Review, 75*, 711–722. https://doi.org/10.1111/puar.12423

Hoogman, M., Stolte, M., Baas, M., & Kroesbergen, E. (2020). Creativity and ADHD: A review of behavioral studies, the effect of psychostimulants and neural underpinnings. *Neuroscience and Biobehavioral Reviews, 119*, 66–85. https://doi.org/10.1016/j.neubiorev.2020.09.029

Hopkins, M. and Bilimoria, D. (2008). Social and emotional competencies predicting success for male and female executives, *Journal of Management Development, 27*(1), 13–35. https://doi.org/10.1108/02621710810840749

Horn, J. L. (1976a). Human abilities: A review of research and theory in the early 1970s. In M. R. Rosenzweig & L. W. Porter (Eds.), *Annual Review of Psychology* (pp. 437–485). Annual Reviews, Inc. https://doi.org/10.1146/annurev.ps.27.020176.002253

Horn, J. L. (1976b). Personality and ability theory. In R. B. Cattell & R. M. Dregers (Eds.), *Handbook of modern personality theory* (pp. 139–165). Hemisphere.

Horn, J. L., & Cattell, R. B. (1966). Refinement and test of the theory of fluid and crystallized general intelligences. *Journal of Educational Psychology, 57*(5), 253–270. https://doi.org/10.1037/h0023816

Horton, J., & Walsh, W. B. (1976). Concurrent validity of Holland's theory for college degreed working women. *Journal of Vocational Behavior, 9*(2), 201–208. https://doi.org/10.1016/0001-8791(76)90078-6

Hough, L. (1990). *Personality variables and criterion-related validity: Construct confusion* [Paper presentation]. Personnel Testing Council of Southern California Annual Conference, Newport Beach, CA, United States.

Hough, L., & Dilchert, S. (2017). Personality. Its measurement and validity for employee selection. In J. L. Farr & N. T. Tippins (Eds.), *Handbook of employee selection* (2nd ed., pp. 298–325). Routledge/Taylor & Francis Group. https://doi.org/10.4324/9781315690193-13

Hough, L. M., Oswald, F. L., & Ock, J. (2015). Beyond the Big Five: New directions for personality research and practice in organizations. *Annual Review of Organizational Psychology and Organizational Behavior, 2*(1), 183–209. https://doi.org/10.1146/annurev-orgpsych-032414-111441

House, R. J., & Singh, J. V. (1987). Organizational behavior: Some new directions for I/O Psychology. *Annual Review of Psychology, 38*, 669–718. https://doi.org/10.1146/annurev.ps.38.020187.003321

Houston, D. J. (2000). Public-service motivation: A multivariate test. *Journal of Public Administration Research and Theory, 10*(4), 713–728. https://doi.org/10.1093/oxfordjournals.jpart.a024288

Houston, J. M., Harris, P. B., Howansky, K., & Houston, S. M. (2015). Winning at work: Trait competitiveness, personality types, and occupational interests. *Personality and Individual Differences, 76*, 49–51. https://doi.org/10.1016/j.paid.2014.11.046

Howard, A., & Bray, D. W. (1988). *Managerial lives in transition: Advancing age and changing times*. Guilford Press.

Howard, K. A. S., Carlstrom, A. H., Katz, A. D., Chew, A. Y., Ray, G. C., Laine, L., & Caulum, D. (2011). Career aspirations of youth: Untangling race/ethnicity, SES, and gender. *Journal of Vocational Behavior, 79*(1), 98–109. https://doi.org/10.1016/j.jvb.2010.12.002

Howarth, E. (1986). What does Eysenck's psychoticism scale really measure? *British Journal of Psychology, 77*(Pt 2), 223–227. https://doi.org/10.1111/j.2044-8295.1986.tb01996.x

Howell, W., & Fleishman, E. A. (1981). *Human performance productivity: Information processing and decision making.* Erlbaum.

Howland, A. C. (2015). *Inter-domain profiles of persons in social and enterprising careers and majors* (UMI No. 3640266) [Doctoral dissertation, Alliant International University]. ProQuest Dissertations and Theses Global.

Hughes, H. M., Jr. (1972). Vocational choice, level, and consistency: An investigation of Holland's theory for an employed sample. *Journal of Vocational Behavior, 2*(4), 377–388. https://doi.org/10.1016/0001-8791(72)90013-9

Hunt, E. (2010). *Human intelligence.* Cambridge University Press. https://doi.org/10.1017/CBO9780511781308

Hunt, T. (1928). The measurement of social intelligence. *Journal of Applied Psychology, 12*(3), 317–334. https://doi.org/10.1037/h0075832

Hunt, T. (1936). The measurement of mechanical aptitude. In T. Hunt (Ed.), *Measurement in psychology* (pp. 162–171). Prentice-Hall, Inc., https://doi.org/10.1037/11336-009

Hunt, T., Moss, F. A., Omwake, K. T., & Woodward, L. G. (1955). *George Washington University Social Intelligence Test–Revised Form* (2nd ed.). Center for Psychological Service.

Hunter, J. E. (1986). Cognitive ability, cognitive aptitudes, job knowledge, and job performance. *Journal of Vocational Behavior, 29*(3), 340–362. https://doi.org/10.1016/0001-8791(86)90013-8

Hunter, J. E., & Hunter, R. F. (1984). Validity and utility of alternative predictors of job performance. *Psychological Bulletin, 96*(1), 72–98. https://doi.org/10.1037/0033-2909.96.1.72

Hurt, D. J., & Holen, M. C. (1976). Work values in vocational interest exploration. *Journal of Vocational Behavior, 8*(1), 89–93. https://doi.org/10.1016/0001-8791(76)90037-3

Hurtz, G. M., & Donovan, J. J. (2000). Personality and job performance: The Big Five revisited. *Journal of Applied Psychology, 85*(6), 869–879. https://doi.org/10.1037/0021-9010.85.6.869

Hyland, A. M., & Muchinsky, P. M. (1991). Assessment of the structural validity of Holland's model with job analysis (PAQ) information. *Journal of Applied Psychology, 76*(1), 75–80. https://doi.org/10.1037/0021-9010.76.1.75

Iachan, R. (1984). A measure of agreement for use with the Holland classification system. *Journal of Vocational Behavior, 24*, 133–141. https://doi.org/10.1016/0001-8791(84)90001-0

Iachan, R. (1990). Some extensions of the Iachan congruence index. *Journal of Vocational Behavior, 36*, 176–180. https://doi.org/10.1016/0001-8791(90)90025-W

Institute for Personality and Ability Testing Staff. (1986). *Administrator's manual for the 16 Personality Factor Questionnaire.*

Irvine, S. H., & Berry, J. W. (1988). Abilities of mankind: A reevaluation. In S. H. Irvine & J. W. Berry (Eds.), *Human abilities in cultural context* (pp. 2–59). Cambridge University Press. https://doi.org/10.1017/CBO9780511574603.002

Ispa, M. M., Gray, M. M., & Thornburg, K. R. (1984). Childrearing attitudes of parents in person-oriented and thing-oriented occupations: A comparison. *Journal of Psychology, 117*(2), 245–250. https://doi.org/10.1080/00223980.1984.9923685

Itzkoff, D. (2019, January 14). Sara Gilbert balances her lives on 'The Conners' and 'The Talk.' *New York Times*. https://www.nytimes.com/2019/01/14/arts/television/sara-gilbert-the-conners-the- talk.html

Jacklin, C. N., Wilcox, K. T., & Maccoby, E. E. (1988). Neonatal sex-steroid hormones and cognitive abilities at six years. *Developmental Psychobiology, 21*(6), 567–574. https://doi.org/10.1002/dev.420210607

Jackson, D. N., Ahmed, S. A., & Heapy, N. A. (1976). Is achievement a unitary construct? *Journal of Research in Personality, 10*(1), 1–21. https://doi.org/10.1016/0092-6566(76)90079-9

Jackson, D. N., Holden, R. R., Locklin, R. H., & Marks, E. (1984). Taxonomy of vocational interests of academic major areas. *Journal of Educational Measurement, 21*(3), 261–275. https://doi.org/10.1111/j.1745-3984.1984.tb01033.x

Jackson, D. N., Paunonen, S. V., & Rothstein, M. G. (1987). Personnel executives: Personality, vocational interests, and job satisfaction. *Journal of Employment Counseling, 24*(3), 82–96. https://doi.org/10.1002/j.2161-1920.1987.tb00221.x

Jackson, D. N., & Williams, D. R. (1975). Occupational classification in terms of interest patterns. *Journal of Vocational Behavior, 6*(2), 269–280. https://doi.org/10.1016/0001-8791(75)90053-6

Jacobs, A., & Dunlap, D. N. (1976). The clinical interpretation of the GZTS Scales. In J. S. Guilford, W. S. Zimmerman, & J. P. Guilford (Eds.), *The Guilford-Zimmerman Temperament Survey handbook* (pp. 287–301). Edits Publishers.

Jain, N., Youngblood, P., Hasel, M., & Srivastava, S. (2017). An augmented reality tool for learning spatial anatomy on mobile devices. *Clinical Anatomy, 30*(6), 736–741.

Jamison, K. R. (1989). Mood disorders and patterns of creativity in British writers and artists. *Psychiatry: Interpersonal and Biological Processes, 52*(2), 125–134.

Jamison, K. R. (1996). *Touched with fire: Manic-depressive illness and the artistic temperament*. Free Press.

Jaskolka, G., Beyer, J. M., & Trice, H. M. (1985). Measuring and predicting managerial success. *Journal of Vocational Behavior, 26*(2), 189–205. https://doi.org/10.1016/0001-8791(85)90018-1

Jeng, H., & Liu, G. (2016). Test interactivity is promising in promoting gender equity in females' pursuit of STEM careers. *Learning and Individual Differences, 49*, 201–208. https://doi.org/10.1016/j.lindif.2016.06.018

Jenkins, S. R. (1987). Need for achievement and women's careers over 14 years: Evidence for occupational structure effects. *Journal of Personality and Social Psychology, 53*(5), 922–932. https://doi.org/10.1037/0022-3514.53.5.922

Jenkins, S. R. (1994). Need for power and women's careers over 14 years: Structural power, job satisfaction, and motive change. *Journal of Personality and Social Psychology, 66*(1), 155–165. https://doi.org/10.1037/0022-3514.66.1.155

Jensen, A. R. (1998). *The g factor: The science of mental ability*. Praeger.

Jeske, D., & Shultz, K. S. (2016). Using social media content for screening in recruitment and selection: Pros and cons. *Work, Employment and Society, 30*(3), 535–546. https://doi.org/10.1177/0950017015613746

Jiménez, K. M., Pereira-Morales, A. J., & Forero, D. A. (2017). Higher scores in the extraversion personality trait are associated with a functional polymorphism in the *PER3* gene in healthy subjects. *Chronobiology International, 34*(2), 280–286. https://doi.org/10.1080/07420528.2016.1268149

Johansson, C. B. (2003). *Career Assessment Inventory: The Vocational Version (CAI)*. Pearson Assessments.

Johnson, J. A. (1987). Influence of adolescent social crowds on the development of vocational identity, *Journal of Vocational Behavior, 31*, 182–199. https://doi.org/10.1016/0001-8791(87)90056-X

Johnson, J. A., Germer, C. K., Efran, J. S., & Overton, W. F. (1988). Personality as the basis for theoretical predilections. *Journal of Personality and Social Psychology*, *55*(5), 824–835. https://doi.org/10.1037/0022-3514.55.5.824

Johnson, J. A., & Hogan, R. (1981). Vocational interests, personality and effective police performance. *Personnel Psychology*, *34*(1), 49–53. https://doi.org/10.1111/j.1744-6570.1981.tb02176.x

Johnson, J. F., Barron, L. G., Rose, M. R., & Carretta, T. R. (2017). Validity of spatial ability tests for selection into stem (science, technology, engineering, and math) career fields: The example of military aviation. In M. Khine (Ed.), *Visual-spatial ability in STEM education*. Springer. https://doi.org/10.1007/978-3-319-44385-0_2

Johnson, R. C., & Nagoshi, C. T. (1985). Parental ability, education and occupation in Hawaii and Korea. *Personality and Individual Differences*, *6*(4), 413–423. https://doi.org/10.1016/0191-8869(85)90133-3

Johnson, R. W. (1965). Are SVIB interests correlated with differential academic achievement? *Journal of Applied Psychology*, *49*(4), 302–309. https://doi.org/10.1037/h0022411

Johnson, W., & Bouchard, T. J., Jr. (2005). The structure of human intelligence: It is verbal, perceptual, and image rotation (VPR), not fluid and crystallized. *Intelligence*, *33*(4), 393–416. https://doi.org/10.1016/j.intell.2004.12.002

Johnson, W., & Bouchard, T. J., Jr. (2009). Linking abilities, interests, and sex via latent class analysis. *Journal of Career Assessment*, *17*(1), 3–38. https://doi.org/10.1177/1069072708325738

Joint Task Force for the Development of Telepsychology Guidelines for Psychologists. (2013). Guidelines for the practice of telepsychology. *American Psychologist*, *68*(9), 791–800. https://doi.org/10.1037/a0035001

Jones, K. S., Newman, D. A., Su, R., & Rounds, J. (2020). Black-White differences in vocational interests: Meta-analysis and boundary conditions. *Journal of Business and Psychology*. Advance online publication. https://doi.org/10.1007/s10869-020-09693-5

Joyce, J. (1947). *The portable James Joyce*. The Viking Press.

Judd, T. (1988). The varieties of musical talent. In L. K. Obler & D. Fein (Eds.), *The exceptional brain: Neuropsychology of talent and special abilities* (pp. 127–155). Guilford Press.

Judge, T. A., & Bono, J. E. (2001). Relationship of core self-evaluations traits—self-esteem, generalized self-efficacy, locus of control, and emotional stability—with job satisfaction and job performance: A meta-analysis. *Journal of Applied Psychology*, *86*(1), 80–92. https://doi.org/10.1037/0021-9010.86.1.80

Judge, T. A., Jackson, C. L., Shaw, J. C., Scott, B. A., & Rich, B. L. (2007). Self-efficacy and work-related performance: The integral role of individual differences. *Journal of Applied Psychology*, *92*(1), 107–127. https://doi.org/10.1037/0021-9010.92.1.107

Judge, T. A., Rodell, J. B., Klinger, R. L., Simon, L. S., & Crawford, E. R. (2013). Hierarchical representations of the five-factor model of personality in predicting job performance: Integrating three organizing frameworks with two theoretical perspectives. *Journal of Applied Psychology*, *98*(6), 875–925. https://doi.org/10.1037/a0033901

Judge, T. A., Thoresen, C. J., Bono, J. E., & Patton, G. K. (2001). The job satisfaction-job performance relationship: A qualitative and quantitative review. *Psychological Bulletin*, *127*(3), 376–407. https://doi.org/10.1037/0033-2909.127.3.376

Jung, C. G. (1971). *The collected works of C. G. Jung: Vol. 6. Psychological types* (H. Read et al., Eds.; R. F. C. Hull, Trans.). Princeton University Press. (Original work published 1921)

Jung, R. E., Grazioplene, R., Caprihan, A., Chavez, R. S., & Haier, R. J. (2010). White matter integrity, creativity, and psychopathology: Disentangling constructs with diffusion tensor imaging. *PLOS ONE, 5*(3), e9818. https://doi.org/10.1371/journal.pone.0009818

Juni, S., & Koenig, E. J. (1982). Contingency validity as a requirement in forced-choice item construction: A critique of the Jackson Vocational Interest Survey. *Measurement and evaluation in Guidance, 14*, 202–207. https://doi.org/10.1080/00256307.1982.12022274

Kaiser, R. B., LeBreton, J. M., & Hogan, J. (2015). The dark side of personality and extreme leader behavior. *Applied Psychology, 64*(1), 55–92. https://doi.org/10.1111/apps.12024

Kandler, C., Bleidorn, W., Riemann, R., Angleitner, A., & Spinath, F. M. (2011). The genetic links between the Big Five personality traits and general interest domains. *Personality and Social Psychology Bulletin, 37*(12), 1633–1643. https://doi.org/10.1177/0146167211414275

Kantamneni, N. (2014). Vocational interest structures for Asian Americans, Middle-Eastern Americans and Native Americans on the 2005 Strong Interest Inventory. *Journal of Vocational Behavior, 84*(2), 133–141. https://doi.org/10.1016/j.jvb.2013.11.003

Kantamneni, N., & Fouad, N. (2011). Structure of vocational interests for diverse groups on the 2005 Strong Interest Inventory. *Journal of Vocational Behavior, 78*(2), 193–201. https://doi.org/10.1016/j.jvb.2010.06.003

Kapes, J. T., & Martinez, L. (1999). *Career assessment with special populations: A survey of national experts.* Education Resources Information Center. https://eric.ed.gov/?id=ED438399

Karma, K. (1983). Selecting students to music instruction. *Bulletin of the Council for Research in Music Education, 75*, 23–32.

Karma, K. (1985). Components of auditive structuring: Towards a theory of musical aptitude. *Bulletin of the Council for Research in Music Education, 82*, 1–13.

Kass, R. A., Mitchell, K. J., Grafton, F. C., & Wing, H. (1983). Factorial validity of the Armed Services Vocational Aptitude Battery (ASVAB), Forms 8, 9, and 10: 1981 Army applicant sample. *Educational and Psychological Measurement, 43*(4), 1077–1087. https://doi.org/10.1177/001316448304300417

Katz, D., & Kahn, R. L. (1978). *The social psychology of organizations* (2nd ed.). Wiley.

Kaub, K., Karbach, J., Spinath, F. M., & Brünken, R. (2016). Person-job fit in the field of teacher education—An analysis of vocational interests and requirements among novice and professional science and language teachers. *Teaching and Teacher Education, 55*, 217–227. https://doi.org/10.1016/j.tate.2016.01.010

Kaufman, J. C. (2001). Genius, lunatics and poets: Mental illness in prize-winning authors. *Imagination, Cognition and Personality, 20*(4), 305–314. https://doi.org/10.2190/M3W0-AT3T-GTLE-0L9G

Kaufman, J. C. (Ed.). (2014). *Creativity and mental illness.* Cambridge University Press. https://doi.org/10.1017/CBO9781139128902

Kaufman, J. C., Pumaccahua, T. T., & Holt, R. E. (2013). Personality and creativity in realistic, investigative, artistic, social, and enterprising college majors. *Personality and Individual Differences, 54*(8), 913–917. https://doi.org/10.1016/j.paid.2013.01.013

Kaufman, S. B., Quilty, L. C., Grazioplene, R. G., Hirsh, J. B., Gray, J. R., Peterson, J. B., & DeYoung, C. G. (2016). Openness to experience and intellect differentially predict creative achievement in the arts and sciences. *Journal of Personality, 84*(2), 248–258. https://doi.org/10.1111/jopy.12156

Kell, H. J., & Lubinski, D. (2015). Intellectual abilities for counseling interventions, practice, and theory: Dismissing their significance for learning and work constitutes malpractice. In P. J. Hartung, M. L. Savickas, & W. B. Walsh (Eds.), *APA handbook of career intervention: Vol. 1. Foundations.* (pp. 303–326). American Psychological Association. https://doi.org/10.1037/14438-017

Kelly, A. (1988). Sex stereotypes and school science: A three year follow-up. *Educational Studies, 14*, 151–163, https://doi.org/10.1080/0305569880140203

Kelso, G. I., Holland, J. L., & Gottfredson, G. D. (1977). The relation of self-reported competencies to aptitude test scores. *Journal of Vocational Behavior, 10*(1), 99–103. https://doi.org/10.1016/0001-8791(77)90046-X

Kepler, E., & Shane, S. (2007). *Are male and female entrepreneurs really that different?* Office of Advocacy, U.S. Small Business Administration.

Kern, M. L., Friedman, H. S., Martin, L. R., Reynolds, C. A., & Luong, G. (2009). Conscientiousness, career success, and longevity: A lifespan analysis. *Annals of Behavioral Medicine, 37*(2), 154–163. https://doi.org/10.1007/s12160-009-9095-6

Kernan, M. C., & Lord, R. G. (1988). Effects of participative vs. assigned goals and feedback in a multitrial task. *Motivation and Emotion, 12*(1), 75–86. https://doi.org/10.1007/BF00992473

Kessler, R. C., Angermeyer, M., Anthony, J. C., De Graaf, R., Demyttenaere, K., Gasquet, I., De Girolamo, G., Gluzman, S., Gureje, O., Haro, J. M., Kawakami, N., Karam, A., Levinson, D., Medina Mora, M. E., Oakley Browne, M. A., Posada-Villa, J., Stein, D. J., Adley Tsang, C. H., Aguilar-Gaxiola, S., . . . Üstün, T. B. (2007). Lifetime prevalence and age-of-onset distributions of mental disorders in the World Health Organization's World Mental Health Survey Initiative. *World Psychiatry, 6*(3), 168–176.

Kessler, R. C., Berglund, P., Demler, O., Jin, R., Merikangas, K. R., & Walters, E. E. (2005). Lifetime prevalence and age-of-onset distributions of DSM-IV disorders in the National Comorbidity Survey Replication. *Archives of General Psychiatry, 62*(6), 593–602. https://doi.org/10.1001/archpsyc.62.6.593

Kessler, R. C., Chiu, W. T., Demler, O., & Walters, E. E. (2005). Prevalence, severity, and comorbidity of 12-month DSM-IV disorders in the National Comorbidity Survey Replication. *Archives of General Psychiatry, 62*(6), 617–627. https://doi.org/10.1001/archpsyc.62.6.617

Kets de Vries, M. F. R. (1985). The dark side of entrepreneurship. *Harvard Business Review, 63*, 160–168.

Kihlstrom, J. F., & Cantor, N. (2011). Social intelligence. In R. J. Sternberg & S. B. Kaufman (Eds.), *The Cambridge handbook of intelligence* (pp. 564–581). Cambridge University Press. https://doi.org/10.1017/CBO9780511977244.029

Kilianski, S. E. (2003). Explaining heterosexual men's attitudes toward women and gay men: The theory of exclusively masculine identity. *Psychology of Men & Masculinity, 4*(1), 37–56. https://doi.org/10.1037/1524-9220.4.1.37

Kincel, R. L., & Murray, S. C. (1984). Kinaesthesias in perception and the experience type: Dance and creative projection. *British Journal of Projective Psychology and Personality Study, 31*(1), 19–26.

King, A. S. (1985). Self-analysis and assessment of entrepreneurial potential. *Simulation & Games, 16*(4), 399–416. https://doi.org/10.1177/104687818501600402

Kinslinger, H. J. (1966). Application of projective techniques in personnel psychology since 1940. *Psychological Bulletin, 66*(2), 134–149. https://doi.org/10.1037/h0023609

Kirkcaldy, B. (1988). Sex and personality differences in occupational interests. *Personality and Individual Differences, 9*(1), 7–13. https://doi.org/10.1016/0191-8869(88)90025-6

Klein, K. L., & Wiener, Y. (1977). Interest congruency as a moderator of the relationships between job tenure and job satisfaction and mental health. *Journal of Vocational Behavior, 10*(1), 92–98. https://doi.org/10.1016/0001-8791(77)90045-8

Klemp, G. O., & McClelland, D. C. (1986). What characterizes intelligent functioning among senior managers. In R. J. Sternberg & R. K. Wagner (Eds), *Practical intelligence: Nature and origins of competence in the everyday world* (pp. 31–50). Cambridge University Press.

Klimoski, R., & Brickner, M. (1987). Why do assessment centers work? The puzzle of assessment center validity. *Personnel Psychology, 40*(2), 234–260.

Kline, P., & Lapham, S. L. (1992). Personality and faculty in British universities. *Personality and Individual Differences, 13*(7), 855–857. https://doi.org/10.1016/0191-8869(92)90061-S

Knapp, R. R., Knapp, L., & Knapp-Lee, L. (1985). Occupational interest measurement and subsequent career decisions: A predictive follow-up study of the COPSystem Interest Inventory. *Journal of Counseling Psychology, 32*(3), 348.

Knudsen, K. S., Bookheimer, S. Y., & Bilder, R. M. (2019). Is psychopathology elevated in Big-C visual artists and scientists? *Journal of Abnormal Psychology, 128*(4), 273–283. https://doi.org/10.1037/abn0000416

Kofodimos, J. R., Kaplan, R. E., & Drath, W. H. (1986). *Anatomy of an executive. A close look at one executive's managerial character and development* (Technical Report #29). Center for Creative Leadership.

Kogan, N. (1990, August 10–14). *The performing artist: Some psychological observations* [Paper presentation]. The 98th Annual Convention of the American Psychological Association, Boston, MA, United States.

Kogan, N. (2002). Careers in the performing arts: A psychological perspective. *Creativity Research Journal, 14*(1), 1–16. https://doi.org/10.1207/S15326934CRJ1401_1

Korman, A. K. (1968). The prediction of managerial performance: A review. *Personnel Psychology, 21*(3), 295–322. https://doi.org/10.1111/j.1744-6570.1968.tb02032.x

Kotter, J. P. (1982). *The general managers*. Free Press.

Kowalski, R. M. (2001). Aversive interpersonal behaviors: On being annoying, thoughtless, and mean. In R. M. Kowalski (Ed.), *Behaving badly: Aversive behaviors in interpersonal relationships* (pp. 3–25). American Psychological Association. https://doi.org/10.1037/10365-001

Krefting, L. A., Berger, P. K., & Wallace, M. J. (1978). The contribution of sex distribution, job content, and occupational classification to job sextyping: Two studies. *Journal of Vocational Behavior, 13*(2), 181–191. https://doi.org/10.1016/0001-8791(78)90043-X

Krug, S. E. (1981). *Interpreting 16PF profile patterns*. IPAT.

Kuder, G. F. (1948). *Kuder Preference Record—Personal*. Science Research Associates.

Kuder, G. F. (1991). *Occupational Interest Survey, Form DD*. CTB McGraw-Hill.

Kumar, P., & Mutha, D. N. (1985). Teacher effectiveness as related with intelligence, anxiety and ascendance-submission. *Journal of Psychological Researches, 29*(1), 24–29.

Kunce, J. T., Decker, G. L., & Eckelman, C. C. (1976). Strong Vocational Interest Blank basic interest clusters and occupational satisfaction. *Journal of Vocational Behavior, 9*(3), 355–362. https://doi.org/10.1016/0001-8791(76)90063-4

Kuncel, N. R., & Sackett, P. R. (2014). Resolving the assessment center construct validity problem (as we know it). *Journal of Applied Psychology, 99*(1), 38–47. https://doi.org/10.1037/a0034147

Kyaga, S., Landén, M., Boman, M., Hultman, C. M., Långström, N., & Lichtenstein, P. (2013). Mental illness, suicide and creativity: 40-year prospective total population study. *Journal of Psychiatric Research, 47*(1), 83–90. https://doi.org/10.1016/j.jpsychires.2012.09.010

Ladda, A. M., Wallwork, S. B., & Lotze, M. (2020). Multimodal sensory-spatial integration and retrieval of trained motor patterns for body coordination in musicians and dancers. *Frontiers in Psychology, 11*, 3201. https://doi.org/10.3389/fpsyg.2020.576120

Laing, J., Swaney, K., & Prediger, D. J. (1984). Integrating vocational interest inventory results and expressed choices. *Journal of Vocational Behavior, 25*(3), 304–315. https://doi.org/10.1016/0001-8791(84)90053-8

Lamb, R. R., & Prediger, D. J. (1980). Construct validity of raw score and standard score reports of vocational interests. *Journal of Educational Measurement*, *17*(2), 107–115. https://doi.org/10.1111/j.1745-3984.1980.tb00819.x

Lancaster, S. J., Colarelli, S. M., King, D. W., & Beehr, T. A. (1994). Job applicant similarity on cognitive ability, vocational interests, and personality characteristics: Do similar persons choose similar jobs? *Educational and Psychological Measurement*, *54*(2), 299–316. https://doi.org/10.1177/0013164494054002005

Landy, F. J. (2005). Some historical and scientific issues related to research on emotional intelligence. *Journal of Organizational Behavior*, *26*(4), 411–424. https://doi.org/10.1002/job.317

Larsen, R. J., & Buss, D. M. (2008). *Personality psychology: Domains of knowledge about human nature* (3rd ed.). McGraw-Hill.

Larson, L. M., & Borgen, F. H. (2002). Convergence of vocational interests and personality: Examples in an adolescent gifted sample. *Journal of Vocational Behavior*, *60*(1), 91–112. https://doi.org/10.1006/jvbe.2001.1821

Larson, L. M., Rottinghaus, P. J., & Borgen, F. H. (2002). Meta-analyses of Big Six interests and Big Five personality factors. *Journal of Vocational Behavior*, *61*(2), 217–239. https://doi.org/10.1006/jvbe.2001.1854

Latona, J. R. (1989). Consistency of Holland code and its relation to persistence in a college major. *Journal of Vocational Behavior*, *34*(3), 253–265. https://doi.org/10.1016/0001-8791(89)90018-3

Lattimore, R. R., & Borgen, F. H. (1999). Validity of the 1994 Strong Interest Inventory with racial and ethnic groups in the United States. *Journal of Counseling Psychology*, *46*(2), 185–195. https://doi.org/10.1037/0022-0167.46.2.185

Laufer, W. S. (1981). The vocational interests of homeless, unemployed men. *Journal of Vocational Behavior*, *18*(2), 196–201. https://doi.org/10.1016/0001-8791(81)90007-5

Lauronen, E., Veijola, J., Isohanni, I., Jones, P. B., Nieminen, P., & Isohanni, M. (2004). Links between creativity and mental disorder. *Psychiatry: Interpersonal & Biological Processes*, *67*(1), 81–98.

Law, L. N. C., & Zentner, M. (2012). Assessing musical abilities objectively: Construction and validation of the profile of music perception skills. *PLOS ONE*, *7*(12), e52508. https://doi.org/10.1371/journal.pone.0052508

Leach, M. M., & Oakland, T. (2007). Ethics standards impacting test development and use: A review of 31 ethics codes impacting practices in 35 countries. *International Journal of Testing*, *77*(1), 1–88. https://doi.org/10.1080/15305050709336859

Lee, C. I. S. G., Bosco, F. A., Steel, P., & Uggerslev, K. L. (2017). A metaBUS-enabled meta-analysis of career satisfaction. *Career Development International*, *22*(5), 565–582. https://doi.org/10.1108/CDI-08-2017-0137

Lee, H. W., Bradburn, J., Johnson, R. E., Lin, S. J., & Chang, C. D. (2019). The benefits of receiving gratitude for helpers: A daily investigation of proactive and reactive helping at work. *Journal of Applied Psychology*, *104*(2), 197–213. https://doi.org/10.1037/apl0000346

Lee, K., & Ashton, M. C. (2004a). Psychometric properties of the HEXACO personality inventory. *Multivariate Behavioral Research*, *39*(2), 329–358. https://doi.org/10.1207/s15327906mbr3902_8

Lee, K., & Ashton, M. C. (2004b). Scale descriptions. In *The HEXACO Personality Inventory—Revised. A measure of the six dimensions of personality*. http://hexaco.org/scaledescriptions

Lehman, P. R. (1968). *Tests and measurements in music*. Prentice-Hall.

Lemos, G. C., Abad, F. J., Almeida, L. S., & Colom, R. (2013). Sex differences on g and non-g intellectual performance reveal potential sources of STEM discrepancies. *Intelligence*, *41*(1), 11–18. https://doi.org/10.1016/j.intell.2012.10.009

Lent, R. W., Larkin, K. C., & Brown, S. D. (1989). Relation of self-efficacy to inventoried vocational interests. *Journal of Vocational Behavior*, *34*, 279–288. https://doi.org/10.1016/0001-8791(89)90020-1

Leong, F. T. L., & Hartung, P. J. (2000). Cross-cultural career assessment: Review and prospects for the new millennium. *Journal of Career Assessment*, *8*(4), 391–401. https://doi.org/10.1177/106907270000800408

Leong, F. T. L., & Leung, S. A. (1994). Career assessment with Asian-Americans. *Journal of Career Assessment*, *2*(3), 240–257. https://doi.org/10.1177/106907279400200304

Lester, D. (1983). Why do people become police officers: A study of reasons and their predictions of success. *Journal of Police Science and Administration*, *11*(2), 170–174.

Leutner, F., & Chamorro-Premuzic, T. (2018). Stronger together: Personality, intelligence and the assessment of career potential. *Journal of Intelligence*, *6*(4), 49, 1–10. https://doi.org/10.3390/jintelligence6040049

Leuty, M. E., & Hansen, J.-I. C. (2013). Building evidence of validity: The relation between work values, interests, personality, and personal values. *Journal of Career Assessment*, *21*(2), 175–189. https://doi.org/10.1177/1069072712466714

Leuty, M. E., & Hansen, J.-I. C. (2014). Teasing apart the relations between age, birth cohort, and vocational interests. *Journal of Counseling Psychology*, *61*(2), 289–298. https://doi.org/10.1037/a0035341

Leuty, M. E., Hansen, J.-I. C., & Speaks, S. Z. (2016). Vocational and leisure interests. *Journal of Career Assessment*, *24*(2), 215–239. https://doi.org/10.1177/1069072715580321

Levanon, A., England, P., & Allison, P. (2009). Occupational feminization and pay: Assessing causal dynamics using 1950–2000 U.S. Census Data. *Social Forces*, *88*(2), 865–891. https://doi.org/10.1353/sof.0.0264

Leventhal, A. M. (1966). An anxiety scale for the CPI. *Journal of Clinical Psychology*, *22*(4), 459–461. https://doi.org/10.1002/1097-4679(196610)22:4<459::AID-JCLP2270220426>3.0.CO;2-U

Levin, N., Braunstein-Bercovitz, H., Lipshits-Braziler, Y., Gati, I., & Rossier, J. (2020). Testing the structure of the Career Decision-Making Difficulties Questionnaire across country, gender, age, and decision status. *Journal of Vocational Behavior*, *116*(Part A). https://doi.org/10.1016/j.jvb.2019.103365

Levine, S. S., Bernard, M., & Nagel, R. (2017). Strategic intelligence: The cognitive capability to anticipate competitor behavior. *Strategic Management Journal*, *38*(12), 2390–2423. https://doi.org/10.1002/smj.2660

Levy, M. F., Reichman, W., & Herrington, S. (1979). Congruence between personality and job characteristics in alcoholics and nonalcoholics. *Journal of Social Psychology*, *107*(2), 213–217. https://doi.org/10.1080/00224545.1979.9922701

Lievens, F., & Chan, D. (2017). Practical intelligence, emotional intelligence, and social intelligence. In J. L. Farr & N. T. Tippins (Eds.), *Handbook of employee selection* (2nd ed., pp. 342–364). Routledge/Taylor & Francis Group. https://doi.org/10.4324/9781315690193-15

Likert, R., & Quasha, W. H. (1970). *Revised Minnesota Paper Form Board Test*. Psychological Corporation.

Lindley, R. H., Smith, W. R., & Thomas, T. J. (1988). The relationship between speed of information processing as measured by timed paper-and-pencil tests and psychometric intelligence. *Intelligence*, *12*(1), 17–25. https://doi.org/10.1016/0160-2896(88)90020-7

Link, B. G., & Phelan, J. C. (2013). Labeling and stigma. In C. S. Aneshensel, J. C. Phelan, & A. Bierman (Eds.), *Handbook of the sociology of mental health* (2nd ed., pp. 525–541). Springer Science + Business Media. https://doi.org/10.1007/978-94-007-4276-5_25

Lipman-Blumen, J., Handley-Isaksen, A., & Leavitt, H. J. (1983). Achieving styles in men and women: A model, an instrument, and some findings. In J. T. Spence (Ed.), *Achievement and achievement motives. Psychological and sociological approaches* (pp. 147–204). W. H. Freeman.

Lipman-Blumen, J., Leavitt, H. J., Patterson, K. J., Bies, R. J., & Handley-Isaksen, A. (1980). A model of direct and relational achieving styles. In L. J. Fyans (Ed.), *Achievement motivation* (pp. 135–168). Plenum. https://doi.org/10.1007/978-1-4757-8997-3_7

Lippa, R. A. (2005). *Gender, nature, and nurture* (2nd ed.). Routledge. https://doi.org/10.4324/9781410612946

Lippa, R. A. (2006). The gender reality hypothesis. *American Psychologist, 61*(6), 639–640. https://doi.org/10.1037/0003-066X.61.6.639

Livneh, H., & Livneh, C. (1989). The five-factor model of personality: Is evidence of its cross-measure validity premature? *Personality and Individual Differences, 10*(1), 75–80. https://doi.org/10.1016/0191-8869(89)90181-5

Logue, C. T., Lounsbury, J. W., Gupta, A., & Leong, F. T. L. (2007). Vocational interest themes and personality traits in relation to college major satisfaction of business students. *Journal of Career Development, 33*(3), 269–295. https://doi.org/10.1177/0894845306297348

Lohman, D. F. (1979). *Spatial ability: A review and reanalysis of the correlational literature* (Technical Report No. 8). Stanford University.

Lord, T. R. (1985). Enhancing the visuo-spatial aptitude of students. *Journal of Research in Science Teaching, 22*(5), 395–405. https://doi.org/10.1002/tea.3660220503

Lounsbury, J. W., Foster, N., Patel, H., Carmody, P., Gibson, L. W., & Stairs, D. R. (2012). An investigation of the personality traits of scientists versus nonscientists and their relationship with career satisfaction. *R&D Management, 42*(1), 47–59. https://doi.org/10.1111/j.1467-9310.2011.00665.x

Low, K. S. D., Yoon, M., Roberts, B. W., & Rounds, J. (2005). The stability of vocational interests from early adolescence to middle adulthood: A quantitative review of longitudinal studies. *Psychological Bulletin, 131*(5), 713–737. https://doi.org/10.1037/0033-2909.131.5.713

Lowenkopf, E. L., & Vincent, L. M. (1982). The student ballet dancer and anorexia. *Hillside Journal of Clinical Psychiatry, 4*(1), 53–64.

Lowman, R. L. (1987). Occupational choice as a moderator of psychotherapeutic approach. *Psychotherapy: Theory, Research, & Practice, 24*(4), 801–808. https://doi.org/10.1037/h0085782

Lowman, R. L. (1989). *Pre-employment screening for psychopathology: A guide to professional practice*. Professional Resource Exchange.

Lowman, R. L. (1991). *The clinical practice of career assessment: Interests, abilities, and personality*. American Psychological Association. https://doi.org/10.1037/10091-000

Lowman, R. L. (1993a). *Counseling and psychotherapy of work dysfunctions*. American Psychological Association. https://doi.org/10.1037/10133-000

Lowman, R. L. (1993b). The inter-domain model of career assessment and counseling. *Journal of Counseling and Development, 71*(5), 549–554. https://doi.org/10.1002/j.1556-6676.1993.tb02240.x

Lowman, R. L. (1993c). Malpractice of what and by whom? Will the real straw theory please stand up. *Journal of Counseling and Development, 71*(5), 558–559. https://doi.org/10.1002/j.1556-6676.1993.tb02242.x

Lowman, R. L. (2003). Interest. In R. Fernandez-Ballesteros (Ed.), *Encyclopedia of psychological assessment* (pp. 477–480). Sage.

Lowman, R. L. (Ed.). (2013). *Internationalizing multiculturalism: Expanding professional competencies in a globalized world*. American Psychological Association. https://doi.org/10.1037/14044-000

Lowman, R. L. (2018). Ethical and legal concerns in internet-based testing. In J. C. Scott, D. Bartram, & D. H. Reynolds (Eds.), *Next generation technology-enhanced assessment: Global perspectives on occupational and workplace testing* (pp. 350–374). Cambridge University Press.

Lowman, R. L., & Carson, A. D. (2012). Conceptualization and assessment of interests. In J. R. Graham & J. A. Naglieri (Eds.), *Handbook of psychology* (2nd ed.). Wiley. https://doi.org/10.1002/9781118133880.hop210020

Lowman, R. L., & Cooper, S. E. (2018). *The ethical practice of consulting psychology*. American Psychological Association. https://doi.org/10.1037/0000058-000

Lowman, R. L. & Leeman, G. E. (1988). The dimensionality of social intelligence: Social interests, abilities and needs. *Journal of Psychology, 122*(3), 279–290. https://doi.org/10.1080/00223980.1988.9915516

Lowman, R. L., & Ng, Y. (2010). Interest, ability and personality characteristics of two samples of employed Realistic males: Implications for management and assessment. *Psychologist Manager Journal, 13*(3), 147–163. https://doi.org/10.1080/10887156.2010.500259

Lowman, R. L., Palmer, L. K., Santana, R., & Abbott, J. (2003). Executive and career assessment. Can alternative occupational interest measures be used interchangeably? *Psychologist Manager Journal, 6*(2), 65–78. https://doi.org/10.1037/h0095927

Lowman, R. L., & Schurman, S. J. (1982). Psychometric characteristics of a Vocational Preference Inventory short form. *Educational and Psychological Measurement, 42*(2), 601–613. https://doi.org/10.1177/001316448204200225

Lowman, R. L., & Williams, R. E. (1987). Validity of self-ratings of abilities and competencies. *Journal of Vocational Behavior, 31*(1), 1–13. https://doi.org/10.1016/0001-8791(87)90030-3

Lowman, R. L., Williams, R. E., & Leeman, G. E. (1985). The structure and relationship of college women's primary abilities and vocational interests. *Journal of Vocational Behavior, 27*(3), 298–315. https://doi.org/10.1016/0001-8791(85)90038-7

Lubinski, D., Benbow, C. P., & Ryan, J. (1995). Stability of vocational interests among the intellectually gifted from adolescence to adulthood: A 15-year longitudinal study. *Journal of Applied Psychology, 80*(1), 196–200. https://doi.org/10.1037/0021-9010.80.1.196

Lubinski, D., & Dawis, R. V. (Eds.). (1995). *Assessing individual differences in human behavior: New concepts, methods, and findings*. Davies-Black Publishing.

Lubinski, D., Tellegen, A., & Butcher, J. N. (1983). Masculinity, femininity, and androgyny viewed and assessed as distinct concepts. *Journal of Personality and Social Psychology, 44*(2), 428–439. https://doi.org/10.1037/0022-3514.44.2.428

Lucas, R. E., & Donnellan, M. B. (2011). Personality development across the life span: Longitudinal analyses with a national sample from Germany. *Journal of Personality and Social Psychology, 101*(4), 847–861. https://doi.org/10.1037/a0024298

Ludwig, A. M. (1998). Method and madness in the arts and sciences. *Creativity Research Journal, 11*(2), 93–101. https://doi.org/10.1207/s15326934crj1102_1

Lundin, R. W. (1949). The development and validation of a set of music ability tests. *Psychological Monographs, 63*(10), i–20. https://doi.org/10.1037/h0093616

Lundin, R. W. (1967). *An objective psychology of music* (2nd ed.). Ronald Press.

Lunneborg, P. W. (1975). Interest differentiation in high school and vocational indecision in college. *Journal of Vocational Behavior, 7*(3), 297–303. https://doi.org/10.1016/0001-8791(75)90071-8

Lunneborg, P. W. (1979). The Vocational Interest Inventory: Development and validation. *Educational and Psychological Measurement, 39*(2), 445–451. https://doi.org/10.1177/001316447903900226

Lunneborg, P. W., & Gerry, M. H. (1977). Sex differences in changing sex-stereotyped vocational interests. *Journal of Counseling Psychology, 24*, 247–250. https://doi.org/10.1037/0022-0167.24.3.247

Lykken, D. T., Bouchard, T. J., Jr., McGue, M., & Tellegen, A. (1993). Heritability of interests: A twin study. *Journal of Applied Psychology, 78*(4), 649–661. https://doi.org/10.1037/0021-9010.78.4.649

Lynn, R., & Gault, A. (1986). The relation of musical ability to general intelligence and the major primaries. *Research in Education, 36*(1), 59–64. https://doi.org/10.1177/003452378603600107

Lynn, R., & Hampson, S. (1987). Further evidence on the cognitive abilities of the Japanese: Data from the WPPSI. *International Journal of Behavioral Development, 10*(1), 23–36. https://doi.org/10.1177/016502548701000102

Lyons, M. J., Panizzon, M. S., Liu, W., McKenzie, R., Bluestone, N. J., Grant, M. D., Franz, C. E., Vuoksimaa, E. P., Toomey, R., Jacobson, K. C., Reynolds, C. A., Kremen, W. S., & Xian, H. (2017). A longitudinal twin study of general cognitive ability over four decades. *Developmental Psychology, 53*(6), 1170–1177. https://doi.org/10.1037/dev0000303

Maccoby, E. E., & Jacklin, C. N. (1974). *The psychology of sex differences*. Stanford University Press.

Mackinnon, D. W. (1962). *The personality correlates of creativity: A study of American architects*. In G. Nielson (Ed.), *Proceedings of the XIV International Congress of Applied Psychology. Vol. 2. Personality research* (p. 11–39). Munksgaard.

Mackinnon, D. W. (1970). The personality correlates of creativity: A study of American architects. In P. E. Vernon (Ed.), *Creativity: Selected readings* (pp. 289–311). Penguin.

MacLeod, C. M., Jackson, R. A., & Palmer, J. (1986). On the relation between spatial ability and field dependence. *Intelligence, 10*(2), 141–151. https://doi.org/10.1016/0160-2896(86)90011-5

MacQuarrie, T. W. (1927). A mechanical ability test. *Journal of Personnel Research, 5*(9), 329–337.

Maguire, E. A., Woollett, K., & Spiers, H. J. (2006). London taxi drivers and bus drivers: A structural MRI and neuropsychological analysis. *Hippocampus, 16*(12), 1091–1101. https://doi.org/10.1002/hipo.20233

Maitra, A. K. (1983). Executive effectiveness: Characteristic thematic phantasy. *Managerial Psychology, 4*, 59–68.

Malafouris, L. (2020). Thinking as "thinking": Psychology with things. *Current Directions in Psychological Science, 29*(1), 3–8. https://doi.org/10.1177/0963721419873349

Marco, C. D., Hartung, P. J., Newman, I., & Parr, P. (2003). Validity of the decisional process inventory. *Journal of Vocational Behavior, 63*(1), 1–19. https://doi.org/10.1016/S0001-8791(02)00018-0

Marcus, B., Goffin, R. D., Johnston, N. G., & Rothstein, M. G. (2007). Personality and cognitive ability as predictors of typical and maximum managerial performance. *Human Performance, 20*(3), 275–285. https://doi.org/10.1080/08959280701333362

Margolis, A., Bansal, R., Hao, X., Algermissen, M., Erickson, C., Klahr, K. W., Naglieri, J. A.,& Peterson, B. S. (2013). Using IQ discrepancy scores to examine the neural correlates of specific cognitive abilities. *Journal of Neuroscience, 33*(35), 14135–14145. https://doi.org/10.1523/JNEUROSCI.0775-13.2013

Markham, S., & Sugarman, L. (1978). The Connolly Occupational Interests Questionnaire: Some psychometric data and comments on its use in counselling. *British Journal of Guidance and Counselling, 6*(1), 75–81. https://doi.org/10.1080/03069887808256324

Markman, G. D. (2007). Entrepreneurs' competencies. In J. R. Baum, M. Frese, & R. A. Baron (Eds.), *The psychology of entrepreneurship* (pp. 67–92). Lawrence Erlbaum Associates Publishers.

Marmor, G. S., & Zaback, L. A. (1976). Mental rotation by the blind: Does mental rotation depend on visual imagery? *Journal of Experimental Psychology: Human Perception and Performance, 2*(4), 515–521. https://doi.org/10.1037/0096-1523.2.4.515

Martin, J. D., Blair, G. E., Dannenmaier, W. D., Jones, P. C., & Asako, M. (1981). Relationship of scores on the California Psychological Inventory to age. *Psychological Reports, 49*(1), 151–154. https://doi.org/10.2466/pr0.1981.49.1.151

Matarazzo, J. D. (1972). *Wechsler's measurement and appraisal of adult intelligence* (5th ed.). William & Wilkins.

Matheson, K., & Strickland, L. (1986). The stereotype of the computer scientist. *Canadian Journal of Behavioural Science / Revue Canadienne Des Sciences Du Comportement, 18*(1), 15–24. https://doi.org/10.1037/h0079953

Mayberry, P. W., & Carey, N. B. (1997). The effect of aptitude and experience on mechanical job performance. *Educational and Psychological Measurement, 57*(1), 131–149. https://doi.org/10.1177/0013164497057001010

Mayer, D. M. (2018). How men get penalized for straying from masculine norms. *Harvard Business Review Digital Articles*, 7–11. https://hbr.org/2018/10/how-men-get-penalized-for-straying-from-masculine-norms

Mayer, J. D., Caruso, D. R., Zigler, E., & Dreyden, J. I. (1989). Intelligence and intelligence-related personality traits. *Intelligence, 13*(2), 119–133. https://doi.org/10.1016/0160-2896(89)90011-1

Mayer, J. D., Salovey, P., & Caruso, D. R. (2002). *Mayer–Salovey–Caruso Emotional Intelligence Test (MSCEIT) user's manual*. MHS Publishers.

Mayer, J. D., Salovey, P., & Caruso, D. R. (2008). Emotional intelligence: New ability or eclectic traits? *American Psychologist, 63*(6), 503–517. https://doi.org/10.1037/0003-066X.63.6.503

Mayer, J. D., Salovey, P., Caruso, D., & Cherkasskiy, L. (2011). Emotional intelligence. In R. J. Sternberg & J. Kaufman (Eds.), *The Cambridge handbook of intelligence* (3rd ed., pp. 528–549). Cambridge University Press.

Mayer, J. D., Salovey, P., Caruso, D. R., & Sitarenios, G. (2003). Measuring emotional intelligence with the MSCEIT V2.0. *Emotion, 3*(1), 97–105. https://doi.org/10.1037/1528-3542.3.1.97

Mayer, R. E. (2011). Intelligence and achievement. In R. J. Sternberg and S. B. Kaufman (Eds.). *Cambridge handbook of intelligence* (738–747). Cambridge University Press.

McCall, M. W., & Lombardo, M. M. (1983). *Off the track: Why and how successful executives get derailed* (Tech. Rep. No. 21). Center for Creative Leadership.

McClelland, D. C. (1961). *The achieving society*. Van Nostrand. https://doi.org/10.1037/14359-000

McClelland, D. C. (1975). *Power: The inner experience*. Irvington-Wiley.

McClelland, D. C. (1985). *Human motivation*. Scott Foresman.

McClelland, D. C. (1987). Characteristics of successful entrepreneurs. *Journal of Creative Behavior, 21*(3), 219–233. https://doi.org/10.1002/j.2162-6057.1987.tb00479.x

McClelland, D. C., & Boyatzis, R. E. (1982). The leadership motive pattern and long-term success in management. *Journal of Applied Psychology, 67*(6), 737–743. https://doi.org/10.1037/0021-9010.67.6.737

McClelland, D. C., & Burnham, R. E. (1976). Power is the great motivator. *Harvard Business Review, 81*(1), 117–126.

McClelland, D. C., & Winter, D. G. (1969). *Motivating economic achievement*. Free Press.

McCrae, R. R. (1987). Creativity, divergent thinking, and openness to experience. *Journal of Personality and Social Psychology, 52*(6), 1258–1265. https://doi.org/10.1037/0022-3514.52.6.1258

McCrae, R. R. (1994). Openness to experience: Expanding the boundaries of Factor V. *European Journal of Personality, 8*(4), 251–272. https://doi.org/10.1002/per.2410080404

McCrae, R. R., & Costa, P. T., Jr. (1985a). Comparison of EI and psychoticism scales with measures of the five-factor model of personality. *Personality and Individual Differences, 6*(5), 587–597. https://doi.org/10.1016/0191-8869(85)90008-X

McCrae, R. R., & Costa, P. T., Jr. (1985b). Updating Norman's "Adequate Taxonomy": Intelligence and personality dimensions in natural language and in questionnaires. *Journal of Personality and Social Psychology, 49*(3), 710–721. https://doi.org/10.1037/0022-3514.49.3.710

McCrae, R. R., Costa, P. T., Jr., & Piedmont, R. L. (1993). Folk concepts, natural language, and psychological constructs: The California Psychological Inventory and the five-factor model. *Journal of Personality, 61*(1), 1–26. https://doi.org/10.1111/j.1467-6494.1993.tb00276.x

McCrae, R. R., & Sutin, A. R. (2009). Openness to experience. In M. R. Leary & R. H. Hoyle (Eds.), *Handbook of individual differences in social behavior* (pp. 257–273). Guilford Press.

McCutchen, D. (1986). Domain knowledge and linguistic knowledge in the development of writing ability. *Journal of Memory and Language, 25*(4), 431–444. https://doi.org/10.1016/0749-596X(86)90036-7

McDonough, I. M., Bischof, G. N., Kennedy, K. M., Rodrigue, K. M., Farrell, M. E., & Park, D. C. (2016). Discrepancies between fluid and crystallized ability in healthy adults: A behavioral marker of preclinical Alzheimer's disease. *Neurobiology of Aging, 46*, 68–75. https://doi.org/10.1016/j.neurobiolaging.2016.06.011

McGee, M. G. (1979). *Human spatial abilities. Sources of sex differences.* Praeger.

McGue, M., Bouchard, T. J., Jr., Lykken, D. T., & Feuer, D. (1984). Information processing abilities in twins reared apart. *Intelligence, 8*(3), 239–258. https://doi.org/10.1016/0160-2896(84)90010-2

McKay, D. A., & Tokar, D. M. (2012). The HEXACO and five-factor models of personality in relation to RIASEC vocational interests. *Journal of Vocational Behavior, 81*(2), 138–149. https://doi.org/10.1016/j.jvb.2012.05.006

McLeish, J., & Higgs, G. (1982). Musical ability and mental subnormality: An experimental investigation. *British Journal of Educational Psychology, 52*(3), 370–373. https://doi.org/10.1111/j.2044-8279.1982.tb02524.x

Mebert, C. J., & Michel, G. F. (1980). Handedness in artists. In J. Heron (Ed.), *The neuropsychology of left-handedness* (pp. 273–279). Academic Press.

Megargee, E. I. (1972). *The California Psychological Inventory handbook.* Jossey Bass.

Megargee, E. I., & Carbonell, J. L. (1988). Evaluating leadership with the CPI. In C. D. Spielberger & J. N. Butcher (Eds.), *Advances in personality assessment* (Vol. 7, pp. 203–210). Erlbaum.

Mehta, M., & Agrawal, R. (1986). Effect of need for achievement and repression sensitization dimension upon job satisfaction of bank employees. *Indian Journal of Applied Psychology, 23*(1), 39–44.

Meier, N. C. (1928). A measure of art talent. *Psychological Monographs, 39*(2), 184–199.

Meier, N. C. (1939). Factors in artistic aptitude. *Psychological Monographs. 51*(5), 1–158.

Meier, N. C. (1942). *Art in human affairs.* McGraw Hill.

Meir, E. I. (1988). The need for congruence between within-occupation interests and specialty in mid-career. *Career Development Quarterly, 37*(1), 63–69.

Meir, E. I., Rivka Bar, R., Gabi Lahav, G., & Shalhevet, S. (1975). Interest inventories based on Roe's classification modified for negative respondents. *Journal of Vocational Behavior, 7*(1), 127–133. https://doi.org/10.1016/0001-8791(75)90039-1

Melamed, S. & Meir, E. T. (1981). The relationships between interests, job incongruity and selection of avocational activity. *Journal of Vocational Behavior, l8*(3), 310–325. https://doi.org/10.1016/0001-8791(81)90018-X

Mell, J. C., Howard, S. M., & Miller, B. L. (2003). Art and the brain: The influence of frontotemporal dementia on an accomplished artist. *Neurology, 60*(10), 1707–1710. https://doi.org/10.1212/01.WNL.0000064164.02891.12

Melville, H. (1977). *Moby Dick*. Easton Press. (Original work published 1851)

Metzler-Brennan, E., Lewis, R. J., & Gerrard, M. (1985). Childhood antecedents of adult women's masculinity, femininity, and career role choices. *Psychology of Women Quarterly, 9*(3), 371–381. https://doi.org/10.1111/j.1471-6402.1985.tb00887.x

Meudell, P. R., & Greenhalgh, M. (1987). Age related differences in left and right hand skill and in visuo-spatial performance: Their possible relationships to the hypothesis that the right hemisphere ages more rapidly than the left. *Cortex, 23*(3), 431–445. https://doi.org/10.1016/S0010-9452(87)80005-9

Midorikawa, A., & Kawamura, M. (2015). The emergence of artistic ability following traumatic brain injury. *Neurocase, 21*(1), 90–94. https://doi.org/10.1080/13554794.2013.873058

Miller, B. L., Cummings, J., Mishkin, F., Boone, K., Prince, F., Ponton, M., & Cotman, C. (1998). Emergence of artistic talent in frontotemporal dementia. *Neurology, 51*(4), 978–982. https://doi.org/10.1212/WNL.51.4.978

Miller, B. L., & Hou, C. E. (2004). Portraits of artists: Emergence of visual creativity in dementia. *Archives of Neurology, 61*(6), 842–844. https://doi.org/10.1001/archneur.61.6.842

Miller, D., & Droge, C. (1986). Psychological and traditional determinants of structure. *Administrative Science Quarterly, 31*(4), 539–560. https://doi.org/10.2307/2392963

Miller, L. K. (1999). The Savant Syndrome: Intellectual impairment and exceptional skill. *Psychological Bulletin, 125*(1), 31–46. https://doi.org/10.1037/0033-2909.125.1.31

Miller, M. J., McKee, T., Springer, T. P., & Soper, B. (1985). Vocational interest patterns among varsity football athletes. *College Student Journal, 19*(2), 144–151.

Mills, J. I. (1984). The "pitch" subtest of Bentley's Measures of Musical Abilities: A test form the 1960s reconsidered in the 1980s. *Psychology of Music, 12*(2), 94–105. https://doi.org/10.1177/0305735684122003

Miner, J. B. (1978). Twenty years of research on role-motivation theory of managerial effectiveness. *Personnel Psychology, 31*(4), 739–760. https://doi.org/10.1111/j.1744-6570.1978.tb02122.x

Miner, J. B. (1985). Sentence completion measures in personnel research: The development and validation of the Miner Sentence Completion Scales. In H. A. Bernardin & D. A. Bownas (Eds.), *Personality assessment in organizations* (pp. 145–176). Praeger.

Minogue, B. M. (1923). A case of secondary mental deficiency with musical talent. *Journal of Applied Psychology, 7*(4), 349–352. https://doi.org/10.1037/h0073149

Mintzberg, H. (1973). *The nature of managerial work*. Harper & Row.

Mischel, W. (2014). *The marshmallow test: Why self-control is the engine of success*. Little, Brown.

Mittelstädt, J. M., Pecena, Y., Oubaid, V., & Maschke, P. (2016). Psychometric personality differences between candidates in astronaut selection. *Aerospace Medicine and Human Performance, 87*(11), 933–939. https://doi.org/10.3357/AMHP.4548.2016

Mohan, V., & Brar, A. (1986). Motives and work efficiency. *Personality Study & Group Behaviour, 6*(2), 37–45.

Moloney, D. P., Bouchard, T. J., Jr., & Segal, N. L. (1991). A genetic and environmental analysis of the vocational interests of monozygotic and dizygotic twins reared apart. *Journal of Vocational Behavior, 39*(1), 76–109. https://doi.org/10.1016/0001-8791(91)90005-7

Monahan, C. J. (1987). Construct validation of a modified differentiation index. *Journal of Vocational Behavior, 30*(3), 217–226. https://doi.org/10.1016/0001-8791(87)90001-7

Moore, T. E., Richards, B., & Hood, J. (1984). Aging and the coding of spatial information. *Journal of Gerontology, 39*(2), 210–212. https://doi.org/10.1093/geronj/39.2.210

Morey, L. C., Hopwood, C. J., Markowitz, J. C., Gunderson, J. G., Grilo, C. M., McGlashan, T. H., Shea, M. T., Yen, S., Sanislow, C. A., Ansell, E. B., & Skodol, A. E. (2012). Comparison of alternative models for personality disorders, II: 6-, 8- and 10-year follow-up. *Psychological Medicine, 42*(8), 1705–1713. https://doi.org/10.1017/S0033291711002601

Morris, L. W. (1979). *Extraversion and introversion. An interactional perspective*. Hemisphere Publishers.

Morris, M. L. (2016). Vocational interests in the United States: Sex, age, ethnicity, and year effects. *Journal of Counseling Psychology, 63*(5), 604–615. https://doi.org/10.1037/cou0000164

Morrow, R. S. (1938). An analysis of the relations among tests of musical, artistic, and mechanical abilities. *Journal of Psychology, 5*(2), 253–263. https://doi.org/10.1080/00223980.1938.9917566

Moscoso, S., & Salgado, J. F. (2004). "Dark side" personality styles as predictors of task, contextual, and job performance. *International Journal of Selection and Assessment, 12*(4), 356–362. https://doi.org/10.1111/j.0965-075X.2004.00290.x

Mosing, M. A., Madison, G., Pedersen, N. L., Kuja-Halkola, R., & Ullén, F. (2014). Practice does not make perfect: No causal effect of music practice on music ability. *Psychological Science, 25*(9), 1795–1803. https://doi.org/10.1177/0956797614541990

Moss, F. A., Hunt, T., & Omwake, K. T. (1930). Social Intelligence Test. *PsycTESTS*.

Mount, M. K., Barrick, M. R., Scullen, S. M., & Rounds, J. (2005). Higher-order dimensions of the Big Five personality traits and the Big Six vocational interest types. *Personnel Psychology, 58*(2), 447–478. https://doi.org/10.1111/j.1744-6570.2005.00468.x

Mount, M. K., Oh, I.-S., & Burns, M. (2008). Incremental validity of perceptual speed and accuracy over general mental ability. *Personnel Psychology, 61*(1), 113–139. https://doi.org/10.1111/j.1744-6570.2008.00107.x

Muchinsky, P. M. (1993). Validation of intelligence and mechanical aptitude tests in selecting employees for manufacturing jobs. *Journal of Business and Psychology, 7*(4), 373–382. https://doi.org/10.1007/BF01013752

Muchinsky, P. M. (2004). Mechanical aptitude and spatial ability testing. In J. C. Thomas (Ed.), *Comprehensive handbook of psychological assessment: Vol. 4. Industrial and organizational assessment* (pp. 21–34). Wiley.

Mumford, M. D., & Gustafson, S. B. (1988). Creativity syndrome: Integration, application, and innovation. *Psychological Bulletin, 103*(1), 27–43.

Mumford, M. D., & Owens, W. A. (1982). Life history and vocational interests. *Journal of Vocational Behavior, 21*(3), 330–348.

Murakami, H. (2000). *Norwegian wood*. Knopf Doubleday Publishing Group.

Murray, H. A. (1938). *Explorations in personality*. Oxford University Press.

Murray, H. A. (1943). *Thematic Apperception Test*. Harvard University Press.

Mursell, J. L. (1939). Intelligence and musicality. *Education, 59*(9), 559–562.

Mussel, P., Winter, C., Gelléri, P., & Schuler, H. (2011). Explicating the openness to experience construct and its subdimensions and facets in a work setting. *International Journal of Selection and Assessment, 19*(2), 145–156. https://doi.org/10.1111/j.1468-2389.2011.00542.x

Myers, I. B. (1980). *Gifts differing*. Consulting Psychologists Press.

Myers, I. B. (1987). *Introduction to type*. Consulting Psychologists Press.

Myers, I. B., McCaulley, M. H., Quenk, N. L., & Hammer, A. L. (1998). *MBTI manual: A guide to the development and use of the Myers-Briggs Type Indicator* (3rd ed.). Consulting Psychological Press.

Nafziger, D. H., Holland, J. L., & Gottfredson, G. D. (1975). Student-college congruency as a predictor of satisfaction. *Journal of Counseling Psychology, 22*(2), 132–139. https://doi.org/10.1037/h0076340

Naglieri, J. A. (2003). Naglieri Nonverbal Ability Tests. In R. S. McCallum (Ed.), *Handbook of nonverbal assessment* (pp. 175–189). Springer. https://doi.org/10.1007/978-1-4615-0153-4_9

Naglieri, J. A., & Ford, D. Y. (2015). Misconceptions about the Naglieri Nonverbal Ability Test: A commentary of concerns and disagreements. *Roeper Review, 37*(4), 234–240. https://doi.org/10.1080/02783193.2015.1077497

Nagoshi, C. T., & Johnson, R. C. (1987). Cognitive abilities profiles of Caucasian vs. Japanese subjects in the Hawaii Study of Cognition. *Personality and Individual Differences, 8*(4), 581–583. https://doi.org/10.1016/0191-8869(87)90223-6

Naoumenko, S. I. (1982). Individual differences in musical ability. *Voprosy Psychologii, 5*, 85–93.

National Academies of Sciences, Engineering, and Medicine. (2020). *Promising practices for addressing the underrepresentation of women in science, engineering, and medicine: Opening doors*. National Academies Press. https://doi.org/10.17226/25585

National Career Development Association. (2015). 2015 NCDA code of ethics. https://www.ncda.org/aws/NCDA/asset_manager/get_file/3395

National Center for Education Statistics. (2013). *Bachelor's, master's, and doctor's degrees conferred by postsecondary institutions, by sex of student and discipline division: 2011–12*. Digest of Education Statistics. https://nces.ed.gov/programs/digest/d13/tables/dt13_318.30.Asp

National Center for O*NET Development. (2018a). Abilities. *O*NET OnLine*. Retrieved September 20, 2018, from https://www.onetonline.org/find/descriptor/browse/Abilities/

National Center for O*NET Development. (2018b). Search results for "mechanical abilities". *My Next Move*. Retrieved August 29, 2018, from https://www.mynextmove.org/find/search?s=mechanical+abilities

National Center for O*NET Development. (2018c). Search results for "spatial abilities". *My Next Move*. Retrieved August 29, 2018, from https://www.mynextmove.org/find/search?s=spatial+abilities

National Center for O*NET Development. (2018d). Skills. *O*NET OnLine*. Retrieved September 20, 2018, from https://www.onetonline.org/find/descriptor/browse/Skills/

National Center for O*NET Development. (2018e). Social skills. *O*NET OnLine*. Retrieved November 1, 2018, from https://www.onetonline.org/find/descriptor/browse/Skills/2.B.1/

National Center for O*NET Development. (2019a). Search results for "visual artists". *O*NET OnLine*. Retrieved June 24, 2019, from https://www.onetonline.org/find/quick?s=visual+artists

National Center for O*NET Development. (2019b). Sensory abilities. *O*NET OnLine*. Retrieved June 24, 2019, from https://www.onetonline.org/find/descriptor/browse/Abilities/1.A.4/

National Center for O*NET Development. (2019c). Summary report for: 11-1021.00 - General and operations managers. *O*NET OnLine*. Retrieved September 25, 2019, from https://www.onetonline.org/link/summary/11-1021.00

National Center for O*NET Development. (2019d). Summary report for: 27-2011.00 - Actors. *O*NET OnLine*. Retrieved June 25, 2019, from https://www.onetonline.org/link/summary/27-2011.00

National Center for O*NET Development. (2019e). Summary report for: 27-2031.00 - Dancers. *O*NET OnLine*. Retrieved June 24, 2019, from https://www.onetonline.org/link/summary/27-2031.00

National Center for O*NET Development. (2019f). Summary report for: 27-3022.00 - Reporters and Correspondents. *O*NET OnLine*. Retrieved June 25, 2019, from https://www.onetonline.org/link/summary/27-3022.00

National Center for O*NET Development. (2019g). Summary report for: 27-3041.00 - Editors. *O*NET OnLine*. Retrieved June 25, 2019, from https://www.onetonline.org/link/summary/27-3041.00

National Center for O*NET Development. (2019h). Summary report for: 27-3043.05 - Poets, Lyricists and Creative Writers. *O*NET OnLine*. Retrieved June 25, 2019, from https://www.onetonline.org/link/summary/27-3043.05

National Center for O*NET Development. (2021a). Abilities: Number facility. *O*NET OnLine*. Retrieved March 12, 2021, from https://www.onetonline.org/find/descriptor/result/1.A.1.c.2

National Center for O*NET Development. (2021b). Abilities: Perceptual speed. *O*NET OnLine*. Retrieved March 12, 2021, from https://www.onetonline.org/find/descriptor/result/1.A.1.e.3?a=1

National Center for O*NET Development. (2021c). Cognitive abilities. *O*NET OnLine*. Retrieved March 12, 2021, from https://www.onetonline.org/find/descriptor/browse/Abilities/1.A.1/

National Institute for Occupational Health and Safety. (2017). *Healthcare workers*. Retrieved June 19, 2019, from https://www.cdc.gov/niosh/topics/healthcare/default.html

National Institute of Mental Health. (2017). *Mental health*. Retrieved July 7, 2019, from https://www.nimh.nih.gov/health/statistics/mental-illness.shtml

National Research Council. (2015). *Measuring human capabilities. An agenda for basic research on the assessment of individual and group performance potential for military accession*. The National Academies Press. https://doi.org/10.17226/19017

National Science Foundation, National Center for Science and Engineering Statistics. (2019). *Women, minorities, and persons with disabilities in science and engineering: 2019* (Special Report NSF 19-304). https://www.nsf.gov/statistics/wmpd

Natsopoulos, D., Kiosseoglou, G., & Xeromeritou, A. (1992). Handedness and spatial ability in children: Further support for Geschwind's hypothesis of "pathology of superiority" and for Annett's theory of intelligence. *Genetic, Social, and General Psychology Monographs, 118*(1), 103–126.

Nauta, M. M. (2010). The development, evolution, and status of Holland's theory of vocational personalities: Reflections and future directions for counseling psychology. *Journal of Counseling Psychology, 57*(1), 11–22. https://doi.org/10.1037/a0018213

Neisser, U. (1983). Components of intelligence or steps in routine procedures? *Cognition, 15*(1–3), 189–197. https://doi.org/10.1016/0010-0277(83)90039-2

Neisser, U., Boodoo, G., Bouchard, B. J., Jr., Boykin, A. W., Brody, N., Ceci, S. J., Halpern, D. F., Loehlin, J. C., Perloff, R., Sternberg, R. J., & Urbina, S. (1996). Intelligence: Knowns and unknowns. *American Psychologist, 51*(2), 77–101. https://doi.org/10.1037/0003-066X.51.2.77

Nettle, D. (2006a). Psychological profiles of professional actors. *Personality and Individual Differences, 40*(2), 375–383. https://doi.org/10.1016/j.paid.2005.07.008

Nettle, D. (2006b). Schizotypy and mental health amongst poets, visual artists, and mathematicians. *Journal of Research in Personality, 40*(6), 876–890. https://doi.org/10.1016/j.jrp.2005.09.004

Neubert, D. A., Danehey, A. J., & Taymans, J. M. (1990). Vocational interests, job tryouts and employment outcomes of individuals with mild disabilities in a time-limited transition program. *Vocational Evaluation & Work Adjustment Bulletin, 23(1)*, 17–23.

Ng, T. W. H., Sorensen, K. L., & Eby, L. (2006). Locus of control at work: A meta-analysis. *Journal of Organizational Behavior, 27*(8), 1057–1087. https://doi.org/10.1002/job.416

Nicholls, J. G. (1984). Achievement motivation: Conceptions of ability, subjective experience, task choice, and performance. *Psychological Review*, *91*(3), 328–346. https://doi.org/10.1037/0033-295X.91.3.328

Nichols, R. C. (1985). Review of Comprehensive Ability Battery. In J. V. Mitchell, Jr., (Ed.), *The ninth mental measurements yearbook* (Vol. 1, pp. 376–377). Buros Institute of Mental Measurements.

Nilsson, C., Leanderson, J., Wykman, A., & Strender, L.-E. (2001). The injury panorama in a Swedish professional ballet company. *Knee Surgery, Sports Traumatology, Arthroscopy*, *9*(4), 242–246. https://doi.org/10.1007/s001670100195

Nobo, J., & Evans, R. G. (1986). The WAIS—R Picture Arrangement and Comprehension subtests as measures of social behavior characteristics. *Journal of Personality Assessment*, *50*(1), 90–92.

Noice, H., & Noice, T. (2006). What studies of actors and acting can tell us about memory and cognitive functioning. *Current Directions in Psychological Science*, *15*(1), 14–18. https://doi.org/10.1111/j.0963-7214.2006.00398.x

Noice, T., & Noice, H. (2013). Practice and talent in acting. In S. B. Kaufman (Ed.), *The complexity of greatness: Beyond talent or practice* (pp. 309–332). Oxford University Press. https://doi.org/10.1093/acprof:oso/9780199794003.003.0015

Nolting, E., & Taylor, R. G. (1976). Vocational interests of engineering students. *Measurement and Evaluation in Guidance*, *8*, 245–251. https://doi.org/10.1080/00256307.1976.12022698

Norman, W. T. (1963). Toward an adequate taxonomy of personality attributes: Replicated factors structure in peer nomination personality ratings. *Journal of Abnormal and Social Psychology*, *66*(6), 574–583. https://doi.org/10.1037/h0040291

Norton, A., Winner, E., Cronin, K., Overy, K., Lee, D. J., & Schlaug, G. (2005). Are there pre-existing neural, cognitive, or motoric markers for musical ability? *Brain and Cognition*, *59*(2), 124–134. https://doi.org/10.1016/j.bandc.2005.05.009

Nye, C. D., Perlus, J. G., & Rounds, J. (2018). Do ornithologists flock together? Examining the homogeneity of interests in occupations. *Journal of Vocational Behavior*, *107*, 195–208. https://doi.org/10.1016/j.jvb.2018.04.004

Nye, C. D., Su, R., Rounds, J., & Drasgow, F. (2012). Vocational interests and performance: A quantitative summary of over 60 years of research. *Perspectives on Psychological Science*, *7*(4), 384–403. https://doi.org/10.1177/1745691612449021

Nye, C. D., Su, R., Rounds, J., & Drasgow, F. (2017). Interest congruence and performance: Revisiting recent meta-analytic findings. *Journal of Vocational Behavior*, *98*, 138–151. https://doi.org/10.1016/j.jvb.2016.11.002

Nykodym, N., & Simonetti, J. L. (1987). Personal appearance: Is attractiveness a factor in organizational survival and success? *Journal of Employment Counseling*, *24*(2), 69–78. https://doi.org/10.1002/j.2161-1920.1987.tb00950.x

O'Boyle, E. H., Jr., Forsyth, D. R., Banks, G. C., & McDaniel, M. A. (2012). A meta-analysis of the Dark Triad and work behavior: A social exchange perspective. *Journal of Applied Psychology*, *97*(3), 557–579. https://doi.org/10.1037/a0025679

O'Boyle, E. H., Forsyth, D. R., Banks, G. C., Story, P. A., & White, C. D. (2015). A meta-analytic test of redundancy and relative importance of the dark triad and five-factor model of personality. *Journal of Personality*, *83*(6), 644–664. https://doi.org/10.1111/jopy.12126

O'Connor, J. (1927). *Born that way*. The Williams & Wilkins Co.

O'Connor, J. (1941). *The too many aptitude woman*. Human Engineering Laboratory, Inc.

O'Connor, J. (1943). *Structural visualization*. Human Engineering Laboratory, Inc.

O'Connor, N., & Hermelin, B. (1987). Visual memory and motor programmes: Their use by idiot-savant artists and controls. *British Journal of Psychology*, *78*(3), 307–323. https://doi.org/10.1111/j.2044-8295.1987.tb02249.x

O'Shea, A. J., & Harrington Jr., T. F. (1974). Measuring the interests of male and female students with the SVIB for men, *Measurement and Evaluation in Guidance, 7*, 112–117, https://doi.org/10.1080/00256307.1974.12022629

O'Sullivan, M., & Guilford, J. P. (1966). *Tests of social intelligence*. Sheridan Psychological Services.

O'Sullivan, M., & Guilford, J. P. (1975). Six factors of behavioral cognition: Understanding other people. *Journal of Educational Measurement, 12*(4), 255–271. https://doi.org/10.1111/j.1745-3984.1975.tb01027.x

O'Sullivan, M., & Guilford, J. P. (1976). *Four factor tests of social intelligence (behavioral cognition): Manual of instructions and interpretations*. Sheridan Psychological Services.

Oda, M. (1982). An analysis of relation between personality traits and job performance in sales occupations. *Japanese Journal of Psychology, 53*(5), 274–280.

Oda, M. (1983). Predicting sales performance of car salesmen by personality traits. *Japanese Journal of Psychology, 54*, 73–80.

Oldfield, R. C. (1971). The assessment and analysis of handedness: The Edinburgh inventory. *Neuropsychologia, 9*(1), 97–113. https://doi.org/10.1016/0028-3932(71)90067-4

Olson, P. D., & Bosserman, D. A. (1984). Attributes of the entrepreneurial type. *Business Horizons, 27*(3), 53–56. https://doi.org/10.1016/0007-6813(84)90027-2

Omvig, C. P., & Thomas, E. G. (1974a). A socioeconomic comparison of vocational interests: Implications for counseling. *Journal of Vocational Behavior, 5*(1), 147–155. https://doi.org/10.1016/0001-8791(74)90016-5

Omvig, C. P., & Thomas, E. G. (1974b). Vocational interests of affluent suburban students. *Vocational Guidance Quarterly, 23*(1), 10–16. https://doi.org/10.1002/j.2164-585X.1974.tb02132.x

Ones, D. S., Anderson, N., Viswesvaran, C., & Sinangil, H. K. (2018). *The SAGE handbook of industrial, work, and organizational psychology: Personnel psychology and employee performance*. SAGE Publications.

Ones, D. S., Dilchert, S., Viswesvaran, C., & Judge, T. (2007). In support of personality assessments in organizational settings. *Personnel Psychology, 60*(4), 995–1027. https://doi.org/10.1111/j.1744-6570.2007.00099.x

Ones, D. S., Dilchert, S., Viswesvaran, C., & Salgado, J. F. (2017). Cognitive ability. Measurement and validity for employee selection. In J. L. Farr & N. T. Tippins (Eds.), *Handbook of employee selection* (2nd ed., pp. 251–276). Routledge/Taylor & Francis Group. https://doi.org/10.4324/9781315690193-11

Opdebeeck, C., Martyr, A., & Clare, L. (2016). Cognitive reserve and cognitive function in healthy older people: A meta-analysis. *Neuropsychology, Development, and Cognition: Section B. Aging, Neuropsychology and Cognition, 23*(1), 40–60. https://doi.org/10.1080/13825585.2015.1041450

Ormerod, M. B., & Asiedu, K. (1991). The psychological profiles of physical and biological science oriented pupils at 16+. *Personality and Individual Differences, 12*(5), 437–443. https://doi.org/10.1016/0191-8869(91)90061-F

Orpen, C. (1983). The development and validation of an adjective check-list measure of managerial need for achievement. *Psychology: A Quarterly Journal of Human Behavior, 20*(1), 38–42.

Osborn, H. H. (1983). The assessment of mathematical abilities. *Educational Research, 25*(1), 28–40. https://doi.org/10.1080/0013188830250104

Osipow, S. H., & Fitzgerald, L. F. (1995). *Theories of career development* (4th ed.). Allyn and Bacon.

Osipow, S. H., & Gati, I. (1998). Construct and concurrent validity of the career decision-making difficulties questionnaire. *Journal of Career Assessment, 6*(3), 347–364. https://doi.org/10.1177/106907279800600305

Oswald, F. L., & Ferstl, K. L. (1999). Linking a structure of vocational interests to Gottfredson's (1986) Occupational Aptitude Patterns Map. *Journal of Vocational Behavior, 54*(1), 214–231. https://doi.org/10.1006/jvbe.1998.1647

Palan, K. M., Areni, C. S., & Kiecker, P. (1999). Reexamining masculinity, femininity, and gender identity scales. *Marketing Letters, 10*(4), 357–371. https://doi.org/10.1023/A:1008110204546

Pallrand, G. J., & Seeber, F. (1984). Spatial ability and achievement in introductory physics. *Journal of Research in Science Teaching, 21*(5), 507–516. https://doi.org/10.1002/tea.3660210508

Papworth, M. A., Jordan, G., Backhouse, C., Evans, N., Kent-Lemon, N., Morris, J., & Winchester, K. J. G. (2008). Artists' vulnerability to psychopathology: Towards an integrative cognitive perspective. *Journal of Creative Behavior, 42*(3), 149–163. https://doi.org/10.1002/j.2162-6057.2008.tb01292.x

Park, G., Lubinski, D., & Benbow, C. P. (2007). Contrasting intellectual patterns predict creativity in the arts and sciences: Tracking intellectually precocious youth over 25 years. *Psychological Science, 18*(11), 948–952. https://doi.org/10.1111/j.1467-9280.2007.02007.x

Parsons, F. (1909). *Choosing a vocation*. Houghton Mifflin Company.

Parvathi, S., & Natarajan, P. (1985). A study of the drawing abilities of children as related to abstract intelligence. *Journal of the Indian Academy of Applied Psychology, 11*(2), 21–24.

Pässler, K., Beinecke, A., & Hell, B. (2014). Gender-related differential validity and differential prediction in interest inventories. *Journal of Career Assessment, 22*(1), 138–152. https://doi.org/10.1177/1069072713492934

Patel, A. D., & Demorest, S. M. (2013). Comparative music cognition. In D. Deutsch (Ed.), *The psychology of music* (pp. 647–681). Academic Press. https://doi.org/10.1016/B978-0-12-381460-9.00016-X

Patterson, D. G., Elliott, R. M., Anderson, L. D., Toops, H. A., & Heidbreder, E. (1930). *Minnesota Mechanical Ability Tests*. The University of Minnesota Press.

Paul, S. M. (1986). The Advanced Raven's Progressive Matrices: Normative data for an American university population and examination of the relationship with Spearman's g. *Journal of Experimental Education, 54*(2), 95–100. https://doi.org/10.1080/00220973.1986.10806404

Paulhus D. L., Bruce M. N., Trapnell, P. D. (1995). Effects of self-presentation strategies on personality profiles and their structure. *Personality and Social Psychology Bulletin, 21*(2), 100–108. https://doi.org/10.1177/0146167295212001

Paulhus, D. L., & Williams, K. M. (2002). The dark triad of personality: Narcissism, Machiavellianism, and corporate psychopaths. *Journal of Research in Personality, 36*(6), 556–563. https://doi.org/10.1016/S0092-6566(02)00505-6

Pawlik, K. (1966). Concepts in human cognition and aptitudes. In R. B. Cattell (Ed.), *Handbook of multivariate experimental psychology* (pp. 535–562). Rand McNally.

Pearlman, K., Schmidt, F. L., & Hunter, J. E. (1980). Validity generalization results for tests used to predict job proficiency and training success in various occupations. *Journal of Applied Psychology, 65*(4), 373–406. https://doi.org/10.1037/0021-9010.65.4.373

Peiser, C., & Meir, E. I. (1978). Congruency, consistency, and differentiation of vocational interests as predictors of vocational satisfaction and preference stability. *Journal of Vocational Behavior, 12*(3), 270–278. https://doi.org/10.1016/0001-8791(78)90015-5

Peraino, J. M., & Willerman, L. (1983). Personality correlates of occupational status according to Holland types. *Journal of Vocational Behavior, 22*(3), 268–277. https://doi.org/10.1016/0001-8791(83)90012-X

Peterson, J. M. (1979). Left-handedness: Differences between student artists and scientists. *Perceptual and Motor Skills, 48*(3), 961–962. https://doi.org/10.2466/pms.1979.48.3.961

Peterson, J. M., & Lansky, L. M. (1980). Success in architecture: Handedness and/or visual thinking. *Perceptual and Motor Skills, 50*(3 Suppl.), 1139–1143. https://doi.org/10.2466/pms.1980.50.3c.1139

Phillips, S. D., & Bruch, M. A. (1988). Shyness and dysfunction in career development. *Journal of Counseling Psychology, 35*(2), 159–165. https://doi.org/10.1037/0022-0167.35.2.159

Pickman, A. J. (1987). Career transitions for dancers: A counselor's perspective. *Journal of Counseling & Development, 66*(4), 200–201. https://doi.org/10.1002/j.1556-6676.1987.tb00848.x

Piechowski, M. M., & Cunningham, K. (1985). Patterns of overexcitability in a group of artists. *Journal of Creative Behavior, 19*(3), 153–174. https://doi.org/10.1002/j.2162-6057.1985.tb00655.x

Pinkney, J. W. (1985). A card sort interpretive strategy for flat profiles on the Strong-Campbell Interest Inventory. *Vocational Guidance Quarterly, 33*(4), 331–339. https://doi.org/10.1002/j.2164-585X.1985.tb01327.x

Pittenger, D. J. (2005). Cautionary comments regarding the Myers-Briggs Type Indicator. *Consulting Psychology Journal, 57*(3), 210–221. https://doi.org/10.1037/1065-9293.57.3.210

Plotkin, H. M. (1987). What makes a successful salesperson? *Training and Development Journal, 41*(9), 54–56.

Polderman, T. J. C., Benyamin, B., de Leeuw, C. A., Sullivan, P. F., van Bochoven, A., Visscher, P. M., & Posthuma, D. (2015). Meta-analysis of the heritability of human traits based on fifty years of twin studies. *Nature Genetics, 47*(7), 702–709. https://doi.org/10.1038/ng.3285

Poltrock, S. E., & Brown, P. (1984). Individual differences in visual imagery and spatial ability. *Intelligence, 8*(2), 93–138. https://doi.org/10.1016/0160-2896(84)90019-9

Portegal, M. (Ed.). (1982). *Spatial abilities. Development and physiological foundations.* Academic Press.

Post, F. (1996). Verbal creativity, depression and alcoholism. An investigation of one hundred American and British writers. *British Journal of Psychiatry, 168*(5), 545–555. https://doi.org/10.1192/bjp.168.5.545

Posthuma, A. B., & Navran, L. (1970). Relation of congruence in student-faculty interest to achievement in college. *Journal of Counseling Psychology, 17*(4), 352–356. https://doi.org/10.1037/h0029687

Powell, C. S. (1994). Nobel notes. *Scientific American, 270*(2), 16–20.

Powell, G. N., & Greenhaus, J. H. (2010). Sex, gender, and decisions at the family → work interface. *Journal of Management, 36*(4), 1011–1039. https://doi.org/10.1177/0149206309350774

Power, R. A., Steinberg, S., Bjornsdottir, G., Rietveld, C. A., Abdellaoui, A., Nivard, M. M., Johannesson, M., Galesloot, T. E., Hottenga, J. J., Willemsen, G., Cesarini, D., Benjamin, D. J., Magnusson, P. K., Ullén, F., Tiemeier, H., Hofman, A., van Rooij, F. J., Walters, G. B., Sigurdsson, E., . . . Stefansson, K. (2015). Polygenic risk scores for schizophrenia and bipolar disorder predict creativity. *Nature Neuroscience, 18*(7), 953–955. https://doi.org/10.1038/nn.4040

Pozzebon, J. A., Visser, B. A., Ashton, M. C., Lee, K., & Goldberg, L. R. (2010). Psychometric characteristics of a public-domain self-report measure of vocational interests: The Oregon Vocational Interest Scales. *Journal of Personality Assessment, 92*(2), 168–174. https://doi.org/10.1080/00223890903510431

Prabhu, V., Sutton, C., & Sauser, W. (2008) Creativity and certain personality traits: Understanding the mediating effect of intrinsic motivation, *Creativity Research Journal, 20*(1), 53–66, https://doi.org/10.1080/10400410701841955

Prada, M. F., & Urzúa, S. (2017). One size does not fit all: Multiple dimensions of ability, college attendance, and earnings. *Journal of Labor Economics, 35*(4), 953–991. https://doi.org/10.1086/692477

Preckel, F., Golle, J., Grabner, R., Jarvin, L., Kozbelt, A., Müllensiefen, D., Olszewski-Kubilius, P., Schneider, W., Subotnik, R., Vock, M., & Worrell, F. C. (2020). Talent development in achievement domains: A psychological framework for within-and cross-domain research. *Perspectives on Psychological Science, 15*(3), 691–722. https://doi.org/10.1177/1745691619895030

Prediger, D. J. (1980). The determination of Holland types characterizing occupational groups. *Journal of Vocational Behavior, 16*(1), 33–42. https://doi.org/10.1016/0001-8791(80)90035-4

Prediger, D. J. (1981). Mapping occupations and interests: A graphic aid for vocational guidance and research. *Vocational Guidance Quarterly, 30*(1), 21–36. https://doi.org/10.1002/j.2164-585X.1981.tb01072.x

Prediger, D. J. (1982). Dimensions underlying Holland's hexagon: Missing link between interests and occupations? *Journal of Vocational Behavior, 21*(3), 259–287. https://doi.org/10.1016/0001-8791(82)90036-7

Prediger, D. J. (1989). Ability differences across occupations: More than g. *Journal of Vocational Behavior, 34*(1), 1–27. https://doi.org/10.1016/0001-8791(89)90061-4

Prediger, D. J. (2002). Abilities, interests, and values: Their assessment and their integration via the World-of-Work Map. *Journal of Career Assessment, 10*(2), 209–232. https://doi.org/10.1177/1069072702010002006

Prediger, D. J., & Hanson, G. R. (1974). The distinction between sex restrictiveness and sex bias in interest inventories. *Measurement and Evaluation in Guidance, 7*(2), 96–104. https://doi.org/10.1080/00256307.1974.12022627

Prediger, D. J., & Hanson, G. R. (1976a). Holland's theory of careers applied to women and men: Analysis of implicit assumptions. *Journal of Vocational Behavior, 8*(2), 167–184. https://doi.org/10.1016/0001-8791(76)90019-1

Prediger, D. J., & Hanson, G. R. (1976b). A theory of careers encounters sex: Reply to Holland (1976). *Journal of Vocational Behavior, 8*(3), 359–366. https://doi.org/10.1016/0001-8791(76)90051-8

Prediger, D. J., & Swaney, K. B. (1985). *Role of counselee experiences in the interpretation of vocational interest scores* (Research Report No. 86). American College Testing.

Prediger, D. J., & Swaney, K. B. (1999). *Career counseling validity of Discover's Job Cluster scales for the Revised ASVAB Score Report* (ACT Research Report 92-2). American College Testing.

Pryor, R. G., & Taylor, N. B. (1986). On combining scores from interest and value measures for counseling. *Vocational Guidance Quarterly, 34*(3), 178–187. https://doi.org/10.1002/j.2164-585X.1986.tb01121.x

Pufal-Struzik, I. (1992). Differences in personality and self-knowledge of creative persons at different ages: A comparative analysis. *Gerontology & Geriatrics Education, 13*(1–2), 71–90. https://doi.org/10.1300/J021v13n01_06

Puglisi, J. T., & Morrell, R. W. (1986). Age-related slowing in mental rotation of three-dimensional objects. *Experimental Aging Research, 12*(4), 217–220. https://doi.org/10.1080/03610738608258571

Puts, D. A., McDaniel, M. A., Jordan, C. L., & Breedlove, S. M. (2008). Spatial ability and prenatal androgens: meta-analyses of congenital adrenal hyperplasia and digit ratio (2D:4D) studies. *Archives of Sexual Behavior, 37*(1), 100–111. https://doi.org/10.1007/s10508-007-9271-3

Rachman, D., Amernic, J., & Aranya, N. (1981). A factor-analytic study of the construct validity of Holland's Self-Directed Search. *Educational and Psychological Measurement, 41*(2), 425–437. https://doi.org/10.1177/001316448104100221

Radecki, C., & Walstedt, J. J. (1980). Sex as a status variable in work settings: female and male reports of dominance behavior. *Journal of Applied Social Psychology, 10*(1), 71–85. https://doi.org/10.1111/j.1559-1816.1980.tb00694.x

Rahman, Q., Sharp, J., McVeigh, M., & Ho, M.-L. (2017). Sexual orientation-related differences in virtual spatial navigation and spatial search strategies. *Archives of Sexual Behavior, 46*(5), 1279–1294. https://doi.org/10.1007/s10508-017-0986-5

Rainey, H. G. (2000). Work motivation. In R. T. Glombiewski (Ed.). *Handbook of organizational behavior* (2nd ed., pp. 19–42). Routledge/Taylor & Francis.

Randahl, G. J. (1990). *A typological analysis of the relationship between measured vocational interests and abilities* [Unpublished doctoral dissertation]. University of Minnesota.

Randahl, G. J. (1991). A typological analysis of the relations between measured vocational interests and abilities. *Journal of Vocational Behavior, 38*(3), 333–350. https://doi.org/10.1016/0001-8791(91)90034-J

Raskin, R., Novacek, J., & Hogan, R. (1991). Narcissism, self-esteem, and defensive self-enhancement. *Journal of Personality, 59*(1), 19–38. https://doi.org/10.1111/j.1467-6494.1991.tb00766.x

Rao, S., & Murthy, V. N. (1984). Psychosocial correlates of locus of control among college students. *Psychosocial Studies, 29*(1), 51–56.

Rao, T. V. (1981). Sales effectiveness. *Managerial Psychology, 2*(2), 1–12.

Ratcliffe, G. (1982). Disturbances of spatial orientation associated with cerebral lesions. In M. Portegal (Ed.), *Spatial abilities: Development and physiological foundations* (pp. 301–331). Academic Press.

Raven, J. C., Court, J. H., & Raven, J. (1992). *Raven manual: Section 3. Standard progressive matrices.* Oxford Psychologists Press Ltd.

Raven, J. C., Court, J. H., & Raven, J. (1994). *Raven manual: Section 4. Advanced progressive matrices.* Oxford Psychologists Press Ltd.

Reardon, R. C., & Lenz, J. G. (2015). *Handbook for using the Self-Directed Search: Integrating RIASEC and CIP theories in practice.* PAR Inc.

Reeve, J., Olson, B. C., & Cole, S. G. (1987). Intrinsic motivation in competition: The intervening role of four individual differences following objective competence information. *Journal of Research in Personality, 21*(2), 148–170. https://doi.org/10.1016/0092-6566(87)90004-3

Reiter, S., Friedman, L., & Molcho, M. (1985). Motivation, vocational interests and job satisfaction of mentally retarded adults. *International Journal of Rehabilitation Research, 8*(1), 19–28. https://doi.org/10.1097/00004356-198503000-00002

Resnick, L. B. (1989). Developing mathematical knowledge. *American Psychologist, 44*(2), 162–169. https://doi.org/10.1037/0003-066X.44.2.162

Resnick, S. M., Berenbaum, S. A., Gottesman, I. I., & Bouchard, T. J. (1986). Early hormonal influences on cognitive functioning in congenital adrenal hyperplasia. *Developmental Psychology, 22*(2), 191–198. https://doi.org/10.1037/0012-1649.22.2.191

Reuman, D. A. (1982). Ipsative behavioral variability and the quality of thematic apperceptive measurement of the achievement motive. *Journal of Personality and Social Psychology, 43*(5), 1098–1110. https://doi.org/10.1037/0022-3514.43.5.1098

Révész, G. (1953). *Introduction to the psychology of music.* Longmans, Green Company.

Revelle, W., Dworak, E. M., & Condon, D. (2020). Cognitive ability in everyday life: The utility of open-source measures. *Current Directions in Psychological Science, 29*(4), 358–363. https://doi.org/10.1177/0963721420922178

Rhoads, B. A. (2013). *Artistic creativity and mental health: Relationships among creativity, mood, and hardiness in visual artists* (UMI No. 3544454) [Doctoral dissertation, Chesnut Hill College]. ProQuest Dissertations and Theses Global.

Riggio, R. E. (1989). *Social Skills Inventory manual* (Research ed.). Consulting Psychologists Press.

Riggio, R. E., & Sotoodeh, Y. (1987). Screening tests for use in hiring microassemblers. *Perceptual and Motor Skills, 65*(1), 167–172. https://doi.org/10.2466/pms.1987.65.1.167

Rimfeld, K., Shakeshaft, N. G., Malanchini, M., Rodic, M., Selzam, S., Schofield, K., Dale, P. S., Kovas, Y., & Plomin, R. (2017). Phenotypic and genetic evidence for a unifactorial structure of spatial abilities. *Proceedings of the National Academy of Sciences of the United States of America, 114*(10), 2777–2782. https://doi.org/10.1073/pnas.1607883114

Ritchie, R. J., & Moses, J. L. (1983). Assessment center correlates of women's advancement into middle management: A 7-year longitudinal analysis. *Journal of Applied Psychology, 68*(2), 227–231. https://doi.org/10.1037/0021-9010.68.2.227

Ritchie, S. J., & Tucker-Drob, E. M. (2018). How much does education improve intelligence? A meta-analysis. *Psychological Science, 29*(8), 1358–1369. https://doi.org/10.1177/0956797618774253

Robbins, P. I., Thomas, L. E., Harvey, D. W., & Kandefer, C. (1978). Career change and congruence of personality type: An examination of DOT-derived work environment designations. *Journal of Vocational Behavior, 13*(1), 15–25. https://doi.org/10.1016/0001-8791(78)90067-2

Roberts, B. W., Jackson, J. J., Fayard, J. V., Edmonds, G., & Meints, J. (2009). Conscientiousness. In M. R. Leary & R. H. Hoyle (Eds.), *Handbook of individual differences in social behavior* (pp. 369–381). Guilford Press.

Roberts, M. A. (2015). The testing industrial complex. Incarcerating education since 2001. In M. Abendroth & B. J. Porfilio (Eds.), *Understanding neoliberal rule in K12 Schools: Educational fronts for local and global justice* (Vol. 1, pp. 153–178). Information Age Publishing.

Roe, A. (1946). The personality of artists. *Education and Psychological Measurement, 6*, 401–408.

Roe, A. (1951). A psychological study of eminent biologists. *Psychological Monographs, 65*(14).

Roe, A. (1952). *The making of a scientist*. Dodd Mead.

Roe, A. (1956). *The psychology of occupations*. Wiley. https://doi.org/10.1037/13192-000

Rogers, C. R. (1959). A theory of therapy, personality and metapersonal relationships, as developed in the client-centered framework. In S. Koch (Ed.), *Psychology, a study of a science: Vol. 3. Formulations of the person and the social context*. McGraw-Hill.

Rohe, D. E., & Athelstan, G. T. (1985). Change in vocational interests after spinal cord injury. *Rehabilitation Psychology, 30*(3), 131.

Rose, M. (2014). *Mind at work: Valuing the intelligence of the American worker* (10th anniv. ed.). Penguin.

Roselli, C. E. (2018). Neurobiology of gender identity and sexual orientation. *Journal of Neuroendocrinology, 30*(7), e12562. https://doi.org/10.1111/jne.12562

Rosen, J. C. (1955). The Barron-Welsh Art Scale as a predictor of originality and level of ability among artists. *Journal of Applied Psychology, 39*(5), 366–367. https://doi.org/10.1037/h0042340

Rosenblatt, E., & Winner, E. (1988). Is superior visual memory a component of superior drawing ability? In L. K. Obler & E. Fein (Eds.), *The exceptional brain* (pp. 341–363). Guilford Press.

Rossen, E., Kranzler, J. H., & Algina, J. (2008). Confirmatory factor analysis of the Mayer–Salovey–Caruso Emotional Intelligence Test V 2.0 (MSCEIT). *Personality and Individual Differences, 44*(5), 1258–1269. https://doi.org/10.1016/j.paid.2007.11.020

Rothstein, M. G., & Goffin, R. D. (2006). The use of personality measures in personnel selection: What does current research support? *Human Resource Management Review, 16*(2), 155–180. https://doi.org/10.1016/j.hrmr.2006.03.004

Rotter, J. B. (1966). Generalized expectancies for internal versus external control of reinforcement. *Psychological Monographs, 80*(1), 1–28. https://doi.org/10.1037/h0092976

Rottinghaus, P. J., Coon, K. L., Gaffey, A. R., & Zytowski, D. G. (2007). Thirty-year stability and predictive validity of vocational interests. *Journal of Career Assessment, 15*(1), 5–22. https://doi.org/10.1177/1069072706294517

Rounds, J. (1990). The comparative and combined utility of work value and interest data in career counseling with adults. *Journal of Vocational Behavior, 37*(1), 32–45. https://doi.org/10.1016/0001-8791(90)90005-M

Rounds, J. (1995). Vocational interest: Evaluating structural hypotheses. In D. Lubinsky & R. V. Dawis (Eds.), *Assessing individual differences in human behavior. New concepts, methods, and findings* (pp. 177–232). Davies-Black Publishing.

Rounds, J., & Su, R. (2014). The nature and power of interests. *Current Directions in Psychological Science, 23*(2), 98–103. https://doi.org/10.1177/0963721414522812

Rounds, J., Walker, C. M., Day, S. X., Hubert, L., Lewis, P., & Rivkin, D. (1999). *O*NET Interest Profiler: Reliability, validity, and self-scoring*. National Center for O*NET Development. https://www.onetcenter.org/dl_files/IP_RVS.pdf

Rudocy, R. E., & Boyle, J. D. (1979). *Psychological foundations of musical behavior*. Thomas.

Ryan, J. C. (2014). The work motivation of research scientists and its effect on research performance. *R&D Management, 44*, 355–369. https://doi.org/10.1111/radm.12063

Ryan, J. J., Bartels, J. M., Morris, J., Cluff, R. B., & Gontkovsky, S. T. (2009). WAIS-III VIQ–PIQ and VCI–POI discrepancies in lateralized cerebral damage. *International Journal of Neuroscience, 119*(8), 1198–1209. https://doi.org/10.1080/00207450902889219

Rychlak, J. F. (1982). *Personality and lifestyle of young male managers: A logical learning theory analysis*. Academic Press.

Sackett, P. R., & Lievens, F. (2008). Personnel selection. *Annual Review of Psychology, 59*(1), 419–450. https://doi.org/10.1146/annurev.psych.59.103006.093716

Sackett, P. R., Lievens, F., Van Iddekinge, C. H., & Kuncel, N. R. (2017). Individual differences and their measurement: A review of 100 years of research. *Journal of Applied Psychology, 102*(3), 254–273. https://doi.org/10.1037/apl0000151

Sadana, D., Rajeswaran, J., Jain, S., Kumaran, S. S., Thennarasu, K., Ravi, S., & Sundar, N. (2017). The neuropsychology of creativity: A profile of Indian artists. *Acta Neuropsychologica, 15*(2), 143–160. https://doi.org/10.5604/01.3001.0010.2406

Sagiv, L. (2002). Vocational interests and basic values. *Journal of Career Assessment, 10*(2), 233–257. https://doi.org/10.1177/1069072702010002007

Saksvik, I. B., & Hetland, H. (2011). The role of personality in stress perception across different vocational types. *Journal of employment counseling, 48*(1), 3–16.

Sala, G., & Gobet, F. (2017). When the music's over. Does music skill transfer to children's and young adolescents' cognitive and academic skills? A meta-analysis. *Educational Research Review, 20*, 55–67. https://doi.org/10.1016/j.edurev.2016.11.005

Sala, G., Signorelli, M., Barsuola, G., Bolognese, M., & Gobet, F. (2017, 9 June). The relationship between handedness and mathematics is non-linear and is moderated by gender, age, and type of task. *Frontiers in Psychology, 8*, 948. https://doi.org/10.3389/fpsyg.2017.00948

Salgado, J. F., Moscoso, S., & Berges, A. (2013). Conscientiousness, its facets, and the prediction of job performance ratings: Evidence against the narrow measures. *International Journal of Selection and Assessment, 21*(1), 74–84. https://doi.org/10.1111/ijsa.12018

Salthouse, T. A. (1984). Effects of age and skill in typing. *Journal of Experimental Psychology: General, 113*(3), 345–371. https://doi.org/10.1037/0096-3445.113.3.345

Salthouse, T. A. (1986a). Effects of practice on a typing-like keying task. *Acta Psychologica, 62*(2), 189–198. https://doi.org/10.1016/0001-6918(86)90068-5

Salthouse, T. A. (1986b). Perceptual, cognitive, and motoric aspects of transcription typing. *Psychological Bulletin, 99*(3), 303–319. https://doi.org/10.1037/0033-2909.99.3.303

Salthouse, T. A. (1996). The processing-speed theory of adult age differences in cognition. *Psychological Review, 103*(3), 403–428. https://doi.org/10.1037/0033-295X.103.3.403

Sampson, J. P., Jr., & Osborn, D. S. (2015). Using information and communication technology in delivering career interventions. In P. J. Hartung, M. L. Savickas, & W. B. Walsh (Eds.), *APA handbook of career intervention: Vol. 2. Applications* (p. 57–70). American Psychological Association. https://doi.org/10.1037/14439-005

Sampson, J. P., Jr., Peterson, G. W., Lenz, J. G., Reardon, R. C., & Saunders, D. E. (1996). *Career Thoughts Inventory (CTI): Professional manual.* Psychological Assessment Resources

Samuel, D. B., & Widiger, T. A. (2008). A meta-analytic review of the relationships between the five-factor model and *DSM-IV-TR* personality disorders: A facet level analysis. *Clinical Psychology Review, 28*(8), 1326–1342. https://doi.org/10.1016/j.cpr.2008.07.002

Sandberg, D. E., Ehrhardt, A. A., Mellins, C. A., Ince, S. E., & Meyer-Bahlburg, H. L. (1987). The influence of individual and family characteristics upon career aspirations of girls during childhood and adolescence. *Sex Roles, 16*(11–12), 649–668.

Sanders, B., Wilson, J. R., & Vandenberg, S. G. (1982). Handedness and spatial ability. *Cortex, 18*(1), 79–89. https://doi.org/10.1016/s0010-9452(82)80020-8

Sarason, S. (1972). *The creation of change and future societies.* Jossey-Bass.

Saucier, G. (2008). Measures of the personality factors found recurrently in human lexicons. In G. J. Boyle, G. Matthews, & D. H. Saklofske (Eds.), *The SAGE handbook of personality theory and assessment: Vol. 2. Personality measurement and testing* (pp. 29–54). SAGE Publications. https://doi.org/10.4135/9781849200479.n2

Savickas, M. L. (2019). *Career counseling* (2nd ed.). American Psychological Association.

Savickas, M. L., & Hartun, P. (1996). The Career Development Inventory in review: Psychometric and research findings. *Journal of Career Assessment, 4*(2), 171–188. https://doi.org/10.1177/106907279600400204

Savickas, M. L., Taber, B. J., & Spokane, A. R. (2002). Convergent and discriminant validity of five interest inventories. *Journal of Vocational Behavior, 61*(1), 139–184. https://doi.org/10.1006/jvbe.2002.1878

Saw, G., Chang, C.-N., & Chan, H.-Y. (2018). Cross-sectional and longitudinal disparities in STEM career aspirations at the intersection of gender, race/ethnicity, and socioeconomic status. *Educational Researcher, 47*(8), 525–531. https://doi.org/10.3102/0013189X18787818#

Scarr, S. (1969). Social introversion-extraversion as a heritable response. *Child Development, 40*(3), 823. https://doi.org/10.2307/1127191

Schacter, S. C., & Galaburda, A. M. (1986). Development and biological associations of cerebral dominance: Review and possible mechanisms. *Journal of the American Academy of Child Psychiatry, 25*(6), 741–750. https://doi.org/10.1016/S0002-7138(09)60191-6

Schellenberg, E. G., & Weiss, M. W. (2013). Music and cognitive abilities. In D. Deutsch (Ed.), *The psychology of music* (pp. 499–550). Academic Press. https://doi.org/10.1016/B978-0-12-381460-9.00012-2

Schilit, W. K. (1986). An examination of individual differences as moderators of upward influence activity in strategic decisions. *Human Relations, 39*(10), 933–953.

Schlickum, M., Hedman, L., & Felländer-Tsai, L. (2016). Visual-spatial ability is more important than motivation for novices in surgical simulator training: A preliminary study. *International Journal of Medical Education, 7,* 56–61. https://doi.org/10.5116/ijme.56b1.1691

Schmidt, F. L. (2014). A general theoretical integrative model of individual differences in interests, abilities, personality traits, and academic and occupational achievement: A commentary on four recent articles. *Perspectives on Psychological Science, 9*(2), 211–218. https://doi.org/10.1177/1745691613518074

Schmidt, F. L. (2015). Select for ability. In E. A. Locke (Ed.), *Handbook of principles of organizational behavior: Indispensable knowledge for evidence-based management* (2nd ed., pp. 3–18). Wiley.

Schmidt, F. L., & Hunter, J. E. (2004). General mental ability in the world of work: Occupational attainment and job performance. *Journal of Personality and Social Psychology, 86*(1), 162–173. https://doi.org/10.1037/0022-3514.86.1.162

Schmitt, N. (2014). Personality and cognitive ability as predictors of effective performance at work. *Annual Review of Organizational Psychology and Organizational Behavior, 1*, 45–65. https://doi.org/10.1146/annurev-orgpsych-031413-091255

Schneider, B. (1987). The people make the place. *Personnel Psychology, 40*(3), 437–453. https://doi.org/10.1111/j.1744-6570.1987.tb00609.x

Schneider, B., & Schmitt, N. (1986). *Staffing organizations* (2nd ed.). Scott, Foresman.

Schneider, D. E. (1979). *The psychoanalyst and the artist*. The Alexa Press, Inc.

Schoon, C. G. (1978). The structure of interests as a structure of occupational stimuli and as a structure of affective responses. *Journal of Vocational Behavior, 12*(1), 109–118. https://doi.org/10.1016/0001-8791(78)90012-X

Schroth, M. L. (1987). Relationships between achievement-related motives, extrinsic conditions, and task performance. *Journal of Social Psychology, 127*(1), 39–48.

Schroth, M. L., & Andrew, D. F. (1987). Study of need-achievement motivation among Hawaiian college students. *Perceptual and Motor Skills, 64*(3 Suppl.), 1261–1262. https://doi.org/10.2466/pms.1987.64.3c.1261

Schulenberg, J., Goldstein, A. E., & Vondracek, F. W. (1991). Gender differences in adolescents' career interests: Beyond main effects. *Journal of Research on Adolescence, 1*(1), 37–61.

Schutz, W. (1978). *FIRO Awareness Scales Manual*. Consulting Psychologists Press.

Schwaba, T., Luhmann, M., Denissen, J. J. A., Chung, J. M., & Bleidorn, W. (2018). Openness to experience and culture-openness transactions across the lifespan. *Journal of Personality and Social Psychology, 115*(1), 118–136. https://doi.org/10.1037/pspp0000150

Scott, J., Bartram, D., & Reynolds, D. H. (Eds.). (2018). *Next generation technology-enhanced assessment: Global perspectives on occupational and workplace testing* (pp. 350–374). Cambridge University Press.

Seashore, C. E. (1939). *Psychology of music*. McGraw-Hill.

Seashore, C. E., Lewis, D., & Saetveit, J. G. (1960). *Seashore Measures of Musical Talent* [Test manual]. Pearson Assessments.

Sechrest, L., & Jackson, D. N. (1961). Social intelligence and accuracy of interpersonal predictions. *Journal of Personality, 29*(2), 167–182. https://doi.org/10.1111/j.1467-6494.1961.tb01653.x

Sedge, S. K. (1985). A comparison of engineers pursuing alternate career paths. *Journal of Vocational Behavior, 27*(1), 56–70. https://doi.org/10.1016/0001-8791(85)90052-1

Seesjärvi, E., Särkämö, T., Vuoksimaa, E., Tervaniemi, M., Peretz, I., & Kaprio, J. (2016). The nature and nurture of melody: A twin study of musical pitch and rhythm perception. *Behavior Genetics, 46*(4), 506–515. https://doi.org/10.1007/s10519-015-9774-y

Seligman, M. S., & Schulman, P. (1986). Exploratory style as a predictor of productivity and quitting among life insurance sales agents. *Journal of Personality and Social Psychology, 50*(4), 832–838. https://doi.org/10.1037/0022-3514.50.4.832

Sexton, D. L., & Bowman-Upton, N. (1990). Female and male entrepreneurs: Psychological characteristics and their role in gender-related discrimination. *Journal of Business Venturing, 5*(1), 29–36. https://doi.org/10.1016/0883-9026(90)90024-N

Shah, S. (2016). *Young disabled people aspirations, choices and constraints*. Routledge.

Shahnasarian, M. (2011). Career rehabilitation: Integration of vocational rehabilitation and career development in the twenty-first century. *Career Development Quarterly, 49*(3), 275–283. https://doi.org/10.1002/j.2161-0045.2001.tb00571.x

Sheehan, E. P., & Smith, H. V. (1986). Cerebral lateralization and handedness and their effects on verbal and spatial reasoning. *Neuropsychologia, 24*(4), 531–540. https://doi.org/10.1016/0028-3932(86)90097-7

Sheppard, A. (1985). Funny women: Social change and the audience response to female comedians. *Empirical Studies of the Arts, 3*(2), 179–195. https://doi.org/10.2190/6F5G-6L8U-VH7M-NQCB

Sherman, G. D., Lerner, J. S., Josephs, R. A., Renshon, J., & Gross, J. J. (2016). The interaction of testosterone and cortisol is associated with attained status in male executives. *Journal of Personality and Social Psychology, 110*(6), 921–929. https://doi.org/10.1037/pspp0000063

Shettel-Neuber, J., & O'Reilly, J. (1983). Handedness and career choice: Another look at supposed left/right differences. *Perceptual and Motor Skills, 57*(2), 391–397. https://doi.org/10.2466/pms.1983.57.2.391

Shuter, R. (1968). *The psychology of musical ability*. Methuen.

Shuter-Dyson, R., & Gabriel, C. (1981). *The psychology of musical ability* (2nd ed.). Methuen.

Sid, A. K., & Lindgren, H. C. (1982). Achievement and affiliation motivation and their correlates. *Educational and Psychological Measurement, 42*(4), 1213–1218. https://doi.org/10.1177/001316448204200430

Silver, E. M., & Bennett, C. (1987). Modification of the Minnesota Clerical Test to predict performance on video display terminals. *Journal of Applied Psychology, 72*(1), 153–155. https://doi.org/10.1037/0021-9010.72.1.153

Simonton, D. K. (1988). *Scientific genius: A psychology of science*. Cambridge University Press.

Simonton, D. K. (2014). More method in the mad-genius controversy: A historiometric study of 204 historic creators. *Psychology of Aesthetics, Creativity, and the Arts, 8*(1), 53–61. https://doi.org/10.1037/a0035367

Sincoff, J. B., & Sternberg, R. J. (1987). Two faces of verbal ability. *Intelligence, 11*(4), 263–276. https://doi.org/10.1016/0160-2896(87)90010-9

Sipps, G. J., Berry, W., & Lynch, E. M. (1987). WAIS-R and social intelligence: A test of established assumptions that uses the CPI. *Journal of Clinical Psychology, 43*(5), 499–504. https://doi.org/10.1002/1097-4679(198709)43:5<499::AID-JCLP2270430513>3.0.CO;2-7

Slaney, R. B. (1978). Expressed and inventoried vocational interests: A comparison of instruments. *Journal of Counseling Psychology, 25*(6), 520–529. https://doi.org/10.1037/0022-0167.25.6.520

Slaney, R. B. (1980). An investigation of racial differences on vocational variables among college women. *Journal of Vocational Behavior, 16*(2), 197–207. https://doi.org/10.1016/0001-8791(80)90050-0

Slaney, R. B., & Russell, J. E. (1981). An investigation of different levels of agreement between expressed and inventoried vocational interests among college women. *Journal of Counseling Psychology, 28(3)*, 221–228. https://doi.org/10.1037/0022-0167.28.3.221

Slaney, R. B., & Slaney, F. M. (1986). Relationship of expressed and inventoried vocational interests of female career counseling clients. *Career Development Quarterly, 35(1)*, 24–33. https://doi.org/10.1002/j.2161-0045.1986.tb00758.x

Sleep, C. E., Hyatt, C. S., Lamkin, J., Maples-Keller, J. L., & Miller, J. D. (2018). Examining the relations among the *DSM-5* alternative model of personality, the five-factor model, and externalizing and internalizing behavior. *Personality Disorders, 9*(4), 379–384. https://doi.org/10.1037/per0000240

Smith, I. M. (1964). *Spatial ability. Its educational and social significance*. Robert R. Knapp.

Smith, K. E. (1986). Sex-typed occupational roles and self-image among teachers. *Psychological Reports, 58*(1), 73–74. https://doi.org/10.2466/pr0.1986.58.1.73

Smith, T. J., & Campbell, C. (2009). The relationship between occupational interests and values. *Journal of Career Assessment, 17*(1), 39–55. https://doi.org/10.1177/1069072708325740

Sneider, J. T., Hamilton, D. A., Cohen-Gilbert, J. E., Crowley, D. J., Rosso, I. M., & Silveri, M. M. (2015). Sex differences in spatial navigation and perception in human adolescents and emerging adults. *Behavioural Processes, 111*, 42–50.

Snyder, A. W., & Thomas, M. (1997). Autistic artists give clues to cognition. *Perception, 26*(1), 93–96. https://doi.org/10.1068/p260093

Snyder, H. R. (2013). Major depressive disorder is associated with broad impairments on neuropsychological measures of executive function: A meta-analysis and review. *Psychological Bulletin, 139*(1), 81–132. https://doi.org/10.1037/a0028727

Solan, H. A. (1987). The effects of visual-spatial and verbal skills on written and mental arithmetic. *Journal of the American Optometric Association, 58*(2), 88–94.

Solso, R. L. (2000). The cognitive neuroscience of art: A preliminary fMRI observation. *Journal of Consciousness Studies, 7*(8–9), 75–86.

Soto, C. J., & John, O. P. (2009). Using the California Psychological Inventory to assess the Big Five personality domains: A hierarchical approach. *Journal of Research in Personality, 43*(1), 25–38. https://doi.org/10.1016/j.jrp.2008.10.005

Spangler, W. D. (1992). Validity of questionnaire and TAT measures of need for achievement: Two meta-analyses. *Psychological Bulletin, 112*(1), 140–154. https://doi.org/10.1037/0033-2909.112.1.140

Spearman, C. (1904). "General intelligence," objectively determined and measured. *American Journal of Psychology, 15*(2), 201–292. https://doi.org/10.2307/1412107

Spearman, C. (1927). *The abilities of man*. Macmillan.

Spelke, E. S. (2005). Sex differences in intrinsic aptitude for mathematics and science? A critical review. *American Psychologist, 60*(9), 950–958. https://doi.org/10.1037/0003-066X.60.9.950

Spence, J. T., & Helmreich, R. L. (1978). *Masculinity and femininity: Their psychological dimensions, correlates, and antecedents*. University of Texas Press.

Spence, J. T., & Helmreich, R. L. (1983). Achievement-related motives and behaviors. In J. T. Spence (Ed.), *Achievement and achievement motives: Psychological and sociological approaches* (pp. 7–74). W. H. Freeman.

Spritzer, M. D., Daviau, E. D., Coneeny, M. K., Engelman, S. M., Prince, W. T., & Rodriguez-Wisdom, K. N. (2011). Effects of testosterone on spatial learning and memory in adult male rats. *Hormones and Behavior, 59*(4), 484–496. https://doi.org/10.1016/j.yhbeh.2011.01.009

Staggs, G. D., Larson, L. M., & Borgen, F. H. (2007). Convergence of personality and interests: Meta-analysis of the Multidimensional Personality Questionnaire and the Strong Interest Inventory. *Journal of Career Assessment, 15*(4), 423–445. https://doi.org/10.1177/1069072707305760

Stahl, M. J., & Harrell, A. M. (1982). Evolution and validation of a behavioral decision theory measurement approach to achievement, power, and affiliation. *Journal of Applied Psychology, 67*(6), 744–751. https://doi.org/10.1037/0021-9010.67.6.744

Stajkovic, A. D., Bandura, A., Locke, E. A., Lee, D., & Sergent, K. (2018). Test of three conceptual models of influence of the Big Five personality traits and self-efficacy on academic performance: A meta-analytic path-analysis. *Personality and Individual Differences, 120*, 238–245. https://doi.org/10.1016/j.paid.2017.08.014

Stanek, K. C., & Ones, D. S. (2018). Taxonomies and compendia of cognitive ability and personality constructs and measures relevant to industrial, work, and organizational psychology. In D. S. Ones, N. Anderson, C. Viswesvaran, & H. K. Sinangil (Eds.), *The Sage handbook of industrial, work and organizational psychology: Vol. 1. Personnel psychology and employee performance* (2nd ed., pp. 366–407). SAGE Publications. https://doi.org/10.4135/9781473914940.n14

Stankov, L., & Horn, J. L. (1980). Human abilities revealed through auditory tests. *Journal of Educational Psychology, 72*(1), 21–44. https://doi.org/10.1037/0022-0663.72.1.21

Steel, Z., Marnane, C., Iranpour, C., Chey, T., Jackson, J. W., Patel, V., & Silove, D. (2014). The global prevalence of common mental disorders: A systematic review and meta-analysis 1980–2013. *International Journal of Epidemiology, 43*(2), 476–493. https://doi.org/10.1093/ije/dyu038

Steinberg, R., & Shapiro, S. (1982). Sex differences in personality traits of female and male Master of Business Administration students. *Journal of Applied Psychology, 67*(3), 306–310. https://doi.org/10.1037/0021-9010.67.3.306

Stericker, A., & LeVesconte, S. (1982). Effect of brief training on sex-related differences in visual-spatial skill. *Journal of Personality and Social Psychology, 43*(5), 1018–1029. https://doi.org/10.1037/0022-3514.43.5.1018

Stern, B. B., Barak, B., & Gould, S. (1987). Sexual Identity Scale: A new self-assessment measure. *Sex Roles, 17*(9–10), 503–519. https://doi.org/10.1007/BF00287732

Sterne, D. M. (1974). The Kuder Ois and rankings of vocational preference. *Educational and Psychological Measurement, 34*(1), 63–68. https://doi.org/10.1177/001316447403400109

Sternberg, R. J. (1982). A componential approach to intellectual development. In R. J. Sternberg (Ed.), *Advances in the psychology of human intelligence* (Vol. 1, pp. 413–463). Lawrence Erlbaum.

Sternberg, R. J. (1997a). Managerial intelligence: Why IQ isn't enough. *Journal of Management, 23*(3), 475–493. https://doi.org/10.1016/S0149-2063(97)90038-6

Sternberg, R. J. (1997b). The triarchic theory of intelligence. In D. P. Flanagan, J. L. Genshaft, & P. L. Hanson (Eds.), *Contemporary intellectual assessment: Theories, tests, and issues* (pp. 92–104). Guilford Press.

Sternberg, R. J. (2004). Culture and intelligence. *American Psychologist, 59*(5), 325–338. https://doi.org/10.1037/0003-066X.59.5.325

Sternberg, R. J., & Kaufman, S. B. (Eds.). (2011). *The Cambridge handbook of intelligence*. Cambridge University Press. https://doi.org/10.1017/CBO9780511977244

Sternberg, R. J., & Wagner, R. K. (Eds.). (1986). *Practical intelligence: Nature and origins of competence in the everyday world*. Cambridge University Press.

Stewart, D. W., & Latham, D. R. (1986). On some psychometric properties of Fiedler's contingency model of leadership. *Small Group Behavior, 17*(1), 83–94. https://doi.org/10.1177/104649648601700107

Stoll, G., Rieger, S., Lüdtke, O., Nagengast, B., Trautwein, U., & Roberts, B. W. (2017). Vocational interests assessed at the end of high school predict life outcomes assessed 10 years later over and above IQ and Big Five personality traits. *Journal of Personality and Social Psychology, 113*(1), 167–184. https://doi.org/10.1037/pspp0000117

Stoltz, K., & Barclay, S. (2019). *A comprehensive guide to career assessment* (7th ed.). National Career Development Association.

Storms, M. D. (1978). Attitudes toward homosexuality and femininity in men. *Journal of Homosexuality, 3*(3), 257–263. https://doi.org/10.1300/J082v03n03_08

Strahan, R. F., & Severinghaus, J. B. (1992). Dealing with ties in Holland-type consistency measures. *Journal of Vocational Behavior, 40*(2), 260–267. https://doi.org/10.1016/0001-8791(92)90074-A

Strang, R. (1930a). Measures of social intelligence. *American Journal of Sociology, 36*(2), 263–269. https://doi.org/10.1086/215342

Strang, R. (1930b). Relation of social intelligence to certain other factors. *School and Society, 32,* 268–272.

Strauss, V. (2014, June 9). Blue collar and service work takes more smarts than you may think-author. *The Washington Post.* https://www.washingtonpost.com/news/answer-sheet/wp/2014/06/09/blue-collar-and-service-work-takes-more-smarts-than-you-may-think-author/

Stricker, L. J., Rock, D. A., & Bennett, R. E. (2001). Sex and ethnic-group differences on accomplishments measures. *Applied Measurement in Education, 14*(3), 205–218. https://doi.org/10.1207/S15324818AME1403_1

Strong, E. K., Jr. (1931). *Change of interests with age.* Stanford University Press.

Strong, E. K., Jr. (1935). Predictive value of the vocational interest test. *Journal of Educational Psychology, 26*(5), 331–349. https://doi.org/10.1037/h0062498

Strong, E. K., Jr. (1938). *Vocational interest blank for men.* Stanford University Press.

Strong, E. K., Jr. (1943). *Vocational interests of men and women.* Stanford University Press.

Strong, E. K., Jr. (1951a). Interest scores while in college of occupations engaged in 20 years later. *Educational and Psychological Measurement, 11*(3), 335–348. https://doi.org/10.1177/001316445101100302

Strong, E. K., Jr. (1951b). Permanence of interest scores over 22 years. *Journal of Applied Psychology, 35*(2), 89–91. https://doi.org/10.1037/h0054643

Su, R., Rounds, J., & Armstrong, P. I. (2009). Men and things, women and people: A meta-analysis of sex differences in interests. *Psychological Bulletin, 135*(6), 859–884. https://doi.org/10.1037/a0017364

Subich, L. M. (1992). Holland's theory: "Pushing the envelope." *Journal of Vocational Behavior, 40*(2), 201–206. https://doi.org/10.1016/0001-8791(92)90068-B

Subich, L. M., Cooper, E. A., Barrett, G. V., & Arthur, W. (1986). Occupational perceptions of males and females as a function of sex ratios, salary, and availability. *Journal of Vocational Behavior, 28*(2), 123–134. https://doi.org/10.1016/0001-8791(86)90045-X

Super, D. E. (1973). The Work Values Inventory. In D. G. Zytowski (Ed.), *Contemporary approaches to interest measurement* (pp. 189–205). University of Minneapolis Press

Super, D. E., & Crites, J. O. (1962). *Appraising vocational fitness by means of psychological tests* (Rev. ed.). Harper & Brothers.

Swan, K. C. (2005). Vocational interests (The Self-Directed Search) of female carpenters. *Journal of Counseling Psychology, 52*(4), 655–657. https://doi.org/10.1037/0022-0167.52.4.655

Swanson, H. L. (2017). Verbal and visual-spatial working memory: What develops over a life span? *Developmental Psychology, 53*(5), 971–995. https://doi.org/10.1037/dev0000291

Swanson, J. L. (1992). The structure of vocational interests for African-American college students. *Journal of Vocational Behavior, 40*(2), 144–157. https://doi.org/10.1016/0001-8791(92)90062-5

Swanson, J. L. (2013). Assessment of career development and maturity. In K. F. Geisinger, B. A. Bracken, J. F. Carlson, J.-I. C. Hansen, N. R. Kuncel, S. P. Reise, & M. C. Rodriguez (Eds.), *APA handbook of testing and assessment in psychology: Vol. 2. Testing and assessment in clinical and counseling psychology* (pp. 349–362). American Psychological Association. https://doi.org/10.1037/14048-020

Swanson, J. L., & Hansen, J. I. (1988). Stability of vocational interests over 4-year, 8-year, and 12-year intervals. *Journal of Vocational Behavior, 33*(2), 185–202. https://doi.org/10.1016/0001-8791(88)90055-3

Takeuchi, A. H., & Hulse, S. H. (1993). Absolute pitch. *Psychological Bulletin, 113*(2), 345–361. https://doi.org/10.1037/0033-2909.113.2.345

Talamini, F., Altoè, G., Carretti, B., & Grassi, M. (2017). Musicians have better memory than nonmusicians: A meta-analysis. *PLOS ONE, 12*(10), e0186773. https://doi.org/10.1371/journal.pone.0186773

Talamini, F., Carretti, B., & Grassi, M. (2016). The working memory of musicians and nonmusicians. *Music Perception, 34*(2), 183–191. https://doi.org/10.1525/mp.2016.34.2.183

Talboy, A. N. (2011). Evaluation of the Armed Services Vocation Aptitude Battery (ASVAB). *Journal of Young Investigators, 22*(11), 81–84.

Tan, Y. T., McPherson, G. E., Peretz, I., Berkovic, S. F., & Wilson, S. J. (2014). The genetic basis of music ability. *Frontiers in Psychology, 5*, 658. https://doi.org/10.3389/fpsyg.2014.00658

Tay, L., Su, R., & Rounds, J. (2011). People–things and data–ideas: Bipolar dimensions? *Journal of Counseling Psychology, 58*(3), 424–440. https://doi.org/10.1037/a0023488

Taylor, C. W., & Barron, F. (Eds.). (1963). *Scientific creativity: Its recognition and development.* John Wiley.

Taylor, D. (2018, November). *Americans with disabilities: 2014* (Current Population Reports, Report No. P70-152). U.S. Census Bureau. https://www.census.gov/content/dam/Census/library/publications/2018/demo/p70-152.pdf

Taylor, G. A., Bidus, D. R., & Collins, H. A. (1977). The vocational interests of drug-dependent patients. *Psychological Reports, 41*(3), 959–963. https://doi.org/10.2466/pr0.1977.41.3.959

Taylor, J., Hunt, E., & Coggan, P. (1987). Effect of diazepam on the speed of mental rotation. *Psychopharmacology, 91*(3), 369–371. https://doi.org/10.1007/BF00518193

Teevan, R. C., Heinzen, T. E., & Hartsough, W. R. (1988). Personality correlates between need for achievement and subscales of the F-scale of authoritarianism. *Psychological Reports, 62*(3), 959–961. https://doi.org/10.2466/pr0.1988.62.3.959

Teig, S., & Susskind, J. E. (2008). Truck driver or nurse? The impact of gender roles and occupational status on children's occupational preferences. *Sex Roles, 58*(11–12), 848–863. https://doi.org/10.1007/s11199-008-9410-x

Tellegen, A., & Ben-Porath, Y. S. (2011). *Minnesota Multiphasic Personality Inventory–2: Restructured form* (Technical manual). University of Minnesota Press.

Tellegen, A., & Waller, N. G. (2008). Exploring personality through test construction: Development of the Multidimensional Personality Questionnaire. In G. J. Boyle, G. Matthews, & D. H. Saklofske (Eds.), *The SAGE handbook of personality theory and assessment: Vol. 2. Personality measurement and testing* (pp. 261–292). SAGE Publications. https://doi.org/10.4135/9781849200479.n13

Tenopyr, M. L. (1967). Social intelligence and academic success. *Educational and Psychological Measurement, 27*(4), 961–965. https://doi.org/10.1177/001316446702700444

Terman, L. M. (1925). *Genetic studies of genius: Vol. 1. Mental and physical traits of a thousand gifted children.* Stanford University Press.

Terpstra, D. E. (1983). An investigation of job-seeker preferences through multiple methodologies. *Journal of Employment Counseling, 20*(4), 169–178. https://doi.org/10.1002/j.2161-1920.1983.tb00777.x

Tetlock, P. E., Peterson, R. S., & Berry, J. (1993). Flattering and unflattering personality portraits of integratively simple and complex managers. *Journal of Personality and Social Psychology, 64*(3), 500–511. https://doi.org/10.1037/0022-3514.64.3.500

Tétreau, B., & Trahan, M. (1988). Sexual identification and the maturing vocational interests of pre-adolescent girls. *Applied Psychology, 37*(2), 165–181. https://doi.org/10.1111/j.1464-0597.1988.tb01134.x

Tett, R. P., & Christiansen, N. D. (2008). Personality assessment in organizations. In G. J. Boyle, G. Matthews, & D. H. Saklofske (Eds.), *The SAGE handbook of personality theory and assessment: Vol. 1. Personality theories and models* (pp. 720–742). SAGE Publications.

Tett, R. P., Simonet, D. V., Walser, B., & Brown, C. (2013). Trait activation theory: Applications, developments, and implications for personality-workplace fit. In

N. Christiansen & R. P. Tett (Eds.), *Handbook of personality at work* (pp. 71–100). Routledge.

Thomas, L. E. & Robbins, P. I. (1979). Personality and work environment congruence of mid-life career changes. *Journal of Occupational Psychology, 52*(3), 177–183. https://doi.org/10.1111/j.2044-8325.1979.tb00452.x

Thompson, C. E. (1942). Motor and mechanical abilities in professional schools. *Journal of Applied Psychology, 26*(1), 24–37. https://doi.org/10.1037/h0059177

Thompson, R. A. (1985). Vocational interests of vocational/technical and non-college bound students using the Career Assessment Inventory. *Journal of Research & Development in Education, 18*(4), 61–67.

Thomson, K. (2012, June 15). How many musicians are there? *Future of Music Coalition*. http://money.futureofmusic.org/how-many-musicians-are-there/

Thomson, P., & Jaque, V. S. (2016). *Creativity and the performing artist: Behind the mask*. Academic Press.

Thorndike, E. L. (1920). Intelligence and its use. *Harper's Magazine, 140*, 227–235.

Thorndike, R. L. (1936). Factor analysis of social and abstract intelligence. *Journal of Educational Psychology, 27*(3), 231–233. https://doi.org/10.1037/h0059840

Thorndike, R. L. (1985). The central role of general ability in prediction. *Multivariate Behavioral Research, 20*(3), 241–254. https://doi.org/10.1207/s15327906mbr2003_1

Thorndike, R. L., & Stein, S. (1937). An evaluation of the attempts to measure social intelligence. *Psychological Bulletin, 34*(5), 275–285. https://doi.org/10.1037/h0053850

Thornton, G. E., III, Johnson, S. K., & Church, A. H. (2017). Executives and high potentials. In J. L. Farr & N. Tippins (Eds.), *Handbook of employee selection* (2nd ed., pp. 833–852). Taylor & Francis.

Thornton, G. E., III, Rupp, D. E., & Hoffman, B. J. (2015). *Assessment center perspectives for talent management strategies* (2nd ed.). Routledge.

Thurstone, L. L. (1936). The isolation of seven primary abilities. *Psychological Bulletin, 33*, 780–781.

Thurstone, L. L. (1938). *Primary mental abilities*. The University of Chicago Press.

Thurstone, L. L. (1948). Primary mental abilities. *Science, 108*(2813), 585.

Tiebout, C., & Meier, N. C. (1936). Artistic ability and general intelligence. *Psychological Monographs, 48*(1), 95–125. https://doi.org/10.1037/h0093367

Tiffin, J. (1947). Mental ability and mechanical aptitude tests. In J. Tiffin (Ed.), *Industrial psychology* (pp. 82–121). Prentice-Hall, Inc. https://doi.org/10.1037/12233-004

Tinker, M. A. (1944). Speed, power, and level in the Revised Minnesota Paper Form Board Test. *Journal of Genetic Psychology, 64*, 93–97.

Tinsley, D. J., & Faunce, P. S. (1978). Vocational interests of career and homemaker oriented women. *Journal of Vocational Behavior, 13*(3), 327–337. https://doi.org/10.1016/0001-8791(78)90059-3

Tipton, R. M. (1976). Attitudes towards women's roles in society and vocational interests. *Journal of Vocational Behavior, 8*(2), 155–165. https://doi.org/10.1016/0001-8791(76)90018-X

Toker, Y. (2011). *Non-ability correlates of the science-math trait complex: Searching for personality characteristics and revisiting vocational interests* (UMI No. 3451383) [Doctoral dissertation, Georgia Institute of Technology]. ProQuest Dissertations and Theses Global.

Toossi, M. (2002). A century of change: The U.S. labor force, 1950–2050. *Monthly Labor Review, 125*, 15–28.

Torpey, E. (2017). Women in management. *Career Outlook*. U.S. Bureau of Labor Statistics. https://www.bls.gov/careeroutlook/2017/data-on-display/women-managers.htm

Torrance, E. P. (1965). *Rewarding creative behavior*. Prentice-Hall.

Tosto, M. G., Hanscombe, K. B., Haworth, C. M. A., Davis, O. S. P., Petrill, S. A., Dale, P. S., Malykh, S., Plomin, R., & Kovas, Y. (2014). Why do spatial abilities predict mathematical performance? *Developmental Science, 17*(3), 462–470. https://doi.org/10.1111/desc.12138

Townsend, A. (1986). The inner critic, the creative, and the feminine. *Psychological Perspectives, 17*(1), 49–58. https://doi.org/10.1080/00332928608408706

Tracey, T. J. G. (2002). Personal Globe Inventory: Measurement of the spherical model of interests and competence beliefs. *Journal of Vocational Behavior, 60*(1), 113–172. https://doi.org/10.1006/jvbe.2001.1817

Tracey, T. J. G., & Robbins, S. B. (2005). Stability of interests across ethnicity and gender: A longitudinal examination of Grades 8 through 12. *Journal of Vocational Behavior, 67*(3), 335–364. https://doi.org/10.1016/j.jvb.2004.11.003

Tracey, T. J. G., & Rounds, J. B. (1993). Evaluating Holland's and Gati's vocational-interest models: A structural meta-analysis. *Psychological Bulletin, 113*(2), 229–246. https://doi.org/10.1037/0033-2909.113.2.229

Tracey, T. J. G., & Rounds, J. B. (1997). Circular structure of vocational interests. In R. Plutchik & H. R. Conte (Eds.), *Circumplex models of personality and emotions* (pp. 183–201). American Psychological Association. https://doi.org/10.1037/10261-008

Tracey, T. J. G., & Sodano, S. M. (2008). Issues of stability and change in interest development. *Career Development Quarterly, 57*(1), 51–62. https://doi.org/10.1002/j.2161-0045.2008.tb00165.x

Tracey, T. J. G., & Sodano, S. M. (2015). Assessing children: Interests and personality. In P. J. Hartung, M. L. Savickas, & W. B. Walsh (Eds.), *APA handbook of career intervention: Vol. 2. Applications.* (pp. 113–124). American Psychological Association. https://doi.org/10.1037/14439-009

Tracey, T. J. G., Wille, B., Durr, M. R., II, & De Fruyt, F. (2014). An enhanced examination of Holland's consistency and differentiation hypotheses. *Journal of Vocational Behavior, 84*(3), 237–247. https://doi.org/10.1016/j.jvb.2014.01.008

Trahan, L. H., Stuebing, K. K., Fletcher, J. M., & Hiscock, M. (2014, September). The Flynn effect: A meta-analysis. *Psychological Bulletin, 140*(5), 1332–1360. https://doi.org/10.1037/a0037173

Tryon, G. S. (1983). Differentiation between counseled and noncounseled students on the general occupational themes of the Strong Campbell Interest Inventory. *Journal of College Student Personnel, 24*, 51–54.

Tsay, C. J., & Banaji, M. R. (2011). Naturals and strivers: Preferences and beliefs about sources of achievement. *Journal of Experimental Social Psychology, 47*(2), 460–465. https://doi.org/10.1016/j.jesp.2010.12.010

Tuck, B. F., & Keeling, B. (1980). Sex and cultural differences in the factorial structure of the self-directed search. *Journal of Vocational Behavior, 16*(1), 105–114. https://doi.org/10.1016/0001-8791(80)90042-1

Tupes, E. C., & Christal, R. E. (1961). Recurrent personality factors based on trait ratings. *Journal of Personality, 60*(2), 225–251. https://doi.org/10.1111/j.1467-6494.1992.tb00973.x

Turner, R. G., & Hibbs, C. (1977). Vocational interest and personality correlates of differential abilities. *Psychological Reports, 40*(3), 727–730. https://doi.org/10.2466/pr0.1977.40.3.727

Turner, S., Unkefer, C., Cichy, B. E., Peper, C., & Juang, J.-P. (2011). Career interests and self-estimated abilities of young adults with disabilities. *Journal of Career Assessment, 19*(2), 183–196. https://doi.org/10.1177/1069072710385651

Turnipseed, D. L. (2018). Emotional intelligence and OCB: The moderating role of work locus of control. *Journal of Social Psychology, 158*(3), 322–336. https://doi.org/10.1080/00224545.2017.1346582

Twenge, J. M. (1997). Changes in masculine and feminine traits over time: A meta-analysis. *Sex Roles, 36*(5–6), 305–325. https://doi.org/10.1007/BF02766650

Twenge, J. M., Zhang, L., & Im, C. (2004). It's beyond my control: A cross-temporal meta-analysis of increasing externality in locus of control, 1960-2002. *Personality and Social Psychology Review, 8*(3), 308–319. https://doi.org/10.1207/s15327957pspr0803_5

Tyler, L. E. (1951). The relationship of interests to abilities and reputation among first-grade children. *Educational and Psychological Measurement, 11*(2), 255–264. https://doi.org/10.1177/001316445101100209

Urist, J. (2014, September 24). What the marshmallow test really teaches about self-control. *The Atlantic.* https://www.theatlantic.com/health/archive/2014/09/what-the-marshmallow-test-really-teaches-about-self-control/380673/

U.S. Census Bureau. (2013). Men in nursing occupations. *American Community Survey Highlight Report.* Retrieved July 16, 2019, from https://www.census.gov/content/dam/Census/library/working-papers/2013/acs/2013_Landivar_02.pdf

U.S. Department of Labor. (1970). *Manual for the USES General Aptitude Test Battery: Section III. Development.*

U.S. Department of Labor. (1979). *Manual for the USES General Aptitude Test Battery: Section II. Occupational aptitude pattern structure.*

U.S. Employment Service. (1957). *Estimates of worker trait requirements for 4,000 jobs.* United States Government Printing Office.

Uttal, D. H., Meadow, N. G., Tipton, E., Hand, L. L., Alden, A. R., Warren, C., & Newcombe, N. S. (2013). The malleability of spatial skills: A meta-analysis of training studies. *Psychological Bulletin, 139*(2), 352–402. https://doi.org/10.1037/a0028446

Utz, P., & Korben, D. (1976). The construct validity of the occupational themes on the Strong–Campbell Interest Inventory. *Journal of Vocational Behavior, 9*(1), 31–42. https://doi.org/10.1016/0001-8791(76)90004-X

Vacc, N. A., & Hinkle, J. S. (1994). Review of the Career Assessment Inventory—Enhanced Version and Career Assessment Inventory—Vocational Version. In J. T. Kapes, M. M. Mastie, & E. A. Whitfield (Eds.), *A counselor's guide to career assessment instruments* (3rd ed., pp. 145–150). National Career Development.

Van Iddekinge, C. H., Putka, D. J., & Campbell, J. P. (2011). Reconsidering vocational interests for personnel selection: The validity of an interest-based selection test in relation to job knowledge, job performance, and continuance intentions. *Journal of Applied Psychology, 96*(1), 13–33. https://doi.org/10.1037/a0021193

Van Iddekinge, C. H., Roth, P. L., Putka, D. J., & Lanivich, S. E. (2011). Are you interested? A meta-analysis of relations between vocational interests and employee performance and turnover. *Journal of Applied Psychology, 96*(6), 1167–1194. https://doi.org/10.1037/a0024343

Van Lange, P. A., De Bruin, E. M., Otten, W., & Joireman, J. A. (1997). Development of prosocial, individualistic, and competitive orientations: Theory and preliminary evidence. *Journal of Personality and Social Psychology, 73*(4), 733–746. https://doi.org/10.1037/0022-3514.73.4.733

Vandenberg, S. G., & Kuse, A. R. (1979). Spatial ability: A critical review of the sex-linked major gene hypothesis. In M. A. Wittig & A. C. Petersen (Eds.), *Sex-related differences in cognitive functioning: Developmental issues* (pp. 67–95). Academic Press.

Venable, M. A. (2010). Using technology to deliver career development services: Supporting today's students in higher education. *Career Development Quarterly, 59*(1), 87–96. https://doi.org/10.1002/j.2161-0045.2010.tb00132.x

Verbeke, W., Dietz, B., & Verwaal, E. (2011). Drivers of sales performance: A contemporary meta-analysis. Have salespeople become knowledge brokers? *Journal of the Academy of Marketing Science, 39*(3), 407–428. https://doi.org/10.1007/s11747-010-0211-8

Vernon, P. E. (1950). *The structure of human abilities.* Methuen & Co.; Wiley.

Vernon, P. E. (2014). *The structure of human abilities*. Routledge (Psychology Revival series). (Original work published 1961)

Vinchur, A. J., Schippmann, J. S., Switzer, F. S. III, & Roth, P. L. (1998). A meta-analytic review of predictors of job performance for salespeople. *Journal of Applied Psychology, 83(4)*, 586–597. https://doi.org/10.1037/0021-9010.83.4.586

Vinitsky, M. (1973). A forty-year follow-up on the vocational interests of psychologists and their relationship to career development. *American Psychologist, 28(11)*, 1000–1009. https://doi.org/10.1037/h0035603

Viscott, D. S. (1970). A musical idiot savant: A psychodynamic study, and some speculations on the creative process. *Psychiatry, 33(4)*, 494–515. https://doi.org/10.1080/00332747.1970.11023647

Visser, B. A., Ashton, M. C., & Vernon, P. A. (2006). Beyond "g": Putting Multiple Intelligences Theory to the test. *Intelligence, 34(5)*, 487–502. https://doi.org/10.1016/j.intell.2006.02.004

Vocational Rehabilitation Association of Canada. (2021). *Code of ethics for vocational rehabilitation professionals*. https://members.vracanada.com/wp-content/uploads/VRA-Canada-Code-of-Ethics-June-2-2021.pdf

Vogel, J. J., Bowers, C. A., & Vogel, D. S. (2003). Cerebral lateralization of spatial abilities: A meta-analysis. *Brain and Cognition, 52(2)*, 197–204. https://doi.org/10.1016/S0278-2626(03)00056-3

Volodina, A., Nagy, G., & Köller, O. (2015). Success in the first phase of the vocational career: The role of cognitive and scholastic abilities, personality factors, and vocational interests. *Journal of Vocational Behavior, 91*, 11–22. https://doi.org/10.1016/j.jvb.2015.08.009

Waddell, C. (1998). Creativity and mental illness: Is there a link? *Canadian Journal of Psychiatry, 43(2)*, 166–172. https://doi.org/10.1177/070674379804300206

Waddell, F. T. (1983). Factors affecting choice, satisfaction, and success in the female self- employed. *Journal of Vocational Behavior, 23(3)*, 294–304. https://doi.org/10.1016/0001-8791(83)90043-X

Wagner, J., Lüdtke, O., & Robitzsch, A. (2019). Does personality become more stable with age? Disentangling state and trait effects for the Big Five across the life span using local structural equation modeling. *Journal of Personality and Social Psychology, 116(4)*, 666–680. https://doi.org/10.1037/pspp0000203

Wagner, R. K., & Sternberg, R. J. (1985). Practical intelligence in real-world pursuits: The role of tacit knowledge. *Journal of Personality and Social Psychology, 49(2)*, 436–458. https://doi.org/10.1037/0022-3514.49.2.436

Wai, J., Lubinski, D., & Benbow, C. P. (2009). Spatial ability for STEM domains: Aligning over 50 years of cumulative psychological knowledge solidifies its importance. *Journal of Educational Psychology, 101(4)*, 817–835. https://doi.org/10.1037/a0016127

Wai, J., Lubinski, D., Benbow, C. P., & Steiger, J. H. (2010). Accomplishment in science, technology, engineering, and mathematics (STEM) and its relation to STEM educational dose: A 25-year longitudinal study. *Journal of Educational Psychology, 102(4)*, 860–871. https://doi.org/10.1037/a0019454

Wall, J. E. (2018). Qualifying for military service as an enlistee and the importance of the ASVAB for military and civilian work. *Career Planning and Adult Development Journal, 34(1)*, 46–52.

Wallace, T., & Walberg, H. J. (1987). Personality traits and childhood environments of eminent essayists. *Gifted Child Quarterly, 31(2)*, 65–69. https://doi.org/10.1177/001698628703100204

Waller, N. G., Lykken, D. T., & Tellegen, A. (1995). Occupational interests, leisure time interests, and personality: Three domains or one? Findings from the Minnesota Twin Registry. In D. J. Lubinski & R. V. Dawis (Eds.), *Assessing individual differences in human behavior: New concepts, methods, and findings* (pp. 233–259). Davies-Black Publishing.

Walters, J. M., & Gardner, H. (1986). The theory of multiple intelligences: Some issues and answers. In R. J. Sternberg & R. K. Wagner (Eds.), *Practical intelligence* (pp. 163–192). Cambridge University Press.

Wampold, B. E., Ankarlo, G., Mondin, G., Trinidad-Carrillo, M., Baumler, B., & Prater, K. (1995). Social skills of and social environments produced by different Holland types: A social perspective on person-environment fit models. *Journal of Counseling Psychology, 42*(3), 365–379. https://doi.org/10.1037/0022-0167.42.3.365

Wan, C. Y., & Schlaug, G. (2013). Brain plasticity induced by musical training. In D. Deutsch (Ed.), *The psychology of music* (pp. 565–581). Academic Press.

Wang, L., Cohen, A. S., & Carr, M. (2014). Spatial ability at two scales of representation: A meta-analysis. *Learning and Individual Differences, 36*, 140–144. https://doi.org/10.1016/j.lindif.2014.10.006

Wang, Q., Bowling, N. A., & Eschleman, K. J. (2010). A meta-analytic examination of work and general locus of control. *Journal of Applied Psychology, 95*(4), 761–768. https://doi.org/10.1037/a0017707

Wanzel, K. R., Hamstra, S. J., Caminiti, M. F., Anastakis, D. J., Grober, E. D., & Reznick, R. K. (2003). Visual-spatial ability correlates with efficiency of hand motion and successful surgical performance. *Surgery, 134*(5), 750–757. https://doi.org/10.1016/S0039-6060(03)00248-4

Ward, C. M., & Walsh, W. B. (1981). Concurrent validity of Holland's theory for non-college-degreed Black women. *Journal of Vocational Behavior, 18*(3), 356–361.

Ward, G. R., Cunningham, C. H., & Wakefield, J. A., Jr. (1976). Relationships between Holland's VPI and Cattell's 16PF. *Journal of Vocational Behavior, 8*(3), 307–312. https://doi.org/10.1016/0001-8791(76)90046-4

Warrier, S. K. (1982). Values of successful managers: Implications for managerial success. *Management and Labour Studies, 8*, 7–15.

Watson, S., & Watson, T. S. (2014). *Review of the Emotional and Social Competence Inventory Lincoln*. Buros Testing Institute, University of Nebraska.

Watts, T. W., Duncan, G. J., & Quan, H. (2018). Revisiting the marshmallow test: A conceptual replication investigating links between early delay of gratification and later outcomes. *Psychological Science, 29*(7), 1159–1177. https://doi.org/10.1177/0956797618761661

Webb, R. M., Lubinski, D., & Benbow, C. P. (2007). Spatial ability: A neglected dimension in talent searches for intellectually precocious youth. *Journal of Educational Psychology, 99*(2), 397–420. https://doi.org/10.1037/0022-0663.99.2.397

Wechsler, D. (1975). Intelligence defined and undefined: A relativistic appraisal. *American Psychologist, 30*(2), 135–139. https://doi.org/10.1037/h0076868

Weekley, J. A., & Gier, J. A. (1987). Reliability and validity of the situational interview for a sales position. *Journal of Applied Psychology, 72*(3), 484–487. https://doi.org/10.1037/0021-9010.72.3.484

Weiner, J. A., & Necus, I. (2018). Infrastructure to support technology-enhanced global assessment. In J. C. Scott, D. Bartram, & D. H. Reynolds (Eds.), *Next generation technology-enhanced assessment: Global perspectives on occupational and workplace testing* (pp. 71–101). Cambridge University Press.

Weis, S. E., Firker, A., & Hennig, J. (2007). Associations between the second to fourth digit ratio and career interests. *Personality and Individual Differences, 43*(3), 485–493. https://doi.org/10.1016/j.paid.2006.12.017

Weiss, A., & Deary, I. J. (2020). A new look at neuroticism: Should we worry so much about worrying? *Current Directions in Psychological Science, 29*(1), 92–101. https://doi.org/10.1177/0963721419887184

Weiss, A., King, J. E., & Figueredo, A. J. (2000). The heritability of personality factors in chimpanzees (Pan troglodytes). *Behavior Genetics, 30*(3), 213–221. https://doi.org/10.1023/A:1001966224914

Weiss, L. G., Saklofske, D. H., Coalson, D., & Raiford, S. E. (Eds.). (2010). *WAIS-IV clinical use and interpretation: Scientist-practitioner perspectives.* Academic Press.

Weller, L., Shlomi, A., & Zimont, G. (1976). Birth order, sex, and occupational interest. *Journal of Vocational Behavior, 8*(1), 45–50. https://doi.org/10.1016/0001-8791(76)90032-4

Westbrook, F. D. (1975). High scales on the Strong Vocational Interest Blank and the Kuder Occupational Interest Survey using Holland's occupational codes. *Journal of Counseling Psychology, 22*(1), 24–27. https://doi.org/10.1037/h0076155

Westbrook, M. T., & Nordholm, L. A. (1984). Characteristics of women health professionals with vertical, lateral, and stationary career plans. *Sex Roles, 10*(9–10), 743–756. https://doi.org/10.1007/BF00287385

Whetzel, D. L., McCloy, R. A., Hooper, A., Russell, T. L., Waters, S. D., Campbell, W. J., & Ramos, R. A. (2011). Meta-analysis of clerical performance predictors: Still stable after all these years. *International Journal of Selection and Assessment, 19*(1), 41–50. https://doi.org/10.1111/j.1468-2389.2010.00533.x

White, K. R. (1985). Review of Comprehensive Ability Battery. In J. V. Mitchell, Jr. (Ed.), *The ninth mental measurements yearbook* (Vol. 1, pp. 377–379). Buros Institute of Mental Measurements.

White, P. A. (1988). The structured representation of information in long-term memory: A possible explanation for the accomplishments of "idiots savants." *New Ideas in Psychology, 6*(1), 3–14. https://doi.org/10.1016/0732-118X(88)90019-0

Whitley, M. T. (1932). A comparison of the Seashore and the Kwalwasser-Dykema music tests. *Teachers College Record, 33,* 731–751.

Whittington, J. E. (1988). Large verbal–non-verbal ability differences and underachievement. *British Journal of Educational Psychology, 58*(2), 205–211. https://doi.org/10.1111/j.2044-8279.1988.tb00894.x

Wicherts, J. M., & Vorst, H. M. (2010). The relation between specialty choice of psychology students and their interests, personality, and cognitive abilities. *Learning and Individual Differences, 20*(5), 494–500. https://doi.org/10.1016/j.lindif.2010.01.004

Widiger, T. A. (2009). Neuroticism. In M. R. Leary & R. H. Hoyle (Eds.) *Handbook of individual differences in social behavior* (pp. 129–146). Guilford Press.

Widiger, T. A. (2011). Personality and psychopathology. *World Psychiatry, 10*(2), 103–106. https://doi.org/10.1002/j.2051-5545.2011.tb00024.x

Widiger, T. A., Crego, C., Oltmanns, J., Rojas, S. L., & Oltmanns, R. (2017). Five-factor model and personality disorder. In T. A. Widiger (Ed.), *The Oxford handbook of the five factor model* (pp. 449–478). Oxford University Press.

Widiger, T. A., & Oltmanns, J. R. (2017). Neuroticism is a fundamental domain of personality with enormous public health implications. *World Psychiatry, 16*(2), 144–145. https://doi.org/10.1002/wps.20411

Widiger, T. A., & Trull, T. J. (1992). Personality and psychopathology: An application of the five-factor model. *Journal of Personality, 60*(2), 363–393. https://doi.org/10.1111/j.1467-6494.1992.tb00977.x

Widiger, T. A., & Trull, T. J. (2007). Plate tectonics in the classification of personality disorder: Shifting to a dimensional model. *American Psychologist, 62*(2), 71–83. https://doi.org/10.1037/0003-066X.62.2.71

Wiegand, J. P., Drasgow, F., & Rounds, J. (2021). Misfit matters: A re-examination of interest fit and job satisfaction. *Journal of Vocational Behavior, 125,* 103524. https://doi.org/10.1016/j.jvb.2020.103524

Wiener, Y., & Klein, K. L. (1978). The relationship between vocational interests and job satisfaction: Reconciliation of divergent results. *Journal of Vocational Behavior*, *13*(3), 298–304. https://doi.org/10.1016/0001-8791(78)90056-8

Wiener, Y., & Vaitenas, R. (1977). Personality correlates of voluntary midcareer change in enterprising occupations. *Journal of Applied Psychology*, *62*(6), 706–712. https://doi.org/10.1037/0021-9010.62.6.706

Wiernik, B. M. (2016). Intraindividual personality profiles associated with realistic interests. *Journal of Career Assessment*, *24*(3), 460–480. https://doi.org/10.1177/1069072715599378

Wiernik, B. M., Dilchert, S., & Ones, D. S. (2016). Creative interests and personality: Scientific versus artistic creativity. *Zeitschrift für Arbeits- und Organisationspsychologie*, *60*(2), 65–78. https://doi.org/10.1026/0932-4089/a000211

Wilhelm, O. (2005). Measures of emotional intelligence: Practice and standards. In R. Schulze & R. D. Roberts (Eds.), *Emotional intelligence: An international handbook* (pp. 131–154). Hogrefe & Huber Publishers.

Wilk, S. L., Desmarais, L. B., & Sackett, P. R. (1995). Gravitation to jobs commensurate with ability: Longitudinal and cross-sectional tests. *Journal of Applied Psychology*, *80*(1), 79–85. https://doi.org/10.1037/0021-9010.80.1.79

Wilkinson, G. S., & Robertson, G. J. (2017). *Wide Range Achievement Test* (5th ed.) [Manual]. Pearson Assessments.

Williams, E. D., Winter, L., & Woods, J. M. (1938). Tests of literary appreciation. *British Journal of Educational Psychology*, *8*(3), 265–284. https://doi.org/10.1111/j.2044-8279.1938.tb03132.x

Williams, S. W., & McCullers, J. C. (1983). Personal factors related to typicalness of career and success in active professional women. *Psychology of Women Quarterly*, *7*(4), 343–357. https://doi.org/10.1111/j.1471-6402.1983.tb00849.x

Wills, G. I. (1984). A personality study of musicians working in the popular field. *Personality and Individual Differences*, *5*(3), 359–360. https://doi.org/10.1016/0191-8869(84)90075-8

Wilson, G. D., & Jackson, C. (1994). The personality of physicists. *Personality and Individual Differences*, *16*(1), 187–189. https://doi.org/10.1016/0191-8869(94)90123-6

Wilt, J., & Revelle, W. R. (2009). Extraversion. In M. R. Leary & R. H. Hoyle (Eds.), *Handbook of individual differences in social behavior* (pp. 27–45). Guilford Press.

Wing, H. (1941). A factorial study of musical tests. *British Journal of Psychology*, *31*(4), 341–355.

Wing, H. (1960). *Manual for Standardised Tests of Musical Intelligence*. National Foundation for Education Research.

Wing, H. (1968). *Tests of musical ability and appreciation: An investigation into the measurement, distribution, and development of musical capacity*. Cambridge University Press.

Wink, P., & Gough, H. G. (1990). New narcissism scales for the California Psychological Inventory and MMPI. *Journal of Personality Assessment*, *54*(3–4), 446–462. https://doi.org/10.1080/00223891.1990.9674010

Winner, E. (1996). *Gifted children: Myths and realities*. Basic Books.

Winner, E. (1997). Giftedness versus creativity in the visual arts. *Psychology and the Arts. Gifted and Talented International*, *12*(1), 18–26. https://doi.org/10.1080/15332276.1997.11672861

Winter, D. G. (1973). *The power motive*. Free Press.

Witkin, H. A., Moore, C. A., Goodenough, D. R., & Cox, P. W. (1977). Field-dependent and field-independent cognitive styles and their educational implications. *Review of Educational Research*, *47*(1), 1–64.

Wittkower, R., & Wittkower, M. (1963). *Born under Saturn. The character and conduct of artists: A documented history from antiquity to the French revolution*. Norton.

Wolff, A. S., & Frey, P. W. (1984–1985). A note on the correlation of visual-spatial ability and the acquisition of game skill. *Educational Research Quarterly*, *9*(4), 4–5.

Wolff, S. B. (2005). *Emotional Competence Inventory (ECI) technical manual*. Hay Group, McClelland Center for Research and Innovation. http://www.eiconsortium.org/pdf/ECI_2_0_Technical_Manual_v2.pdf

Wong, P. T., Kettlewell, G. E., & Sproule, C. F. (1985). On the importance of being masculine: Sex role, attribution, and women's career achievement. *Sex Roles, 12*(7–8), 757–769. https://doi.org/10.1007/BF00287869

Wood, W., & Eagly, A. H. (2009). Gender identity. In M. R. Leary & R. H. Hoyle (Eds.), *Handbook of individual differences in social behavior* (pp. 109–125). Guilford Press.

Woodrow, H. (1939). The common factors in fifty-two mental tests. *Psychometrika, 4*(2), 99–108. https://doi.org/10.1007/BF02288489

Woollett, K., & Maguire, E. A. (2009). Navigational expertise may compromise anterograde associative memory. *Neuropsychologia, 47*(4), 1088–1095. https://doi.org/10.1016/j.neuropsychologia.2008.12.036

World Health Organization. (2001). *International classification of functioning, disability and health (ICF)*.

Wortman, J., Lucas, R. E., & Donnellan, M. B. (2012). Stability and change in the Big Five personality domains: Evidence from a longitudinal study of Australians. *Psychology and Aging, 27*(4), 867–874. https://doi.org/10.1037/a0029322

Wroblewski, D. (2008). *The story of Edgar Sawtelle*. Ecco (HarperCollins).

Wrzus, C., Wagner, G. G., & Riediger, M. (2016). Personality-situation transactions from adolescence to old age. *Journal of Personality and Social Psychology, 110*(5), 782–799. https://doi.org/10.1037/pspp0000054

Wu, J., & LeBreton, J. M. (2011). Reconsidering the dispositional basis of counterproductive work behavior: The role of aberrant personality traits. *Personnel Psychology, 64*(3), 593–626. https://doi.org/10.1111/j.1744-6570.2011.01220.x

Xu, H., & Li, H. (2020). Operationalize interest congruence: A comparative examination of four approaches. *Journal of Career Assessment, 28*(4), 571–578. https://doi.org/10.1177/1069072720909825

Yogev, S. (1983). Judging the professional woman: Changing research, changing values. *Psychology of Women Quarterly, 7*(3), 219–234. https://doi.org/10.1111/j.1471-6402.1983.tb00836.x

Yoon, S. Y. (2011). *Psychometric properties of the Revised Purdue Spatial Visualization Tests: Visualization of rotations (The Revised PSVT-R)*. ProQuest.

Zachar, P., & Leong, F. T. (1992). A problem of personality: Scientist and practitioner differences in psychology. *Journal of Personality, 60*(3), 665–667. https://doi.org/10.1111/j.1467-6494.1992.tb00925.x

Zagar, R., Arbit, J., Stuckey, M., & Wengel, W. W. (1984). Developmental analysis of the Wechsler Memory Scale. *Journal of Clinical Psychology, 40*(6), 1466–1473. https://doi.org/10.1002/1097-4679(198411)40:6<1466::AID-JCLP2270400635>3.0.CO;2-5

Zaidel, D. W. (2016). *Neuropsychology of art: Neurological, cognitive, and evolutionary perspectives* (2nd ed.). Routledge/Taylor & Francis Group.

Zajenkowski, M., & Dufner, M. (2020). Why do narcissists care so much about intelligence? *Current Directions in Psychological Science, 29*(3), 261–266. https://doi.org/10.1177/0963721420917152

Zak, I., Meir, E. I., & Kraemer, R. (1979). The common space of personality traits and vocational interests. *Journal of Personality Assessment, 43*(4), 424–428. https://doi.org/10.1207/s15327752jpa4304_17

Zaleznik, A. (1974). Charismatic and consensus leaders: A psychological comparison. *Bulletin of the Menninger Clinic, 38*(3), 222–238.

Zaleznik, A. (1977). Managers and leaders: Are they different? *Harvard Business Review, 82*(1), 74–81.

Zaleznik, A. (1989). *The managerial mystique. Restoring leadership in business*. Harper & Row.

Zaman, R., Agius, M., & Hankir, A. (2011). Manic-depressive illness and the artistic temperament. *European Psychiatry, 26*(S2), 261–261.

Zaval, L., Li, Y., Johnson, E. J., Elke, U., & Weber, E. U. (2015). Complementary contributions of fluid and crystallized intelligence to decision making across the life span. In T. M. Hess, J. N. Strough, & C. E. Löckenhoff (Eds.), *Aging and decision making: Empirical and applied perspectives* (pp. 149–168). Academic Press. https://doi.org/10.1016/B978-0-12-417148-0.00008-X

Zenatti, A. (1985). The role of perceptual-discrimination ability in tests of memory for melody, harmony, and rhythm. *Music Perception, 2*(3), 397–403. https://doi.org/10.2307/40285307

Zettler, I., Thielmann, I., Hilbig, B. E., & Moshagen, M. (2020). The nomological net of the HEXACO model of personality: A large-scale meta-analytic investigation. *Perspectives on Psychological Science, 15*(3), 723–760. https://doi.org/10.1177/1745691619895036

Zhao, H., & Seibert, S. E. (2006). The big five personality dimensions and entrepreneurial status: A meta-analytical review. *Journal of Applied Psychology, 91*(2), 259–271.

Zhao, H., Seibert, S. E., & Hills, G. E. (2005). The mediating role of self-efficacy in the development of entrepreneurial intentions. *Journal of Applied Psychology, 90*(6), 1265–1272. https://doi.org/10.1037/0021-9010.90.6.1265

Zhao, H., Seibert, S. E., & Lumpkin, G. T. (2010). The relationship of personality to entrepreneurial intentions and performance: A meta-analytic review. *Journal of Management, 36*(2), 381–404. https://doi.org/10.1177/0149206309335187

Zickar, M. J. (2018). Using social media for assessment. In J. C. Scott, D. Bartram, & D. H. Reynolds (Eds.), *Next generation technology-enhanced assessment: Global perspectives on occupational and workplace testing* (pp. 171–192). Cambridge University Press.

Ziegler, M., Colom, R., Horstmann, K. T., Wehner, C., & Bensch, D. (2018). Special issue information: The ability-personality integration. *Journal of Intelligence.* https://www.mdpi.com/journal/jintelligence/special_issues/ability_personality_integration

Zimmerman, I. L., Woo-Sam, J. M., & Glasser, A. J. (1973). *Clinical interpretation of the Wechsler Adult Intelligence Scale.* Grune & Stratton.

Zytowski, D. G. (1973). *Contemporary approaches to interest measurement.* University of Minnesota Press.

Zytowski, D. G., & Kuder, F. (1986). Advances in the Kuder Occupational Interest Survey. In W. B. Walsh & S. H. Osipow (Eds.), *Advances in vocational psychology: Vol. 1. The assessment of interests* (pp. 31–53). Lawrence Erlbaum Associates.

INDEX

A

Abilities, 5, 16. *See also* Artistic and Creative abilities; Emotional Intelligence; General intelligence (g); Mechanical abilities; Perceptual Speed and Accuracy; Physical abilities; Social abilities; Social Intelligence; Spatial abilities; Visual Arts abilities; Writing abilities
  acting, 193
  actual vs. perceived, 413
  age and, 256
  analytical and abstract thinking, 219
  associations with work or career outcomes, 127
  broad-brush, 207
  career-relevant, 16, 128, 260
  categories of, 128
  clusters, 387
  cognitive, 132
  combination of, 162
  compensating, 66
  computational mathematical, 228
  correlating interests, 238
  dance, 192
  definition of, 127–128
  differences in, 139
  Enterprising-related, 213
  in entrepreneurs, 218
  facets of, 134
  factor-analytic studies of, 158
  fluid vs. crystallized, 256
  formulation of, 129
  general intelligence, 16, 127
  general mental ability (GMA), 207, 213, 220
  genetic vs. environmental influences on, 135
  groupings, 384
  identified variables, 207
  intelligence and, 132
  interactions of personality and, 392
  interests paralleling, 424
  literature on, 128
  managerial, 207, 212, 215–216
  measures of, 129, 130, 381, 416
  memory, 232–233
  models of, 131
  nature of, 129
  nature of social and interpersonal, 214
  neglect of, 129
  neuropsychological findings of, 131
  non-general-intelligence, 390
  numerical computational, 227–228
  pattern of, 259
  perceived weaknesses and, 22
  predictive power of, 397
  primary, 131–134
  primary variables, 229
  profile of, 132
  psychoacoustical perceptual discrimination, 172
  purpose of assessing, 132
  Realistic-related, 393
  relevant to career success, 232
  required skills for, 231
  results, 236–237

559

Abilities (*continued*)
　role of, 403
　sales, 218
　scores of, 140
　scores of interest groups, 383
　self-estimates of, 129
　self-perceived, 391
　self-rated, 90–91, 130, 389
　sense of, 433
　sex differences, 156
　skills vs., 128
　SRA Primary Mental Abilities Test, 381
　testing of, 130, 413–415
　theories of, 130, 392
　treatment of, 131
　understanding results of, 238
　use of, 421–422
　verbal vs. nonverbal, 243
　vocational interests and, 59
Ability batteries, 171, 181
　Differential Aptitude Test, 171
　General Aptitude Test Battery (GATB), 171
　Multidimensional Aptitude Battery (MAB), 236–237
Ability functions, nonverbal, 157
Ability measures
　Australian Council for Educational Research Higher Test ML-MQ, 384
　Raven's Standard Progressive Matrices, 384
Ability patterns, 96, 157
　in interest groups, 383
Ability profiles, 235, 239–242
　interpretation of, 260
Ability variables
　focus vs. diffusion (FD), 388
　general intelligence (GI), 388
　rotation vs. verbal (RV), 388
Absolute pitch (AP), 172
　training of, 173
Achievement motivation, 314–321
　achievement variable, 277
　career relevance, 318–319
　conceptual issues, 314–316
　dimensionality and facets, 317
　measure, 277
　measurement issues, 319–321
Acting
　emotional maladjustment, 194
　employment uncertainty, 194
　personality vs. ability, 194
　psychological difficulties in, 194
Acting abilities, 193
　intelligence and, 193
　physical, 193
Action, 201
Activity patterns, 64
Affective disorders, 200

Age, 49–51, 152
　cohort differences and, 50
　Conscientiousness and, 289
　decline in abilities and, 256
　distributions, 152
　intelligence and, 138
　managerial hierarchy and, 221
　personality variables and, 268
　spatial ability and, 166
　specific norms for, 268
　tests and, 221
Agreeableness, 301
　alternative approaches to, 303
　autonomy vs. submissiveness, 304
　counterproductive workplace behavior (CWB) and, 301
　definitions of, 301, 303
　intentional motivation (IM) and, 303
　interest correlation, 373
　issues with, 304
　literature on, 303
　measures of, 303, 304
　negative aspects of, 304
　organizational citizenship behavior (OCB) and, 301
　polarities of, 302
　predicting work and career outcomes and, 302–303
　self-deception (SD) and, 303, 304
Ambition, 433
　facets of, 284
Ambiverts, 281, 355
American College Testing (ACT), 31
　Program's Interest Inventory, 92
　UNIACT, 46
American Psychological Association (APA), 263
Americans With Disabilities Act of 1990, 294
Analysis of latent class, 388
Anxiety, 21, 82, 296. *See also* Neuroticism
　Leventhal Scale of, 297
　measures of, 297
Application goals, 227
Aptitudes, 64, 127–128, 147
　translations of, 127
Arithmetic, 229
Armed Services Vocational Aptitude Battery (ASVAB), 227
Artistic activities, 73
Artistic and Creative abilities, 169. *See also* Dance abilities; Musical abilities; Visual Arts abilities; Writing abilities
　battery, 196
　brain dysfunction and, 169
　intelligence and, 186
　measure of, 171
　profiles, 183
Artistic assessments, 72

Artistic interests, 44, 73
  characteristics of, 71
  correlating abilities, 390–391
  creativity and, 169
  devotion and willingness, 73
  distribution of, 71
  female groups and, 44
  norm questioning and, 351
Artistic occupations, 70, 108
  acting, 70
  characteristic conditions, 74
  dance, 70
  diversity of, 169
  educational level, 71
  generalizations vs. themes, 71
  nature of, 71
  prestige level, 71
  settings, 74
  spatial abilities and, 162
  visual arts, 70
  writers, 70
Artistic performance, 183
  types of, 196
Artistic talent, 183
  distribution, 74–75
Artistic types, 72
  career courses, 96
  cognitive brain processes, 73
  research, 73
  stereotypes, 71, 73
Assembling Objects (AO), 163
Assessment centers, 207
  components of, 221
  methodologies, 220
Assessment instruments, 30
  culture specific, 47
Assessment process resistance, 95
Assessments, 5
  of ability, 91, 96
  of artistic-related abilities, 196
  batteries, 167
  career exploration, 413
  exercises and measures, 206
  focal issues of, 409
  goals and, 5
  guardedness, 121
  Guilford's six major factors, 30
  of interests, 29–30
  modalities, 167, 207
  of physical abilities, 151, 153
  of personality, 270
  purposes of, 339
  reasons for, 367, 431
  of social abilities, 206
  standards for, 413
  value before, 409
  of visual artistic talent, 190
Atlas of Individual Differences, 388–389

Australian Council for Educational Research Higher Test ML-MQ, 384
Autistic spectrum, 200
Automation, 66
Averages, 84

B

Barron-Welsh Art Scale (BWAS), 190
Behavioral abnormalities and affective disorders, 200
Behavioral cognition, 198
Behavioral etiquette, 66
Behavioral evidence, 343
  test results and, 345
Behavioral patterns, 65
Behavior and personality, 345
Bennett Mechanical Comprehension Test, 149
Big Five personality variables, 79, 271. *See also* Five-Factor Personality Model; Personality variables
  Aspects Scale, 309
  trait pairings, 377
Big Six RIASEC types, 36, 63. *See also* RIASEC model
  connections with personality, 376
Block Design subtest, 160
Blue-collar positions, 63–64
Blue-collar work, 148
Brain
  disorders, 184
  functioning, 156
  lateralization, 157
  mechanisms, 73
  patterns, 157
Bright side personality, 321–327
Bureau of Labor Statistics (BLS), 70, 178
Burnout, 90
Business Interest, 30

C

California Occupational Preference System Interest Inventory (COPS II), 92
California Psychological Inventory (CPI), 267, 271. *See also* Extraversion/Introversion
  Achievement through Conformity (Ac), 317
  Achievement through Independence (Ai), 317
  Communality (Cm), 343, 356
  Dominance (Do), 302, 417
  Empathy (Em), 302
  Femininity/Masculinity (F/M) scale and, 331
  Flexibility (Fx), 307, 309

California Psychological Inventory (*continued*)
   Good Impression (Gi), 297, 343, 347, 351, 355
   Independence (In), 348
   Managerial Potential (Mp), 276
   Masculinity (Mf), 402
   Norm Favoring vs. Norm Questioning (v2), 290, 307
   norms for occupational samples, 276
   related constructs, 290
   second-order variables, 276, 347
   Sociability (Sy), 302
   Social Presence (Sp), 302
   structural types. *See* Personality types
   structural vectors of, 276
   test interpretation, 339
   validity scales, 363
   variables, 290
   vectors, 296
   Well-Being (Wb), 295–297, 351, 359
   Work Orientation (Wo), 276
California Psychological Inventory (CPI) test manual, 340
Career
   aspirations vs. reality, 8
   characteristics, 7
   choice and personality preferences, 4
   conflicts, 352
   contemporary searches for, 3–5
   counseling, 87, 422
   counselors, 417
   data in practice, 407
   desired direction, 88
   direction, 95
   fit. *See* Occupational fit
   guidance, 12
   guidance issues, 419
   happiness, 84
   history, 94
   identities, 3, 74
   importance of, 3, 7
   indecision, 97, 375
   individual fit, 398
   motivations, 94
   opportunities, 64
   path characterization, 117
   productivity, 84
   readiness for, 409, 410
   relevance of personality, 270, 339
   satisfaction, 97
   stress, 3
   studies, 148
   success, 52
   typical concerns about, 8–12
Career assessment professionals, 8
   offerings from, 8
   scope of, 4
Career assessments
   across multiple domains, 431
   applications, 267
   basis for practice, 475
   considerations of, 91, 418
   contextualization of the process, 19–23
   core questions addressing, 19–22
   of creative occupations, 195
   data in practice, 67
   discrepancies in, 417
   domains of, 4, 14
   for Enterprising types, 79
   ethical considerations in, 464, 474–477
   ethical requirements, 470–472
   family pressure and, 9
   final report, 434
   foundational literature and, 13
   goals of, 203, 408–409
   group models and, 13
   guidelines for, 421
   individualized models and, 13
   informed consent in, 468
   integration across domains, 18
   integration of findings, 419
   Interdomain Model of Career Assessment, 5, 14–19
   interpretation of personality, 291
   issues with technology, 480
   job-finding vs., 20
   legal matters in, 463
   level of practice, 83
   measured variables of, 412–413
   measures and differential validity, 47–48
   measures of personality in, 271
   memory, 233
   mental health and, 410
   methodologies of, 407
   modifications in, 410
   motivation and readiness for, 4, 410
   multiculturally diverse clients, 476
   neglected areas in, 200
   performance in, 127
   personality variables for, 267
   practice, 97
   preassessment process, 21
   problems in, 411
   process vs. content, 409
   psychological factors affecting, 21
   purpose of, 94–95, 409, 466
   racial/ethnic groups and, 48–49
   readiness for, 20–21
   reasons for, 19
   regulations on, 464
   report preparation, 438–439
   results of, 430, 432
   service delivery, 482
   spatial abilities and, 162
   summary of, 430
   technology in, 479
   understanding of process, 430
   usefulness of, 18, 23, 411–412

variables of, 413
virtual, 479
written reports, 433–434
Career assessors, 66. *See also* Career assessment professionals
  duties of, 419
  feedback and, 18–19, 23
  goals for, 410–411, 422
  integration across domains and, 18
  mental health professionals and, 21
  new measures of interest and, 94
  resources for, 84
  skills needed by, 12
  sorting alternatives, 90
  understanding aspects of interests, 82
Career choices, 7
  consistency and, 56
  Extraversion/Introversion impact, 286
  major questions affecting people considering, 14–15
  personality variables and, 22
Career concerns
  anxiety and, 21
  depression and, 21
  intrapersonal and interpersonal contexts of, 12
  personal concerns vs., 11
  psychopathology and, 21
Career decision making, 409
  in the context of personal situations, 422
  literature on, 410
  measures of, 410
  prescreening, in-depth exploration, and choice model, 409
  readiness for, 20, 409
Career fit. *See* Occupational fit
Career Occupational Preference System (COPS), 57
Case profiles, 98
Cattell, Horn, and Carroll (CHC) Three Stadium Model, 134, 392
Census approach, 284–285
Central tendency, 84
Challenges
  with clients, 87
  in interest measures, 87
  in interpretation, 87
Character disorders, 294
Characteristics
  of interest-ability-personality, 402
  structures of, 398
  of work, 267
Choosing a Vocation, 29
C-index, 53
Circular structural models, 38
Clark's Drawing Abilities Test, 191
Classification systems, 65, 75
  Job Zone, 65
Clerical aptitude analysis, 225

Clerical Interest, 30
Clients
  aspirations, 95
  data, 96
  feedback, 18–19
  relationships with, 94
Clinical Analysis Questionnaire (CAQ), 285
Closure speed, 159
Codes, 84
  consistencies, 88
  Holland's system, 97
  inconsistencies, 90
  permutations of, 90, 96
  summary of, 89
  tertiary, 117
Cognition, 201
Cognitive abilities, 96, 155, 172, 243, 386
  computational mathematics, 223
  demands for, 223
  measures, 151
  models of, 227
  perceptual speed and accuracy (PSA), 223–225
  social intelligence and, 198
  tests of, 227
Cognitive brain processes, 73
Cognitive science, 73
Cognitive systems, 162
Cohort differences, 50
Combinations
  ability and personality, 202
  atypical, 90
  Enterprising–Conventional–Social (ECS), 90
  Enterprising–Realistic–Conventional (ERC), 90
  of interest and personality, 344
  Investigative–Artistic (I–A), 88
  Social–Conventional–Enterprising (SCE), 90
Comparisons
  with criterion groups, 84
  of FFM factors and facet scores, 369
  individual–group occupational, 84
  of interest profiles, 84
Compensating abilities, 66
Competence, 476–477
Complexity, 86
Composite Creativity Index, 73. *See also* creativity, measures
Compound traits, 267. *See also* Emotional intelligence (EI), Extraversion
  ambition, 267
  anxiety, 267
  borderline personality disorder (BPD), 283
  cross-scale items and, 267
  extraversion, 267
  generalized self-efficacy, 283

Compound traits (*continued*)
  identification of, 267
  independence, 267
  passive aggressiveness, 283
  self-control, 267
  tough-mindedness, 267
Comprehensive Ability Battery (CAB), 227
Computational mathematics, 223
Computational skills, 231
Confidentiality, 472–474
  ethical and legal issues of, 474
Congenital adrenal hyperplasia (CAH), 35
Congruence, 52–55
  C-index for measuring, 53
  comparisons among, 54
  job satisfaction and, 52–55
  leisure activities and, 55
  measurement of, 53–54
  M index for measuring, 53
  as a predictive tool, 55
  Zener-Schunelle index for measuring, 53
Conscientiousness, 79, 287. *See also* Personality factors
  age and, 289
  aspects of, 289
  career issues of, 287
  career success and, 288
  conceptualization and method of measuring, 292
  definitions of, 287
  dimensionality of, 289
  facets of, 290
  Industriousness, 290
  interest correlations, 372, 373
  low scores of, 287, 288
  measures of, 289–292
  Orderliness, 290
  perceptions of, 287
  personality tests and, 292
  personal outcomes and, 291
  problems associated with, 288
  relationship to work, 291
  scores, 292
  stability in, 289
  validity coefficients, 290
  work outcomes and, 291
Consent, 470
Consideration (C), 219
Consistency, 55
  career choice and, 56
  of interest findings, 83
Conventional interests, 89
  anxiety and, 82
  associations, 82
  attitudes and behaviors, 81
  career assessments, 82
  correlating abilities, 234, 391
  correlating skills, 389
  model employee, 81
  patterns, 81
  personal preferences, 82
  sex differences, 81
  for women, 81
Conventional occupations
  characteristics of, 223
  duties in, 223
  educational levels, 81–82
  examples, 223
  representative jobs, 81
Conventional types
  characteristics, 80
  correlated abilities, 389
  settings, 80, 82
  structure, 82
  work improvement, 81
Core Questions, 19
Correlations
  between abilities and interests, 381, 389
  between abilities and personality, 396, 400
  between interests scales, 389
  between interests and personality, 376–377, 400–401
  between Neuroticism and RIASEC scales, 370
  between RIASEC interests and FFM personality, 370
  between variables, 377
  zero order, 372
Costs of administering multiple measures of interest, 93
Counselors. *See* Career assessors
Counterproductive Workplace Behavior (CWB), 54
Course of actions, 433
Creative artists, 72
Creative interests and psychological adjustment, 298
Creative productivity, 72
Creativity, 72, 98, 170, 233
  abilities cross-over, 233
  association with mental illness, 299
  basis for, 170
  Compound Remote Associates Task (CRAT), 402
  criteria for, 371
  measures, 73
  mental illness and, 371
  Openness and, 308
  psychopathology and, 371
  syndrome, 194
Criterion
  group, 84
  measures, 267
Cross-domain
  comparisons, 419
  findings, 415
  patterns, 418

Cultural differences, 157
Cultural validity, 47
Culture specific assessment instrumentation, 47

D

Dance abilities
 career challenges, 193
 physical, 192
 requirements, 192
Dark side personality, 321–327
Data
 administering and interpreting, 425
 career implications of, 416
 for career patterns, 407
 of clients, 96
 command of, 431
 differentiation, 398
 in domains, 415
 examination on an interdomain basis, 418
 identification of, 84
 idiographic, 425
 integration of, 399
 interest-ability-personality, 398–399
 interpretation of, 415
 negative, 429
 occupational census, 307
 occupational normative, 165
 personality, 369
 psychological assessment, 407
 vocational profile, 83
Decidedness. *See* Career decision making readiness
Department of Labor, 84
Dependency, 79
Depression, 21
Differential Aptitude Tests (DAT), 227
 spatial subtests, 165
Differential validity
 career assessment measures and, 47–48
 group differences and, 47
 structural studies and, 47
Differentiation, 55
Dimensions of Extraversion/Introversion, 284
Discrepancies
 in career assessment, 417
 evidence for, 87
 explanation of, 87
 expressed vs. measured interests, 97
 in interest measures, 90
 of norms, 355
 in personality measures, 344
 sources of, 97
 in vocational interests, 87
Dissimulation, 295

Domains, 15. *See also* Abilities; Interests; Personality
 career and work outcomes, 401
 consideration of other, 91
 cross-domain relationships, 367
 data in each, 415
 hypotheses for, 425–427
 integration across, 399
 integration of, 398
 overlap between, 392
 separation of, 371
 summarizing findings, 423–425
 variance in, 401
Dominance, 214, 332–338

E

Edinburgh Handedness Inventory, 166
Educational levels
 of Artistic occupations, 71
 of Conventional occupations, 81–82
 of Enterprising occupations, 78
 job zones and, 108
 level 5, 105
 of investigative occupations, 68
 of Realistic occupations, 64
 of Social occupations, 75
Educational samples
 groupings of, 276
 norms for, 276
Effort, 158
Emotional Intelligence (EI), 16, 197, 218. *See also* Social abilities; Social Intelligence
 career-relevant aspects of, 203
 dimensions of, 203
 literature on, 199–200
 Mayer-Salovey-Caruso Emotional Intelligence Test (MSCEIT), 201, 205
 measures of, 202, 205
 models of, 206
 rejection of, 202
 research on, 199, 202
 self-ratings of, 202
Emotional Stability, 79, 299
 correlating personality variables, 395
 interest correlation, 373
Empathy, 193, 218. *See also* Social abilities
Empirical studies, 84
Enterprising
 abilities, 213
 behavior, 77
 definition of, 77
 individuals, 77
 settings, 78
Enterprising interests, 38, 89
 correlating abilities, 390–391
 managerial interest and, 79
 pattern of, 77

Enterprising interests (*continued*)
  power and control, 76
  sex differences, 80
  for women, 78
Enterprising occupations
  educational level, 78
  prestige, 78
  representative jobs, 76–77
Enterprising types, 76
  characteristics, 76–78, 80
  character pathology, 79
  correlated abilities, 389
  emotional intimacy, 77
  expectations, 77
  extremes, 78
  extrinsic rewards, 77
  introspection, 77
  leadership, 80
  personal control maintenance, 79
  personal counseling avoidance, 79
  personal preferences, 78
  relationships, 77–78
Entrepreneurial self-efficacy (ESE), 79
  intentions, 79
  performance, 79
Entrepreneurs, 218
  abilities of, 218
  characteristics of, 218
  literature on, 218
Ethical standards, 464
  examples of, 465–466
  related to competence, 467–468
  of technology in career assessments, 482
Ethics, 19
  concepts, 465
  conduct, 463
  conflict, 463
  maleficence and nonmaleficence, 465
  requirements in professional work, 466
Ethics codes, 463, 464, 468–470
  in career assessment work, 464
  confidentiality, 472
  cultural and multicultural competence, 476
  diversity factors, 476
  guidelines and, 484
Ethnicity. *See* Race/Ethnicity
Experiences, 152
  interest-relevant, 97
Expressed interests, 97
Extraversion, 17, 75, 77. *See also* Extraversion/Introversion; Introversion
  definition of, 280
  division of work with, 282
  group characteristics, 281–282
  interest correlation, 373
  introversion vs., 279
  measures of, 344
  predictions of, 285

Scarr's formulation of, 281
Extraversion/Introversion. *See also* Extraversion; Introversion
  16PF variables related to, 284
  arousal theory of, 281–282
  career assessments and, 286
  correlations between, 283
  dichotomous split of, 284
  dimensions of, 283–284
  facets of, 284
  heritable components to, 281
  impact on career choice and satisfaction, 286
  interest correlations, 372
  job performance and, 285
  literature on, 282
  measures of, 284, 286–287
  occupational groupings and, 284
  occupational limitations of, 285
  occupational preference of, 283
  other personality variables and, 283
  as a personality trait, 281
  reward valences in, 282
  self-identity, 286
  Sociability and, 283
  Social Introversion scale, 286
  stimuli and rewards and, 281
  subjective well-being of, 282
Eysenck Personality Inventory, 295, 300
Eysenck Personality Questionnaire (EPQ), 298

F

Facets
  6-2-1 model, 268, 269
  measures of, 269
  scores, 369
  traits of, 268
  use and interpretation of scores, 292
Fear of success, 11
Feedback, 429. *See also* Client feedback
  explanation of, 470
  face-to-face, 430
  findings and recommendations of, 430
  focal in, 430
  follow-up sessions, 439
  goal of, 432, 440
  individual vs. group, 430
  influence of, 430
  information in, 431
  other documents in, 439
  presentation of information, 432
  principles of, 430–433
  processing and integrating findings of, 433
  reactions to, 433
  reminders in, 431
  reports, 434–438

resistance to, 432
types of, 429
typical process of, 432
verbal vs. written, 434
virtual, 479
Femininity/Masculinity (F/M) scale, 331
FFM (five-factor personality model).
  See Five-factor personality model
  (FFM)
Field dependence, 252
Fit. *See* Occupational fit
Five-factor personality model (FFM), 17,
  265, 269, 376. *See also* Personality
  Agreeableness, 266, 301
  alternatives to, 268
  Conscientiousness, 266
  culture, 266
  Emotional Stability, 266
  Extraversion or surgency, 266
  factors, 279, 369
  limitations and omissions of, 266, 270
  NEO measures, 277, 344
  Openness, 305
  variables of, 270
Flexibility of Closure, 393
Fundamental Interpersonal Relations
  Orientation-Behavior (FIRO-B), 348,
  355, 363, 424
  expressed control vs. wanted control, 359

G

General Aptitude Test Battery (GATB), 140,
  382
  Finger Dexterity test, 382
  limitations of, 383
  spatial subtests, 165
General intelligence (g), 16, 132. *See
  also* Abilities; Cognitive abilities;
  General Mental Ability
  major issues in, 132
General learning ability, 382
General Mental Ability (GMA), 191, 207,
  213, 220, 386
  importance of, 260
General trends, 83
Genetics
  contribution of, 148
  development and expression of musical
    talent, 171
  in music ability, 172
  musical tasks and, 172
  role in specific abilities, 170
Goals in career assessments, 203, 408–409
Gold standard of managerial behavior, 222
Group differences, 83
  differential validity and, 47
  interest measures of, 44–46
  vocational interests and, 43–45

Groupings, 388
  interest-ability, 388
  of personality variables, 394
Group interest, 84
Guidance, career-relevant, 279
Guilford Zimmerman Temperament Survey
  (GZTS), 298

H

Handedness, 157, 166
  in visual artists, 185
Harrington and O'Shea's Career
  Decision-Making System Revised, 93
HEXACO model, 302, 376
Hierarchy, managerial, 221
Higher-order structure, 374
Hogan Personality Inventory (HPI), 278,
  289, 417. *See also* Five-factor personal-
  ity model (FFM)
  Adjustment factor, 297
  advantages and limitations of, 278
  Inquisitive factor, 306, 308
  Intellectance factor, 306
  Interpersonal Sensitivity, 302
  Personnel Selection Series, 265
  seven-factor model, 283
  validity scales, 363
Holland interest types and their correspond-
  ing abilities, 382
Holland, John L., 15–16, 30–31
Holland personality types, 54
Holland's interest codes, 84
Holland's Occupations Finder, 369
Holland's RIASEC model. *See* RIASEC model
Hormone exposure, 148

I

Icelandic Interest Inventory, 377
Idiographic traits, 13
Impostor syndrome, 11
Independence, 344
  field independence, 371
Independent Imagery (IM), 159
Indexes
  Infrequent Responses (IR), 94
  Strong's Like, Indifferent, and Dislike, 94
Individual differences, 12
  in interests, 83
  literature on, 13
  stability of over time, 13
  variables, 13
  work relevance and, 13
Individual difference variables
  age and, 49–51
  race/ethnicity, 42–49
  sex, 40–42
Individual variation, 86

Industrial–Organizational (I–O) psychologists, 17, 208, 285, 392–393
Influences, genetic and hormonal, 156
Information and communication technology (ICT), 479
Infrequent Responses Index (IR), 94
Initiation of structure (IS), 219
Innovations in management, 219
Instrument administration and interpretation procedures, 94
Instruments of interest measurement
    choice of, 93
Integrated Postsecondary Education Data System (IPEDS), 78
Intelligence, 390. *See also* Emotional intelligence (EI); Social intelligence (SI)
    abstract, 67
    aesthetic intelligence, 186
    age and, 138
    artistic ability and, 186, 188
    aspects of, 388
    averages of, 138
    concept of, 134
    definitions of, 132
    examination of, 201
    factors of, 133
    general vs. specific, 134
    interpersonal, 200–201
    intrapersonal, 200
    levels of, 433
    managerial, 222
    managerial approach to, 213
    measures of, 131, 188, 206, 383
    models of, 133, 135, 388
    multiple, 135
    music, 171
    musical abilities and, 177
    nature of, 133
    occupational outcomes and, 53
    personal intelligence, 199
    pragmatic, 213
    predictors of job performance and, 236
    relationship to occupational performance, 140
    role in work effectiveness, 393
    strategic, 219
    subfactors of, 383
    theories of, 131, 134
    types of, 197
    verbal, 193
    verbal measure of, 386
    verbal vs. nonverbal, 139, 149
    Wechsler test, 198
    writing and, 192
Intelligence tests
    Johansson's Career Assessment Inventory Vocational, 92
Interdomain. *See also* Interdomain relationships
    examination of data, 418
    integration, 22
    literature on, 407
    overlap of variables, 378
    predictive research, 398
    profile, 421
    profile vs. real-world career choices, 22
    relationship studies, 402
    research on, 391
Interdomain Model of Career Assessment, 5
Interdomain relationships, 368, 398
    abilities and personality, 368
    interest and abilities, 368
    interests, abilities, and personality, 368
    interests and personality, 368, 369
    literature on, 368
Interest-Ability-Personality (Interdomain) Career Assessment Model, 14–19
    abilities and, 16
    client feedback and, 18–19
    contextualization of, 19–23
    ethics and, 19
    occupationally relevant personality characteristics and, 16–18
    vocational interests and, 15–16
Interest codes, 83. *See also* Interest measures
    Conventional, 223
Interest combinations, 91. *See also* Combinations
Interest measures. *See also* American College Testing (ACT); Self-Directed Search; Strong Interest Inventory; Strong Vocational Interest Blank; Vocational Preference Inventory
    age, 49–51
    alternatives, 93
    anomaly, 90
    approaches to, 83
    assurance of, 91
    basis of, 95
    challenges, 87
    complexity of combining results, 91
    convergent validity, 92
    differential validity and, 47
    discrepancies, 90–92
    for groups, 44–46
    inconsistencies in, 83
    instruments of, 92
    interchangeability, 92
    Interest Profiler, 84
    Jackson Vocational Interest Survey, 92
    results, 83
    Rothwell-Miller Interest Blank, 384
    scales and subscales, 94
    summary codes, 118
    validity indicators, 95
    variability, 90, 92
Interest patterns, 95
    genetic factors and, 35
    hormonal influences on, 35

measures of, 67
in occupational groups, 84
overinterpretation, 122
validity of, 96
Interest-personality
correlations between, 369
results, 369
sex differences, 369
Interest Profiler, 84, 93
tools, 93
Interest profiles, 60, 83
flat vs. peaked, 97
interpretation of, 63, 96
pattern analysis of, 60
validity of, 95
Interest reliability, 95
consistency, 95
Interest results comparisons, 92
Interests, 5. *See also* Vocational interests
absence of, 88
activities correlated to, 95
age and, 50–51
area of, 83
avocational, 94
codes vs. measured, 416
conflict of, 418
congruence and, 53
consistency and, 55, 83
in context, 29
differentiation in, 55
discrepancies, 97
diversity of, 97
endorsement, 92
expression of, 87
factors, 96
fulfillment outside of work, 91
group differences in endorsement of, 43–45
individual difference variables and, 40–51
intellectual vs. aesthetic, 309
interpretation of, 415
intersection of personality variables and, 368
inventories of, 31–32
job performance and, 52
occupational environments and, 39
origins of, 96
perceptions of, 95
personality and, 58, 417
personality vs., 53
presentation of, 95
prioritization of, 90
psychotropic medication and, 57
race/ethnicity and, 49
rediscovery of, 393
research, 83
review of, 96
secondary, 114
self-ratings of, 97, 369
social abilities and, 385–386
stability of, 50–51
structure of, 35–38
theories and research on, 122
types of, 59
values and, 58
variables, 35
Interest scales, 389
associated characteristics, 96
Interest scores, 89
clarification of, 90
context of, 86
Interest structures, cross-cultural adaptations of, 46–47
Interest types
Artistic, 63, 70–74
Conventional, 80–82
Enterprising, 76–80
Investigative, 67–70
Realistic, 63–67
Social, 74–76
Interindividual stability, 33
International Classification of Functioning, Disability and Health, 56
Interoccupational differences, 275
Interpersonal Problem Solving Ability Test (IPSAT), 198. *See also* Social abilities, measures of
Intra-individual stability, 33
Introversion, 17. *See also* Extraversion/Introversion
definition of, 280
division of work with, 282
extraversion vs., 279
group characteristics, 281
literature on, 282
Scarr's formulation of, 281
Inventoried interests, 97
Investigative environments, 68
Investigative interests, 38, 67
correlating abilities, 390, 391
male Asian American groups and, 44
nature of, 418
reward pattern, 68
sex differences, 69
Investigative Interests, 67
Investigative occupations, 67
educational requirement, 69
minority underrepresentation, 69
representation of women, 69–70
representative jobs, 67–68
spatial abilities and, 162
Investigative people
characteristics of, 67
profiles of, 68
Investigative personality variables, 69
Investigative types, 67, 69
perceptions, 70
self-perceptions, 67
subtypes, 68

Iowa Tests of Educational Development Quantitative Thinking subtest (Test Q), 232

J

Jackson Vocational Interest Survey, 92
Job criteria, 152
Job database, 84. *See also* O*Net
Job duties
  influence of personality measures, 303
  of managers, 209–211, 219
  necessary abilities and skills of, 211
Job-finding vs. career assessment, 20
Job performance
  interests and, 52
  Introversion/Extraversion dichotomy, 285
  key predictors of, 52
  literature on, 141
  personality traits as predictors of, 268
  predictors of, 16, 224, 287
  psychopathology and, 17
Job satisfaction, 51–52
  congruence and, 52–55
  facets of, 52
Job Zones, 65, 78. *See also* Classification systems
  educational levels and, 108
  of identified occupations, 118
  Level 5, 106
Johansson's Career Assessment Inventory Vocational, 92
Johns Hopkins University, 31
Journal of Applied Psychology, 52

K

K factor. *See* Spatial abilities
Knowledge (Spatial, Perceptual, and Mechanical), 150. *See also* Intelligence
Kuder Occupational Interest Survey (KOIS), 49, 93
  interest areas in, 50

L

Latency measures, 159
Law of effect, 197
Leadership, 217
Learning approach, 278
Legal issues, 463
  licenses and certifications, 463
Leventhal Scale, 297. *See also* Anxiety
Lexical approach, 295
Locus of Control, 311–314. *See also* Career-Related Self-Efficacy

M

MacQuarrie tests, 149
Making Vocational Choices: A Theory of Vocational Personalities and Work Environments, 36
Management, aspects of, 379
Managers. *See also* Abilities, managerial
  abilities of, 212, 215–216, 222
  as a career group, 208
  characteristics of, 212
  duties and characteristics of, 211
  entrepreneurs vs., 219, 222
  gold standard of, 222
  influencing competencies of, 212
  intellectual competencies of, 212, 213, 215
  job definition, 208–209
  job duties of, 209–211, 214, 219
  leaders vs., 217, 222
  literature on, 208
  measurement of abilities in, 220–221
  measures of dominance in, 214
  on Neuroticism scales, 298
  personality styles, 215
  profile of, 214
  public vs. private, 217
  sales vs., 217
  self-confidence of, 212
  sex differences of, 221
  skill sets needed by, 211
  studies on, 214
  subtypes of, 216
Marker variables, 155
Match approach validity, 48
Mathematical Reasoning, 228–229
Mathematics
  abilities, 228
  measures of ability, 231
  types of competency, 228
Mayer-Salovey-Caruso Emotional Intelligence Test (MSCEIT), 205, 386
McAdory Art Test, 189
Measurement
  customization of, 377
  of interest and personality, 377
Measurement factors
  age, 166
  speed, 166
Measures. *See also* Tests
  accuracy of, 159
  of artistic ability, 191
  of Introversion/Extraversion, 286–287
  limitations of, 476
  of musical ability, 174
  outcomes, 403
  of personality variables, 269
  selection of, 92
  of social abilities, 198

of social and interpersonal ability, 204
  variation in, 339
Measures of artistic talent
  issues with, 190
  Meier Art Judgment Test, 185
Measures of Music Audiation (MMA), 181
Measures of social intelligence (SI)
  Social Insight Scale, 198
  Social Intelligence Test, 198
  Social Participation Scale, 198
  Test of Social Intelligence, 198
Mechanical abilities, 147
  applications of, 151
  aptitude, 149–150
  assessment of, 154
  comprehension, 152
  controversies, 148
  of cotton mill machine fixers, 150
  definition of, 147
  factors of, 150
  factor structure, 149
  genetic basis of, 147
  interests and, 30
  measures of, 148, 151
  objects, 150
  occupations, 150–151
  personnel selection, 148
  real-world outcomes, 149
  reasoning, 149
  sex differences, 148, 152
  skills, 66, 149
  and social importance, 147
  strengths, 149
  studies on, 148
  test development, 148
  test results, 150
  tests of, 151
  thinking, 147
  treatises on, 147
Mechanisms, genetic and hormonal, 156
Meier Art Judgment Test (MAJT), 185, 189
Memory, 232
  acquisitions, 232
  in career assessment, 233
  literature on, 232
  measures of, 233
  mechanisms of, 232
  skills, 232
  in work applications, 232
Mental disorders, 293, 294
  prevalence of, 298
Mental health
  assessment and treatment of, 299
  career assessment and, 410
  professionals, 21
Mental illness
  any mental illness (AMI), 293
  association with creativity, 299
  creativity and, 371

stigmatization of, 298
Methodology, 202
Method variance, 417
Military
  behavioral etiquette, 66
  work, 66
M index, 53
Miner Sentence Completion Scale, 265
Minnesota Clerical Test, 225, 227, 229
Minnesota Mechanical Ability Tests, 149
Minnesota Multiphasic Personality
  Inventory-2-Restructured Form
  (MMPI-2-RF), 286
Minnesota Study of Twins Reared Apart, 388
Minority underrepresentation, 69
Misfits, 380
Moderators, 374, 387
Motivations
  by outside factors, 96
  for social interactions, 280
Multidimensional Aptitude Battery (MAB), 236–245
Multidimensional Personality Questionnaire (MPQ), 373
Musical abilities, 171
  absolute pitch (AP), 172
  age and, 171–172
  conceptualization of, 175
  evaluation of, 182, 183
  factors of, 174–176
  factor structures of, 176
  genetics and, 171
  genetics in, 171–172
  identification of, 181
  intelligence and, 177
  markers for, 172
  maturation of, 173
  measures of, 173, 174, 179–180, 180
  models of, 175
  naturals vs. strivers, 171
  nonmusical factors, 176
  other abilities and, 177
  profiles, 178
  psychoacoustical measures, 174
  relevant abilities, 176
  research in, 174
  spatial abilities and, 177
  stabilized vs. developmental, 175
  tests of, 174, 179
  training and, 172
Musical aptitudes, 173, 175
  definition of, 173
Musical education, 173
Musical factors
  Advanced Measures of Music Audiation (AMMA), 175
  auditory cognition of relationships (ACoR), 175

Musical factors (*continued*)
  auditory immediate memory (MSa), 175
  discrimination among sound patterns (DASP), 175
  judicious-musical factor, 174
  listening verbal comprehension (Va), 175
  maintaining and judging rhythm (MaJR), 175
  Measures of Music Audiation (MMA), 175
  mechanical-acoustical, 174
  Musical Aptitude Profile (MAP), 175, 181
  speech perception under distraction/distortion (SPUD), 175
  temporal tracking (Tc), 175
Musical tasks, 175
  factors from, 175
  genetics and, 172
Musical training, 172. *See also* Absolute pitch (AP)
Music aptitude tests, 177
Music-related jobs, 178
Music unions
  American Federation of Musicians (AFM), 178
  American Federation of Television and Radio Artists (AFTRA), 178
Myers-Briggs Type Indicator (MBTI), 284, 307. *See also* Extraversion/Introversion
  Intuitive (N) vs. Sensing (S), 307

N

National Center for Educational Statistics, 78
Negative Emotionality (NEM), 297
Neuropsychology and artistic abilities, 183
Neuroticism, 17, 269, 292, 344. *See also* Emotional Stability
  acting and, 194
  Anxiety, 295–296
  aspects of, 293, 297
  associations with, 297
  connotations, 292–293
  contextualization of, 293
  correlating abilities, 396
  definition of, 295
  facets and scales for, 297
  harm-avoidance, 372–373
  interest correlations, 372
  managers and, 298
  measures of, 296
  mental disorders and, 293
  NEO Personality Inventory, 295
  polarities, 293
  psychopathology and, 293
  RIASEC variables and, 370
Nomothetic work, 13
Nonverbal intelligence. *See* Abilities
Norms
  age-specific, 221, 227
  discrepancies of, 355
  general population, 221
  questioning direction of, 351
  sex-specific, 227
Number Aptitude, 228
Number Facility, 228–229
Numerical abilities, 157, 228
Numerical fluency, 227

O

Occupation. *See* Career
Occupational
  choices, 84
  clusters, 164
  comparisons, 84
  daydreams, 108, 117, 243, 424
  history, 166
  implications, 165
  interests and environments, 39
  norms, 275
  personalities, 86
  prestige, 39
  profiles, 275
  relevance, 280
  samples, 276
Occupational differences, 162
  in writing, 192
Occupational fit, 84, 88, 267
  conflicts in, 421
  determination of, 231
  domain satisfaction, 421
  measurement of, 52
  nonwork activities and, 55
  Openness and, 308
  other factors and, 422
  personality profile and, 279
  personality variables (occupationally relevant) and, 17
Occupational groups, 84
  ability patterns of, 225
  alpha-dominant, 276
  associated abilities, 388
  beta-dominant, 276
  delta-dominant, 276
  Extraversion/Introversion, 283–284
  gamma-dominant, 276
  modal incumbent of, 212
  outliers of, 276
  varying interest patterns, 84
Occupational Information Network (O*Net). *See* O*Net
Occupational interests, 122. *See also* Vocational interests
  inconsistencies, 87
  measures, 92
Occupational outcomes
  congruence and, 53
  personality vs. interests vs. intelligence, 53

vocational interests and, 51–56
Occupational preferences
    and spatial abilities, 155
    working alone vs. working with others, 285
Occupations
    feminization of, 41
    interest-congruent, 97
    required social abilities, 204
    status level of, 369
    task-oriented vs. socially oriented, 283
    war-related, 148
Occupations Finder, 84
O'Connor's Wiggly Blocks, 149
O*Net, 84, 128, 150, 479
    abilities of, 203
    career searches, 91
    database, 93
    Interest Profiler, 93
    Number Facility, 229
    occupational matches, 122
    occupation listings, 105
    perceptual speed and accuracy (PSA) and, 224, 225
    profile coding, 84
    social abilities on, 203
    social skills on, 203
Openness, 79
    approaches to, 306
    correlating abilities of, 396
    creativity and, 308
    dimensionality of, 307
    to experience, 305–306
    extremes of, 309
    facets of, 308
    factors of, 307
    intellect and, 306
    interest correlations, 372–373
    issues of, 305, 308
    measures of, 308–309
    occupational fit with, 308
    perceptual vs. epistemic, 308
    polarities of, 306
    predicting work and career outcomes, 308
Organizational factors
    impact on individuals, 270
    occupational stress, 270
    toxic work environments, 270
Outdoor-Work interest, 30
Overestimation, 97
Overexcitability, 299
Overlaps, 378, 392
    interest-ability, 383

P

Patterns
    of abilities, 259
    analysis of, 60

    contextualization of, 379
    cross-domain, 418
    managerial, 208
    recognition, 218
    typological, 399
Perceptual speed and accuracy (PSA), 159, 223, 225, 247
    Armed Services Vocational Aptitude Battery (ASVAB), 227
    career and work implications of, 224
    Comprehensive Ability Battery (CAB), 227
    context of clerical aptitude and, 224
    definition of, 224
    Differential Aptitude Tests (DAT), 227
    general mental ability (GMA) and, 225
    importance of, 224
    information processing and, 225
    measures of, 225, 227
    Minnesota Clerical Test, 227
    number correct score (NC), 225
    number wrong score (NW), 225
    platforms for administering tests, 227
    prediction of work outcomes, 227
    as predictors, 224
    in relationship to other variables, 225
    sex differences of, 227
    spatial processing and, 225
    stability of, 224
    test format, 227
    verbal ability and, 229
    working memory and, 225
Performance
    abilities, 194
    divergence of abilities, 195
    improvement, 158
    prediction, 167
Performance rights organizations
    American Society of Composers, Authors, and Publishers (ASCAP), 178
    Broadcast Music Inc. (BMI), 178
Personal intelligence, 199
    interpersonal aspects, 199–201
    intrapersonal aspects, 199–201
    social intelligence and, 200
Personality, 5, 263. *See also* Five-factor personality model (FFM); Personality disorders; Personality factors
    alternative models of, 266
    approaches to, 277
    assessments, 276
    behavior and, 345
    Bright side and Dark side, 321–327
    in career and work domain, 265
    career relevance and, 267, 270
    changes over time, 270, 348, 378
    characteristics of, 91, 267, 270
    comparative neglect of, 264
    consideration of scores, 344

Personality (*continued*)
  data on, 369
  definition of, 263–264
  dimensions of, 269, 339, 375
  disorders, 294
  environmental influences on, 270
  facets and factors, 268, 397. *See also* Compound traits
  factor models of, 266
  genetics and, 270
  importance of, 264
  instruments, 277
  interests and, 58
  issues with models, variables, and measures of, 268
  limitations of scales, 275
  literature on, 264, 265, 268
  long-term health problems and, 270
  measures in career assessment, 271
  measures of, 264, 270, 292, 416
  nature of, 263
  occupational applications and, 265
  occupational outcomes and, 53
  PEN (Psychoticism, Extraversion, and Neuroticism, respectively) model, 294–295
  predictive power of, 264
  profile, 424
  psychopathology and, 264, 294
  rediscovery of, 265
  related to applications, 264
  reputation and, 381
  research on, 264
  results of interest and ability testing, 339
  role of, 265
  self-esteem and, 413
  self-rated, 369
  social abilities and, 206
  spousal ratings of, 369
  stress exposure and, 270
  test interpretation, 339
  understanding findings, 291
  variations of, 264
  vocational interests and, 368
  in work-related assessments, 264
Personality assessment devices
  in clinical or educational contexts, 265
  Hogan Personnel Selection Series, 265
  Miner Sentence Completion Scale, 265
Personality factors. *See also* Five-factor personality model
  Achievement, 355
  Adjustment, 269, 276
  Agreeableness, 266, 301
  Anxiety, 348
  Communality, 351, 355
  Conscientiousness, 266, 287, 348
  Dominance, 355
  Emotional Stability, 266
  Extraversion–Introversion, 348
  higher-order, 374
  Independence, 344, 348
  interest relationships, 374
  Neuroticism, 269
  Openness, 266, 348, 351
  Realization, 351
  Responsibility, 348
  second-order factors, 276
  Self-Control, 348
  Sensitivity, 348
  Tough Poise, 344, 348
  Well-Being, 348
Personality measures. *See also* Sixteen Personality Factor Questionnaire (16PF); California Psychology Inventory (CPI); NEO
  discrepancies in, 344
  validity indicators on, 347, 351
Personality profiles, 340–364
  career fit and, 279
Personality traits
  approaches to identifying, 269
  Introversion/Extraversion, 281
  as predictors of job performance, 268
  problems with identifying, 269
Personality types, 276
  Alpha, 276, 290, 343, 359, 363
  Beta, 276, 348, 355
  Delta, 276, 296, 351
  Gamma, 276
Personality variables, 16–18, 22, 264–265, 393. *See also* Achievement Motivation; Five-factor personality models (FFM); Personality factors
  abilities vs., 265
  age and, 268
  for career assessment, 267
  career fit and, 17
  career-related Self-Efficacy, 311–314
  career-relevant, 267, 339
  challenges in applying interpretations of, 277
  change over time, 270
  conceptualization of, 17
  dark side, 321–326
  Dominance, 332–338
  extraversion and, 17
  five factor model (FFM) and, 17
  Gender Identity, 327–332
  interpretations of, 277
  intersection of interests and, 368
  introversion and, 17
  learning approach, 278
  Locus of Control, 311–314
  Masculinity-Femininity, 327–332
  measures of, 17, 270–271
  neuroticism and, 17
  overall vs. work-related, 17
  predicting work outcomes with, 265

research about, 17
role of, 265
second-order factors of, 276
test results of, 340
unreliability in, 396
Personal satisfaction, 398
Person-environment fit, 60. *See also* Occupational fit
Physical abilities, 152
assessment of, 151, 153, 154
factor model, 153
in personnel selection, 153
requirements, 154
Polarities
Introversion/Extraversion, 281
positive ends of, 282
Polygenic risk scores, 73
Positive Emotionality (PEM), 297
Potential, 344
leadership, 345
supervisory, 345
Predictability, 66
Predictive factors of occupational pursuits, 384
Predictors
of career indecision, 375
Conscientiousness, 291
of general intelligence, 225
in job finding, 372
of work outcome, 227
Prediger's World-of-Work Map, 92
Preferences, exploration of, 344
Prestige (occupational), 39
Probabilistic reasoning, 73
Productivity, 398
Professional training, 468
Profiles
of abilities, 132, 235
ability-personality, 394
analysis of, 86, 371
associated occupations, 367
codes, 84
cross-ability, 160
interdomain, 421
interest-ability-personality, 402–403
personality, 424
review of, 419
subtypes, 419
Property Vector Fitting, 375
Protected classes, 43
Protective mechanisms, 298–299
Psychological disorder, 295
denial of, 347
Psychological dysfunctions, 73, 343
in particular occupations, 298
Psychological functioning
idealized model of, 306
Psychometric measures, 201
Psychometric properties in interest measurements, 92

Psychomotor ability tests, 153
Psychopathology, 69, 72
career concerns and, 21
creativity and, 371
in occupations, 264
personality and, 264, 294
work performance and, 17
Psychotropic medication, 57

R

Race/Ethnicity, 42–49
career assessment and counseling and, 48
protected classes and, 43
service delivery and, 43
structural differences and, 46–48
Raven's Advanced Progressive Matrices (RAPM), 386, 445
Raven's Standard Progressive Matrices (RSPM), 177, 384
Reading-Free Vocational Interest Inventory, 57
special populations and, 57
Realistic interests
correlating abilities, 391, 393
decline of endorsement, 64
endorsement of, 64
female lack of endorsement of, 44
male Latinos and Caucasians and, 44
occupational groups, 65
patterns, 65
personal preferences, 66
sex differences, 66
work history and, 66
Realistic, Investigative, Artistic, Social, Enterprising, and Conventional (RIASEC) model. *See* RIASEC model
Realistic occupations, 39, 63, 147
average educational level, 64
characteristics, 66
difficulties, 65
physical abilities, 149
representative jobs, 63–64
required educational levels, 64
Realistic types, 65, 68
for males, 65
Realistic world, 65
Reasoning, probabilistic, 73
Referral questions, 413
Relationships. *See also* Interdomain relationships
ability-personality, 392
examination of, 389
importance of, 215
interest-ability, 381, 387, 390
interest-ability-personality, 398, 399, 401
interest-personality, 371, 372, 374
personality-ability, 393, 401
typologies of, 396

Relevance
    practical, 82
    theoretical, 82
Research
    ability-interest findings, 382
    bases, 93
    controversy, 156
    on interest-personality findings, 379
    about interests, 83
Responders
    high, 95
    low, 95
Results, 94
RIASEC model, 36, 375. *See also* Interest types
    codes, 88
    consistency and, 55
    contemporary U.S. occupations and, 38
    data vs. ideas dimension, 38–39
    different approaches to, 38
    differentiating characteristics of interests in, 36–37
    examination of codes, 92
    hexagonal representation of, 37
    interests, 82
    interest scores, 84
    measures, 93
    metadimensions underlying, 38
    origins of, 31
    prestige ratings, 39, 75
    RIASEC types, 36–38, 63, 83
    scale scores, 94
    sex differences and, 38, 42
    special populations and, 57
    specified relationship among the six interest types in, 37
    theory, 381
    things vs. people dimension, 38–39
    variables, 370
Role prescription theory, 212
Rothwell-Miller Interest Blank, 384

S

Sales abilities, 218
Satisfaction, 403
Scientific Interest, 30
Scientific-professional model of psychological practice, 30
Seashore Measures of Musical Talent (SMMT), 174
Self-concepts, 97
Self-confidence, 344
    in managers, 212
Self-Directed Search (SDS), 36, 57, 89, 92, 369
    intention, 91
    Like, Indifferent, and Dislike indexes, 94
    measurements, 89
    special populations and, 57
    subparts (Activities, Competencies, Occupations, and Self-Estimates), 91
Self-efficacy, 410
Self-exploration process, 87
Self-identity, 286
    of Introversion/Extraversion, 286
Self-perceptions, 432
Self-presentations, 343, 363, 416
    tendencies in, 345
Self-rated abilities, 90–91
Self-ratings, 369
    limitations on, 389–390
Self-realizations, 295
    levels of, 355
Self-report measures, 95
Self-sufficiency vs. dependency, 348
Serial Integration, 159
Service requests, 430
Sex differences, 40–42, 155
    age and, 41
    consideration of, 166
    in Conventional interests, 81–82
    and cultural differences, 157
    discrimination, 69
    in Enterprising types, 80
    in interest-ability-personality relationships, 401
    in interest-ability relationships, 389
    in interest-personality correlations, 369, 376
    of managers, 221
    in mechanical abilities, 148
    in PSA tests, 227
    in Realistic types, 66
    in spatial abilities, 156–157
Sex role preferences, 156
Sexual orientation, 156
Situational judgement tests (SJTs), 222
Sixteen Personality Factor Questionnaire (16PF), 277, 280, 340, 368
    Anxiety, 359
    Cattell's factor C, 295
    Clinical Analysis Questionnaire (CAQ), 351, 352
    Dominance scale, 417
    Extraversion, 283
    Extraversion/Introversion factor, 280
    fake bad scale, 347, 355
    fake good scale, 343, 355, 363
    five second factors, 277
    impression management, 356
    Independence vs. Accommodation, 302
    Introversion, 283
    primary factors, 296
    second-order factors, 344, 348
    Self-Control vs. Lack of Restraint, 289
    variables related to Extraversion/Introversion, 284, 286

Skills
  mastery of, 227
  self-rated, 389
Sociability, 283–284
Social abilities, 207. *See also* Emotional Intelligence; Social Intelligence
  assessment of, 206
  complexity of, 200
  construct of, 201
  interests and, 201, 385–386
  measures directed to behavior, 198
  measures of, 198
  multiplicity, 200
  in O*Net, 203
  personality and, 206
  sensitivity, 201
  social disabilities vs., 200, 204
  types required, 204
Social acuity in writing, 191
Social coping skills, 386
Social deficits, 200
  affective disorders and, 200
Social discomfiture, 65
Social Intelligence (SI), 197, 215. *See also* Emotional Intelligence; Social abilities
  abilities of, 203
  career-relevant aspects of, 203
  cognitive ability and, 198
  constructs related to, 198
  correlating personality variables, 394
  definition of, 197
  dimensions of, 203
  empirical research on, 198
  four-factor measure of, 198
  interest-ability-personality relationships related to, 399
  literature on, 199–200
  measures of, 198, 202, 205
  mechanical and abstract intelligence vs., 197
  personal intelligence and, 200
  Social Insight Scale, 198
  Social Intelligence Test, 198
  Social Participation Scale, 198
  Test of Social Intelligence, 198
Social interactions
  difficulties in, 200
  types of, 204
Social interests, 35, 38, 44, 52
  African American groups and, 44
  characteristics, 74
  correlating abilities, 390–391
  factors, 75
  female endorsement of, 44
  finger lengths and, 35
  orientations, 75
  personal preferences, 75
  preferences, 378
Social occupations, 74, 75
  educational requirements, 75
  end product, 75
  female composition, 75
  financial rewards, 75
  prestige, 75
  representative jobs, 74
  societal importance, 75
  subordination of personal goals, 75
  work conceptualization, 75
Social skills
  coping, 386
  deficits in, 200
  problem-focused, 386
  problem-solving, 386
  type matching, 204
Social types, 75
Social Welfare, 30
Socioeconomic Index (SEI), 369
Socioeconomic issues, 69
Socioeconomic status (SES) and STEM careers, 44
Sociopathy, 215
Spatial. *See also* Spatial abilities; Spatial factors
  aptitude, 158
  intelligence, 186
  measures, 159
  orientation, 159–160
  scanning, 159
  tasks, 159
Spatial abilities, 16, 139, 147, 155, 172, 381
  acquisition of, 156
  age and, 158
  in Artistic occupations, 164
  conceptual and structural issues, 160
  correlating personality variables, 393
  cultural differences and, 157
  definition of, 155
  educational success, 163
  factors, 159–160
  handedness, 157
  importance in occupational applications, 166
  interpreting results, 157
  lateralization of, 156
  marker for, 160
  measures of, 160, 164–165, 238
  multidimensionality, 155
  musical talent and, 177
  neuropsychology, 156
  oblique factors, 159
  occupational success, 160
  occupations, 161
  other abilities and, 160
  patterns of, 158
  practice and, 158, 164
  scores, 158
  sex differences, 156

Spatial abilities (*continued*)
   strategies, 157
   structure of, 158
   study results of, 159
   training and, 158
   visual arts and, 160
   in youth, 162
Spatial factors, 159. *See also* Independent Imagery (IM)
   intrinsic vs. extrinsic, 159
   occupational outcomes and, 165
   Perceptual Speed–Closure Flexibility, 159
   static vs. dynamic, 159
   Visualization, Speeded Rotation, Speed of Closure, and Visual Memory, 159
Spatial, Perceptual, and Mechanical Knowledge, 150
Spatial visualization, 134, 159
   subfactors of, 159
Special populations
   Career Occupational Preference System (COPS) and, 57
   Reading-Free Vocational Interest Inventory and, 57
   RIASEC model and, 57
   Self-Directed Search (SDS) and, 57
   underemployed of, 56
   vocational interest measurement in, 56–58
Speed of closure
   correlating personality variables, 393
Spouse ratings, 369
SRA Primary Mental Abilities Test, 381
   Verbal, Perceptual, Quantitative, Motor, and Spatial subtests, 381
Stability
   children and, 33
   genetic influences and, 34
   interests and age and, 49–50
   interindividual, 33
   intra-individual, 33
   longitudinal study of, 34
   over time, 378
   profile order, 33
   structural, 33
   vocational interests and, 32–37
Standard Self-Directed Search, 36
Standards for Educational and Psychological Testing, 413
STEM careers and socioeconomic status (SES), 44
Stenquist's Picture Matching Test, 149
Stress, 355
   measure of tolerance, 295
   medical problems related to, 90
   occupational, 3
   tolerance of, 215
Strong Interest Inventory (SII), 29, 35, 46, 84, 89, 92, 100
   Basic Interest scales, 106, 113, 115, 122, 376

   compatible activities, 113
   General Occupational Theme (GOT), 385
   measures of, 34, 44–46, 64
   Social Skills Inventory (SSI), 385, 386
   Strong Campbell Interest Inventory (SVIB-SCII), 382
Structural stability, 33
Structural studies and differential validity, 47
Studies
   on ability-personality, 395
   empirical, 84
   on interest-ability-personality, 398
   on interest-ability relationships, 381, 384
   of interest-personality, 371, 373, 377
   neglect in, 398
Success
   abilities related to, 218
   predictors of, 207
   strategies for, 141
Superego controls, 348
Supervisory influence, 344

T

Talents, 208
   bias, 171
Technical expertise, 66
Tellegen's Multidimensional Personality Questionnaire, 292
Testing
   circumstances, 206
   considerations, 95
   distortion of responses, 95
   exaggerations, 95
   expenses, 171
   purpose of, 94
   questions to validity, 95
   self-presentation, 95
Test of Social Intelligence subtests, 198
Tests. *See also* Measures
   of ability, 382, 414–415
   accurate representation of scores, 344
   Appreciation of Phrasing, 179
   Assembling Objects (AO), 163
   behavioral evidence and results, 345
   Block Design, 160
   Differential Aptitude Test, 165
   General Aptitude Test Battery (GATB), 165
   influence of age, 221
   of interests, 382
   MacQuarrie tests, 149
   measures and results of, 235
   Minnesota Mechanical Ability Tests, 149
   Multidimensional Aptitude Battery (MAB), 236–245
   for musical abilities, 174, 179
   music aptitude, 177

O'Connor's Wiggly Blocks, 149
order of administration, 414
of personality and interest, 414
properties of, 414
purpose of, 415
reactions to, 415
of social intelligence, 198
Stenquist's Picture Matching Test, 149
used for screening, 396
Test-taking orientation, 94, 95
atypical, 99
consideration of distress in, 356
fake good direction, 363
scales, 94
validity indicators, 339
Test-taking "set", 96
Traits
activation, 267
complexes, 399
orientations, 286
Turnover intent, 403
Typical intellectual engagement (TIE), 387

U

Underlying model of intelligence (g-VPR), 388
Universal Index (UI), 155. *See also* Spatial abilities
Upward mobility, 221
U.S. National Institute of Mental Health (NIMH), 293

V

Validity evidence, 179, 181
for emotional and social intelligence, 202
indicators, 95
match approach, 48
for social intelligence measures, 198
studies of, 149
Values
measurement of, 58
Work Aspect Preference Scale and, 58
Variables
aggregation of, 379
of career assessment, 413
classes of, 392
comparable, 417
individual approach, 418
interdomain, 213
isolation of, 418
measurement of, 396
separation of, 214
socioeconomic status (SES), 403
Variance
between abilities and interest variables, 382
between interests and personality, 375

Verbal ability and perceptual speed and accuracy (PSA), 229
Verbal intelligence, 193
aspects of, 388
Verbal-Perceptual-Image Rotation (g-VPR), 388
Verbal vs. visual strategies, 157
Visual artistic performance components, 187
Visual Arts
occupations, 183
tasks, 185
Visual Arts abilities, 183
aesthetic discrimination and, 186
aesthetic judgment and, 186, 187
assessment of, 190
biological and neurological bases, 189
brain structures of functions, 184
characteristics of, 185
deterioration of, 188
dimensions of, 187
early emergence of, 185
factor structures of, 186
gestalt perception and, 186
identification of, 189
incidental visual memory, 187
intelligence and, 188
manifestation of, 185
measures of, 185, 188, 191
other abilities and, 188
representational drawing ability, 186
reproductive drawing, 185
research on, 183, 186
screening of, 189
spatial intelligence and, 186
spatial visualization, 186
speed of perception, 186
visual thinking, 185, 186
Visual memory, 159
Visual thinking, 186
Vocational interests, 15–16, 22. *See also* Interest types
abilities and, 59
assessment devices for, 29–30
career success and, 52
complexity of, 59
cross-sectional study of, 33
definitions of, 28
discrepancies in, 87, 96
early youth and, 33
empirical measures of, 36
expressed, 97
genetic influences and, 34
group differences and, 43–45
history of, 29–50
hormonal influences on, 35
inconsistent codes, 90
interdomain relationships and, 58–59
interindividual stability and, 33
intraindividual stability and, 33

Vocational interests (*continued*)
  inventories of, 40, 92
  job satisfaction and, 51–52
  matching process and, 28
  measures of, 15, 29, 92, 94
  as measures of personality, 368
  motivation and, 27
  occupational outcomes and, 51–56
  practice perspective and, 59–60
  prestige level of occupations and, 39
  race/ethnicity differences and, 42–49
  sex differences and, 40–42
  special populations and, 56–58
  stability of, 32–37
  trait-like, 32–33
  unified theory of, 16
  variables in relationship to, 29
Vocational Preference Inventory (VPI), 36, 58, 89, 92, 368
  Infrequency scale, 94
  Infrequency score, 99
  Status scale, 423
Vocational preferences, 84
  measures of, 93. *See also* Self-Directed Search (SDS); Strong Interest Inventory (SII); Vocational Preference Inventory (VPI)
  misfit, 86
Vocational profiles data, 83
Vocational researchers, 29–30
Vocational/Technical educational programs, 65
Vocational titles, 90

W

Weaknesses, self-perceived, 107
Wechsler Adult Intelligence Scale-Revised, 160
Wide Range Achievement Test, 231
  Arithmetic factor, 229
  components of, 231
Windelband, Wilhelm, 13
Wing Standardised Tests of Musical Intelligence, 180, 181
Wink-Gough Scale for Narcissism, 297
Women
  in Enterprising occupations, 78
  in Realistic occupations, 64
Work. *See also* Career
  applications, 232
  dissatisfaction with, 3
  fit. *See* Occupational fit
  radical change in the nature of, 4–6
  rough division of, 282
  unhappiness, 7
Work Aspect Preference Scale, 58
Work effectiveness and general intelligence, 393
World Health Organization, 56
Writing abilities, 191
  creative writing, 192
  factors of, 191–192
  intelligence scores, 191
  nonability factors, 191–192
  occupational differences in, 192
  profiles of, 192

Y

Young adults
  interest sorting, 91
  retesting, 91

Z

Zener-Schnuelle index, 53, 92

ABOUT THE AUTHOR

Rodney L. Lowman, PhD, ABAP, consulting psychologist and author, is president of Lowman & Richardson/Consulting Psychologists and Distinguished Professor Emeritus, California School of Professional Psychology, Alliant International University in San Diego, California. He has also held academic appointments at the University of Michigan, University of North Texas, Duke University Medical School, and the University of South Africa. Dr. Lowman is the author or editor of 13 books and monographs, has published over 130 peer-reviewed articles and chapters, and has made hundreds of professional presentations all over the world. He is fellow of seven APA Divisions: 1 (Society for General Psychology), 10 (Society for the Psychology of Aesthetics, Creativity and the Arts), 12 (Society of Clinical Psychology), 13 (Society of Consulting Psychology), 14 (Society for Industrial and Organizational Psychology), 17 (Society of Counseling Psychology), and 52 (International Psychology). He currently edits the Fundamentals of Consulting Psychology book series published by the APA and has edited two APA-published journals, *Consulting Psychology Journal: Practice and Research* and *The Psychologist-Manager Journal*. Currently he is coeditor of *Diversity Business Review*. His books include *The Ethical Practice of Consulting Psychology* (with Stewart Cooper); *An Introduction to Consulting Psychology: Working With Individuals, Groups, and Organizations*; *Internationalizing Multiculturalism: Expanding Professional Competence in a Globalized World*; *The Ethical Practice of Psychology in Organizations* (2nd ed.); *The California School of Organizational Studies Handbook of Organizational Consulting Psychology: A Comprehensive Guide to Theory, Skills and Techniques*; *The Clinical Practice of Career Assessment: Interests, Abilities, Personality*; and *Counseling and Psychotherapy of Work Dysfunctions*. He is past president of the Society of Consulting Psychology and of the Society of Psychologists in Leadership and has held a number of leadership roles in the APA and in several universities. He is a widely recognized authority on professional ethics and on career assessment and interventions. He has consulted with a large number of career and organizational clients. For additional information, visit his website (http://rodneylowman.com).